THE BOOK OF JOB

The Text of the Hebrew Bible, 1

Series Editor
David J.A. Clines

The Book of Job

John Gray

Edited by David J.A. Clines

Sheffield Phoenix Press
2015

First published in hardback, 2010
First published in paperback, 2015

Published by Sheffield Phoenix Press
Biblical Studies, University of Sheffield
45 Victoria Street
Sheffield S3 7QB

www.sheffieldphoenix.com

A CIP catalogue record for this book
is available from the British Library

Typeset by Forthcoming Publications Ltd.
Printed by Lightning Source Inc.

ISBN 978-1-909697-91-1 (paperback)
ISBN 978-1-905048-02-1 (hardback)

ISSN 1747-9622

CONTENTS

Preface ix
Abbreviations x

Part I
GENERAL INTRODUCTION

Chapter 1
INTRODUCTION 3

Chapter 2
JOB IN THE CONTEXT OF NEAR EASTERN WISDOM LITERATURE 5

Chapter 3
JOB IN HEBREW WISDOM 21

Chapter 4
DATE AND PROVENANCE 32

Chapter 5
LITERARY FORMS IN THE BOOK OF JOB 39

Chapter 6
THE COMPOSITION OF THE BOOK OF JOB 56

Chapter 7
TEXT AND VERSIONS 76

Chapter 8
THE LANGUAGE OF THE BOOK OF JOB 93

Chapter 9
THE ARGUMENT 108

Part II
COMMENTARY

Job 1 and 2
THE PROLOGUE 119

Job 3
JOB'S EXPOSTULATION 138

Job 4 and 5
Eliphaz's First Address 148

Job 6 and 7
Job's First Rejoinder to Eliphaz (Chapter 6)
and his Expostulation with God (Chapter 7) 167

Job 8
Bildad's First Expostulation 183

Job 9 and 10
Job's Second Rejoinder 190

Job 11
Zophar's First Address 206

Job 12–14
Job's Statement 213

Job 15
Eliphaz's Second Reply: A Remonstration
to Job's Obstinacy in Questioning the Theodicy 235

Job 16 and 17
Job's Rejoinder to Eliphaz 247

Job 18
The Reply of Bildad 261

Job 19
Job's Rejoinder to Bildad 267

Job 20
The Reply of Zophar 279

Job 21
Job's Rejoinder to Zophar 289

Job 22
Eliphaz's Statement 301

Job 23
Job's Response to Eliphaz: His Ardent Desire
for Confrontation with God 310

Job 24
Job's Response to Eliphaz (continued, vv. 1-12),
with Two Citations from Wisdom Poetry (vv. 13-18, 19-25) 314

Job 25 and 26
THE INTRODUCTION OF BILDAD'S THIRD ADDRESS:
INTRODUCED BY 26.2-4, CONTINUED BY 25.2-6
AND CONCLUDED BY 26.5-15 325

Job 27
JOB'S FINAL RESPONSE TO HIS FRIENDS 333

Job 28
AN INDEPENDENT POEM ON THE TRANSCENDENCE OF WISDOM 340

Job 29
JOB'S REVIEW OF HIS FORMER PROSPERITY 351

Job 30
JOB'S PLAINT 363

Job 31
JOB'S GREAT OATH OF PURGATION 376

Job 32–37
INTERPOLATION 392

Job 32
ELIHU'S FIRST ADDRESS (VV. 6-22)
AFTER THE PROSE INTRODUCTION (VV. 1-5) 393

Job 33
ELIHU'S FIRST STATEMENT 399

Job 34
ELIHU'S SECOND STATEMENT 412

Job 35.1; 33.31-33; 35.2–36.25
ELIHU'S THIRD ADDRESS 423

Job 36.26–37.13
ELIHU'S CITATION OF A HYMN OF PRAISE 435

Job 37.14-24
CONCLUSION OF THE ELIHU SECTION: ADDRESS TO JOB 447

INTRODUCTION TO JOB 38–41 451

Job 38
THE DIVINE DECLARATION: PART I 455

Job 39 and 40.25-30 (EVV 41.1-6)
THE DIVINE DECLARATION: CONTINUED 469

Job 40.2, 7-14
THE DIVINE DECLARATION: CONCLUSION 482

Job 40.3-5; 42.2-6
JOB'S SUBMISSION 485

Job 40.15–41.26 (EVV 34)
WISDOM POEMS ON NATURAL THEMES 489

Job 42.7-17
THE EPILOGUE 503

Bibliography 508

PREFACE

At his death in 2000, John Gray, who was Professor of Hebrew and Semitic Languages in the University of Aberdeen, left a complete manuscript of a commentary on the Book of Job. It came into my hands through the good offices of Professor William Johnstone, Gray's successor at Aberdeen, and was entrusted to Sheffield Phoenix Press by his daughter Mrs Jean Reynolds, who, with a certain degree of trepidation, personally conveyed the sole typescript copy of the book to Sheffield.

The very lengthy manuscript had to be completely retyped, a heroic task which Duncan Burns undertook with his characteristic skill and enthusiasm. It needed nevertheless a number of readings of the proofs and very many editorial interventions to remove inconsistencies and minor blemishes, not least in standardizing and checking the transliteration of the Hebrew. I was glad to have the opportunity of doing the editorial work, which could not be farmed out to a copy-editor, but needed the expertise of a fellow-commentator on the Book of Job. I apologize for the unconscionable delay in completing the work, which was sadly competing for time with various other projects.

The chief interest of the present volume lies in its philological observations, all of them worthy of consideration. Gray brought to his work on the Hebrew text of Job a lifetime of experience with Arabic and Ugaritic texts, and made many original suggestions for the meaning of passages. When it came to emendations of the text, which the Book of Job is sorely in need of at many places, Gray's instinct everywhere was to accept only those where he could show that the original text had been corrupted in the old script. This was an unusual self-imposed limitation, but it had striking results.

In addition, Gray conceived his work on Job as an all-purpose commentary, prefixing a substantial General Introduction to the book as a whole and prefacing each section of translation and critical notes with an essay displaying his own special form-critical and theological interests. In all these essays his own distinctive approach is evident.

I believe that this outstanding commentary will be a fitting tribute to the sound judgment and innovative scholarship of its author.

David J.A. Clines
October 2010

ABBREVIATIONS

11QtargJob	Targum of Job from Qumran Cave 11
AB	Anchor Bible
AV	Authorized Version
Aq.	Aquila
AfO	*Archiv für Orientforschung*
AJSL	*American Journal of Semitic Languages and Literatures*
Akk.	Akkadian
ALUOS	Annual of Leeds University Oriental Society
AnatSt	*Anatolian Studies*
ANEP	James B. Pritchard (ed.), *Ancient Near East in Pictures Relating to the Old Testament* (Princeton: Princeton University Press, 1954)
ANET	James B. Pritchard (ed.), *Ancient Near Eastern Texts Relating to the Old Testament* (Princeton: Princeton University Press, 1950)
AO	*Der Alte Orient*
AnOr	Analecta orientalia
Arab.	Arabic
Aram.	Aramaic
ARW	*Archiv für Religionswissenschaft*
ASTI	*Annual of the Swedish Theological Institute*
AuS	G. Dalman, *Arbeit und Sitte in Palästina*
ATANT	Abhandlungen zur Theologie des Alten und Neuen Testaments
ATD	Das Alte Testament Deutsch
ATR	*Anglican Theological Review*
BA	*Biblical Archaeologist*
BASOR	*Bulletin of the American Schools of Oriental Research*
BDB	Francis Brown, S.R. Driver and Charles A. Briggs, *A Hebrew and English Lexicon of the Old Testament* (Oxford: Clarendon Press, 1907)
BKAT	Biblischer Kommentar: Altes Testament
Bib	*Biblica*
BotAT	Die Botschaft des Alten Testaments
BSO(A)S	*Bulletin of the School of Oriental (and African) Studies*
BZAW	Beihefte zur *ZAW*
CB	The Century Bible
CBQ	*Catholic Biblical Quarterly*
EHAT	Exegetisches Handbuch zum Alten Testament
EchB	Echter Bible
ET	*Expository Times*
ETL	*Ephemerides theologicae lovanienses*
ETR	*Études théologiques et religieuses*
EVV	English Versions

GB	Gesenius-Buhl, *Hebräisches und aramäisches Handwörterbuch über das Alte Testament*
GHAT	Göttinger Handkommentar zum Alten Testament
Gk.	Greek
GKC	*Gesenius' Hebrew Grammar* (ed. E. Kautzsch; revised and trans. A.E. Cowley; Oxford: Clarendon Press, 1910)
HAT	Handbuch zum Alten Testament
Hebr.	Hebrew
HSAT	Die Heilige Schrift des Alten Testaments
HTR	*Harvard Theological Review*
HUCA	*Hebrew Union College Annual*
ICC	International Critical Commentary
JAOS	*Journal of the American Oriental Society*
JBL	*Journal of Biblical Literature*
JJS	*Journal of Jewish Studies*
JMEOS	*Journal of the Manchester Egyptian and Oriental Society*
JNES	*Journal of Near Eastern Studies*
JPOS	*Journal of the Palestine Oriental Society*
JPTh	*Jahrbücher für protestantische Theologie*
JQR	*Jewish Quarterly Review*
JR	*Journal of Religion*
JRAS	*Journal of the Royal Asiatic Society*
JSS	*Journal of Semitic Studies*
JTS	*Journal of Theological Studies*
KAT	Kommentar zum Alten Testament
KB	Ludwig Koehler and Walter Baumgartner (eds.), *Lexicon in Veteris Testamenti libros* (Leiden: E.J. Brill, 1953)
KD	*Kerygma und Dogma*
KEH	Kurzgefasstes exegetisches Handbuch zum Alten Testament
KHC	Kurzer Hand-Commentar zum Alten Testament
KS	A. Alt, *Kleine Schriften zum Alten Testament*, I (1953); II (1959); III (1959)
LXX	Septuagint
MGWJ	*Monatsschrift für Geschichte und Wissenschaft des Judentums*
MT	Masoretic Text
NCB	New Century Bible
NEB	New English Bible
NICOT	New International Commentary on the Old Testament
OTL	Old Testament Library
OTS	*Oudtestamentische Studiën*
PEFQS	*Palestine Exploration Fund, Quarterly Statement*
PEQ	*Palestine Exploration Quarterly*
PR	*Le palais royal d'Ugarit*
RA	*Revue d'assyriologie et d'archéologie orientale*
RB	*Revue biblique*
RE	*Realencyklopädie für protestantische Theologie und Kirche*
RevQ	*Revue de Qumran*
RGG	*Die Religion in Geschichte und Gegenwart: Handwörterbuch für Theologie und Religionswissenschaft* 3 (ed. K. Galling; Tübingen: J.C.B. Mohr, 1957–65)

RHPR	*Revue d'histoire et de philosophie religieuses*
RHR	*Revue de l'histoire des religions*
RQ	*Revue de Qumran*
RS	Ras Shamra
Theod.	Theodotion
ThLZ	*Theologische Literaturzeitung*
TRu	*Theologische Rundschau*
RSV	Revised Standard Version
S	Syriac (Peshitta)
SBLMS	SBL Monograph Series
SBOT	The Sacred books of the Old Testament
SBT	Studies in Biblical Theology
Sem	*Semitica*
SGV	Sammlung Gemeinverständlicher Vorträge und Schriften aus dem Gebiet der Theologie und Religionsgeschichte
SSEA	Society for the Study of Egyptian Antiquities. Publications
Sym.	Symmachus
Syr.	Syriac
T	Targum
Ug.	Ugaritic
UT	Cyrus H. Gordon, *Ugaritic Textbook* (AnOr, 38; Rome: Pontifical Biblical Institute Press, 1965)
V	Vulgate
VT	*Vetus Testamentum*
VTSup	*Vetus Testamentum*, Supplements
WBC	Word Biblical Commentaries
WO	*Die Welt des Orients*
ZAW	*Zeitschrift für die alttestamentliche Wissenschaft*

Part I

General Introduction

Chapter 1

Introduction

In the grandeur of its conception, its daring questioning of the traditional faith, its noble defence of 'an honest man, the noblest work of God', and in the existential solution of the acute problem of the relation of human justice to the justice of God in the human confrontation with 'the dreadful yet alluring mystery' (*mysterium tremendum et fascinans*) of the divine presence, and in the wonderful range of poetic diction and imagery and the rich variety of literary forms, each with its own peculiar significance in the argument, the book of Job well deserves the appraisal of Thomas Carlyle: 'One of the grandest things ever written with pen' (Carlyle 1908: 67). In view of the limitations of Carlyle's knowledge of Hebrew and cognate Semitic languages and literatures, and especially in view of the relatively uncritical view of the structure and notoriously difficult text of Job, Carlyle's judgment, 'There is nothing, I think, in the Bible or out of it, of equal literary merit', may be an intuitive rather than a critical assessment, but it is also the assessment of Hebrew specialists. Cornill (1892: 229), for instance, considered it 'the crown of the Hebrew Wisdom-writings and one of the most wonderful products of the human spirit, belonging to the literature of the ancient world like Dante's *Divina commedia* and Goethe's *Faust*, and, like both these mighty all-embracing works, striving to explain the deepest secrets of existence, to solve the ultimate mysteries of life'. The assessment of even a Semitist like Cornill and his contemporaries, however, was but a glimpse of the truth. As we may appreciate one of our magnificent mediaeval abbeys from the ruins in which there is still something of the nobility of the original which defies spoliation and decay, so in the book of Job the imperishable beauty and truth, which still delight and inspire, lay upon us the obligation to restore with renewed energy whenever new scientific insights give us the means of doing so. In the case of the book of Job, the moment is ripe for such restoration.

First this is demanded by fresh insights into analogous texts from Mesopotamia[1] and a new appraisal of Egyptian Wisdom literature.[2] G. Fohrer's

1. Stamm 1946; Nougayrol 1952; van Dijk 1953: 119ff.; Kramer 1953; Kuschke 1956; Gese 1958: 63ff. Relevant texts are conveniently published by Lambert 1960. See further below.

recognition of the use and adaptation of Hebrew literary forms in Job is a significant new contribution, affecting not only the argument of the author but also the composition of his work and the recognition of redaction (Fohrer 1963a). The discovery of an Aramaic targum of Job at Qumran (11QtargJob) from the latter half of the second century BCE (van der Ploeg and van der Woude 1971), the earliest known version of the book of Job, permits a reassessment of the Hebrew text and of the later versions. C.J. Gadd's study of the inscriptions of the Neobabylonian King Nabona'id at Harran (Gadd 1955) has given evidence for the presence of the king and probably Jewish garrisons in the oases of the Hejaz already established by the time of the appearance of the book of Job, which is supported by an Aramaic fragment from Qumran published by J.T. Milik (1956) that refers to the association of Nabona'id with Jews in the Hejaz. We would question A. Guillaume's use of this evidence to support his thesis of the provenance of the book of Job from this community in the Hejaz and the reflection of their Hebrew–Arabic bilingualism in the many Arabic cognates in the book (Guillaume 1944 and 1963), which must certainly be modified by the recognition of cognates in Akkadian, Assyrian, Ugaritic, Aramaic and Syriac often in common with Guillaume's 'Arabisms'. Nevertheless, those texts widen the horizon reflected in the book of Job, which in fact we expect in the dispersion of the Jews after the Babylonian Conquest. The time is ripe, too, to apply our new knowledge of the literature of Canaan from Ras Shamra, with its grammatical features, poetic diction and imagery, to the many linguistic and textual problems in Job. The contribution of such Ugaritic experts as M.J. Dahood (1962) and M.H. Pope (1965) to the specific problems of Job is most welcome, though all Ugaritic experts would admit that this matter should be very critically handled.

These are the outstanding, though not the only, advances in the scientific field of OT language and literature and related studies which have permitted an impressive reconstruction of this great memorial of Hebrew thought and literature. It is the conviction that it is now possible to effect this reconstruction to such a remarkable degree of fullness and enhanced elucidation that prompts the present study.

2. For a survey of the Egyptian material with full appraisal, see Schmid 1966: 8-84, 202-23.

Chapter 2

Job in the Context of Near Eastern Wisdom Literature

Jewish tradition associated wisdom with Solomon, and it is significant that this period is characterized by a marked degree of humanism and cosmopolitan interest in Israel. Solomon ruled a kingdom which lay athwart lines of communication between Mesopotamia and Egypt and included the head of the Gulf of Aqaba, which was so vital to the mercantile kingdoms of South Arabia and Egypt, as evidenced by the visit of the Queen of Sheba. It was important that an official class should be trained to deal with foreign correspondence in affairs of state both at home and in diplomatic activity abroad. The marriage of Solomon and a daughter of the Pharaoh is evidence of this new involvement of Israel. Consequently the 'wise men' (*ḥ^{a}ḵāmîm*), on whom the training of the administrative class devolved, were more and more interested in the educational traditions of Mesopotamia and Egypt, both in the methods and objectives of the older sages and in their works.

Characteristic of the sapiential tradition both of Mesopotamia from the Sumerian domination in the third millennium BCE and of Egypt was the scientific interest in nature and society, which is attested by lists of phenomena according to their classification. Thus plants, animals, minerals, tools, equipment, clothes, adornment, food, drink, buildings, etc., are so listed, and society is classified according to professions both in Sumerian[1] and Egyptian texts (Gardiner 1947). Such texts had doubtless great value in giving young scribes practice in writing in the complicated cuneiform syllabic script and ideogram and in hieroglyphics, but they had a deeper significance. They are evidence of belief in a divinely appointed Order in nature and society, which the Egyptians called *ma'at*, and of a serious effort to recognize evidences of this Order and inculcate a respect for it. H.H. Schmid in fact speaks of such lists and wisdom texts compiled under the same presupposition as having the purpose of initiation of the students into this Order (Schmid 1966: 21-22). The use of

1. Chiera 1929; Matous 1933; Schmid 1966: 95ff. The actual classification is the contribution of the Sumerians. The Semitic Akkadians used the lists on the basis of Sumerian-Akkadian lexical tables.

classified lists of phenomena of this type in Israel is no doubt the factual source of the tradition of Solomon's encyclopaedic nature-lore (1 Kgs 5.12-13 [EVV 5.32-33]) (Alt 1937).

In the Book of Job the citation of instances of God's power and providence in the earth (38.4-7) and sea (38.8-11), the disposition of the day (38.12-15), and floods and storms (38.35-38), and in certain animals grouped according to their particular properties, such as the freedom of the wild ass (39.5-8), the untameable nature of the wild ox (39.9-12), the speed of the ostrich (39.13-18), etc., is probably a poetic development of such a classified list. In this case, in view of the belief in a Divine Order which underlies such lists in the Sumerian, Egyptian and Hebrew wisdom tradition, the implication of the Divine Declaration in Job 38.2–39.30 and its relevance to the problem of the relation of Job in his unmerited suffering to the Divine Order which his faith assumed is obvious.

The grouping of phenomena in nature and society according to their affinities made sages in Mesopotamia and Egypt aware also of their differentiae. Such a preoccupation with the differentiae as a problem in the context of belief in the Divine Order may be reflected in the controversial dialogue between different parties such as Summer and Winter (van Dijk 1953), Dumuzu and Enkidu, the shepherd and the farmer (*ANET*, 41ff.), and the Palm and the Tamarisk (Lambert 1960: 150ff.), where each vaunts its own advantages and criticizes the attributes and assets of the other. This reflects the exercise of value judgments and the tendency to seek evidence for the Divine Order not only in harmony but in tension between opposites. The dispute between the Palm and the Tamarisk suggests at once a rough analogy in Jotham's fable of the trees in Judg. 9.7-15, which is probably not an isolated instance of such a text in Israel.

Not only natural phenomena might be collated according to their affinities and differentiae; situations in human relationships might be also so presented. This was done in proverbs, where situations might be presented with or without imagery, usually with respect to the relationship of cause and effect. A general truth might be so expressed or a collection of proverbs might express various facets of the truth that are mutually complementary, as often in the presentation of proverbs in antithetic couplets in the Book of Proverbs, especially in Proverbs 10–15. This convention was employed to a very much more limited extent in Mesopotamia.

Proverb collections are numerous in the Sumerian sapiential tradition in Southern Mesopotamia (Kramer 1956: 152-59; Gordon 1959), where again they attest the recognition of the Divine Order and the effort to adjust the philosophy and behaviour of society to conform to it in the developing situation. In the OT even in an early section of Proverbs, for instance chs. 10–15, we notice in the sharp antithesis between wisdom and folly, and between good and evil conduct and their consequences, a sharper challenge to the individual and a more determined effort not only to recognize God's Order, but to bring humans into conformity with it.[2] This doubtless is a consequence of the adaptation of the wisdom tradition of the Near East to the ethos and faith of the Covenant community by emphasizing empiric moral facts and experiences.

The stability of the existing order is also the concern of certain texts from Mesopotamia, such as the Instruction of the antediluvian Shuruppak to his son Ziusudra the survivor of the Flood (Lambert 1960: 92-95), or the Counsels of Wisdom (pp. 96-107), and from Egypt the Instruction for the Pharaoh Merikare (Thomas 1958: 155-61), the Precepts of Anii (*ANET*, 420ff.), the Pleading of the Eloquent Peasant (*ANET*, 407-10) and the Teaching of Amenemope (*ANET*, 421-25). These either advocated to the ruler the principles to be observed in government or made clear to future administrators the Order in nature and society which they were to labour to realize.

In all this matter a Divine Order was accepted, *ME* in Sumerian, *ma'at* in Egyptian, which might have been expressed in Hebrew either by *ṣeḏeq*, 'what is right and proper',[3] and secondarily 'justice', or by *mišpāṭ*, properly 'the government', or 'order' sustained by the divine ruler.[4] In this context in proverbs and precepts emphasis was laid on the general principle of cause and effect, sin and retribution, virtue and reward, as in the conventional wisdom tradition in the OT represented by Proverbs and by Job's interlocutors.

However, from an early age, sages in Egypt and Mesopotamia were embarrassed by the fact that in actual experience the Order in which they believed (and of which they saw so much evidence in nature and society) was apparently disrupted by occasional vicissitudes. In Egypt for instance the security and assurance concerning the Order, of which the state and cult in the Old Kingdom (third millennium BCE) was held to be the expression, was disrupted by the eclipse of the state at the Amorite Invasion in the First Intermediate Period of Egyptian history (c. 2300–2050 BCE). This uncertainty is reflected in such a text as the Dialogue of a Man with his Own Soul (*DOTT*, 162-67), partly in prose and partly in verse, on the apparent lack of moral order in the world and the pointlessness of life, the note on which the Dialogue in Job opens (ch. 3), with Job's abjuration of the day he was born. There is of course an essential difference; the two texts are in dialogue form, but the Egyptian text, where the man is tempted to commit suicide—which Job never contemplates—is prompted by the general social situation, while the Book of Job expresses the intense personal agony of one deeply involved in an acute

2. This is well emphasized by Schmid 1966: 150ff.

3. Ringgren (1947: 49, 58) recognizes the correspondence of *ma'at* to Hebrew *ṣᵉḏāqāh*; so Horst (*RGG*³, 1404) and Schmid (1966: 159), who notes the correspondence of Hebrew *'āśāh ṣeḏeq* to, for example, *'ry ma'at*, signifying the creative function of humanity and society in the upholding of *ma'at* order.

4. This translation of Hebrew *mišpāṭ* must be emphasized as basic in view of the significance of the cognate *ṯpṭ* in Ugaritic in parallelism with *mlk* ('king') and *zbl* ('prince') in the Ras Shamra texts.

crisis of personal belief. Fundamentally, however, the problems of the writers of both texts were the same, the discrepancy between experiential facts and the Divine Order in which both believed.

In Mesopotamia too this discrepancy was felt, and it is expressed in several texts which recall the theme and indeed the diction of the Book of Job. One of these in fact is popularly known as 'the Babylonian Job', though the affinity is more formal and superficial than real.[5]

This work (Lambert 1960: 21-62), which begins with the words *ludlul bēl nēmeqi* ('I will praise the lord of wisdom'), is known from copies of a text of four tablets (c. 500 lines) from Ashurbanipal's library at Nineveh, the original probably going back to the fifteenth century BCE. This is not a dialogue, but a song of praise for deliverance from various troubles. The list of these, to be sure, is reminiscent of the sufferings of Job, and the phraseology of both works has much in common. Thus the sufferer complains like Job that he is forsaken by his gods though he has been scrupulous in his religious and social duties. Arguing from his sufferings to sin, like Job's orthodox friends, he complains:

> I wish I knew that these things were pleasing to one's god!
> What is proper to oneself is an offence to one's god,
> What in one's own heart seems despicable is proper to one's god. Who knows the will of the gods in heaven?
> Who understands the plans of the underworld gods?
> Where have mortals learned the way of a god?

The sufferer is popularly shunned like Job under the impression that he is under the divine curse, which was anciently believed to be infectious:

> My city frowns on me as an enemy;
> Indeed my land is savage and hostile.
> My friend has become foe,
> My companion has become a wretch and a devil.
> In his savagery my comrade denounces me,
> Constantly my associates furbish their weapons.
> My intimate friend has brought my life into danger;
> My slave has publicly cursed me in the assembly.
> My house (   ) the mob has defamed me,
> When my acquaintance sees me, he passes me by on the other side.
> My family treats me as an alien.

5. This is generally recognized. Thus M. Buttenwieser (1922: 10) rightly states 'this text lacks all the essential points that give the Job story its distinctive character'. But his criticism refers only to the narrative framework of the Book of Job, and so fails to reckon seriously with the real affinities of this and other Mesopotamian texts of this type. Those texts are of the utmost value for a comparative study of the literature and thought of Israel in the ancient Near East, but it is of the essence of comparative study that more than one instance should be cited, and that due significance should be attached to such affinities as may be established, so that the distinctive characteristics may be appreciated. J.J. Stamm (1946: 19) shows a better appreciation as well as due reserve in asking if this work brings us into the forecourt of the OT, especially the Book of Job.

Compare Job 19.13-17:

> My brothers have withdrawn far,
> My acquaintances are strangers to me,
> My kinsmen and friends have deserted me,
> The sojourners in my house have forgotten me,
> Yea, my slave-girls treat me as an outsider,
> I am a stranger in their eyes.
> I have called to my slave, and he does not answer me,
> I have to entreat him with my own mouth.
> My breath is repugnant to my wife,
> And I am putrid to my own children.

Another feature common to the two works is the statement of innocence:

> Yet I myself was thinking only of prayer and supplication;
> Supplication was my concern, sacrifice my rule;
> The day of the worship of the gods was my delight,
> The day of my goddess's procession was my profit and wealth… (cf. Job 29.7-17).

This close correspondence incidentally may indicate that the author of the Book of Job was familiar with this and similar Mesopotamian texts, for example the 'Babylonian Theodicy' (see below, pp. 10-15), but the explanation is that in this particular both these texts and the Book of Job reflect the conventional language of the Plaint of the Sufferer in fast-liturgies in Mesopotamia and Israel, and are variants of this common literary type.[6] The Babylonian sufferer in such texts is never confronted by God except through a dream-revelation, nor does he, like Job, challenge such an encounter. In fact his hope of relief is quickened by a dream, and in the text cited he is freed from all his diseases by 'the lord of wisdom', that is Marduk, the lord of exorcism. This sudden relief may have suggested the complete rehabilitation of Job in the epilogue to the book (Job 42.7-17), which of course is quite external to the theological substance of the complete Book of Job.[7] In this Babylonian text the essential difference from the Book of Job is obvious in spite of undeniable affinities. The closest affinity of the Babylonian text with the OT is with the Plaint of the Sufferer in the Psalms, both in form and in content. These list the sufferings of the subject in similar hyperbole, posing also the problem of the suffering of one who can confidently state his

6. So Dhorme (1926: lxxxvi), who, however, fails to recognize all the characteristic elements in the Mesopotamian genre and the possibility that the author of Job deliberately adapted it.

7. H. Gese (1958: 63ff.), recognizing the 'happy ending', categorizes such texts as *Klagehörungs*-paradigms ('the type "the Plaint of the Sufferer" heard'). He recognizes three main elements, the statement of the sufferer's unhappy situation, his plaint and his relief, and goes on to suggest that the Job-tradition which was the source or the extant Book of Job conformed to this type, the author retaining the theme of the first and final components of the prototype, but adapting the plaint as a controversy in the Dialogue in the book.

exemplary conduct. Both record their deliverance by God, to whom vows are made and paid (see Lambert 1960: 61, ll. 91ff.; cf. Ps. 107.22), and thanks are rendered. The theme of such Mesopotamian texts in fact is that of Psalm 107 with its list of sufferings and its refrain:

> They cried unto the Lord in their trouble,
> And he delivered them from their distress.

Significantly, both these texts include a hymn of praise to God for his deliverance and all his great works (Ps. 107.32ff.; cf. Lambert 1960: 59-61, ll. 33ff.). More specifically, since like the Mesopotamian texts and Job it is conscious of the problem of the theodicy, Psalm 34 may be cited, beginning like the Mesopotamian text with the theme of praise:

> I will bless the Lord at all times,
> His praise shall continually be in my mouth.

The discussion of the moral problem of an innocent orphan wronged in an order believed to be under the government of just gods is presented in dialogue in the 'Babylonian Theodicy' (Lambert 1960: 63-91), known from texts in Ashurbanipal's library but dating from c. 1000 BCE.

The text opens with the miserable case of the orphan bereft of his parents by the act of God, which recalls the problem stated by Job (3.23):

> (Why is light given) to a man whose way is hidden,
> And about whom God has set obstructions?

The answer in the 'Babylonian Theodicy' is that of orthodox theology: death is the common lot of all, but

> He who waits on his god has a protecting angel,
> The humble man who fears his god accumulates wealth...

Compare the words of Eliphaz in Job 4.7-8:

> Recall, what man if innocent ever perished?
> Or where were the upright ever cut off ?

In contradiction, the Babylonian sufferer cites his sufferings in all their varied detail, with which we are familiar in Job and the Plaint of the Sufferer in the Psalms and in Mesopotamian fast-liturgies. This evokes a rebuke from his friend:

> But you (   ) your balanced reason like a madman,
> You make (your   ) diffuse and irrational...

Compare the preface to the speech of Eliphaz in Job 4.4-5:

> Your words would raise the fallen,
> Would strengthen bowing knees;
> But now when it reaches you you cannot bear it,
> And when it comes to you you are non-plussed.

Like Job's friends the friend of the Babylonian sufferer can simply reiterate the traditional doctrine of retribution and reward, which the sufferer counters by citing the fact of the prosperity of the impious:

> The savage lion who devoured the choicest flesh,
> Did it bring its flour-offering to appease-the goddess's anger?
> ( ) the nouveau riche who has multiplied his wealth,
> Did he weigh out precious gold for the goddess Mami?
> (Have I) held back offerings? I have prayed to my god,
> (I have) pronounced the blessing over the goddess's regular sacrifice...

Compare Job 21.7-13:

> Why do the wicked live,
> Prosper and grow mighty in power?
> Their seed is established in their presence,
> And their offspring stand fast before their eyes;
> Their houses are safe from fear,
> No rod of God is on *them*;
> Their bull engenders without fail,
> Their cow calves and does not cast her calf.
> They send forth their little ones like a flock,
> And their children skip about;
> They sing to the timbrel and the lyre,
> And make merry to the sound of the pipe.
> They finish their days in prosperity,
> And go down to Sheol in peace.

The friend of the Babylonian sufferer nevertheless reasserts the principle of reward and retribution and urges that the ways of God are beyond scrutiny:

> You are as stable as the earth; but the plan of God is remote...

Compare Job 36.26–37.24:

> Behold God is great, and we know him not;
> The number of his years is unsearchable.
> Lo, God is great beyond our knowledge,
> The number of his years is unsearchable...
> To the Almighty we cannot attain,
> Great in power and justice...
> Wherefore let men fear him;
> He does not regard any who are wise in their own conceit.

The debate in the 'Babylonian Theodicy' ends with the friend's concession that the social disorders are the result of human nature created and tolerated by the gods, and the sufferer is content with the prospect of his friend's sympathy and the hope of the god's eventual mercy. The ultimate result is the same as in Job, but is much more facile. The Mesopotamian sage with academic detachment acquiesces in the situation; the theologian in Job agonizes over the paradox of the suffering of the innocent and the Order of God, and finally finds satisfaction in the fact that though God gives no answer which is intellectually satisfying he is not aloof from the sufferer. The traditional view that suffering implied sin and alienation from God was exploded in the conclusion of Job, and when the sufferer in Job rose above this traditional fatalism he found fresh hope in the living fellowship of God:

> As the ear hears I had heard of you,
> But now my eye has seen you.

Another such text is that published by J. Nougayrol (1952) as 'Une version ancienne du "Juste Souffrant" ', hereafter cited according to its enumeration in the Louvre AO 4462. This text, from the sixteenth century, is fragmentary. Nougayrol considers that it began with a description of the prosperity of the subject, the loss of which he deplores, and with the description of his calamity. This would suggest an analogy with the Prologue in Job. The actual text begins with a statement by his friend supporting the description of the subject's sufferings. The sufferer then states his innocence, mentioning the support of his friend in his affliction:

> Does brother not belong to brother?
> Is a friend not bitten when his friend is bitten?

Job may refer to this traditional role of the friend in such a text as this in his animadversion on his friends' lack of sympathy in 6.14ff.:

> He who withdraws his loyalty from his friend
> Forsakes the fear of the Almighty.

The sufferer then states that in spite of his adversity he has remained faithful to his god. He acknowledges his god's blessings which he has enjoyed and of which he is now deprived, as Job remembers his former blessing (ch. 29), with which he contrasts his present misery (ch. 30). In this also the Babylonian sufferer is supported by his friend.

Then the sufferer's plaint is heard and his faith vindicated in a Divine Declaration:

> Thy démarche is worthy of a man.
> Thy heart is innocent.

This strikingly recalls the divine approval of the words of Job in 42.7, referring, we believe, to the source material of the Dialogue of the present Book of Job, which the writer has adapted. The god continues:

> The years are fulfilled, the days have redeemed thy suffering.
> Hadst thou not been called to life, how wouldst thou have come
> to the end of this serious illness?
> Thou hast known anguish, fear in its full extent.
> Until the end hast thou borne thy heavy load.
> The way was blocked; it is open to thee.

> The road is levelled; grace is granted to thee.
> In the future forget not thy god,
> Thy creator when thou hast recovered thy health.

Nougayrol considers that the text ended with a description of the rehabilitation of the sufferer, but here the text is fragmentary. Apart from the affinities of thought and expression with the Book of Job which have been noted above, there is a striking affinity in pattern in the initial disaster after prosperity, the plaint of the sufferer describing his grief in detail, the protestation of innocence and the Divine Declaration heralding the rehabilitation of the sufferer. The differences between this text with its happy ending and the Book of Job are at once apparent, of course, but the epilogue in the Book of Job (42.11-12) agrees with the Mesopotamian text, and the divine approval of the words of Job in 42.7 indicates that the present Dialogue has been considerably adapted from a source which after H. Gese we believe to have been the literary prototype of the source of the Book of Job, probably mediated through the Plaint of the Sufferer,[8] which is attested in the OT in the Psalms, notably, so far as concerns this subject Psalms 37 and 73, and in Jeremiah and Lamentations. That there was such a literary type to serve as an ultimate source for the Book of Job is indicated by a Sumerian text from c. 2000–1700 published by J.J.A. van Dijk in 1953 (see van Dijk 1953 and Kramer 1955).

Like the text *ludlul bēl nēmeqi* ('I will praise the lord of wisdom') and Psalm 34, the text opens with the exhortation to the man to praise constantly the exaltation of his god, which suggests Job's sentiment (1.21):

> Yahweh gave, Yahweh has taken;
> Blessed be the name of Yahweh,

and the advice of Elihu to Job (36.24):

> Remember to extol his work
> Of which men have sung.

The text continues with the call to the sufferer, 'a man' (cf. Job 1.1, 'There was a man…'), to state his plaint to God. He is aided by his wife and friends, as the wife and friends of Job in the source used by the writer of our present Book of Job may have abetted Job in his occasional questioning of God's moral order, as Job 2.9 and 42.7 indicate—though, as 42.7 suggests, Job, like the Mesopotamian sufferer, resists the temptation to let this note predominate. As in the other texts cited above, the sufferer, like Job in ch. 31, exculpates himself of social sins, and addresses his plaint to his god, hoping for relief.

8. This well exemplifies the peculiar adaptation of literary types in the book of Job from the situation with which they were traditionally associated, which Fohrer has noted as an original feature of the method of the author of the Book of Job in his *Studien zum Buch Hiob* (1963b: esp. pp. 70ff.), which may certainly be said to have given a new orientation to the study of the book with very fruitful results.

The text ends with the statement that his god had 'heard the right words of the suppliant' and had rehabilitated him, turning his sufferings into joy. The Mesopotamian prototype indicates that the epilogue in Job is simply a survival of the writer's source which he did not adapt as he did the Dialogue, conscious no doubt of the value of his source for those not sufficiently mature to appreciate the searching philosophy of the Dialogue.

H. Gese (1958) has admirably emphasized the affinity and difference between the Book of Job and those wisdom texts of Mesopotamia. The connection between the situation of the sufferer and sins of omission and commission which they emphasize according to the conventional ethical theory of the day is voiced by Job's friends (4.8ff.; 5; 8; 15.17ff.; 18.1ff.; 20), even though the divine economy in the moral order is admitted to be inscrutable; Job's friends also represent the Mesopotamian wisdom tradition in emphasizing the limitation of humans before the Almighty and Omniscient (4.17–21; 15.2-16; 25), and in their urge to Job to cast himself on God's mercy (5.8-22; 22.21ff.). All these traditional positions are disputed by the author of Job. He questions the conventional faith in the theodicy (Job 6.15ff.; 13.1ff.; 16.2ff.; 19; 21); the insignificance of a human before God reflects on God, who condescends to inquisition and affliction with such a one (7; 9-10), and whether Job must finally abase himself before the Almighty and inscrutable. If Job must do this he has at least maintained his innocence (16.18-19; 31) and won the assurance that he is not beneath the notice of God.

Those texts from the sages of Egypt and Mesopotamia by no means exhaust the sapiential material available to the sages of Israel; they are only those most relevant to the Book of Job. Affinities of thought and phraseology are striking, though the sense of the whole differs markedly from Job's bold, almost blasphemous questioning of the divine economy. What is most important, however, is the affinity between the Mesopotamian texts and the Book of Job in literary form or pattern, within which the writer of Job adapted the tenor of what we believe to be his prototype. This will be largely the theme of our study of the Composition of the Book of Job (see below, pp. 56-75).

Common to those Mesopotamian texts, as to the other sapiential texts we have cited both from Mesopotamia and Egypt, is the assumption of a Divine Order in which all in nature and society is integrated. Those texts that most resemble the Book of Job reveal in some degree the embarrassment of their authors in face of reality, for instance the suffering of the innocent with the consequent impairing of their moral potential, which seems to contradict the Divine Order. The unpalatable fact of the suffering of the innocent, which contradicts the ethical principle of retribution and reward in the Divine Order, is not equally prominent in all the Mesopotamian texts cited. The emphasis on this element seems to depend on the nature of the text. In *ludlul bēl nēmeqi*, for instance, the opening and conclusion obviously suggest a text intimately related to the cult, that is to say not a wisdom text proper. Here the suffering of the innocent and the moral problem it raises is frankly admitted, but it is connected with the confession, or in this case the protestation, of the worshipper's innocence, and serves to emphasize his dependence on the grace of God. On the other hand, the problem of the suffering of the innocent is much more emphasized in the 'Babylonian Theodicy', where the sufferer to be sure finally depends on God's grace, but that dependence is acquiescence rather than real faith. This, as the sharp dialectic indicates, is a wisdom text proper. It is not so easy to decide the nature of the other two, though the introduction of the sufferer in 'the Sumerian Job' as 'a man' rather indicates a wisdom text serving a philosophic discussion of a hypothetical case, even though, like certain wisdom psalms in the OT, for example Psalms 22, 37 and 73, it takes the form of a cultic text. In this case, as in those psalms in the OT, the fact that the emphasis falls not on the problem of the suffering of the innocent but on the revelation of God's grace indicates that the purpose of the text was not to accentuate the problem but to defend the belief in God's Order by seeking a solution beyond philosophy in religion. This is the solution also in the Book of Job, though both the problem and the religious experience in which a solution is found are much more intensive than in any of the Mesopotamian texts. All those texts indicate how intimately wisdom in the ancient Near East was connected with religion. The 'Babylonian Theodicy', which is so strongly critical and most humanist in character, still concludes with acquiescence to the Divine Order. The text *ludlul bēl nēmeqi*, which is the most liturgic, seeks first, like the author of the Book of Job, to solve the moral problem by humanistic argument before finally seeking the answer in religion. The problem is posed, as we have seen, by the observation:

> What is proper to oneself is an offence to one's god...
> Where have mortals learnt the way of a god?

But this is also a statement of the relative nature of humanity and its system of values, a philosophic argument cited in defence of the Divine Order, which is accepted as absolute.

It is to be noted that Job, though embarrassed by the discrepancy between the justice of humans (with its principle of sin and retribution and virtue and reward) and the justice of God, does not quite abandon his belief in the Order of God and the validity of the human conception of justice within it. Otherwise there would be no point in his reiterated appeal for a hearing in open tribunal with God. Like the Mesopotamian writers, the author of Job finds the final solution in religion. Only in Job is the orthodox doctrine of the theodicy subjected to a more thorough and severe criticism, so that the sufferer is isolated with his God beyond all social conventions and doctrine to find the solution of his moral problem in that living confrontation and communion beyond the limitations of tradition in religion. Again the answer to the problem of Job, as in its Mesopotamian counterparts, is given in the Divine Declaration, where the sufferer is assured of communion with God. But, as distinct from the Mesopotamian texts, God in Job so far respects the capacity of the sufferer as to give him sufficient evidence to make a solution of his problem at least partly intelligible intellectually, though full conviction is the result of his existential experience of the living God.

The Mesopotamian matter which we have cited suggests such a prototype for the source of the Book of Job, though the saga style of the Prologue and Epilogue rather suggest a popular version of such a work. That literary works of this character from Mesopotamia were not unknown in Palestine is now indicated by a fragment of the Gilgamesh Legend from the thirteenth century found at Megiddo.[9] More relevant to the present subject, Mesopotamian sapiential texts are among more recent discoveries at Ras Shamra. Akkadian and Sumerian wisdom texts have been found in the vicinity of the palace at Ras Shamra. The texts found include proverbs (Nougayrol 1968: 273-300), fragments of the Gilgamesh Legend (pp. 300-10), which is also a sapiential text despite its epic form, and, what is particularly relevant to our problem of the innocent sufferer, a text from c. 1300 in Akkadian script and language (pp. 264-73) which carries it back to the age of Hammurabi in the opinion of Nougayrol (pp. 266f.).

The new text most closely resembles *ludlul bēl nēmeqi* among the Mesopotamian texts cited. It opens by presenting the sufferer as non-plussed; neither oracles nor the consulting of livers and entrails nor omens nor dreams explain his sufferings with relation to his deserts nor indicate an end to them. His nearest kinsmen implore him to bow to his fate (cf. Job's wife), while at the same time offering him solace. Nevertheless they mourn him as one whose ill is irremediable.

Significantly, in view of the affinity with *ludlul bēl nēmeqi*, the sufferer anticipates revival through the grace of Marduk. The anticipated relief suggests again the theme of his sufferings, and here the language is reminiscent of Job and the Plaint of the Sufferer in the Psalms:

> I knew no more dreams, and sleep no longer embraced me,
> I lay all the night awake;[10]
> In the midst of my dreams the grave ever dogged me;
> I was ever the prey of the ill I had suffered...[11]
> For sustenance I had tears instead of food.[12]

As Job blesses the name of the Lord even under the stroke of calamity (Job 1.20), the sufferer, like the author of *ludlul bēl nēmeqi*, praises Marduk, without whom, he confesses, he would have had no breath to voice his plaint.

9. See Goetze and Levy 1959. The Gilgamesh Epic, despite its form and entertainment value, is nevertheless a humanist text on the sapiential subject of the natural limitations of humans despite the high aspirations of 'the glory, jest and riddle of the world'.

10. Cf. Job 7.4.

11. Cf. Job 7.13-15.

12. Cf. Job 3–24; Ps. 42.3.

The very consciousness of suffering is evidence of the care of his god. Job never makes this declaration of faith in the biblical book, but it is voiced by Eliphaz in his argument 'Happy is the man whom God reproves...' (Job 5.17-21), which like the Ugaritic text freely admits the ill to which humanity is subject, but holds firm faith in the grace of God. The intensification of suffering as evidence of the persistent grace of God is also the theme of Elihu's argument in the addendum to the Book of Job (chs. 32–37) in Job 33.14-30, culminating in the declaration (33.29-30):

> Behold, God has done all these things,
> Twice, three times with a man,
> To bring back his soul from the pit
> That he may see the light of life.

The declaration of faith leads on to praise of the sufferer's god.

The conception of the sufferer finding the solution to his troubles, even against the evidence of facts, in praise of God is familiar in the Book of Job, not only in Job's heroic blessing of the name of God in his utter destitution (Job 1.20), but in the speech of Elihu (32.6–37.4), in the undertones of hymns of praise inspired by the New Year liturgy with its central theme of the Kingship and Ordered Government of God (36.5-23; 36.26–37.13) and the explicit injunction (36.24):

> Remember to extol his works
> Of which men have sung.

Though Job is not named in any such text from Ras Shamra, the antiquity of the tradition of the worthy sufferer attested in this sapiential text seems to corroborate the antiquity of the Job-tradition, as indicated in Ezek. 24.14, 20, where Job is associated with Dan'el, now known from the Ugaritic Legend of Aqht as a figure of the heroic past in the second millennium BCE. This association, moreover, is not only an argument for the antiquity of the Job-tradition, but also for its currency in the urban culture of Canaan.

The affinities of the Book of Job with the sophisticated sapiential tradition of Mesopotamia are not to be denied. But what of the characteristics of folk-tale,[13] saga or epic[14] in the Prologue and Epilogue?

13. J. Wellhausen (1914: 207 n. 2) proposed a folk-saga; K. Budde (1896) envisaged this as a *Volksbuch*, but K. Kautzsch (1900) more cautiously proposed that the narrative framework of the Book of Job was the modification of an older folktale rather freely adapted by the author of the Book of Job; so also Hölscher 1937: 4f.

14. N.M. Sarna (1957) in particular noted the regular cadence, verbal repetition, conventional round numbers and rare vocabulary and forms familiar in the poetic epic in the Ras Shamra texts. The same conventions, however, with the exception of the last two features, are also characteristic of the prose of the earlier narrative sources of the Pentateuch, which in turn may have been influenced by the oral tradition of the Canaanite epic.

The view has been widely canvassed that the original of the Book of Job was a popular tradition of a worthy man reduced to destitution, yet maintaining his faith despite the dissuasions of wife and friends until his eventual vindication. This of course is to reverse the roles of Job and his friends in the Dialogue of the extant book (as the divine appraisal of the words of Job and the condemnation of those of his friends in 42.7 may indicate), and to lay the emphasis in their assumed original less on the problem expressed in the Dialogue than on the edifying theme of the fortitude and faith of Job and his final vindication. The Mesopotamian texts we have cited, however, though emphasizing the final deliverance of the sufferer, do not minimize the trial of his faith, with which we are familiar in the arguments of Job. Those texts thus suggest the possibility that the author of the Book of Job had at least available a more sophisticated prototype than the popular folk-tale. This is further suggested by the form of those Mesopotamian texts, the worthy man reduced from his former comfort, his moral impasse, the divine intervention, or theophany, the sufferer's acknowledgment of divine grace. The recognition of those essential elements in the Mesopotamian texts on the same problem as the Book of Job is most important in the debate on the authenticity and significance of corresponding elements in the structure of the Book of Job, particularly the theophany and Divine Declaration, which has been taken as secondary.[15] Nor is the analogy between the Book of Job and the comparable Mesopotamian texts remote and fortuitous. The new text from Ras Shamra is evidence that the Mesopotamian tradition was cultivated also in Canaan two centuries before the time of Solomon, when particularly Israel was introduced to the sapiential prototype. At least one Egyptian wisdom text, the Protest of the Eloquent Peasant on social injustice (*ANET*, 407-10) and the Aramaic Proverbs of Ahiqar (Cowley 1923: 204-48; *ANET*, 427-30) are introduced by an engaging story in narrative prose, though to be sure the Prologue and Epilogue of Job show more characteristic features of oral saga or folk legend. Those are familiar in the stories of the patriarchs in the older narrative sources (J and E) in the Pentateuch, with which the narrative framework of Job has been compared. Such features in the stories of the patriarchs, however, do not preclude their sober, edifying purpose. Thus the story of Joseph, communicated in simple, dramatic, colourful prose, is none the less a wisdom text on the subject of God's providence in the vindication of a worthy sufferer (von Rad 1953; 1958: 272ff.). In view of the theme of the ordeal of the worthy sufferer in the Mesopotamian sapiential tradition as known from the evidence of the new text from Ras Shamra and of the features of popular folk-narrative in the Prologue and Epilogue to the Book of Job, it is possible that there was a

15. Alleging that the Divine Declaration is inconclusive P. Volz (1921) took the Divine Declaration as secondary. J. Hempel (1930: 179) came to the same conclusion on the grounds that it does not sufficiently answer Job's appeal in ch. 31. In the nature of the case, however, in such a critical work as the Book of Job no such simple and satisfying answer can be expected.

popular version of the tradition of the ordeal of the worthy sufferer current in Canaan, probably first adapted as an edifying legend on the theme of the sufferer's fortitude and the final vindication of his faith.

The sapiential original may have been transmitted in oral tradition in the two centuries when the culture of Egypt and Mesopotamia in the cities of Canaan suffered eclipse between the Philistine and Aramaean irruptions (c. 1200 BCE) and the renaissance under Solomon. In this popular form the Job legend was apparently first adapted in Hebrew tradition and may have gained currency along with the patriarchal traditions, particularly that of Joseph, with the teachings of the sages of Israel. The citation of Job as a figure of remote antiquity like Noah and Dan'el, of exemplary righteousness (Ezek. 14.14) and of saving efficacy (Ezek. 14.20; cf. Job 42.8), indicates that the popular version of Job, including Prologue and Epilogue, at least to 42.11, was current until the middle of the sixth century BCE. However, the sages also knew the literary prototype in the Mesopotamian tradition of the worthy sufferer, which they elaborated with emphasis rather on the moral problem of the Dialogue than the final vindication in the Epilogue. The role of Job in the Dialogue as first adapted in the Hebrew tradition (Job 42.7, on which Alt based his view that the roles of Job and his friends in the present form of the book were reversed) is quite ambiguous. The passage might indeed indicate that Job maintained his faith and the orthodox doctrine against the criticisms of the friends; but it might equally well indicate the divine disgust at the too facile acceptance of the traditional faith and ethic, with the friends' wilful dismissal of the facts in defence of orthodox doctrine, which was actually a limitation of the government of God (Gordis 1965: 305), and the divine approval of Job's franker approach and deeper concern. It is significant that in the new text from Ras Shamra the friends of the sufferer, in urging him to bow to his fate, comforting him and mourning for him as if foredoomed to death, play the same role as in the Prologue and Dialogue in Job. The fact that the sufferer's spiritual agony, though not so acute or sustained as in the Book of Job, was already expressed in the Mesopotamian texts we have cited, and indeed was familiar in the tradition of Israel in the Plaint of the Sufferer in the fast-liturgy, suggests that this is seriously to be reckoned with in the immediate source of the present Book of Job. In the latter the greater intensity of the author's concern for the moral problem of the suffering of the worthy man is expressed by the concentration of the criticism of the orthodox position in the person of Job in the Dialogue, and of the arguments for the conventional faith in the ripostes of Job's friends. This quasi-dramatic arrangement, which results in a more systematic marshalling of theses and antitheses, is peculiarly the contribution of the author of Job and is symptomatic of the tradition of the sages which finds more pointed expression in the Elihu addendum (Job 32–37).

The Mesopotamian texts end in rehabilitation or the revelation of the divine favour; in the theophany in Job no such rehabilitation is visualized, but God's answer is a challenge. This in itself is sufficient evidence that the subject is not alienated by his suffering as the orthodox ethic assumed. So long as humans are confronted by God their suffering is bearable in the purpose of the eternal, which they may glimpse in the prospect of wonders beyond wonders that speak of the concern of God for all his creation and leave even the fullest revelation of God that humans have experienced unexhausted and inexhaustible.

Chapter 3

JOB IN HEBREW WISDOM

The Book of Job is included in the third part of the OT canon, the Writings, where, with Proverbs and Ecclesiastes, it is regarded as comprising that part of Hebrew Wisdom which was accepted as canonical.

The humanistic character of wisdom (*ḥoḵmāh*) in Israel has often been stressed. It is the technical skill of the craftsman such as Bezalel and those associated with him in the building and furnishing of the Tabernacle (Exod. 28.3; 35.25, 31; 36.1) and goldsmiths (Jer. 10.9) and sailors (Ezek. 27.8; Ps. 107.27). It applies to women skilled in lamentation, implying improvisation (Jer. 9.16 [EVV 17]), and to music and psalm-composition (1 Kgs 5.10-12, cf. 1 Chron. 15.19; Ps. 49.4-5 [EVV 3-4]) and soothsaying where real sagacity and resource were usually cloaked under the guise of traditional superstition (Gen. 41.8; Isa. 44.25). Skill in politics in war and peace is also denoted by *ḥoḵmāh* (Isa. 10.13; 29.14; Jer. 49.7). The essentially humanistic or intellectual character of *ḥoḵmāh* is clearly indicated in the account of Solomon's reign. In the tradition of Solomon's dream at Gibeon and its sequel (1 Kgs 3.4ff.), the famous judgment between the two mothers, it denotes the capacity of discernment and the ability to decide a case, like the Arabic verb *ḥakama*, with its participle *ḥākimu(n)* ('governor'). At this time in fact the 'wise' (*ḥ^{a}ḵāmîm*) probably first acquired status in Israel in association with the new governing class in Solomon's administration, and as those engaged, like the scribes in the Egyptian bureaucracy, in preparing young men to succeed them. In the Egyptian analogy, practical knowledge of the details of administration, conduct towards superiors and inferiors and prudential advice to secure and maintain success and to help in emergency were all communicated as the ripe fruits of experience and mature reflection. The ability to observe and classify according respectively to differentiae and affinities was cultivated in Egypt by the observation of natural phenomena and their classification, which is probably the source of the tradition that Solomon 'spoke of the trees, from the cedar that is in Lebanon to the hyssop that grows out of the wall; he spoke also of beasts, and of birds, and of reptiles, and of fish' (1 Kgs 5.13 [EVV 4.33]).[1] This

1. Alt 1953. R.B.Y. Scott (1955) emphasizes rather the significance of Hezekiah's reign in this connection (cf. Prov. 25.11), but admits the possibility of an earlier origin under Solomon.

scientific classification according to common characteristics, which extended beyond nature to society, is exemplified notably in the numerical clusters of common cases in Prov. 30.15-16, 18-19, 21-23, 24-28, 29-31 and in Job in the list of nocturnal criminals (Job 24.13-17) and of the creatures provided for and endowed by God irrespective of human economy (Job 38.39–39.30). In all this discipline the empiric familiarity with facts is essential, and to this extent wisdom was a secular asset, a gift of God perhaps, but to be cultivated by human ingenuity and industry. This wisdom might be in the calculating prudence of the careerist or political opportunist, the *savoir faire* or often the unashamed expediency of the man whom Noth well characterizes as *klug* ('astute') rather than *weise* ('wise'), *ja vielleicht schlau* ('indeed perhaps even cunning') (Noth and Thomas [eds.] 1955: 233), a notable instance of which was the cold cunning of Solomon to which David commended Shimei for vengeance (1 Kgs 2.9). But the 'wise men' (*ḥ^{a}ḵāmîm*) who passed on the fruits of their experience in the Davidic monarchy, for all their worldly wisdom, were really interested in a stable society which was still, in spite of secular developments in the monarchy, a development of the sacral community of Israel. Thus they inculcated the well-tried social virtues of industry, moderation, sexual temperance and religious conformity, which best equipped the individual to be successful because he was responsible and trusted in the community, but also above all preserved that stability of society which was the aim of the state. It must be emphasized that the questioning of the principles conventionally recognized in religion and ethics, which is so distinctive a feature respectively of Ecclesiastes and Job, was no part of Wisdom in this early period of the history of Israel. People must accept the situation in state and society as they found it, seeking by personal example to keep them true to the traditional standards. Insofar as the situation might deteriorate, Ecclesiastes and Job did not vainly inveigh, but counselled patience by sobriety and self-control so that people might survive what they could not immediately amend, or accept the situation with dignity, or even perhaps by their perseverance turn the situation to legitimate account. This is the attitude of Job in the Prologue to the Book, and of his friends in the Dialogue. The writer of the Dialogue through Job is of course much more critical, since he has a much deeper personal involvement.

In animadverting upon the fabric of society towards the end of the monarchy in Judah, Jeremiah (18.18) and Ezekiel (7.26) refer to revelation, divine direction and 'counsel' from prophets, priests and wise men (*ḥ^{a}ḵāmîm*) respectively as vital to the guidance and indeed existence and coherence of the state. Israel had come into being as a sacral community, a covenanted people chosen as the instruments of God's purpose. Its development therefore, whatever secular factors it necessarily involved, was conditioned by the will of its God interpreted through traditional experience conserved and expressed through the institutions of religion, which was the function of the priests, or by fresh revelation from God relevant to the contemporary situation, which was experienced by the prophet and communicated by him to the people. The function of the sage (*ḥāḵām*) was humanistic. He was not the intermediary between humans and God either objectively within the context of the cult as the priest, nor as the direct mediator of an inspired dynamic word as the prophet. To be sure, he felt that he, like the prophet, was guided by the Spirit of God, which gave him insights beyond the common knowledge and prejudices of others; but his experience of the spirit of God did not, as in the case of the prophet, involve him in the compulsive communication of an oracle. His role was to analyse and assess the situation in society, primarily in Israel, but also in a wider context. He was of course heir to the tradition of Israel as a sacral community (von Rad 1958–61: I, 431) with its religious institutions and prophetic communication of the will of God, and his function was to preserve the well-tried social institutions and values, of which the sages of Israel gave due notice in the dictum 'the fear of the Lord is the beginning of wisdom' (Prov. 1.7; 9.10; cf. Job 28.28). However, he was neither ecclesiastic nor prophet, but a shrewd, observant humanist in whom the spirit of God took the form of sanctified sobriety. He studied society, deduced principles of conduct both social and individual, and he related society to its environment in nature, from which he deduced many sound principles which could be profitably applied in society. The references in Jeremiah and Ezekiel attribute 'counsel' (*'ēṣāh*) to the sage as the divine direction (*tôrāh*) was the function of the priest and the divine word (*dāḇār*) was the province of the prophet. 'Counsel' (*'ēṣāh*), however, means more than 'advice' though that is included. Counsel relates also to the purpose of God and may actually denote it, as in Isa. 5.19; 19.17; 46.10; Psalm 33; Job 38.2; 42.3. It denotes also the ability to ascertain it and mediate it and to carry it out. This was ideally the function and privilege of the ancient king as God's vassal or vice-gerent, so that *yô 'ēṣ* may be a royal title (Pedersen 1926: 128), as in the royal titulary in Isa. 9.5 (EVV 6). Insight into the divine plan and purpose and the function of carrying it into effect in the community, though the duty of the royal vice-gerent, might also be discharged by prophets admitted into God's intimate counsel or by sages, who at least in the Davidic monarchy worked to sustain the order in the state and community of Israel, which was of course basically a sacral community. This sober religious undertone in the wisdom of Israel which, for all its wealth of utilitarian precepts, was formerly considered to be the characteristic of Hebrew wisdom (Fichtner 1933: 87ff., 95ff., 123; Baumgartner 1933: 27), has been well emphasized by Ringgren (1947: 127ff.; 1962: 10), von Rad (1958–61: I, 415ff.), Gese (1958: 33ff.) and H.H. Schmid (1966: 3ff.). It is well illustrated in the Book of Job, where the writer, for all his trenchant criticism of the answer of conventional wisdom and piety, feels his way to a solution in the traditional religious experience of Israel.[2] This is reflected in his use of the

2. Baumgartner cites Job as an instance of later Hebrew Wisdom, which was strongly impregnated with religion (1933: 27-29).

forms in which that experience was expressed, the Hymn of Praise, the Oath of Purgation before God and the Plaint of the Sufferer,[3] in the framework of which his problem is posed and answered.

Thus the sage (*ḥāḵām*) in Israel sought by analysis of society in the context of nature and history to discover the purpose of life, or perhaps we should say to verify what religion revealed of that purpose, and to promote and coordinate all forces conducive to it and to discourage all that militated against it.[4] Thus, in their own society of ancient Israel, the sages did what the priests did through the law and what the prophets did through the word, all seeking, each in their own way, to conserve an integrated society according to the will of its God. The sages, however, were more involved in the practical and often mundane problems of the realization of the integrated society. Heirs of the spiritual tradition of Israel, they yet imposed on themselves the limitation of scientific humanism in their moral philosophy, so far as that was possible for sober persons in Israel, where the sage's provision for a sound society had so largely been anticipated by the priest and prophet since the settlement of Israel in Palestine.

In spite of the involvement of the 'wise men' of Israel in the practical problems of the training of an administrative class, they were keenly interested in the moral philosophy of the empiric order, both in the context of their practical function and through their own interest in the fundamental problems of life—an interest which they shared with the professional sages of Egypt. Thus they looked at nature and society in broad perspective and, though aware of the fact of suffering and unrequited sin in a world believed to be under the wise and benevolent government of God Almighty, saw more to support the traditional belief in God's order (*mišpāṭ*) than to contradict it.

So long as the state survived, the community integrated under the king as God's executive was a visible token of God's order, where the traditional communal ethic was upheld. However, on the collapse of the state and the social order this traditional ethic with its balance in favour of the principle of reward and retribution within God's order could no longer be maintained on traditional evidence. But customary views of life die hard, and the long-inured sense of solidarity now found expression as a guilt-complex under which, after the catastrophe of 586 BCE, people were content to accept fatalistically the fact that they were doomed to suffer for their fathers' sins. This attitude, which paralysed moral effort, was apprehended by Ezekiel (ch. 18) as an outstanding danger of his time, and his effort to emancipate the individual from the

3. A. Weiser (1959: 12) relates the thought of the writer in these to the religion of the covenant-community of Israel, speaking of them as the reflection of the writer's 'personal Drama of Salvation' (*persönlicher Heilsgeschichte*). This is none the less true even where those forms are adapted, or even parodied, in Job.

4. So in Egypt de Buck (1922) stresses the purpose of wisdom to recognize and sustain *ma'at*, or Order. H.H. Schmid (1966: 20-24) goes further, maintaining that the cultivation and propagation of wisdom had a creative function with respect to *ma'at*.

trammels of this morality must have been supported by the rediscovery of the Prophets with their critical attitude to institutions, their moral discrimination and their qualification of the current social ethic by their doctrine of the responsive remnant as the object of God's grace in the general doom of the people.

It was natural that in this period Hebrew Wisdom should have endeavoured to apply the principles of the traditional Hebrew ethic, with its insistence on condign rewards and punishments to the individual, as Ezekiel had done in his modification of the principle 'the fathers have eaten sour grapes and the children's teeth are set on the edge'. But however generally applicable this principle might be in effect, even in the case of the individual, its universal validity was obviously impaired by the sufferings of individuals beyond their deserts. The fate of the Jews after the fall of Jerusalem and the triumph of the materialistic power and policy of paganism itself suggests the final inadequacy of the traditional doctrine of reward and punishment.

The inadequacy of the traditional ethic, already felt in certain psalms of the type the Plaint of the Sufferer and by Jeremiah (e.g. 12.1-2), was exposed notably by the writer of the Book of Job, which marks a new departure in Hebrew Wisdom. The writer reaches the positive conclusion that suffering beyond one's deserts bears no invariable relationship to the traditional doctrine of the theodicy and implies no alienation from God, who is still accessible to humans. The sage in Job is sufficiently faithful to the sapiential tradition to counsel not rebellion on the basis of human ego-centric interest and limited knowledge and experience, but acceptance of the situation under the providence of God (of which nature beyond human control or interest provides so many instances) and is prepared to move forward to the ever-fresh encounter with God in response to which humans gain fuller knowledge of the divine nature and purpose. For this purpose, God's intelligent master-plan which motivated his creation (the *ḥokmāh* of Prov. 8.22-31; Job 11.6, 13, 20; 15.8; 28.12ff.) was the business of the sage in Israel to discern in nature and society not only as a clue to the ultimate truth, but as the guide to the practical fulfilment of the life of the individual and society by the legitimate use of life's opportunities in maximum cooperation with the Creator. But the master-key to the knowledge of the purpose of God insofar as it could be known to humanity was the living experience of God himself.

Job is associated with Proverbs and Ecclesiastes in the Wisdom literature of the OT. Apart from a general affinity between the poem on Wisdom in Job 28, which is an interpolation in the Book of Job, and the poem on Wisdom as God's instrument in creation in Prov. 8.22-31 in the latest section of Proverbs, there is little matter for comparative dating common to Job and Proverbs. Nowhere in Proverbs is there a strenuous and sustained preoccupation with a fundamental theme as in Job. Generally such coherence as there is in Proverbs is in the praise of Wisdom, which in the pre-exilic sections of the book is that empirical ability to assess a situation which on its more mundane level amounts to practical *savoir faire* as a key to success in business or administration and on its higher level keeps a person patient in adversity and prevents one compromising one's ideals in a hasty judgment which may abet moral perversity. With this prudential wisdom the writer of Job, with his agonizing problem, has little in common, though as a result of his experience and his ultimate confrontation with God we see that the writer of Job knew the significance of patience in suffering which the sages of Israel taught. From the criticisms of Ecclesiastes we may gather that there were various schools of wisdom among the Jews and various methods of philosophic engagement and communication. Ecclesiastes at the end of the fourth century BCE certainly had its more orthodox contemporaries, whose views are represented probably in the first book of Proverbs (chs. 1–9). Possibly there were more critical views at all periods when wisdom flourished, but in the pre-exilic sections of Proverbs there is no evidence of them, and the view of sin and retribution, virtue and reward which dominates Proverbs is probably a fair index to the dominant philosophy of the sages throughout the Hebrew monarchy. On the basis of experience, the author of Job, like Ecclesiastes, questions the hitherto predominating wisdom tradition, exposing its inadequacy in ruthless dialectic. To hymns of praise extolling God's order in nature and society Job opposes hymns of praise emphasizing the destructive aspect of the rule of God; to didactic poems on the end of the wicked he opposes similar poems on the prosperity of the wicked and the hopeless misery of the poor. He cites edifying proverbs on the theme of sin and retribution and exposes their inadequacy in the light of hard facts. The self-sufficiency of the sages in Proverbs, however, in their practical commission, should not disguise the fact that they were aware of the ultimate imponderables in God's purpose for his creation. To say nothing of the implications of the hymn on Wisdom as God's instrument in creation (Prov. 8.22-31), the theme recurs even in the wisdom of the monarchic period that humans may propose and strive for an end with all their resources and energies but it is God who ultimately disposes in his higher wisdom (Prov. 12.15; 16.1, 2, 25; 21.2). But the preoccupation of the sages with the practical task of education led to their emphasis on the pragmatic potentiality of humans in society. The preoccupation with the problem of the worthy sufferer in Job, however, which called the doctrine of condign punishment and reward in question, occasions a greater emphasis on the ultimate purpose of God's creation which is ultimately beyond human knowledge and control. In the arguments of Job's three friends this is invoked as an argument for patience in suffering and suspension of judgment in the situation of the worthy sufferer or the apparent impunity of the wicked, or it is used as a rebuke to the presumption of Job to criticize the prevailing doctrine of the theodicy. It is used in the statements of Job in the Dialogue to emphasize the transcendence of God beyond all meaningful contact with humans. But ultimately in the author's conclusion in the Divine Declaration it is used, illustrated by instances of God's beneficent providence in nature beyond human control and apart from his convenience, to inspire in the worthy sufferer a new hope, beyond the salutary but inadequate doctrine of retribution and reward, that in the living encounter with the Creator one may discover more of the purpose of life and new tokens of the care of one's God.

Faith in God's moral government and the optimism of current piety had already been questioned, probably during the monarchy, in the psalms which voice the plaint of the community or of the individual on behalf of the community, and which may have been part of the royal liturgy in public fast and penitence. Here the sufferings of the subject were stated, usually with a protestation of innocence; the subject then turned to God and declared one's faith, rendered thanks either for deliverance or in anticipation of it, or else would vow a vow of thanksgiving. The detailed and cumulative enumeration of sufferings, often figurative and hyperbolic, probably derives ultimately from primitive counter-incantations, which are extant in Mesopotamian texts, an essential feature of which was the counteraction of malicious spells by the use of corresponding terms. In the context of the Hebrew Psalms, however, the detailed list of the sufferings enhances the power and grace of God in deliverance experienced or hoped for. Often, however, they express the agony of the subject not merely under the stroke of sufferings, but in doubt of God's moral government. This is the problem of the author of Job, who makes extensive use of the literary type we have just described, a fact which should warn us against the literalistic or biographical interpretation of the poetic dialogue in the book. Unfortunately, it is not possible to date the psalms of this type precisely and while the convention was established during the monarchy (e.g. Ps. 44) it continued long after the Exile.

Psalms of this type, which pose a moral problem to conventional faith, were peculiarly suited to the moral philosophy of the sages of Israel, and Psalms 37 and 49, which like Job show concern about the suffering of the innocent and the prosperity of the wicked, are either sapiential productions or individual thanksgivings, psalms and prayers which have been influenced by the thought and form of wisdom literature. Here, however, the moral problem is not a scandal to faith as in the argument in Job. The prosperity of the wicked is admitted, but it is only for a season and their end is miserable. This is echoed in the arguments of Job's friends, for example, Bildad in the figure of the plant on stony ground which wilts with sunrise (8.16-18) and the statement of Zophar 20.4ff.:

> That the jubilation of the wicked is but for a short time,
> And the joy of the impious but for a moment.

Compare Prov. 24.19-20:

> Fret not yourselves because of evil-doers,
> And be not envious of the wicked,
> For the evil man has no future,
> And the lamp of the wicked is put out.

The last saying is cited by Bildad with approval (Job 18.5-6) and questioned by Job as belied by experience (21.17). The moral scandal of the prosperity of the ungodly, which Job states at length (e.g. 21.7-21), is posed as a problem to the pious in Psalm 73, who confesses that it has been a problem only to humanist philosophy (Ps. 73.2-3, 15-16, 21-22), to be solved in communion with God in worship and in sacrament (Ps. 73.17). The intensely personal character of this psalm suggests a comparatively late period after the rebuilding of the Temple in 516 BCE. It is thus of limited use for the dating of the Book of Job, but the two indicate the intensification of the moral problem of the prosperity of the wicked and the suffering of the innocent, and though the psalmist poses the problem and finds the solution within the context of the cult, which the author of the Book of Job as a humanist denies himself, both reach assurance in communion with God.

The problem of the suffering of the innocent had thus been already set in focus and all the adaptation required by the author of Job was simply to withhold the statement of faith and thanksgiving characteristic of the Plaint of the Sufferer. He thus questions traditional piety as well as traditional ethics, orthodox religion as well as orthodox philosophy, which is done with less intensity, but with more finesse, in Ecclesiastes. The tremendous seriousness of the challenge of the writer of Job to orthodox faith and wisdom and his intense concentration and involvement in contrast to the scientific detachment and diffuse interest of the 'gentle cynic' Ecclesiastes suggests the priority of the writer of Job as the first major thinker seriously to challenge orthodox belief in Israel.

Although the Book of Job is rightly grouped with Proverbs and Ecclesiastes in the OT and is as practical as the former and as critical of orthodox faith and ethics as the latter, it transcends the limits of a strictly sapiential work. Like Ecclesiastes and unlike Proverbs Job is concentrated on a single theme, a man's reaction to unmerited suffering, believed to be caused directly by God. The problem of Job is the paradox of a man created in the image of God, tried beyond endurance yet not allowed to understand the reason or purpose of his suffering or to enjoy the relief of death he so earnestly desired, the natural object of God's special care yet the butt of affliction (Job 7.17-21; cf. Ps. 8), a potential blessing to society (ch. 29), yet having his effectiveness crippled by his calamity which encourages the worst elements, who defy God's order (ch. 30). But, unlike the Book of Ecclesiastes, Job is not the reflection of lectures in the schools in spite of the form of sapiential controversy in which much of the book is cast. There is in fact a distinctive character about the Book of Job that has led a number of scholars[5] to question its nature as a typical sapiential

5. E.g. P. Volz (1911: 25ff.), J. Fichtner (1933), J. Baumgartner (1933: 187ff.). M. Buttenwieser (1922: 38-40) characterized Job as a drama of the human soul rather than a wisdom text, and C. Kuhl (in *RGG*[3], col. 359) declares that the Book of Job is not primarily a wisdom text but '*carmen sui generis*, expressing the experience of its author'. The same

work. If, as Ecclesiastes, Job poses a problem, the fact of suffering in what faith declares to be the wise and beneficent economy of Almighty God, that is not suffering as such nor even the suffering of a worthy man objectively considered; it is rather, as Westermann (1956: 2ff.) has noted, the agonizing of a worthy man on his personal sufferings, and to this the academic question is strictly secondary, a situation which is reflected in the literary form which predominates in these parts of the book where Job expresses himself, namely the Plaint of the Sufferer, which Volz so strongly stressed in stating 'the poet has not written a treatise but a plaint' (Volz 1911: 26). This is cited with approval by Westermann (1956: 3), who goes on to emphasize the character of Job's statement in chs. 3 and 29–31 as a Plaint of the Sufferer, which is mainly the character of Job's part in the Dialogue proper in chs. 4–27, which Westermann after Bentzen characterizes as the 'dramatization of the Plaint of the Sufferer', as envisaged in Pss. 41.10 and 51.13ff. (1956: 5f.).[6]

We should agree with this general assessment, though in its minimizing the element of disputation in the speeches of Job in favour of the Plaint of the Sufferer we must not be influenced by the mere lack of theses and antitheses in the Dialogue according to the method of Western logic. This is after all not the method of Oriental disputation, which depends on repeated and increasing emphasis of its point with variation of expression rather than on logical argument, as Köhler rightly observed (1953: 153), and though Job's statements are predominantly in the style of the Plaint of the Sufferer they are nonetheless poignant citations of fact in indictment of the traditional doctrine of the divine economy urged by the friends. Nevertheless it is fair to say that the sapiential controversy, conducted often in the style of forensic debate, is more distinctive of the speeches of the friends and of God's reply than of the statements of Job, though even here the convention of legal or sapiential disputation is more marked in the introduction to the statements of the three friends and of God than in the substance, as Köhler has done well to note (p. 156). As the book proceeds, the statements of Job give increasingly the impression less of a disputation than of the audible reflection of the author, who at all points reflects his nurture in the religion of Israel, thinking aloud and voicing his experience in great spiritual travail. Thus Job's replies to his friends repeatedly terminate in questions, expostulations and prayers to God (e.g. 7; 9.25-31; 10; 13.20-28; 14.13-22). Even in the first round of debate (chs. 4–13), where Job

appraisal is given by C. Westermann (1956) and S. Terrien, who states 'le héros se rebelle et devient un prophète' (1963: 41).

6. Westermann, correctly in our opinion, understands the speeches of Job's three friends, despite their predominant literary character of sapiential disputation, as intended for Job's comfort and so understood by him throughout (13.4; 16.25; 21.2, 24; 26.2-4), giving the sufferer the opportunity to relieve his feelings and, we should add, being apologetic for the divine economy in moral principles even in suffering, which despite its limitations in the mechanical doctrine of retribution offers more encouragement than the view that humanity is at the mercy of blind chance.

srebuts the orthodox arguments of his friends, the writer is more and more concerned with Job's relationship to God and less with doctrine about God and human suffering. The friends and their doctrine recede more and more into the background, leaving Job increasingly in isolation with God, who alone and in such concentrated and exclusive fellowship can give the answer to the innocent sufferer.

Here we may profit from the study of Baumgärtel (1933), who, though rather too severely limiting what he terms 'the original dialogue' to one round of debate between Job and his three friends (which is included in the first round of the extant book, with a monologue from Job of which Baumgärtel finds vestiges in 16.6, 9, 12-17, 18-21; 19.1-29; 23.2-7, 10-17; 31.35, 37), has succeeded in bringing the problem of the book into clear focus. As a result we see that the book has both an academic and an existential aspect, reflecting the influence of the current doctrine of retribution on the thinking and faith of the author. His mouthpiece Job thinks as much in the context of that doctrine as his friends, as was natural considering the fact that it was of the essence of the faith of Israel inculcated in the tradition of the will and nature of God revealed in the covenant experience and sacrament and expressed in the message of the prophets and in the fast-liturgy. Thus the author through Job accepts the fact that in the divine economy sin occasions suffering. Maintaining his innocence, Job in effect exposes the logical fallacy of his friends in concluding that *all* suffering is occasioned by the sin of the sufferer, supporting his thesis by sharp criticism of the traditional view of the theodicy expressed in current proverbs and didactic poems in the sapiential tradition on the basis of the known facts both of unmerited suffering and unrequited sin. Job, however, holding, as he and his contemporaries did, that God was immediately responsible for his sufferings, commits the same logical error as his friends in arguing from his sufferings to, if not sin, then what God had imputed to him as sin, falsely as his conscience assures him. It is this logical fallacy in the application of the current doctrine of retribution that raises the academic problem of the book. However, on the same principle, Job's consciousness of his innocence leads him to appeal to God for a direct confrontation in the firm conviction that, from all that tradition had taught him of the nature of God, he would be acquitted and indeed that God himself would sanction his vindication (16.19f.; 19.25f.; 23.6f.). Though this is a logical conclusion to the premises of the traditional belief in the nature of God on the basis of what was believed to be his own revelation and of Job's innocence, it was, in the face of the former conclusion, equally logical, that God who had afflicted him had unjustly condemned him, an act of faith. It is this persistent, growing faith that makes the Book of Job more than a sapiential exercise, richer and more serious than a mere academic criticism of the current doctrine of the theodicy.

It is in Job's final appeal to God (chs. 29–31), to whom also ch. 3 is less directly addressed, as Westermann well emphasizes (1956: 6), that the true character of the Book of Job is to be recognized. The sapiential disputations of

Job's three friends, though sustained rather by intensifying emotion than by progressive argumentation, the introduction to Job's statements in the same literary convention, his replies in the same style and in ch. 29 the forensic form of his final appeal to God, put the book into the formal category of sapiential literature, which is recognized by its expansion in the poem on wisdom (ch. 28) and the review and supplementation of arguments in the Elihu addendum (chs. 32–37). But within this category the book is *sui generis*; the author is personally committed to a degree unparalleled in Hebrew Wisdom literature. His book is no didactic treatise, however earnest; it is the direct reflection of the most intense spiritual experience of a soul in ordeal, beyond the help of any impersonal system of theology, whose life and hope can be renewed only in renewed fellowship with God himself. Well may Weiser describe the Book of Job as 'this unique book which the poet has written in his own heart's blood'.[7]

The personal involvement of the sage moreover has elated the poet, so that 'we have in this book no mere transcript of some polemical discourses of wise men… The book gives rather a sublimation of that sort of thing. There were poets at that time in Israel, and one of them touched the experience of such a crisis with his magic wand' (Kraeling 1938: 24). The result is a singular monument of poetic genius, which in its detail and general impression has continued to arrest thinking people and to evoke admiration throughout the ages.

7. Weiser 1959: 10; cf. J. Strahan 1913: 13: 'His theology is charged with whitehot emotion, and emits flashes of prophecy', an appraisal which recalls that of S. Terrien (see above, n. 6).

Chapter 4

Date and Provenance

The obvious *terminus post quem* for the Book of Job is the conception of the *śāṭān* in the Prologue, still a supernatural figure in an official capacity of 'public prosecutor' under the permissive will of God as in Zech. 3.1 and an intelligence agent who ranges through the world (cf. Zech. 1.10), which is verbally reflected in Job 1.7. This establishes a *terminus post quem* for the narrative framework of the book c. 520 BCE. The affinity of 42.12ff. with the Pentateuch in its P recension might suggest a later date, in the fifth or even the fourth century.[1] This, however, is a midrashic expansion to the Epilogue, of which 11QtargJob from the latter half of the second century BCE[2] takes no notice, so that it is of no relevance for the date of the definitive Book of Job. If the Prologue gives evidence of a *terminus post quem* both for the narrative and for the Dialogue, however, it is not so easy to date the Dialogue precisely. If indeed 19.23f. refers to the inscription of Darius I (521–486 BCE) on the rock of Behistun, the evidence would carry us no further than the reference to the *śāṭān* in the Prologue. Given the likelihood of an Israelite version of an older Job tradition of the narrative framework (see below, pp. 56-75), with which Ezekiel (14.20) was familiar[3] in the early half of the sixth century BCE, it is likely that the final version if the present Prologue was the work of the sage who developed the Dialogue.

The language of the Dialogue does not settle the question of the date. Granted, there is a substantial element of Aramaic in grammatical forms and vocabulary, which might be expected in the Persian period in the sixth century BCE. However, the Aramaic and Syriac words (which elucidate Hebrew words which as such are out of place in the context by the canons of what was

1. O. Eissfeldt (1965: 208) dates the P recension of the Pentateuch after the Deuteronomistic History and Malachi (c. 470 BCE) but before Chronicles (c. 350 BCE) and the whole Pentateuch including P by the time of Nehemiah on the evidence of Neh. 8–9 (398 BCE).

2. Van der Ploeg and van der Woude 1971. A study of the script indicated a date in the first half of the first century CE, while a comparison of grammatical forms with Daniel and the Genesis Apocryphon from Qumran (first century CE) indicates a date for the work as distinct from the manuscript in the first half of the second century BCE.

3. Suggested by the association of Job with Noah and Dan'el [*sic*], hence with the Ugaritic tradition.

familiar in Hebrew philology) and Arabic and Ugaritic words (which have the same effect) indicate that such cases need signify no more than homonyms in Hebrew which have not so far been recognized in the substantial, though limited, range of Classical Hebrew.

The thought of the Dialogue with relation to other parts of the OT may possibly suggest a date, though this question must be handled with reservation. The OT, despite a certain unity of outlook, is not a book bearing on one theme progressively developed in which the parts are merely in disarray, but a library which reflects the predominating interests of its various authors with relevance to their several situations. Nevertheless, at certain times crucial issues emerge. Thus the attitude of the writer of Job to the doctrine of sin and retribution suggests a time when that was being questioned. Ezekiel's questioning of the traditional view of communal as distinct from personal retribution (Ezek. 18.2-4) seems to be re-echoed in Job 21.19-21, quoting the conventional doctrine that 'God stores up iniquity for their sons' and adding 'Let him requite the man himself that he may feel it'. The mitigation of the traditional mechanical view of sin and retribution in the more positive conception that 'God has no pleasure in the death of the wicked' but 'that he should turn from his way and live' (Ezek. 18.2) indicates the same conclusion. The disciplinary significance of suffering towards amendment is also emphasized in Isa. 40.2 (cf. Job 5.17 and 33.16ff. in the Elihu addendum). Ezekiel's preoccupation with those questions became more urgent after the fall of the state in 586 BCE, and the mood of the time is reflected in the Deuteronomistic History, which was completed after 561 BCE.[4] The problem of the suffering of the object of God's particular notice would certainly have particular point after the liquidation of the Covenant community,[5] and the nostalgic picture of the security and prosperity of the community integrated in the blessing of the chief so movingly drawn in Job 29[6] reflects the sense of loss so acutely felt after the fall of Jerusalem, when the poet in Lam. 4.20 declares:

> The breath of our nostrils, the Lord's anointed
> Was taken in their pits,
> He of whom we said, 'Under his shadow
> We shall live among the nations!'

The urgency of the problem of the suffering of the innocent and the prosperity of the ungodly, which upset the belief in the doctrine of sin and retribution, virtue and reward, finds piquant expression in Jeremiah and Habakkuk (e.g. 1.3), and imagery in certain passages in Job (3.3ff.; 10.18-22; 21ff.) and Jeremiah (20.14-18; 12.1-3) might suggest a date for the Book of

4. Indicated by the reference in 2 Kgs 25.27 to the accession of Awil-Marduk in that year.

5. Cf. the view that Job is the personification of Israel in the Exile, supported by Kraeling 1939–40; Susman 1946.

6. J. Pedersen's fine study of this passage (1926: 213-16) should be noted.

Job near the time of Jeremiah (first half of the sixth century BCE or soon after). But both writers drew on a common source, the Plaint of the Sufferer (e.g. Ps. 10.12-22) and the fast-liturgy with application in the Wisdom tradition (e.g. Pss. 37, 49 and 73), which were familiar in Israel throughout the Monarchy and were attested in Mesopotamia since the second millennium BCE.[7]

On the problem of the suffering of the innocent in Job Terrien has stressed that no notice was taken of vicarious suffering, which finds its classical expression in the servant Songs in Deutero-Isaiah (especially Isa. 52.13–53.12), and concludes that the book of Job was anterior to this passage (Terrien 1963: 28f.). However, the prophet addresses a challenge to the community to exploit its humiliation by fulfilling in itself the former function of the king in rites of penance for the community; the author of Job is agonizing over a personal problem. He is concerned with the reason and the significance of suffering only insofar as he rejects the mechanical doctrine that it is the natural and inevitable consequence of sin. True to the traditional function of the sage in Israel and the Near East, he is interested primarily in the practical question of the reaction of a worthy man to suffering in a world believed to be under the wise, just and beneficent rule of God. He is concerned with the discipline of the individual to avoid hasty and impassioned judgment and to maintain one's faith and dignity even under the stroke of unmerited affliction, realizing that there were tokens of a higher Order under Providence by faith in which one might learn to endure one's lot. We cannot then admit the absence of the doctrine of atonement through vicarious suffering in the Book of Job as a reason for dating the Book before Deutero-Isaiah.

Dhorme adduces the analogy between the Book of Malachi (c. 450 BCE) and Job in the embarrassment of even the pious before the prosperity of the ungodly, for instance, in Mal. 2.17 and 3.13-15:

> You have said, 'It is vain to serve God.
> And what is the good of our keeping his charges,
> Or of walking in mourning before Yahweh of Hosts?'
> Henceforth we consider the arrogant blessed,
> Yea, evil-doers prosper,
> Yea, they even put God to the test and escape.

This is, significantly, the prophet's complaint of the faithless conduct of commonalty, and not the daring questioning of the critical philosopher. Orthodoxy represented by Job's friends had not yet dared to press the embarrassing fact of the prosperity of the wicked. This might suggest a *terminus ante quem* for Job's daring démarche, before the addition of the Elihu speeches (chs. 32–37) and probably the poems on Behemoth (40.15-24, 31-32; 41.1-3) and Leviathan (40.25-30; 41.4-26 [EVV 40.25-30; 41.1-6, 12-34]).

If we may revert to the evidence of the *śāṭān* in the Prologue, we would stress that, sinister as he may be, he is not yet *śāṭān* of 1 Chron. 21.1, which

7. See above, pp. 5-20.

would suggest a *terminus ante quem* for the Book of Job c. 350 BCE. We might further suggest that Job's trenchant criticism of the doctrine of sin and retribution, virtue and reward, mark a protest against the tendency to over-stress the doctrine, which crystallizes in its mechanical application in Chronicles in the untimely fate of the good King Uzziah whose leprosy was said to be the consequence of his infringement of priestly offices (2 Chron. 26.16-19), the captivity of the reprobate Manasseh (2 Chron. 33.1-11) and his restoration to Judah after prayer (2 Chron. 33.12f.) and the untimely death of the reforming King Josiah since he refused, the Chronicler alleges, to believe the claim of his antagonist Pharaoh Necho of a divine commission from Yahweh in his expedition against the Babylonians (2 Chron. 38.21-24).

On such evidence we conclude that the Book of Job, excluding the later addenda of the Elihu section (chs. 32–37), and the poems on Behemoth and Leviathan, and 42.12ff., which we regard as a midrashic expansion, was substantially composed between 450 and 350 BCE. Such amplifications as the Elihu speeches and the midrashic expansion indicate continued preoccupation with the definitive Book. This may be reflected in the Wisdom poems (e.g. 24.13-18) and hymns of praise (e.g. 25.2-6; 26.5-14) and the poem on Wisdom (ch. 28), which intervenes between Eliphaz's arraignment of Job (ch. 22) and Job's reply (ch. 23), Job's final protest of innocence to his friends on oath (ch. 27), his apologia *pro vita sua* (ch. 29), his final plaint (ch. 30) and his oath of purgation (ch. 31) before the Divine Declaration (38.2–39.30; 40.1, 7-14).

Beside the date of the Book in relation to the general literary deposit and particular sapiential tradition of Israel, the question of local provenance is rather academic. To limit the evidence to the Prologue, Dialogue and Divine Declaration, the references to vines and olives (24.10f.), the migrant stork (39.13) and hawk (39.26) would indicate Palestine. The writer's familiarity with snow, ice, hail (38.22-38) and winter torrents swollen with melting snow might suggest the Lebanon or Anti-Lebanon. Tur-Sinai, unduly, we consider, claiming an Aramaic original subsequently rendered into Hebrew, claimed a Mesopotamian provenance. To be sure, there are many references to Mesopotamian mythology throughout the book, for example Marduk's mastery of Rahab and monstrous allies (9.13), 'the land of no return' (10.21), with the gates and gate-keepers of death (38.17), the foundation of the earth on the lower deep (38.4) and the possible reference to the inscription of Darius I on the rock of Behistun (19.23f.). This Mesopotamian matter, however, was known to Hebrew poets and finds expression more and less in the prophets and Psalms, while familiarity with the Behistun inscription may be owing to Jewish merchants on their trading ventures.

A. Guillaume contended for provenance from the Hejaz (1963, 1964a, 1964b). The setting is indeed in 'the land of Uz', conceivably in the Hejaz, with the imminent possibility of the sudden ghazzu, which left Job destitute (1.15-17), with other flock-masters in the Dialogue (15.21). The possible identification of the Sabaeans (1.15) with tribesmen from the Wadi Shebā in the

Hezaz and the raid by the Kasdim, possibly garrison troops such as Nabona'id actually settled in the Hejaz, seems to reflect a historical situation, if only to lend verisimilitude to the setting in 'the land of Uz'. This land was traditionally associated with Edom and with wisdom, selected by the Hebrew sage to emphasize the independence of the cult and revealed religion in Israel in the solution of moral problems. The writer is obviously familiar with the landscape of the desert and its oases, with his references to the caravans of Teima and Sheba (6.18-20), the ibex (39.1) and the onager (39.13-18). There was certainly a Jewish settlement at Teima in the sixth century BCE, to which the Prayer of Nabona'id from Qumran refers (Milik 1956), which was highly populated and influential in the Hejaz in the time of Muhammad. But here again all detail can be explained on the assumption of caravan trade through the region, to which Ps. 107.4 refers. In fact all those local references necessarily do no more than indicate that the writer of Job and his circle were one way and another familiar with the Near East from the Hejaz to Egypt and Syria and even Iran, which was traversed by caravans, with which the writer or some of his circle may have travelled.

We must, to a certain extent, admit Guillaume's case for the very substantial number of words in Job, where the meaning of the text, obscure by the canons of Classical Hebrew, has been elucidated through Arabic cognates, especially in pairs of seemingly identical words in parallelism. However, in such cases the Arabic word which restores the obvious sense may be no more than the cognate of a Hebrew homonym so far unknown, or at least unrecognized by scholars in the limited corpus of extant Hebrew literature. Such Hebrew words, not only in Job but throughout the OT, may be elucidated by the recognition of cognates in Akkadian, Aramaic, and Syriac and Ugaritic. Not only so, but the recognition of Arabic cognates to Ugaritic words from the fourteenth century BCE severely modifies Guillaume's conclusion. For instance, the stock title of El in the Ras Shamra texts *lṭpn 'il dp'id* corresponds verbally to Arabic *'allāhu 'l-laṭīf dhū fā'id* (Allah the Kindly, the Compassionate).

A stronger case might be made for the composition of the Book in Egypt. From the latter days of Jeremiah, Egypt was known as the home of most of the influential Jews who remained after the deportations to Babylon, and here Jewish literature tradition flourished, including the Wisdom tradition represented by the grandson of Ben Sira, who settled in Egypt and translated his grandfather's work after 132 BCE. By the same token of course the work of Ben Sira himself attests the activity of sapiential circles in Palestine in the third century. Given the activity of Jeremiah in Egypt and the interest in the preservation of his work it may be no coincidence that Job's curse on the day of his birth (3.3-11) should so clearly echo Jer. 20.14-18. The conception of sleep and repose in the grave for which Job longs recalls the plaint of him who was weary of life (*ANET*^{3}, 407, cf. 33). Job's puzzling declaration, 'Naked I came from my mother's womb and naked I shall go back thither (*šammāh*)', finds its best explanation in our opinion in the Egyptian reference to death as 'yon place' (*ANET*³, 34). The same passage in Job (3.14f.) refers to the burial of 'kings and counsellors', who built *ḥªrābôṯ* for themselves, possibly 'places in the desert', the pyramids on the desert plateau beyond the cultivable strip of the Nile Valley or the well-furnished tombs ('houses of eternity')[8] of the Pharaohs and their officials in the desert Valley of the Kings at Luxor. In view of the age-old profession of grave-robbing, the rich contents of such tombs (3.15) might be familiar to the author of Job. The watch kept over the tombs of the notables (21.32) is also explicable in view of tomb-robbery. The allusion to the long cortège of such a burial (21.32) could well reflect specifically the Egyptian wisdom text which contrasts the cortège of the dead notable, including rich grave-offerings, with the corpse of the poor man carried out without ceremony on a reed mat. Again Job's wish to be 'weighed in a just balance' that God might know his integrity might well reflect the scene from the Egyptian Book of the Dead, where the soul of the defunct is weighed against the feather of Maat, Truth (*ANEP*, pl. 639). In the figure of the reed (papyrus) flourishing so long as it is rooted in the marsh Egyptian words are used—*gōme'* (Egyptian *km'i*) and *'aḥu* (Egyptian *ꜣ hꜣ h*)—and the reference to reed-skiffs (9.26; cf. Isa. 18.2) surely refers to such craft on the Nile, which are well attested in ancient Egyptian painting and tomb sculpture (Breasted 1917). The reference to the 'wisdom' of *ṭuḥôṯ*, for which the parallel *śeḵwî* ('cock') indicates a bird, the ibis sacred to the wise god Thoth (Egyptian *dhwṭi*), the activity of which is associated with the vital Nile flood, points in the same direction, though the plethora of creatures of the desert and the migrant birds of Palestine suggests an origin in a comprehensive bestiary of the same category as the classified lists of natural phenomena such as those including Solomon's encyclopaedic nature lore (1 Kgs 4.33), which probably derived from such lists in Egypt.[9] In the description of the nature and habitat of the hippopotamus (Behemoth) and the crocodile (Leviathan), the name *bᵉhēmoṯ* is not as generally in Hebrew 'beasts' or 'beast *par excellence*'; it is a Hebrew transliteration of Egyptian *pꜣ'ihmw* ('river-ox'), while in the introduction to the passage on Leviathan 'Can you draw out (*timšōḵ*) Leviathan?' (40.25 [EVV 41.1]) there is probably a wordplay between the Hebrew verb and the ancient Egyptian word for 'crocodile', which has survived in Coptic *'imsaḥ*, whence the loanword in Arabic *timsaḥ*. Finally, in a description of the crocodile's eyes like the beams of the rising sun (41.10 [EVV 18]) we note Fohrer's observation that the crocodile's eyes were the hieroglyphic sign for the beams of the rising sun (Fohrer 1989: 530 n. 9). Moreover, à propos of the statement that the crocodile is king over other beasts (41.26 [EVV 34]) it is significant that the

8. So Dhorme, *ad loc*., who, with Budde, Duhm, G.B. Gray, Stevenson, Weiser and Fohrer, thinks of the pyramids. G.R. Driver (1950d: 349) however, cites Ethiopic and S. Arab. *mḥrb* ('castle').

9. Gardiner 1949. For similar lists see Matous 1933 and von Soden 1934.

crocodile was the hieroglyphic sign for 'king' (Erman 1894: 180). Although the passages on Behemoth and Leviathan are later addenda to the definitive Book of Job, which may indicate a recension in Egypt, there is strong evidence for Humbert's view of the Egyptian provenance of the definitive Book (1929: 75-105).

When all this is said, however, we should emphasize strongly that the local provenance has but superficial bearing on the distinctive thought of the book. There were by the Persian period settlements of Jews in Egypt, Mesopotamia, Syria and Lebanon and the caravan towns of the Hejaz, with known literary interests in Mesopotamia and Egypt. But, wherever they might be and whatever calling they might adopt as holding no land, like the Murashu Sons of Nippur with their far-flung trading and financial interests, or those with similar interests in the Hejaz, like the later Arab Quraish in Mecca, their real cultural and spiritual home was the tradition of their Hebrew scriptures. In comparison with the odd reflection of possible physical background, the familiarity with the Law, the Prophets and their own Wisdom tradition (attested in verbal citation, literary types, their characteristic expressions and association of ideas), used so naturally to reinforce the arguments of Job and his interlocutors, and the development of the mature thought of their Hebrew forebear, reduces any influence of their physical environment to the minimum and makes the question of the local provenance of the Book of Job merely academic.

Chapter 5

LITERARY FORMS IN THE BOOK OF JOB

The Book of Job has an aesthetic appeal and an arresting power far beyond any other known work of Hebrew Wisdom. Like Ecclesiastes, but unlike Proverbs, the Wisdom of Solomon or Ben Sira, it is preoccupied by a single central theme and it arrests by its bold and realistic challenge to accepted dogma. In Job, however, unlike Ecclesiastes, the challenge is presented not in academic detachment with the faint personal note of mild regret or of gentle cynicism, but as the expression of intense personal conflict between faith and experience. This tension finds dramatic expression in work which by its dramatic form, its deep concern with a central issue, its serious and realistic questioning of conventional thought and faith, has been aptly compared to the tragedies of Euripides.[1]

Job is a sapiential work dramatically presented in which the interest of the reader is engaged by the literary art of the drama, the swift succession of scenes in the Prologue set alternatively in heaven and earth, with the crescendo account of Job's calamities, culminating in his exemplary declaration of faith (2.10):

> If we accept good from God
> Shall we not accept calamity?

We find the good man at the nadir of his experience cursing the day he was born and content to renounce life as meaningless (ch. 3). In response Eliphaz intervenes in the normal role of the sage who seeks to adjust others to their circumstances and convince them that calamity is not a fortuitous accident to which they are helplessly and hopelessly exposed, but betokens God's government according to regular moral principles, according to which humans may protect themselves (chs. 4–5). The drama is continued in the cut and

1. So H.M. Kallen (1918), who regarded the book as the imitation of a tragedy of Euripides. Since the first tragedy of Euripides was produced in 455 BCE it is unlikely that the influence of Euripides had time or opportunity to penetrate to the Near East during the Persian period in which we should date the definitive Book of Job and probably its recensions. Actually in Mesopotamian Wisdom literature and in the Hebrew Plaint of the Sufferer there were native Semitic prototypes, so that in our opinion the affinity claimed with the tragedies of Euripides, though striking—without being complete—is fortuitous.

thrust of the Dialogue between Job and his friends (chs. 4–23).[2] As Job makes it increasingly plain that his friends' assertions of orthodox doctrine are inadequate to his case, the event of a third party is adumbrated, that of God, to whom Job makes a dramatic appeal in his apology for his blameless life (ch. 29), the statement of his sufferings and the consequent crippling of his potential in society (ch. 30) and the ultimate appeal in his oath of purgation (ch. 31). Finally there is the dramatic entry of God in the Theophany and Divine Declaration, which, far from giving a dogmatic answer, sustains the interest of the reader by giving simply glimpses into ultimate truth and by consequent assurance and rebuke, leaving Job in a state of tension as to his adequacy to question God in view of the limitations of his experience and reason and his grasp of the boundless possibility of the grace of God in the scope of his own dimension. However, the drama of the Book of Job is never merely formal. In the statements of Job throughout, the personal note prevails. It is a strange reader indeed who, whatever his or her interest, philosophical, aesthetic or even critical, fails to be engaged in the intensely existential thinking of the author, which transcends the limits of logical debate and the canons of formal drama. This clamant personal experience of the author of Job must be borne in mind in our consideration of the question of the formal character of the book, which we shall find to be conditioned, though limited, by the literary tradition of Israel.

Views which regard Job as a tragedy on the Classical Greek model,[3] or a dialogue like Plato's Dialogues (Fries 1904), or even an epic like Homer's, fail entirely to recognize the literary forms of Israel and the ancient Near East, which offer much closer analogies, and date mainly from the time when the higher levels of culture in antiquity were arrogated for Greece through lack of knowledge of, or even interest in, the culture of the further East.

Appreciative of the native milieu of the book, H. Richter suggests that its structure reflects the process of ancient law in Israel.[4] This he reconstructs as the preliminary efforts of the parties and assessors to settle the matter out of court by getting one party to admit his liability, helping him to make this admission without loss of face rather than forcing him. This failing, the next step is to arraign him before the court with the help of witnesses, the process being completed when the accused has admitted the evidence against him and

2. On our delimitation of the Dialogue to two rounds of debate involving Job and his three friends, and a third section involving Job and Eliphaz in chs. 22–23, with Job's final dismissal of his friends with an oath of purgation and his declaration of the consequences of perjury (ch. 27), and an assembly of miscellaneous fragments and poems (chs. 24, 25, 26), see pp. 56-75.

3. This was the view of Theodore of Mopsuestia. Affinities with Aeschylus, particularly *Prometheus*, have been emphasized by M. Jastrow (1920: 185ff.), J.J. Slotki (1927–28), J. Lindblom (1939: 280ff.) and H.G. May (1952: 240ff.); with Sophocles by R. Lowth 1847: 372ff. (but dependence rejected).

4. Richter 1959: 11-58. This view is developed from the theses of L. Koehler (1930–31).

accepted the sentence of the judge. This admission may be expressed, as eventually Job admits that he had no reply to God's challenge to his presumption to dispute the divine economy on equal terms (40.4-5; 41.2-6), or it might be signified by his silence (40.4-5). But if the defendant was not convinced of his guilt and in turn could not convince his accusers of his innocence, and in default of actual evidence, he might still appeal to God, reinforcing his appeal by an oath of purgation (as Job does in chs. 29–31). Finally in the Book of Job God replies to this appeal, convicting Job of seeking to subject him to the limitations of temporal social conventions and dogmas against the evidence of his free grace and power, humanity in its familiar environment being but one object of his concern (38.2–40.14). To the final verdict of God here implied Job declares his submission (40.4-5; 42.2-6) and the case according to the legal form postulated by Richter is closed.

This legal procedure is conjecturally reconstructed from Babylonian texts from the second millennium BCE, from texts from Ptolemaic Egypt and from passages in the OT admittedly sporadic and formally as widely divergent as the patriarchal narratives and the Plaint of the Sufferer among the Psalms, where Richter follows Hans Schmidt in his view that such psalms as Pss. 4; 5; 7; 26; 27.1-6, 7-14; 31.1-9 (EVV 1-8); 52; 109; 142 and possibly Pss. 11; 13; 54; 55.1-19 (EVV 1-18); 56; 59; 94.16-23 and 140 are relevant to the final appeal to God when a case proved inconclusive in secular justice.[5] His schema of the structure of the Book of Job certainly recognizes the dramatic character of the work, for which the forensic case would be an admirable medium, and it does full justice to the use of legal forms and diction. Richter's emphasis on the forensic pattern, however, seems to us to do less than justice to the full significance of other literary forms in the book, the recognition of which, in all their rich variety and peculiar adaptation in Job, is the great merit of Fohrer (1963b: 68-86) and to a lesser extent of Westermann (1956).

The recurrence of the forensic convention, so readily adaptable to sapiential disputation, in the speeches of Job's three friends, in the introductions to Job's statements, his argument in chs. 12 and 21 and in his final appeal to God (chs. 29–31), and in the introduction to the Divine Declaration (38.1-2) is not to be denied. Against this formal aspect of the Book, however, is to be set the substance of the definitive Book, Job's despairing wish for death and oblivion (ch. 3), the expostulations and arguments of his friends and his rejoinders (chs. 4–23), Job's increasing orientation to God and his final impassioned appeal (chs. 29–31) and the Divine Declaration (38.2–40.14). In Job's statements here

5. Schmidt 1928. In the psalms adduced by Schmidt the subject protests his innocence in contrast to 'penitential psalms', where the sufferer acknowledges that his suffering is caused by his sin. The relevance of the latter to the fast-liturgy is likely, though the former also may have relevance to the same situation, expressing the humiliation of the innocent sufferer and his dependence on divine deliverance. Here the motif of the accusers, which Schmidt took literally, may be a figurative expression of the popular conception that suffering is the consequence of sin.

Westermann rightly recognizes features characteristic of the Plaint of the Sufferer, and feasibly suggests that the arguments of the three friends are less designed to provoke disputation than to give Job an opportunity to relieve his feelings, which he does mainly in the literary convention of the Plaint of the Sufferer (Westermann 1956: 5ff.). But throughout Job's plaint, as in his initial curse of the day of his birth (ch. 3), there is an undeniable note of controversy in his setting the grim facts of his experience against God's purposeful creation and moral economy, which finally succeeds in revealing the inadequacy of orthodox doctrine and traditional morality in the existential situation of the sufferer, who is thus eventually brought into confrontation with God for his answer. Nor is the Theophany and Divine Declaration foreign to the Plaint of the Sufferer, formally corresponding to the divine response or oracle, which is either expressed or implied in certain of the plaints of the sufferer in the Psalms, and is an even more regular feature of Mesopotamian texts on the subject of the worthy sufferer, the affinities of which with the Book of Job we have noted (see above, pp. 5-20). But being a rebuke leading to conviction rather than merely an assurance, its affinity with the legal convention must not be excluded. The role of Job's three friends might be regarded as the amplification of the theme of the sufferer's alienation from his friends which is more vaguely mentioned in the plaints of the sufferer in Pss. 41.10 and 51.13. Or it may correspond to the role of the friends of the sufferer in the Mesopotamian texts who, either by contradiction or agreement, help the sufferer to express his plaint. This may indicate that the definitive Book of Job is the 'dramatization of the Plaint of the Sufferer', as Westermann and Bentzen (Westermann 1956: 11; Bentzen 1959: 177) term it. This certainly does more justice to the peculiar nature of the work, with its intensity, which is unique in Hebrew Wisdom literature. This is the view of the book that we prefer, though we should beware of applying it too mechanically in view of the rich variety of literary forms each with its own characteristic implications to those in ancient Israel familiar with such forms in their traditional *Sitz im Leben.* Nor can anyone familiar with such forms in Hebrew literature be unaware that forensic language and forms are frequently used in the Plaint of the Sufferer, just as the harrowing details from the Plaint of the Sufferer are used in presenting a case at law, the protestation of innocence being common in both conventions. Thus we admit Richter's emphasis on the forensic features in Job, though finding that Westermann's view of the Book as the dramatization of the Plaint of the Sufferer does fuller justice to its nature, which seems to us to be confirmed by the Mesopotamian wisdom texts with which Job has affinity. Steinmann, speaking more generally, describes Job as 'a voluminous legal dossier in an abortive case', where the accused is interrogated before he is judged guilty,[6] but when he verges on blasphemy, is acquitted and rehabilitated. The work, he

6. Steinmann 1955: 289: 'Par un étrange paradoxe ce volumineux dossier juridique est celui d'un procès avorti'.

suggests, did not conform to any preconceived pattern, but developed as a reflection of the writer's own dialectic (Steinmann 1955: 270ff.), embellished by a rich variety of literary forms, particularly the Hymn of Praise and the Plaint of the Sufferer (pp. 56ff.). This view is largely the consequence of Steinmann's conception of the present Book of Job as composed in four stages: the first consisting of Prologue, Dialogue and Job's monologue, ending at ch. 31, the second an expansion of this by the speeches of Elihu (chs. 32–37) as the answer to the problem of the Dialogue, the third a parallel edition of the second, but with the answer in the Divine Declaration and the Epilogue instead of in the Elihu section, and the fourth, the present book, the fusion of those editions (pp. 273ff.).[7] However, we prefer to think of the definitive Book, without the addendum of the Elihu speeches, the poem on Wisdom (ch. 28) and perhaps a secondary expansion with inserted poems in chs. 24–27 (see below, pp. 56-75), as conceived according to a literary prototype, either as legal process or, as we prefer, the Plaint of the Sufferer or the Mesopotamian wisdom texts on the subject of the worthy sufferer—however this may need to be qualified. Thanks, however, to the poetic genius of the author and particularly to his intense involvement in his problem, we have a work which transcends the limitations of any traditional literary type and which in consequence has been justly described as *sui generis*.

The framework of the book in the Prologue (chs. 1–2) and Epilogue (42.7ff.) is the vivid narrative form of the *saga* or *popular folk-tale* with edifying purpose. The use of such narrative to introduce a more sophisticated wisdom text has analogies in the Protest of the Eloquent Peasant (*ANET*[3], 407-10) in Egyptian Wisdom literature and in the introduction to the Aramaic Proverbs of Ahiqar (*ANET*[3], 427). The narrative, however, as used by the author of Job was adapted from an earlier work and has retained many features of oral saga or folk-legend. Of those we may note round numbers in the account of Job's wealth, seven thousand sheep, a thousand camels, five hundred yoke of oxen and five hundred she-asses (1.3), which were doubled on Job's rehabilitation (42.12); the quick succession of the bringing of bad news, with verbal reiteration while the previous messenger 'was yet speaking'; and the total loss of Job's oxen and asses (1.14), sheep and shepherds (1.16), camels and herdsmen (1.17) and family (1.19), with the messengers as sole survivor in each case. The crescendo effect of this account and the further account of Job's bodily affliction hold the hearer in suspense and key one up for the sufferer's reaction, uncertain whether that is to be the fortitude of faith, as in the source (1.21; 2.10), or the despair of the realist, which Job's wife counselled (2.9). The hearer is also held in suspense for the solution of the sufferer's problem. These features are familiar in Hebrew tradition in the patriarchal narratives in the older sources of the Pentateuch, with which the narrative framework of Job has been compared. The E source particularly,

7. This is the view of the composition of Job proposed by van Hoonacker.

with its moralizing tone, is reminiscent of the Prologue and Epilogue of Job. This suggests the art of the professional story-teller, of the Arab *rāwi*, a conspicuous figure in the coffee-halls of the East before the advent of gramophone, radio and television. Thus Muhammad introduced the Surah of Yussuf in the Qur'an: 'We will recount to you the best of stories'. The story itself, however, had an edifying value like the story of Joseph in Genesis, emphasizing the guidance of providence in the vicissitudes of a worthy man (von Rad 1953: 120ff.). The saga features we have noted in the narrative framework of Job, however, are also features of the Ugaritic Legends of Krt and Aqht in the fourteenth century, and the association of Job with Dan'el [*sic*] in Ezek. 14.14, 20, may well point to a Canaanite popularization of a Mesopotamian wisdom text such as we have noticed at Ugarit in the fourteenth century BCE (see above, pp. 5-20) as N.M. Sarna has suggested (Sarna 1957; Spiegel 1945), with a Hebrew version reflecting the early patriarchal narratives in the ninth century. Whatever the respective roles of Job and his friends may have been, the present book gives no certain clue, and it must suffice for us to recognize the saga and edifying tale as the survival of the source-material in the narrative framework of the Book of Job in the Prologue and Epilogue (chs.1–2; 42.1-11), with Midrashic addenda much later than the completion of the book. The narrative source so developed in the Israelite monarchy was adapted in the Persian period in the scenes with the *sāṭān* and his trials of Job in the Prologue, probably by the author of the Book (Fohrer 1963b: 26ff.), but preserving the character of the source.

The moral problem in the Dialogue of the Book was no novelty in Israel. As has already been noted, it is implicit in the Plaint of the Sufferer, where it is particularly poignant, as for example in Ps. 73.3-12, and while such psalms cannot be dated precisely, the adaptation of this literary type by Jeremiah in the sixth century indicates that it was already familiar in Israel. Assyrian analogies indicate that this literary category was an element in the ritual of fast and penance, where the king represented the community (Frankfort 1948: 260ff.; Mowinckel 1962: I, 46, 61, 225ff.), so that the sufferer in the Hebrew psalms of this type was quite possibly the king as a 'societary figure'.[8]

The Plaint of the Sufferer, whether communal or individual, follows a well-defined pattern. The sufferings are stated usually both literally and figuratively, and this cumulative list is followed by a cry for help. Here, as in Mesopotamian laments, it is to be noted that the plaint is not a querulous questioning of God's order, but emphasizes the worshipper's dependence on God.[9] A marked feature of the Book of Job, which it is the merit of Fohrer (1963b: 70ff) to have recognized and duly emphasized, is the originality—and

8. The phrase coined by H.W. Robinson.

9. The cumulative list of sufferings was possibly developed from the counter-incantation, the principle feature of which, as is evident from counter-incantations from Mesopotamia, the systematic countering of malicious incantations be the verbal repetition of the various evils which had been wished upon the sufferer; see e.g. Jastrow 1898: 272.

indeed daring—with which this and other traditional forms are applied to circumstances quite other than those with which they were originally and traditionally associated. Thus the writer of Job adapts the Plaint of the Sufferer as an indictment of God's moral government. In the traditional Plaint of the Sufferer, God's former mercies may be recalled, either as the grounds of hope in extremity or, as in the Communal Plaint in Psalm 44, as a foil to present distress. This is the significance of Job 29. But in association with Job's plaint in ch. 30 the emphasis on the social potential of Job's prosperity makes the plaint less of a lament than an arraignment of his divine opponent. Another feature of the Plaint of the Sufferer is a confession of guilt, which is rather general (e.g. Pss. 38.5, 18; 51.5; 79.8; 130.3), or perhaps a protestation of innocence, which may in fact be elaborated as a separate psalm, as in Psalm 131. This latter element is naturally elaborated in Job. There is also a statement of faith in the providence of God, in which the finest example, again elaborated as an independent psalm, is Psalm 23. This has its counterpart in Job's trusting submission to God in 40.3-5 and 42.2-6, though in form this reproduces rather the legal convention of the acceptance of the verdict, as Richter contends.[10] The relief anticipated in the Plaint of the Sufferer may be heralded by a reassuring oracle, as in the Communal Plaints (Pss. 60.8-11 [EVV 6-9]; 85.9ff. [EVV 8ff.]), mediated by a cultic prophet on behalf of God. This last element is represented in the Book of Job by the answer of the Lord in person,[11] though characteristically it is adapted by the author as a challenge rather than an assurance of the relief sought by the sufferer. As the experience of God's presence, however, seen now 'with the eye' rather than merely heard (42.5), with infinite possibilities of new insight, new life, new hope, this is even fuller than the oracle in the Plaint of the Sufferer. While the whole of the Book of Job may be regarded as an expansion of the theme of the Plaint of the Sufferer[12] (all the characteristic features of which it employs or adapts), there are certain passages in it which conform in detail to this type, such as those just noted and particularly 16.7-17; 19.7-20 and 30.9-31. The Plaint of the Sufferer, however, in the Book of Job has not the same significance as in the Psalms or in the Mesopotamian fast-liturgies and such wisdom texts as *ludlul bēl nēmeqi* and the others cited above. There its purpose is to signify the abasement of the subject and his dependence on the mercy of God, which he either anticipates or has experienced. In Job, as H. Gese (1958: 76) has well observed, Job's plaint is not designed to evoke the mercy of God except in

10. Richter 1959: 125f. Fohrer also admits this (1963b: 23), though as an alternative to the view that Job's statement here corresponds to the assurance of the sufferer that he will be heard in the conclusion to the plaint.

11. The failure to notice all the formal characteristics of the Plaint of the Sufferer in the Book of Job led Dhome (1929: xlviii) to treat the Divine Declaration as a later insertion, like the Elihu speeches.

12. A. Gese (1958: 63ff.) suggested that the book of Job is an adaptation of the *Klagehörersparadigma*.

death or vindication. Thus it has a controversial note, which is foreign to the Plaint of the Sufferer in its cultic *Sitz im Leben*. We may add that, as well as highlighting the contrast with Job's righteous conduct, the list of his accumulated sufferings is adduced as an excuse for his questioning of the moral order of God. This particular application of the Plaint of the Sufferer, with its characteristic elements in Mesopotamian and Hebrew literature (the Psalms), agrees with the adaptation by the author of Job of other literary forms proper to a particular *Sitz im Leben*, where he uses the traditional association of ideas not always to reinforce those ideas, but also to contradict them in the light of experience. Dhorme, in his otherwise excellent commentary, has failed to notice this tendency in his cavalier dismissal of the influence of Mesopotamian wisdom texts, to which he sees only a superficial resemblance in the Book of Job (Dhorme 1929: lxxxvi). The appreciation of the significance of the Plaint of the Sufferer and of other literary forms in the Book of Job and the writer's highly original adaptation of them to his argument is the great contribution of G. Fohrer (1963a) to the study of Job and the nerve of his magisterial commentary on the Book.

We may consider the particular significance of such passages in the context of the Book of Job. In 16.7-17 and 19.8-13 Job describes the intensity of his suffering in a series of highly colourful and concrete figures characteristic of the Plaint of the Sufferer. In the Plaint of the Sufferer, the afflictions at the hands of the sufferer's enemies are a prominent feature. In Job, however, God is the persecutor. He has worn the sufferer out and shrivelled him up so that his emaciation attests his sufferings and the enmity of God (cf. 19.20; 30.30; Pss. 22.15 [EVV 14]; 18 [EVV 17]; 102.4 [EVV 3]); opponents take up the hue and cry against him and gape at him (cf. Pss. 22.8 [EVV 7]; 35.21); he is buffeted on the cheek (cf. Lam. 3.30); he has sown sackcloth on his skin (cf. Pss. 35.13; 69.12, EVV 11); and in spite of all this, Job declares he is innocent (cf. Ps. 73.13). In the context of Job 16 this citation from the Plaint of the Sufferer emphasizes the intense suffering of Job, which justifies the urgency of his questioning of God's moral Order to which his friends object with unseasonable philosophic detachment (16.1-6), and the protest of innocence with which it closes leads naturally to Job's claim that even if his sufferings, as they are likely to do, prove fatal, his case be still left open for vindication (16.18-22). In 19.7-20, in continuation of his complaint that God has prejudged his case (vv. 7ff.), Job emphasizes his sufferings at the divine hand in a list of sufferings typical of the Plaint of the Sufferer (vv. 7ff.). All his friends are estranged from him and even his family (vv. 13-19; cf. 30.10a; Ps. 38.12 [EVV 11]), and he is reduced to skin and bone (v. 20, cf. 30.30; Ps. 22.15, 18 [EVV 14, 17]). In the sequel Job questions the right of his friends to pursue him like God, and, claiming perhaps the same indulgence as the mentally ill, who are regarded as 'touched by God' (cf. v. 21), he claims pity rather than censure. Job's lament in 30.9-31 describes his sufferings in an accumulation of figures familiar in the Plaint of the Sufferer. He is a byword to all, even the lowest of society (v. 9; cf. Pss. 44.15 [EVV 14]; 69.12 [EVV 11]); good people are appalled; he is surrounded by enemies; they spit upon his face (vv. 10ff.); God has loosed his tent-cord (v. 11; cf. Jer. 10.20); he is prey to terrors (v. 15); night racks his bones (v. 17); God has cast him in the mire (v. 19; cf. Ps. 69.3 [EVV 2]); he goes about black (v. 28; cf. Pss. 38.7 [EVV 6]; 42.10 [EVV 9]), the companion of jackals and ostriches (v. 29); his lyre and his pipe are turned to mourning (v. 31). So Job described his persistent misery as a contrast to his prosperity in ch. 29. The subject is introduced by the popular attitude to suffering, which reflects the conventional view of suffering as the natural consequence of sin and the withdrawal of the divine blessing. This is the attitude of persons who share the leader's loss of the blessing (30.1-8) as they had previously enjoyed his share of the blessing (ch. 29).

Here it must be emphasized that the recognition of the incorporation of typical passages from the literary category of the Plaint of the Sufferer does not necessarily militate against the authenticity of these passages in Job, but it does suggest that the various references to suffering need not be literal and biographical.

There are other passages of this nature, which Baumgärtel (1933) regards as secondary to the Dialogue (e.g. 3.3-12, 13-19, 20-26; 7.1-10, 12-21; 8.12-19; 9.4-10, 25-31; 10.1-22; 12; 13.23-27; 14.1-22). It is difficult to see why 3.3-27, Job's curse of the day of his birth (vv. 3-12) and the advantages of non-existence (vv. 13-19) and the questioning of the purpose of life in misery (vv. 20-26), should be removed and the statement retained in v. 1 that Job cursed the day of his birth. The following speech of Eliphaz (chs. 4–5) has as much relevance to the one as to the other, and if 3.3-26 had not stood in the Book of Job critics would certainly have demanded an opening speech from the protagonist. From a dramatic point of view Job's explosive curse of his life is natural after this pent-up emotion (1.20-22; 2.9-13). Job's speech is also the introduction to the sage's argument deploring the life of the wretched vv. 3ff., and questioning the purpose of life in misery in two passages (vv. 13-19, 20-26), each introduced by 'Why?' (*lāmmāh*) like the Egyptian Dispute over Suicide (*ANET*[3], 405-407) and the Babylonian Theodicy (Lambert 1960: 63-91). Actually 3.1 is to be taken with the prose narrative in ch. 2 and, as 3.2 indicates, 3.3-26 is the introduction to the Dialogue.

The fact that the Book of Job is the production of a poet of original genius and one well versed in the native literature of Israel and probably also in the wisdom literature of the Near East, who was also a philosopher engaged not in presenting a preconceived conclusion but in experimental and creative thought, must seriously modify any view of such passages as secondary. The imprecation with elaboration of the calamity invoked is a well-known literary category, best known in the OT in Balaam's oracles on Edom (Num. 24.18), Amalek (Num. 24.21-22) and developed in the folk-oracles in Amos (1.3–2.3). As applied to the subject's own life it is paralleled in Jer. 20.14-18, but it is questionable if this can be regarded as a distinct literary category, in spite of the close verbal correspondence between Job 3.3-12 and Jer. 20.14-18.

In vv. 1-10, which Baumgärtel also regards as secondary, vv. 1-2 deals generally with the brevity of human life, proceeding then to the particular misery of Job (vv. 3-6) and then, with apparently an apostrophe to God, to the brevity of his life and the imminence of death. This adds point to Job's appeal for the sympathy of his friends rather than their censure, which is the theme of 6.14-30, and to his claim on God for mercy and relief rather than apparently pointless persecution as if he were not a man responsive to God, the sea or sea-monster (*tannīn*), known in the Ras Shamra texts as the inveterate enemies of God's Order. The sequel, Bildad's reply that God does not pervert justice, but that suffering implies sin (8.2-4), might seem to connect directly with 6.29-30, but his insistence on the availability of God's mercy on repentance (8.5-7, 21-22) and humanity's vital need of it (vv. 11ff.) is the direct reply to Job's complaint of the pointless brevity of human life and the indiscriminate hostility of God. The author adopts the Plaint of the Sufferer with its enumeration of sufferings in 7.1-10 as the traditional appeal to God, specifically in the sequel (vv. 11-21), since his case has proved beyond the understanding and sympathy of his friends.

The passage 9.25-31, in the tradition of the Plaint of the Sufferer on the theme of the brevity of life and the agonizing problem of God's apparent indifference to human righteousness, does seem to be a self-contained passage which breaks the sequence of thought between v. 24 (which states that God is indifferent to justice) and v. 31 (which states that he is inaccessible to the innocent sufferer who claims justice). After the statement that God destroys innocent and wicked alike, sudden death mocking the innocent (9.22-23), vv. 25-31 seems tautological. The explanation is possibly that the latter passage, a Plaint of the Sufferer, was suggested secondarily by vv. 22-23.

10.1-22, in contrasting the sufferer's relationship to God with his relationship in arbitration or in inquisition with humanity (vv. 4-6, cf. 9.23), reverts to the theme of 3.11-13 (10.18-19), and echoes the theme of the pointless brevity of human life (v. 20, cf. 9.25-26), which may suggest that 9.25-31 is secondary. Verses 8-17 introduce fresh argument that God's creation and providential care for humans as moral beings (v. 12) are inconsistent with human sufferings in spite of their merit. In 10.2-20, as in many passages which have been regarded as secondary, Job addresses not the friends but God, and so, it is claimed, they do not relate directly to the Dialogue. There is nevertheless usually some connection with the thought of the context and allowance must be made for the intensity of the author's thought, which all the while was creative, questing for a solution of his major problem beyond the strict confines of the orthodox arguments advanced by Job's friends.

Other passages in Job have been regarded as secondary because they are self-contained expressions of general truth, including 3.20-23, 7.1-2 and 14.1-12, 18-22. These may well be citations from wisdom literature which in the sequel are applied to Job's own case. Thus the general truth of 7.1-12 is particularized in Job's case in vv. 3-10. 14.1-2 expresses, perhaps in citation, a general truth, which the author uses to question God's censorious judgment of mortals (v. 3); v. 4 implies humans' limitation, and v. 5 God's determination of the human life-span; v. 5 states the author's claim that in the brief life which God has given humans he should, it is implied, if his creation of them has any point, allow them to live in peace since, the passage continues (vv. 7-12), death brings annihilation and oblivion. The author continues his argument that if he could hope for life beyond the grave with a correspondence with God, he would be content to endure all the hardships of life (vv. 13-17). This hope sinks with the final declaration of the mortality and final annihilation of humans (chs. 18–22). Here, though the argument points the statement of a general truth with the author's own experience in the role of Job, it is impossible to determine whether ch. 14 is a later expansion from wisdom literature supported by the general statement of human evanescence in 13.28, or a number of citations to which the author adds his own annotations, or whether the whole (both general truths and particular elaborations) are the work of the author as poet and philosopher. The references throughout the book and the variety of literary forms indicates the author's wide repertoire, and there is no indication that his work was confined to the strict dialogue and his adaptation of his source. At any point he may well have inserted a passage of his own work, either composed *ad hoc* or an independent piece, which he considered appropriate in the context.

Another distinctive literary category in the Book of Job is the *Hymn of Praise*, in, for example, 5.9-16, 9.4-10, 12.7-10, 13-25, which Baumgärtel regards as secondary, and 26.5-14. The Hymn of Praise is well known in Mesopotamian liturgy, a characteristic being the flattering invocation of the god by all his conceivable titles or epithets and references to his exploits, which ensured that, whatever his mood, the worshipper could not fail to use the proper means of address. In the Hebrew version of the Hymn of Praise, in place of this plethora of divine titles God was addressed as the Creator, or, in the adaptation of the liturgy of the Canaanite New Year festival, as the one who, like the Canaanite Baal in the Ras Shamra texts, had prevailed over the powers of Chaos, exemplified in the unruly waters of the sea or river floods or in the water-monsters such as Rahab, Tannin or Leviathan, or in the sustaining of nature or the social order, or as the God who had overthrown the Egyptians and delivered Israel from the land of bondage. This in the liturgy of the New Year festival was a means of engendering fresh faith in God's providential Order as well as being an expression of homage to God. In Israel the reference to such exploits took the place of divine titles in the Mesopotamian counterpart, but a formal correspondence remained in the Hebrew Hymn of Praise in the reference to the divine exploits by a series of participles of the verb (cf. Ps. 104; Amos 4.13; 5.8-9). These characteristic features distinguish the Hymn of Praise in the Book of Job.

The Hymn of Praise in the context of Wisdom literature is nothing extraordinary. Its theme, as in the Psalms, being generally the providence of God in creation and history, it might be cited in Wisdom literature either for criticism or in support of argument for the divine economy. Thus for instance a Hymn of Praise is cited in the wisdom Psalm 8 on the theme of humanity so insignificant in the universe yet the consummation of God's works (cf. Ps. 144.3, a Royal Psalm). The Hymns of Praise in Job are very apposite in their context whether in support or in criticism of the divine economy.

Thus in 5.9-16 Eliphaz checks Job's wild lament and nihilistic philosophy in ch. 3, where incidentally Job uses the form of the Hymn of Praise to extol death and oblivion (3.17-19). So Eliphaz maintains the doctrine of God's Order in nature and society and commends Job to commit his case to God by the traditional confession of faith whereby the worshippers approached God in confidence and hope. The Hymn of Praise in 9.4-10 is plainly relevant to its context. Bildad has just advanced the orthodox view of the providence of God expressed in the doctrine of sin and retribution, holding out the hope of the divine mercy on human repentance. Job's reply is to admit the might and unfathomable wisdom of God in nature. But by the same token God is inscrutable and inaccessible in the personal need of humans, as the immediate context states (vv. 3, 11-12). In reply (in 12.7-10, 13-25) to Zophar's presentation of the orthodox view of God's providence and the possibility of grace (ch. 11) Job admits the doctrine of Divine Providence in the same literary convention but emphasizes the destructive rather than the constructive aspect of providence (vv. 13-25). This section, which is actually a parody of a Hymn of Praise, is particularly characteristic of the author's originality in adapting familiar literary forms to new significance according to their context in his argument.

In Scripture the citation of a verse or even a phrase is often evocative of a much larger passage and its characteristic context. Thus Job's question 'Am I Sea or Tannin?' (7.12) is to be understood as evoking a well-known theme of the Hymn of Praise, God's triumph over the primeval powers of Chaos. Thus the author animadverts on the providence of God who would thus treat a righteous person, a moral being who aspired to realize the image of God within oneself, and on the abuse of his almighty power in breaking a mere mortal who might more fittingly have been the object of his mercy.

Certain forms of *prophetic communication* are also adapted in the Book of Job. The communication of Eliphaz, for instance, in 4.12-16 employs the form of the prophetic declaration of a theophany and the ensuing oracle adapted as a sapiential statement (4.17-21). The apparent indictment of Job for palpable sins (22.6-9), and the punishment for them introduced by the formula 'Therefore' (*lākēn*) is the traditional prophetic form of indictment, probably adapted from the controversy (*rîḇ*) originally sustained by an advocate for God in the sacrament of the Covenant (Gemser 1955: 128ff.) (cf. Judg. 6.7-10 and, with a detailed list of offences, Amos 2.6-12; Hos. 4.1-2; Ps. 50.17-21). This passage, however, is not, as in the true prophetic tradition, directed at a particular person or community, least of all Job, of whom Eliphaz alleges no particular sins here, upbraiding him not for sin but for impatience and despair (4.3-6). Eliphaz does eventually charge Job with particular sins, mainly of omission (ch. 22), but this is the forensic tradition, and is to be understood as giving Job a concrete charge to answer and in preparation of his oath of purgation (ch. 31).

Throughout the book, where the theodicy is called in question and Job asserts his claim to be allowed to state his case at the bar and be answered in open court by God, the figures, phraseology and literary *forms of law* abound, duly emphasized by Richter, perhaps overemphasized at the expense of the wide range of other literary forms equally prominent in Job. Nevertheless the legal forms and figures are impressive, as we should expect in a book of this kind, which opens with the activity of the 'public prosecutor' in the heavenly court and ends with God's counter-challenge to Job:

> Gird up your loins like a warrior
> That I may question you and you shall declare to me... (38.3)

The most striking and significant of the legal forms is Job's great oath of purgation. This convention was well attested in antiquity. In cases between two parties where no witness was available, an oath was taken at the sanctuary by which the parties invoked grave penalties upon themselves. This was known in Mesopotamian law (The Code of Hammurabi §§103, 106, 107, regarding claims of merchants and travelling agents; §249, where a hired ox is alleged to have died a natural death; and §266, when a shepherd claims to have lost beasts entrusted to his care by the attack of beasts of prey). The last case was settled also in Israel by oath of purgation at the sanctuary (Exod. 22.9), like alleged adultery (Num. 5.16-28) and other unspecified cases (1 Kgs 8.31ff.; 2 Chron. 6.22ff.). A particularly close formal correspondence with Job 31 may be observed in Psalm 7. See further H.H. Schmidt (1928). Nearer the time of Job the oath of purgation at the sanctuary was known in the Judaeo-Aramaean colony at Elephantine by Aswan.[13] The negative confession of various sins in similar context was projected into the judgment in the hereafter in the Egyptian Book of the Dead (*ANET*^{3}, 34-36), in connection with the ceremony of weighing the heart of the defunct against the feather of *ma'at* (Order, Truth), which Dhorme cites (1928: 412) à propos of Job 31.6:

> Then may (God) weigh me with just balance,
> And let him know my innocence.

Actually Job's oath of purgation itself shows a variety of literary forms, which Fohrer (1963a: 84 n. 24) has classified as:

13. Volz 1912. The passage is in Pap. 27 of Sachau's edition.

1. the solemn assertion of innocence, invoking a covenant to which the subject is a party (31.1-4),
2. an adjuration stating the conditions under which the specified curses would be operative (vv. 5-35, 38-40b, 16-17, 18, 19-20, 21-22).
3. an adjuration stating the conditions under which the curse would be operative, but not specifying the curse (vv. 24-34).

In view of our arrangement of the text here, however (see below, Introduction to ch. 31), we should include vv. 24-35 in the second category, thus eliminating Fohrer's third class.

The enumerations of twelve different sins is significant here, having an exact analogy in the twelve sins upon which a curse was endorsed by the sacral community at the Covenant Sacrament in the tradition of Shechem (Deut. 27.15-26). The sins of course are not the same as in the days when the community was thus safeguarded against absorption into the life and religion of Canaan; they relate to the individual, defining his duties as the Decalogue (Exod. 20.2-17; Deut. 5.6-21) had defined them, as a member of the covenant-community of Israel. The passage is valuable as indication of the relevance and development of such codes as the Decalogue among Jews in about the middle of the fifth century BCE.

Formally ch. 31 is a self-contained unit, but its adaptation in the Book of Job indicates clearly that it is integral to the structure of the book. It fittingly marks the culmination of Job's repeated appeal from the opinion of conventional morality to God himself. In the law of Israel and the ancient Near East the sanctuary was the final court of appeal in the oath of purgation. This invoked the immediate activity of God. In the context of the author's literary model, the Plaint of the Sufferer, God intervenes to help the sufferer who had implored his mercy. In the author's adaptation of his prototype God intervenes in response to Job's daring challenge in his oath of purgation. As the culmination of Job's dearest desire for confrontation with God and as anticipating the theophany and divine address (38.1–40.2, 6-14), Job's great oath of purgation in ch. 31 is indispensable in the structure of the book. By the same token the speeches of Elihu (chs. 32–37), whatever the value of their content and their representation of continued thought in the circle of the author of Job, are an intrusion which barbarously disregards the dramatic climax of the book.

Throughout the book, by his highly original adaptation of traditional literary types to reinforce ideas traditionally associated with them, but more often with the opposite significance in the style often of parody, the author has kept the reader on the alert. So he does to the end. Here, where we expect the Divine Declaration as an assurance in the convention of the Plaint of the Sufferer, or an acquittal or condemnation in the legal response to Job's oath of purgation, we have instead a counter-challenge, introduced by the language and literary form of a legal summons (38.1-3; 40.2, 7-8).[14] But here again the writer shows

14. The language is probably the reminiscence of belt-wrestling as a legal ordeal, which is attested in a legal document from Nuzu cited by Gordon 1950–51.

his familiarity with the wide range of literary forms. God's argument and counter-challenge is not sustained in legal forms, but in *forms familiar in the sapiential tradition*, where students were trained both to discriminate and recognize affinity by means of classified lists of natural phenomena, each item elaborated as a little Hymn of Praise to the Creator and all combining to praise his providence which reaches to realms beyond human power or comprehension, but into which they have a glimpse which may encourage them to hope beyond the full evidence of experience. The passages, on the various natural phenomena moreover in their interrogative form, have affinity with a form of controversy in Egyptian wisdom literature.

In a sapiential work like Job characteristic literary forms of wisdom literature are naturally used. The whole argument is in the form of the philosophic dialogue with thesis and antithesis as in the Egyptian Dialogue of a Man with his Own Soul (Thomas [ed.] 1958: 162-67) and the Babylonian Theodicy.[15] The Book of Job is the only example of Hebrew Wisdom in the form of a dramatic dialogue, but it has a variation in the experimental method of Ecclesiastes, where the sage states hypotheses and then proceeds critically to test them.

This is the method adopted in Job 21.17ff., where a number of proverbs typical of the conventional moral philosophy are cited—for example, 'How often is the lamp of the wicked put out?' (cf. Prov. 13.9; 20.20) and 'God stores up iniquity for their sons'—and are then exploded by the citation of actual experience.

The didactic poem is used to emphasize the principle of sin and retribution in Zophar's speech in 20.4-29. This may have been incorporated en bloc from a different context, but Job's riposte (21.7ff.), with a parody on the impunity of the wicked and the indiscriminate fate of wicked and innocent in death, clearly indicates that the passage was integral to the book. This passage recalls the question of the prosperity of the wicked which is cited as a scandal to the faithful sufferer in the psalms of the type the Plaint of the Sufferer (Pss. 10.5ff; 73.3-9; 17.17; 49.7; 52.9b), as Fohrer observes (1963a: 74).

The didactic declaration on the fate of the wicked and the blessing of the upright is familiar in couplets and in antithetic parallelism in Proverbs, e.g. 14.11:

> The house of the wicked will be destroyed,
> But the tent of the upright will flourish.

This theme may be amplified in an elaborate figure like the antithetic figures in Ps. 1.3ff., where the Homeric simile in v. 3 recalls that in Job 6.15-21. So the blessing of the righteous who has sought God's pardon and the fate of the obdurate wicked are set in antithesis in 11.14-20. Thus in Job there are didactic declarations at length and with a wealth of concrete detail and imagery on the wicked and their fate (in Job 4.8-11; 5.2-7; 8.8-19; 11.20; 15.17-35; 18.5-21

15. See above, p. 7.

and 20.4-29), which Job parodies, describing the prosperity of the wicked (21.7-16), and on the blessing of the righteous (in 5.17-27; 8.5-7; 11.13-19 and, after this model, ch. 29). Such passages are generally used respectively as sober admonition or as encouragement by Job's friends in support of the theodicy, but, as has been indicated, the author may characteristically give them an original turn in the mouth of Job. Here as in his use of other literary types he is not bound by the circumstances with which the literary form was traditionally associated, but it is only by the recognition of the traditional *Sitz im Leben* that the particular point of his usage of the literary type is appreciated.

The hymn on the fundamentality of Wisdom ('Where shall Wisdom be found?') in Job 28 is already known as a distinct literary type from the Hymn to Wisdom as God's instrument of creation in Prov. 8.22-31. In another context in the book, for instance, in the context of God's speeches, the passage might have been considered original, but in its actual context it must be regarded as secondary, a commentary on the limitations of traditional wisdom.

The classification of rebels against the light in Job 24.13-17 has its literary prototype in the classified categories in Prov. 30.18-19 (things which leave no trace of their course), 30.24-28 (creatures small but effective), 30.29-31 (beings stately in their gait) and 30.21-23:

> Under three things the earth trembles,
> Under four it cannot bear up:
> A slave when he becomes king,
> And a fool when he is filled with food,
> An unloved woman when she gets a husband,
> And a maid when she supplants her mistress.

Such classified lists of natural phenomena and social categories have already been noted as a feature of Mesopotamian and Egyptian wisdom literature (see above, pp. 5-8). The citation of classified instances of God's creation in the Divine Declaration (38.2–40.2, 6-14) shows the same influence of this sapiential type, being reminiscent particularly of the Onomesticon of Amenemope (probably thirteenth century BCE) (Gardiner 1947) 'on all the works of Ptah (the creator-god) in the sky and what pertains thereto, on the earth and what is in it', the affinities of which, with the Divine Declaration, have been particularly stressed by von Rad.[16]

The same ultimate influence of Egyptian wisdom tradition may be noticed in the interrogative form of the passages on the works of the Creator which constitute a challenge to Job in the Divine Declaration. Von Rad (1955: 298-301) cites the analogy of the Egyptian Papyrus Anastasi I (thirteenth century

16. Von Rad 1955; Richter 1958a. Richter would include the passages on the hippopotamus and the crocodile in this category, their fuller categorizations being of the same nature as the lists of natural phenomena according to their characteristics, their fulness being justified by their position as the culmination of the classified lists in ch. 39.

BCE) (*ANET*³, 477-78), where the scribe Hori humiliates a rival scribe by addressing a series of ironical questions, and challenges him on knowledge of details of scribal expertise and knowledge. A feature of this text is the challenge couched in the imperative as well as in the interrogative, as in Job 40.10-14:

> Pray deck yourself with pride and exaltation,
> And put on glory and splendour!
> Pour out your overflowing anger
> And lay low every haughty man you see.
> If you see any proud man abase him,
> Pull down the wicked from their place;
> Hide them in the dust together,
> Imprison their persons on the lowly ground;
> And I will render you praise
> That your right hand has wrought deliverance for you.

The use of the challenge in the imperative, along with the ironical question in the Egyptian sapiential prototype in Papyrus Anastasi I and the extension in the Onomasticon of Amenemope from the world of nature to society, might be cited as a strong argument for the view that in Job there is but a single Divine Declaration and not, as in the extant text, two speeches.

Apart from the formal affinity of the Divine Declaration in Job with the Egyptian prototypes there is common to both Hebrew and Egyptian texts the interest in the Divine Order in nature and society (Egyptian *ma'at* and Hebrew *ṣᵉḏāqāh* or *mišpāṭ*; see above, pp. 5-7), which the sufferings of the innocent have brought into question. God's government (*mišpāṭ*), a consequence of his sovereignty, was traditionally the theme of the Hymn of Praise in the liturgy of the New Year festival in Israel with its Canaanite prototype reflected in the Baal Myth of Ras Shamra. Thus the statement of God's activity in creation is impregnated with Canaanite mythology, especially in 38.4-11 which refers to God's triumph over Chaos, represented by the sea (38.8-11). Compare the Ras Shamra text Gordon *UT* 68, which was a prelude to the establishment of Baal as King and the imposition of his government in nature. The total effect of the divine address, then, is that of the traditional Hymn of Praise.

Thus the author of the Book of Job moved easily through the wide range of 'Hebrew life and literature'.[17] Preoccupied with his main moral problem, he was too skilful a teacher and a poet to present a colourless philosophic discussion, but introduced a rich variety of language, figures and literary forms, which enlivened his argument and extended the scope of his message beyond the schools of the sages to the whole of the life of his people.

17. The use and adaptation of those literary forms with their specific significance in the tradition of Israel is a strong indication that the Book of Job was intended for a Jewish audience and not, as Tur-Sinai suggests (1957: xxvii; 2nd edn 1967: xxxvii), to convince the Gentiles in Mesopotamia.

Chapter 6

The Composition of the Book of Job

The Narrative Framework

Having discussed the possibility of a popular version of the ordeal of an innocent sufferer and his tenacious endurance in faith, which possibly developed from such a text as we have noticed in Mesopotamia, which is actually attested at Ras Shamra in the fourteenth century BCE (see above, p. 18), we have argued for a didactic version in rhythmic narrative prose in Israel in the early monarchy (see above, p. 18). The tradition survives in the Prologue and Epilogue, with the editor's adaptation to theological conceptions in Judaism in the fifth century BCE. This serves the author as a basis for his more mature sapiential work in the intervening Dialogue and its sequel in Job's *apologia pro vita sua* (ch. 29), his plaint (ch. 30) and his oath of purgation (ch. 31), the Divine Declaration (38.1–40.14), and Job's submission (40.3-5; 42.2-6). In the Epilogue it serves also as a counterpoise to the very sharp criticism of the orthodox teaching of the sages of Israel in Proverbs and Wisdom Psalms expressed in the addresses of Job's friends in the Dialogue, as the final statement, or addendum, in Ecclesiastes (12.13f.) counterbalances the work of 'the gentle cynic'.

Job's Curse on the Day of his Birth

Before the Dialogue proper (chs. 4–27),[1] ch. 3 takes up the suggestion of Job's wife in the Prologue to 'curse God and die!' (2.9). Job does not succumb to this temptation, but in cursing the day of his birth and the futility of a life exposed to unremitting suffering, he seriously questions God's Order, a recurrent theme of the Dialogue. This chapter then serves as a bridge between the Prologue and the Dialogue.

The Dialogue

The Dialogue in the MT is limited to chs. 4–27, though we will question what has been generally regarded as a debate in three rounds of addresses and

1. Fohrer (1989: 34) treats this chapter as part of the Dialogue.

responses from each of the four speakers in which Zophar's expected third address is wanting or wrongly attributed to Job (see below, pp. 59ff.).

There is no question about the first two cycles of the Dialogue, which we may tabulate:

First Cycle (chs. 4–14)

4–5	Eliphaz's remonstrance to Job's curse (4.2–5.7) and encouragement (5.8-27)
6–7	Job's response
8	Bildad's expostulation (8.2-19) and encouragement (8.20-27)
9–10	Job's response
11	Zophar's expostulation (11.2-12) and encouragement (11.13-20)
12–13	Job's response (12.2–13.19) and direct appeal to God (13.20-27)
14	Job's direct address to God continued, ending the first cycle of the Dialogue

Second Cycle (chs. 15–21)

15	Eliphaz's expostulation
16–17	Job's response, emphasizing his sufferings in the language and imagery of the Plaint of the Sufferer (16.6-17; 17.1-2, 6-8, 11-16), with a plea for direct confrontation with God (16.18-20), direct appeal to God (17.3.4) and final statement of his integrity (17.9)
18	Bildad's expostulation
19	Job's response
20	Zophar's expostulation
21	Job's response

Conclusion of the Dialogue (chs. 22–27)

22	Eliphaz's expostulation and arraignment of Job (22.5-8) in anticipation of Job's *apologia* (ch. 29) and oath of purgation (ch. 31), with encouragement to come to terms with God and be restored to favour (22.21-30)
23; 24.1-12	Job's response, amplified by a wisdom poem on the conduct of the wicked (24.13-17), with possible interpolation of a Wisdom poem on their eventual retribution (24.18-25)
25; 26.5-14	Hymn of Praise to God transcendent (ch. 25 attributed, perhaps secondarily, to Bildad), secondarily introduced by 26.2-4, secondarily attributed to Job
27	Job's final dismissal of his friends' case, with an oath of purgation (27.2-6) and elaboration of the consequences to him of perjury (27.7ff.)

With this the Dialogue ends

29–31	Job's Oath of Purgation and Prelude Job's *apologia*, with its social potential (ch. 29) Job's Plaint, implying the impairing of that potential (ch. 30) Job's Oath of Purgation (ch. 31); this is at once a response to Eliphaz's particular accusations in 22.5-8 and a prelude to the Divine Declaration

38.1–39.30; 40.25-30 (EVV 1-6); 40.7-14	The Divine Declaration
40.3-5; 42.1-6	Job's Submission
42.7-11	Epilogue

Interpolations

24.13-17	Wisdom poem on nocturnal criminals
24.18-25	Wisdom poem on the eventual retribution of the wicked
25.2-6; 26.5-14	Hymn of Praise to God Transcendent
28	Sapiential poem on Wisdom
32–37	Elihu addendum, addressed to the arguments of Job and his friends, culminating in Hymn of Praise to the Divine Creator (36.26–37.12)
40.15-24 (EVV 41.7-11)	Poem on Behemoth, the Hippopotamus
41.4-26 (EVV 41.12-34)	Poem on Leviathan, the Crocodile, secondarily prefaced by 40.25-30 (EVV 41.1-6)
42.12ff.	Midrashic Expansion

The Dialogue

The Dialogue proper opens with Eliphaz's response with mild yet firm censure of Job's impassioned reaction to his suffering. He urges the current doctrine of the sages that suffering implied sin, which he advises Job accept, and by due contrition to return to the divine favour. From this point the Dialogue proceeds with addresses to the same effect by the three friends, with diminution of the element of encouragement which marks the end of the addresses by Eliphaz (5.8-27), Bildad (8.20-22) and Zophar (11.13-20) in the first cycle of the Dialogue and the intensification of their insistence on the theme of the invariable connection of sin and suffering, which Job refuses to admit in his case, becoming more and more vehement in his protestation throughout the first cycle of the Dialogue. The intensity of Job's response to his friends is marked by direct address to God (7.7-21; 10.2-22; 13.20-29), and in the final colourful soliloquy on the mortality of humanity in ch. 14 (vv. 2-6, 15-17), which ends the first cycle of the Dialogue. Here also emerges Job's appeal to God to state the charges against him (10.2) that might explain and justify his affliction, with an urgent appeal for confrontation with God and a fair chance to reply to actual charges (13.20-23).

In the second round of the Dialogue (chs. 15–21) the friends intensify their censure of Job for opposing their arguments and the tradition which emphasized the mutual relevance of suffering and sin to his resentment directed to God and his daring demand for a confrontation. Their theme is sustained by what traditional Wisdom taught of the ultimate end of the wicked in striking figures (15.17-35, Eliphaz; 18.5-21, Bildad; 20.5-29, Zophar) with the added notice that even in the heyday of the wicked, retribution is anticipated by the hazards of their conduct: 'the wicked are racked by anxiety all their days' (15.20; 18.11-12). To Eliphaz, Job replies in the style and figure of the Plaint of the Sufferer (16.8-17; 17) and similarly to Bildad (19.11-20), emphasizing the alienation of his friends (16.8–17.5), with particular reference to Eliphaz and his colleagues (16.7; 19.2-6), which leaves him but the prospect of vindication before a divine tribunal (16.18-22; 19.25-27). To Zophar's declaration on the downfall of the prosperous wicked (ch. 20), and generally to the friends' arguments in support of the theodicy, Job concludes the second cycle of the Dialogue by elaborating the flourishing of the wicked without retribution, culminating in an honoured burial and incidentally exploding what Bildad has claimed as the universal validity of well-worn proverbs (18.5ff.).

We consider it questionable that the author conceived a third cycle of the Dialogue corresponding to the first two. Volz (1911: 66ff.) long ago expressed this doubt. It is not to be denied that sentiments attributed to Job in the MT are more characteristic of the views already expressed by the friends and this has suggested disruption of the text.[2] Buhl considered that chs. 25–28 is a collection of short passages of varying origin adapted to the author's work secondarily with the intention of depicting Job as eventually conforming to the orthodox view of the theodicy which he has so sharply criticized (Buhl 1925). This view has been revived with modification by Snaith, who proposes that the section consists of distinct fragments not indeed of various origin but possibly written by the author himself, though never quite integrated with the Dialogue.[3] Westermann has developed the thesis of Volz. Starting from the assumption that a third round of the Dialogue contains only one speech of Eliphaz's and none of Bildad and Zophar, closing with Job's statement in ch. 23, Westermann proposes that chs. 24–27 consist of fragments comprising parts of earlier speeches and later additions which have not been fully integrated into the book (Westermann 1956: 102-104). Thus he would associate 24.1-17, on the instances of oppression unchecked by God, with Job's earlier statements on this subject, and would associate 24.18-21, on the condign end of the wicked, with one of the friends' earlier statements. Again 24.5-8, 10-11, describing the wretchedness of the oppressed, and 24.13-17, a series of vignettes classifying malefactors hostile to the light in the tradition of the listing of manifestations of a common principle in sapiential literature (e.g. Prov. 10.15f., 18f., 21-23,

2. Sentiments attributed to Job in the MT more characteristic of the views already expressed by his friends have suggested the disruption of the text (so Tournay 1957; Pfeiffer 1953: 171; *inter alios*).

3. According to Snaith (1968: 61-63), 'the most probable solution to the literary problem of cc. 24-26 is that in these chapters we have the further speculations of the author himself concerning the whole problem of God in his heaven and man on the earth, and that either he began to fit these ideas into his scheme, but died before he proceeded very far, or found them too difficult, if not impossible, to fit into his scheme, and gave up'.

24-28, 29-31), may be excerpts from some sapiential source listed for incorporation into the Book of Job but never quite integrated with it.[4] Westermann gets over the difficulty of the exceptionally short statement attributed to Bildad in ch. 25 in the form of a Hymn of Praise to the majesty and righteousness of God by assuming that, with 26.5-14 in the same tenor, it belongs to Bildad's statement in ch. 8, an arrangement which Volz had already proposed (1911: 34). This is feasible insofar as it might explain Job's riposte to the citation of a Hymn of Praise to God as sustainer of creation in 9.5-10 and the passage on God's sublime indifference to Job's outraged innocence in 9.11-24. Westermann further proposes that 26.1-4 and its heading was the introduction to Job's statement in ch. 9 which lacks the customary sapiential introduction. In ch. 27 he takes vv. 2-6, in which adjuration predominates, as probably the introduction to Job's oath of purgation in ch. 31, and proposes that 27.8-10, 13-25, which is counter to Job's declarations hitherto, as the end of Zophar's statement in ch. 11, while 27.11-12, which is in the characteristic style of the introduction to statements of the disputants, is, Westermann suggests, the introduction to Elihu's speech in ch. 32 or to the poem on Wisdom in ch. 28. Fohrer also would find disruption of any dialogue in chs. 24–27 by displacement of text, adjustment and insertion (1989: 34-36), particularly of independent poems from the Wisdom tradition. In what he regards as the third cycle of the Dialogue (chs. 21–27), though incomplete, he admits Job's statement in ch. 21 and Eliphaz's statement in ch. 22 as original and in place. From the exceptionally short statement attributed to Job in ch. 23, Fohrer assumes that a longer statement was intended, indicated by the statement in 27.11 'I will teach you concerning the power of God', a promise which is apparently not realized. He suggests that Job's statement in ch. 23 and perhaps in 27.11 was possibly interrupted by the secondary insertion of Wisdom poems, four in ch. 24 (10.12, 22-23; 5-8; 13-17; and 18ff., with glosses and secondary expansion); a Hymn of Praise to the Creator, attributed in the MT to Bildad, probably secondarily, in ch. 25 and continued in 26.5-14, 26.2-4 and 27.2-6 as Job's last statement in the Dialogue; and 27.7-10, 13-23 on the end of the wicked as a sapiential poem.

While subject-matter in the various parts of chs. 22–27 might with considerable adjustment afford material for the reconstruction of a third cycle of dialogue involving all four disputants according to sentiments already associated with each, form-criticism, we would contend, indicates that this is unlikely. The fixed points that must guide us are Eliphaz's statement in ch. 22, the main point of which is his indictment of Job, alleging his failure to fulfil the responsibilities of his prosperity and high standing. This directly anticipates, and is specifically related to, Job's great oath of purgation (ch. 31),

4. Volz 1911: 45; Fohrer (1989: 367, 370) resolves this chapter into four separate Wisdom poems, of which only the first, vv. 1-4, 10-12, 22-23, on his arrangement, represents Job's view as in his statements in ch. 23.

preceded by his prosperity and its benefits to society (ch. 29), all of which have been lost in his ruin (ch. 30).This passage, taken in conjunction with ch. 29 is tantamount to an indictment of Job's divine antagonist at law. The next stage is the divine response (38.2–39.30; 40.25-30 (EVV 41.1-6), and Job's submission (40.4-5; 42.2-6).

Between Eliphaz's indictment (ch. 22) and chs. 29–31 is Job's insistence on the justice of his case if only he could gain a hearing from God (23; 27.2-6) in the personal tone of dialectic and forensic idiom, which is proper to that context, where Job's case rapidly approaches its climax in the divine confrontation. The intervening passages (24.1-25; 25.2-6 and 26.5-14) are markedly impersonal and of a different literary form. Chapter 24 as a whole is a sapiential poem, or, according to Fohrer, four sapiential poems on the cruelty of oppressors, and their eventual retribution; 25.2-6 is a Hymn or part of a Hymn of Praise to God transcendent, beyond the questioning of humanity, a mere worm (25.6); it is continued in 26.5-14 in the theme of God's sovereignty in creation, which the poet describes as 'but the outskirts of his ways', of which humans apprehended only 'a whisper'. 27.7-10, 13-23 is a sapiential poem on the miserable end of the sinner, which, however, we consider that the author adapted as imprecation to Job's oath in 27.2-6 in his final dismissal of his friends. And finally, to support the view that between ch. 22 and chs. 29–31 there has been substantial interpolation of secondary matter, is the poem on Wisdom (ch. 28), which is generally taken as independent, and the Elihu addendum (chs. 32–37).

Assuming the secondary nature of those poetic passages in the Dialogue, we may ask what prompted their inclusion between 22; 23; 26.1-4; 27.1-6, 11-12. In ch. 24 the detailed list of abuses of power amplify Eliphaz's allegation of Job's sins of omission and failure to fulfil his responsibilities. In the same context the passage on nocturnal criminals, surely the citation of a sapiential categorization, may be prompted by Eliphaz's imputation to Job of the question, 'What does God know?' (22.14).

The hymnic statement ascribed to Bildad (25.2-6), setting the question of human justification before God in the context of his transcendent might, obviously relates to Job's persistent assertion of innocence and confidence of acquittal if only he had a fair hearing. This is the adaptation to Job's case of a Hymn of Praise continued in 26.5-14, as is indicated by the assertion of God's sovereignty 'on high' (25.2) and in the underworld (26.5f.), and is an instance of citation *in extenso*[5] which recurs in such passages cited to reinforce dialectic arguments throughout the Dialogue. The ascription of ch. 25 to Bildad in the MT may reflect the secondary effort to construct a full-scale third cycle of the Dialogue comparable to the first two. 26.2-4, which we consider redactionally

5. Tur-Sinai (1957: liiif.) duly notes this citation *in extenso*, which he explains as intended to certify the citation of a certain sentiment or sentence as coming from an authoritative source and not simply an expression of the author's personal opinion.

ascribed to Job, probably belongs to a tentative third address by Bildad reflecting the introduction to Eliphaz's first address (4.3ff.).

With the admission of a possible third statement of Bildad, though tentative, however, we would not see in 27.7-10, 13-23 a third statement of Zophar, whose sentiments it admittedly expresses though it does seem to be a Wisdom poem, as Fohrer maintains, but, we consider, not independent and incorporated by a redactor endeavouring to construct a third cycle of the Dialogue, where Job wishes upon his antagonists in the Dialogue the fate of the wicked, the theme of the poem quoted. We regard it as belonging to Job's adjuration in 27.2-6.

We propose a form-critical approach to the problem of ch. 27 in favour of the whole in the order of MT as the statement of Job as the heading states. The statement asserting his innocence is in the form of an oath (vv. 2-6); what follows is a Wisdom poem adapted by the author as an imprecation. In his strenuous protestation of his innocence Job includes in his imprecation 'his enemy', that is any who is alienated from him on the assumption that the sufferer is guilty and alienated from God, including by implication his friends. In this and what follows we should find a formal affinity with the curse on those opposed to the sufferer in the Plaint of the Sufferer (e.g. Pss. 35.26; 55.16, 24 [EVV 15, 23]; 58.7-10 [EVV 6-9]; 59.11-14 [EVV 10-13]; 69.23-29 [EVV 22-28]; 139.19-22).

In pursuance of the theme of 'the fate of the wicked', which he wishes upon his antagonists (27.7-10), the author introduces a sapiential poem on the retribution of the wicked (vv. 13-23). This is introduced by an address to the friends, whom Job undertakes to teach the 'purpose of the Almighty (vv. 11f.). What follows seems at first sight nothing new to the friends. But in the mouth of Job, who had dissociated himself from their conclusion from his suffering to his guilt and their elaboration *ad nauseam* of the fate of the wicked under the divine economy, it was calculated to surprise, and indeed shock, them. We consider it in effect an elaboration of Job's imprecation not only on his antagonists but on himself if guilty of perjury in his oath in vv. 2-6. With this oath of purgation Job terminates his case with his friends. In thus dismissing them he uses their own theme of the fate of the wicked, 'which they themselves have seen' (v. 12a), but in a much less impersonal and even superficial way ('Why then this empty vapouring?'), holding himself liable to the same fate if he is perjuring himself.

Job's Great Oath of Purgation and Prelude

Job's *apologia* (ch. 29) is an effective reply to his arraignment by Eliphaz and is complementary to his oath of purgation (ch. 31). The solemn oath with its imprecations is his preparation for his final confrontation with God for which he has been continuously pressing in the Dialogue. He has been directing his case progressively from his friends to God and now, having dismissed them in his sworn statement in ch. 27, he makes his final appeal to the divine tribunal. This demands response from God either in condemnation or acquittal. The prelude, moreover, in the glowing picture of the social benefits of the divine favour which Job had enjoyed and shared (ch. 29) and of the great social potential crippled by the suffering he endured (ch. 30) is in itself a case against God who had permitted this situation to develop. On this account the divine response is surely imperative.

The Divine Declaration

The Divine Declaration, which we take as a unity (38.1-39; 40.25-30 [EVV 41.1-6; 40.2, 6-14]), with displacement of 40.25-30 (EVV 41.1-6) on Leviathan (the crocodile) and Job's submission in 40.4-5 from before 42.2-6, with the poems on Behemoth, the hippopotamus, (40.15-24, 31-32; 41.1-3) and Leviathan (41.4-26 [EVV 12-34]) as a later addition, has been rejected by some as part of the original Book of Job.[6] Suffice it to say that the narrative source of the Book in 42.7 implies a Divine Declaration. In the context of the author's version this was demanded by Job's challenge in his oath of purgation and its prelude. On the analogy of the theophany and oracle in the Plaint of the Sufferer, in the form of which Job's hard case is so often presented, such a Divine Declaration is expected, as also in the Mesopotamian texts on the same subject which we have noticed (see above, p. 9). The answer is not a formal acquittal in the legal tradition, as the source in the epilogue implies, nor formally assurance as in the Plaint of the Sufferer. In the developed work of the author of Job it relates to the Order in nature and society for which Job's friends have contended against Job's sharp criticism and indeed parody (ch. 12) with relation to his own case. Thus it takes the form of a magnificent statement of Divine Omnipotence and Wisdom in creation beyond human control or comprehension (ch. 38) and of Divine Providence for the wild creatures apart from human control or convenience (ch. 39). However, this statement in itself, though properly emphasizing that humans are not the measure of the universe so that they may call God's economy in question, is not so obviously related to the human predicament in the Dialogue, and so called for the challenge to Job to match God in the effective control of the social Order (40.2, 6-14).

Thus, in the author's development of his source, we would admit the Divine Declaration, as we have delimited it, in its universal scope. Less would not have been expected of God in reply to Job's contention in the Dialogue; nor would we expect less of the poet in such a monumental work. Moreover, while we cannot ignore the rebuke to human presumption to criticize God's economy despite their limited knowledge and experience, we cannot agree

6. E.g. Studer 1875; Staples 1925: 11f.; Rankin 1936: 93; Irwin 1937: 45ff.

with Cornill's opinion that the Divine Declaration was savagely ironical.[7] The irony, which is not to be mistaken, was more kindly, 'the expression of a concealed severity and calm superiority' and 'the effective and benevolent incisiveness of a higher insight', according to Ewald (1882: 294). It is at the same time an encouragement to mortals in citing the many instances of God's daily providence besides the spectacular evidence of his rule and Order expressed in the Hymn of Praise familiar in the history of Israel in the liturgy of the New Year festival (Westermann 1956: 91ff.).

The question remains as to the extent of the Divine Declaration, apart from what we consider addenda, the poems on Behemoth (40.15-24, 31-32; 41.1-3) and Leviathan (41.4-26 [EVV 12-34]). The double introduction 'And Yahweh answered Job out of the whirlwind' (38.1 and 40.6), in both cases with the challenge 'Brace yourself like a man and I will question you and you shall declare to me' (38.3; 40.7), would seem to indicate two declarations[8] or perhaps two versions which have been unskilfully fused. The double submission of Job in the MT (40.3-5 and 42.1-6) might indicate the same. The substance of 40.2, 6-14, however, stressing the limitations of Job in the moral Order, which more distinctly connects with the attitude of Job assumed in the Dialogue, might justify a repetition of the formal challenge to Job in 40.7, unless with Fohrer it is taken, like 40.1, after 38.1, as a redactional gloss. The assertion of God's omnipotence in the moral Order, however, is the natural complement to the declaration of his power and providence in the natural Order, as well as being directly relevant to the debate in the Dialogue. We would therefore retain it as an integral part of a single Divine Declaration,[9] whether we regard 40.7 as a fresh challenge to Job, to whose case 40.2, 6-14 is particularly relevant, or Fohrer is right in regarding it as a redactional gloss.

Job's Submission

In the interest of a single Divine Declaration we would agree with Fohrer in assuming a single submission of Job, assuming the displacement of 40.4-5 from immediately before 42.2-6.

7. Quoted by Strahan 1914: 14.
8. So Le Fèvre 1949: 1081; Skehan 1964; Gordis 1965: 122f.
9. So Bickell, Budde, Duhm, Steuernagel, Sellin, Lods, Hölscher, Siegfried, Fullerton, Lindblom, Lévêque, Fohrer. Westermann regards the Divine Declaration as *substantially* one though *formally* divided. Others propose the omission of 38.1–39.30 (e.g. Kraeling 1938: 144). Eissfeldt (1965: 459) also finds 40.6-14, with Job's reply in 42.1-6, more closely linked with the main theme of the Dialogue than anything else in the Divine Declaration; cf. K. Fullerton (1924), who rejected 40.3-4, presumably since God's control of his order in nature in 38.1–40.2, to which Fullerton would confine the Divine Declaration along with 40.3-4, involves also his control of the moral Order. S.R. Driver and G.B. Gray (1921: 160) omit 40.6-14, a modification of Gray's earlier view that both parts of the Divine Declaration were secondary (G.B. Gray 1913).

Major Addenda

The Poem on Wisdom

Between the complex chs. 22–27 and Job's oath of purgation and its prelude in chs. 29–31 stands the Poem on Wisdom (ch. 28). This has formal affinity with the sapiential tradition of instruction by question and answer (e.g. Prov. 23.29; Eccl. 8.1ff.; etc.), the question being a refrain,[10] 'As for Wisdom, whence comes she...?' The answer is deliberately withheld by statements of inaccessibility by the most strenuous effort of humans and the inestimable value of Wisdom, which emphasizes the final answer that God alone understands the way to Wisdom, his instrument in creation (cf. Prov. 8.23-31).

In the present book it follows ch. 27, which is headed as a statement of Job, and being itself without a heading it has been taken as a continuation of Job's statement (so Budde). But in the detached academic tradition, as distinct from the dramatic Dialogue with its heavy borrowing from forensic idiom, the Plaint of the Sufferer and the Hymn of Praise, to say nothing of Job's agonized pleas to God, it is obviously *sui generis* and is suspect as a secondary insertion. This suspicion is confirmed by the fact that the statement that Wisdom is the property of God alone (and is unattainable to any human) would unduly anticipate the main point of the Divine Declaration.[11]

As a sober limitation to the confident claim of traditional Wisdom that Wisdom could be acquired according to the repeated exhortations in Proverbs, this passage would be admittedly a fitting conclusion to the inadequate efforts of Job's friends to explain the sufferings of the worthy man by the traditional doctrine of the theodicy, as well as an animadversion on Job's negative and humanistic arguments. This evidently persuaded Westermann and Tournay that the passage belonged to the original conception of the book of Job (Westermann 1956: 107; Tournay 1957: 31), but in view of the interruptions to the dramatic movement of the work by the incorporation of wisdom poems and hymns of praise between chs. 23 and 29–31 we would regard ch. 28 as also redactional. It may be an insertion by one of the author's circle, and we are prepared to admit that it was by the author himself, perhaps available to a later redactor.[12]

However fitting the poem may have been as a conclusion to the Dialogue and as a corrective to the assurance of Job's sapiential friends and of himself,

10. Fohrer suggests that the same question or a variation of it may have introduced the poems; so A. Weiser (1968: 198), J. Lindblom (1945: 79) and C. Kuhl (1953: 1. 281) regard the introduction as the fragment displaced to 27.11.

11. M. Jastrow (1920: 136), C.J. Ball (1922: 8), P. Szczygiel (1931: 233), J. Lindblom (1945: 91) and N.H. Tur-Sinai (1957: 395) regard the poem as displaced from after the Divine Declaration, not as a comment on the inadequacy of the wisdom of Job's friends in the Dialogue, but as a supplement to the Divine Declaration.

12. So Gordis 1965: 102. We hardly agree with Gordis, however, in his assessment of the poem as 'probably a youthful effort'.

its inclusion in this particular context, where the text has suffered disturbance, may have been through its association with other independent poems assembled for inclusion at some point or other in the Book of Job, and was perhaps specifically suggested by the couplet in 27.11:

> I will teach you concerning the power of God,
> The purpose of the Almighty I will not hide.

The Elihu Passages

Those passages (chs. 32–37), which intervene awkwardly to break the dramatic sequence between Job's invocation of the immediate activity of God in his great oath of purgation (ch. 31) and the theophany and Divine Declaration (38.1ff.), are certainly an intrusion, and are so treated by practically all modern commentators, though a number have regarded them as integral to the book.[13]

There are certain very significant features in the Elihu passages which suggest an origin independent of the rest of the Book of Job. Elihu is not mentioned among Job's friends in the Prologue, the Epilogue or the Dialogue. Nor does Job reply to him as he does to his three friends, and in the Divine Declaration which immediately ensues at 38.1 it is to Job in his final appeal in ch. 31 that God replies. The section is disproportionately long, a lecture or learned treatise rather than a round of argument or lively debate as in the statements of Job and his friends in the Dialogue, with their striking figures of speech.[14] Elihu is not committed as Job and his friends, but theologically detached. A number of new words appear in Elihu's statements which occur nowhere else in Job, and Wagner's statistics show about half as many Aramaisms again than in the rest of Job excluding the Prologue and Epilogue (Wagner 1966: 139-43).

It is often objected that the Elihu passages add nothing to the argument. That is true in so far as strict relevance to the main theme of Job is concerned, but Elihu has his insights, notably the disciplinary purpose of suffering, particularly in the case of the worthy man, as a preventative of spiritual pride (33.12-30). Much indeed of this section is a recapitulation of the arguments of Job and his friends, with specific citation of Job's statements, but new points are made and new emphasis laid. The significant contribution of the Elihu passages is the emphasis laid on the urgency of God's grace beyond the anxiety or expectancy of humans (33.14ff.; 35.10) and on the attitude of praise to God for the signal tokens of his providence, which will leave humans no time for recrimination but will help them to adjust themselves to realities. But so far as Elihu's arguments elicit no response from Job, and since his insistence

13. Cornill 1907: 426ff.; Wildeboer 1905: 380f., 382ff.; so also Van Hoonacker 1903; Pedersen 1926: 531; Humbert 1955; Peters 1928: 23-29; Szczygiel 1931: 23ff.; Dennefeldt 1939; Eerdmans 1939: 16f.; Dubarle 1946: 84ff.; Guillaume 1964b: 27-35.

14. This was already emphasized by E. Renan (1889: 37); cf. S. Mowinckel (1955: 313): 'He has the whole discussion in his head and takes up particular propositions, partly in verbal citation, partly in contradicting them in the tone of a schoolmaster'.

on God's providential order in nature beyond the understanding of humanity is simply a statement of God's own declaration,[15] it must be said that, whatever fresh insights the Elihu passages present, they contribute nothing to the dialectic progress of the debate as such, but in the nature of commentary they must be regarded as intrusive. The fact remains, however, that Elihu seems less concerned to help Job to adjust himself to his situation and own his guilt and so find pardon than with the *raison d'être* of suffering as an academic. Recognizing this, Rowley argues that since the reason for Job's suffering is already known as a test of his piety, this concern of Elihu indicates the secondary nature of the passage.

The unity of the Elihu passages has been questioned. Thus H.H. Nichols (1910–11) proposed that chs. 32–33, 34 and 35–37 were from different hands, a view which was developed by Jastrow, who distinguished four quite distinct compositions in the Elihu section,[16] and W.A. Irwin (1937: 36ff.) who regarded chs. 32–33 as the original ending to the Book of Job according to a hand later than the author of the Dialogue and chs. 34–37 as later comments from sapiential tradition between c. 400 and 100 BCE. More recently Westermann maintained that the Elihu speeches are artificially composed from an unfinished draft of supplementary arguments to the Dialogue (1956: 109). This view was developed by D.N. Freedman, who concluded that the Elihu passages, already elaborated as several speeches in their present form, were composed by the author of the book of Job with the intention of re-organizing his work, a project which he gave up because it would have disrupted unduly the existing form of the Book. The theme of the conclusion of the Elihu passages, however, expressed in the Hymn of Praise (36.22ff.), was developed in the Divine Declaration, especially in ch. 38. The Elihu passages were then added subsequently in their present place by a later hand (Freedman 1968). But whether the material assembled according to Freedman was the work of the author of the Book rather than an independent supplement is a matter which seems to defy solution. In the view of the detached academic interest which we have noted in contrast to the more intense involvement of the speakers in the Dialogue we consider the latter explanation of the Elihu passages the more likely. It can well be imagined that the Book of Job became a favourite text in sapiential circles, and it is not unlikely that the Elihu section is a crystallization of theses from the Book of Job originally debated piecemeal in such circles, like the theses in Ecclesiastes. If this is so, we may expect considerable disagreement among critics as to the order in which the matter was composed in the Elihu speeches or the order in which it has been transmitted in the MT.

15. Lévêque concludes from Elihu's verbal citations of Job's statements that the author of the Elihu section had a written text of the Dialogue before him and that the challenge in interrogatory form on the subject of created nature in 37.15-20 is a conscious imitation of the Divine Declaration, which was included in this written text.

16. Jastrow 1920: 77ff.; so also Buttenwieser and Kraeling.

The Passages on Behemoth and Leviathan

Anyone who has experience of speaking or writing for effect knows the importance of making a decisive conclusion. Thus after the passage on the sovereignty of God and the limitations of Job in society, in direct reply to the problem of Job, the reversion to the theme of creatures in nature beyond human control in the long descriptive passages on Behemoth and Leviathan must surely make a first impression of a later expansion.[17] Considering the possible relevance of those passages, Westermann suggests that Behemoth and Leviathan are treated as historical forces hostile to God, as Egypt was depicted as *tannîn*, the monster of the Nile, possibly envisaged as the crocodile, in Ezek. 29.3.[18] However, this is questionable. Leviathan in the eschatological passage in Isa. 27.1 and Rahab in Isa. 51.9, which Westermann cites, are rather the cosmic forces traditionally overcome by God in the establishment of his effective rule, the theme of the liturgy in the New Year festival in Mesopotamia and Canaan, where *ltn* (Hebrew *liwyāṯān*) is known in the Ras Shamra texts with this significance. The historification of this theme, as for instance in Ezek. 29.3, is secondary to the cosmic theme and a particularization of it. The description of Behemoth and Leviathan undoubtedly refer respectively to the hippopotamus and the crocodile, but the designation of the latter as 'Leviathan' is extraordinary since the Hebrew and Ugaritic traditions describe the monster as 'serpent' (*naḥas/bṯn*). Hence H.H. Schmidt has contended for mythological overtones in the passage on Leviathan[19] which may claim the support of the LXX, which renders Leviathan as *ho drakōn*. The same may be said for Behemoth, Egyptian *pꜣ'iḥmw*, the hippopotamus, which was the symbol of chaos ritually slain by the Pharaoh in the cult of Horus at Edfu.[20] Thus the passages on Behemoth and Leviathan have recently been defended as authentic by a number of scholars on the grounds mainly that those two monstrous instances of destructive power beyond human control, with their undertones of the myth of the conflict of cosmos and chaos, are a fitting climax to the Divine Declaration that even the suffering of the innocent, the helplessness of humanity and the apparent inadequacy of human justice are under the

17. Dhorme, having defended the originality of those passages in his commentary (1928: lxiii-lxxv), rejected them as later accretions in *La Bible* (1959: cxxxii). Lévêque (1970: 502f.) rejects the passages mainly on stylistic grounds. Hertzberg, Kuhl and Kissane consider them as addenda. Others have regarded them as compositions of the author but inserted later by him (so Larcher 1957: 13) or by a later scribe (so Steuernagel 1953: 382).

18. Westermann (1956: 87) contends that Leviathan has this significance in Isa. 27.1, like Rahab in Isa. 51.9; cf. Isa. 30.9, where the historical application of the mythological theme is more obvious.

19. Schmidt 1966: 183n. H. Gunkel also (1922: 41-49) regarded the significance of Behemoth and Leviathan in Job as wholly mythical; so more recently Pope 1965 and Gibson 1985: 251ff.

20. Fohrer 1989: 523, citing T. Säve-Söderbergh 1953: 55f.

divine control,[21] or, as J.C.L. Gibson has contended (1985: 254ff.), that those sinister forces beyond human control continue to challenge the Order of God, who alone is able to hold them in control though they demand his constant effort and vigilance. However, if this were so it would surely have been stated more explicitly in those passages.

There are significant stylistic differences between those passages in 40.15-24, 31-32; 41.1-3 (EVV 40.15-24; 41.7-11) and 41.4-26 (EVV 12-34) and the Divine Declaration in 38.1–39.30 and 40.25-30 (EVV 41.1-5) which militate against the original association of the two passages. The detailed and lengthy description of Behemoth and Leviathan is certainly far different from the artistic economy with which the works of God in nature are treated in 38.1-30–39.30; 40.25-30 (EVV 41.1-6), where significant characteristics are noted selectively in the broadest outline. H. Richter has taken this discrepancy to be the design of the author, who permitted himself this latitude at the end of his account of the works of God (Richter 1950: 253). There are, however, other objections to the authenticity of those passages which are not so readily explained. The passage on Behemoth is not introduced by the interrogative as the rest of the natural phenomena except the passage on the ostrich (39.13-18), and that passage, to be sure, is suspect either as a secondary insertion or a fragment wanting an introduction, and is moreover noted in Origen's Hexapla as lacking in the original LXX, being supplied from Theodotion's translation.[22] God is moreover referred to in 40.19 in the third person, which suggests a citation from a poem independent of the Divine Declaration, possibly drawn from a sapiential poem classifying and describing natural phenomena including the beasts. Thus we consider the passages on Behemoth and Leviathan, which we have delimited, addenda to the Divine Declaration which ended at 40.14.

The passage on 'Leviathan' in 40.25-30 (EVV 41.1-6) is introduced and sustained like the rest of the passages on the beasts (except that on the ostrich) by questions, and like them emphasizes either the intractable nature of the beasts and/or the inability of humans to have any advantage from them. This indicates that it belongs to the original Divine Declaration, being displaced after the passage on Behemoth to provide an introduction to the passage on the crocodile (41.4-26 [EVV 12-34]).

21. Lods 1934: 514; Hertzberg 1950: 253; MacKenzie 1959 emphasizes the cosmic significance of Behemoth and Leviathan as representing the historical forces inimical to the Order of God.

22. Dhorme (1928: 551) explained the omission of the passage in the LXX as owing to the difficulty of translation and, we might add, to an imperfect text which was occasioned by difficulties of vocabulary, with further complication by efforts to understand it. Lévêque (1970: 503) regards the passage on the ostrich and the horse (vv. 19-25) as original, though he regards the order of the passages as reversed by the redactor in order to associate the two because of the comparison in the passage on the ostrich with the speed of the horse (v. 18).

The descriptive passages on Behemoth and Leviathan, as indicated by the name Behemoth (Egyptian *pꜣ 'iḥmw*, 'hippopotamus') and the word-play on *timšōḵ* and Egyptian *'emsḥ*, and Coptic *'emsḥ* ('crocodile') indicate the Egyptian provenance of the passage, which may be further indicated by the significance of the hippopotamus in the myth and ritual of Edfu and by the reference to the crocodile as 'king', its significance in Egyptian hieroglyphics.[23]

'Adjustments' to the 'Original Dialogue'

Within the Dialogue proper (chs. 4–27) there is considerable difference of opinion as to how much is original. As in any book of antiquity a number of expressions, glosses, and short commentaries on the text, usually fairly obvious and often quite prosaic in a poetic context, may be noticed, and the Dialogue is really not affected by their admission as secondary. The case is not quite so simple for a number of longer passages, which E. Bruston (1928: 297-305) segregated as expressing generalities, thus, he claims, departing from the strict dialectic of the debate and from the particular case of Job. Those include hymns of praise (e.g. 5.9-16 from Eliphaz, 9.5-10 from Job on God in creation to emphasize his aloofness, and 12.13-25 from Job emphasizing rather the destructive aspect of God's government in nature and in society) and didactic passages (e.g. 5.12-26 from Eliphaz). He segregates also a numerical cluster of statements of preservation in seven emergencies (cf. Prov. 30.15-31), with affinities also with prophetic blessing after pardon (11.13-19 from Zophar on the requital of the pious, 15.20-35 from Eliphaz, 18.5-21 from Bildad on the end of the wicked, a theme which is also found in the Plaint of the Sufferer, and 27.13-23, which is attributed to Job in chs. 24–27 on the same theme). He includes in addenda citation of popular aphorisms, for example 8.11-19 from Bildad and the Plaint of the sufferer in 19.7-20 from Job, which interrupts his complaint against God's injustice and his friends' misunderstanding (19.1-6) and his appeal to his friends' sympathy and his statement that his case shall yet be heard (vv. 21-27).

Here, however, the plaint emphasizing God's hostility (19.8-12) and Job's isolation in his trouble (vv. 13-20) obviously emphasizes Job's statement of his case, and is therefore the author's own citation. Even in the strictly dialectic passages the language and imagery reveal the author as a poet, and, as poet and sage, familiar with the whole range of his people's literature. In view of his interest in the suffering of the innocent and the problem of the theodicy which it raised it is inconceivable that he should not have been steeped in the Plaint of the Sufferer, which was projected against the background of the Hymn of Praise on the government of God, (e.g. Ps. 89.6-15, 39-52 [EVV 5-14, 38-51]). Again it is quite natural that illustrations of God's order

23. Fohrer 1989: 531, citing Erman 1894: 180.

in the homely aphorisms of didactic literature should have been cited to assure Job that human suffering was not fortuitous nor the effect of the caprice of an arbitrary divine tyrant, leaving humans with no hope or opportunity to profit from their experience. It was natural for Job's friends to supplement their arguments with such citations, and indeed the book of Job would have been a singularly *jéjune* production without such passages. Thus reduced it would have an interest for the moral philosopher or theologian, but would have lacked the general appeal and arresting power that is the hallmark of a great piece of literature. Those who would divest the Dialogue in Job of such passages in the interests of strict dialectic ignore the fundamental principle that Lindblom so justly emphasized,[24] that argument among Orientals does not depend merely on logic, but on the vehemence, persistence, emphasis and variation of expression with which it is presented, and the more pleasing the rhetorical style, choice of diction and imagery the stronger is the appeal of the argument. The passages on which Bruston animadverted might be ruled out of order in Western debate, but would be expected in the East. Even if they do interrupt the strict dialectic they are never unapt. They are in fact citations, and are noted as such in their dialectic context at 8.8-10; 12.12; 15.18f., which indicate that they are citations by the author of the definitive book and are not secondary. Had they been of the limited proportion of citations familiar in Western debate they would have been generally admitted; but Orientals, though they may cite by limited quotation and even by allusion, is also fond of citing at length as we have personally found frequently in discussion with Arabs, where the relish of a quotation from the Qur'an would often carry them far beyond the bounds of the strictly relevant.

Baumgärtel likewise took exception to the Hymn of Praise, the didactic passages on the blessing of the righteous and the end of the wicked noted by Bruston, and other such passages in the Dialogue (Baumgärtel 1933: 159f.). He reduces (pp. 160ff.) the original Dialogue to one round of debate, 4.1–5.7, 27 (Eliphaz); 6.1-30 (Job); 8.1-11, 20-22 (Bildad); 9.1-3, 11-23, 32-35 (Job); 11.1-5, 10-20 (Zophar) and 13.1-9 (Job) with a monologue from Job (16.6-9, 12-17, 18-21; 23.2-7, 10-17; 29). This, Baumgärtel's 'original dialogue', he considered to be developed from an original monologue in the style of the Plaint of the Sufferer like Psalm 73, which may be conjectured in 17.2-20; 21.7-18; 22.12-16; 24.2-4, 9, 12, itself to be developed in a further compilation in three rounds of debate using the 'original dialogue' for the first round and the 'original monologue' for the second and third rounds. It was at this point, according to Baumgärtel, that the scope of the work, which, like that of the Plaint of the Sufferer, concerned the sufferer's relationship to God, developed

24. Lindblom 1945: 40ff. Tur-Sinai (1957: liiif.) admits such citation *in extenso*, which he explains as intended to certify the citation of a certain sentiment or as coming from an authoritative source and not simply an expression of the author's personal opinion.

more as a sapiential work on the more general question of the theodicy. He rightly emphasized the predominance of the theme of the end of the wicked, though delayed, in the second round of the debate in the present form of the book. The original work, however, was considerably modified in Baumgärtel's estimation, especially in his third round of the debate, so that it can no longer be recognized. He regarded this compilation as further modified by the inclusion of chs. 28–31. Over and above, the passages from hymns of praise, plaints and didactic poems, which Baumgärtel would segregate as secondary, have to be accommodated, but at what stage he is uncertain. In his view we must further reckon with displacements, intentional or unintentional, losses of text, amplifications, omissions, and finally with revision by a redactor, who brought in insertions for the sake of conformity with the rest of the Dialogue, including the divine names *'ēl* and *'ᵉlôah* in parallel with *šadday*, which we should rather consider only one of the various stylistic features that support a less complicated view where the passages in question are citations made by the author of the definitive Book himself.

Baumgärtel distinguished between the statements both of Job and of his friends which were partly addressed to the personal and particular case of Job and partly to the general question of the government of God, the theodicy. The latter, he claims, interrupt the current of thought in the context, being expressed in different literary categories, the Hymn of Praise and didactic poetry or dicta. Such passages fall significantly at the end of statements of the friends, who have already made their point in the debate on the specific subject of Job's complaint and, it is claimed, add nothing to the argument. Besides such passages, Baumgärtel under similar considerations segregated as secondary Job's oath of purgation (ch. 31) excepting vv. 35 and 37, and 27.2-12, where Job protests his innocence (vv. 2-10) and undertakes to instruct his friends about God's purpose (vv. 11f.), which he regards as part of the Dialogue in the author's source which he modified in the definitive book.

Baumgärtel's whole argument for the secondary nature of the passages he notices is based on his excessively mechanical application of form criticism and the assumption that the Dialogue was confined to the consideration of the personal problem of Job. However, in a sapiential text, where the universal interest is emphasized by the international character of the disputants and by the generic names of God, it is most unlikely that Job's case should not be considered in the wider context of the theodicy, the current interpretation of which the Book of Job challenged. The fact that the passages in question fall at the end of the friends' statements need not mean that they are secondary insertions. This place is not only suitable for the insertion of secondary matter; it is even more so for apt citation as an appeal to higher authority in a literary work which gives evidence at every point that it is more than the report of an actual disputation of a particular case. In reply to the claim of the worthy sufferer that his case was not adequately met by the doctrine of the theodicy current in Judaism of the author's time there was no better expression of this doctrine than the Hymn of Praise to the Creator and Sustainer of Order in nature and society and the didactic poem, and no stronger expression of the agony of Job alienated from God than the Plaint of the Sufferer. Such passages round out and clinch the arguments of Job's friends, as is recognized by Kraeling, Westermann and Fohrer. Kraeling, to be sure, was hesitant about ascribing them to the author of the extant book either as his own work or citations from other sources or as anonymous compositions inserted by a redactor (Kraeling 1938: 29-94), but Westermann and Fohrer have no hesitation in admitting them as citations by the author, and Kuhl aptly cites the analogous citation of the Hymn of Praise in the doxologies in Amos and in Deutero-Isaiah as well as in the First Book of the Maccabees (Kuhl 1953: 287).

In the Hymns of Praise in Job's statements in 9.4-10 and 12.13-25, the regular theme of the Hymn of Praise, the omnipotence and beneficence of God as creator and ruler, his majesty and government, is presented in an unusual light by the realism of the sufferer emphasizing rather the terrible and destructive aspects of the rule of God or, as in 9.4-10, his transcendence and aloofness from the predicament of the worthy sufferer. They thus clinch Job's arguments against his friends by citations similar to their own in form but with quite a different and quite legitimate application in the criticism of orthodox doctrine. We may notice the same relationship to the didactic poem on the end of the wicked which rounds out Zophar's last statement (20.5-28) in Job's statement on the prosperity and peaceful end of the wicked in 21.7-26, which is too obviously a parody of the didactic poem to be from any hand but the author of the Book of Job. In view of the later adjustments in the interest of orthodoxy, notably in the Elihu addendum, it is unlikely that a redactor would have elaborated the trenchant parody of 20.5-28 and 21.7-26.

Baumgärtel further notes the double nature of most of Job's statements not only in respect of length but also of character. Besides Job's long description of his sufferings in the style of the Plaint of the Sufferer, he turns from the address to his friends' arguments to direct address to God (e.g. 7; 9.25-31; 10.2-27; 13.20-27; 14). Certain of such passages, like the hymns of praise and didactic passages in the statement of the friends, fall at the end of Job's statements (e.g. 10.2-22; 13.20-27; 14), of which the first and the last are not strictly related to the thought of what precedes. In 9.25-31, too, the direct address to God contrasts with the reference to God in the third person in 9.1-24, 32-35. But such passages could be rejected as secondary only on the assumption that the Book of Job was a severely academic work limited to strictly logical dialectic instead of the highly dramatic expression of the existential situation of the worthy sufferer who believes in what tradition has told him of the nature of a just God yet knows that what he suffers cannot be reconciled with traditional doctrine. The personal involvement of the author in this situation forces him to seek an answer in the presence of the living and beyond all traditional doctrine and the arguments of its representatives, and that finds expression in the direct address to God in the interjections of a soul in anguish.

The edifying narrative of Job which Ezekiel (14.14, 20) knew was probably dominated by Job's expression of faith and the maintenance of his integrity despite the counsels of despair of his associates, but in his delimitation of the Dialogue of the present Book by his drastic surgical operation Baumgärtel is open to Baumgartner's criticism that his work is vitiated by *petitio principis* (Baumgartner 1951: 219). The sceptical aspect of the work before us is not the result of a second hand in the definitive Book of Job, as Baumgärtel contends, but characteristic of the author's own work. Indeed the questioning of the condign significance of the suffering of the worthy man may well have been expressed in some degree even in the author's source, as it was expressed in the Mesopotamian texts on the same subject, one of which was known in Syria at Ugarit. Kraeling developed Baumgärtel's thesis and carried it further. In the immediate source of the present work which he dates c. 800 BCE he assumes a dialogue where Job upheld his faith in divine justice and beneficence despite all doubts cast by his friends. The Dialogue, he suggests, was rewritten with perhaps a more determined challenge to God from Job in confidence of his innocence. At this point Kraeling regarded the passages of the Plaint of the Sufferer-type which admitted the sin of the sufferer (e.g. 7.1-10, 12-21; 9.25-31; 10.1-22; 13.23-27) as accretions made to tone down Job's challenge, a view which does not admit the possibility, indeed the probability, that the sin mentioned is hypothetical. With Job's determined attack on the traditional doctrine of God's order in society in ch. 21, which provokes Eliphaz's charges in ch. 22, a sceptical note is introduced according to Kraeling (1938: 197) which appears again in ch. 24. Accordingly he took chs. 21–26 as part of a sceptical redaction. There was, however, he suggests, a final orthodox adjustment, represented by the inclusion of 27.2-12, this having been drawn from a lost dialogue, the statement of the doctrine of retribution in 27.13-23, and the independent poem on wisdom in ch. 28. He suggests that the final effort to counteract the scepticism which had crept into the Job tradition was the Divine Declaration and Job's final submission, and, in view of the final divine acceptance of Job, chs. 29–31 were introduced, according to Kraeling, possibly from the 'original dialogue' as distinct from the 'earlier dialogue', that is Baumgärtel's *verdrängte Dialog*. The whole was, he maintains, set in the framework of the narrative in chs. 1–20 and 42.10-17 from an earlier version of the Job tradition.

We find no reason to doubt that the *cause célèbre* of Job was much debated over a considerable period in sapiential circles among the Jews with varying emphasis, but we doubt Kraeling's conclusion that the book, apart from the major intrusions which we have noted (see above, pp. 52, 66), was not the work of a single author, but 'the final harvest of a number of books' about the ancient figure of Job (1938: 198). There seems no good reason why the artistic achievement of a great creative poet and thinker should be made to disappear in favour of such a complicated theory of adjustments and readjustments so radical as to present a new and independent work.[25]

25. Gordis (1965: 110) objects to the view of extensive adjustments in the interests of orthodoxy, stating that an offensive book would simply have been consigned to the *geniza*. The Book of Job, however, was exceptional insofar as it represented an old traditional work of orthodoxy which had been adapted by the author of the definitive Book in a much more mature critical work. In view of the original tradition which survived as the framework of the late sapiential work and of the divine approval of Job in the Epilogue there was no need to adjust the Dialogue as a corrective to the criticism of orthodoxy.

Chapter 7

Text and Versions

The extant authority for the Hebrew text of the OT is admittedly late, not indeed until the Aleppo Codex from the first half of the tenth century CE. This represents the same textual tradition as the Leningrad Codex from the Ben Asher family of manuscripts, which is dated in 1008 CE. Variants in other manuscripts from the same textual tradition have been noted by Kennicott and de Rossi, but though those are extensive they are of relatively minor significance, and in the Book of Job, where the MT raises many difficulties and doubts, seldom of themselves help to recover the original text. Standardization in the MT was, evidently at least, well on course by the middle of the first century CE on the evidence of such biblical portions as have survived at Qumran, such as the Book of Isaiah from Cave 1 (1QIs[a]), which contains variants though minor. Of two fragments of Samuel, however, from Cave 4, one (4QSam[a]) mainly agrees with the MT, while the other (4QSam[b]) differs from the MT more widely, agreeing with the LXX (Cross 1956), where it varies from MT. Unfortunately too little of Job has survived to serve our purpose. However, the general situation indicates that, while the Masoretic tradition of Job must be respected, we must admit the possibility of variation of greater or less significance, as indicated in 4QSam[b] and the fragmentary targum of Job (11QtargJob).

In assessing the value of the LXX variants for the appraisal of MT Job we must consider the possibility of an early variant of the Hebrew text, as in 4QSam[b]. But our judgment must be modified owing to the known tendency of the Greek translators to adjust the text in accordance with Greek literary tradition, pruning long repetitive passages in the interest of logical argument, or adjustments in the interests of theological orthodoxy (e.g. 1.5; 5.18; 7.20; 9.4f.; 10.13; 12.6; 21.22; 22.2, 17; 23.15; 24.12; 27.2; 30.20-23; 31.35-37; 32.2; etc.).

Older Greek versions are available, extant in Origen's Hexapla (c. 240 CE), including the Hebrew text, Greek versions of Aquila, an Anatolian proselyte to Judaism (c. 130 CE), of Symmachus, possibly an Ebionite or Jewish sectary (c. 170 CE) and of Theodotion, a converted Jew (c. 200 CE). The last two, being from Jews, have their own value; that of Aquila, if somewhat inelegant and excessively literal, has by the same token a certain value for the recognition of the text he translated.

The Latin Vulgate produced by Jerome in Bethlehem between 390 and 405 CE from Hebrew but with reference to the LXX and other Greek versions has significance as a direct translation from Hebrew and because of Jerome's local knowledge of the Semitic milieu through long residence in Palestine and his preoccupation with commentaries in the rest of the OT.

The Syriac version, or Peshitta, is attested in the Codex Ambrosianus (sixth or seventh century CE). Produced as it was for a public in northern Syria and Mesopotamia of kindred language, thought-forms and ethos to the Jews, it has a significant value for the assessment of the MT, and, especially in vocabulary, provides a key to the solution of many an outstanding problem in Job.

The standard Aramaic version of Job in rabbinic Bibles is comparatively late in the first half of the first millennium CE. This, however, is of limited value as a clue to the reliability of the MT. As a development of oral rendering and exposition of Scripture, targums are an indirect rather than a direct witness to the original Hebrew text, and, with a fair amount of paraphrasing, they are generally fuller than the MT. Aiming at edification in their own day, they reflect theological developments from the original text, the careful avoidance of anthropomorphism in statements about God and in attitudes and reactions natural to humans which the MT attributes to God, and many expressions of human contention with God, as throughout Job, which even formally imply anything other than God's absolute transcendence and majesty are avoided, even when that involves considerable variation from the Hebrew *Vorlage*. Topical interests are also reflected, and even in a sapiential work like Job references to the history of Israel are found which were not in the intention of the original. Thus for instance in 4.10,

> The lion may roar, the roarer cry aloud,
> But the teeth of the great lions are done away,

the standard Targum equates the lions with Esau and Edom, like the 'robbers' in 12.6. In 5.5 'His harvest is eaten by the hungry' is amplified by a specific reference to the Egyptians and Amalekites, a tradition possibly developed from the role of the Amalekites in the introduction to the Gideon cycle (Judg. 6.3f.). In 5.23,

> But with the waste stones you will make your pact,
> And the weeds of the field will be brought into concord with you,[1]

it relates the stones to the stone tablets of the Law and the weeds, which it renders 'beasts', to the Canaanites. In 7.12,

> Am I Sea or Tannin
> That you set a guard over me?,

1. Suspecting *śāḏeh* in colon a as a homonym of *śāḏeh* ('field') in colon b, the style of Job, we take it as cognate with Arab. *sada(y)* ('forsaken, useless') and *ḥayyat* as 'weeds', cognate with Arab. *ḥayyun*, which means both cultivated plants and weeds (Driver 1933: 44). See Commentary *ad loc.*

the symbolic significance of Sea and Tannin, the powers of Chaos in the classical conflict resulting in the demonstration of the effective Kingship of God and the imposition of his government or order (*mišpāṭ*) in its development in the argument of Job, is quite lost in the Targum owing to its preoccupation with the themes of the Pentateuch. Thus the Targum renders:

> Am I guilty like the Egyptians who for their guilt were bound to be sunk in the Reed Sea, or like Pharaoh who was drowned in the midst thereof for his sins?

Similar references to the episode at the Reed Sea are found in 14.11 and 26.13. Indeed in a quite neutral reference to the sudden end of the wicked (34.20) those are specified as Sodomites and Egyptians.

Again the Targum may reflect current postexilic tradition, as when the occasion of the heavenly court in the Prologue is specified as 'the judgment day at the New Year', reflecting the tradition noted in *Tosefta Rosh Hash-Shanah* that the New Year was the occasion when all were judged and the fate for the year settled. Similarly in Job's curse on 'his day' (3.6b),

> Let it not be associated[2] with the days of the year,

the Targum reads:

> Let it not be included in the good days of the year!

This evidently reflects the observance of memorable days in Jewish history recorded in *m. Taanith* II.8 as days when mourning was forbidden (Dalman 1927: 1-3).

Midrashic accretions to Scripture are also reflected. Thus the Shebans in the Prologue (1.15) are specifically associated with 'the Queen of Zemargad', a tradition possibly developed from the tradition of the Queen of Sheba of Solomon's time. Job's wife is actually named in the Targum to 2.9 as Dinah, and in 2.11 the disasters of Job and his family are specified as the blasting of his orchards, his wine turned to blood and his meat to living flesh. In 32.2 Elihu is specified as a descendent of Abraham, and on 3.1,

> The small and the great are there,
> And the servant is free from his master,

the Targum is quite expansive:

> Jacob, who was called the Young, and Abraham, who was called the Aged, are there, and Isaac the servant of Yahweh who came out free from the place of sacrifice from the grasp of his hand.

And 25.2,

> Dominion and fear are with him,
> He makes all well in/from his heights,

2. Reading *yēḥad* with Sym, V, T, and S for MT *yiḥadd* ('rejoice').

is amplified by a passage which depicts Michael at God's right hand and Gabriel on his left.

In such passages in the Targum, however, and in the case of the avoidance of anthropomorphisms, it is usually simple to detect the Masoretic text to which the adjustment or amplification is made.

There is a reference to a targum of Job before the middle of the first century CE (*b. Shab.* 115a).[3] The use of an Aramaic targum on Job at this early date is confirmed by the Qumran targum (11QtargJob), which antedates the abandonment of the settlement c. 68 CE, and has been dated by the editors on palaeographic grounds and by comparison of grammatical forms in the Aramaic parts of Daniel as composed in the latter half of the second century (van der Ploeg and van der Woude 1971: 2f.). On this dating 11QtargJob must be as old as, if not older than, the LXX on Job, since the Greek translation of the Law itself was effected c. 250 BCE.

This new text is fragmentary though fairly substantial, containing wholly or partly the following sections of Job: 17.14–18.4; 19.11-19; 19.29–20.6; 21.2-10, 20-27; 22.3-9, 16-22; 24.12-17; 24.24–26.2; 26.10–27.4; 27.11-20; 28.4-13, 20-28; 29.7-16; 29.24–30.4; 30.13-20; 30.25–31.1; 31.8-16, 26-32; 31.40–32.3; 32.10-17; 33.6-16, 24-32; 34.6-17, 24-34; 35.6-15; 36.7-16, 23-33; 37.10-19; 38.3-13, 23-34; 39.1-11, 20-29; 40.5-14, 23-31; 41.7-17; 41.25–42.6; 42.9-11.

Fragmentary as it is, giving in the earlier parts only half couplets, but towards the end whole couplets, for instance 33.10-17 and particularly from 37 to 42.11, it is possible to assess the nature and value of the targum and its witness to the MT and to the LXX.

By comparison with the official Targum, 11QtargJob is much more of a direct translation, without specific references to the history or traditions of Israel, current custom or Midrashic expansion, though it too has the tendency to avoid anthropomorphism and anthropopathism in statements about God and in demythologizing mythological references. Thus for instance in 38.7, where MT reads,

> When the morning stars cheered together
> And all the divine beings shouted acclaim,

11QtargJob renders more soberly,

> When the morning stars shone all together,
> And all the angels of God shouted acclaim,

3. This relates that R. Gamaliel, the master of St Paul, who was so ill-pleased with a targum of Job that he ordered a workman who was carrying out some repairs to build it into a wall. This may reflect his rejection of the targum as occasionally differing from the Hebrew *Vorlage* or a prejudice against Job which was not yet admitted to the same status as the Law and the Prophets, particularly in view of Job's trenchant criticism of current orthodoxy.

to which we may compare the LXX:

> When the stars were brought into being,
> And my angels praised me with a loud voice.

In aiming at a direct translation for the most part 11QtargJob represents rather the translation and exegesis which emerges as that of the Jewish community of Alexandria in the LXX. It has in fact peculiar relevance to the debate on the relation of the MT to the LXX and particularly the LXX before Origen's supplementation from Theodotion.[4]

The significance of 11QtargJob for the appraisal of LXX and the relation of both to the MT or to a variant Hebrew *Vorlage* may be now illustrated in detail at some length, to which the reader is referred in the textual notes to our translation and in our commentary.

In MT 17.16, *baddê šᵉ'ôl tēraḏnāh 'im-yaḥaḏ 'al-'āpār nāḥaṯ* (read *nēḥaṯ*), the problematic *baddê* ('bars') is called into question by LXX *ē met' emou* and by 11QtargJob *h'my* ('with me'), which respectively understand and express the interrogative particle, which is omitted in MT. G.B. Gray had already conjectured *hᵃ'immāḏî* ('with me?'). LXX and the Qumran targum may have read this in a *Vorlage* different from MT, which in turn read *bᵉyāḏî* or *bîḏî*, which is used in this form in Phoenician inscriptions meaning 'with me' as in Ass. *'ina idi* (lit. 'by my hand') 'beside me', which is cited by Dhorme. This modification of MT *baddê* may be retained on the principle *lectio difficilior potior*, especially as it gives the obvious sense of the context which both versions support and is graphically feasible as the original of MT *baddê*. The interrogative particle *hᵃ*, included in 11QtargJob, was either omitted by haplography after the final *h* of the preceding word or was *'im* as evidently read by LXX and taken to mean 'or' (*eti*).

In 18.2 MT *'aḏ-'ānāh tᵉśîmûn qinṣê lᵉmillîn* the singular of the verb is read by LXX and the Qumran targum, which is appropriate in view of Bildad's address to Job in vv. 4ff. We suggest the dittograph of *n* with corruption to *w*, the verb being the energic imperfect in *scriptio defectiva*. The phrase *qinṣê lᵉmillîn* is suspect. *qnṣ* would be a *hapax legomenon* in the OT though it might be a cognate of Ass. *qinṣu* ('fetter') as proposed by Zimmern (so Gesenius–Buhl, Friedrich Delitzsch, Dhorme, Hölscher, Kissane, Stevenson, Weiser, Terrien); cf. Gordis and Pope, who propose, with less probability, Arab. *qanaṣa* ('to hunt'), rendering respectively 'go hunting for words' and 'set word-snares'. The construct before the noun with the proposition is indeed attested in the OT before *lᵉ* and *bᵉ*, for example 24.5, *mᵉšahᵃrê laṭṭārep̄* and the more frequent *yōšᵉḇê bā'āreṣ* (GKC, §130a), but is still suspect. LXX and

4. Theodotion about the end of the second century BCE is thought to have revised one of the current Greek translations, either the immediate predecessor of LXX (so A. Rahlfs) or another (so P. Kahle), such as is exemplified by the Greek fragments of the Prophets and Writings, but not Job, from the Wadi Murabba'at, which have been dated on palaeographic evidence not later than the middle of the first century BCE.

11QtargJob agree in rendering 'stop (speaking)', *mechri ti ou pausē* (LXX) and *tśwy swp* (11QtargJob). Therefore both, and the latter verbally, indicate a reading *qēṣ* in the *Vorlage*, so understood by Ball and by Fohrer, who, however, retains the construct plural ending. We suggest that *qinṣê* may be a scribal corruption of *qēṣ* through dittography of *n* before *ṣ* in the text represented the linear script of the sixth to the second century BCE.[5] And that *y* of *qinṣê* is the corruption of an original in the same script, to be read before *lmlyn*, thus *qēs 'el-millîn*.

In MT 18.3, *maddûa' neḥšab̲nû kabbᵉhēmāh niṭmînû bᵉ'ênêkem*, LXX omits the verb in colon a and renders *niṭmînû* or a variant in the *Vorlage* as 'we are silent'. In a fragmentary passage 11QtargJob indicates what this variant may have been, reading *lm'* (*lb*) *'yr' dmyn* ('Why are we likened to brutes?'). This gives the required three beats in colon b, necessitating the third beat that MT requires in the verb omitted in LXX. *dmyn* of the Qumran targum indicates that LXX may have read *dammōnû* ('we were silent') or *nᵉdammōnû* ('we were put to silence') in the *Vorlage*. MT *niṭmînû*, however, may be a scribal corruption of *nᵉṭammōnû*, the Niphal perfect of *ṭāmam*, unattested in the OT, but cognate with Syr. *ṭmam* ('to be dull, obtuse'), which occurs in this sense in Middle Hebrew. Both versions may have attempted to render the rare verb *ṭāmam* by the general sense through the assonance (but not phonetic correspondence) of *ṭm* and *dm*. The parallelism with *neḥšab̲nû* suggests that, failing *nᵉṭammōnû* in the *Vorlage*, 11QtargJob *dmynw* is a more likely clue to *nid̲mînu* ('we are likened to') in the *Vorlage*, which, in fact, was conjectured by Bickell, Beer and G.B. Gray. It is significant that neither version supports the reading of the verb in MT as *ṭāmē* ('unclean'), of which Fohrer takes MT *ṭāmāh* as a byform.

In MT 19.12, *yaḥad̲ yāb̲ō'û gᵉd̲ûd̲āyw wayyāsōllû* (read *wᵉyāsōllû*) *'ālay darkām wayyaḥᵃnû* (read *wᵉyaḥᵃnû*) *sāb̲îb̲ lᵉ'ohᵒlî* ('his troops come on in mass; they raise their ramp against me; they camp round my tent'), for *gᵉd̲ûd̲āyw* LXX reads *peiratēria* ('raiding parties') and 11QtargJob *ḥtpwhy* ('his robbers'). The context, with reference to a siege-ramp, supports MT *gᵉd̲ûd̲āyw* rather than 'robbers'. LXX *peiratērion* rendering MT *gᵉd̲ûd̲* in Gen. 49.19 supports MT *gᵉd̲ûd̲āyw*.

In the MT version of 19.17, *rûḥî zārāh lᵉ'ištî* ('my breath is repugnant to my wife'), LXX reads 'I supplicate my wife' and 11QtargJob 'I have bowed my spirit before my wife', both agreeing in general sense. They seem to have read *gārāh* in the *Vorlage*, meaning 'fear' with the nuance of 'reverence' or at least 'deference' (cf. *yāḡûrû* // *kabbᵉd̲û* in Ps. 33.8). *ḥannōtî lib̲ᵉnê biṭnî* ('I am putrid to my own sons') in the parallel colon, however, supports MT *zārāh* ('is repugnant'), cognate with Ass. *zîru*, which Haupt cited as expressing the repugnance of a wife for her husband. The evidence of the two versions is that in the *Vorlage gārāh* was a scribal corruption of *zārāh*, though here, given the

5. E.g. the Lachish ostraca (588–586 BCE), Aramaic papyri from Abu Sinjeh in the Wadi Daliyeh (fourth century BCE) (Cross 1969) and Jewish coins from 135 BCE to 44 CE.

early date of the versions and the still earlier date of the Vorlage, we admit graphic difficulties.[6]

In MT 22.17, *hā'ōmᵉrîm lā'ēl sûr mimmennû ûmah-yyip'al šadday lāmô* (read *lānû*) ('who say to God, "Turn away from us", and "What can the Almighty do to us?"'), LXX reads 'who say, "What will the Lord do to us?", and "What will the Almighty bring upon us?"' and the Qumran targum in a fragmentary text 'who say [ ] God [ ] to us'. Both versions support *lānû* in the *Vorlage*, MT *lāmô* being an obvious scribal corruption of *n* to *m* in the Old Hebrew script from the fifth to the second century BCE. Both make theological adjustments vis-à-vis MT.

In MT 24.24, *wᵉhummᵉḵû ḵakkol* ('and they droop like all'), LXX reads 'but he withers like the mauve plant (*malakē*) in the heat'; compare 11QtargJob [ ] *pᵉpw kybl'*. LXX suggests the singular of the verb, which would generally agree with the context. This would indicate *wᵉhummaḵ* in the *Vorlage*, suggesting that final *w* in MT is a dittograph after *k* in the linear script of the fifth to the fourth century BCE. A plant is surely denoted in colon b, as indicated in LXX. The Qumran targum specifies *kybl*, surely the dog-tooth *kîḇālāh*, identified by I. Löw (1881: 230), of which MT *kkl* is a corruption of the *Vorlage* of the Qumran version.

MT 25.2 exemplifies a case where the Qumran targum confirms the MT, while the LXX seems to suggest a different *Vorlage*, though the difference is more apparent than real. MT reads *hamšēl wāpāḥaḏ 'immô* ('effective rule[7] and terror are in his power [lit. "with him"]'). This is confirmed by 11QtargJob which reads, *'šlṭn wrbw 'm 'lh'*, provided we understand *rbw* as cognate with Arab. *rāba, yārūb* (cf. Ass. *rîbu*, 'to quake'), rendering 'With God is authority and terror', which would agree with LXX *phobos*. But this meaning of *rb* has yet to be attested in Aramaic, and the probability is, we consider, that *rbw* means 'greatness', complementary to *šlṭn*. This would be a paraphrase rather than direct translation which generally characterizes 11QtargJob. LXX offers the strange reading, *ti gar prooimion ē phobos par' autou* ('For what prelude or fear proceed from him?'). Strangely enough, *prooimion* may support MT *hamšēl*, the infinitive absolute Hiphil of *māšal* ('to rule'), since it is a synonym of *archē* ('beginning' and 'rule'), though we suspect that it is a variant or a corruption in the transmission of LXX of *paroimion* ('proverb' or 'example'), Hebrew *māšāl*. This is not the only case where an apparently widely divergent Greek rendering in LXX really supports the view that the Hebrew *Vorlage* was MT and not a variant Hebrew text.

MT 25.3 reads *hᵃyēš mispār ligᵉḏûḏāyw wᵉ'al-mî lō'-yāqûm 'ôrēhû* ('Is there any counting of his troops? And against whom does his light not rise?'), which the LXX renders 'Has anyone supposed (*hupolaboi*) that there is escape

6. But cf. the corruption of *z* to *g* in Amos 7.1: MT *gizzê hammeleḵ* ('the king's mowings') to 'King Gog' in LXX (Hebrew *gōḡ hammeleḵ*).

7. Literally 'imposition of rule'.

(*parelkusis*) from his troops?' In colon a 11QtargJob reads *rḥṣn* for MT *mispār*. *rḥṣn* means 'trust' or 'promise', hence 'hope', Hebrew *sbr*, of which MT *mispār* may be a corruption. In colon b *'w 'l mn l' tqwm kmntw* supports LXX *enedra* ('ambush'), indicating *'ōrᵉḇēhû*, of which MT *'ôrēhû* is a corruption, with omission of *b* after *r* through haplography in the script attested in Egyptian papyri of the fifth to first century BCE.

An emendation of MT 30.17 is suggested by the agreement of the Qumran targum with LXX before corruption of the latter. MT *layᵉlāh 'aṣāmay niqqar mē'ālāy* gives no feasible sense in the context. The Qumran text is fragmentary in the passage, but reads *gmry yqdwn* ('My bones are inflamed'). LXX reads *nukti de mou ta ostea sugkechutai* ('At night my bones are dissolved'). But the verb may be a corruption of *sugkekautai*, which is preferred by A. Rahlfs, thus establishing agreement with 11QtargJob and indicating the corruption of *niqqad* to *niqqar* in MT. This in turn suggests the emendation of MT *mē'ālāy* ('from upon me') to *mē'ᵃlî* ('than a cauldron') as suggested by Dahood, assuming *'ᵃlî* as a cognate of Arab. *ġala(y)*, *ġalayatu(n)* ('cooking-pot'); compare *'ālāh* in this sense noticed by G.R. Driver (1954: 304) in Ezek. 38.18, thus giving the passage the excellent sense 'at night my bones are hotter than a cauldron'.

MT 34.9 reads *lō' yiskon-* (read *yissākēn*) *geḇer birᵉṣōṯô 'im-'ᵉlōhîm* ('A man has no advantage by his giving satisfaction to God'), for which 11QtargJob offers the reading *l' yšnh gbr my* though it is too fragmentary to indicate the *Vorlage* of *yšnh* ('changes' or 'attains eminence') or its restoration or adjustment. But in LXX *ouk estin episkopē andros* the noun *episcopē* ('oversight'), corroborates the consonants *skn* of MT; cf. Hebrew *sōḵēn* ('steward', Isa. 22.15).

In MT 35.10 *'ayyēh 'ᵉlōah 'ōśāy* (read *'ōśî*) *nōṯēn zᵉmirôṯ ballāyᵉlāh* the noun *zᵉmirôṯ* has caused misapprehension in English translations, the reading 'songs in the night' perhaps unduly influenced by the experience of Paul and Silas at Philippi (Acts 16.25) and the meaning of the root in Amos 5.23; Pss. 81.9; 95.2, and so on, and Arab. *zamara* ('to play music, specifically on a wind-instrument'). Alternatively the noun is taken as 'strength', 'courage', cognate of Arabic *ḏāmira*, or, as suggested by D.W. Thomas (1936–37: 478), 'protection'. The root in Hebrew *zmr* in such a sense is surely a component of the proper names cited by James Barr (1968: 182), *b'lzmr* and *zmryhw* from the Samaritan ostraca and Zimri. The sense 'protection' is understood in LXX, which renders *phulakas* ('guards'), evidently misunderstanding the Hebrew feminine plural as signifying the abstract singular, and in 11QtargJob *'lh' dyḥlq ln l* [ ] *lnṣbt' hlyly'*. The context and LXX *phulakas* indicate that the Aramaic *nṣbt* is cognate with Hebrew *nᵉṣṣîḇ in* 2 Sam. 8.6, 14; 1 Chron. 18.13 and 2 Chron. 17.2, which denotes watchposts or detachments posted by David in occupied territory and in the homeland for defence, being rendered *phroura* in LXX. This sense of Hebrew *zmr* in Exodus 15 was recognized by LXX in the translation of *'ozzî wᵉzimᵉrāṯ yh* (read *'ûzî wᵉzimᵉraṯî yh*) as *boēthos kai skepastēs* ('a help and protector'), where *'ûz*, as well as its complement *zim^e^raṯî*, has an Arabic cognate *'awaḏu(n)* ('protection'); compare the exclamation *na'ūḏu billāhi* ('May God protect us!').

In MT 37.13 *'im-l^e^šēḇeṭ 'im-l^e'arṣô* (read *'arṣû*) *'im-l^e^ḥeseḏ* ('Whether for chastisement [lit. "a rod"] or for favour or in token of steadfast grace'), for *l^e^sēḇeṭ* the versions are more specific, the Qumran targum reading *lmktš* ('to bruise', or 'beat') and LXX *eis paideian* ('for discipline'); compare *šēḇeṭ* in Prov. 22.14; 29.15. But for MT *l^e'arṣô* LXX renders 'for his land', which the Qumran targum also evidently understood, in rendering *l'r''*, thus misunderstanding *'arṣû* ('favour') as a cognate of Arabic *raḍwu(n)*; compare the Palmyrene deity *'arṣû*, *Monimus* in the Latin translation (cf. Arabic *munā'im*, 'gracious'; see Commentary *ad loc*). LXX *eis eleos* is a direct translation of MT *l^e^ḥeseḏ*, but the Qumran targum reads *l...ḥsrhh* ('for our want'), amplifying by *lkpn* ('for famine'). The divergence from MT, however, is readily comprehensible on the assumption of the mistaking of the final *d* of *ḥeseḏ* for *r*.

In MT 39.10, *h^a^ṯiqšor-rym b^e^ṯelem '^a^ḇōṯô 'im-y^e^śaddēr '^a^māqîm 'ah^a^reyḵā*, we suspect the meter as too long; the collocation of *b^e^ṯelem '^a^ḇōṯô* is also suspect, as is *'^a^ḇōṯô* if, as LXX assumes, it means 'ropes', lacking as it does a preposition and having the singular pronominal suffix with the plural noun. *rym*, pointed in MT as if *r^e^ēm*, is suspect on two counts—the spelling and the repetition of the noun after *r^e^ēm* in the preceding verse. The evidence of LXX and 11QtargJob may now be adduced. LXX reads:

> Will you bind his yoke with thongs?
> Or will he draw your furrows in the plain?

The Qumran targum reads *htqṭr r'm' btryh wylg(wn) bbq' btryk*. Both versions omit explicit mention of 'furrow' (*ṯelem*) in colon a, where it probably crept into MT as an explanatory gloss on a rare word in the bicolon, which we suspect to be Aram. *ḥ^a^rāṯeykā* (cf. Syr. *ḥrat*, 'to split'). The verb *w^e^ylg(wn)* in 11QtargJob, if it means to make a narrow track, the meaning of Aram. *lagnā'* given by M. Jastrow (1903), may render the verb in colon b *y^e^śaddēḏ*, a rare word, found only here and in Isa. 28.24 and Hos. 10.11, where it is parallel to, and probably a synonym of *ḥāraš* ('to plough'), possibly with the sense of drawing a straight furrow; compare Arab. *śadda* ('to be straight'). Still in colon b, MT *'aḥ^a^reyḵā*, which is not indicated in LXX, is assumed by 11QtargJob to mean 'after you', which disagrees with ploughing. We suggest that it is a corruption of *ḥ^a^rāṯeykā* (Aram. 'your furrows'), the object of the verb *y^e^śaddēḏ*. To revert to colon a, with the removal of *ṯelem* as a gloss, the regular three-beat metre would be restored and *ḇ^e^* then be attached to *'^a^ḇōṯ*, which, without a preposition, is a problem. LXX understands this word, without a preposition and significantly without the pronominal suffix, as 'thongs' or 'ropes', which may have been suggested by Isa. 5.18. But here the pronominal suffix with the plural is suspect. We suggest therefore that *'^a^ḇōṯ* is the verbal noun of *'āḇāh* ('to be thick'), with which the pronominal suffix would be regular, meaning 'his thickness' or 'his massive bulk', with specific reference to the 'bull-neck' of the animal, the forequarters of the bull including the neck, which is markedly more massive than the hind quarters. This may possibly be suggested by 11QtargJob *btwryh*, possibly 'his bull-like strength'. MT *rêm* is also omitted in LXX, where 'his yoke' suggests an original *nîr* of which *rm* may be a scribal error of metathesis, with corruption of *n* to *m* in the Old Hebrew script. The *Vorlage* of LXX would then have been *h^{a}ṯiqšor-nîr ba'^{a}ḇōṯô* ('Will you bind a yoke on his massive bulk?'). This and other variations in LXX and the Qumran targum in this passage alone indicate that each used a different Hebrew *Vorlage* with substantial variations from MT. In conclusion we propose an original reading of the couplet:

> *h^{a}ṯiqšor-nîr ba'^{a}ḇōṯô*
> Will you bind a yoke on his massive bulk?
>
> *'im-y^{e}śaddēd bā'ēmeq ḥ^{a}rāṯeyḵā*
> Will he plough your furrows straight in the plain?

MT 40.26 reads *h^{a}ṯāśîm 'agmôn b^{e}'appô*. LXX and 11QtargJob differ from MT *'agmôn* in reading respectively *krikon* ('a ring') and *zmm* (cf. Syr. *zmāmā'* and Arab. *zamāmu*[*n*], 'bridle'), which would give an excellent sense in the context. MT *'agmôn* is not an impossible corruption of *zāmām* or *zāmôn*; compare LXX *gôḡ hammeleḵ* for *gizzê hammeleḵ* in Amos 7.2. So long as the crocodile's mouth can open, a ring (LXX) or hook (T) is pointless. Hence the snout must first be bound. It is important to note that the text refers not to the crocodile's mouth (*pîw*) but to his snout (*'appô*).

In 41.26 the crocodile is described as *meleḵ 'al-kol-b^{e}nê-šāḥaṣ* ('king over all the big game'); compare *b^{e}nê-šāḥaṣ* in 28.8 (see Commentary *ad loc*.). LXX and the Qumran targum agree in disagreeing with MT, reading respectively 'king over all those that are in the water' (cf. T 'little fishes') and '...over all the reptiles' (*'al kl rḥš* [Syr. *raḥšā'*]); compare S *šērēṣ*. While a naturalistic description of the crocodile, the scribal corruption of *rḥš* or *šrṣ* is not graphically feasible. It is less than what MT says, which may reflect the allusion to the crocodile as the beast *par excellence* implied in the crocodile as the hieroglyphic sign for 'king', as Fohrer notes (1989: 531) after A. Erman (1894: 180). It would appear that the targums and LXX missed this point in their *Vorlage* or that their *Vorlage* differed from MT. 11QtargJob shows an interesting correspondence with LXX, apparently as against MT, in 42.11, where Job's kinsmen, visiting him after his rehabilitation, present him with a lamb (Aram. *'mr*, LXX *amnōn*, cf. MT *q^{e}śîṭāh*). Since a hundred *q^{e}śîṭôṯ* are given as the price of the ground acquired by Jacob at Shechem (Gen. 33.19), Job 42.11 is probably a case of conscious archaizing. On the basis of LXX, now supported by the Qumran targum, Dhorme (*ad loc.*) elaborated the view that a *q^{e}śîṭāh* was a lamb as a unit of exchange, citing the semantic analogy of Latin *pecunia* ('money') from *pecus* ('cattle).

MT 42.6 reads *'al-kēn 'em'as w^e^niḥamtî 'al-'āp̄ār wā'ēp̄er* ('therefore I despise/reject and repent on dust and ashes'). As indicated by the *athnaḥ* in *w^e^niḥamtî* the Masoretes understood this verb to end colon a. In this case colon b must be admitted as deficient of a beat. If, *pace* MT, *w^e^niḥamtî* or its original is taken as the first word in colon b, the verb required before *'al-'āp̄ēr w^e^'ēp̄er*, this leaves colon a short of a beat, while according to MT the transitive Qal *'em'as* is without an object. It might be assumed that as an object 'my words' might be implied when Job rejected his case, but this still does not meet the objection to the short meter if *niḥamtî* or its original is taken with colon b, and the same would apply to the reading *'emmā'ēs*, which would avoid the difficulty of the transitive verb in the Qal without an object. The metrical difficulty would be met by assuming the reading *himmā'ēs 'emmā'ēs* ('I utterly demean myself'), which would agree with Job's repentance '(sitting) on dust and ashes'.

Here we may cite the evidence of LXX and 11QtargJob. LXX reads *ephaulisa emauton kai etakēn hēgēmai de egō emauton gēn kai spodon* ('I demean myself and am dissolved, I consider myself dust and ashes'); compare 11QtargJob, *'l kn 'tnsk w'tmh' w'hw' l'pr wqṭm* (lit. 'Therefore I am poured out and reduced [lit. "diluted"[8]] and I have become dust and ashes'). Here LXX *ephaulisa emauton* supports the reading *'emmā'ēs*, while *etakēn* indicates *'emmas* from *māsas* ('to melt, dissolve'), which was in fact conjectured by Beer, who proposed *himmēs 'emmas*, thus restoring the three-beat meter in colon a, omitting *w^e^niḥamtî* or its original. The verb *māsas* in the Niphal is indicated in the Qumran targum, which reads colon a *'l kn 'tnsk w'tmh'* (lit. 'I am poured out and diluted'). This suggests an original of MT *w^e^niḥamtî* as *w^e^nimhē'tî*, cognate of Aram. *m^e^hā* or an Aramaism in Job. The sense of this verb in 11QtargJob and LXX *etakēn* would support Beer's conjecture. But LXX *ephaulisa emauton* supports MT *'em'as* read *'emmā'ēs*. Our conclusion in colon a is that in view of the familiar word-play so dear to the author of Job, the original of this colon was *'al-kēn 'emmā'ēs w^e^'emmas* ('Therefore I demean myself and yield', lit. 'melt, lose coherence', hence 'yield' in the physical sense). Both versions supply the verb required in colon b, LXX 'I considered myself' and the Qumran targum 'I have become', both of which we find in the context quite colourless. The original may have been *nihmē'ṯî* (corrupted to *niḥamtî* in MT), which the Qumran targum read and included in colon a. We suggest an original text:

> *'al-kēn 'emmā'ēs w^e^'emmas*
> *w^e^nimhē'ṯî 'al-'āp̄ār w^e^'ēp̄er*

> Wherefore I demean myself and yield,
> and am reduced to dust and ashes.

Possibly the targumist took *'emmā'ēs* and *'emmas* as alternative readings and omitted *'emmā'ēs* and included *w^e^nimhe'tî* of his *Vorlage* in colon a supplying

8. See Dalman 1938: 226a.

the verb *'hw'* in colon b (*metri causa*), while LXX took *'emmas* and *nimhē'ṯî* as alternatives and omitted the latter, supplying the missing beat in colon b with *kai hēgēmai*.

Finally in the Epilogue 11QtargJob makes a valuable contribution to the problem of the composition and transmission of the Book of Job, in ending at 42.11 of MT. Here there is no question of a fragmentary text since the targum ends here in the middle of column 38 of the scroll and nothing further is written in this line or in the space left in the column. The rather naive reference to Job's material restitution, which has always offended spiritual sensibilities, may, of course have been omitted for theological reasons. But it probably indicates that the Book of Job as the targumist knew it in the late second century BCE ended at 42.11, the rest being a later midrashic expansion, like 'the Syriac book' to which LXX refers (ed. Swete, 42.17 b-e), indicating a certain fluidity of the Job tradition at this point. The necessity for the LXX version of the Hebrew Scripture and the translation of Ben Sira's work into Greek indicates that since c. 250 BCE and probably earlier the Jews in Egypt were more familiar with Greek than with Hebrew, and particularly with the less familiar words in a poetic work like Job, such as the many homonyms which characterize the book. Indeed, even among Hebrew speakers in Palestine it is not to be expected that all nuances of the living language of c. 450 BCE, when we should date the Book of Job, should have been familiar even three centuries later any more than most average English speakers should know what the Authorized Version meant by 'earing' ('ploughing') in Exod. 34.21. But, produced in Palestine, where Hebrew and Aramaic were living languages, the Qumran targumist was on more familiar ground and is noticeably more faithful to the Hebrew *Vorlage*.

In Job, which so fully exploits the resources of Hebrew language and current Aramaic, students of the book, from the starting point of the more familiar content of Hebrew language, soon find it necessary to have recourse to the versions where an unfamiliar word occurs or where the sense seems to break down. If directly or indirectly they do not solve the problem they may have recourse to Comparative Semitic Philology, using the increasing resources of cognate Semitic languages, Akkadian, Amorite from Mari, Assyrian, Ugaritic, Phoenician, Aramaic, Syriac, Arabic and Ethiopic with South Arabian dialects from the latter half of the first millennium BCE. This may at once solve the problem, giving the obvious sense in the context and agreeing with other passages in the OT. This is particularly the case where, as often in Job, apparently the same word is used in a couplet in parallelism, a solecism which the poet would surely never have committed even occasionally.

Failing such help, we may have recourse to emendation, and here again the ingenuity of the scholar must be subject to control. A version, even where it does not give direct help, may yet give a clue to the original which it has misunderstood, and here the deficiency of one version may, and indeed must, be checked against another, as we have noticed in our citation of LXX and

11QtargJob. Subject to such controls, conjectural emendation must be graphically feasible, its characters relating to those of the dubious text, for scribal corruption did occur. The corruption may be a wrong arrangement of consonants as in 42.6, where on the clue of 11QtargJob which reads *w'tmh'* we may suspect such a corruption with the further corruption of *h* to *ḥ*, MT *wᵉniḥamtî* being suggested to the scribe by *'emmā'ēs* in colon a. The emendation to *wᵉnimhē'ṯî* suggested by the Qumran targum and read in colon b, together with LXX and 11QtargJob supports Beer's conjecture *'emmas* for MT *'em'as* in colon a, where, reading MT *wᵉniḥamtî* in colon b, he supplied the metric deficiency in colon a by proposing *himmēs 'emmas*. This conjecture, however, must be modified by the support for MT *'em'as*, read *'emmā'ēs* ('I demean myself') in LXX. Finally, in support of the reading *'al-kēn 'emmā'ēs wᵉ'emmas wᵉnimhē'ṯî 'al-'āpār wᵉ'ēp̄er*, appeal to the general style of the poetic author of Job in his fondness for word-play exemplified in the collocation of *'emmā'ēs* and *'emmas* (lit. 'demean myself and am dissolved', sc. 'lose coherence'). The sense of the second member of such a pair is amplified in the next verb *wᵉnimhē'ṯî* (lit. 'and I am diluted', sc. 'reduced') in a convention well known in Arabic poetry and rhetoric as *tawriya*, cited by Guillaume (1963) in the case of homonyms, to which *'emmā'ēs* and *'emmas*, though not homonyms, vocally approximate. Beer's conjecture is thus controlled by metrical considerations, but modified by the support of LXX, for MT *'emmā'ēs* in the consonantal text, and with due recognition of the poetic style of Job, MT *wᵉniḥamtî* read by the Masoretes in colon a and conjectured to belong to colon b is a corruption of *wᵉnimh'ētî*, suggested by 11QtargJob, and supported by the meaning of the sense of *'emmas* in colon a on the analogy of *tawriya* in Arabic poetry.

In considering the graphic feasibility of an emendation we must reckon with the origin and transmission of a text. If the definitive Book of Job was composed c. 450 BCE with later addenda until c. 400 BCE it is reasonable to suppose that it was written in the Old Hebrew script attested in the Lachish Ostraca (588–586 BCE) and in Aramaic Papyri from the Wadi Daliyeh (fourth century BCE). At Qumran from the last quarter of the second century BCE, this script was replaced by one not far removed from that familiar in our printed Bibles. But the older Hebrew script is still attested at Qumran in certain fragments from Caves 1 and 4 and was used in Jewish coinage from 135 BCE to 44 CE and in coins from the revolt of Bar Coseba (132–135 CE). Thus it might be supposed that if the Book of Job was composed and transmitted in Palestine, it may have had currency in the Old Hebrew script, while, if it was composed and transmitted in Egypt, we must reckon with the development of this script as attested in the development of that script as attested in Egyptian papyri from the fifth century BCE. On the other hand, the direct ancestor of the developed Hebrew alphabet, which betrays its origin among the exiles in Mesopotamia by the term 'the Assyrian script', known also as 'the square script', generally adapted at Qumran, was evidently brought to Palestine by Jews returning from Exile from the middle of the sixth century BCE. Developed by Jewish intelligentsia in Mesopotamia keenly concerned to conserve their scriptural heritage, this may well have set the pattern in the west for scriptural manuscripts, including the Book of Job. Be that as it may, we shall find obvious cases where the recovery of the original text is graphically explicable on the assumption of scribal corruption in the Old Hebrew script, while other cases indicate the square script as attested in its development in the bulk of the Qumran manuscripts or later, while that of the Egyptian papyri is not out of the reckoning.

Some emendations of the consonantal text by the application of epigraphy or calligraphy will be relatively simple and obvious, but in the case of others which are more complex we must apply the checks we have mentioned, always mindful that once corruption has occurred, especially in a difficult text—and those are any which baffled the versions in Job—corruption may proliferate. A notable example of this we would find in the description of the splendid burial of the prosperous wicked in 21.33: *māṯᵉqû-lô rigᵉḇê naḥal* ('Sweet to him are the clods of the wadi'), which we find quite unHebraic and not apt in the context. We have suggested the emendation *miṯqōnēn bᵉ 'ûgāḇ wᵉḥālîl* ('Having provided for his elegy to the accompaniment of flute and pipe'). We find it significant in the context that in the elaborate funeral this essential element is the sole omission. Here we may note the correspondence of most of the consonants to MT. Others in the emendation, such as *n* for *w* and *m* for *n* are simple scribal errors in the Old Hebrew script, and *w* for *y* in *'ûgāḇ wᵉḥālîl* in the square script; equally simple is dittography as in *miṯqōnēn*. This leaves ' in *'ûgāḇ* as the outstanding difficulty, for which there is no obvious graphic relation to the MT at any stage of the script, and this we explain as a case of proliferating corruption of an already corrupted text. Here the most helpful 11QtargJob is unfortunately fragmentary.

We must notice the contribution of comparative philology to the assessment of the MT, with special reference to conjectural emendation. This resort, once so freely exercised, seemed to find a fruitful field in Job with its outstanding abundance of *hapax legomena* and words formally known in Hebrew but in their familiar sense incongruous with the context. This applies particularly to the apparent repetition of a word in corresponding position in parallel cola. In the frequency of such cases in Job we may be sure that this was no literary lapse, but was a deliberate stylistic convention, which Guillaume did well to note as a feature of Arabic poetry and rhetoric. That such word-play was known in Israel is evidenced by Samson's riddle (Judg. 14.14),

> Out of the eater came forth meat,
> Out of the strong came forth sweet,

with its answer,

> What is sweeter than honey (*'ᵃry*)?[9]
> What is stronger than a lion (*'ᵃrî*)?,

and Judg. 15.16,

> With the jawbone of an ass (*ḥᵃmôr*), heap upon heap (*ḥᵃmōrāṯāyim*)…

The formally identical words in parallelism in Job prove to be such homonyms, formally identical yet quite different in meaning, like the English 'sole', meaning part of a foot, a fish, and 'only'. In Hebrew the unfamiliar member of such a pair is to be recognized from a cognate either in Aramaic, Syriac, Northern Arabic, or Ethiopic or one of the Southern Arabian dialects which would indicate the obvious sense in the context, which must of course be the final criterion. The recognition of this stylistic feature in Job and the application of comparative Semitic philology has severely limited the exercise of conjectural emendation of the MT.

The order of the MT has often been called in question by practically every serious commentator on Job, and usually a displacement of text is taken to have occurred, as for instance in a tricolon where a colon is out of accord, or seems to be, with its context and where it gives more sense in another position. Such an exercise can be quite subjective if we may judge by the difference of opinion as to where the assumed 'errant block' originally belonged. Such a question may often be objectively settled by the appreciation of the style of the poet, who, like the poets in the Ras Shamra myths and legends, used the tricolon occasionally to punctuate their text which was usually in bicola. Thus in Job we find that the tricolon frequently marks the end of a theme, as we find regularly once we have resolved the various chapters into strophes, either thematically or on form-critical grounds, as Fohrer has so admirably done. Thus, while an odd colon in a prevailing arrangement of bicola may suggest to the critic a rearrangement of the text of the MT exercised, one would hope, in accord with the sense of the context and with the minimum of subjective judgment, this tendency is modified if not minimized by the real significance of the odd tricolon among the predominant bicola.

In cases where displacement of text is assumed it must be admitted that this is proposed *ad sensum*, but a significant criterion is also the style of the author. For instance in 20.10 between the statement of the evanescence of the wicked and his prosperity in vv. 9 and 11 the MT reads,

> *bānāyw yᵉraṣṣû ḏallîm wᵉyāḏāyw tāšēḇnāh 'ônô*

> His sons crush the poor but his hands will give back his wealth,

while in the statement of the prosperous wicked to enjoy his profits in 20.19 MT reads:

> *kî-riṣṣēs 'āzaḇ dallîm bayiṯ gāzal wᵉlō' yiḇenēhû.*

9. Cognate of Arab *'aryu(n)*.

For the unintelligible *'āzab̲* we propose *'ōzām* ('by force'). The fondness of the poet for word-play suggests the emendation of *yᵉraṣṣû* in v. 10, *yirᵉṣû* ('they will make restitutions'), a parallel to *yāḏāyw tāšēb̲nāh*, with further word-play between *bānāhû* (MT *yib̲enēhû*). This suggests that vv. 19 and 10 belong together in that order:

> 19. *kî-riṣṣēs 'ōzām dallîm bayit̲ gāzal lō' bānāhû*
> 10. *bānāyw yirᵉṣû dallîm wᵉyādāyw tāšēbnāh 'ônô*

> Since he has crushed the poor by force, plundered a house which he had not built,
> His sons will have to make restitution to the poor, and his own hands give back his wealth.

The word-play between *bānāyw* and *bānāhu* indicates the chiastic arrangement of the two bicola, which we would place after v. 18.

With the multiple aid of all such disciplines, the study of versions, epigraphy and calligraphy, comparative philology, prosody and the appreciation of the stylistic idiom of the author, we may and must make our approach to the assessment of the MT or to the recovery of the original after scribal corruption in transmission. At certain disputed points the MT will be supported against proposed conjectural emendation; at others a more meaningful original will be recovered. In all cases both support and emendation of the MT must be under strict and indeed multiple control.

Chapter 8

The Language of the Book of Job

The Book of Job, a masterpiece in Hebrew literature, exhibits a wide range of language, with an extraordinary number of rare words and *hapax legomena.* These have always been a problem to commentators, together with passages either obscure in themselves or through scribal corruption, which have occasioned copious emendation often more ingenious than controlled. Such passages are sometimes reconstructed from Hebrew diction, phraseology or sentiment familiar elsewhere in the OT preferably in similar contexts; more often they proceed from the assumption of a hitherto unknown or doubtful Hebrew word as cognate with one in one of the kindred Semitic languages or even as not a Hebrew word at all but an import—an 'Aramaism' for instance, or an 'Arabism'. Some of such suggestions, like conjectural emendation, have reflected the interest and expertise more or less in those languages rather than deep appreciation of Hebrew language and literature.

All such attempts to arrive at the form and meaning of the original must employ all available checks. The proposed reconstruction must be assessed with relation to its immediate context and other parts of the work studied and other parts of the OT reflected or consciously cited or alluded to, as particularly in Job, where the writer makes such ample use of known literary forms with their conventional diction, imagery and association of thought (see above, pp. 39-55). The ancient versions, the LXX, S, V, T and now the earliest known version, the Aramaic targum from Qumran, 11QtargJob, may supply a measure of the desired control. When in addition the effort is made to solve an outstanding problem or to elucidate a text in the OT by the citation of cognate Semitic languages, words cited from such sources must be cited wherever possible with due regard to their native context.

Here we are fortunate to possess such a volume of material from Akkadian texts of various character from southern Mesopotamia, early in the second millennium BCE, from Mari just before the middle of that millennium in an Amorite dialect, Assyrian texts contemporary with the history of Israel, Canaanite citations and glosses in the Amarna Tablets from Syria and Palestine from the fourteenth century BCE, and administrative texts and poetic myths and legends from Ras Shamra with vocabulary, grammar, figures and forms of prosody so close to Hebrew (particularly Hebrew poetry) that a

Hebrew prophet could speak of his language as 'the language of Canaan' (Isa. 19.18). Contemporary with the appearance of the Book of Job, Aramaic, the *lingua franca* of Persian administration in western Asia and Egypt is well attested in documents both administrative and domestic, from Elephantine and in letters found in the Wadi Daliyeh and dated in the fourth century BCE (Cross 1969). From the Christian era there is a great volume of Syriac in the targum to the OT and the direct translation of the Testament, and original works such as patristic literature, mediaeval history and a work on agriculture (*Geoponicum*). Any commentary on Job teems with citation of Arabic, either conjectures as to the meaning of *hapax legomena* or rare or doubtful words unattested in what is known of Hebrew or its obvious cognates. Many of these will be supported by citation of cognates in one or more of the kindred Semitic languages just mentioned, though regrettably this has not always been done. Despite occasional over-emphasis and exclusive application of Arabic it does occupy a very significant place in a philological approach to the linguistic problems of Job.

The Arabic element in Job was first suggested by the mediaeval Jewish commentator ibn Ezra, who suggested that the linguistic peculiarities of the Book of Job, which had long been the despair of Jewish rabbis, arose from its character as a translation. This was taken up and argued by D.S. Margoliouth and F.H. Foster, who argued for an Arabic original (Margoliouth 1924; Foster 1932–33: 21-45). However we may evaluate Arabic in the study of Job, this explanation is most unlikely. R. Gordis (1965: 210), rightly in our opinion, argues that there is nothing known in Arab culture in the pre-Christian era which could have given birth to such a work as Job or which could have evoked such emulation in an advanced Hebrew society as to demand translation.

'Arabisms' in Job were more recently claimed by the late A. Guillaume[1] in explanation of the many cases where apparently identical words are used in parallelism. With this great wealth of vocabulary it is rightly argued that it is inconceivable that the poet should have lapsed to this extent in the short compass of a couplet. In qualification it must be noticed that occasionally identical words in parallelism do occur in Ugaritic poetry in the cuneiform texts where there is no question of textual corruption. In such cases the word is repeated for the sake of emphasis. In Job, however, this is relatively rare. In such cases Guillaume recognized that the words were not synonyms but homonyms. He took the first as Hebrew and the second as Arabic with a different meaning. This is a conscious word-play exemplified outside Job in Ps. 137.5f.:

'im-'eškāḥēḵ yᵉrûšālāyim	If I forget thee, O Jerusalem,
tiškaḥ yᵉmînî	Let my right hand wither away.[2]

1. Guillaume 1954: 1-12; 1963; 1965: I, 3-35; II, 5-35; III, 1-10; IV, 1-18.

2. The verb *šāḵaḥ* in this sense, in our opinion, has an Ugaritic cognate, for example, in Gordon *UT* 67 I.4, 30f., *ṯḵḥ ttrp šmm* ('the heavens will dry up, yea languish'); so also Driver 1956a; Gibson, *ad loc.* ('burnt up'); cf. Pope 1966: 240.

This literary convention is used much more frequently in Arabic poetry and rhetoric, and is found in Job more often than in any other book in the OT. From this fact Guillaume goes on to argue that the writer and his circle were bilingual and indeed that the book was produced in the Hejaz (see above, p. 4). Though the clue to one or other of the homonyms—usually the second—is frequently found in Arabic, this does not mean that the word is an Arabism, as Guillaume concluded; it may have an Aramaic cognate as well as, or even rather than, an Arabic one or a cognate in Ugaritic, which Guillaume persistently ignored. In this case the word in question is probably genuinely Hebrew, an element in fact of *s*^{e}*p̄āṯ k*^{e}*na'an* (Isa. 19.18). We are even less convinced by Guillaume's conclusion that his 'Arabisms' indicate the provenance of the Book of Job from the Hejaz.

The weakness of Guillaume's thesis of extensive Arabic influence in Job is that his alleged 'Arabisms' are cited from Classical Arabic at least a millennium after the composition of Job, and there is nothing contemporary except possibly short inscriptions, little more in fact than mere graffiti of uncertain and probably much later date.[3] That, of course, does not exclude Arabic as the medium of communication in daily life and in oral tradition. In fact the full flowering of Arabic poetry with its elaborate structure and polished, precise diction in the pre-literary period just before Islam in the seventh century CE implies a long period of currency of Arabic in the peninsula, while in the south the language is attested in its local expression in numerous inscriptions in the ruinfields of the south Arabian kingdoms from the tenth century BCE.[4]

When all this is said, however, of all the resources of comparative Semitic philology, the significance of Arabic must be admitted. North or Hejazi Arabic, attested in sophisticated poetry before the seventh century CE, is used in all its fullness and fluency in the Qur'an and in traditions of early Islam and subsequently in jurisprudence, history and science to modern times, with current books, periodicals and newspapers. There are of course specific developments in the meaning of words to say nothing of coinage, which, however, in the immense resources of the language, are relatively rare and readily detected. In invoking Arabic in explication of passages in the OT, however, due regard must be paid to the use of Arabic words and roots in their living context, as in the profuse citations in the lexica of Lane–Poole (1863–93) and Freytag (1830–37) and authoritative works of native Arab

3. Van den Branden 1956. On the basis of his understanding of the development of the Old Arabian script F.V. Winnett proposed to date such inscriptions from Teima and its vicinity not later than the sixth century BCE. This date is supported by no local evidence from northern Arabia, but a closely related script from southern Iraq in an archaeological context dated to the eighth or seventh century was found; see Driver, 1944b: 124; Albright 1965. Relatively to this, Winnett dates his inscriptions in the 'Taymanite script'; see Winnett and Reed 1970: 99-103.

4. On the application of Southern Arabic and Ethiopic in Semitic Philology, see Ullendorff 1956 and Beeston 1962.

lexicographers.[5] There is furthermore the opportunity to hear and communicate in spoken Arabic in a living Semitic milieu, particularly, from the point of view of the Hebraist, in the local dialects of Palestine and Syria. Here we may pay tribute to Gustaf Dalman, our teacher in the University of Greifswald, in his monumental *Arbeit und Sitte in Palastina* (1928–39), where he cites verbal communications to him in the practical situations of peasants and humble folk, with profuse citation of relevant passages in the OT, Targum, Talmud and Midrash which makes this work an invaluable supplement to his *Aramäisch-neuhebräisches Handwörterbuch zu Targum, Talmud und Midrasch* (1938).

Thus the many words in Job where the familiar sense of Hebrew is not applicable may reasonably be invested with meaning on the assumption of an Arabic cognate, always, however, subject to congruity with the context. This has informed an impressive series of studies by G.R. Driver from 1922 to 1955,[6] which are reflected in NEB, and by I. Eitan (1924), J. Reider[7] and D.W. Thomas.[8] In many, if not indeed most cases, however, Arabic does not offer the only cognate with a Hebrew word. Cognates in other Semitic languages suggest themselves, which may indeed confirm the evidence of Arabic adduced, but may occasionally modify it. We find that this applies particularly to the work of Guillaume. Notwithstanding his many brilliant insights, he declared, in defence of the MT in Job against what he alleged to be 'deliberate falsification of the evidence in an appalling degree' that he would be determined to read it as an Arabic work (Guillaume 1963: 108).

In discussing the Aramaic element in Job we would dismiss Tur-Sinai's thesis of an Aramaic original and Hebrew translation (Tur-Sinai 1957). This is surely exploded by the fluent application of literary forms with relation to their *Sitz im Leben*, and the characteristic language, imagery and themes of Hebrew literature. Moreover the ample evidence we shall cite of the elements of Ugaritic, a dialect of 'the tongue of Canaan' with which the prophet classified Hebrew (Isa. 19.18), surely militates against the thesis of an Aramaic original and a subsequent Hebrew translation. Such an original would never have exhibited such features, nor would the alleged Hebrew translation in the fifth century BCE. In this respect the Book of Job is a natural development of biblical, particularly the Wisdom, tradition and idiom and in the language and literary tradition of ancient Canaan to which Hebrew poets were heirs. Moreover in Mesopotamia, where Tur-Sinai has suggested that the book was produced in Aramaic (at a period of activity in assembling and editing the considerable literary deposit of Hebrew from before the Exile and when and

5. Ibn Manẓur, *Lisānu 'l-'arab*, 1232–1311; al-Fīrūzābādī, *al-Qāmūsu 'l-Muḥīṭ*, 1326–1414; Murtaḍā 'z-Zabīdī, *Tāju 'l-'arūs*, 1732–91.

6. Driver's work is cited throughout the Commentary; cf. also his 'Hebrew Poetic Diction' (1956b).

7. J. Reider, articles in *HUCA* from 1925 to 1953; *VT* 4 (1954); *JJS* 3 (1956).

8. D.W. Thomas 1938: 374, 402 and articles in *ZAW*, *ETL*, *JTS*, *VT* and VTSup. from 1934 to 1944.

where the massive prophetic work of Ezekiel was produced) it seems odd that a work which so fully develops the sapiential tradition of the Hebrew sages should appear in Aramaic.

Given the currency of Aramaic as the administrative *lingua franca* of Palestine and the western provinces of the Persian Empire when the Book of Job was produced and the extent to which it had penetrated popular Hebrew, Aramaic elements in vocabulary and grammar are but to be expected in Palestine and in Egypt, as is indicated by the records of the Jewish or perhaps North Israelite community of Elephantine (Cowley 1923) and elsewhere in Egypt on the evidence of epigraphic matter (Gibson 1975: 113-47).

N.H. Snaith has supplemented the deficiencies of Guillaume's work in citing the same list of 'Aramaisms' from Driver–Gray and Kautzsch[9] and in giving a more just notice of their use in Aramaic and Syriac, in Akkadian and often in Ugaritic (Snaith 1968: 104-12). Here we may note that many an Akkadian root has a direct descendant in Aramaic and Syriac. The case for an assumed Aramaism in Job being a genuine Hebrew word, the rarity of which in Hebrew literature is simply accidental, is much stronger when a Ugaritic cognate is validly adduced. Thus Snaith rightly adduces evidence of Ugaritic cognates to Kautzsch's 'Aramaisms'. Thus, for instance, *mākak̲* ('to be low, humiliated', Job 24.24), which has Aramaic and Arabic cognates and is attested in a Hebrew context in Eccl. 10.18 and probably earlier in Ps. 102.43, occurs in Ugarit in the physical sense 'to collapse' (Gordon *UT* V.68.2, 17). *'āṯaq* ('to be advanced in years', lit. 'to pass on', Job 21.7) occurs in Ugaritic (Gordon *UT* 49 II.5, 26; 125.16, 19; 126 VI.1, 13) in the physical sense 'to pass on'; compare Job 9.5; 14.18; 18.4, where the verb is possibly Hebrew rather than Aramaic. *qibbēl* ('to receive', Job 2.10) is regular in Aramaic but exceptional in Hebrew, occurring only in late Hebrew works, for example, Esther (4.4; 9.27), Chronicles (1 Chron. 12.19; 21.12; 2 Chron. 29.16, 22), Ezra (8.31) and Ben Sira (12.5). Here despite its incidence in Ugaritic in the fourteenth century BCE we are entitled to accept it in Job as an Aramaism. Despite the affinities with Hebrew we must remember that Ugaritic was a northern Canaanite dialect,[10] so that a word like *qibbēl* in this sense evidently

9. Kautzsch 1902: 101; Gray and Driver 1921: xlvi-xlvii. For Guillaume it is sufficient that a word has a possible Arabic cognate to rule out the possibility of Aramaism. N.H. Snaith (1968) also follows this line, though adducing certain instances where the assumed Aramaisms have Ugaritic cognates. It is significant that Pope, whose Ugaritic equipment is much superior to Snaith's, while no more convinced than the writer by Tur-Sinai's main thesis, treats his demonstration of the Aramaic element in Job with much more respect than Snaith (Pope 1965: livf.).

10. This was emphasized by J. Cantineau (1932; 1940: 59-61), J. Aistleitner (1937: 38f.), J. Friedrich (1933: 27; 1951), and A. Goetze (1936: 142), who regard Ugaritic as a new language hitherto unattested which lay between Biblical Hebrew and Akkadian, characterized by H. Bauer as 'Saphonisches' (1935), by Goetze as 'Amorite' and by Aistleitner as 'altmesopotamisches Westsemitisch', which recognized the Amorite, or North-West Semitic features characteristic of the dialect of Mari in the early second

survived in Aramaic in the region, but not in Classical Hebrew before the fifth century BCE. In Job 22.28 Snaith rightly claims that the verb *gāzar* in the basic sense 'to cut' is attested in Ugaritic as well as Arabic, from which the sense it has in Job and Est. 2.1, 'to decree', is derived. The word has this sense in the Mishnah, Talmud and modern Hebrew, but here it is probably influenced by the usage in those late Hebrew passages. The fact remains that it is in Aramaic that it has the regular sense 'to decree', and its incidence in the late Hebrew passages surely indicates Aramaism. The same may be said for *ḥ*^{e}*mēh* ('beware!'), which should probably be read in Job 36.18 for MT *ḥēmāh*. It is true that this has cognates in Arabic *ḥama(y)* ('to protect') and Ugaritic *ḥmyt* in the phrase *gr ḥmyt* ('an alien in sanctuary', Gordon *UT* 2.27f.); compare Akkadian *ḫamatu* ('sanctuary, protection'). This is obviously the root of Hebrew *ḥômāh* ('wall') so that it is only a matter of chance that the verb is unattested in Hebrew except possibly in Job 36.18. Here again the exceptional incidence in the late Hebrew work and the relative frequency of *ḥ*^{a}*mēh* and *ḥ*^{a}*mā'* in Aramaic must indicate Aramaism in the passage. In a case like *ma'*^{a}*lîm 'ēṣāh* ('obscuring [God's] purpose', Job 42.3) the first radical consonant of the verb may suggest the Aramaic variation of Hebrew *ṣ*. Here, however, Ugaritic *ġlm* ('darkness', *UT* Krt 10; 125, 50) may indicate a Classical Hebrew root *'ālam* ('to be dark'), which Dahood would recognize in Eccl. 3.11 (Dahood 1952: 38). The verb *'ālam*, however, is well attested in pre-exilic Hebrew works in the sense of 'to hide', which is not unconnected with the sense 'to be dark' or Ugaritic *ġlm*, which is the sense of the verb in Job 42.3 and possibly in Eccl. 3.11. Since we are unable to attest the root in the sense 'to be dark' in Aramaic or Syriac, the passages in Job 42.3 and Eccl. 3.11 may indicate Aramaic influence on the pronunciation of Hebrew rather than an Aramaic root.

In his study 'Hebrew Poetic Diction', G.R. Driver cautions us against concluding from Aramaic roots in a Hebrew work which are known only through Aramaic sources that that of itself is evidence for the late date of the work. Contending that Aramaic is by far the largest single extraneous element in the Hebrew language (Driver 1953a), he has noted strong Aramaic influence in the Elohistic narrative source of the Pentateuch and Hosea in northern Israel, with which we may compare Aramaic forms which characterize certain narratives of Elisha in Kings, for example 2 Kgs 4.1-7, 8-37; 5.8-23; 6.24; 7.20, also from northern Israel (Burney 1903: 420ff., 440ff.).

Gordis repeats this caution (1965: 162), classifying Aramaic elements in the OT in four categories. He admits first an Aramaic element, which is reasonable in view of the provenance of the patriarchs from northern Mesopotamia.

millennium BCE and the Canaanite glosses in the Amarna Tablets. Greater emphasis was placed on the Canaanite element by J.A. Montgomery and Z.S. Harris (1935: 10ff.), R. de Langhe (1938), C.H.W. Brekelmans (1962: 6ff.) and particularly C.H. Gordon (1965: 147f.) and M. Dahood (1952; 1962; 1963c; 1964b; besides current articles in *Biblica* and *CBQ*).

Secondly he reckons with borrowing from Aramaic in the pre-exilic period, especially from Syria during the days of the kingdom of Damascus, with which Israel had relations friendly and more often unfriendly until the eighth century BCE. In the Northern Kingdom with its interest in the northern part of Transjordan, a border land itself, it is natural to expect affinity of language with Aramaic which was spoken just over the border, just as in the English marches of Northumberland and Cumberland we find closer affinity in vocabulary and pronunciation with the dialect of the Scottish borders than the English of Oxford or London. Thirdly, in and after the exile, when communities of Jews were isolated in Aramaean communities in Mesopotamia and particularly when Aramaic became the official administrative language in the western provinces of the Persian Empire from the middle of the sixth century BCE, Hebrew was particularly exposed to Aramaic influence. This is the period in which, on grounds other than language, the Book of Job is usually dated. Finally the current Aramaic is attested increasingly in the targums, Mishnah and the Talmud in the early Christian era.

The same case is developed at greater length and depth by Max Wagner in his important monograph,[11] where he examines possible Aramaisms in vocabulary, roots and forms, meanings and phonetic variations in the various books in the OT. He reaches the conclusion that Aramaic contributed at all times to the vocabulary and grammatical forms in Hebrew either by the influence of Old Aramaic in local dialects in Palestine or, in the case of late books like Job, through the currency of Aramaic from the sixth century BCE to the Masoretic standardization of the text of the OT, which in fact it may to a great extent have determined.[12]

In Wagner's tabulated summary of his survey and conclusions on vocabulary (Wagner 1966: 139-43) we find that though there are Aramaisms of one or other of those classes in every book of the OT (except possibly Nahum) they are particularly frequent in exilic or postexilic books, especially Esther,[13] Song of Songs, Ecclesiastes, the Hebrew section of Daniel and, to a lesser extent than those, Job, especially in the Elihu section.[14] From the considerable evidence of Aramaisms of various categories in the earlier books of the OT we should not be prepared to take automatically all Aramaic words and forms as reflecting the Aramaic of the exilic or postexilic period. Nevertheless their

11. Wagner 1966. Wagner cordially endorses Driver's views of the influence of Aramaic on Hebrew throughout the OT, which had already been expressed by D. Winton Thomas in *Record and Revelation* (1938: 386-91). Wagner specifies more particularly what constitutes an Aramaism.

12. So Meyer 1957: 139ff.; 1958: 45ff.; Baumgartner 1959: 209.

13. Wagner includes Persian loanwords through Aramaic.

14. Wagner gives the percentage of Aramaisms in the whole vocabulary of Job excluding the Prologue and Epilogue and the Elihu sections as 1.6%, of the Elihu sections as 2%, of Song of Songs as 2.2%, of Ecclesiastes as 3.1%, of Daniel 1.75%, and of Esther as 5.3% (excluding Persian loanwords through Aramaic 4%).

exceptional frequency in Job in contrast to pre-exilic works and in comparison to postexilic books makes it probable that they do reflect the currency of Aramaic at that time, when Wagner demonstrates that even on the most generous estimate of Aramaisms in the earlier sources, this element increased six-fold (1966: 149f.). Granted that the number of Aramaisms Wagner finds in Job may require to be reduced in the light of Ugaritic elements with affinity with the Canaanite rather than the Aramaic substratum of Hebrew, there is still a comparatively substantial element of Aramaism in Job, though, in comparison with the Song of Songs, Ecclesiastes and Esther, not enough to suggest that the book was a translation of an Aramaic original. In conclusion, we may note that that *nota accusativa 'et*, which is regular in Classical Hebrew, is limited to the prose narrative in the Prologue and Epilogue and certain introductions to the various addresses in the Dialogue, but occurs only thrice in the Dialogue where the MT is questioned in the versions (5.17; 14.3 and 26.4). Elsewhere in the poetic Dialogue, where the *nota accusativa* is used sparingly, it is always the Aramaic *l*[e]. We would note also the Aramaic masculine plural termination *-în* which appears invariably in *millîn* ('words'). This noun, incidentally, though occurring in earlier Hebrew works (2 Sam. 23.2), Prov. 23.9 (monarchic) and in the undateable Ps. 139.3, 4, is found in the late postexilic Ps. 19.5 and recurs over 30 times throughout Job from 4.2 to 38.2.

The survival of Aramaic elements in Classical Hebrew is understandable in view of the Mesopotamian antecedents of the *'ᵃrammî 'ōḇēḏ*, the 'forwandered Aramaean', and later contacts between northern Israel and northern Transjordan with the Aramaean populations of Syria and the borderlands. What then of the Canaanite substratum of Hebrew evidenced by Ugaritic?

In the Late Bronze Age when Egypt claimed suzerainty over Palestine and southern Syria (Canaan) we are familiar with citations and glosses in the Amarna Tablets which have affinity with Hebrew and more particularly with Ugaritic. The repeated deportations of the populations of Palestine and southern Syria to which Egyptian records of that time refer, must have resulted in a large Canaanite population in Egypt, particularly in the north, which was a ready material for exploitation in forced labour, of which the Exodus tradition has preserved vivid reminiscence (Exod. 1.9-14). There is no reason to believe that the 'mixed multitude' that traditionally Moses led out of Egypt (Exod. 12.38) was limited to the family of Jacob, the Aramaean forbears of Israel. The majority of those who survived detention in Egypt were probably those deported to Egypt and their descendants. Nor do we find it likely that Palestine was occupied in the Early Iron Age by a conquering minority of Aramaean stock. We have no doubt that Moses or some such figure with a natural gift of leadership and spiritual charisma was able to weld a 'mixed multitude' into a religious community which penetrated into Palestine. In an analysis of the names, local settlement and characteristics of the conventional 'tribes' of Israel in Palestine and Transjordan we have contended for the accretion from the nucleus of such a sacral community to a larger sacral confederacy through attraction of 'second-class citizens' disaffected under the petty kings and oligarchies of the small city-states of the land (J. Gray 1988: 439-55) in agreement with the thesis of G. Mendenhall (1962). This symbiosis was put on a firm political basis by David with the emergence of the historic Israel. The linguistic result was the Hebrew of the early narrative sources of the Pentateuch and certain of the Psalms and subsequent literature in 'the language of Canaan'.

We are now prepared to assess the language of the Book of Job on the evidence of the fullest extant representative of Canaanitish, Ugaritic, bearing always in mind that it represents the most northerly of the Canaanite dialects, with affinity with Akkadian and Aramaic dialects in northern Syria and Mesopotamia,[15] though the affinity of Ugaritic with other Canaanite dialects in the southern Syria and Palestine including their development in Hebrew was stronger.

The Ras Shamra texts, particularly the poetic myths and legends, attest many words which not only formally suggest a cognate with Hebrew, but, being in parallelism with others often in the same combination as in Hebrew,[16] give indication of a more precise nuance in the latter than is often the case with cognates cited from other Semitic languages. This in itself is very impressive evidence of the value of Ugaritic for understanding Hebrew texts and in the solution of many problems that abound in such a book as Job. But it is when we study the grammar of the Ras Shamra texts that its pre-eminence for the appreciation of the language of such a book, whether in support or emendation of the MT, is really manifest.

To begin with the verb, we encounter here the optative perfect, for example in *UT* 76 II.20: *ḥwt 'aḫt* ('May you live', sc. flourish, 'O sister'). This is found also in Arabic, but on the strength of its incidence in Ugaritic, taken with the mass of evidence that may be cited for the affinity of Hebrew and Ugaritic, its closest neighbour, we may confidently see Canaanite influence rather than Arabic in Job's exclamation on the fateful night of his parents' marriage (3.3): *hōrāh gāḇer* ('May a man-child be conceived!'). The imperfect is used in graphic narrative, though this may express rapid succession of actions in the past like the Akkadian preterite. Like Hebrew and Arabic the jussive and imperfect indicative has often an energic ending, which we must be prepared to find more often in Hebrew than has been recognized. Thus in Bildad's second address he opens with the statement: *'aḏ-'ānāh ṯᵉśîmennā qēṣ 'el-millîn*[17] ('How long until you put an end to speaking?', 18.2). Here the recognition of the energic imperfect suggests the emendation of the verb in MT, where the plural is contrary to Bildad's address to Job. The final *n* of the restoration of the text has been corrupted to *w* in the Old Hebrew script.

15. See above p. 77.
16. Gevirtz 1963; Craigie 1971; 1977; 1979a; 1979b. Watson 1988.
17. MT emended after LXX and 11QtargJob. See above p. 92.

The imperfect is also used in Ugaritic to express purpose after the imperative in anacoleuthon, for example in Gordon *Krt* 37:

> *rd lmlk 'amlk*
> *ldrktk 'aṯbnn*
>
> Come down from the kingship that I may be king,
> From your administration that I may occupy the throne.

Compare Job 34.28:

> *lᵉḇābî' 'ālāyw ṣa'ᵃqaṯ-dāl*
> *wᵉṣa'ᵃqaṯ 'ᵃniyyîm yišmā'*
>
> To bring before him the cry of the poor,
> That he may hear the cry of the distressed.

This Ugaritic text also illustrates 'the energic imperfect' and the root *drk* expressing 'rule' or ordered government; compare Arabic *darkatu(n)* with the same sense, which we shall have occasion to note in Job as distinct from the usual sense of *dereḵ* ('way') in passages expressing the ordered government of the divine king.

The verb in Ugaritic is often introduced by a proclitic *l* with asseverative force, for example in Gordon *UT* 51 V.65-66:

> *rbt 'il lḥkmt*
> *šbt dqnk ltṣrk*
>
> Thou art aged, O El, thou art indeed wise,
> Surely the grey hairs of your beard instruct thee.

In this passage, almost pure Hebrew, we may note *rb* in the sense not of 'great', as usually in Hebrew, but, as the parallel indicates, 'aged', as in Job 32.9:

> *lō'-rabbîm yᵉḥkāmû*
> *ûzᵉqēnîm yāḇînû mišpāṭ*
>
> It is not (just) the aged who are wise,
> And the old who are discriminate in judgment.

However, it is the asseverative sense of the proclitic *l* in the Ugaritic text that is really significant. This we find to have been repeatedly misunderstood by Hebrew scribes who pointed it in many a passage as the negative *lō'* possibly because it was pronounced *lo* in Ugaritic, as Gordon suggested. In the MT the effect was to give such passages the diametric opposite of the sense the context demands. One out of many such instances, perhaps the most striking, is in Job's *apologia pro vita sua* in 29.24:

> *'eśḥaq 'ᵃlēhem lᵉ* (MT *lō'*) *ya'ᵃmînû*
> *wᵉ'āru* (MT *wᵉ'ôr*) *pānay lᵒyaḇlîqû* (MT *lō' yappîlûn*)

If I smiled to them then indeed they gained confidence,
And if my face shone they fairly beamed.

Confronted by the difficulty of the negative *lō'* in the MT Mowinckel and Fohrer cut the Gordian knot by omitting it as a scribal error, while G.R. Driver understood it as interrogative for the more normal *hᵃlō'*, the rhetorical question as a strong asseverative. But other instances of MT *lō'* which give the converse of the sense of the context do not support this explanation, for example Job's objection to his inquisitor in 14.16:

kî-'attāh ṣᵉ'āḏay tispôr
lᵉtišmôr 'al-ḥaṭṭā'ṯî (reading *lᵉ* for MT *lō'*)

But as it is thou dost keep account of my steps,
And dost surely mark my transgression.

Here incidentally the parallel *ṣᵉ'āḏay* indicates that *ḥaṭṭā'ṯî* is, as Eitan proposed (1924: 38-42), probably cognate of Arabic *ḫaṭwatu(n)* ('a step'), which the Masoretes pointed as the more familiar Hebrew *ḥaṭṭ'aṯ*. By happy coincidence we may recognize both senses of the noun by the English translation 'transgression'.

Another usage to emerge in Ugaritic is the significance of *'al* introducing the imperfect. It is already familiar in Hebrew as the negative particle introducing the jussive and occasionally has this force in Ugaritic. In Ugaritic, however, it may also introduce the imperfect indicative, for example in Gordon *UT* 51.VIII.1:

'idk 'al ttn phm 'm ġr

Then indeed did they direct themselves to the mountain.

The Masoretes evidently recognized this usage in Ps. 121.3:

'al-yittēn lammôṭ raḡlekā
'al-yānûm šōmᵉrekā

He will not suffer your foot to stumble,
Your keeper will not sleep.

This solves an outstanding difficulty in Job 13.20, where the sufferer makes his request:

'aḵ-šᵉttayim 'al-ta'aś 'immāḏî

Grant me but two requests.

The Ras Shamra texts familiarize us with the conjunction or proclitic *k* introducing the verb in the final position in a sentence, which is thus emphasized, for example in Gordon *UT* Aqhat V.15:

gm l'intṯh kyṣḥ

Aloud he cries to his wife.

This is also found in Hebrew though possibly not recognized by the Masoretes or even earlier scribes, for example in the refrain in Ps. 118.10-12:

> *b^{e}šēm yhwh kî '^{a}mîlēm*
>
> in the name of Yahweh I will drive them away.

It may even introduce and so emphasize a final sentence, for example in Deut. 32.9:

> *kî ḥēleq yhwh 'ammô*
> *ya'^{a}qōḇ ḥeḇel naḥ^{a}lāṯô*
>
> Yahweh's portion was his people,
> Jacob the lot which he inherited.

Another phenomenon with the verb in Ugaritic is the final enclitic *m*, for example apparently with the participle or infinitive absolute in Gordon *UT* V.10:

> *my b'ilm ydy mrṣ*
> *gršm zbln*
>
> Who among the gods will drive out the sickness,
> Expelling the disease?.

In such cases *m* may have an adverbial sense. A final *m* with a verb has caused commentators on the OT some perplexity, which might, of course, be resolved by assuming scribal corruption of a final *n* or, in the case of the masculine plural, *w* to *m* in the Old Hebrew script. Now emendation is obviated in the light of Ugaritic usage, for example in Job 12.27:

> *y^{e}maš^{e}šû-ḥōšeḵ* (MT *w^e*) *lō'-'ôr*
> (MT *wayyaṯ'ēm*) *kaššikkôr*.

Here in colon b the LXX read the Niphal *wayyittā'û*, assuming the same subject as for the verb in colon a, and it must be admitted that the final *m* in the MT *wayyaṯ'ēm* must have been taken as *w* in the *Vorlage* of the LXX. But the Masoretes must have found final *m* in the text they transmitted, which was probably in *scriptio defectiva*. They then took the final *m* as the pronominal suffix, pointing accordingly, so changing the subject, converting the Niphal of the verb into the Hiphil.

Final *m* appears also in Ugaritic as a substitute for a preposition, for example in Gordon *UT* Krt 265-66:

> *ṯnh kspm 'atn*
> *wṯlṯ ḫrṣm*
>
> Two (thirds) of her I will give in silver,
> Yea, a third in gold.

Or final *m* may be used as a supplement to the preposition, for example *km* ('as'), *bm* ('in, with, at, on, from'), *lm* ('to, for, from'), which evidently survived in Hebrew *kᵉmô*, *bᵉmô*, *lᵉmô*. Final *m* attached to a noun, as in *gm* ('aloud', lit. 'with a voice'), or to a verb, either participle or infinitive absolute as in *gršm* ('driving away'), may have an adverbial sense. This usage has survived in Hebrew in the adverbs *ḥinnām* ('in vain'), *piṯ'ōm* ('suddenly'), *'omnām* ('truly'), *rêqām* ('empty-handed') and *yômām* ('by day') (de Langhe 1946).

Certain prepositions in Ugaritic have meanings beyond the usual sense of their Hebrew equivalents. Thus *b*, as well as meaning 'at, by, with, in, on' as in Hebrew, may mean 'from', for example Gordon *UT* 1 Aqht. 75, 113:

bph rgm lyṣ'a
bšpth hwt

Word passed from her lips,
Declaration from her lips.

Incidentally, this attests a word *hāwāh* (Akkadian *awatu*) which must be recognized in Job 6.30: *'im-ḥikkî lō'-yāḇîn hawwôt* ('Can my palate not discriminate words?'). The sense of 'from' is illustrated in Job 12.10:

'ᵃšer bᵉyāḏô nep̄eš kol-ḥāy
wᵉrûaḥ kol-bᵉśar-'îs.

Here *'îs* in the sense of 'man', assumed in the pointing of the MT, is unapt. The chiastic parallelism demands something corresponding to *bᵉyāḏô*. So MT *'îs* is probably a corruption in the square script attested at Qumran of an original *'ûš* ('gift'), cognate with Arabic *'awśu(n)* and Ugaritic *'ušn* and the verbal element in the theophoric name Jehoash. This being so *bᵉyāḏô* means not 'in his hand' but 'from his hand'. The passage incidentally illustrates another distinctive feature of Ugaritic poetry which survived in Hebrew, the pronominal suffix doing double duty in a couplet. The passage in Job may then be rendered:

From whose hand are all who live,
And whose gift is all flesh?

Another case of *bᵉ* meaning 'from' as well as *lᵉ* with this sense is Job 20.20b-21a:

bᵉḥomᵉḏô (MT *baḥᵃmûḏô*) *lō' yᵉmmālēṭ*
'ên-śārîḏ lᵉ'oḵᵉlô

No one escapes from his greed,
There is no survivor from what he devours.

We find another case of *bᵉ* meaning 'from' in Job 19.19:

ta'ᵃḇûnî kol-mᵉ ṯê sôḏî
wᵉzeh-'āhaḇtî nehpᵉḵû-ḇî

All the men of my society have shown their abhorrence of me,
And those I moved have turned from me.

This passage illustrates another correspondence with Ugaritic, *zeh* corresponding to Ugaritic *d*, which is the regular relative pronoun in Aramaic. This may be a feature of Ugaritic as a northern Canaanite dialect with affinities with the Semitic dialects of northern Syria and Mesopotamia, which emerge to our notice as Aramaic. That the sense of l^e ('from') was once more familiar in Hebrew is indicated by the compound preposition *mill*^{e} and l^e*min*.

In the OT the preposition *'al* means normally 'against', like *'im*, or 'upon', but is found where the meaning 'to' is expected, for example in Job 31.5:

> *'im-hālaḵtî 'im-šāw'*
> *wattaḥaš 'al-mirmāh raglî*
>
> If I have gone to evil,
> And my foot has hastened to treachery.

Compare Gordon *UT* 127.39:

> *'l 'abh y'rb*
>
> To his father he enters.

It is significant, however, that this is not a regular usage in Ugaritic, but is used exceptionally in this passage in the Krt Legend of being admitted to the presence of a dignitary, here the king, who would of course be seated while the one who entered stood 'above' him. Despite the evidence of *'al* in this sense from Ugarit, its recurrence in Aramaic passages in Dan. 2.24; 4.31, 33, 6.7, 18; Ezra 4.12, 23 and so on indicates that in such a passage in Job as the one we have cited this may be an Aramaism.

The preposition *'m* as well as meaning 'to' as in Aramaic and Syriac but not in Hebrew, and 'with', which is regular in Hebrew, evidently was at one time patient of the meaning 'from', to judge from the compound preposition in Hebrew *mē'im*. We are not able to attest this meaning in Ugaritic, but the compound preposition may indicate this sense of *'im* in a southern Canaanite dialect from which Hebrew developed. However this may be, this seems to be the sense of *'im* in Job 27.13 in the MT:

> *zeh ḥēleq (-'āḏām) rāšā' 'im-'ēl*
> w^e*naḥ*^{a}*laṯ 'ārîṣîm miššadday yiqqāḥû*
>
> This is the portion of the wicked man from God,
> And the lot of the violent which he will receive from the Almighty.

Here the parallel with *'*^{a}*rîṣîm* may indicate the plural *r*^{e}*šā'îm* in colon a, and the collocation of *'* and *m* might suggest the more familiar preposition *mē'im*, with haplography of *m*.

Impressive as we find these correspondences between Ugaritic and Hebrew poetry in vocabulary and grammar, the instances we have cited are a mere fraction of what must be cited in any commentary on Job, as the publications of the late M. Dahood, including one specially on Job, have shown, even if one must occasionally qualify his conclusions.[18] In the passages we have cited, beyond the features we have especially mentioned, the close correspondence with Hebrew, especially Hebrew poetry, will have been noticed, indicating a correspondence far exceeding that of any other cognate language, which is mainly confined to vocabulary. The correspondence of Hebrew with Ugaritic extends much further, to style in the parallelism of members symmetric, antithetic, cumulative and chiastic and to the plethora of imagery common to both and the wealth of mythology in Israelite literature which is invested with a new meaning in the new medium, the significance of which is to be fully understood in the light of its *Sitz im Leben* in Ugarit.

However we may appreciate the Canaanite substratum of Hebrew and the extent to which the author of Job drew upon the poetic tradition of Canaan, we must recognize that Hebrew language was no arrested development. Thought and expression in Israel developed and matured with political development and contact with the outside world, Egypt in the time of Solomon and the Aramaeans of Syria. With those widening horizons in Solomon's reign, and under his patronage, professional administrators and their instructors came into contact with the sapiential works and traditions of Egypt and probably Mesopotamia and found their own expression of Wisdom so stimulated. New expressions were occasioned by the spiritual development promoted by the liturgy of the Temple and evidenced by the Psalms and by the great prophets. The Book of Job is poetry of the highest quality, which drew generously upon the resources of Canaanite poetry and used a wealth of language often beyond the scope of current Hebrew, at least so far as it is attested, the meaning of which we may gather from cognates in kindred Semitic languages, subject always to the test of congruency with the context and the parallelism of members in Job. However, the more we know of Hebrew literature the more we are impressed with the fluency of the author of Job in Hebrew language as it had developed through the history of Israel, his natural application of its idiom, thought and literary forms. With consummate ease and mastery he adapted the literary forms and their associated themes and expressions. This he does sometimes in support of the orthodox theology of Job's friends in the Hymn of Praise and the proverbial wisdom they cite and represent or in the declarations on the fate of the wicked from Wisdom psalms. He may on the other hand adapt this material in his criticism of current orthodoxy. He even daringly parodies Psalm 8 (at 7.17-18), while the thought, vocabulary and imagery of the Plaint of the Sufferer in the Psalms echo throughout the book, with verbal and thematic echoes of Jer. 20.14-18 and Lam. 3.8-9 in 3.3-10 and 19.5-8 respectively. Job's *apologia pro vita sua* in ch. 29 reflects the Israelite ideal of social responsibility expressed in the psalms and prophets, while his

18. Cf. the just yet critical appraisal of Dahood's use of Ugaritic material in his AB commentary on *Psalms* by P.C. Craigie in the latter's excellent commentary on Psalms 1–50 (1983).

Oath of Purgation reflects such a declaration of integrity as is expressed in Psalm 15, a liturgy of access to worship in the Temple, and more particularly in substance, the social demands of the Decalogue, and in form, the Twelve Adjurations in Deut. 27.10-26. From such correspondences then we have little doubt that in language, thought and form, the Book of Job is in the mainstream of traditional Hebrew which had developed until the fifth century BCE, with other linguistic elements, like Aramaic, strictly secondary.

Chapter 9

The Argument

In the Prologue the author's adaptation of his source poses the problem of the reaction of a person to what Hebrew thought ascribes to a beneficent and just God in the vicissitudes of life. The tradition of Israel in cult, prophecy and Wisdom encouraged humans to expect that in conformity to the revealed nature and will of God they might expect material expression of his favour as they might expect defiance of the divine will for society to result in condign punishment. This expression of divine justice, or theodicy, is notably inculcated in the Book of Proverbs with its many graphic illustrations of the principle in salutary admonition to prospective leaders of society. As a result, the overall impression is that of a utilitarian morality, which must lead one to question the motivation of the approved conduct of 'a man perfect and upright, fearing God and shunning evil' (1.8). This is done by the agency of the *śāṭān* in the Prologue, and the stage is set to assess God's faith in humanity as the apex of his creation, his 'servant', one devoted to and governed by the divine will and the recipient of his favour, by the acid test of faith in adversity. From this trial the sufferer emerges with faith unimpaired in what the author has retained of his source in Job's classical response (1.21):

> Naked I came out of my mother's womb
> And naked shall I go away again whither I shall go;
> Yahweh gave and Yahweh has taken,
> Blessed be the name of Yahweh.

In this declaration God's faith in humanity is gloriously justified in his fortitude in adversity, which the Wisdom tradition of Israel inculcated, and which is one of the cardinal elements in the Arab ideal of manhood (*murū'atu[n]*).

With the dialogue and its prelude in Job's curse on the day of his birth the author's proper contribution begins. Despite the sturdy faith of the sufferer in Job's declaration in 1.21 and 2.10 the reader may well be disturbed by the suffering of the exemplary Job by the permissive will of God, which, to be sure, seriously modifies the teaching of the sages in Proverbs. This is shared by the author in his controversial adaptation of his source, reflected in Job's curse on the day of his birth (ch. 3). Though in the Prologue he has firmly rejected his wife's advice to 'curse God and die' (2.9), Job, though not cursing his creator, curses his creation in his curse of the day he was born (3.3ff.). The very purpose of life is questioned in the light of his unmitigated suffering (3.20, 23):

> Why is life given to one in trouble...
> To a man whose way is hidden
> And about whom God has set obstructions?

We have little doubt that this is more than a general academic question, but regard it as reflecting the personal agony of the author in contrast to the dismissal of life and its experiences and aims as 'vanity' by 'the gentle cynic'. This intimate personal involvement characterizes Job's arguments in response to his friends throughout the Dialogue with progressive intensity, where the arguments of traditional Wisdom on the mutual relationship of God and humanity are subjected to the author's keen and controversial criticism.

In the opening of the Dialogue Job's impassioned personal reaction in questioning the meaning of the life of a person like himself tormented by unrelieved suffering is rebuked by Eliphaz (4.3-6; 5.2) as the betrayal of the unimpassioned reaction of a human to the vicissitudes of life commended by Hebrew Wisdom:

> Your words would raise the fallen,
> You would strengthen bowing knees;
> But now when it reaches you, you cannot bear it,
> And when it comes to you, you are non-plussed...
> For resentment kills the fool,
> And passion is the death of the simpleton.

Significantly, in his questioning of the meaning of life in face of his suffering (ch. 3), Job has not introduced the subject of his innocence. One's sufferings are indeed related to the will of God, who circumscribes one's freedom (3.23), though the controversial note has been sounded by Job's wife:

> Are you still unshaken in your integrity?
> Curse God and die!

In Job's curse on the day he was born, with his harrowing plaint of his sufferings, there is no question of their relation to his conduct. This is introduced by Eliphaz, insisting on the doctrine of the theodicy represented in traditional Hebrew theology, as in the Deuteronomistic history, prophecy and proverbs. This is the reply of Wisdom to Job's bleak pessimism in ch. 3.

The kindliest and most mature of Job's three friends and probably the one who shares his spiritual problem, Elihu, edges the argument *ad hominem*. He advances from his rebuke of Job's impassioned expostulation in ch. 3 to God's animadversion on his failure as a sage and pious man to appreciate God's Order in his upholding of the innocent and the discomfiture of the wicked (4.7f.):

> What man if innocent ever perished,
> Or where were the righteous cut off?

For as far as I have seen, those who plough in mischief
And sow trouble reap it.

Implying rather than explicitly asserting the culpability of the sufferer, Eliphaz proceeds to argue a *maiore ad minus* that as the celestials are imperfect with relation to God, a mortal is even more morally defective (4.17-19):

Is a man just vis-à-vis God?
Is a man pious vis-à-vis his maker?
If he does not commit himself wholly to his servants,
And charges even his angels with error,
Much more those that inhabit houses of clay,
Whose foundations are in the dust.

Eliphaz uses the same argument with more pointed allegation of the culpability of the sufferer in 15.14-16, and, with probably more than a mere hint at Job's culpability, he states (5.6f.):

Mischief does not grow out of the soil,
Nor trouble spring from the earth.
Trouble is innate in a man
As soaring flight in Reshef's brood.[1]

The sufferer is more overtly indicted by Zophar in the first cycle or the Dialogue (11.6), and from this point, provoked by Job's pointed criticisms of the friends' arguments for the theodicy as applied to his particular case, their indictment intensifies until Eliphaz's specific charges in 22.4-11, which, however, we prefer to regard as in the design of the author to introduce specific charges to answer in anticipation of Job's *apologia* (ch. 29) and oath of purgation (ch. 31).

Meanwhile Eliphaz commends Job to God's mercy in anticipation of relief from his suffering enhanced by material favour (5.8, 17-26), and this is, significantly, at this stage of the Dialogue the approach of Bildad (8.5-7) and even the acrimonious Zophar (11.13-19), in whose statement, in anticipation of the indictment pressed against Job, the relationship between sin and suffering is more directly implied (11.4-6). However, while the plea to God which Eliphaz recommends might be understood as one for relief from unmerited suffering, the drift of the friends' argument indicates rather that it is the plea of the penitent sinner and not the man of whom God approved without qualification in the Prologue.

Apart from the arguments of the friends for the suffering of humans in the divine economy as retributive, which they support by all too familiar experience (5.3-7, 13-16; 8.8-22; 15.20-35; 20.5-29) and by graphic aphorism (18.5-21), Eliphaz proposes the explanation of suffering as discipline which betokens the favour or God, not, however, without the implication that such

1. Vultures. See Commentary *ad loc.*

chastisement is for some degree of sin. This view is propounded in the Elihu addendum, which suggests that such discipline as well as being therapeutic to a sinner may also be preventative (33.14-30).

In reply to Eliphaz's mild rebuke to his impassioned outburst on the curse of the day of his birth Job's despair is not assuaged by Eliphaz's generalities regarding the limitations of humans and their natural propensity to trouble (active or passive). He is not encouraged by Eliphaz's observations of the effective justice of God in the retribution of the wicked and his blessing on the righteous and the repentant sinner. Indeed, Eliphaz's recommendation of an appeal for God's mercy (5.8), coupled with his declaration that trouble is innate in humans, surely implies the belief in a necessary connection between sin and suffering, which dominates the argument of Job's friends throughout the Dialogue. Many obvious instances of such a connection may be adduced, though the realist may cite all too obvious modifications in the case of blatant materialists (21.7-15).

Granted, however, the general experience that sin in more and less degree results physically, mentally and spiritually in suffering, we may not infer that in every case suffering is the consequence of sin. This logical fallacy impairs the argument of Job's friends from first to last in the Dialogue. Nor indeed can Job, despite his clear conscience, divest himself of the fallacy, imputing his suffering to God's allegation of sin. The logical fallacy is finally exposed in the divine rebuke that Job convicts the Almighty while exculpating himself (40.8). Firm in the conviction that his suffering was unmerited at the hand of God (7.12-21) the sufferer breaks out in apostrophe to God (7.12):

> Am I Sea or Tannin
> That you set a watch over me?

Alluding to the traditional theme of God's effective conflict with the forces of chaos, Job animadverts on the Order established by God in creation culminating in the creation of humanity in the image of God, capable of response to him according to the revelation of the divine nature and will expressed in society governed by his Order. The sufferer thus rejects Eliphaz's citation of the Divine Order in nature and society (5.5-16) in his encouragement to convince Job that humans are not the victims of blind chance of an arbitrary divine power but, under the divine economy, may look for relief and favour beyond their present suffering, just as sinners may expect retribution (5.11-27).

The significance of this expression of faith may be grasped by the recognition of its place in the faith of Israel in Hymns of Praise to God as King in the great autumn festival (e.g. Pss. 29; 65; 93; 97; etc.), as the ground of assurance in the Plaint of the Sufferer both communal (e.g. Pss. 44; 74) and individual (e.g. Pss. 22.4, 29 [EVV 3, 28]; 102.13, 16 [EVV 12, 15]; 103.20ff. [EVV 19ff.]), and in its application in the prophets in hope (Nah. 1.3-5; Hab.

3.8-15; and particularly Deutero-Isaiah, 51.9 and 40.12-14, the latter of which enumerates the cosmic exploits of the Divine Creator in a series of questions reflecting the sapiential tradition, as in the Divine Declaration on the same theme in Job 38.1-39; 40.25-30 [EVV 41.1-6]). So in the recurrence of the theme in the statements of Job's friends and its corollary in the assertion of God's Order in society (e.g. 8; 15.20ff.; 18.5ff.) we have matter which might lift the sufferer beyond his nihilistic despair, his obsession with his unmerited suffering and his doubt of the interest and of the justice of God. Or again the application of the theme in prophecies of doom (e.g. Jer. 10.12-16; Isa. 26.22; 27.1) is made by Job's friends in their reply to his intensified challenge to the traditional doctrine they represent. But this the author counters in Job's parody of Ps. 8.4f. in Job 7.17 and his sarcastic criticism (12.10-23), with emphasis on the destructive activity of God in his otherwise ordered creation in nature and society (9.4-24), with particular reference to the case of the worthy sufferer (9.11ff.), whom God condemns to torture without a fair hearing (9.14-20, 32-35). So in his response to the encouragement or censure of his friends the sufferer either relapses into the nihilistic prospect of ch. 3, recurring in 7.1-10, 14-21; 10.18-22; 14; 17.11-16, or aspires, too often in vain, to a hearing in confrontation with God, when he may state his case, confident in his innocence, thus challenging the justice of the Almighty, the traditional belief which, however, he cannot quite renounce despite all apparent evidence to the contrary which his sufferings suggest (13.14-22; 16.18-21). In such a confrontation Job might expect God to state his grounds of complaint which occasion Job's suffering (10.22; 13.23f.):

> I will say to you, 'Do not condemn me,
> Inform me of your case against me...
> Then call, and I will answer,
> Or let me make a statement, and you answer.

Besides natural disasters cited by Job (10.5-7; 12.14-22), which impair God's Order that Job's friends allege, the sufferings of the worthy man, such as disease and at the hands of oppressors or traducers, recur in Job's lamentations (7.5-10; 16.8-16; 19.15-20) in the language and imagery familiar in the Plaint of the Sufferer in the Psalms. There, however, in the context of the cult they are incidental to the rehabilitation of the sufferer in God's Order either in anticipation or in thanksgiving. The author of the book of Job, true to sapiential tradition, faces life's problems independently of the cult, and the sufferings of the worthy man are presented in all their stark simplicity, indeed in the context of a Job's *apologia pro vita sua* (chs. 29–30) the disruption of God's Order without qualification is clearly implied in the fatal impairing of the social potential of the worthy and willing man. In this context then ch. 29 is not a plaint in anticipation of deliverance nor a statement of sufferings from which deliverance is already experienced, but is the statement of a plaintiff with a just cause which he sustains by an oath of purgation (ch. 31).

As humanists, Job's sage friends support the doctrine of the theodicy, re-echoing the summary dismissal of the wicked who seem to disrupt God's Order in Proverbs. Thus they allege that the wicked may flourish but, like the grass in Ps. 37.2-10, this will be but for a time, when their end will be complete (Job 5.3; 8.11-19; 15.20-35; 18.5-21; 20.5-29). In Job's statements there is no such prospect. It is true that, apart from obvious retribution, the physical effects of over-indulgence and the anxiety of the violent malefactor in his constant apprehension of retaliation (18.11ff.) may be cited in support of the arguments of Job's friends. However, the miscreant too often defies justice until his death, going down to an honoured burial (21.31-34). In his reply to the confident assertion of the certain end of the wicked in the aphorisms cited by Bildad, the author seriously questions their universal validity (21.17f.). Nor, in his explosion of the current doctrine of the theodicy, does the author admit that the sin of the wicked who die with impunity may be entailed with condign retribution on his descendants (e.g. Exod. 21.5), a communal ethic already modified in Israel by the time of the book of Job (Deut. 24.6; Ezek. 19.18; Job 21.19). Thus the realist rejects the arguments of his orthodox friends and invites, indeed compels, serious consideration of life's experiences.

The author of the Book of Job puts the problem of suffering beyond the scope of theory and objective discussion in relating his unmitigated sufferings to God (3; 6.4-9; 9.11-24; 19.6-12; 21), his problem being more acute in that his sufferings are out of all proportion to his exemplary life noticed in the Prologue. Thus the poet heightens the drama of his work, but such passages, and particularly Job's apostrophes to the Almighty (7.12-21; 9.25-31; 10; 14.16f.), which come as interjections in the debate, surely reflect the personal agony of the author, which prompted his great work. This personal agony is intensified in Job's appeals to God for a hearing where he may sustain his case of a life corresponding to what was recognized in his society as the declared nature and will of God (13.14-17; 16.19-22; 17.3), which prompts the confident, though to be sure only momentary, hope of ultimate vindication (19.25-27):

> But I myself am sure, the one who will vindicate me is vital,
> And one who is final authority will prove himself effective on this earth,
> And though my skin is stripped from my flesh,
> Even after that I shall come face to face with God,
> Whom I myself shall see,
> Whom I shall see with my own eyes, himself and no stranger.

Here the author ventures into a realm peculiarly personal and beyond the scope of traditional Wisdom and current theology.

Job's objections to his friends' defence of the current conception of the theodicy in its strictly mechanical application on which they insist and his claimant appeals to defend himself before the divine tribunal elicit their response that God is transcendent, beyond the conception and aspiration of mortals and even the celestials (4.17-21; 11.8-10; 15.7f., 15f.; 22.12). The transcendence of God is the ultimate solution of the problem of Job, as is indicated in the Divine Declaration (38.1–39.30; 40.25-30 [EVV 41.1-6]), which Job finally accepts (40.4-5; 42.2-6). But he does so in the light of its full implications, which are not revealed until the theophany and Divine Declaration. However, in response to his friends' appeal to the transcendence of God, Job, far from being silenced, considers the transcendence of God an obstacle to his faith in a God who would, according to his essential character that is just and merciful, treat him according to his own norm of justice as the servant of God, as his blameless conduct deserved, or bring to his notice the case which he apparently had against the sufferer, and admit him to a fair hearing. Yet Job's reaction to his friends' assertion of the transcendence of God as their ultimate argument is an oscillation between hope and despair. Thus to the prospect of God standing surety for him in the encounter which he so ardently desires (17.3) or to his appeal to God backed by celestial support (16.19f.) and his sanguine hope of vindication by the living God (19.25-27) we may counterpoise his statement that even if a petitioner's case could be presented no one could win it nor indeed would God consent to answer 'one question in a thousand' (9.2f.), nor could a sufferer in such a case expect either response to his just case or mercy (9.15). The alternation of sapiential dialectic and impassioned plaint of suffering by the will of God and particularly direct appeal to him emphasizes the theme of the book as the conflict between theological formulation and existential experience, between theology and religion. Thus it culminates in the nearest approach to the confrontation with God which Job has wished, his direct appeal to God in his oath of purgation (ch. 31) prefaced by his *apologia pro vita sua* (ch. 29) and his plaint (ch. 30), which in such a context is tantamount to a charge against God for permitting the impairment of the social potential indicated in ch. 29, and God's response in the Divine Declaration. Here the author leaves the controversial field of the Dialogue for the final solution of his problem, significantly between Job himself and God, whom he has been apostrophizing throughout the debate with his friends in the Dialogue.

In the theophany in thunder, where the poet uses the imagery of the revelation of the sovereignty of God in the Enthronement Psalms (Pss. 29; 46; cf. Amos 1.2; Joel 3.16), and in the Divine Declaration Job finally 'sees' God. That is to say he is brought to an overwhelming sense of the presence and power of God, tremendous beyond the full comprehension and scope of human competence, yet of compelling attraction and compelling response as in the call of Isaiah (Isa. 6.5, 9):

> Woe is me! For I am lost…
> For my eyes have seen the King, the Lord of Hosts…
> And I answered, 'Here am I; send me'.

The Divine Declaration is not the answer Job would expect. It is in fact a rebuke, and as such it is a reply to Job's allegation of divine injustice in his suffering, which, through the logical fallacy we nave noticed, he regarded as the consequence of sin imputed to him by God. To the logical fallacy God's condemnation of Job's 'words without knowledge' (38.2b) might specifically refer. The gist of the divine reply, however, exposes the inadequacy of the mechanical application of the humanly formulated doctrine of the theodicy with relation to the eternal counsel, or purpose (*'ēṣāh*) of God (38.2a). The latter theme is elaborated in an impressive series of ironical questions which pose the limitations of humans in contrast to the manifold evidences of the power and wisdom of the creator, all of which attest His positive purpose. These ironical questions culminate in the passage 40.7-14, which asserts God's Order in society and exposes, or at least implies, human limitations to make that order effective, even though he might acknowledge it.

The rebuke, however, is tempered by the emphasis on the Providence of God as evidenced by the regulation of nature to the benefit of humans (38.31-37) even apart from human advantage, with rain upon the uninhabited desert (38.26f.) and his provision for the beasts of the wild (38; 39; 40.25-30 [EVV 41.16]) with their characteristics beyond humans' control for their convenience. Humanity, we are thereby reminded, is not the measure of God's universe, and if humans are chastened by being reminded of this, a wider prospect is thereby opened which enables them to emancipate themselves from the limitations of a deterministic theodicy as formulated by current doctrine and to renew their faith in the Divine Creator and his inexhaustible providence. The fact that Job has the grace to acknowledge this justifies God's faith in them, which is explicitly expressed in the Epilogue, which is accepted and adapted by the author as more than the happy ending of a popular story.

However, apart from the wider prospect of the divine purpose disclosed to the perplexed sufferer to lift him from his self-pity and rebuke his self-righteousness, raising him into a realm where he may expect ever fresh disclosure of the divine power and grace, the mere fact of God's self-manifestation to Job is the effective answer to his real problem. It is this that dispels for him 'the dark night of the soul'. His suffering does not betoken the alienation of the sufferer from God as though he were, as the friends alleged, a sinner. The traditional theology, the systematization of thought about God on the basis of humans' limited experience and understanding is not commensurate with religion, the encounter with and response to the living God. Having 'seen God' (42.5a), possibly with the nuance of the courtly idiom in ancient Israel, having been admitted to the presence of God, Job is relieved of his burden and freed from his ordeal. With a new assurance to face life and its problems, he regains his composure. It is only in the personal encounter, granted at length to Job, that his problem may be solved and he and all humans may be adjusted to bear his suffering, like the sufferer in Psalm 73, who agonized over the same problem and found peace of mind in communion with God (Ps. 73.26):

> My heart and my flesh may fail,
> But God is my portion for ever.

Here, the sage author of the Book of Job may fulfil the ideal of Wisdom in maintaining patience in affliction but, like those rallied by the great prophet of the restoration from the exile, he is prepared to wait upon the Lord that he might renew his strength (Isa. 40.31).

Part II

COMMENTARY

Job 1 and 2

The Prologue

As an introduction to the Dialogue (4-27), Job's curse on the day of his birth (3), his oath of purgation and its prelude (29–31), the Theophany and Divine Declaration (38.2–40.2, 6-14) and Job's response (40.3-5; 42.2-6), the author of the Book of Job reworks his source in the popular Hebrew form recast in a patriarchal setting, but showing evidence of elaboration, probably by the author of the book as late as the end of the sixth century BCE. See further, General Introduction, pp. 56-75. The narrative prologue to a sapiential work recalls the Protest of the Eloquent Peasant on social injustice (*ANET*, 407-10), the Aramaic Proverbs of Ahiqar (*ANET*, 427-30) and the Book of Tobit.

The literary form of the Prologue is the oral saga or folk legend, with quick succession of dramatic events, dramatic direct speech, verbal repetition, round numbers, seven, three, five and their multiples, and the remarkable survival of one man only in all the disasters. This indicates the author's familiarity with the Job tradition in popular oral form on the subject of a man's faith in God's just and beneficent providence in face of all appearances to the contrary. The narrative is reminiscent of the narratives of the Hebrew patriarchs in the earliest sources of the Pentateuch, but the cadence is more regular and is often almost as regular as poetry. The assonances, word-plays, rare vocabulary and forms are more characteristic of poetry than of prose.

The Prologue falls into two parts:

1. Job's prosperity (1.1-5), his faith impugned (6-12), the test of adversity (13-19), Job's declaration of steadfast faith (20-22).
2. Further impugning of Job's faith (2.1-6), the intensification of the test of his faith (7-8), Job's faith despite counsels of despair (9-10), the visit of his friends (11-13).

The scenes in the heavenly court (1.6-12; 2.1-6), which are each followed by tests of Job's faith (1.13-19; 2.7-8), are particularly significant as emphasizing that, however critical the sage intends to be in the Dialogue, he is a constructive writer who is prepared to consider human contingencies *sub specie aeternitatis*, which is the view eventually expressed in the Divine Declaration in the Dialogue (38.2–40.2, 7-14). As Fohrer (1963b: 69) rightly stresses, the Prologue emphasizes not the question of the theodicy, but that of human reaction to the vicissitudes of life, where the attitude of traditional wisdom is going to be critically examined in the Dialogue.

Chapter 1

1. There was a man in the land of Uz whose name was Job. And that man was perfect and upright, fearing[1] God and shunning evil.
2. And seven sons and three daughters were born to him,
3. and his property was seven thousand sheep, three thousand camels, and five hundred yoke of oxen, five hundred she-asses and a great many servants; and that man was greater than all the peoples of the East.
4. His sons used to go and hold a feast in one another's houses day about, and they would send and invite their three[2] sisters to eat and drink with them.
5. And when the feast-days were over, Job would send and have them purified. He would get busy in the morning and offer up sacrifices for each of them, for Job said:
Perhaps my sons have sinned
And cursed[3] God in their mind.
So did Job on all the occasions.
6. Now one day the celestials came and presented themselves before Yahweh and
among them came also the *śāṭān*. 7. And Yahweh said to the *śāṭān*, 'Where are you
coming from?' And the *śāṭān* answered Yahweh and said:
'From going to and fro in the earth
And walking about in it.'
8. Then Yahweh said to the *śāṭān*:
'Have you considered[4] my servant Job,
How there is none like him in the earth,
A man perfect and upright,
Fearing God and shunning evil?'
9. And the *śāṭān* answered Yahweh and said:
'Is it for nothing that Job fears God?
10. Have you not yourself set a hedge[5] completely
About him and his house
And about all that he has?
His undertakings[6] you have blessed,
And his cattle have passed all bounds in the land.
11. But stretch forth your hand
And touch whatever he has,
And he will assuredly curse[7] you to your face.'
12. Then Yahweh said to the *śāṭān*:
'Lo, all he has is in your power;
Only on himself do not put forth your hand.'
And the *śāṭān* went out from the presence of Yahweh.
13. And one day his sons and daughters were eating and drinking[8] in their eldest
brother's house, 14. when a messenger came to Job and said:
'The cattle were ploughing
And the she-asses were grazing beside them,[9]
15. When the Sabaeans made a raid and took them,
And smote the lads with the edge of the sword,
And I alone escaped to tell you.'
16. While he was yet speaking another came and said:
'Lightning fell from the sky
And blasted the sheep and the lads[10] and consumed them,
And I alone escaped to tell you.'

17. While he was yet speaking another came and said:
'The Chaldaeans laid an ambush in three bands,
And broke out against the camels and took them;
The lads they smote with the edge of the sword,
And I alone escaped to tell you.'
18. While[11] he was yet speaking another came and said:
'Your sons and daughters were eating and drinking[12]
In the house of their eldest brother,
19. When, lo, a great wind
Came from across the desert
And struck[13] the four corners of the house
And it fell on the young people and they were killed,
And I alone escaped to tell you.'
20. Then Job rose up and tore his robe and shaved his head and fell on the ground and did obeisance, 21. and said:
'Naked I came out[14] of my mother's womb
And naked shall I go away again whither I shall go.
Yahweh gave; Yahweh has taken;
Blessed be the name of Yahweh.'
21. In all this Job did not sin, nor did he ascribe lack of moral discrimination[15] to God.

Textual Notes to Chapter 1

1. Reading *y^e^rē'* for MT *wîrē* as in v. 8 with T and two Heb. MSS, omitting *w* as a dittograph before *y* in the first stage of the Hebrew square script as in the Qumran texts.
2. Reading *šālôš* for MT *š^e^lōšeṯ* as in v. 2, according to the regular grammar of Classical Hebrew and with 1 Heb. MS.
3. MT *ûḇēr^a^ḵû* (lit. 'and blessed'), a regular euphemism of the orthodox scribes, to whom 'curse God' was intolerable.
4. Lit. 'applied your heart (sc. mind) to'. For MT *'al* we may read *'el* with many Heb. MSS as in 2.3, a common scribal confusion characteristic of the time when Aramaic was displacing Hebrew as the spoken dialect in the last pre-Christian centuries.
5. MT *śaḵtā* is perhaps a scribal error from *śakkoṯā* from *sāḵaḵ* ('to screen'), but MT may denote a verb *śûḵ* meaning 'to set a thorn hedge or barrier'. See Commentary *ad loc.*
6. Reading *ma'^a^śê* with LXX, S and T for the singular *ma'^a^'śēh.*
7. Lit. 'bless', a scribal euphemism; cf. n. 3.
8. Omitting *yayin* with S and one Heb. MS as a dittograph of *y* and *m* in the preceding word *šōṯîm* in the Hebrew script; cf. 1.4, where eating and drinking is mentioned without *yayin* ('wine').
9. Reading the pronominal suffix *-hen* for MT *-hem* with five Heb. MSS in agreement with the feminine participles.
10. A possible reading is *ûḇārō'îm* ('and [on] the shepherds'), so LXX and S, but we retain MT, which agrees with the reading in v. 17 in a similar context, where there is no question of a variant in the versions.
11. For MT *'aḏ* read *'ôḏ* as in vv. 16 and 17, with many Heb. MSS.
12. Omitting MT *yayin* with LXX, S and two Heb. MSS; cf. n. 8.

13. Reading *wattigga'* for MT *wayyigga'* in agreement with the subject *rûaḥ*, which is generally feminine. Alternatively, Tur-Sinai suggests that *wayyiggā'ᵃḇû 'arba' pinnôṯ habbayiṯ* should be read, 'and the four corners of the house were overthrown'; cf. Arab. *ja'aba* ('to throw down').
14. Reading *yāṣā'ṯî* for MT *yāṣāṯî*.
15. For MT *tip̄lāh*, LXX reads 'folly', which probably reflects a reading *nᵉḇālāh*, a word which means lack of discrimination between right and wrong, the subject of the Dialogue in Job being just this in God's moral Order according to the orthodox faith. See further note on v. 22.

Commentary to Chapter 1

1. The opening of Job, *'îš hāyāh* ('there was a man'), recalls the opening of the narrative prologue in the Mesopotamian wisdom text commonly known as 'the Sumerian Job' (van Dijk 1953: 29ff.; Kramer 1955). See above, pp. 1-15.

On 'the land of Uz' in the N. Hejaz see above, pp. 35-36.

Various proposals have been made to explain the name Job (*'iyyôḇ*) in agreement with the subject of the book, for example, the man with whom God was at enmity or 'the enemy' (*'ōyēḇ*) of God, or 'the man who eventually returned' (cf. Arab. *'āba*) to God. The name, however, is not *ad hoc*, as such views suggest, but is widely attested in the Near East in the second millennium, for instance, in the Egyptian Execration texts from Luxor in the nineteenth century (*'ybm*), the Brooklyn Papyri from Egypt in the eighteenth century (*hybi'ilu*), the Mari texts from the eighteenth or seventeenth centuries (*Ha-a-ia-a-ba-m*), the Alalakh tablets from the fifteenth to the fourteenth centuries (*Ayabi*), administrative texts from the palace of Ras Shamra from the fourteenth century (*Hy'abu*), the Amarna Tablets in the fourteenth century (*A-ya-ab*). The significance of the name is probably 'Where is (God) the Father?' This, to be sure, would agree with the theme of the book, recalling the gibe of the Bedouin to the disconsolate Doughty, 'Where is thy God?' More relevant to the Book of Job is the taunt of the ungodly to the sufferer in Ps. 42.2, 11 (EVV 3, 10).

tām wᵉyāšār and *yᵉrē' 'ᵉlōhîm* ('perfect and upright' and 'fearing God') is characteristic phraseology of wisdom literature; see above, pp. 21-31.

2. Seven sons is the conventional number of saga. Thus in the royal legend of Krt in the Ras Shamra texts it is promised to the king:

'aṯt tqḥ ykrt	The wife thou takest, O Krt,
'aṯt tqḥ bbtk	The wife thou takest into thy house,
ġlmt tš'rb ḥzrk	The damsel thou bringest into thy court,
tld šb' bnm lk	Will bear thee seven sons,
wṯmn tṯmn lk	Yea eight times will she bear to thee,

Cf. the psalm in 1 Sam. 2.5 ('The barren woman has borne seven sons') and Ruth 4.15. In the Semitic community, however, daughters were economically and morally a liability, hence in the ideal family they were relatively fewer than the sons; here they are three, to make up the round number of ten children. In his family and property Job is richly blessed, the due reward for his conduct according to the retributory view of morality, which is to come under such severe criticism in the Dialogue.

3. *miqneh* is ambiguous, meaning both property in general and cattle in particular, in which a man's wealth was reckoned in the patriarchal age and society in which the narrative framework of the source of the Book of Job was cast. Note again the round numbers 10,000 (7000 and 3000) and 1000 (2 × 500). Job is depicted as a paramount sheikh. The association of camels and ploughing oxen suggests a semi-nomad milieu such as S. Palestine between Gaza and Beersheba, where the semi-nomadic Isaac is said to have sown and reaped (Gen. 26.12). The collective singular *'ᵃḇuddāh* is, like *miqneh*, ambiguous, meaning either servants or slaves. Never at any time had the Israelites any inhibitions against slavery, whether the slaves were acquired as prisoners of war (Deut. 21.11-14; cf. Num. 31.26-47) or aliens bought from slave-dealers (Exod. 12.44; Lev. 22.11; 25.44-45; Eccl. 2.7) or taken in mortgage for debt (Exod. 21.7ff.; Num. 5.1-5), the only case in which an Israelite could hold a fellow-Israelite as a slave, it being necessary to release him in the seventh year if the slave wished to go free (Exod. 21.2-11; Deut. 15.13-14; Jer. 34.14). Slave-trading by Israelites, however, was condemned as the enterprise of foreign Phoenicians (Amos 1.9; Ezek. 27.13), Edomites (Amos 1.6, 9) and of the Greeks (Joel 4.6 [EVV 3.3]). The slave had a certain personal status in Israel, being protected in the Book of the Covenant against personal injury by the master (Exod. 21.20, 26-27) and being admitted to the Passover meal if circumcised (Exod. 12.43) The category of Job's *'ᵃḇuddāh* is not specified, but in the context of the account of his wealth they were probably slaves. The wealth of Isaac as a semi-nomad sheikh in the Negeb is similarly described, with slaves mentioned *after* cattle, in Gen. 26.14 (J). This enumeration is to be noted also in administrative tablets from the palace of Ras Shamra (Thureau-Dangin 1937: 246ff.).

'The people of the East' (*bᵉnê-qeḏem*), is vague here as in Gen. 29.1, where it refers to Aramaeans of N. Mesopotamia, Judg. 3.33; 7.12; 1 Kgs 5.10 (EVV 4.30); Isa. 11.14; Jer. 49.28; Ezek. 25.4, 10. Job's wisdom is associated with that of the 'people of the East' whose wisdom was proverbial (1 Kgs 5. 10 [EVV 4.30]), namely the Edomites (Obad. v. 8).

4. In *wᵉhālᵉḵû*, *waw* consecutive with the perfect denotes habitual action. *mišteh*, lit. 'a drinking feast', though indicating conviviality, need not exclude a cultic occasion; cf. Amos 2.8. *'îš yômô*, lit. 'each (on) his day', might denote an auspicious day, possibly his birthday, but probably means 'in his turn'. In *hiqqîpû yᵉmê ham-mišteh*, in v. 5, it has been feasibly contended that a feast of several days was denoted, possibly on an annual occasion like the seven days

of the New Year Feast of Tabernacles (Deut. 16.13-15). The sheikh among the Arabs has always kept open house, establishing his good name by generosity (Arab. *karmu* [*n*]), one of the cardinal Arab virtues. Each one of Job's sons must have a like opportunity. The presence of the daughters is exceptional and indicates the status of Job's family and the consciousness of a higher ethical standard in the Jewish community. Convention demanded that Job could not compromise his dignity by being entertained in his sons' houses.

In *šelōšeṯ 'aḥyōṯêhem* the feminine numeral with the feminine plural noun is exceptional, being instanced only in Gen. 7.13, 1 Sam. 10.3 and Ezek. 7.2—so exceptionally, that is, as to be questionable. Here, however, *šelōšeṯ* may be the abstract noun 'trio'.

5. On *hiqqîpû yemê ham-mišteh* see on v. 4. The verb *nāqap̄*, 'to come full circuit' (of time), is found only here in the Hiphil, and in Isa. 29.1 in the Qal; cf. *nqpt* in the Ras Shamra texts, for example Gordon *UT* 52.66-67:

šb' šnt tmt	Seven whole years,
ṯmnt nqpt 'd	An eighth circuit besides.

Cf. Gordon, *UT* 75, 45-46.

As in Arab tribal society the father so long as he lived was head of the household, so Job assumed responsibility for the conduct of his sons though they were sufficiently adult to have houses of their own. Thus he had his sons 'sanctified' (*wayeqaddešēm*), that is, purified from whatever was incompatible with the sacral society, which every community in antiquity was. This he effected here and in 42.8 by offering up whole burnt offerings as the patriarchs had done, an office which during the history of Israel was increasingly restricted to Levites and later priests of the house of Aaron. Again the lavish sacrifice of a whole beast for each of the family (*mispar kullām*) is a feature of saga. *mispar* in this phrase is used adverbially, like the verbal accusative in Arabic.

wehiškîm babbōqer is generally rendered 'he would rise early in the morning'; Pope aptly renders 'he bestirred himself in the morning', observing that when 'morning' is explicitly mentioned the verb denotes urgency as here, or, as Jer. 7.13; 25; 11.7; 25.4; 26.5; 32.33; 35.14, 15; 44.4 and Zeph. 3.7 indicate, persistency. The Hiphil indicates a denominative verb from *šekem* ('shoulder') and is a survival, like many expressions in Classical Hebrew, from the nomad past, when the first task in the morning was the striking of camp and the loading of baggage on the shoulders of beasts of burden. It thus comes to denote the bestirring of oneself to any enterprise.

ḥāṭe'û may denote unwitting offence, either moral or ritual, as well as conscious sin. It has been suggested that for MT *bilebāḇām* ('in their heart') we should read *beṭûḇ lelāḇām*, 'in the exuberance of their heart' (Joüon 1937: 322), but in this letter-complex the omission of such a distinctive letter as *ṭ* either in the Old Hebrew or the square script is unlikely. The meaning here is that though convention might forbid articulate defiance of God, 'cursing him' or 'making light of him', for which MT gives the euphemism 'blessed', the mood ('heart') of the revellers might have implied such an insult or blasphemy.

6. *wayᵉhî hayyôm* followed by *waw* consecutive and the imperfect of the verb is the regular expression for 'there came a day' (cf. v. 13; 2.1; 1 Sam. 1.4; 14.1; 2 Kgs 4.8, 11, 18; etc.), the definite article signifying in anticipation the particular day when the event happened, that is to say 'a *certain* day' (GKC, §126s) specifies the day as the New Year day, the second day, when the heavenly court is held (2.1), being specified as the Day of Atonement, ten days later then the New Year day according to P. The New Year was associated with judgment in the postexilic tradition reflected in T, but this was not fortuitous. In ancient Canaan, as indicated in the Baal myth from Ras Shamra, the New Year festival in late autumn was the great crisis of the peasant's year when the kingship of Baal and his establishment of Order in nature was celebrated. This occasion was celebrated also in Israel as an agricultural festival, but owing to the precaution in the days of the settlement to have such festivals celebrated at the central sanctuary of the sacral confederacy, where the tribes expressed their solidarity by the sacramental experience of the Exodus and the Covenant, the kingship of Baal in nature was supplanted by the kingship of Yahweh in nature, in history and in the social order expressed by the religious and social demands of the Covenant. Throughout the monarchy this was the theme of the New Year festival and the source of the postexilic conception of that as the occasion of the great judgment. It was possibly the recurrent questioning of God's moral Order (*mišpāṭ*) throughout the Dialogue in the Book of Job that led the Targumists to consider this as the occasion of the heavenly assize.

bᵉnê hā'ᵉlōhîm, lit. 'the sons of God', denotes divine beings, 'sons' signifying those who belonged to a certain category, or circle, like 'the sons of the prophets', or members of prophetic guilds. It originally, as in the Ras Shamra texts, denoted members of the divine family, and appears in this sense in the earliest passages in the OT, signifying the gods of other peoples over whom Yahweh was supreme in Israel, as, for example, in Deut. 32.8:

> When the most High assigned the peoples their portion,
> When he separated the sons of men,
> Fixing the boundaries of the peoples,
> According to the number of the gods (*bᵉnê 'ēl*, so LXX for MT *bᵉnê yiśrā'ēl*).

The same situation, implying the worship of Yahweh alone in Israel, but admitting the existence of other gods in other communities, is implied in Exod. 15.11, which was incorporated into J in the early monarchy:

> Who is like you among the gods, O Yahweh?
> Who is like you, lordly in holiness?

Cf. Pss. 29.1; 89.7 (*b^enê 'ēlîm*). The present passage reflects more closely the settlement of decisive affairs in the government of the world in a heavenly court, or assembly (*pḥr bn'il*, Gordon *UT* 51.III.14; cf. *puḫur ilani*, known in the Babylonian Creation Myth, *Enuma Elish*, and *mpḫrt bn'il* in ritual texts from Ras Shamra, Gordon *UT* 2.17, 34; 107.3, and an inscription from Byblos, and *'dt 'ilm* in Gordon *UT* 128.II.7, 11). This conception was adopted in Israel with the theme and imagery of the liturgy of the New Year festival of Canaan, celebrating the kingship and government (*mišpāṭ*) of God, and this is a feature of the Enthronement Psalms. The conception, however, was so adapted in Israel that the heavenly court served as a foil to the sole efficacy of Yahweh; cf. Pss. 96.4-5; 97.7, and particularly Ps. 82.1-5. Later 'the sons of God' were identified with supernatural forces disposed by God, like 'the host of heaven' (1 Kgs 22.19) and later the stars, which were beyond the control of humans, of which there is a reminiscence in Job 38.7 (H.W. Robinson 1943; Cross 1953; Meyer 1961). Eventually when Israel emerged from monolatry to monotheism the gods associated with Yahweh were conceived of as angelic forces subservient to him, executors of his will, like the *śāṭān* in Job, or witnesses of the divine decree, or as intercessors for humans before God; cf. 33.23-24. The conception of angelic assessors and executives of God in Judaism became firmly established after the Jews' contact with Persian Zoroastrianism in the late sixth century BCE, though the beginning of this conception may be seen in the vision of the heavenly court in the episode of Micaiah ben Imlah before Ahab at the gate of Samaria (1 Kgs 22.19-23) from a prophetic source which may be dated to the eighth century BCE. In a juncture which concerns the moral government of God as in the Book of Job, the scene in the divine assembly retains something of its old significance in Canaan and in the liturgy of the New Year festival in Israel.

hiṯyaṣṣēḇ here denotes taking an acknowledged place; cf. Ps. 82.1, also depicting the heavenly court, *'^elōhîm niṣṣāḇ ba'^aḏaṯ-'ēl*, 'God takes his place in the divine assembly' (actually Yahweh takes his place among the other gods in the Assembly of El, the senior god of the Canaanite pantheon, with whom Yahweh God of Israel was eventually assimilated as the universal Most High God). The verb is used in the sense of executives reporting personally to God for his orders in Zech. 6.5.

On *haśśāṭān*, God's 'public prosecutor', as in Zech. 3.1, and not yet as in 1 Chron. 21.1 the personal arch-enemy of God and humanity, and the relevance of this passage for the date of Job see above, pp. 32-38. For the development of the conception of Satan in late Judaism see Bousset and Gressmann (1926).

7. In the reply of the *śāṭān* to God's question,

> From going about (*miššûṭ*) in the earth
> And walking up and down in it,

there is what at first sight seems to be a word-play between *śāṭān* and *šûṭ*, which describes the activity of God's agents in terms of the intelligence service of the Persian Empire, 'the Eyes of Yahweh', in Zech. 4.10. *śāṭān*, however, as the final *n* indicates, is more naturally connected with the verbal root *śāṭan*, 'to oppose' (Pss. 38.2; 71.13; 109.20), than with *šûṭ*, and indeed the *śāṭān* in Job exceeds his commission as a mere intelligence agent and is rather the Adversary. The verb *šûṭ* is used of going to and fro, as of the people gathering manna in Num. 11.8, of the officers in David's census of Israel in 2 Sam. 24.2, of the people wandering about seeking water in a drought in Amos 8.12 (in Polel) and of the eyes of the Lord which range all the earth in Zech. 4.10. The complementary verb *hiṯhallēḵ* in the sense of patrolling, or going about inspecting, recalls the patrols of Zech. 1.10-11; 6.5-7. The description in 1 Pet. 5.8 of Satan 'going about like a roaring lion' is reminiscent of the passage in Job.

8. 'Have you considered?' (*haśamtā libbekā*) means 'Have you set your heart to?', that is, applied your mind to, the heart being to the Hebrews the seat not of affection but of cognition. On the reading *'el* for MT *'al* ('upon'), see textual note. Job is designated as the servant (*'eḇeḏ*) of God. The word is ambiguous, denoting servant, slave and worshipper. Certain persons are singled out as God's 'servants' *par excellence*, for example, kings in ancient Canaan, as, for instance, Krt in the Ras Shamra texts and David in Israel, or prophets, as Moses and others in Israel, and the community which will effect the divine purpose in atonement in Isa. 52.13–53.12. The term expresses the dependence of the servant on the master and the identity of their interests.

Job is again described as *tām weyāšār yerē' 'elōhîm wesār mērā'*; cf. v. 1. His innocence is thus emphasized and singled out as the subject of testing.

9. The question is raised of the disinterested nature of Job's reverence of God ('Is it for nothing MT [*ḥinnām*] that Job, fears God?). *ḥinnām* is composed of *ḥēn* ('free grace') with the adverbial ending in *-m*, which is found in Akkadian and Ugaritic as reinforcing, or as a substitute for, the preposition (de Langhe 1946); cf. *'omnām*, *yômām*, *piṯ'ōm*, *rêqām*.

10. The personal pronoun *'attā* is included for emphasis; Job was the special object of divine favour. *śaḵtā* as it is pointed in MT is from *śûḵ*, used in Hos. 2.8 (EVV 6) of putting a barrier of thorns in the way of a straying beast. Here it denotes doing the same to protect property, that is, crops or grain on the threshing-floor, against beasts. See further, textual note *ad loc. missāḇîḇ*, generally in Hebrew meaning 'around', here probably, like Akk. *ana siḫirti*, adduced by Dhorme, 'completely'.

pāraṣ means not only 'abounded' but rather 'has broken all bounds'; cf. Jacob's flocks (Gen. 30.30).

11. The conditional sentence with the ellipse of the oath in the apodosis and with the negative after the conditional particle in the protasis is the common Hebrew idiom for the strong asseverative.

14. The use of the definite article in *hammal'āḵ*, now introduced for the first time, indicates the focus of the narrator's attention; cf. *happālîṭ* (lit. 'the survivor') in Gen. 14.13; see GKC, §126q, r.

bāqār is collective singular and masculine, which makes the feminine plural participle *ḥōrᵉšôṯ* strange. A. Guillaume emphasizes ploughing with cows and uses this as an argument for the provenance of the Book of Job from the Hejaz, citing Doughty's mention of ploughing with 'kine' there.

We think this an extremely tenuous argument. Doughty's 'kine' is as general as Hebrew *bāqār*, with no implication of sex. The feminine plural ending of *ḥōrᵉšôṯ* is probably a scribal inadvertency through the influence of the following two words. She-asses were more numerous than males and more docile and valuable for breeding, where grazing had to be husbanded for the more productive females with the minimum of males for stud. The asses were at hand by the ploughing oxen, being used to ride to the fields and to carry the implements and also to facilitate watching against the sudden razzia.

15. The Sabaeans (*šᵉḇā'*) are to be distinguished from the Shebans of the S. Arabian mercantile kingdom, which flourished from the tenth century to the fifth century BCE (W.F. Albright 1956: 6-10; Van Beek 1956: 6-9). The Sabaeans are a N. Arabian people who have possibly left their name in the Wadi 'shaba NE of Medinah. *wattippōl* suggests the Hebrew verb *nāp̄al* ('to fall') and is taken as 'fell upon'. There is only one clear instance in the OT of *nāp̄al* with the preposition *bᵉ* in this sense, namely Josh. 11.7, and the verb in Job may well have the meaning of 'plunder'; cf. Arab. *nafala* ('to assign booty'), cited in BDB. This may be conveyed by the translation 'made a raid'. The survival of a single individual in a general disaster is part of the stuff of the popular folk-tale; cf. the survival of the Hebrews' cattle in two of the plagues of Egypt (Exod. 9.6, 25-26) in the popular elaboration of cult-legend.

16. The popular saga passes on swiftly from one incident to another, and dramatic effect is heightened by the arrival of one messenger of disaster before the other has done speaking. This suits the purpose of the sapiential author admirably as it allows him to come to his proper subject without delay and to emphasize the cumulative suffering of the innocent man. *'ēš 'ᵉlōhîm*, lit. 'fire of God', is lightning; cf. *'ēš yhwh* in the ordeal between Elijah and the devotees of Baal on Carmel (1 Kgs 18.38; cf. Num. 11.1) and *'ēš 'ᵉlôhîm* in 2 Kgs 1.12. *'āḵal*, lit. 'ate' and so 'consumed', is regularly used with *'ēš*; cf. 15.34; 20.26, 22.30; etc., and in the Ras Shamra texts, for instance, Gordon *UT* 75.I.10, *kbd k'iš t'ikln*, 'The liver like fire they consumed'.

17. *kaśdîm*, read *kaldîm* in Aq., Sym. and V, is the Hebrew term for the Chaldaean, Aramaic, dynasty of Babylon founded by Nabopolassar. The Kaldu were Aramaean tribesmen NW of the Persian Gulf, who menaced S. Mesopotamia like the Arabs in the early seventh century CE, and like them,

finally, overran it. *kaśdîm* probably visualizes the Babylonians rather that the tribal Kaldu. This may reflect a late recension of the narrative source, with a reminiscence of Chaldaean, Aramaean, Moabite and Ammonite raiding parties against Judah in the last days of the monarchy (2 Kgs 24.2). The situation might well have encouraged raids by predatory tribes like the 'Sabaeans' from the N. Hejaz. Alternatively the association of the *kaśdîm* with the N. Arabian 'Sabeans' might refer to Nabona'id's occupation of the oases of the Hejaz, which must have made heavy demands on his commissariat. Jewish settlement in the region, well attested in the time of Muhammad, was not unlikely after the disasters under Jehoiakim, Jehoiachim and Zedekiah, and consequent deportations of leading citizens. See further General Introduction, p. 4.

śāmû, lit. 'they put', denotes an ambush as in 1 Sam. 15.2, where the verb is transitive. In this case MT *š^{e}lōšāh rā'šîm* ('three hands', lit. 'three heads') is an adverbial accusative and not the direct object of *śāmû*. This sense of *śām* is supported by the verb *pāšaṭ* which is used of deploying from an ambush in Judg. 9.33f.; 20.37; 1 Sam. 23.27; 30.14. The verb is probably cognate with Arab. *baśaṭa* ('to open out, extend'), which is also the meaning of Aram. and Syr. *p^{e}šaṭ*.

19. *mē'ēḇer hammiḏbār* may simply mean 'from the direction of the desert'; cf. *rûaḥ hammiḏbār* (Jer. 13.24). A whirlwind is probably visualized associated with dust devils, which thus might convey the impression of 'striking the four corners of the house' simultaneously.

20. *mē'îl*, as the derivation from *'ālāh* indicates, means the great robe, Arab. *'abayya*, which is worn over the tunic, being distinctive of the dignity or wealth of those who had not to strip for work; cf. 1 Sam. 18.4; 24.5, 12; Ezek. 26.16. The rending of the mantle may be a modification of the laceration of the skin as a mourning rite, known in Canaan in the fourteenth century BCE; cf. the mourning of El in the Baal myth of Ras Shamra (Gordon *UT* 67.VI.11-22):

'apnk lṭpn 'il dp'id	Then the kindly One, El the Merciful,
yrd lks'i yṯb lhdm	Came down from the throne, he leapt to the footstool,
wlhdm yṯb l'arṣ	And from the footstool he sat on the ground.
yṣq 'mr 'un lr'iš	He let down his turban in grief from his head;
'pr plṯt lqdqdh	On his head was the dust in which he wallowed;
lps yks m'izrtm	He tore asunder the knot of his girdle;
ġr b'abn ydy	He scraped his skin with a stone;
psltm by'r	With a chipped flint for a razor;
yhdy lḥm wdqn	He shaved his side-whiskers and beard;
yṯlṯ qn zr'h	The humeral joint of his arm he scored;
yḥrṯ kgn 'aplb	He scored his chest like a garden,
k'mq yṯlṯ bmt	As a valley-bottom his back he lacerated.

The shaving (*gāzaz*) of the head is already known as a rite of mourning (Jer. 2.29; Amos 9.10; Mic. 1.16; etc.). It is one of the rites of separation whereby a person suspends his normal behaviour and appearance in the interim period necessary to the readjustment of the community or family, when it is more than normally exposed to supernatural influences with evil potential. For the shaving of the head as a rite of separation, cf. the treatment of a captive woman before remarriage (Deut. 21.11-12). Such rites were eventually forbidden in Israel because of their association with the superstitions of Canaan (cf. Deut. 14.1; Lev. 19.27-28), but survivals persisted.

In *wayyištāḥû* the explanation of the form as the Hithpael of the verb *šāḥā*(*w*) has been questioned since Albright's recognition of the reflexive of the causative Shaphel in Ugaritic corresponding to the Xth form of the Arabic verb *iśtaqṭala*. This is formally possible, but must be doubtful so long as the assumed root *ḥāwā*(*w*) is not attested in the simpler forms in Ugaritic, Hebrew or Arabic, whereas *šāḥā*(*w*) is attested (Isa. 51.23). The meaning, however, is not doubted, 'to prostrate oneself', lit. to touch the ground with one's forehead, the gesture of total submission to humans or God.

21. Job's submission to the will of God, expressed in obeisance, is declared in his citation of a proverb:

> Naked I came out of my mother's womb,
> And naked I shall go away again whither I shall go.

This and the following couplet,

> Yahweh gave; Yahweh has taken;
> Blessed be the name of Yahweh,

are the classical expression of the truth that mortals hold life and all that it can give on a terminable lease from God. Occasionally the Hebrew thought scientifically of birth, occasionally poetically of the origin of humanity (*'āḏām*) from the dust of the earth (*'ᵃḏāmāh*) or of being fashioned in the hidden depths of the earth (Ps. 139.15). The two conceptions are combined in Ps. 139.13, 15, and so too possibly in Job 1.21 (so Tur-Sinai), where *šāmāh* cannot refer literally to the womb, where a human does not return. It has been thought that the reference is to a return to 'mother earth' (so Mowinckel, Larcher [JB]; cf. Ben Sira 40.1), or that here is a reminiscence of burial in a crouched position like the embryo in the womb, which may once have reflected the conception of the earth as the mother of humans (so Ricciotti 1955). Buttenwieser and Hölscher see an echo of the Egyptian euphemism for death, 'those who are yonder'. *šamāh* may be used here with a demonstrative sense independent of 'my mother's womb', as in Eccl. 5.14:

> Even as he has come forth from his mother's womb
> Naked shall he depart as he came.

šāmāh may then be admittedly vague, indicating the ultimate uncertainty of the ancients as to the end of life (so Horst, Fohrer). The verb *šûḇ* does not necessarily mean that *šāmāh* is identical with the place of origin. It may rather denote here the going back not to but from a certain estate, 'to go away again'.

In v. 21b the use of the divine name Yahweh as distinct from El, Eloah, Shaddai ('the Almighty') and Elohim in the poetic Dialogue is characteristic of the Prologue and Epilogue. It has been noticed as characteristic of the prose as distinct from the poetic portions of the book. The latter distinction does not apply here, where Job's declaration is in poetry, but in the general context of the Prologue it is admissible, in any case probably reproducing a well-known formula from a fast-liturgy, the context of the Plaint of the Sufferer. The phraseology is re-echoed among the Arabs, where A. Musil cites the acknowledgment of the next of kin among the Bedouin of the Hejaz, 'the Lord gave him; the Lord has taken him' (1927: 427). The last phrase too recalls the Arabic *'al-ḥamdu 'lillāhi* ('Praise be to Allah!'), which is added to the report of ill as well as good, in which case *'ala*(*y*) *kulli ḥāli* ('in any condition') will be added.

22. *ḥāṭā'* signifies 'missed the mark', hence 'sinned, offended', wittingly or unwittingly.

tip̄lāh suggests *tāp̄ēl* ('insipid'), hence our translation 'lack of moral discrimination'. It has been suggested that the word is cognate with Arab. *tafala* ('to spit') (Tur-Sinai, Pope), giving a meaning 'reprehensible'. But in view of the obvious meaning of *tāp̄ēl* in 6.6 we prefer the meaning derivative from 'insipid'. On the LXX variant *n*ᵉ*ḇālāh*, see textual note *ad loc*. The moral sense of *tip̄lāh* is attested in Jer. 23.13 of the prophets of Samaria who prophesied by Baal and misled people, and possibly in Ps. 109.4.

Chapter 2

1. Then one day the celestials came and presented themselves before Yahweh and among them came also the *śāṭān* to present himself before Yahweh.[1] 2. And Yahweh said to the *śāṭān*, 'Where do you come from?', and the *śāṭān* answered Yahweh and said:
'From going to and fro in the earth
And from walking about in it.'

3. Yahweh said to the *śāṭān*:
'Have you considered my servant Job,
How there is none like him in the earth,
A man perfect and upright,
Fearing God and shunning evil,
And holding fast to his integrity,
Though you have moved me against him to hurt him without cause?'

4. And the *śāṭān* answered Yahweh and said:
'Skin for skin;
All that a man[2] has
Will he give for his life.

5. But stretch out your hand
And touch his bone and his flesh,
And he will assuredly curse you[3] to[4] your face.'
6. And Yahweh said to the *śāṭān*:
'Here he is, in your power,
Only spare his life.'
7. Then the *śāṭān* went out from Yahweh's presence and struck Job with a bad pox from the sole of his foot to his head; 8. and he took a potsherd to scrape himself, and sat in the ashes.[5]
9. And his wife said to him:
'Do you still hold to your integrity?
Curse God and die!'
10. But Job said to her:
'You speak like one[6] of the obtuse women.
Are[7] we to accept good from God
And not accept ill?'
In all this Job did not sin with his lips.
11. Now Job's three friends heard of all the calamity which had befallen him and they came from their several places, Eliphaz the Temanite, Bildad the Shuhite and Zophar the Na'amathite. They arranged to meet together and go and condole with him and console him.
12. And they lifted up their eyes from the distance but did not recognize him, and they raised their voices and wept, and each tore his robe and they sprinkled dust on their heads (casting it up).[8] 13. And they sat with him (on the ground)[9] for seven days and seven nights, and no one spoke a word to him, for they saw that his grief was very great.

Textual Notes to Chapter 2

1. MT *l^ehiṯyaṣṣēḇ 'al-yhwh* ('to present himself before God') is omitted in the original version of LXX, being included in Origen's recension from the versions of Theod. and Aq. It is thought that it should be omitted here as a scribal inadvertency since it is not included in 1.6. But since the *šāṭān* was reporting back to Yahweh after his first trial of Job it may be retained.
2. Reading *l^e'îš* for MT *lā'îš* with LXX, S and T.
3. A scribal euphemism as in 1.5; see textual note *ad loc.*
4. Reading with certain Heb. MSS *'al* for MT *'el*, as in 1.11.
5. LXX has a long addition here. See Commentary *ad loc.*
6. Reading *min* after *'aḥaṯ* with two Heb. MSS, S and T.
7. As the text is set out in BH[3], *gam* is taken with what precedes, in which case it demands *'att* ('you') after it, the pronoun being omitted by haplography before the following *'eṯ*. It was taken by the ancient versions with what follows in MT (so Dhorme; G.B. Gray). Ball proposed to read the interrogative particle *'im* for *gam*, introducing the rhetorical question, which LXX indicates, reading the sequel as a conditional sentence.
8. MT *haššāmāy^emāh* should probably be omitted with LXX; see Commentary *ad loc.*
9. MT *lā'āreṣ* should probably be omitted with LXX and two Heb. MSS. Strictly, if the friends sat with Job they would sit on the refuse heap.

Commentary on Chapter 2

3. The verb *bāla‘* is most familiar in the OT meaning ‘to swallow up’, and may mean total annihilation. But Job is not totally annihilated, so we take the verb as a cognate of Arab. *balaġa* (‘to reach’) in the same hostile sense as *nāḡa‘* (lit. ‘to touch’) in v. 5. Arab. *balaġa* means also ‘to hurt’ or ‘attack’. This meaning would be more apt than ‘to swallow’ at 8.18; 10.8; 2 Sam. 20.19; Ps. 52.6, ‘harmful words/false tongue’.

4. The *śāṭān* possibly cites a proverb in reply. *‘ôr bᵉ‘aḏ-‘ôr* has been the subject of much speculation and debate. It is generally regarded as the citation of a proverb reflecting the practice of barter (so Calmet, Duhm), where ‘skin’ is used as our ‘head of cattle’, the point being equivalence in moral dealing. In support of this interpretation Hölscher cites the Arab proverb *rā’ś birā’ś*; cf. *bîta kîma bîti* in an Ugaritic deed of exchange (RS 16.283) published by J. Nougayrol (1955: RS 16.383) and cited by Horst. The difficulty in this interpretation is that the preposition would not normally be *bᵉ‘aḏ* but *taḥaṯ*, which means ‘in place of’. *bᵉ‘aḏ* means usually ‘about’ or ‘for the sake of’. Following the first sense of *bᵉ‘aḏ*, the phrase is translated ‘one skin is over another’, or, as we might say ‘under the skin there is still the quick’ (so Schultens, Budde, Merx, Jastrow, Lindblom). Pope’s objection that as yet Job’s skin has not yet been touched ignores the figurative sense of ‘skin’. Tur-Sinai takes ‘skin’ as denoting the various layers protecting the heart, the seat of life, hence Pope translates ‘skin after skin’. Following the second sense of *bᵉ‘aḏ*, T and Rashi understood the phrase to mean that one will risk and suffer injury to one part of the body to protect a more vital part, or to acquiesce in the loss of property and children to ‘save one’s own skin’ (St Thomas Aquinas). The phrase is not to be considered apart from the following: ‘All that a man has will he give for (*bᵉ‘aḏ*) his life’. Dhorme suggests that *‘ôr bᵉ‘ad-‘ôr* is a figure drawn not from commerce but from law, reflecting the principle ‘an eye for an eye, a tooth for a tooth, etc.’ (Exod. 21.24ff.), where, incidentally the preposition is not *bᵉ‘aḏ*, but *taḥaṯ*. The sense according to Dhorme would be that as in retaliation a skin wound only is allowed for a skin wound, what Job has so far suffered cannot be expected to provoke violent reaction, but if his life, or at least the full capacity to enjoy it, were threatened Job’s faith would be really tried. In view of the meaning of *bᵉ‘aḏ*, ‘for the sake of’, in *kōl ’ᵃšer lā’îš yittēn bᵉ‘aḏ napšô* this is a feasible interpretation. Alternatively we might propose the emendation *‘ôḏ bᵉ‘āḏô ‘ôrô* of which the assumption that MT is a corruption is graphically feasible, and even more so if *w* of MT *wᵉḵōl* is attached to the preceding *‘ôr* resulting in the reading

> *‘ôḏ bᵉ‘āḏô ‘ôrô*
> *kōl ’ᵃšer lā’îš yittēn bᵉ‘aḏ napšô*
>
> His skin is still about him;
> All that a man has will he give for the sake of his life.

This is admittedly a conjecture, with no support in the ancient versions, but it has the merit of congruity with the sequel and it gives an extra beat, which the meter, such as it is in the passage, demands. Nevertheless we prefer Dhorme's interpretation.

nep̄eš should be noted here. The word does not mean 'soul' as distinct from body as in the Greek or Christian conception of life, but the life-breath or life itself. It may also denote the full capacity to enjoy life, English 'vitality', the impairment of which is denoted in certain passages of the OT as 'death' (*māweṯ*) which is considered as invading life to various degrees in human suffering.

7. Various suggestions have been made, generally with a certain amount of medical support, to diagnose more particularly Job's skin disease (see bibliography in Rowley 1958: 169-70), but the evidence in Job is insufficient. Since the case is hypothetical, to serve as an introduction to the moral problem of the book, we refrain from more precise speculation as to whether the disease be visualized as black, or tubercular, leprosy or elephantiasis, eurythema, chronic eczema, or, as Terrien suggests (1963: 59) *pamphigus foliaceus*. The only clue is that Job erupted in boils. *šeḥîn*, from a root attested in Akkadian, Ugaritic, Aramaic and Arabic meaning 'to be hot, or inflamed', is rendered in S as 'ulcers', which, so far as may be specified, suggests 'the Nile rash' as Job's disease; cf. 'the Egyptian boil' as one of the plagues threatened in Deut. 28.27, and as one of the plagues of Egypt in Exod. 9.8ff.

qoḏqōḏ, lit. 'skull', is usually poetic for 'head' in Hebrew, as, for example, in Deut. 28.35; 2 Sam. 14.25, but regularly means 'head' in Ugaritic texts. Job's potsherd (*ḥereś*) may have been not to relieve his itch, but rather to scrape off running matter, as the verb *hiṯgārēḏ* suggests (so LXX).This verb is a *hapax legomenon*, and is cognate with the Arabic verb *jarada* which is used of scraping hair off a hide or peeling the bark off a tree.

In *hā'ēp̄er* the refuse of baking ovens, cooking hearths and broken pots and generally the village midden (Arab. *mazbala*) is visualized, as particularly in LXX, which translates *kopria*. This steadily mounting heap of refuse in Arab villages is periodically burnt, and the mound outside the settlement is often a place where the natives take the evening air. It was a natural place of isolation outside the settlement for such as Job (cf. the lepers in 2 Kgs 7.3), but it did not absolutely deny him the company of such as his three friends.

9. Christian dogmatics has made capital out of the role of Job's wife, whom St Augustine calls 'the Devil's Abettor' (*Diaboli adjutrix*); cf. Calvin, 'the instrument of Satan' (*organum Satanae*). St Thomas Aquinas after Chrysostom and St Augustine regards woman as the natural intermediary between a man and the tempter as Eve was the intermediary between the man and the serpent. The Rabbis note the parallel between Eve and Job's wife, but remark that Job unlike Adam resisted the temptress.

'Curse (MT 'bless') God and die' may mean either 'Curse God, since in any case you are going to die' or 'since God has deprived you of blessing and made your life void as a dead man, accept the fact of alienation from him and make it final'. This touches the central problem of the book. Did suffering mean alienation from God? Or was it to be borne in hope and faith that expected response in suffering, where God was ready to help the sufferer in his own time and manner?

The role of the wife, abetted by Job's friends, as 42.7 may imply, to undermine the faith of Job in God's beneficence was probably part of the immediate source of the present Book of Job. LXX has a considerable expansion here in the style of midrash (Swete, 2.9, 9a-d):

> After the lapse of a long time (his wife said to him), 'How long will you hold out saying, "See, I will wait a little longer, looking for the hope of my salvation?" See, your memory is already wiped out from the earth, sons and daughters, the pains and labours of my womb, for whom I laboriously strove for nothing. You yourself sit in wormy decay, the whole night in the open, while I roam as a drudge from place to place and from house to house, waiting for the sun to go down, that I may rest from my labours and pains which grip me. But say some word against the Lord and die.' But he looked on her and said to her...

This is part of the very substantial elaboration of the Job legend, which emphasizes the patience of the sufferer, ignoring his embarrassing questioning of the faith of orthodox wisdom in the Dialogue as distinct from the Prologue and Epilogue of the Book of Job.

10. *nāḇāl*, a synonym of *k^esîl* ('fool') in Prov. 17.21, means generally 'churlish' and contrasts with 'wise' and 'prudent'. It signifies one whose conduct is governed by regard for reason or popular repute. In Isa. 32.5ff., it is contrasted with *šôa'*, 'noble', a gentleman who behaves as such, to whom the community looks to uphold its fair ethic, like the good man of birth on whom the community depends on Job 29. The *nāḇāl* is animated by none of the finer susceptibilities, which attest the spirit of God in a person. He is the moral 'deadwood' of society, as the possible connection with *n^eḇēlāh* ('a dead body') may indicate. The aspect of *nāḇāl* as 'godless' is emphasized by W.W.M. Roth (1960).

The Piel of *qāḇal* in the sense 'receive' is attested in Ugaritic and in the OT only once before the Exile, in Prov. 19.20. The regularity of the verb in Aramaic and Syriac and its recurrence in Ezra, Chronicles, and Esther suggests that there as in the present passage it may be a Hebrew usage which fell into desuetude but revived under the influence of Aramaic in the postexilic period.

ra' in this context means 'ill' or 'calamity' without the moral implication of 'evil'. In 'from God' note the Hebrew emphasis on primary causes. In an original, pre-Israelite source God may have been represented by the guardian spirit of the individual, whose alienation is betokened by the afflictions of the sufferer in the Mesopotamian plaint *ludlul bēl nēmeqi* I.43-46, designated either as the sufferer's god or his 'good daemon' (*šēdu dimqi*) or his 'protecting genius' (*lamassu*).

11. Here Job's three interlocutors in the Dialogue are introduced. It is thought by Alt (1937; so too Fohrer 1989: 104) that they are secondary, being introduced by the author of the Book in its present form in place of Job's own community (cf. 42.11), who like his wife sought to assail his orthodox faith.

habbā'āh, but for the Masoretic punctuation, which indicates the perfect after the definite article with the force of the relative pronoun, might be a participle, which, however, does not alter our translation.

Eliphaz is given as the son of Esau (Gen. 36.4) and father of Teman (Gen. 36.11), hence an Edomite; cf. Teman as a place-name in Edom in Amos 1.12; Ezek. 25.13 (Edom from Teman to Dedan); Obad. 8f. and particularly Jer. 49.7 in his oracle on Edom, 'Is wisdom no longer to be found in Teman?' Bildad is unknown elsewhere in the OT, but Shuah is given as the son of Abraham by Qeturah (Gen. 25.2), who with her other sons was sent to the East. Fohrer after Albright suggests a connection of 'Shuhite' with *šûḥu* by the mid-Euphrates. Zophar is not mentioned elsewhere in the OT, but his designation as 'the Naamathite' may refer to Jebel Na'ameh east of Tebuk in the N. Hejaz. All are chosen by the Israelite redactor of the source as representative of the reputedly wise 'people of the East', and particularly, in the case of Eliphaz, with Edom.

wayyiwwā'ᵃḏû denotes both agreement and meeting by appointment. 'To condole with him' (*lānûḏ-lô*) means lit. 'to shake the head', or 'rock the body to and fro for him'.

12. In MT 'and they sprinkled dust on their heads (to the sky)', LXX omits 'to the sky'. Dhorme posits a conflation of two variants, 'they sprinkled dust on their heads', a mourning rite (cf. 1 Sam. 4.12; Ezek. 27.30; Lam. 2.10), and the mourning rite mentioned in the citation from the Baal myth from Ras Shamra (see note on 1.20), 'and they threw dust up into the sky so that it fell on their heads', or as intervening between them and God to indicate alienation in suffering. The letter would recall the gesture of the Jews at the martyrdom of Stephen (Acts 22.23), where, however, it is rather designed to register horror at what was regarded as blasphemy and so to rid the subjects from the attention of God. On this assumption Buttenwieser (1922: 43) takes it to refer to the friends' condemnation of Job, arguing from his suffering to his sin. This strangely ignores the statement in 2.11 that the friends come to condole and console (*lᵉnaḥᵃmô*). Tur-Sinai suggests that *haššāmāyᵉmāh* is a corruption of the infinitive absolute of the Hiphil, a verbal noun used adverbially, *hašmēm* ('dumbfounded'), which was inadvertently omitted from the following verse (cf. Ezek. 3.15; Ezra 3.3-4), and added in the margin, then displaced and repointed. The verb *zāraq* is that used of the rite whereby Moses cast up ashes to induce the plague of boils in Egypt (Exod. 9.8f.).

12. The gesture of the friends, sitting silently with Job in his ritual isolation, whether or not 'on the ground' is read with MT or omitted with LXX and two Heb. MSS, is a striking token of their sympathy. They too for the conventional mourning period of 'seven days and seven nights' (cf. Gen. 50.10; 1 Sam. 31.13) were prepared to consider themselves under the cloud of the divine displeasure through their association with the sufferer and so alienated from the community and its association with God. Their tactful silence is designed not to provoke a hasty retort on the subject of the divine economy. Job himself, quite unprovoked, first broke silence in his curse of his existence, to which his wife had first provoked him (2.9). This (3.1) is the culmination of the Prologue as well as the immediate introduction to the Dialogue.

Job 3

Job's Expostulation

Job's curse on his existence, to which the whole of the chapter is devoted, while not directly the curse of God which his wife had urged on him (2.9), comes very near to it, in the implicit animadversion on the Giver of life. Significantly, Job does not yet question the justice of God in the suffering of the innocent in his personal case. His concern is a general problem of the meaningfulness of a life lived in unrelieved suffering, as of course exemplified in his own. In any case his impassioned outburst, contravening the sapiential ideal of calm resignation, serves to introduce Eliphaz's mild rebuke (4.3-6) and the subsequent censure of all the friends. It further sets Job's problem beyond academic discussion into the domain of existential experience, which characterizes Job's subsequent declarations as distinct from those of the friends in the Dialogue and his ultimate appeal directly to God.

The chapter is divided into three strophes, vv. 3-10, 11-19, 20-26. After the statement in v. 1 that Job cursed the day he was born, which is the culmination of the Prologue as adapted by the author of the Book, the first strophe (vv. 3-10) expresses the despair of the sufferer in the literary form of a curse. This leads in the second strophe (vv. 11-19) to the question of the meaning of his life when he is in such hard case, and in the third strophe (vv. 20-26) to the question of the meaning of human life in general, in which suffering is such a common lot. Thus while vv. 11-19 express the subject's sufferings within the common convention of the literary prototype of the Plaint of the Sufferer, vv. 20-26 open up the philosophic question of the meaning of life itself, where experience often affords so little support to faith in Providence. In the last section the apparent shift from the general case in vv. 20-23 to the particular in the first person in vv. 24-26 may be explained by assuming that vv. 24-26 is a citation from the Plaint of the Sufferer. The curse on a particular day including the day on which the sufferer was born is familiar in Arab society (Dhorme), and, as applied by the sufferer himself has its counterpart in Jer. 20.14-18, which recalls the language and thought of much of Job 3.3-10, particularly in the wish that he might have been still-born and the reference to the announcement of his birth. The curse is more elaborate in Job with notable wealth of mythological imagery.

The arrangement of MT may be questioned. In vv. 4, 5 and 6 it is important to realize that the arrangement is not in bicola but tricola, the threefold curse perhaps reflecting a convention of incantations. We should thus defend MT against the view that the passage is interpolated by later insertions, for example, v. 4a and v. 6a according to Bickell, Beer, Stevenson and Hölscher, but admit that v. 6 was possibly followed by the tricolon in v. 9 (so Dhorme, Pope). Verse 16, which interrupts the thought of vv. 15-17, may be displaced from after v. 11 (so Dhorme), in which case MT *lō'* would require to be emended to *lû* ('would that').

1. After this Job opened his mouth and cursed the day he was born.
2. Then Job spoke up[1] and said:

3. 'Perish the day on which I was born
And the night on which one declared, "Let a man-child be conceived."
4. That day—let it be darkness;
Let God from above not care for it,
Nor let light shine on it.
5. Let darkness and utter gloom claim it as its own.[2]
Let cloud settle upon,
May eclipse surprise it.
6. That night—let darkness seize it,
Let it not be associated with[3] the days of the year,
Nor be entered into the number of the months.
9. May the stars of its twilight be darkened,
Let it wait for light which shall never be,
And let it not be seen[4] by the eyes of the dawn.
7. [5]That night—let it be barren,
Let no joyful shout come therein.
8. Let those curse it who curse day (light),
Who are skilled to rouse Leviathan,
10. Because I did not close up the doors of the womb that bore me
And hide trouble from my eyes.

11. Why did I not die at birth,
Emerge from the womb—to expire?
16. [6]Would that[7] I were as a still-born child,
Like babes that never saw the light![6]
12. Why did the knees receive me?
And what was the significance of breasts to suck?
13. For now I should have been lying down quiet,
I should have slept and had rest,
14. Just as kings and counsellors of the earth,
Who built themselves palaces,
15. Or as princes who had gold,
Who filled their houses with silver.
17. There the wicked cease from troubling
And the weary are at rest;
18. Prisoners are at ease together,
Hearing no taskmaster's voice.

19. Small and great are the same there,
And slave is free from master.

20. Why is light given[8] to one in trouble,
Life to those whose life is bitter,
21. Who long in vain for death,
And seek for it as[9] for hidden treasure,
22. Who rejoice to reach the burial-heap,[10]
Are happy to have found a grave?
23. (Why is light given) to a man whose way is diverted,
And about whom God has set obstructions?
24. For instead of my food comes my sighing;
My groans are poured out as water.
25. For what I feared has come to me,
And what I dreaded comes upon me.
26. I have no rest nor quiet,
Nor repose, but disturbance has come upon me.'

Textual Notes to Chapter 3

1. LXX and V omit MT *wayya'an* through a misunderstanding of the verb, which they take in the sense common in Classical Hebrew 'and he answered'. Job, of course, does not answer, but speaks for the first time. Actually the verb is common in the myths and legends of Ras Shamra, where there is no question of 'answering', and where it means 'spoke up'.
2. We take *gā'al* to signify figuratively the claim exercised by darkness for its kindred manifestations over against the kindred manifestations of light. The verb *gā'al* means 'to stain', which is spelt as *gā'al* in Zeph. 3.1; Lam. 4.14; Isa. 59.3; 63.3; Mal. 1.7; Ezra 2.62 = Neh. 7.64; Dan. 1.8. The dates of those passages from the late seventh century to the second century BCE indicates that this meaning is possible in Job without emending to *gā'al*. See further Commentary *ad loc.*
3. For MT *yiḥadd*, from *ḥāḏā* ('to rejoice') read the jussive Qal *yēḥaḏ*, from *yāḥaḏ* ('to be united'), with Sym., V, T and S.
4. Reading the Niphal *yērā'eh* for MT *yir'eh.*
5. Omitting MT *hinnēh metri causa* with LXX, S, V and one Hebrew MS.
6. The couplet breaks the sense of vv. 15-17, and obviously goes with v. 11, either as part of the original text or a marginal gloss expanding v. 11, which would more easily account for its transposition to after v. 15 in MT. *'ô*, which is superfluous to the meter, was probably added after the transposition.
7. Reading the optative particle *lû* for MT *lō'.*
8. Reading the passive *yuttan* with LXX, S, T and V for MT active *yittēn.*
9. Reading *k^e^maṭmônîm* ('as hidden treasure') for MT *mimmaṭmônîm*, which would mean 'more than for hidden treasure'. This is possible, but the simile is more natural. We assume a scribal error of *m* for *k* in the Old Hebraic script.
10. *gîl* may originally have been written in *scriptio defectiva*, which would be intentionally ambiguous, *gîl* ('joy') or *gal* ('burial heap').

Commentary on Chapter 3

1. It has been suggested that 'his day' (*yômô*) is not the day he was born but 'his fate' (so Tur-Sinai), but in view of the immediate reference to 'the day of my birth', etc., and of Jeremiah's similar curse on the day of his birth (Jer. 20.14-18), 'his day' probably refers to the day of Job's birth as indicated by the immediate sequel.

3. In *yôm 'iwwāleḏ bô* the omission of the definite article before *yôm* and of the relative particle *'ᵃšer* before the relative clause are features of poetry. Dhorme notes the imperfect as 'a veritable Aorist'. This may be equated with the Akkadian preterite, which had the same significance as the Greek Aorist. The so-called narrative imperfect in the Ras Shamra myths and legends has the same significance.

MT *hallayᵉlāh 'āmar hōrāh gāḇer* has been questioned on the grounds that the indefinite subject of *'āmar*, unlike the announcer of the birth, could not tell the sex of the child conceived, and so it is proposed either to emend *hōrāh* to *hᵃrēh*, the Aramaic interjection, 'Behold!' (so Beer, Budde, Stevenson, after LXX) or to take *hallayᵉlāh* (masc. as in v. 6) as the subject of *'āmar* (so Horst, Fohrer, Pope). MT, however, might feasibly be defended on three counts. If the subject of *'āmar* is indefinite the reference might be to an anniversary celebration of the conception of a man (so Hölscher), or if the reference is to the actual night of conception the perfect might be optative as often in Ugaritic and regularly in Arab., 'the night on which one said, "Let a man-child be conceived"', referring to the consummation of the Oriental wedding with its embarrassingly public celebration. Alternatively the subject of the verb might be God, who could determine both conception and sex. Our preference is for the optative sense of the Pual *hōrāh*. The preposition with the resumptive pronominal suffix in the relative clause is probably omitted *metri causa*, being in any case understood after the preposition and pronominal suffix in v. 3a.

4. In *'al-yiḏrᵉšēhû* the verb has the same meaning 'to care for' as in Deut. 11.12, where it is used of the land of Canaan as the special object of God's attention, and in Isa. 62.12, where it is used of Jerusalem in antithesis to the neglected (*'ᵃzûḇāh*) city. *nᵉhārāh*, 'light', a *hapax legomenon* in the OT, from the verbal root *nāhar*, 'to shine' (Isa. 60.5; Ps. 34.6), is more common in Aramaic; cf. *nᵉhôrā'* (Dan. 2.22). Here it may have the meaning 'daylight'; cf. Arab. *nahāru(n)*.

5. In *yiḡ'āluhû* Aq., T, Dhorme, Stevenson and Tur-Sinai read *yiḡ'ᵃlûhû*, 'may the darkness stain it', a sense which *gā'al* also has in Zeph. 3.1; Lam. 4.14; Isa. 59.3; 63.3; Mal. 1.7; Ezra 2.62 = Neh. 7.64; Dan. 1.8. Theod. renders *anchisteusato* ('performed the kinsman's part') and Sym *antepoiēsato* ('ransomed'), hence 'claim as its own' (so Hölscher, Horst, Fohrer, Pope). S and

the Arab. versions render 'obfuscate' or 'cover up', which, with the meaning 'protect', is the primary sense claimed for *gā'al* ('to play the kinsman's part') by A.R. Johnson, 'The Primary Meaning of *ga'al*', *VTS* 3 (1953), pp. 67-77. While this meaning claimed by Johnson would suit Job 3.5 and the phrase *gō'ēl haddām*, he suggests no etymology, and the question is still open as to whether the verb is primarily denominative, signifying 'to discharge a kinsman's duties', which was primarily rehabilitation to an acknowledged status or affinity within a given group—which would be intelligible at Job 3.5—or a pure verb such as Johnson assumes, of which 'to play the kinsman's part' is secondary. We favour the former alternative, taking *gā'al* on the evidence of the OT to mean not simply protection from something that menaces the subject, but rehabilitation to a status one has actually lost; cf. Snaith (1963), who maintains that the primary meaning of the verb denotes restoration to proper ownership, to which we should add affinity. We understand *ṣalmāweṯ* as a compound noun, *māweṯ* having a superlative significance.

ʿanānāh is a *hapax legomenon* in the OT, being the particular noun (*nomen unitatis*) from the more common generic *ʿānān*. The verb *šāḵan*, used of the cloud, recalls the cloud which signified the abiding Divine Presence (*šeḵînāh*) over the Tabernacle in the Exodus tradition (Exod. 40.35; Num. 9.17).

yeba'aṯuhû is generally taken to mean 'terrify'. It may rather be cognate of Arab. *baġata* ('to come suddenly upon, surprise'), a more apt description of a solar eclipse, the first of which to be scientifically predicted was that on 28 May 585 BCE by Thales of Miletus. For this sense of *bā'aṯā*, cf. 18.11; 33.7.

For MT *kimerîrê yôm* we should probably read *kamrîrê yôm* ('blackness of day') (Dhorme); cf. Stevenson, who proposed to read *kamrîrîm*, omitting *yôm* as a dittograph. The plural of *kamrîr* has cognates with the same sense in Akk. and Syr. Dhorme suggested the obscurity of the sirocco, but the Akk. cognate *kamāru* ('to cover') suggests rather the eclipse, which is supported by the verb *yeba'atû* ('to come suddenly upon, surprise').

6. *yēḥad* ('let it be associated with') is obviously demanded by the context instead of MT *yiḥadd* ('rejoice').

9. *nešep̄* is the twilight both of dawn (Ps. 119.147) and evening (Job 7.4; 24.15; etc.). *kôḵeḇê* ('stars') in the context may be dual rather than plural, the Venus star in its twin role of morning and evening star, *šḥr* ('dawn') and *šlm* ('completion', sc. of day) in Canaanite mythology (Gordon *UT* 52). Here and at 41.10 *ʿap̄ʿappê šaḥar* ('the eyes of dawn') is intelligible as a reflection of Canaanite mythology in Hebrew poetry. The dual *ʿap̄ʿappê* means 'eyes' rather than 'eyelids' of NEB, as is indicated by *ʿpʿp* in parallel with *ʿq* ('eye ball') in the Ugaritic text (Gordon *UT* Krt 148, 295). NEB renders the phrase at 41.18 'the shimmer of dawn', connecting *ʿap̄ʿappê* with a verb cognate with Syr. *ʿap̄ā'* ('to shine').

7. For *galmûd̲*, meaning here and at 15.34 'barren', Dhorme cites Isa. 49.21, where *galmûd̲āh* is parallel to *šᵉkûlāh* ('with no children'); cf. *galmûd̲āh* in the Talmud, signifying a wife who must live apart without relations with her husband. Arab. *jalmûdu(n)* denotes rocky, sterile ground, as in Job 30.3; cf. a wife as a fertile field in the correspondence of Ribaddi of Byblos in the Amarna Tablets (Knudtzon 1908–15: 74.17; 75.15; 81.51), 'My land is like a woman without a husband, for it has not been ploughed', and in the Ras Shamra text Gordon *UT* 77.22-23, referring to the marriage of the Moon-god and the Moon-goddess:

> I will make her fallow land into a vineyard,
> The fallow field of her love into orchards.

Cf. Song 1.6; 4.12-16; 8.12; and probably the original of the Song of the Vineyard, 'my lovesong' (*šîr dôd̲î* cited by Isa. 5.1-7). *rinnāh* signifies a ringing shout of joy.

8. *yiqqᵉb̲û* is the imperfect not of *nāqab̲* ('to mark, pierce'), but of *qāb̲ab̲*, here a synonym of *'ārar* ('to curse'), and denotes a specific curse such as Balaam was requested to pronounce against Israel (Num. 22.11, 17; 23.8, 11, 13, 25, 27; 24.10), where the verb *qāb̲ab̲* is uniformly used. Professional mourners are not denoted, as Calmet proposed, but possibly sorcerers who might make a day inauspicious, and Dhorme connected it with Job's curse in v. 1, considering it as relating to all unfortunates, citing the drab curse 'on the day' of an adversary. MT *yôm*, however, has been questioned, though it is unanimously supported by the Hebrew MSS and ancient versions. Leviathan in the parallel colon indicates a mythological reference. In view of the significance of Leviathan as a primaeval monster, the power of Chaos *par excellence*, like the Sea (*yām*), Gunkel (1895: 59 n. 1) suggested that MT *yôm* ('day') should be pointed *yām* ('sea'), a suggestion adopted by Beer, Cheyne, Horst, Pope, Lévêque and G.R. Driver, who cites an Aramaic incantation 'I will cast spells upon you with the spell of the Sea and the spell of the dragon Leviathan' (1955: 72); so too C.H. Gordon (1966). Horst and Pope invoke the evidence of the Ras Shamra texts, where this significance of Sea and Leviathan is well attested. But the same texts refer to 'day (of battle) of the Sun and the Many-headed One', even the dragon (*tnn*), in a hymn to the Sun (Gordon *UT* 62.44-52), so interpreted by A. Caquot (1959: 93ff.). This would support MT *yôm* (so Hitzig, Budde, Hölscher, Fohrer, Tur-Sinai, Mowinckel), the reference being to an eclipse of the sun, which according to Egyptian mythology was the result of the serpent Apophis swallowing the sun. In support of this interpretation we might cite the incantation text from Ras Shamra against snake-bite, where the power of the sun is invoked and there is, on our interpretation,[1] reference to

1. See the writer's study of this text in the official publication in *Ugaritica* VI (Schaeffer [ed.] 1969: 79-97).

the Apophis myth in its Canaanite counterpart. The conception of the Primaeval monster of Chaos temporarily subdued but still capable of being roused (cf. *'ōrēr liwyāṯān*) is familiar from Amos 9.3. *'āṯîḏ* means 'ready' as in Aram. and Syr., but the Arab. cognate means 'with all equipment prepared', hence here 'able and having the relevant incantations and ritual', so 'skilled'.

10. *biṭnî*, lit. 'my belly', obviously means 'the womb that bore me'. For MT *wayyastēr* ('and it hid'), LXX, in rendering 'it turned away' (trans.), read either *wayyāsar* or perhaps misunderstood MT *wayyastēr* as the Iphteal of *sûr*, namely *wayyistar*, a verbal form attested in the Mesha inscription and in the Ugaritic texts. This would be rather an intransitive reflexive, and the direct object 'eyes' supports MT.

11. Note *'āmûṯ* in parallelism with the perfect *yāṣā'ṯî* being imperfect in form, but preterite in sense, like the narrative imperfect in the Ras Shamra texts; see above on v. 3. The perfect *yāṣā'ṯî* is used before the imperfect *'eḡwā'* to denote that the action is prior to that of the second verb, which may be taken as the verb in a final clause.

16. On the reading of v. 16 after v. 11 see Introduction to ch. 3.

nēp̄el, from the root *nāp̄al*, which is used of 'dropping' from the womb (Isa. 26.18), is specifically used of abortions (Ps. 58.9, 'which have not seen the sun'); cf. Eccl. 6.3. *ṭāmûn*, lit. 'hidden', recalls the fate of the abortion enveloped in darkness in Eccl. 6.4-5.

12. *maddûa' qiddᵉmûnî birkāyim* ('Why did the knees receive me?') implies, according to some commentators (Duhm, Musil, citing the Arab custom among the Hanajira, *Arabia Petraea*, III, 1927, p. 214), the father's acknowledgment of the child (cf. Gen. 50.23). It may, however, simply describe the nursing of the child (so Dhorme, citing the nursing by the city-goddess of Nineveh; so too Budde, Weiser, Horst). For the use of *qiddēm* in parallel with Aram. *qibbēl*, 'to receive' (cf. 2.10), of a mother with her child, Dhorme cites Ben Sira 15.2.

mah, as the parallel *maddûa'* indicates, may mean 'why' as in 7.21, *ûmeh lō'-tiśśā' p̄iš'î*. Grammatically it may mean 'what is the significance of...?'

In *mah-ššādayim kî 'înāq*, the construction *māh* followed by *kî* ('that') is paralleled in 6.11; 7.17; 15.14; Ps. 8.5, *māh 'ᵉnôš kî tizkᵉrennû*; cf. in the Ras Shamra texts Gordon *UT* Krt 39:

m'at krt kybky	Who is Krt that he should weep?

13. In illustration of the conception of death as sleep Dhorme aptly cites the inscription on the bricks of Sennacherib's tomb 'palace of sleep, tomb of rest, eternal dwelling of Sennacherib, King of the World, King of Assur'.

14. In *'im-mᵉlāḵîm wᵉyō'ᵃṣê 'āreṣ*, the preposition is regularly used of comparison in Proverbs, and has probably the same significance here. 'Counsellors' might be synonymous with 'kings', as those who, according to royal ideology in the ancient Near East, are executives of the divine purpose (cf. the royal titulary in Isa. 9.5 [EVV 6]; 11.2), or it may denote statesmen who share the knowledge of the king's purpose and mediate it to the community. In the present context one might think of the statesmen of Egypt, who were favoured with tombs in the vicinity of the pyramids and other tombs of the Pharaohs. But this privilege of spectacular burial was not confined to Egypt, as indicated by the tomb of 'the brother', that is, trusted minister, of the queen of the Nabataeans so designated in an inscription at Petra.

If *ḥºrāḇôṯ* is a sound reading, meaning literally 'ruins', it might refer to the building of monuments, such as tombs, which were subsequently ruins (e.g. Isa. 58.12; 61.4), where *ḥºrāḇôṯ* is the synonymous parallel of *šōmᵉmôṯ*, or as those passages in Isaiah and T and V suggest, the building up of ruined or desert places. Ewald and Stevenson, assuming corruption of MT, understood the reference to be to the pyramids (Arab. *harām*), which we consider unlikely, both on textual grounds and as unattested in Heb., Aram. or Syr. Hölscher and Fohrer retain MT, but in the same sense as Arab. *harām*, the verbal root of which coincides with the regular meaning of Heb. *ḥarēḇ* ('to be ruinous, decrepit'). Olshausen and Daiches (1908: 637ff.) seem nearer the truth in taking *ḥºrāḇôṯ* to mean 'palaces'; so too G.R. Driver (1950d: 349), citing Ethiopic and S. Arab. *mḥrb* ('castle'), which evidently survived in N. Arab., signifying the prestigious quarters of a house, hence a palace. The word in this sense, extant but evidently rare in Hebrew, is used here probably *ad hoc* to suggest *double entendre* in the style of the poet in Job in 'palace' and 'ruin'. In possible support of the interpretation of T and V one might cite tombs in Egypt on the desert edge or in desolate valleys like the Valley of the Kings near Luxor, in which the rich grave furniture (cf. v. 15) was a notorious encouragement to tomb-robbing. The context suggests the decay of former palaces rather than ruins as such or graves on the desert edge.

15. In this context the houses which are filled with gold might be the tombs, which were called 'houses of eternity' in Egypt and Mesopotamia. This, however, is not explicit in the text, and it may refer to the treasures of the kings in their lifetime. Tur-Sinai aptly cites the Aramaic inscription of Bar-Rekub of Sham'al (Cooke 1903: 63.10-11), which refers to 'kings, owners of silver and gold'.

17. *rōḡez* in the OT means generally 'agitation', as of the war-horse (39.24) and of thunder (37.2) and of the agitation to which humans are subject (14.1). In Job 3.17 the word is used of the agitation the subject causes. This usage is familiar in Syr. where the cognate verb denotes the wrath of God; cf. Arab. *rujzu(n)* in the adaptation of the Syriac Christian tradition in the Qur'an.

yᵉgi'ê ḵōaḥ means 'exhausted in strength'. The verb meaning 'to weary out' or 'toil at' is well enough attested in the OT, but the participle is used only here and in Ben Sira 37.12.

18. *nōḡēś* denotes the task-master over slaves (Exod. 3.7; 5.14; etc.; Isa. 14.2, 4; Zech. 9.8). The verb, with an Arab. cognate *najaśa*, means 'to harry' or 'beat up (game)', and is used of the ruler of Abyssinia, the *Negus*; see below, on 40.19.

19. *hû'* means 'the same', 'one and the same'; cf. Ps. 102.28; Isa. 41.4; 43.10, 13; 48.12ff.

ḥop̄šî was a legal term meaning 'quit of burdens' and specifically, as here, of servitude (e.g. Exod. 21.2, 5).

'ᵃḏōnāyw as distinct from the singular, means usually 'his Lord' as distinct from his human master. Here it is a plural of majesty or dignity; cf. GKC, §124g, i.

22. On the reading *'ᵉlê-ḡal* for MT *'ᵉlê-ḡîl* see textual note, adopted by Stevenson, Tur-Sinai, Horst, Fohrer and Pope among modern commentators. Beer, Hölscher and Tur-Sinai connect *gal* with the verb *gālal*, 'to roll', and think of the cylindrical blocking stone rolling in the slot as at the entrance to the tombs of the family of Herod the Great at Jerusalem. But the date of this type of burial is rather late for the Book of Job. *gal* denotes rather a pile of stones (cf. *gal 'ᵃḇānîm*, Josh. 7.24; 8.29; 2 Sam. 18.17), either as marking the grave or as a protection for the corpse against jackals. In Palestine during the British Mandate heavy stones were first piled on the coffin for this purpose before the grave was filled with earth. Horst emphasizes the preposition *'ᵉlê*, signifying the way to the grave, which is a satisfaction to the wretched. This is perhaps preciose. Dhorme retained MT, rendering 'They rejoice to jubilation'. Perhaps the original text read *gîl* without the *mater lectionis y* to suggest the *double entendre gîl* ('joy') and *gal* ('grave-heap'), which is demanded by the parallel 'a grave' in the second colon. The citation of Hos. 9.1 in support of MT *'ᵉlê-ḡîl* is invalid as this is almost certainly a corruption of *'al tāḡēl.*

23. The conception of one's way being diverted recalls 19.8,

> He has walled up my way and I cannot pass
> And he has set thorns on my path.

The phrase *wayyāseḵ ba'ᵃḏô* recalls *śaḵtā ba'ᵃḏô* of 1.10. The different sibilant is to be noted. The verb, which could be Hiphil either of *sûḵ* or *sāḵaḵ*, but is probably from *sûḵ*, means to erect a screen, which obstructed or concealed as well as protected. So *ba'ᵃḏô* ('about him') signifies here obstruction and not protection as in 1.10.

24. The couplet, which resumes the theme of Job's particular misery after the general reflections on the futility of life, reflects the conventional language and imagery of the Plaint of the Sufferer (cf. Ps. 42.4 [EVV 3]). In view of the usage of *lip̄ᵉnê* meaning 'in the character of', 'like' (4.19; 1 Sam. 1.16), there is no need to emend with Beer to *lᵉp̄î* ('in proportion to').

In *laḥmî* the more general sense 'food' is to be noted in Hebrew poetry as regularly in Ugaritic.

25. The verb *'āṯāh* ('to come') is more common in Aramaic than Hebrew, and is common in Arab. and Ugaritic. The retention of the final radical *y* and the direct object after this verb is reminiscent of Arab. usage.

26. On *rōḡez*, here as in v. 17 in the objective sense, see on v. 17.

Job 4 and 5

Eliphaz's First Address

After Job's despairing curse on the day he was born the Dialogue proper begins with a solemn statement of conventional wisdom. The mild rebuke to Job (4.2-6) appeals to him as an exponent of traditional wisdom, aiming at the adjustment of humans to the vicissitudes of life in patience and fortitude. The well-attested fact of retribution for sin encourages a person to hope that life is not meaningless, as Job in his anguish had averred, but that under the theodicy a good person might expect not to be disappointed (vv. 7-11). But the sage is sufficient of a realist to know and be disturbed by human limitations. The sages, though professing reason rather than revelation, were still the heirs of the cultic and prophetic traditions of Israel. Thus Eliphaz shared the realistic view of Jeremiah (17.9) that 'the heart is deceitful above all things and desperately corrupt'. When the angels, though executives of God, cannot fully comprehend the divine plan and purpose in all its scope and may in fact be reprehensible, so even the best of human beings must still die defective in wisdom, that is, in the understanding of life and the proper reaction to life's circumstances (vv. 12-21b). They must then be prepared to suffer the consequences of their lapses under the ordered government of God, which is observable in nature and society (5.3-16) and only a fool who has abandoned the patience and self-discipline practised and counselled by Hebrew wisdom will expostulate with God and yield to despair (5.3). The purposes of God are consistent, and positive even in suffering. Indeed suffering may be a mark of the divine concern (5.17). Therefore the sufferer must take courage, looking to the ultimate deliverance and divine favour, which the sage's study of life attests (5.17-27).

The section falls into nine strophes of five units of bicola and tricola (4.2-6, 7-11, 12-16, 17-20b, 21b + 5.2; 5.3-5b, 4.21a, 5.5c; 5.6-7 + 1 + 8-11, 12-16, 17-20, 22-27). This arrangement suggests that 5.10 is possibly a later expansion (see Commentary *ad loc.*) and 5.2 also is possibly a gloss on 4.21b which has come into the text at the wrong place through the attraction of the word *'ᵉwîl*, which is common to 5.2 and 5.3 (see Commentary *ad loc.*).

The literary types employed in this section are various. Eliphaz opens with some words of apology and the statement of the grounds for his intromission in the convention of sapiential or forensic dialectic, which is a general feature of the opening of the address of Job's interlocutors and also of Elihu (vv. 32-37). The general principle of sin and retribution is stated in the second strophe (vv. 7-11) in the sapiential tradition in figures which recall Proverbs, though the unit is not as in most of Proverbs the couplet, but the strophe. In the following two strophes (vv. 12-16 and 17-20b, 21b + 5.2) this principle is reiterated in the form of a prophetic oracle, though in the language and argument *e fortiori* of wisdom literature. The strophe on the certain discomfiture of the wicked (5.3-5b, 4.21a, 5.5c) by its description of the wicked as 'the fool' betrays its prototype in wisdom literature. The sixth strophe (5.6-7, 1, 8-11), from the same literary tradition, states the antithesis of the retribution of the wicked (vv. 6-7) and the divine vindication of the humble (vv. 8-11), where the divine nature and activity is described in statements in participial form characteristic of the Hymn of Praise on the theme of the establishment of Cosmos by God as King, hence appropriate and evocative of this theme in the argument of Eliphaz for God's Order in society. This hymnic form is developed to the same end in the seventh strophe (5.12-16). In these two strophes the antithesis of the fate of the wicked and the righteous, which is generally stated in the couplet in the wisdom tradition, as in Proverbs, is stated here at greater length in the compass of the strophe. Eliphaz's address ends in two strophes (5.17-20 and 22-27) in the true wisdom tradition. The theme is stated in the aphorism 'happy is the man whom God corrects' in the couplet at v. 17, which is then developed in a poem on the subject of God's discipline and providential care. Repeated instances of this are graphically noted, introduced by the numerical convention 'In six strokes of adversity...yea in seven' (v. 19), which, if not admittedly confined to wisdom literature, was certainly a favourite macronic device of the sages; cf. Prov. 30.15-17, 18-19, 21-23, 24-28, 29-31.

Chapter 4

1. Then Eliphaz the Temanite answered and said:

2. 'If one took up[1] a word with you, could you bear it?
Yet who could refrain from words?
3. Look, you have instructed the tremulous,[2]
And strengthened feeble hands.
4. Your words would raise the fallen,
You would strengthen bowing knees.
5. But now when it reaches you you cannot bear it,
And when it comes to you you are non-plussed.
6. Is not your piety your assurance,
Your perfect conduct[3] your hope?

7. Recall, what man if innocent ever perished,
Or where were the righteous ever destroyed?
8. For as far as I have seen, those who plough in mischief
And sow trouble reap it.

9. Wanting the breath of God they perish,
Wanting the afflatus of his nostrils they are no more.
10. The lion may roar and the roarer may cry loudly,
But the teeth of the great lions are done away,
11. The lion perishes wanting prey,
And the lion-whelps are scattered.

12. But to me a word came quietly,
Yea, a whisper of it caught my ear,
13. In intimate thoughts in night-visions
When deep sleep falls upon men.
14. Terror confronted me and trembling,
And quaking dislocated my bones.
15. And a breath passed over my face,
The hair of my body bristled up.[4]
16. Before me (   ) stood,
But I did not recognize his appearance.[5]
A form was before my eyes,
Silence, then I heard a voice.

17. "Is a man more just than God?
Is a man purer than his maker?
18. If he does not commit himself wholly to his servants,
And charges even his angels with error,
19. How much more those who inhabit houses of clay,
Whose foundations are in the dust,
Who are crushed[6] as the moth,
20. Pulverized between morning and evening,
They perish forever without laying it to heart?[7]
21b [8]They die without attaining to wisdom.
5.2. For vexation kills the fool,
And the death of the simpleton is passion." '[9]

Textual Notes to Chapter 4

1. MT *nissāh* ('put to the test') is a doubtful reading, as is indicated by Aq., Theod., Sym. and apparently also V and S, which read *w*^{e}*niśśā'* (so Böttcher, Beer, Hoffmann, Duhm, Peters, Dhorme, Kissane, Hölscher, Stevenson). *nissāh* means 'to tempt, test' and not 'to venture, attempt' as is assumed by Driver–Gray, Horst, Fohrer and Pope. Hence we read *w*^{e}*nāśā'*.
2. Reading *rāḇîm* (from *rûḇ*) for MT *rabbîm*; see Commentary *ad loc.*
3. The parallelism in this couplet is chiastic, and *w*^{e} should be omitted before *tōm* as a dittograph after *k* in *tiqwāṯ*^{e}*ḵā*. The conjunction might have dropped out before *tiqwāṯ*^{e}*ḵā* by haplography after final *k* in *kislāṯ*^{e}*ḵā* in the Old Heb. script.
4. Reading the Qal *tismar* (intransitive) as the predicate of *śa*^{ʿa}*raṯ* rather than MT *t*^{e}*sammēr* (transitive) as the predicate of *rûaḥ*, which is treated as masculine in v. 15a.
5. In MT the subject of *ya*^{ʿa}*mōḏ* and antecedent of the pronominal suffix in *mar'ēhû* might be *rûaḥ*, which is treated as masculine in v. 15a, the masculine referring to the apparition of a personal agency. In this case if MT is correct the short colon in

v. 16a would include aposeopesis for dramatic effect, but it is more likely that there was explicit reference to a personal agent, which might have been suppressed through motives of orthodoxy.

6. MT *y*^{e}*ḏakk*^{e}*'ûm* ('they crush them') would signify the indefinite subject. S and V read the passive *y*^{e}*ḏukk*^{e}*'û*.
7. Reading *māśîm*, a verbal noun for MT *mēśîm*; see Commentary *ad loc.*
8. On the arrangement of the text, see Commentary on 4.21.
9. The couplet 5.2, which does not connect with 5.1 or with 5.3, may have been displaced to its present position in MT through the incidence of the word *'*^{e}*wîl* in both verses. After 4.21b it explains the statement that one dies unwittingly (*lō' ḇ*^{e}*ḥoḵmāh*) and may be a gloss.

Chapter 5

3. 'I have seen the fool taking root,
And suddenly his homestead was obliterated,[1]
4. His sons abandoned helpless,
And crushed in the gate with none to deliver,
5. His harvest eaten by the hungry;
Men take it away to their own zeriba.[2]
4.21a Is not their abundance plucked from them,[3]
5.5c. And the thirsty[4] gasp for their wealth?

6. Nay, mischief does not grow from the earth,
Nor trouble sprout from the ground,
7. But man is born to trouble
As Reshef's children to soar high.
1. Call, if there is any to answer you.
Yea, to whom of the holy ones will you turn?
8. But I would resort to God,
To God would I refer my case,
9. Who does great things beyond investigation,
Wonders beyond number,
10. Who gives rain on the face of the earth,
And sends water over the surface of the fields,
11. Raising[5] the lowly on high,
The down-stooping[6] are high-established in safety.

12. He frustrates the devices of the crafty,
And their hands do not effect their plan;
13. He takes the clever in their cunning,
And the purpose of the subtle is marred by haste;
14. By day they encounter darkness,
And as at night they grope at high noon;
15. And he has delivered the ruined man[7] from their mouth,
Yea, the poor man from the power of the strong,
16. And there is hope for the poor,
And iniquity has shut her mouth.

17. [8]Happy the man that God corrects!
Spurn not the discipline of the Almighty,

18. For he makes one smart, but he dresses the wound,
He wounds, but his hands also heal.
19. In six strokes of adversity he will deliver you,
Yea, in seven shall no harm touch you.
20. In famine he ransoms you from Death,
And in battle from the power of the sword;
21. When slander is at large[9] you will be hidden,
And you will have no fear of calumny when it comes.

22. At destruction and famine you will laugh,
Yea, you will have no fear of the wild beasts,
23. But with the waste stones you will make your pact,
And the weeds of the field will be bought into concord with you.
24. And you will be assured that your tent is safe,
And will visit your fold and find nothing amiss.
25. And you will know your progeny numerous,
And your issue like the grass of the earth;
26. You will come in full health to the grave,
As a pile of sheaves is brought up to the threshing-floor in its season.
27. Lo, this we have searched out; it is true.
Hear it and know it for yourself.'

Textual Notes to Chapter 5

1. Reading *yûqaḇ*, perhaps in *scriptio defectiva*, from a root cognate with Arab. *waqaba* ('to be obliterated', as the sun in eclipse) or 'to subside', for MT *'eqqōḇ*, from *qāḇaḇ* ('to curse'). See Commentary *ad loc.*
2. Reading *m^{e}ṣinnām* for MT *miṣṣinnîm*. See Commentary *ad loc.*
3. The colon is displaced from v. 21a. See Introduction to chs. 4–5 and Commentary on 4.21.
4. Reading *ṣ^{e}mē'îm* for MT *ṣammîm*.
5. Reading *haśśām* with LXX and V for MT *lāśûm* according to the participial usage characteristic of the Hymn of Praise in vv. 9, 10, 12, 13.
6. Reading *qōḏ^{e}ḏîm* for MT *qōḏ^{e}rîm* as suggested by the parallelism. See Commentary *ad loc.*
7. Reading the Hophal participle *moḥ^{o}rāḇ* for MT *mēḥereḇ*. See Commentary *ad loc.*
8. Omitting *hinnēh metri causa.*
9. LXX, S and V read 'from the scourge' and one Hebrew MT reads *miššôṭ*. MT *b^{e}šôṭ* may retain the Canaanite usage of *b^{e}* meaning 'from', as in the Ras Shamra texts, though the literary influence of Canaanite poetry is most marked in mythological references in the Book of Job. But the consonants of MT may be retained, reading *b^{e}šûṭ hallāšôn* ('when slander is at large'). See Commentary *ad loc.*

Commentary on Chapter 4

2. On the reading *nāśā'* for MT *nissāh* see textual note. The perfect is conditional.

3. Tur-Sinai suggests that *rabbîm* is a Masoretic misunderstanding of a participle *rāḇîm* from *rûḇ*, cognate with Arab. *rāba, yarûbu* ('to take fright, be

confounded'). The parallel with *yāḏayim rāp̄ôt* ('weak hands'), however, indicates the verb *rûḇ* is rather cognate with Akk. *rûbu* ('quaking'). The strengthening of the weak (lit. 'relaxed') hands and the stumbling, or bowing, knees was an ideal of the restoration from Exile in Isa. 35.3-4 in language which practically repeats the passage in Job. The phrase 'to relax the hands', that is, to enervate, is familiar in the OT and denotes pacifist activity in the Lachish Letters (IV, 6) from the end of the Judaean monarchy.

yāsar in Qal or Piel means 'to discipline, admonish, chasten', implying always a positive end and the mind of authority. The parallel with *t^eḥazzēq* ('you have strengthened') makes Ehrlich's proposed reading *yissaḏtā* ('you have supported') at least feasible.

4. In *millîn* the Aram. plural is to be noted, occurring, as Dhorme has pointed out, thirteen times in Job as against ten times when it is *millîm*, surely evidence of Aram. influence in the Book.

5. The verb *lā'āh* means regularly in Hebrew 'to be weary, exhausted', hence 'unable', and may have this meaning here. In Ugaritic it means 'to be strong'; cf. the title of Baal *'al'iyn* ('the mighty'). The usual sense in Hebrew 'to be weary' means 'to have exhausted one's strength'.

The root *nāḡa'*, meaning 'to reach', is usually used in the Hiphil in Classical Hebrew, but is found in the Qal in Isa. 16.8; Jer. 4.10; 48.32; Mic. 1.9.

6. Dhorme notes *yir'āh* ('fear') with the implication 'fear of God' as a peculiarity of the statements of Eliphaz (cf. 15.4; 22.4). It is the regular Hebrew for 'piety'.

8. *ka'^ašer rā'îṯî* ('For as I have seen'), lit. 'according to what I have seen', sc. 'experienced', is particularly frequent in Ecclesiastes in the sage's appeal to empirical fact. The agricultural figure of ploughing in mischief (*'āwen*) and reaping trouble recalls Prov. 22.8 and, at greater length, Hos. 10.13. 'Ploughing mischief' may be a pregnant expression for ploughing the ground for mischief, but it probably refers to ploughing in mischief as seed, which the Arabs in Palestine still sow on the surface and then plough in with their shallow plough (Dalman 1932: II, 184).

9. The couplet may be intentionally ambiguous. *min* may be privative, as in our translation, referring to the animation of humans by the breath of the Creator (Gen. 2.7), on which they totally depend. The preposition may, on the other hand, be causative, 'by the breath of God they perish…' Not only the preposition but also *'appô* is ambiguous, meaning 'his nostril' or 'his anger'. The latter sense is more congruous with the preceding couplet, the former with what follows, which emphasizes the perishing lion-cubs bereft of their provider.

10f. The relevance of this passage is not immediately obvious, and it has been rejected as not original (Duhm), as a marginal note which has crept into the text (Ball) or a secondary addition by a redactor (Strahan). Tur-Sinai (1957: 88-91) regarded it as an exclamation by Eliphaz, animadverting on Job's outburst in ch. 3: 'A lion's roaring: crying of a great beast: (gnashing of) the teeth of lions that roam about, of a lion straying without prey, of a lion's whelps scattered abroad'. Whether the passage refers to Job or not, the mention of lions reflects the figurative reference to the impious who doubt the Order of God in the Plaint of the Sufferer in the Psalms (7.3 [EVV 2]; 22.14 [EVV 13]) or brutes who show their teeth at the sufferer (Ps. 35.17 [EVV 16]). On this interpretation, which we prefer, the passage may well apply to the discomfiture of the wicked in vv. 8f., with a warning to Job to curb his outspoken resentment, which is going to find expression in the Dialogue in his criticism of the current doctrine of the theodicy.

10. *nittā'û* (pausal form) has been taken as an Aram. form of the Niphal of the Classical Hebrew *nāṯaṣ* ('to break down'), which would suit 'teeth' admirably, but would leave 'roar' and 'voice' without a predicate. Israel Eitan (1939: 11ff.) proposed that the verb is a cognate of Ethiopic *nata'a* ('to flee', hence 'to cease, or disappear'); so also Fohrer. The synonyms for 'lion', *'aryeh, šaḥal, k^e^p̄îr, layiš* and *lāḇî'*, make translation impossible without preciosity, as in the innumerable appellations of the camel at various stages of the development of either sex in Arab. poetry. *k^e^p̄îr*, however, possibly refers to the size of the lion, as the word, denoting a great sea-monster in Ezek. 32.2, indicates (so Tur-Sinai).

12. *y^e^gunnaḇ*, here 'came secretly, or furtively', has a parallel in 2 Sam. 19.4, 'and the people came furtively into the city', where the Hithpael of the verb is used.

šemeṣ, known in Hebrew only here and in 26.14 and in the form *šimṣāh* in Exod. 32.25, where the sense seems to be 'malicious rumour', is taken by S and T and by rabbinic commentators as 'a trifle', as possibly in 26.14, but Sym and V render 'a whisper', which suggests that it is probably a cognate of Arab. *šamiṣa*, 'to speak rapidly, or indistinctly' (so Hölscher, Horst).

13. *ś^e^'ippîm* is found in the OT only here and at 20.2 and is variously rendered in the ancient versions, for example, 'thoughts' (T), 'fear' (LXX, Sym., V), 'alternation' (Aq.), 'sleep' (S). No feasible cognate has been suggested for *ś^e^'ippîm*, which we take as a dialectic variant of *s^e^'ippîm* found in 1 Kgs 18.21, where it means 'two minds' (lit. 'forking of a branch'); cf. the variants *śîḡ/sîḡ, śûḡ/sûḡ* and *śāp̄aq/sāp̄aq*. This indicates that 'thoughts' (T) is nearest the meaning, which we render 'diverging thoughts'; cf. 20.2, which we render 'racking thoughts'. Sleep, according to Fohrer (1989: 142f.), indicates the

passive attitude conducive to receptivity when the subjective element is minimized. Eliphaz's terror emphasizes the reaction of the sage to revelation beyond the normal insights of Hebrew wisdom, though of course exaggerated.

14. *qᵉrā'anî* is a byform of *qārāh* ('to light upon, confront'). The subject of *hip̄ḥîḏ* ('made to tremble' or 'dislocated') is usually taken as *paḥaḏ* ('terror'), with *rōḇ 'aṣmôṯay* ('all [lit. "the abundance of"] my bones') as object. MT *rōḇ*, however, may be vocalized as *rîḇ*, a cognate of Akk. *rîbu* ('quaking') as the subject of *hip̄ḥîḏ*; cf. G.R. Driver (1955: 73) ('and quaking shook my bones'). The verb *pāḥaḏ* is taken as cognate with Arab. *faḫaḏa* ('to wound in the thigh', II form, 'to separate'), hence (of bones) 'to dislocate'. The word-play between this verb and *paḥaḏ* ('fear') in v. 14a is a feature of the style of the author of the Book of Job.

15. *ḥālap̄* ('to pass by') is used of a storm-wind in Isa. 21.1. *rûaḥ* is ambiguous. Noticing that the predicate is masculine singular, Duhm took *rûaḥ* to signify a spiritual presence. But *rûaḥ* in Hebrew most normally denotes 'wind', which may be the accompaniment of the advent of God, who presumably speaks in the 'voice' in vv. 17-21. The presence of God, which the word symbolizes, may account for the masculine singular of the verb, though *rûaḥ* is used with the masculine of the predicate in Exod. 10.13, where it means 'a wind'.

On the reading *tismar* (intransitive), meaning 'to bristle up', so used as a predicate of *bāśār* in Ps. 119.120, see textual note.

16. The arrangement of the passage in bicola suggests that part of a colon has been lost, including the more explicit subject of *ya'ᵃmōḏ*, which is probably the antecedent of the pronominal suffix in *mar'ēhû* (see textual note). The mention of the apparition (*tᵉmûnāh*) indicates a supernatural representative of God and not God himself in direct revelation. The whole passage is reminiscent of the revelation to Elijah at Horeb (1 Kgs 19.12), itself reflecting the revelation to Moses at the sacred mountain, particularly the tradition that Moses not only spoke with God face to face, but saw his 'form' (*tᵉmûnāh*, Num. 12.8), a tradition which may be implied in Deut. 4.12-15, which states that the people as distinct from Moses did not see the *tᵉmûnāh* of God, and in Ps. 17.15, where the psalmist declares that he shall see the face of God and be satisfied with his *tᵉmûnāh*. The word may thus denote the exceptionally sure apprehension of the presence of God on the part of rare persons of dedication and spiritual susceptibility. Eliphaz may thus be claiming authority for his statement, as Lévêque (1970: 261) proposes.

'Silence and a voice' (*dᵉmāmāh wāqôl*) may be a hendiadys, but *dᵉmāmāh* may stand pointedly in isolation to indicate the silence, after which the message was heard, as in 1 Kgs 19.12.

18. *hēn* should probably be rendered 'if', as Aram. *'in* (so LXX). *ya'ᵃmîn* signifies reliance upon, implying commitment of one's secrets and interests to the person trusted. The thought is repeated with reference to the 'holy ones' (sc. angels) in 15.15.

The 'angels' of God means lit. his 'messengers'. This was taken by T as the prophets, but in the Book of Job one naturally thinks of heavenly agents as those in the divine court in the Prologue. More particularly the passage recalls 'the saints of the Lord' in Ben Sira, whose immeasurable inferiority to God prevents them from sharing his knowledge of all the wonders of creation (Ben Sira 42.17).

tohᵒlāh is variously rendered in the versions as 'crookedness' (LXX), 'depravity' (Jerome, V, T), 'astonishment' (S), and 'vanity' (Sym., Theod.). The word, if MT is sound, would be a *hapax legomenon*, a verbal noun from a root cognate with Arab. *wahila* ('to commit error'), which has an Ethiopic cognate 'to wander'. So Pope.

19. *'ap̄* is abbreviated from *'ap̄-kî* ('how much less' or 'how much more'); cf. 9.14; 25.6. 'Houses of clay' are bodies of humans created from the earth (*'ᵃḏāmāh*, cf. Gen. 2.6 [J]) or potter's clay (cf. 10.9; 33.6) and figuratively Isa. 64.7 (EVV 8).

On the reading *yᵉḏukkᵉ'û* for MT *yᵉḏakkᵉ'ûm*, assuming dittography of the final *w* mistaken for *m* in the Old Hebraic script, see textual note.

In *lip̄ᵉnê 'āš* ('like a moth', after LXX and V) T and S have misunderstood this sense of the preposition, on which see on 3.24.

20. 'From morning till evening' indicates not continuous affliction but the ephemeral nature of the moth.

yukkattû means lit. 'are reduced to pieces'. In view of the figure 'crushed to powder', 'pulverized' would be a better translation of the verb *kāṯaṯ*; cf. Deut. 9.21, and the pulverization of the Golden Calf. The form *yukkattû* is to be noticed as Aramaic or at least as an Aramaizing form of the Hophal.

miḇᵉlî mēśîm, if correct, assumes the ellipse of *lēḇ* ('heart, understanding'). If this is so, the Hiphil rather than the Qal is suspicious. Pope after Dahood (1962: 55) suggests that the original text may have read *mibbᵉlîm šēm* ('without repute'), the enclitic that reinforces the preposition *min* being mistaken for the preformative of the Hiphil participle in MT *mēśîm* written in *scriptio defectiva*, which is feasible. LXX reads 'without their being able to help themselves', which suggests *mibbᵉlî śîmām lāhem neṣaḥ* (so Beer, Stevenson). But this overloads the metre, and the original of LXX may be *mibbᵉlî môšîa'*, 'without any being able to deliver them' (so Merx, Graetz, Houtsma, Dhorme). Here, however, it is unlikely that such a distinctive letter in the context as *'ayin* should have dropped out at any stage of the script. Tur-Sinai makes the feasible suggestion that MT *mēśîm* is an Aramaic infinitive construct (Qal with the force of a verbal noun; so Horst, who renders 'unbeachtet').

21. On the view that v. 21a is displaced from before 5.5c, see Introduction to chs. 4–5. The transposition of v. 21a to what we believe to be its original position leaves v. 19c parallel to v. 20a, and v. 20b parallel to v. 21b. This supports Tur-Sinai's interpretation of v. 20b as against the various emendations noted above. Here, however, it is important to note that *mēśîm* and *ḥoḵmāh* are not passive, as Horst assumed, but active. This is important in view of the arrangement of the text in the sequel, which is a matter of notorious difficulty.

Commentators differ in the interpretation of the phrase *w^elō' ḇ^eḥokmāh* which is ambiguous, since *ḥokmāh* signifies either the Creator's objective plan and purpose in all things, as in Job 28 and Proverbs 8, or the subjective intelligence or prudence and practical wisdom in the emergencies of life. Horst proposed that it meant that humans die without any intelligent purpose being observable, but that was not in accordance with the orthodoxy of Eliphaz. Budde, Hölscher and Fohrer understood it to mean 'without knowing how'. Ehrlich and Stevenson, after LXX, rendered 'for lack of wisdom', which can scarcely be the meaning in view of death as the common and inevitable fate of all humans. Gray and Driver explain the phrase as 'without having realized the moral limitations of human nature'. In the context of his reply to Job's petulance, Eliphaz, we think, is stating that for lack of self-discipline of wisdom to assimilate the experience of life (v. 20b) and to adjust themselves patiently to circumstances, human beings induce their own destruction by their angry rebellion against circumstances (5.2), which Job has evinced in his cursing of his existence in ch. 3. Note that 5.1, which makes no sense in its position in MT, is displaced from before 5.8 (so Dhorme). See Commentary on Chapter 5.

Commentary on Chapter 5

2. In *le'^ewîl*, *l^e* is the *nota accusativa*, familiar in later Aramaic, but also known in earlier passages in the OT, for example, 2 Sam. 3.30, where it may be a vestige of Old Aramaic. *ka'aś* is an orthographic variant of regular *ka'as*, signifying the emotional strain of resentment with the implication of frustration, which is specifically associated with the fool (*'^ewîl*), which signifies also the 'wicked' in Prov. 27.3.

qin'āh, which usually denotes exclusive and intolerant devotion, in this context denotes rather the overt self-commitment of the simpleton (*pōṯeh*) who is not sufficiently subtle to conceal or restrain his feelings.

3. Noting rightly that the Piel of *šrš* may mean 'to eradicate' as well as 'to take root', Hoffmann interpreted the passage in the former sense, reading the Pual participle *m^ešōrāš*. Dhorme notes that the sudden (*piṯ'ōm*) destruction of the wicked in the second colon indicates the opposite. Actually the Hiphil expresses the denominative sense 'to take root'.

If with Dhorme we take *wā'eqqōḇ* as 'and I cursed' from *qāḇaḇ*, after Aq. and V., this would indicate the endorsement of the divine displeasure by a curse, as for instance the punctilio which the Arabs of Jerusalem used to observe in cursing the reputed tomb of Absalom whenever they passed it. This interpretation is excluded by the adverb *piṯ'ōm*. The reading of the verb, however, is in doubt as indicated by the variations in the versions, for example, 'his livelihood is eaten up' (LXX), 'his abode has perished' (S). The noun *nāweh* is attested in v. 24 and 18.15 as 'abode' or the like. More particularly in Jer. 33.12 it denotes the folds and settlements of shepherds. An Akk. cognate denotes 'encampments' in the Alalakh Tablets (Wiseman 1953: 10). Various emendations have been proposed for MT *wā'eqqōḇ*, for example, *w^erāqēḇ*, 'and (his dwelling) rotted' (Merx, Bickell, Siegfried, Hölscher), or *wayyirqaḇ* (Duhm, Ehrlich, Stevenson, Weiser, Fohrer), with the same meaning. The emendation of Baumgärtel *wayyē'āqer* ('was eradicated'), which is accepted by Horst, is too far removed from the consonants of MT. Perhaps *wayyûqaḇ* should be read, the verb being cognate with Arab. *waqaba* ('to be effaced' or 'to subside'); cf. Israel Eitan's proposal (1939: 9-23) that *wayyûqaḇ* should be read, derived from a verb *qûḇ* cognate with Arab. *qāba*, the II form of which means 'to eradicate'. An interesting proposal is that of J.J. Slotki (1931: 288) that the consonants of T may be arranged without emendation to read *w^e'aqqô b^enāwēhû* ('and the wild goat is in his household'), taking *'aqqô* as 'wild goat' mentioned in Deut. 14.5. But this interpretation also is practically ruled out by the adverb *piṯ'ōm* ('suddenly').

4. 'The gate' is the place of public justice; cf. Prov. 22.22, 'Do not crush the poor in the gate' (*'al-t^eḏakkē' 'ānî baššā'ar*), where the same verb is used as in the present passage. The *locus classicus* for justice and the vindication of the poor 'in the gate' is Ruth 4.1-11.

5. For MT *'^ašer q^eṣîrô rā'ēḇ yō'ḵēl* ('whose harvest the hungry eats') LXX reads, with too abrupt a change of subject, *'^ašer qāṣ^erû rā'ēḇ yō'ḵēl* ('that which they have reaped the hungry shall eat'), understanding 'his sons' as subject.

In v. 5b and c the versions are at variance and give no help beyond attesting MT with only slight variation. *miṣṣinnîm* at first sight suggests 'from the thorns', or possibly 'the place of thorns', though this is not the rendering of any of the versions. The former meaning seems to be contradicted by the preposition *'el* ('to'), but possibly the original reading was *l^emiṣṣinnîm*, with *l^e* signifying 'from' as in Ugaritic, being reinforced by *min*; cf. *mill^eḇô'*. The meaning would be that the hungry took the corn of the wicked from the thorns which, like a *zeriba*, were used, as still among the Arab peasants, to protect the grain from beasts on the threshing-floor until it is brought into storage. Perhaps *'el-m^eṣinnām* ('to their own *zeriba*') may be read as in our translation. G.R. Driver proposes to overcome the difficulty of MT *'el-miṣṣinnîm* by taking *'el* as *'ēl* ('the strong') from the root *'ûl*. Tur-Sinai proposes to read *'ûlām* ('their strength is dearth'), taking *'ûlam* (lit. 'strength', so 'possessions') as parallel to *ḥêlām*. *'ûl*, however, is not attested in the sense of 'wealth'. For his reading *ṣannîm* Tur-Sinai cites the participle *ṣᵉnunôṯ* ('shrivelled'), used of ears of corn in Pharaoh's dream in Gen. 41.23.

The third colon, v. 5c, unless this a case of a tricolon punctuating a passage arranged in bicola to indicate the end of the passage according to sense, is suspect, implying an omission or a displacement of a colon, which is possibly to be found at 4.21a, 'Is not their abundance wrested from them', as Dhorme proposed.

The ancient versions (Aq., Sym., V; cf. S) are unanimous in suggesting that *ṣammîm* is a corruption of an original *ṣᵉmē'îm* ('thirsty'). This involves the reading *wᵉšā'ᵃpû*, possibly written in *scriptio defectiva*. The verb *šā'ap̄*, rendered by Hölscher 'snap after', means 'to pant after', hence 'eagerly desire'. For *ḥayil* a concrete substance such as 'harvest' in v. 5a has been suggested, for example, *ḥᵃlāḇām*, 'their milk' (Hoffmann, Beer, Tur-Sinai), or *ḥallām*, 'their vinegar' (Beer), but *ḥayil* is well attested in the sense of 'substance' or 'wealth'; cf. 20.15, though admittedly after *ṣᵉmē'îm* some liquid would be expected.

6. Here the force of *kî* is corroborative. *yāṣa'* has the specific sense 'grow out'; cf. *ṣe'ᵉṣā'* ('growth').

7. Commentators differ in reading *ywld* as the Niphal as in MT and the ancient versions (Merx, Dillmann, Bickell, G.B. Gray, Ball, Stevenson, Weiser, Horst, Fohrer, Pope, J.C.L. Gibson) or Hiphil *yôlîḏ*, 'begets' (Graetz, Beer, Duhm, Dhorme, Hölscher, Mowinckel, Terrien). Both are possible in the context. The latter might claim the support of Eliphaz's statement in 4.8 that humans plough in mischief (*'āwen*), and sow trouble (*'āmāl*), and more particularly the statement in Ps. 7.15 (EVV 14) that humans conceive mischief (*'āwen*) and bring forth falsehood (*wᵉyālaḏ šeqer*); cf. Job 15.35, and especially Isa. 59.4, where humans 'conceive trouble and beget mischief' (*hārô 'āmāl wᵉhôlêḏ 'āwen*). In this case *lᵉ* in *lᵉ'āmāl* would be the *nota accusativi* as in Aramaic. But the comparison with the young eagles or vultures born to soar high (understanding the imperfect *yaḡbîhû* as the verb in a final clause asyndetically after the verb implied in *yiwwālāḏ* as in Ugaritic poetry) in our opinion supports MT *yiwwālēḏ*, signifying that humans are born to trouble. J.C.L. Gibson (pp. 46ff.) understands this to indicate a decree of sympathy on Eliphaz's part for Job as heir to the burden of humankind after the fall of Adam, reflecting specifically Gen. 3.17-19. In any case, though the entail of Adam's sin might mitigate that of Job, which Eliphaz assumes, Job is not exonerated from a degree of responsibility for the accumulation of trouble in society, particularly in his readiness to venture more than a mortal ought, in pressing his case with the Almighty.

The verb *'ûp̄* suggests that *b^e^nê rešep̄* are birds, and so the phrase is taken in all the versions except T, where it is variously rendered as 'sons of demons' or 'sparks', whence EVV. In support of the interpretation as birds Dhorme suggests that, as Pss. 76.4 (EVV 3), 78.48 and Song 8.6 indicate, *rešep̄* means 'lightning', with which he associated the eagle. Deuteronomy 32.24 and Hab. 3.5, incidentally, do not support this interpretation, since there *rešep̄* is parallel to 'plague', and is therefore the personification of plague or death *en masse*, which was the province of the Canaanite god Rešeph, now well known in this capacity in the Ras Shamra texts (e.g. Gordon, *UT* Krt 18). It is a remarkable fact that in Deut. 32.24 *Targum Onkelos* renders *rešep̄* as 'birds' and Ben Sira 43.14, 17, LXX and V so render the same word, neither, however, specifying eagles or vultures, which none of the versions does in Job 5.7b. LXX in fact renders *rešep̄* as 'vulture', which has suggested the emendation *nešer*, which is graphically feasible. In this case, however, the versions would almost certainly have been specific. We seem to be driven back on the interpretation of *rešep̄* as a forgotten relic of Canaanite mythology. Rešeph was a god who slew humans in mass by war or plague, and is known from a mythological fragment from Ras Shamra as 'Lord of the Arrow' (*b'l ḥṣ*) (RS 15.134.3; Virolleaud 1957: 3ff.). Thus 'the sons of Rešeph' may be arrows, the normal parabolic flight of which may be described. But in view of the association of Rešeph with mass death 'the sons of Rešeph' are probably the vultures ('where the body is there will the vultures gather'). Their high flight enables them to locate their carrion with speed that appears uncanny (39.27-29). Horst suggestively cites the designation *ršp ṣprm* in Azitawadd's inscription from Karatepe (Donner and Röllig 1962: no. 26 A, II, 10-11), where *ṣprm* may mean 'birds', or perhaps more specifically 'birds of prey', lit. 'taloned birds'; cf. *ṣippôr* in Ezek. 39.4. Tur-Sinai comes near to this interpretation, but in the writer's opinion needlessly identifies 'the Rešeph-birds' with the Classical harpies.

5.1. This verse is displaced in MT from before v. 8, to which it is the appropriate introduction, not being relevant in its position in MT, where the theme is the retribution of the fool.

The identity of *q^e^ḏôšîm* in this context is apparently the angels who might intercede for the sufferer, a conception which we encounter again in the speeches of Elihu and which is implied *per contra* by the office of the *śāṭān* as 'public prosecutor' among the 'divine beings' (*b^e^nê '^e^lōhîm*) in the Prologue. The usage and theological background recalls Zech. 14.5 (late postexilic) and Dan. 8.13 (second century BCE). Buttenwieser (1922: 165-67), however, proposes that dead ancestors, notable possessors of divine favour and so effective intercessors, like the Arab. *wālî*, are denoted. In support he cites Saadyah, who renders *gō'ēl* in Job 19.25 as *wālî*, and Isa. 63.16:

> You are our father;
> Abraham does not care for us,
> Nor does Israel acknowledge us.

> You are our father,
> Our Vindicator (*gō'ēl*) has been your name
> From time immemorial.

He takes *'elōhîm* in this sense in Isa. 8.19; cf. 1 Sam. 28.13, where it denotes the dead Samuel. The rhetorical question may, however, rather reflect the limitations of the 'holy ones', the angels of 4.18.

8. This is the natural sequel and contrast to 5.1.

debārāh, familiar in the phrase *'al-dibrat* ('according to the fashion of'), as distinct from *dābār* ('word'), is a forensic or philosophic term denoting 'case'.

9. Here a participle introduces a Hymn of Praise (vv. 9-16), which is sustained by references in the same style and form to praiseworthy acts of God. This form was familiar in psalms celebrating the providence of God in nature, history and society in the liturgy of the New Year festival and is cited here because of its traditional association with this theme and its variations in the argument of Eliphaz (see above, pp. 49-50). This is also the explanation of what are generally described as doxologies in Amos 4.13; 5.8; 8.8; 9.5ff., which, like the chorus of a Greek tragedy, emphasize the main philosophic theme. The use of this hymnic excerpt results in a strophe longer than usual in the context.

niplā'ôt denotes manifestations of God's immediate activity, which, by its very nature, defies human explanation by secondary causes.

10. The mention of the rain and of the distribution of water as the first instance of God's providence reflects the Canaanite origin of the liturgy of the great autumn festival with its theme of the victory of God over the forces of Chaos (J. Gray 1956; 1961). In Canaan this was the exploit of Baal-Hadad, who was manifest in the vital rains and storms of winter. In the Canaanite text celebrating his victory over the power of Chaos represented by the unruly Sea-and-River, which results significantly in the establishment of his kingship (Gordon *UT* 68), Baal is said to drag his defeated adversary away and 'disperse Sea' (*yšt ym*), thereby, we claim, distributing the flood for the good of the land (cf. Ps. 104.6ff.). The verb *šālaḥ* is used of distributing water in an irrigation channel, *šîlōaḥ* (Isa. 8.6).

'The fields' (*ḥûṣôt*), lit. 'places outside', that is, outside the defensive walls of the settlement (Dhorme), is seldom found, but from Ps. 114.13 and Prov. 8.26 its meaning is not in doubt.

11. The operation of God in raising the humble and abasing the haughty is the theme also of Ps. 138.6 and 1 Sam. 2.7; cf. the emphasis on the humbling of the haughty in Isa. 2.9, 11-17 in consequence of the epiphany of God as king (Isa. 2.10, 19, 21).

In v. 11a *haśśām* should probably be read as suggested by LXX and V in keeping with the participial expression of God's great works in vv. 9-13.

'Those who mourn' is a paraphrase of 'those who go black' (MT *qōḏᵉrîm*), either in sack-cloth or with blackened or unwashed faces, as a rite of separation in mourning (cf. Pss. 35.14; 38.7 [EVV 6]; 42.10 [EVV 9] etc.), but in the context this may be a scribal corruption of *qōḏᵉḏîm*, 'those who are bowed down'; cf. Gen. 24.26; Exod. 4.31; 12.27; 34.8; etc. (so Peters, Tur-Sinai, Beer, Stevenson, after S).

12. 'Success' is probably a secondary meaning of *tûšiyyāh*, which is demonstrated by Hebrew wisdom literature to be generally parallel to 'wisdom' (*ḥoḵmāh*, Job 11.6; Prov. 2.7) or 'counsel' *'ēṣāh* (Job 26.3; Prov. 8.14), and 'foresight' (*mᵉzimmāh*, Prov. 3.21). Hence the meaning 'effective wisdom' is proposed (Driver–Gray 1921: 30-32), and in the present passage 'plan' may be the meaning (so Peake, Dhorme, Hölscher). The word is also parallel to 'help' (*'ezrāh*, 6.13) and 'strength' (*'ōz*, 12.16) where 'success' may be the meaning (so Stevenson, Horst). The parallel *maḥšᵉḇôṯ* in the present passage suggests that the meaning here is 'plan', with, however, the implication of the plan realized, or effective.

13. *nip̄tālîm* means 'complicated', lit. 'plaited' or 'twisted' as a rope. *'ēṣāh* means 'counsel' or 'plan', again with the implication of the plan carried through to an effective conclusion, which in this case is frustrated through premature haste (*nimhārāh*).

14. Groping (*yᵉmašᵉšu*) at noon-day reflects the elaboration of the curse of those that contravene the divine commandments in the context of the conclusion of the Covenant-sacrament in Deut. 28.29. This verb would suggest a synonym in the parallel colon, and Tur-Sinai suggests that *pāḡaš* may be a metathetic cognate of Syr. *gᵉšap̄*. But *pāḡaš* in its usual sense of 'encounter' has already the implication of 'stumbling upon', which is a sufficiently apt parallel to *māšaš*.

15. In v. 15a a parallel to *'eḇyôn* ('needy') is demanded. The simplest solution would seem to be to vocalize MT *mēḥareḇ* as *moḥᵒrāḇ*, 'the ruined one' (so Michaelis, Ewald, Friedrich Delitzsch, Dhorme, Terrien), thus respecting the consonants of MT which are attested by all the ancient versions. For the figure of the oppressor devouring the afflicted, cf. Hab. 3.14; Prov. 30.14. This obviates emendations, of which the nearest to MT are that of Stevenson *wayyôša' mᵉḥuyyāḇ mippîhem* ('and he rescued a condemned man from their mouth') and that of Horst *wayyôša' meḥereḇ mupāḥ* ('and he rescued a man from the sword').

16. MT *'ōlātāh* is attested in Ps. 92.16 in the Qere *'ōlāṯāh* or probably *'awlāṯāh*, explained by Dhorme as a poetic form of *'awlāh* on the analogy of *'êpāṯāh*, 'weariness' (10.22) with a similar shift of diphthong to a long vowel and the feminine ending in *-āṯāh*. 'Stop' for *qāp̄ᵉṣāh* perhaps gives the wrong impression. The verb means 'to draw together' (cf. Arab. *qafaṣa*), hence 'to shut by clamping the lips together'; cf. Isa. 52.15, of the powers of the world who desist from speaking against the Servant of Yahweh.

17. On omission of *hinneh metri causa*, with Merx, Dillmann, Beer, Duhm, Ball, Peters, Hölscher and Stevenson, see textual note. So far as sense is concerned the word might be retained as an emphatic enclitic; cf. Arab. *'inna* (so Dhorme, Horst). *hôḵîaḥ* is a forensic term, 'to bring a person's guilt home to one', so in general 'to reprove' (6.25, 26; 32.12; 40.2). The emphasis sometimes falls on the argument for this purpose (13.15) and sometimes on the result, 'correction', as here and at 13.10; 22.4; 33.19. As implying impartial scrutiny of merits and demerits the verb may also denote arbitration between two parties (9.33; 16.21). The parallel *yāsar*, the root of *mûsār*, denotes rather 'correction' or 'discipline'. Here occurs the first of the 31 incidences of *šadday*, generally rendered 'the Almighty', in Job. *'ēl šadday* is the specific name of God in the patriarchal narratives in P (cf. Ezek. 10.5, 4), but may reflect earlier usage (cf. Gen. 43.14 [E] and possibly 49.12 [J] after LXX and the Samaritan Pentateuch). *šadday* has been thought to be connected with the Akk. and Aram. root 'to pour', indicating God as the giver of rain or with Akk. *šadu* ('mountain'); cf. 'the rock' as a divine appellative in Deut. 32.4; etc. A connection with Arab. *šadda* ('to be strong') has also been suggested. The connection with Akk. *šadu* seems probable, if still not certain. The Rabbinical explanation 'He who is sufficient' (Heb. *ša-day*) is an etymological *tour de force*, a theologoumenon rather than serious etymology, and is not seriously to be considered.

In keeping with the universalistic theme of wisdom, the divine name Yahweh, the God of Israel, is confined to the prologue and epilogue to Job and to the few prose passages elsewhere in the book. The names *šadday* and *'ēl* or *'ᵉlôah* are preferred as characteristic of the patriarchal age according to the P tradition and in accordance with the patriarchal setting in which the book is cast. The term *'ᵉlôah* (singular of *'ᵉlōhîm*) is used regularly in Job with *'ēl* and *šadday*, perhaps to emphasize the unity of God. Dhorme (p. xl) suggests that *'ᵉlôah* is an Edomite word, in support of which he cites the use in the psalm in Hab. 3.3, where God is associated with Teman in the vicinity of Edom, but here the choice of *'ᵉlôah* may have been dictated by metric considerations.

'ēl in Amorite theophoric names from the second millennium BCE and in the Ras Shamra texts is both a generic term 'god' and the name of the Amorite and Canaanite high god, known very explicitly from the Ras Shamra texts of

the fourteenth century BCE as the senior god of the Canaanite pantheon, the final authority in all matters in nature and society, but more specifically interested in society (J. Gray 1966). The significance of the Canaanite conception of El for the development of the conception of Yahweh in Israel cannot be overestimated, as Eissfeldt has emphasized (1956: 37), 'He (sc. Yahweh) received from him (sc. El) the impetus to an evolution which meant the supplementation of the traits originally belonging to him...a dangerous and bizarre character and jealous vehemence...by the qualities of discretion, and wisdom, moderation and patience, forbearance and mercy'; cf. Fohrer (1953: cols. 196-97), who also sees in the character of El in the Ras Shamra texts the signs of a monotheistic tendency in Ugarit.

19. In view of the verb *yaṣṣîl^eḵā* ('he will deliver you'), *b^ešēš ṣārôṯ* may mean 'from six troubles', *b^e* meaning 'from' as well as 'in' in Ugaritic; cf. Beer, Duhm, who conjectured *min* for MT *b^e*, but this need not be so, as the parallel colon indicates, where *b^e* indicates the circumstances in which the person will experience God's deliverance. The numerical climax to indicate repetition or an indefinite number is familiar in Hebrew and Ugaritic poetry; cf. Prov. 6.16,

> There are six things that Yahweh hates,
> Yea, seven that he himself abhors...,

and in the Ras Shamra text Gordon *UT* 51.III.17-18:

> There are two sacrifices that Baal detests,
> Three (detested by) Him who Mounts the clouds...

20. *pāḏ^eḵā* is the declaratory perfect, emphasizing the certainty of the divine action proclaimed, particularly common in prophetic utterance, and sometimes called the 'prophetic perfect'. The verb *pāḏāh*, with an Arab. cognate, denotes 'ransom', a familiar practice in tribal warfare raids, in which the blood-feud imposed an economy of life. 'From death' may either denote ransom so that one should not be put to death, or it may denote a personification of death, a reflection, of the anthropomorphic figure of Death and Sterility, the arch-enemy of the life-giving Baal in the Canaanite mythology known in the Ras Shamra texts.

21. *b^ešôṭ lāšôn* might be another case of *b^e* meaning 'from' as in v. 19. The common translation is 'scourge of the tongue', but Tur-Sinai after Saadya takes *šôṭ* as 'to roam'; cf. *šûṭ* in 1.4; 2.2. He might have cited Ps. 73.9, *ûl^ešônām tih^alaḵ bā'āreṣ* (RSV 'And their tongue struts about in the earth') in support of this interpretation, which accords better with the verb 'you shall be hidden' and preserves the parallelism with *šôḏ kî yāḇô'* ('calumny when it comes'). *lāšôn* (lit. 'tongue') has probably the pregnant sense 'calumny' here; cf. the denominative verb *lāšan* in Ps. 101.5; Prov. 30.10, with cognates with this sense in Arabic and Ugaritic (e.g. Gordon *UT* 2 Aqht VI.51). The word

articulated in malice or curse was dreaded as having a potent and palpable force; cf. *qᵉlālāh nimreṣeṯ* in 1 Kgs 2.8, a curse infected with disease, a crippling curse.

The apparent repetition of *šôḏ* in vv. 21 and 22 indicates, as usual in such cases in Job, a word-play with homonyms. Here *šôḏ* with an Arab. cognate comes first and the Hebrew homonym *šôḏ* ('destruction') second, the order being usually the other way round. The parallelism with *šûṭ lāšôn* indicates that the first *šoḏ* is the Arab. *śawādu*(*n*), 'blackness', that is, denigration; cf. *śawwada wajhahu* ('he blackened his face', i.e. calumniated him).

22. *kāpān* ('famine') is an Aram. synonym of Heb. *rā'āb* (v. 20).

'al-tîrā' is usually taken as jussive in prohibition, which is explained (GKC, §109b) as the statement of a conviction that something cannot, or may not, happen. Actually *'al* is found with the imperfect indicative in the Ras Shamra texts, and this may be a vestige of the poetic diction of Canaan in Hebrew literature; cf. 20.17; 40.32; Ps. 121.3.

The menace of wild beasts, such as gazelles, to crops and predatory beasts such as hyenas to flocks and even to human life, was real in the Hejaz, and even till recently in Palestine, where deep ravines, rocks and scrubland and semi-desert regions adjacent to the settled land harboured such creatures.

23. In the context referring to such natural enemies as famine, wild beasts and weeds it is highly unlikely that in 'the stones of the field' there should be any reference to boundary stones. The reference is rather to stones which mar the good land for cultivation either as outcrops of rock or as stony patches (Mt. 13.5) (so Dhorme), or perhaps rock-falls or stones washed over good land by flood or perhaps dry-stone terrace walls washed out by floods. The reading *'ᵃḏōnê haśśāḏeh* ('lords of the field', i.e. local field-spirits) is suggested by K. Kohler, in support of which view Buttenwieser (1922: 170) cites Doughty (1926: I, 177), 'Many have sown here, and awhile, the Arabs told me, they fared well, but always in the reaping time there has died some one of them. A hidden mischief they think to be in all this soil once subverted by divine judgments, that it may never be tilled again or inhabited. Malignity of the soil is otherwise ascribed by the people of Arabia to the ground-demons, *jān*, *ahlu 'l-'ard* or earth-Folk.' The natural nuisances in the context, however, support MT. The marring of cultivable land by stones is noted in war (2 Kgs 3.19, 25), and their removal and use in terracing is a constant and necessary occupation among the hills of Palestine (Isa. 5.2). We accept G.R. Driver's suggestion that *ḥayyaṯ haśśāḏeh* in v. 23b means not 'beasts of the field', but 'weeds of the field', Adam's natural enemies after the Fall (Gen. 2.18 [J]) which by God's grace should be brought into concord with humankind (*hošlᵉmāh*, a form which occurs only here). On Driver's interpretation *ḥayyaṯ* is cognate with Arab. *ḥayyu*(*n*) ('cultivated plants or weeds').

The repetition of *haśśāḏeh* is suspect unless, according to the fondness of the writer of Job for word-play, the one represents the familiar Hebrew and the other a cognate less familiar in Hebrew. Here we suggest that the former is Arabic *suday* ('forsaken, useless'), hence our rendering:

> But with the waste stones you will make your pact,
> And the weeds of the field will be brought into concord with you.

24. MT *šālôm 'ohᵒleḵā* is suspect. We should expect either the noun *šālôm* with a preposition (so evidently read by LXX^A and Jerome) or a stative verb *šālēm*, which LXX evidently read. The same problem is raised in 21.9, *bāttêhem šālôm*, where LXX, V and possibly also S read the verb *šālᵉmû*, indicating perhaps metathesis of *w* and *m*, which closely resemble each other in the Old Hebrew script. But Dhorme cites other instances where *šālôm* is apparently used as a predicate after the subject, for example, Gen. 43.27; 1 Sam. 25.6; 2 Sam. 20.9. If these like the present passage are not simply errors of dittography in the Old Hebrew script, *šālôm* may be the participle of a stative verb *šālôm*, a byform of the more familiar *šālēm* ('to be whole'), specifically denoting 'be at peace'. Alternatively MT *šālôm* in those passages may be *šālûm* ('at ease'), the noun *šālû* with the afformative *m* which is used as a substitute for, or to supplement, the preposition in Akkadian and Ugaritic, having an adverbial force, as in Heb. *yômām*, *piṯ'ôm*, *'omnām* and *ḥinnām*. See further on 21.9.

As *'ōhel*, *nāweh* suggests the desert, not necessarily literally but as a relic of nomadic antecedents, like so much in Hebrew. *nāweh* is the camp and sheepfolds, or corrals, of shepherds on the desert edge (e.g. 2 Sam. 7.8; Isa. 65.10; Jer. 23.3; 33.12; 49.20; Ezek. 25.5; 34.14). The verb *pāqaḏtā* may indicate a periodic 'stock-taking', which is the primary sense of the verb, which only secondarily means 'to visit'.

ḥāṭā' means 'to miss the mark, be the loser' (e.g. 1 Kgs 1.21), with primarily no moral connotation. The meaning 'to be a sinner' is secondary.

26. *bᵉḵelaḥ* has no parallel in Classical Hebrew, and is taken as a scribal error for *bᵉlēḥᵃḵā*, 'in your vigour' (cf. Deut. 34.7) (so Ball after Cheyne), *bᵉḥêlᵉḵā*, 'in your vigour' (Merx), or even *bᵉḵālāh*, 'in the fulness' (of old age) (Dhorme). Rabbinical ingenuity suggests that Job's age is indicated (2+20+30+8 = 60)! *kelaḥ* is probably an Aramaism; cf. Syr. *kᵉlaḥ* ('health') and Arab. *kaliḥa* ('to be stern, firm').

gāḏîš is not a sheaf or 'shock' of corn, but the pile of sheaves that were gathered together in the field as loads to be transported (lit. 'brought up') to the threshing-floor (Exod. 20.5; Judg. 15.5) on an airy height by the village.

27. *ḥᵃqarnûhā* ('we have searched it out') indicates the thoroughness of the sage to investigate the declarations of orthodoxy.

Job 6 and 7

JOB'S FIRST REJOINDER TO ELIPHAZ (CHAPTER 6) AND HIS EXPOSTULATION WITH GOD (CHAPTER 7)

Job's reply to the first round of argument from Eliphaz falls into four parts. In the first (6.2-13) he justifies his resentment under stress of suffering; in the second (6.14-30) he declares his disappointment in his friends, who had failed him with their sympathy in his hour of need; in the third (7.1-15), Job complains of God's unremitting torment of him, a mere mortal to whom death would have been a welcome release; and in the fourth (7.16-21), this theme is sustained, with the addition that even if Job had sinned he could not harm God so as to merit such punishment.

The first two parts are arranged in four strophes each (6.2-4, 5-7, 8-10, 11-13; and 6.14-17, 18-21, 22-25, 26-30), and the last two parts in respectively three (7.1-4, 5-11, 12-15) and two (7.16-19, 20-21).

In the first part, Job replies to Eliphaz's rebuke of his outburst in ch. 3 and his lack of patience under adversity on which Hebrew wisdom insisted, alleging his exceptional suffering at the hand of God. Job's excuse for his reaction is rounded out by two proverbs in the Wisdom tradition (6.5, 6). His sufferings are described in the figurative and hyperbolic language of the Plaint of the Sufferer, but his pleading reflects the forensic controversy, with the significant difference that Job's plea is not for acquittal but for 'easeful death', reflecting 3.11-13 from Job's initial expostulation. This is his response to Eliphaz's exhortation to sue for God's mercy, with the promise of rehabilitation (5.8ff.). This variation of the literary prototype makes the plea particularly poignant.

In the second part the literary form is the forensic controversy, with the disloyal friends in place of the legal opponents of the sufferer. The passage in its subject as well as its figurative language recalls the sufferer's complaint of his friends' alienation in the Plaint of the Sufferer in Pss. 31.12 (EVV 11); 38.12 (EVV 11); 41.10 (EVV 9); 55.13-15 (EVV 12-14; 69.9ff. (EVV 8ff.). More particularly the figure of the friends as a dry wadi (6.15-21) recalls Jeremiah's reproach to God in Jer. 15.18, though the distinctive contribution of the author of the Book of Job must be noted in the expansion of the original to a striking Homeric simile.

In ch. 7 in response to Eliphaz's exhortation to make his petition to God (5.8), with the prospect of a 'happy ending' (5.17-26), with significant change from the plural to the singular of the one addressed, Job directly and simply addresses God; his address, however, is expostulation rather then prayer. The language reminiscent of Eliphaz's reference to the frailty of humans vis-à-vis the angels as prone to sin (4.17ff.), Job cites the hard lot and natural frailty of humans in general and his own hard lot in particular, with the inevitable prospect of death and oblivion to invite the mercy of God to 'let him be' in his miserable life (7.19) or to give him the *coup de grâce* (7.15; cf. 6.8f.). Chapter 7 reflects two sapiential texts, with, however, significant adaptation. First it recalls Hezekiah's prayer in Isa. 38.10-18, with the harrowing recital of sufferings with the grim prospect of Sheol (Isa. 38.10). This, however, is the prelude to the hope of survival as distinct from Job 7, where Sheol is the culmination of Job's sufferings (7.8, 10, 21). Second, again perhaps animadverting on Eliphaz's theme of human frailty in 4.19ff., the passage, particularly 7.17ff., is a parody of Ps. 8.5ff. (EVV 4ff.). The psalmist asks 'What is man?', physically so insignificant in the universe, that God should pay him special attention as the apex of creation; with mortals' limitations in mind Job asks the same question why God should sustain and promote them simply to subject them to inquisition and torment. In this context the citation of the mythological theme of God's inveterate hostility to 'Sea and Tannin', in view of the traditional association with the Hymn of Praise celebrating the victory of God as King confirming the establishment of Order against the menace of Chaos which it naturally evoked in Jewish readers, is tantamount to questioning the justice of 'the Judge of all the earth'.

Chapter 6

1. Then Job answered and said,

2. 'Would that my resentment were weighed
And that they put my ruin[1] with it in the balances;
3. Then it would prove heavier than the sand of the sea;
For this reason are my words impassioned,
4. For the arrows of the Almighty are against me
And my spirit drinks their venom;
The sudden attacks of the Almighty wear me out.

5. Does the wild ass bray over his pasture?
Does the ox low over his fodder?
6. Is that which is insipid eaten without salt?
Is there any taste in bland from cheese?
7. My very being refuses to eat,
My inwards[2] loathe[3] my food.

8. Would that my request were realized,
That God could grant what I hope for!
9. That it would please God to crush me,
To unleash his power and cut me off!

10. Even that would be my consolation,
I would leap for joy in my unremitting anguish,[4]
That I had not concealed declaration concerning the Holy One.[5]

11. What is my strength that I should hold out?
What my appointed end that I should patiently endure?
12. Is my strength the strength of stones?
Is my flesh bronze?[6]
13. Even if I were to increase my help a hundred-fold[7]
My effective power would be driven from me.

14. To one who is in despair[8] ill-will from his friend
Is as though one abandoned the fear of the Almighty.
15. My brothers are fickle as a winter torrent,
Like empty watercourses,[9] which have flowed away,
16. Which are dark by reason of the ice-floe,
And in which snow flows,
17. But when they run off they vanish,
In the heat they are extinguished from their place.

18. The caravans make a detour,[10]
They go off into the desert and perish;
19. The caravans of Tema looked out,
The trains of Sheba set their hopes on them;
20. They were confounded in their trust,[11]
They reached the wadi and were disappointed.
21. Even so[12] you have been to me,[13]
You see a single terror[14] and are afraid.

22. Is it that I have said "Give me something"?
Or "Give a bribe on my behalf from your wealth"'?
23. Or "Rescue me from the power of the enemy"?
Or "Ransom me from brigands"?
24. Instruct me, and I will be silent,
Make me to understand wherein I have erred.
25. How aggravating are the words of rectitude!
But what sort of censure is censure from you?

26. Is it your intention to criticize my words,
The utterances of a desperate man (spoken) for relief?
27. Yea, you would cast lots for an orphan,
And haggle over your friend.
28. Now please face up to me,
Surely I will not lie to your face.
29. Be done.[15] Let there be no injustice;
Relent, for my case is still just.[16]
30. Is there distortion on my tongue?
Can my palate not discriminate words?'

Textual Notes to Chapter 6

1. Reading *hawwāṯî* with LXX, S, V, T and four Heb. MSS for MT *w^{e}hayyāṯî*; see Commentary *ad loc.*
2. Reading *k^{e}ḇēḏî* for MT *kiḏ^{e}wê*; see Commentary *ad loc.*
3. Reading *zih^{a}māh* for MT *hēmmāh* after LXX and supported by the parallelism.
4. Reading *ḥîlî* for MT *ḥîlāh*; see Commentary *ad loc.*
5. The colon after the bicolon which closes the strophe 6.8-10 may refer to Job's satisfaction in stating a case against God's undue persecution of a mere mortal in ch. 7, but in the context of 6.8-10 and 11f. it seems a gloss, as indicated by the term 'the Holy One', the only such designation of God in the Book of Job.
6. Reading *n^{e}ḥušāh*, attaching *h* of the following *ha'im* of MT to the unfamiliar form *nāḥûš*.
7. Reading *ha'^{a}mā'ennā* (*'ezrāṯî ḇî*) for MT *ha'im 'ên 'ezrāṯî ḇî* after Graetz.
8. Reading *lannāmēs* or *l^{e}nāmēs* for MT *lammās*; see Commentary *ad loc.*
9. Reading *ka'^{a}p̄îqîm ḥālîm* for MT *ka'^{a}p̄îq n^{e}ḥālîm*; see Commentary *ad loc.*
10. Reading *y^{e}lapp^{e}ṯû* for MT *yillāp̄^{e}ṯû* to supply the transitive verb which the object *darkām* requires.
11. Reading *bāṭ^{e}ḥû* with S and T for MT *bāṭāḥ*.
12. Conjecturing *kēn* for MT *kî*.
13. Reading *lî* with LXX, S and one Heb. MS for MT *lō'*.
14. Reading *ḥ^{a}ṭā'ṯ 'aḥaṯ* in a four-beat colon to balance the metre of v. 21 after the emendation of MT *kî* to *kēn*.
15. Reading *šobbû*, taking the verb as cognate of Arab. *ṯabba*, 'to be ended' (of a matter) or 'to settle down' (of a person), so we might paraphrase 'rest the case'.
16. Reading *bî* for MT *bāh*, *y* being corrupted to *h* in the Old Heb. script.

Commentary on Chapter 6

2. *lû* introduces an unrealizable wish (GKC, §159.3; §151.2). *hayyāṯî* should probably be emended to *hawwāṯî*, as in 30.13; cf. *hawwōṯ* (Prov. 19.13; Pss. 57.2; 91.3).

3. *kî-'attāh*, which introduces a letter after the greeting, here introduces the apodosis after the protasis which states the condition potentially fulfilled.

Sand was proverbially heavy; cf. Prov. 27.3 and the Wisdom of Ahiqar VII, 112f., *ANET*, p. 429: 'I have lifted sand and I have carried salt, but there is nothing which is heavier than (anger)'. The sand of the sea is hyperbolic. In view of the reference in Prov. 27.3 to the fool as heavier than sand Job 6.3 may specifically allude to Job's impatient expostulation under stress of adversity in 4.5 and 5.3, so out of character in a sage.

The root *lā'āh* is used of rash oaths in Prov. 20.25, though the pointing in that passage suggests a different root, either *lā'a'* or a variant of Arab. *wala'a* ('to be impassioned').

Tur-Sinai evidently takes the verb as a cognate of Arab. *laġa*(*w*) ('to babble'), rendering ('my words) are stammering'. Job's assurance, however, and his articulate argument is far from stammering; though certainly impassioned.

4. For *'immādî*, 'against', we may cite Ugaritic *'im*; cf. Heb. *nilḥam 'im* ('to fight against') and *yāṣā' 'im* ('to make a sortie against'). Wounding by the arrows of God is a conventional figure for affliction in the Plaint of the Sufferer (e.g. Ps. 38.3 [EVV 2]); cf. Job 16.12f., where Job declares that he is the target for the arrows of God. Mowinckel (1955: 325), Steinmann (1955: 111) and Fohrer (1989: 169) think of the arrows of the plague-god Rešeph, called in Phoenician inscriptions *b'l ḥṣ* ('lord of the arrow'); cf. Greek Apollo 'the Far-Shooter', but, as the sequel indicates, the military figure is intended.

rûaḥ in this context probably denotes the spiritual element of God-given reason, patience and self-control which distinguishes humans from the beasts, deriving from their consciousness of affinity with God (cf. 10.12).

We would retain v. 4c to form a tricolon punctuating the strophe vv. 2-4 as against the proposal to treat it as a gloss (so Fohrer). *bi'ûṯîm*, usually rendered 'terrors', is found in the OT only here and in Ps. 88.17, but may rather be connected, as G.R. Driver (1955: 73) suggested, with Arab. *baġata* ('to come suddenly upon'), hence 'sudden attacks', as in 3.5. *ya'arᵉḵûnî* seems at first sight to suggest a connection with *ma'arᵉḵāh* ('battle-line') in the context of a military metaphor; so V, T and S. *'āraḵ* in the sense 'to dress the ranks' is usually transitive, but is used without an explicit object (e.g. Judg. 20.30; Jer. 50.14), but the direct object of the person against whom the ranks are formed is highly suspect. LXX and Jerome in his commentary render 'goad me', which suggested to Siegfried the reading *ya'arᵉqûnî*. Beer, Dillmann, Budde and Hölscher assume metathesis in MT and read *ya'aḵᵉrûnî* ('troubled me'). Peters, following S *sᵉraḏaṯnî* ('has terrified me') proposed the emendation *ya'ᵃrîṣûnî*. MT, however, is defended by G.R. Driver, who takes *'āraḵ* as a cognate of Arab. *'araka* ('to wear out').

5. The verbs *nāhaq* and *gā'āh* ('bray', 'low') are used in parallelism in the Ras Shamra legend of Krt (Gordon, *UT* Krt 120f., 224f.) in a passage relating to beasts in the starvation of a siege (cf. Joel 1.18). This long-attested usage of *nāhaq*, which is used besides only once in the OT (Job 30.7), despite its incidence in Aram. and Arab., should warn us against the assumption that it is either an Aramaism or an Arabism in Job.

pere' is the wild ass, or onager, which defies domestication (39.3-8). It is selected as parallel to the domestic ox to give a comprehensive picture. Fittingly its food is described as *deše'*, natural grass (Gen. 1.11) as distinct from 'fodder' (*bᵉlîl*, lit. 'mixed', i.e. chopped straw [Arab. *tibn*] and corn, Isa. 30.24; cf. *billēl*, 'to give fodder', Judg. 19.21).

6. *tāpēl* is used here in its literal sense, 'insipidness'; see further on 1.22.

The context indicates that *rîr ḥallāmûṯ* denotes an insipid substance. *ḥallāmûṯ* is the doubtful word. The only help given in the ancient versions is in S and T. The former reads 'juice (*rîr*) of the anchusa', or purple plant (*rîrēh daḥlᵉmāṯā'*) (so Terrien), or some other plant (Hölscher, Stevenson, Fohrer,

Gordis, Horst). T renders 'the white and the yolk of an egg'. *rîr* (1 Sam. 21.13) would support one or the other in the sense of 'juice' or 'fluid'. As the more familiar substance the white of an egg (lit. the saliva around the yolk), this might seem more likely in the context. A.S. Yahuda (1903: 702), however, suggested that *ḥallāmuṯ* is cognate with Arab. *ḥalûmu*(*n*) ('soft cheese'). In this case *rîr* would be the insipid fluid left after cheese-making, that is, 'bland' (so Pope).

7. See textual note.

napšî is ambiguous, meaning either 'myself' or 'my appetite' or even 'my throat'. The passage re-echoes 33.20.

lingōa' immediately suggests the well-known Hebrew root *nāga'* ('to touch'), which again, as G.R. Driver suggests (1944a: 168), may be cognate with Arab. *naja'a* ('to eat food to one's advantage'), and would explain the lack of a direct object, which *nāga'* ('to touch') demands. After the reference to insipid food *zihᵃmāh kᵉḇēḏî laḥmî* ('my inwards', lit. 'liver', 'loathe my food'), as Dhorme after Wright, Driver–Gray, Budde, Beer *et al.* for MT *hēmmah kiḏᵉwê laḥmî* ('they are as sickness of my food') is most apposite; cf. 33.20 for support of the emendation.

9. The root *yā'al* is found always in the Hiphil, meaning 'to consent', followed naturally by the jussive. *yattēr* ('let him unleash') is the Hiphil jussive of *nāṯar*, a rare verb in this sense in Isa. 58.6, and meaning 'to set (prisoners) free' in Pss. 105.20; 146.7.

biṣṣā' means 'to cut off' a part from the whole; cf. Arab. *baḍ'atu*(*n*) ('a piece'), *baḍ'u*(*n*) ('divorce').

10. The adverb *'ôd* should be emphasized, meaning 'yet', with the sense of 'nevertheless', as in the Plaint of the Sufferer, Ps. 42.6, 12 (EVV 5, 11).

The root *sālaḏ* is not known elsewhere in the OT, but is known in post-Biblical Hebrew meaning 'to recoil'. LXX and T support the meaning 'would jump for joy'.

The verbal noun (infin. constr.) *ḥîl* means 'writhing', for example, in child-birth (Isa. 26.7) or anguish (Exod. 15.14). The masculine singular preformative in *yaḥmōl* indicates that *bᵉḥîlî* should be read for MT *bᵉḥîlāh*, *y* being corrupted to *h* in the Old Heb. script.

If v. 10c is original it would be the third colon of a tricolon, which might be used for punctuation, as occasionally in the Ras Shamra couplets. Stevenson and Horst see in this verse and particularly in v. 10c a reference to the author's consciousness of his task as a sage of insight not to conceal declarations concerning 'the Holy One', so that the truths he had reached in his ordeal should be communicated as his contribution to final truth (so Weiser). Taking *kiḥēḏ* in the sense of 'efface' or 'deny', which it occasionally has, and *'imrê* as 'commandment' (cf. Prov. 2.1; 7.5; 19.7; Isa. 41.26), Terrien understands

Job to be imploring God's *coup de grâce* that he may die before he is tempted to deny God's commandments. But it is probably a gloss (so Siegfried, Duhm, Beer, Hölscher, Mowinckel, Fohrer). See textual note *ad loc.*

11. The parallelism with *'^{a}yaḥēl* indicates that *'a'^{a}rîḵ nap̄šî* denotes 'patience'; cf. *tiqṣar rûḥî* (21.4) and *qṣr npš* in the Ugaritic Krt text (Gordon *UT* 127.34, 47), meaning 'one whose endurance has been foreshortened'. This passage refutes Dhorme's objection that if patience were denoted in 11b *rûaḥ* and not *nep̄eš* would have been used. He accordingly translates 'I should prolong my life'.

qēṣ denotes the appointed end, or term, rather than simply 'the end' (cf. LXX 'the time'), as the parallel of *middaṯ yāmay* ('the measure of my days') in Ps. 39.5 (EVV 4) indicates. *qēṣ* is familiar in the Dead Sea *Manual of Discipline*, the *War of the Sons of Light* and the *Hymns*, meaning 'the appointed time'; cf. Arab. *qaḍa(y)* ('to decide'). We recall the expression of an Arab guest at the end of a meal *qaḍayt(u)* ('have finished').

13. The double interrogative in MT *ha'im* is awkward, and was felt as such by the ancient versions, which, however, are not in agreement. Modern commentators also disagree, following either S or V in reading *hē' 'im* ('Behold, if...?') (so Hölscher) or LXX 'or had I not trusted in him?' (so Driver–Gray). The former reading points the Aramaic particle *hē'* ('Behold'), which would be an exception in Job. Duhm read *hē' mē'ayin 'ezrāṯî ḇî* ('See, where is my help in me [coming from?]'). LXX suggests a reading *h^{a}lō' 'ên 'ezrāṯî ḇô* ('Is it not that I have no help in him?'); cf. Dhorme, *h^{a}lō' mē'ayin 'ezrāṯî ḇî* ('Is not my help in me a nonentity?'). Horst retains MT, stressing *ha'im* in the only place it occurs in the OT, Num. 17.28, where, however, the text is equally doubtful. After Buttenweiser and Sutcliffe v. 13 begins with the interrogative participle *'im*, *h* being displaced from the end of *n^{e}ḥûšah* (MT *nāḥûš*). Kissane reads *hû'* after *n^{e}ḥûšah* which would include the *aleph* of MT *'im* and permit a reading *mē'ayin 'ezrāṯî ḇî* ('My help in myself is nothing', i.e. 'my own help is nothing'). But see textual note *ad loc.* on Graetz's reading *ha'^{a}mā'ennā 'ezrāṯî ḇî*, taking *'^{a}mā'ennā* as a denominative verb, Piel with the energic ending of the imperfect (so also Dahood 1965: 13). *'ezrāṯî* indicates that the parallel *tûšiyyāh* means 'effective power'. See above on 5.12.

14. MT as it stands might conceivably mean lit. 'to one who is melting loyal love is due from his friends, even though he would abandon the fear of God' (so Weiser and Terrien). *māsas* means secondarily 'to despair' (e.g. Josh. 2.11; 5.1; 7.5; Isa. 13.7; Neh. 2.11), but there the verb is in the Niphal and the subject is 'heart'.

In view of this attested usage MT *lammās* may be a corruption of *l^{e}nāmēs*; alternatively it has been suggested (Hitzig, Friedrich Delitzsch, Snaith 1968: 111) that *ḥeseḏ* here, as in Lev. 20.17 and Prov. 16.34, and in Syr. and Aram., means 'envy' or 'ill-will', giving the meaning 'To one in despair ill-will from his friend is as though one forsook the fear of God'. Assuming that *ḥeseḏ* has its usual meaning 'loyalty', LXX, S, V and T make the further assumption of the reading *māš* ('withdrawing') from *mûš*, generally intransitive, but transitive in Zech. 3.9. This would give the sense 'As for (MT *l*ᵉ) the man who withdraws loyalty from his friend, he abandons the fear of the Almighty', which to be sure accords with the context, but no more than the interpretation of Hitzig and others we have noted. The assumption of *māš* for MT *mās* (possibly *nāmēs*) is very doubtful and the deviation of the versions is caused by their failure to notice that the poet is effecting a word-play with *ḥeseḏ* in the sense opposite to the more familiar one in a convention known in Arab. literature as *'aḍḍād*. Dhorme, Stevenson, Hölscher and Fohrer take v. 14 as a marginal gloss to v. 15, thus, in the opinion of the writer, failing to appreciate the idiom so characteristic of the poet in Job.

15. The figure of the flash flood recalls Jer. 15.18. The repetition of *naḥal* is intolerable in the original and here we would suggest an emendation of *'ᵃp̄îq nᵉḥālîm* to *'ᵃp̄îqîm ḥālîm* ('empty watercourses'); cf. *'ar-rub'u'lḫālī*, the Empty Quarter in SE Arabia. *ya'ᵃḇōrû* is formally, meaning either 'to overflow', or, as here, 'to flow away'. The clause is relative with the omission of the relative particle, as frequently in Ugaritic poetry and in Arab. after an indefinite antecedent; cf. 11.16 *kᵉmayim 'āḇᵉrû* ('as water that has flowed away').

16. In *qōḏᵉrîm minnî-qeraḥ*, Dhorme, after Avronin and Rabinowitz and certain rabbinic authorities, takes *qōḏᵉrîm* to mean 'covered' (lit. 'darkened'), but there is no objection to rendering 'darkened by reason of the (*minnî*) ice-floe'. One suspects that the rabbinic rendering of *qōḏᵉrîm* was prompted by the parallel *yiṯ'allem-šeleḡ*, where the verb was assumed to be the familiar word 'to obscure'. But this may rather be cognate with Arab. *'alima* meaning in the IV form 'to flow'.

17. This couplet caused some trouble to the ancient versions and to modern commentators through the uncertainty as to the meaning of the *hapax legomenon yᵉzōrᵉḇû*. The parallelism with *bᵉḥummô* has suggested *yᵉṣōrᵉḇû*, 'they are scorched' (cf. Prov. 16.27; Ezek. 21.3), the phonetic variation *ṣ/z* being attested in *ṣā'aq/zā'aq*. But *yᵉzōrᵉḇû* may be retained as cognate with the Arab. root from which *mizrab* ('canal') is formed; cf. Late Heb. *marzēḇ* ('gutter'), as recognized by Qimchi, hence the translation 'melt, run off'.

ṣāmaṯ is well attested, meaning 'to annihilate' in the OT and in Ugaritic (Gordon *UT* 'nt II.8); cf. Arab *ṣamata* ('to be silent').

The final *waw* in MT *bᵉḥummô* should probably be attached to the following *niḏ'ᵃḵû* ('they are extinguished').

18. On the reading *y*^{e}*lapp*^{e}*ṯû* (transitive before *darkām*) see textual note. *tōhû*, the description of primaeval chaos (Gen. 1.2 [P]) means here 'desert', and is parallel to *miḏbār* in Deut. 32.10 and used of a trackless wilderness in 12.24 and Ps. 107.40; cf. Arab. *tîhu*(*u*) ('desert'). It aptly describes the tangle of wadis off the beaten track in the desert.

'āḇaḏ means 'to go astray' in 1 Sam. 9.3, 20; Jer. 50.6; Ezek. 34.4, 16 and perhaps Deut. 26.5. Both this meaning and 'to perish' would suit the present context.

19. On Teima and Sheba see above, p. 36. Here Sheba may denote the mercantile kingdom of S. Arabia, and not as in 1.15 a locality in the Hejaz like Teima.

20. Read *bāṭ*^{e}*ḥû*; see textual note.

bōšû means 'they were confounded' or 'disappointed' as in Isa. 1.29; 20.5; Jer. 2.36; 12.13; 48.13; Ezek. 32.30; 36.32, the verb being parallel with *ḥāp̄ar* ('to be abashed', 'disappointed'), as in Pss. 35.26; 40.15.

21. On the reading *kēn*...*lî* see textual note.

ḥ^{a}*ṯāṯ* is a *hapax legomenon* in the OT, perhaps the *nomen unitatis* of *ḥaṯ* ('terror') (41.25; Gen. 9.2); cf. Ass. *ḫattu* ('terror'). Perhaps the singular should be emphasized in the present passage, 'a single terror'. This may refer to the 'infectious' danger of associating with one evidently under the wrath of God, which prompted Job to sit on the ash-heap.

22. *kōaḥ* is used here in the unusual sense of 'wealth', like *ḥayil*; cf. Prov. 5.10.

šiḥ^{a}*ḏû* (lit. 'give a bribe') gives a graphic insight into the ancient Semitic community where friendship extended even to bribing officials in the interest of one's friends.

23. The nature of the oppressor (*ṣār*) is not specified, but *'ārîṣîm* implies high-handed oppressors, such as chiefs of raiding desert tribes and others. In those circumstances ransom (cf. *tip̄dûnî*) must have been often in demand.

25. After T and Rashi *mah-nniml*^{e}*ṣû* ('how sweet') is read by Graetz, Duhm, Dhorme, Hölscher; cf. 119.103. The text and usual sense of *māraṣ* and its Arab. cognate need not be altered, since Job is presenting the correct, but unsympathetic, moralizing of his friends in his distress, which has the same effect as 'a crippling curse' (*q*^{e}*lālāh nimreṣeṯ*) in 1 Kgs 2.8. Hence with Horst we render 'How aggravating are the words of rectitude!'

26. The emphasis in v. 26a lies on *millîm* ('words'), the captious logical arguments of the friends being criticized. The translation of v. 26b 'the

speeches of one that is desperate (*nō'āš*; cf. Arab. *ya'iśa*, "to be desperate") are for the wind' rather misses the point. The sense is rather that the sufferer must find relief in speech; cf. 32.20, *'ᵃḏabbᵉrāh wᵉyirwaḥ- lî*, 'I will speak to find relief'.

27. The sentiment is the disapproval of 'kicking a man when he is down', applying the letter of logic as men apply the law in the case of the orphan sold for his parent's debts instead of exercising sympathy. The Hiphil of *nāp̄al*, understanding *gôrāl* ('lot'), is instanced in 1 Sam. 14.42.

kārāh ('to buy'; cf. Deut. 2.6; Hos. 3.2), has the force of seeking to buy, expressing the activity of merchants, in 40.30, where, as here, it is used with *'al*, and may be translated 'haggle over', here signifying 'chop logic with', or insist impersonally on the moral law of sin and retribution.

28. Now in forensic style Job turns from criticism of his friends to a pointed plea to respond seriously to the justice of his case. *pānāh bᵉ* meaning 'to look at', 'address oneself to', occurs in Eccl. 2.11.

'im 'ᵃkazzēḇ is the strong negative in the truncated oath-formula with the omission of the oath in the apodosis.

29. On our reading of MT *šûbû* in v. 29a, *šōbbû*, cognate of Arab. *ṯabba* ('to be ended', of a matter, 'to settle down', of a person), see textual note. For MT *šuḇî* in v. 29b read *šûḇû* 'withdraw' from the attitude assumed by Job's friends. This is another case of word-play between a more familiar word (here *šûḇû* in colon b) and the less familiar homonym in colon a.

ṣeḏeq is used here in its forensic sense of having a just case.

30. The unexpected collocation of *ḥikkî* ('my palate') and *yāḇîn* ('understands', here in the radical sense 'discriminates') must be noted. Job has not only a discriminating mind, but this is reflected in his speech and arguments, which follow in the Dialogue, despite the allegation of the friends that Job is a loudmouth and a windbag (8.2, Bildad; 11.2f., Zophar; 15.2, Eliphaz). We agree with Pope in taking *hawwôṯ*, not as 'calamity' as in 6.2 and 30.13, but as the plural of Ugaritic *hwt* and Akk. *awatu* ('word'), with a cognate in modern Syrian Arab. The sentiment is reflected in 12.11:

> *hᵃlō-'ōzen millîn tiḇḥān*
> *wᵉḥēḵ 'ōḵel yiṭ'am-lô.*
>
> Does not the ear test words,
> And the palate taste food?

Chapter 7

Job's Expostulation to God

1. 'Has not a man a time of service on the earth?
Are not his days as the days of a hireling?
2. Like a slave that gasps for the shade,
Or like a hireling that longs for his wages,
3. So I have been allotted months of emptiness,
And nights of trouble are assigned to me.
4. Whenever I lie down I say,
"When shall I rise?"
And as night is dragged out
I have my fill of tossing until dawn.

5. My flesh is clothed with corruption
And scab has covered[1] my skin.
(It has broken out and suppurated.[2])
6. My days are swifter than a loom,
They are gone without hope.
7. Remember that my life is but wind,
My eye shall not again see good.
8. The eye that looks for me will not mark me;
Your eyes will be on me, and I shall not be there.
9. A cloud is gone and passes,
Even so he who goes down to Sheol does not come up.
10. He returns to his house no more,
And his place recognizes him no more.
11. But even I will not withold my speech,
I will speak in my anguish of spirit,
Complain in my bitterness of soul.

12. Am I Sea or Tannin
That you set a guard over me?
13. If I say, "My couch will give me comfort,
My bed will ease the burden of my complaint",
14. You terrify me with dreams
And frighten me with hallucinations,
15. So that I would cordially choose strangling,
Death rather than my torment.[3]

16. I have had enough,[4] I shall not live forever;
Hold off from me, for my days are but a vapour.
17. What is man that you rear him
And pay any heed to him,
18. Taking note of him every morning,
Testing him every moment?
19. How long will you refuse to look away from me,
Not letting me alone till I swallow my spittle?

20. If I sin how can I affect you,
You who watch men?
Why do you make me a mark for your attacks?
And why am I a charge upon you?[5]
21. Why not unburden me of my sin,
And pass over my iniquity?
For then I should lie down in the dust,
And you would seek me and I would not exist.'

Textual Notes to the Chapter 7

1. Reading *w^{e}ḡûš ‘āp̄ar ‘ôrî* for MT *w^{e}ḡûš ‘āp̄ār ‘ôrî*; see Commentary *ad loc.*
2. A secondary expansion; see Commentary *ad loc.*
3. Reading *‘aṣṣ^{e}ḇôṯāy* for MT *‘aṣ^{e}môṯāy*; see Commentary *ad loc.*
4. Reading *missattî* for MT *mā’astî*; see Commentary *ad loc.*
5. A scribal adjustment (*tiqqûn sōp̄^{e}rîm*), *‘ālay* being written for *‘āleyḵā* to obviate the theological difficulty of the conception of God as liable to any burden.

Commentary on Chapter 7

1. *ṣāḇā’*, as Aq. and V appreciate, refers to a period of military service, as in 14.14 and Isa. 40.2, though LXX and Jerome in his commentary take it in the more general sense of ordeal, which would also suit Isa. 40.2.

śāḵîr may also be used in the more general sense of 'hired servant' or day-labourer (LXX), but probably denotes a mercenary soldier, as in Jer. 46.21; cf. the verb in 2 Sam. 10.6.

2. *pō‘al* means 'work' and also the reward of work; cf. Jer. 22.13. In this sense *p^{e}‘ullāh* is more common (Lev. 19.13; Prov. 10.16; Ezek. 29.20).

3. LXX, S and V read the passive *munnû* for MT *minnû* ('have been allotted', lit. 'numbered'). MT may nevertheless be retained as an instance of the active verb with indefinite subject with the significance of a passive.

4. *’im* with the perfect is used to express 'as often as'; cf. Gen. 38.9; Num. 21.9; Judg. 6.3; Pss. 41.7; 94.18; Isa. 24.13. In this case it may be followed by *waw* and the perfect, as here. The sentiment re-echoes Deut. 28.67.

middaḏ, if MT is sound, must be the adverbial accusative, 'throughout the length…' LXX has a fuller text, which may have read:

’im šāḵaḇtî w^{e}’āmartî māṯay hayyôm
’āqûm ûmāṯay ‘ereḇ
middê ‘ereḇ śāḇa‘tî n^{e}ḏuḏîm ^{a}ḏê-nāšep̄

As often as I lie down I say, 'When will it be day?'
I rise up (and say), 'When (will it be) evening?'
The whole night long I have my fill of tossing until dawn.

The last colon is abnormally long, and *middê ʿereḇ* may have crept into the text as a variant on MT *māṯay ʿereḇ*. In this case MT represents a telescoped text.

5. In MT *wḡyš ʿāp̄ār*, *gîš* or *gûš* is rendered 'clods' in LXX and T, which would signify in this context the crust of the earth (Dhorme), so figuratively 'scab'. G.R. Driver (1955: 73-76) cites Arab. *jaś'u*(*n*), 'rough skin', and takes *ʿpr* not as a noun *ʿāp̄ār*, as in MT, but as a verb *ʿāp̄ar*, cognate with Arab. *ġafara* ('to cover'), reading the second colon in v. 5 as *w*ᵉ*ḡûš ʿāp̄ar ʿôrî* ('And scab covers my skin'). This is an excellent suggestion, and Driver continues, reading *raḡaʿ wayyimmas* for MT *rāḡaʿ wayyimmāʾēs* and rendering 'It breaks out and suppurates'. *raḡaʿ wayyimmas* or MT *rāḡaʿ wayyimmāʾēs*, however, is suspect as either a defective third member of a tricolon, for which there is no reason here, or as a gloss, as which it is treated by Driver.

6. Tur-Sinai has questioned the usual rendering of *ʾereḡ* as 'a weaver's shuttle', proposing that the word is cognate with Arab. *ʾarija* ('to exhale a smell') and rendering 'smoke', which is noted as being quickly dispelled. This is just possible, but unlikely. The verb *ʾāraḡ* and its participle *ʾōrēḡ* are familiar in the OT, meaning 'to weave' and 'loom' (Exod. 28.32; Judg. 16.13; 1 Sam. 17.7; 2 Sam. 21.19; 2 Kgs 23.7; Isa. 59.5). *ʾereḡ* in the Samson story (Judg. 16.13) means 'loom' rather than 'shuttle' which, however, the present figure particularly visualizes, as the word-play on *tiqwāh* ('hope', thread') indicates.

Dhorme renders *b*ᵉ*ʾep̄es tiqwāh* as 'for lack of thread', *b*ᵉ*ʾep̄es* having this sense in Prov. 26.20. This interpretation had occurred already to ibn Ezra, and there is probably a word-play here between *tiqwāh*, 'thread' (cf. Rahab's scarlet thread in Josh. 2.18, 21), which connects with what precedes, and the more familiar *tiqwāh* which in the word-play so beloved of the author connects with what follows. Unfortunately this cannot be so neatly expressed in translation.

7. 'Remember that my life is but wind (*rûaḥ*)' seems like a quotation of Ps. 78.39, 'And he remembered that they were but flesh, a wind that passes and comes not again'.

8. The verb *šûr* is limited to poetic parts of the OT and found more often in Job than elsewhere (cf. 17.15; 20.9; 24.15; 34.29; 35.5, 13, 14). It means generally 'to regard, mark', and in Hos. 13.7 'to watch' as a lurking leopard. But here it is a synonym of *rāʾāh* ('to see') as in the poetic Balaam-oracles in Num. 23.9; 24.17 (JE).

9. Sheol, thought of as under the earth, as the verb *yāraḏ* indicates, is for the Hebrews as for the Mesopotamians 'the land of no return' (Akk. *ʾarṣu lâ târu*,

cf. Job 10.21). It is nebulous, neuter existence (3.13-19), where humans have no hope of 'seeing good'. It is against this prevailing conception of the afterlife that passages like 19.25-27 must be critically considered.

10. In 'And his place recognizes him no more' (*welō'-yakkîrennû 'ôḏ meqōmô*) the author makes a verbal citation of Ps. 103.16, with the general sentiment of which on the transience of human life without prospect of a hereafter he is in agreement, like contemporary Jewish thought.

11. With the tricolon Job's account of his troubles ends and vv. 12ff. are occupied with his complaint directly to God.

12. Sea (*yām*) and *tannîn* are now known from the Baal myth of Ras Shamra to be powers of Chaos which militated against the Order of God in nature. The nature of *tnn* in those texts is not specified. This imagery was adopted in Israel in the liturgy of the great autumn festival, to which it properly belonged in Canaan. Thus Sea became the inveterate enemy of God and his Order, especially in Enthronement Psalms in the OT (e.g. Pss. 46.2-3 [EVV 1-2]; 74.12-15 [EVV 11-14]; 89.10-11 [EVV 9-10]; 93.3-4; 98.7-8; 104.6-7) with echoes elsewhere in Hebrew literature (e.g. Isa. 51.9-11; Ezek. 29.3; 32.2ff.) where Egypt is equated with Tannin and Rahab 'the Restless One', that is, the Sea. So in Dan. 7.3ff. the great beasts, which militated against God and his people, came up *from the sea*.

In the *Apocalypse of Baruch* after the establishment of the Messiah as King and before his final judgment on all peoples the earth is threatened by a flood of black waters (*2 Bar.* 70.1ff). In the *Psalms of Solomon* (2.28ff.) the providence of God is vindicated in the downfall of Pompey, which is described in the same imagery: 'But thou, O Lord, delay not to recompense them on their own heads, to cast down the insolence of the dragon (Syr. *tanînâ'*) in humiliation'. The setting of a guard (*mišmār*) over the sea refers generally to the conception of the power of Chaos against which God continually has to assert his authority in myth and ritual in Mesopotamia and Canaan and, with its own adaptation, in Israel, and refers perhaps particularly to Marduk's confining the defeated monster Tiamat, the Lower Deep, under bolts, posting guards over it, as is described in the Babylonian New Year liturgy in the myth *Enuma elish*. The consciousness of being watched narrowly by God, 'the watcher of humans' (*nōṣēr 'āḏām*) (v. 20), supports the normal meaning of *mišmār* ('guard').

13. *kî* is employed here as the conditional conjunction by way of variation from the more usual *'im*.

nāśā', meaning 'to share the burden of', followed by *be* is found in Num. 11.17. Here *be* may have the sense of the more regular *min* as in Ugaritic with the partitive force (cf. 21.25; 39.17).

15. Reading *'aṣṣᵉḇôṯāy*, from *'aṣṣᵉḇeṯ* ('sorrow') for MT *'aṣᵉmôṯāy* ('my bones'); cf. 9.28.

16. Fohrer regards MT *mā'astî* as a gloss on v. 15, but the 4:4 meter used in v. 16 as a variation from the regular 3:3 meter is against this. Reiske, Merx, Siegfried and Duhm retain *mā'astî*, connecting it with *māweṯ mē'aṣᵉmôṯāy* in v. 15b, rendering 'I despise death more than my pains', or, as Duhm prefers, 'Death I despise because of my pains'. Driver– Gray (1921: II, 47) object that *mā'as* means 'to reject', but cf. 9.21, 19.18; Amos 5.21; Prov. 15.32; Judg. 9.38 (*hᵃlō' zeh hā'ām 'ᵃšer mā'astāh bô*, 'Is not this the people that you despised?'). Pope proposes that *mā'astî* is the verb in a relative clause without the relative particle, of which the antecedent is *'aṣṣᵉḇôṯāy*, which he renders 'my loathsome pains'. This again, however, ignores the 4:4 meter in v. 16. Tur-Sinai's suggestion, however, may be adapted, to read *missattî* ('I have had enough') from a root *māsaṯ* with this sense, familiar in Aram. and Syr. and attested in Classical Hebrew in Deut. 10.10. It restores the parallelism with *ḥᵃḏal mimmennî* ('hold off from me'). 'My days are but a vapour' (*heḇel*). This noun is used figuratively as 'vanity' in the famous refrain in Ecclesiastes, but means radically 'vapour', as in Arab. *bahlatu*(*u*).

17. The verse which contrasts the significance of ephemeral humans with the scrupulous visitation of a critical God is a parody of Psalm 8, the language of which it re-echoes, and of Ps. 144.3-4, which contrasts the apparent insignificance of humans with God's peculiar love and care for them. As regularly in Hebrew, the heart (*lēḇ*) is the seat of cognition rather than affection.

18. On *pāqaḏ*, here 'to take special note of', see on 5.24.

liḇᵉqārîm means 'every morning'; cf. *lirᵉgā'îm* ('every moment'). This noun (cf. *bᵉregā'*, 21.13) is derived from a verb describing the flickering, that is, of an eyelid (cf. Prov. 12.19 [of the tongue]), and may be a metathetic cognate of Arab. *re'aja* meaning in the VIII form 'to tremble'.

19. *kammāh* means 'how much' (13.23), 'how often' (21.17) and 'how long' (Ps. 35.17, and here). *šā'āh* ('to look steadily at') is used with *min*, 'to look away from', in the sense of overlooking, or averting one's gaze from, in 14.6 and Isa. 22.4, as here.

'Till I swallow my spittle' recalls the Arab. expression cited by Schultens, *'abli'nî rîqi* ('Let me swallow my spittle', i.e. 'Leave me a moment').

20. The metrical arrangement here is suggested by 35.6a, where Elihu quotes Job's arguments ('If you sin now do you affect him?'), as follows: *ḥāṭā'ṯî māh' ep̄'al lāḵ*, where *ḥāṭā'ṯî* is a hypothetical perfect in a conditional sentence (GKC, §159b, h). The following words *nōṣēr hā'āḏām* are thought to give too short a colon in v. 20b, but if they are stressed to give the effect of

bitter irony this difficulty is overcome. In this case there may be *double entendre* in *nōṣēr*, 'watcher', in the sense of 'protector' (cf. Arab. *naṣara*, with this meaning of watching critically, and Arab. *naṭara* 'to watch', e.g. crops; so Prov. 27.18). In the present passage the emphasis falls rather on God as 'Grand Inquisitor'.

'A mark for your attacks', *mip̄gā'*, lit. an object of encounter'; cf. *mip̄gā'îm*, 'the 'targets' of lightning (36.32) and 16.12, 'he has set me up as his target' (*maṭṭārāh*). As the mark of the arrows of God we may render both nouns as 'butt'.

On the scribal adjustment *'ālay lᵉmaśśā'* for *'āleyḵā lᵉmaśśā'* see textual note. Lindblom (1966: 214) makes the interesting suggestion that this couplet refers to two sports or trials of skill, the second to the lifting and heaving of a heavy stone as a trial of strength, to which Ben Sira 6.21 and possibly Zech. 12.3 refer. This is possible, though we prefer the translation 'Why am I a charge upon you?' (i.e. 'are you obliged to punish my sin?').

21. We should see a word-play on *nāśā'* in *maśśā'* in v. 20c, and in *tiśśā'* in v. 21a, the first indicating burdening oneself with the obligation of exacting retribution for sin and the second lifting off the burden of sin. There is a similar polarity of meaning in the verb *šûḇ* 'to return to God', 'repent' and 'to relapse into sin'.

'The dust' here is not merely the synonym of 'ground' (*'ereṣ*), as it often is, but the dust of Sheol.

šiḥēr, used in 24.5 of wild asses looking for their food, denotes anxious search or expectancy. It may be connected with *šaḥar* ('dawn'), hence may mean 'to seek early, or urgently', as, with God as object (Isa. 26.4; Hos. 5.15; Ps. 63.2 [EVV 1]; 78.34 [EVV 33]) and Wisdom (Prov. 1.28).

Job 8

Bildad's First Expostulation

The argument, mainly a sapiential controversy, in support of the theodicy, is arranged in seven strophes of three couplets (8.2-4, 5-7, 8-10, 11-13, 14 + 15 + 19, 16-18, 20-22), of which 8.11-13, 14, 15, 19, 16-18 are figures. The recognition of this arrangement suggests that v. 19 is displaced in MT from after v. 15, where with vv. 14-15 it forms a strophe (so Fohrer).

The first strophe (vv. 2-4), as often in the rejoinders of the friends of Job, is in the form of sapiential controversy. The second (vv. 5-7) has as a formal prototype the prophetic warning of the conditional nature of God's grace, which has its ultimate origin in the public address on the subject of blessings and curses in the context of the Covenant Sacrament at the meeting of the sacral confederacy (Deut. 28). The third strophe (vv. 8-10) asserts the principle of retribution in true sapiential tradition on the basis of traditional experience, and the fourth (vv. 11-13) sustains the theme of the failure of the wicked on the basis of a figure from nature (vv. 11-12), while the fifth (vv. 14, 15, 19) and sixth (vv. 16-18) strophes elaborate the theme by the figure of a spider's web and a blasted plant respectively. The last strophe (vv. 20-22) asserts the theodicy with regard both to the innocent and the wicked in antithesis in the tradition of wisdom literature, which has also a counterpart in the statement of faith in the Plaint of the Sufferer in the Psalms. This has a variation in the promise of relief (v. 21) and the threat of retribution of the wicked (v. 22), the former echoing the promise of relief (*šûḇ šᵉḇûṯ*) from the liturgy of a great public festival, voiced by the prophets, and the latter recalling the curse of the sufferer's adversaries as a token of the theodicy in the general context of the Plaint of the Sufferer, particularly in Pss. 35.8, 26; 40.14-15 (EVV 13-14); 58.6-9.

Bildad upholds the wisdom tradition in animadverting on Job's impatient and impassioned reaction to his misfortune (vv. 1-2), asserting the sapiential dogma of sin and retribution (vv. 3, 20), referring Job to the authority of ancient sages (vv. 9-10), and defending the justice of God (v. 3) against those who would deny it on the evidence of the apparent flourishing of the wicked who ignore God's grace on which they depend, citing the swift withering of the reeds cut from the marsh (vv. 11-13), their substantial and precarious support by the figure of the fragile spider's web (v. 14) and by the withering of a plant rooted among stones (vv. 16-18). He does not charge Job explicitly with his own sin as the cause of his suffering, though that is implied. But significantly he does not abandon belief in this causal connection, assuming the possibility of Job's suffering for the sins of his family (v. 4; cf. 1.5), though to be sure this is only a possibility. But, like Ezekiel (18.4; cf. Deut. 24.16), he advances from communal to personal responsibility (v. 6), and like Eliphaz (5.8) he counsels the sufferer to seek the mercy of the Almighty (v. 5), and like Eliphaz he presents the prospect of hope (vv. 6f., 21) The sapiential tenet of the theodicy in its negative and positive aspects is summarily stated in the concluding strophe (vv. 20f.; cf. Ps. 1).

Chapter 8

1. Then Bildad the Shuhite answered and said:

2. 'How long will you say these things,
And the words of your mouth be as a great bluster?
3. Does God pervert Justice,
Does the Almighty do violence[1] to what is right?
4. If your sons have offended
He has given them over into the power of their sin.

5. If *you* too look earnestly to God
And seek the mercy of the Almighty,
6. If *you* are pure and upright,
Then he will protect you,
And keep your righteous homestead intact.
7. Though your beginning has been insignificant
Your latter end shall be greatly abundant.[2]

8. Nay, but ask a former generation,
Apply yourself to the researches of their fathers,
9. For we are but of yesterday[3] and know nothing,
Our days on the earth are as[4] a shadow.
10. Will they not teach you, declaring to you,
And bring forth words from their minds?

11. Can papyrus grow without marsh,
Reeds abound without water?
12. If it is cut,[5] still fresh as it is,
It withers sooner than any grass.
13. Even so is the latter end[6] of all who forget God,
And the hope of the impious perishes.

14. His confidence is a cobweb,[7]
His trust a spider's dwelling.
15. He leans upon his house, and it does not stand fast,
He grasps it, but it does not stand firm.
19. Lo, this is the dissolution[8] of his way,
And from the dust another springs.[9]

16. He is as a fresh plant before (sc. struck by) the sun,
Its suckers spread over the yard where it grows;
17. Its roots entwine about the stone-heaps,
Taking hold between the stones.[10]
18. Suddenly[11] it is destroyed[12] from where it grew,
(Its place) will deny it, (saying), "I never saw you".

20. Indeed, God does not spurn the innocent,
Nor does he hold the hand of wicked men;
21. He will yet[13] fill[14] your mouth with laughter
And your lips with shouts of joy.
22. Those who hate you will be clothed with shame,
And the tent of the wicked will be no more.'

Textual Notes to Chapter 8

1. Reading *y^{e}'awwēh* for MT *y^{e}'awwēṯ* to obviate the repetition of the verb *'āwaṯ*. See Commentary *ad loc.*
2. Reading *tiśge'* for MT *yiśgeh*. See Commentary *ad loc.*
3. Reading *mitt^{e}môl* with T for MT *ṯ^{e}môl.*
4. Reading *ûḵ^{e}ṣēl* with S for MT *kî ṣēl.*
5. Reading *l^{e}yiqqāṭēp̄* (*l^{e}* enclitic with jussive) for MT *lō' yiqqāṭēp̄.*
6. Reading *'aḥ^{a}rîṯ* with LXX for MT *'or^{e}ḥôṯ.*
7. Reading *qiššurê qayiṭ* for MT *'^{a}šer yāqôṭ*. See Commentary *ad loc.*
8. Reading *m^{e}sôs* for MT *m^{e}śôś*; cf. LXX. See Commentary *ad loc.*
9. Reading *yiṣmāḥ* with LXX, S and one Heb. MS for MT *yiṣmāḥû.*
10. Reading *bên '^{a}ḇānîm* with one Heb. MS.
11. Reading *piṯ'ōm, metri causa* for MT *'im.*
12. Reading the passive imperfect energic *y^{e}ḇull^{e}'ennā* for MT active.
13. Reading *'ôḏ* for MT *'aḏ.*
14. Reading *y^{e}mallē'* with certain Heb. MSS for MT *y^{e}mallēh.*

Commentary on Chapter 8

1. On Shuhite, see above, p. 136.

2. *millēl*, attested in the OT only here and in 33.3; Gen 21.7 (J); Ps. 106.2, is generally taken as an Aramaism. The incidence in Gen. 21.7 might seem to modify that assumption, but that might be an old Aramaism; cf. local features in N. Israelite sources in the Elisha narratives in Kings (J. Gray 1963: 417f.).

The ambiguity of *rûaḥ* is to be noted, meaning 'wind' and 'spirit'; cf. *diḇ^{e}rê rûaḥ* in 16.3.

kabbîr, 'mighty', is confined to Heb. poetry, but is commonly attested in Aram. and Arab., though it has a Phoenician cognate, which may go back to an earlier Canaanite root, so far unattested in the Ras Shamra texts.

3. It is unlikely that a poet such as the author of the Book of Job should have repeated the verb *'awwēṯ* in two parallel cola, and LXX, V and T indicate two

different verbs. The phrase *'awwēṯ mišpāṭ* recurs at 34.12, and the verb is generally found in later passages (e.g. Ps. 119.78 and Eccl. 1.15; 7.13; 12.3), though appearing somewhat earlier in Lam. 3.36 and even in Amos 5. It is likely that MT *'awwēṯ* in v. 3b should be emended to *yᵉ'awwēh* ('do violence to'), possibly cognate with Arab. *'āha ya'ūh*, meaning in the II form 'to bring calamity upon'.

4. Formally *wayᵉšallᵉḥēm* might belong to the protasis of the conditional sentence introduced by v. 4a, in which case vv. 5-7 would be the apodosis, itself containing a condition in vv. 5 and 6a. But we prefer to take the verb introduced by *waw* consecutive as apodosis, concluding the first strophe (cf. Gen. 43.9). In any case the distinction is made between communal and personal responsibility (cf. Deut. 24.16; Ezek. 18.20), which is indicated by the repeated *'attāh* in vv. 5f. Formally, however, *wayyᵉšallᵉḥēm* might continue the protasis in v. 4 before the apodosis in vv. 5-6, itself containing the condition of Job's innocence and plea for mercy (vv. 5-6). In this case Bildad would not have quite rid himself of the conception of the involvement of the innocent man in the sin of his family, though admitting, through upright conduct and conscious dependence on the grace of God, personal emancipation.

5. On the verb *šiḥēr* see above on 7.21.

6. On the incidence of *yāšār* (and *tām*) in wisdom literature see above on 1.1. The adjective *zaḵ* is relatively rare in the OT, where it is usually used in the physical sense 'refined', for example the oil for the lamps of the sanctuary (Exod. 27.20; Lev. 24.2) and the incense in the Tent of Meeting (Exod. 30.34; Lev. 24.7). With a moral connotation it is confined to Job 8.6; 11.4; 16.15; 33.9; Prov. 16.2; 20.11; 21.8, all in wisdom literature.

The verb *hiṯḥannēn* is used of supplication in extreme distress or difficulty, as when Joseph pleads for his life with his brothers (Gen. 42.21), Ahaziah's officer before Elijah (2 Kgs 1.13), and Esther before Ahasuerus (Est. 4.8; 8.3), and less urgently in Solomon's prayer at the dedication of the Temple (1 Kgs 8.59).

6. The collocation of *yā'îr* and *šillam* suggests the formula of greeting in letters from Ras Shamra: *'ilm tġrk tšlmk* ('May the gods protect you and keep you safe!', *PRU* II.9; Gordon *UT* 95; 101; 117; 138; cf. Eissfeldt 1960: 41), but cf. LXX, 'he will listen to your prayer', indicating a reading *kî yē'āṯēr lᵉḵā* ('He will hear your prayer'). The tricolon among bicola has suggested to Bickell, Ball, Dhorme, Hölscher, Horst and Fohrer that one of the cola (v. 6a) is a gloss, or that a colon has been omitted after v. 6c (so Stevenson, Tur-Sinai, Mowinckel). The Ras Shamra poems, however, have familiarized us with the occasional tricolon for punctuation or to vary the monotony of the prevailing bicola, and MT here may well be retained.

7. *waw* with the perfect in *w^e^hāyāh* expresses the protasis in a conditional or concessive sentence, for example, in Gen. 44.22 (GKC, §150g).

śāgāh is a variant of *śāgā'* ('to grow tall, be exalted'), as in v. 11, for example, of a palm tree (Ps. 92.13). The verb should be extended to *tiśge'* or *tiśgeh* in agreement with the subject *'aḥ^a^rîṯ^e^ḵā*.

8. *kônēn*, understanding *lēḇ* ('heart', sc. 'understanding') in the sense of 'fix your attention on', has been thought to be a corruption of the more common *bônēn* ('understand'), but cf. Isa. 51.13.

9. On the text, see textual note.

10. The third masculine plural personal pronoun refers back to 'fathers' in v. 8, alluding to their utterances. This is taken by some commentators as a secondary expansion. The verb *yō'm^e^rû* is weak, and LXX suggests *w^e^yaggîḏû*, which is to be preferred as expressing attendant circumstances.

11. This couplet is doubtless the citation of a popular proverb, perhaps a saying of the ancients mentioned in v. 8, which asserted the principle of cause and effect like the proverbs in Amos 3.3-5. It is not certain, however, that this was the sense in which it was used by the author here, emphasizing the collapse of the wicked who fail to appreciate that their prosperity depended on the sustaining grace of the God they reject.

gā'āh here means 'to grow tall', with the connotation of flourishing (cf. 10.16, of the head) and of God in Exod. 15.1, 21. *gōme'* is used of reeds in the Nile delta (Exod. 2.3) and of reed skiffs of the Nile (Isa. 18.2). It is an Egyptian loanword *kmꜣ*, denoting papyrus, the tallest of reeds, reaching a height of 6 feet. *'āḥu* is also an Egyptian loanword derived from *ꜣ ḫꜣḫ* ('to be green'). It was known to the Ugaritic poets as a feature of the Huleh marshes, *'aḫ smk* in N. Palestine (Gordon *UT* 76.II.9, 12). It was evidently a smaller plant than *gōme'*, as it was grazed by the cows in Joseph's dream (Gen. 42.2, 18).

12. *'ēḇ* is found in the OT only here and in Song 6.11. The word is a cognate of Akk. *ebbu* ('flourish') and Ugaritic *'ib* (Gordon *UT* 1 Aqht 30), meaning 'verdure'; cf. the parallel here, *ḥāṣîr*, 'herbs of pasture', and Arab. *ḫuḍratu*(*n*), lit. 'greens'.

On the reading, *l^e^yiqqāṭēp*, where the emphatic enclitic *l^e^* has been taken by the Masoretes for the negative *lō'*, see textual note; cf. 29.24, *'esḥaq '^a^lēhem lō' ya'^a^mînû*, where the negative contradicts the sense and must therefore be read as the enclitic *le*, 'I smiled at them; they indeed gained confidence'. In 8.12 we take the verb as the jussive in the protasis of a conditional sentence (GKC, §109h, i).

13. On the reading *'aḥ^a^rîṯ*, suggested by LXX, for MT *'or^e^ḥôṯ*, see textual note. This is read by most commentators, but S and V support MT, which is read by Horst. The sense of LXX is supported by v. 12.

The parallel with 'those who forget God' indicates that *ḥānēp̄* may be derived from a verb cognate with Arab. *ḫanafa* ('to turn back, repudiate'). The verb is known to denote a godless, impious act in Jer. 3.1; Ps. 106.38; Isa. 10.6; etc., and is known in Ugaritic in the phrase *ḫnp lb* of a reprobate (Gordon *UT* 3 Aqht rev. 17). A cognate in Syriac denotes 'pagans' most of whom to the Syrian church were Arabs, hence the word may have been used by Muhammad to distinguish Muslims who claimed spiritual descent from Abraham and Ishmael, whom Muhammad declared as the first of the *ḥunafā'u*. The initial guttural *ḥ* will be noticed as distinct from *ḫ* of the cognate we propose for the Hebrew word. It must be remembered, however, that Arab. *ḥunafā'u* in the Qur'an is a loanword from Syriac.

14. If this verb is original, which is denied by Stevenson, MT *yāqûṭ* is either an intransitive verb, either an Aram. form of Heb. *qûṣ*, a byform of *qāṣaṣ* ('to cut off'; cf. Arab *qaṭṭa*, 'to cut off short'), as Weiser proposes, or, as is more likely in view of the figure in the second colon, a noun. Tur-Sinai proposed that *yāqûṭ* is a cognate of Arab. *wāqîṭ* ('a depression where water gathers'), so a puddle quickly evaporating, but this is not a good parallel to the spider's web in v. 14b. Duhm proposed *qûrîm* ('spider's webs') after Isa. 59.5ff.; Budde, wishing to retain *qṭ* of MT, read *qûrê qayiṭ* ('spider's webs in summer'), taking *qayiṭ* as the Aram. form of Heb. *qayiṣ*. Nearer MT is Peters's reading *qiššurê qayiṭ* for MT *'^a^šer yāqûṭ*, meaning 'summer bands'; cf. *Sommerfaden* and Saadya's Arab. *ḥablu's š-šamśi* ('sun cord'); so Hölscher, Horst, Fohrer. For the general sentiment, cf. Qur'an, Surah 29.40 ('The Spider', *'al-'ankabût*; cf. Heb. *'akkāḇîš*), quoted by Driver–Gray, who compare the faith of polytheists to a spider's web for frailty; cf. 27.18; Isa. 59.5.

15. If this is original and not, as Budde and Hölscher maintained, a gloss on v. 14b, *bêṯô* may signify 'his family' rather than 'his house'.

19. The figure of a plant in vv. 16-18 is elaborated in a self-contained strophe. The figure of the spider's web, like the others in vv. 11-12 and 16-18, is best rounded off by a general truth pointing the comparison with the fate of the wicked; hence it probably ends with the displaced v. 19.

MT *m^e^śôś*, 'joy' (so V, T and Bickell, Peake, Driver–Gray), if correct, would be ironical. The more natural sense is 'destruction', as suggested by LXX, which indicates the reading *m^e^šô'āh*, or perhaps 'dissolution' (*m^e^sôs*) (Beer, Hölscher, Horst). More particularly Dhorme suggests that MT may mean 'eaten with maggots', the root *śûś* or *sûs* being cognate with Arab. *śāśa* ('to be eaten with maggots'), which has an Akk. cognate.

For MT *yiṣmāḥû*, for which one Heb. MS reads the singular (so LXX and S), the singular should probably be read. The plural of MT is barely admissible on the understanding that the subject *'aḥēr* is a collective singular; cf. Ezek 28.3, where, however, the text is suspect. In cases of the collective singular with plural verb cited in GKC, §145d the nouns other than in Job 8.19 and Ezek. 28.3 are categories naturally understood as collective singulars.

16. The abrupt change of figure indicates a new strophe. *lip*ᵉ*nê* here mean 'exposed to' rather than 'before the sun' (sc. sunrise). Either sense is comprehensible. The verbal root *rāṭaḇ* is found meaning 'to be wet' in 24.8, but the Arab. cognate means 'to be fresh', e.g. ripe dates.

In this passage there has been much difference of opinion. We would emphasize the reference to the hold (*yeḥ*ᵉ*zeh*) of the plant's roots on stones (*'*ᵃ*ḇānîm*) or 'stone-heap' (*gal*), as in Gen. 31.46, 48, 51, 52; Josh. 7.26; 8.29; 2 Sam 18.17. We propose that *gannô* refers not to 'garden', but enclosed 'yard', of the Oriental house, in which the plant has taken root ('its yarn'), where there would be no cultivated ground. The fortuitous growth is further suggested by the verb *y*ᵉ*subbāḵû*; cf. *sîrîm s*ᵉ*buḵîm* 'tangled thorns' (Nah. 1.10). *Mutatis mutandis* the figure might signify the same as the seed sown on stony ground in the parable. On this interpretation *lip*ᵉ*nê šemeš*, 'before the sun is up', as Dhorme proposed, is possible, though we admit the ambiguity of the phrase.

18. The conditional clause is suspect (so Stevenson), and the first two letters *aleph* and *mem* may be the fragment of *piṯ'ōm* ('suddenly'), which the meter would support. LXX^{A}, 'if one swallow it up', supports MT, but cf. Theod., S and V, 'overpowers', which seems to suggest the root *bā'al*. *bāla'*, however, is attested in the sense 'to overwhelm, or destroy', and may be the cognate of Arab. *balaġa*, 'to reach', with aggressive nuance. The verb is found in the Piel as here in parallelism with *hišḥîṯ* ('to destroy') in 2 Sam 20.19f.

The subject of *kiḥēš* ('to deny') is 'its place'.

21. On the text, see textual note.

Though the assertions of Bildad are the general statements of Wisdom, the opening couplet indicates that Job's questioning of the theodicy is in his mind. Even the hope that he holds out to Job (vv. 6f.) is conditional upon his sincere piety. Bildad's address abates nothing of the firm dogma of sin and retribution, virtue and reward, as emphasized by the *inclusio* in vv. 3, 20-22. In the final colon vv. 20-22 the parallel *śōn'eyḵā* // *r*ᵉ*šā'îm* alludes to the critics of the sufferer, who is assumed to have incurred the wrath of God, which they abet, for example, in Ps. 21.9 (EVV 8). More particularly, both negative and positive aspects of the theodicy are emphasized, as in the assurances at the end of the Plaint of the Sufferer as the person falsely accused, namely the final encouraging oracle (v. 21; cf. Ps. 142.8 [EVV 7]) and the condemnation of the sufferer's critics or opponents (20, 22), which may be amplified by a curse (e.g. Pss. 5.11ff. [EVV 9ff.]; 6.11 [EVV 10]; 141.8f. [EVV 7f.]).

Job 9 and 10

Job's Second Rejoinder

This is arranged in three parts: 9.1-24, on the theme of the transcendence of God; 9.25-35, Job's despairing allegation of God's inaccessibility; and 10.1-22, where Job accuses God of indifference to the sense and purpose of his own creation or of hostility, and anticipates his challenge to God to hear his case (ch. 31).

The passages 9.2-24 and 10.1-22 are composed each of five strophes of unequal length, 9.2-4, 5-10, 11-14, 15-21 and 22-24, and 10.1-2, 3-7, 8-12, 13-17 and 18-22, and the intervening section 9.25-35 of three strophes, 9.25-28, 29-31 and 32-35.

The statement is introduced in the style of controversy at law or in the Wisdom schools (9.2-4). Job then cites a Hymn of Praise on the subject of God's Omnipotence and transcendence, where his exploits and properties are characteristically introduced by participles (9.5-10).

This introduces the more particular statement in the dialectic of the Law-Court and Wisdom school on God's inaccessibility in moral issues (9.11-14), particularly in Job's individual case (9.15-21), which provokes the allegation of God's arbitrary disposition (9.22-24). Job's weakness by contrast is presented with the accumulation of sufferings in a series of figures in the literary convention of the Plaint of the Sufferer (9.25-28, 29-31), while 9.32-35 resumes the theme of the inaccessibility of God and anticipates Job's appeal for direct confrontation and hearing. The theme of an appeal for a hearing is continued in 10.1-2. Job objects to the indifference of God to humans as the object of His own creation and to the compulsive censoriousness which is more human than divine (10.3-7). The former theme in 10.3-7 is developed in the next strophe (10.8-12) and the latter in 10.13-17. The last strophe (10.18-22) resumes the theme of Job's opening statement (esp. 3.11ff.), where he questions God's purpose in creating and sustaining the life of a man destined to misery; and wishes for relief in the remainder of his life before the ultimate oblivion of death.

Chapter 9

1. Then Job answered, and said:

2. 'Truly I acknowledge that this is so.
Yea, how can mere man maintain his right against God?
3. If he pleased to contend with him
(A man) could not answer him one (charge) in a thousand.
4. Be he wise in heart or strong in might,
Who has stubbornly opposed him with impunity?

5. He it is who removes mountains and they are not left undisturbed,[1]
Who overturns them in his anger;
6. Who shakes the earth from its place,
And its pillars quake;
7. Who commands the sun and it does not shine,
And seals up the stars;
8. Who stretches out the heavens Himself
And treads on the back of Sea;
9. Who makes the Bear and Orion,[2]
And the Pleiades and the Chambers of the South;
10. Who does great things beyond investigation,
Yea, wonders beyond number.

11. Lo, he passes by me and I see Him[3] not,
Passes on[4] and I perceive Him not.
12. If he shatters, then who[5] shall restore?
Who can say to him, "What are you doing?"
13. A god could not turn back his anger,
Under him bow the champions of Rahab.
14. How much less then could I answer him
And choose my arguments with him?

15. Since, though in the right, I should not be answered;[6]
I should have to supplicate my opponent;[7]
16. If I were to cite him and he to answer me,
I have no confidence that he would really listen to what I have to say,
17. For he would buffet me with a tempest,
And redouble my blows without cause.
18. He does not let me recover my breath,
But he gives me my fill of bitterness.
19. If it be a matter of strength he is strongest;[8]
And if a matter of justice, who could hold him to an appointment[9]?
20. Though I were in the right, whatever I said would convict me;
Though innocent he would make me out perverse.
21. [10]I care not for myself;
Nay, I despise my existence.

22. "It is all one."[11] So I say,
Innocent and guilty he annihilates.

23. When the scourge slays suddenly,
He mocks at the despair of the innocent.
24. The land is given into the power of the wicked,
He covers the face of the judges therein.
[12]If not he, then who?

25. [13]My days are swifter than a courier;
They flee; I see no good.
26. They pass on like reed-ships,
Like a vulture swooping on its prey.
27. If I think,[14] "I will forget my trouble,
I will compose my features and smile",
28. I dread all my torments,
I know that you will not clear me.

29. Lo,[15] I will be found guilty.
Why then do I labour in vain?
30. Though I were to wash myself in[16] soapweed
And cleanse my hands with lye,
31. You would plunge me in filth,[17]
And my clothes would abhor me.

32. For he is not a man like myself that I could answer,
"Let us go to court together!"
33. Would that[18] there were an arbiter between us
To lay his hand on the two of us.
34. Let him put aside His rod from me,
And let His terror not appal me.
35. Then I should speak and not fear Him,
For have I not a[19] clean conscience?'

Textual Notes to Chapter 9

1. Reading *yuḏāʻû* (pausal) for MT *yāḏāʻû* (see Commentary *ad loc.*)
2. Reading *ûk̲^{e}sîl*, assuming the omission of *w* before *k* in the Old Heb. script.
3. Reading *'er'ēhû* for MT *'er'eh* with S and V.
4. Reading *yaḥ^{a}lōp̄* for MT *w^{e}yaḥ^{a}lōp̄* with two Heb. MSS.
5. Reading *ûmî* for MT *mî* with T and several Heb. MSS.
6. Reading *'ēʻāneh* with LXX, Theod. and S. See Commentary *ad loc.*
7. Conjecturing *l^{e}ḇaʻal mišpāṭî* for MT *lim^{e}šop̄^{e}ṭî*. See Commentary *ad loc.*
8. Reading *'ammîṣ hû'* for MT *'ammîṣ hinnēḥ.*
9. Reading *yôʻîḏennû* for MT *yôʻîḏēnî* after LXX and S.
10. Omitting *tām-'ānî* as a dittograph. See Commentary *ad loc.*
11. LXX omits *'aḥat̲ hî'* of MT which, however, is necessary to the meter, the couplet being 4:4.
12. Reading *'im-lô' hû' mî 'ēp̄ô'* for MT *'im-lō 'ēp̄ô' mî-hû'*, though this may be a gloss.
13. Omitting MT *w^{e}* as a dittograph before *y* in the last stage of the Heb. script before the final form of the square script.
14. Reading *'āmartî* for MT *'om^{e}rî* with LXX, T and one Heb. MS.
15. Reading *hēn 'ānōk̲î* for MT *'ānōk̲î, metri causa.*
16. Reading *b^{e}mô* for MT *b^{e}mēw.*

17. Reading *b^e^śuḥōṯ* (orthographic variant of *suḥōṯ*) for MT *b^e^šaḥaṯ*. See Commentary *ad loc.*
18. Reading *lû'* or *lû* with LXX, S and several Heb. MSS for MT *lō'*.
19. Perhaps reading *kî h^a^lō' ḵēn 'ānōḵî 'immāḏî* for MT *kî lō'-ḵēn...*, assuming the omission of *h* by haplography after *y* in the Old Heb. script. See Commentary *ad loc.*

Commentary on Chapter 9

2. In Job's argument *mah-yyiṣdaq 'e^nôš 'im-'ēl* should be taken in the sense, 'What shall a (mere) man adduce to maintain his right against God?', thus sustaining the legal idiom and understanding that Job is controversially adapting Bildad's thesis of the justice (*ṣeḏeq*) of God (8.3). Here, in view of Job's statement of the might, majesty and transcendence of God (vv. 5-14), the choice of *'enôš* emphasizes the weakness of humanity; cf. *'ānaš* in Isa. 17.11; Jer. 15.18; Ps. 69.21 (EVV 20); Job 34.6; with Ass. and Arab. cognates. The adversative force of *'im* and the forensic sense of *yiṣdaq* is supported by the phrase *lārîḇ 'immô* in v. 3.

3. *yaḥpōṣ*, as in 13.3; 21.14; 33.32; Deut. 25.7f.; 1 Kgs 9.1, means 'is pleased to', with the nuance of condescension as in Est. 6.5.The couplet is formally ambiguous. NEB renders 'If a man chooses to argue with him God will not answer him one question in a thousand'. This might be supported by God's long-deferred answer to Job's complaint and challenge in the Divine Declaration (38.1ff.) and by the fact that there God does not give the expected answer to Job's problem but a rebuke. If we take God as the subject of v. 3a, which the regular meaning of *yaḥpōṣ* ('choose, be pleased to') would suggest, condescending to the confrontation (*rîḇ*) for which Job longs, the inability of a human to answer 'one question in a thousand' might be instanced by the plethora of questions in the Divine Declaration which baffle Job. Under this consideration we prefer the latter interpretation.

4. *hiqšāh*, lit. 'to make hard', sc. *'ōrep̄* ('neck'), means 'to make difficulties' (Exod. 13.15).

5. Verses 5-14, on the subject of the transcendence of God in Creation and in the great catastrophes in nature, has, with the participles, the hall-mark of a Hymn of Praise to the Almighty. It is then not unapt to Job's complaint that God is beyond contention in a human's plea for justice (vv. 2-5, 15ff.), and, to be sure, the theme and style of the Hymn of Praise is used in the addresses of Job's three friends in support of their argument for the sovereignty of God in society (5.9ff., Eliphaz; 11.7ff., Zophar; 25.2, Bildad) and, more extensively, in the Elihu addendum (36.22ff.; 37.1ff.). The form may be used ironically by Job in his arguments against his friends. When that is said, however, formally and thematically it interrupts Job's argument in legal style in vv. 2-4, 15ff., so

that it may be a secondary insertion. Some such explanation is suggested by the fact that vv. 5-7 on the destructive activity of the Almighty, preceded the passage on the positive aspect of His creation in vv. 8-10, which Fohrer (p. 205) takes as possibly two separate fragments of Hymns of Praise. The passage certainly seems secondary, perhaps suggested by the original in vv. 11-14 and particularly v. 12, 'If he shatters then who shall restore?', which may have been elaborated in vv. 5-7, and the passage on God's power over Rahab, the force of chaos *par excellence* in v. 13, which may have been elaborated in vv. 8-10. Alternatively, in pursuance of the theme of the transcendence of God in vv. 2-4, the author may have used a hymn of praise (vv. 8-10); cf. Psalm 104 and the doxologies in Amos 4.13, 5.8f.; 9f., and 5-7 in that order, which was subsequently reversed by a redactor through motives of reverence, like the orthodox conclusion to Ecclesiastes (12.13f.).

'āṯaq in Classical Hebrew means 'to move on' (intrans.) and in Arab. and Aram. 'to grow old'. It is found in the Qal in 14.18 and 16.4 and in the Hiphil as here of mountains being moved. The subject of *yāḏā'û* (pausal) is uncertain. If personal and indefinite, it might indicate the removal of the mountains beyond human powers of anticipation or detection of where they had once stood. The plural, however, suggests rather the subject *hārîm*. In that case as a complement to *he'ᵉṯîq* the verb may rather be cognate of Arab. *wada'a*, 'to leave', sc. undisturbed (as a horse given free rein), cited by W. Johnstone (1991: 54f.) from Lane on the basis of native Arab lexicographers.

hāp̄aḵ is used of drastic overturning, for example, the destruction of Sodom and Gomorrah (Amos 4.11) and similar catastrophes.

rāḡaz is used of earthquake in 1 Sam. 14.15, Amos 8.8 and Isa. 14.16, where it is parallel to *rā'aš*, the regular word for the quaking of the earth. The conception of the earth propped on pillars over the lower deep (*tᵉhôm*) is familiar in Ps. 75.4, where the pillars are said to be kept firm by God; cf. Job 26.11, where the sky also is propped by cosmic pillars. The verb *pālaṣ* occurs only here in the OT, though derivatives are found, e.g. *pallāṣûṯ*, 'shuddering' (Job 21.5; Isa. 21.4; Ezek. 7.18; Ps. 55.6), *mip̄leṣeṯ*, 'something to shudder at', Maacah's cult symbol, perhaps a scribal parody of *mip̄seleṯ*, 'a graven image' (1 Kgs 15.13), and *tip̄leṣeṯ*, 'horror' (Jer. 49.16).

ḥeres is a rare word, found in the OT only here and doubtfully at Judg. 14.18 and in the place-names Timnat-ḥeres in Judg. 2.9 (cf. Josh. 19.20, where the corruption *seraḥ* indicates the consciousness of the scribes that *ḥares* meant 'sun', with associations with a pagan nature-cult at the locality), and *har-ḥeres* (Judg. 1.35), with probably this association with sun-worship, and 'the Ascent of *ḥeres*' in Transjordan in Judg. 8.13.

'āmar in *hā'ōmēr* has probably the Arab. connotation 'to command'. The obscuration of the sun may be the result of eclipse or of the dust-laden sirocco, peculiarly the accompaniment of the theophany of Yahweh as the God of the desert mountain in Sinai.

8. In *nōṭēh šāmayim* the conception is that of stretching out the heavens as the web of a tent is pegged out by Bedouin and stretched on its poles, called in Arab. *'awāmid* (lit. 'pillars'); cf. the 'pillars' (*'ammûḏîm*) of the earth in v. 6b. The phrase 'stretches out the heavens himself' is reiterated with slight variation in Isa. 44.24.

For MT *yām* some Heb. MSS have *'āḇ* ('cloud'). In Heb. *bāmôṯ* means 'humps' usually of earth, such as grave-mounds, or literally 'backs' of humans or animals (Deut. 33.29). Here we should see a reminiscence of the triumph of Baal over the unruly waters in Canaanite mythology, the Canaanite version of the triumph of God over the powers of Chaos and His assumption of kingship which guarantees His Order in nature, which belonged to the liturgy of the autumn festival, and was adapted by Israel in Enthronement Psalms. The specific reference is to the victor setting his foot on the back of the prone enemy, and Marduk's treading upon 'the legs' of the vanquished Tiamat in the cosmic conflict in the Babylonian New Year myth may here be cited.

The image of God treading on the back of Sea or on the summit of the waves may recall the stele of Baal at Ras Shamra, where the god strides out over two registers of undulations, symbolizing perhaps his victory over the waters, now consigned to the sky and under the earth (Schaeffer 1939: pl. xxiii, fig. 2; J. Gray 1964: pl. 28, pp. 127ff., 230).

9. Compare the doxology on the subject of God's creation and ordering of the constellations in Amos 5.8, in support of his general theme of God's sustaining of the moral order, which the prophet understands in the context of His theophany as King and the whole related ideology of the autumn festival. Here it must be noted that LXX reverses the order of the constellations *'āš* and *k^{e}sîl* under the influence of 38.1-32 and Amos 5.8, where the first constellation to be named is *kîmāh*, then *k^{e}sîl*, 'the fool' (cf. 8.14; 31.24) or Orion, called by the Arabs 'the Giant' (*'al-Jabbār*). *'āš* is rendered in Arab. by Saadya as *banāt an-na'aš* ('Daughters of the Coffin'), which signified for the Arabs the Great and the Little Bears. 'The Chambers of the South' (*ḥaḏ^{e}rê ṯēmān*; cf. 37.9), the place from which the whirlwind comes, is rendered 'the intimate places of the South' in T. G.R. Driver (1956b) connects *ḥeḏer* with the root 'to encircle' (Ezek. 21.19) and sees a reference to *circulus Austrinus*.

kîmāh is rendered by LXX here and at 38.31 as 'Pleiades' and so by Sym. and T. In Amos 5.6, Sym. and Theod. render it by the same term. In the present passage Saadya renders it *ṯarîya*, lit. 'the wet' (constellation), i.e. the Pleides. The word is taken generally to signify a cluster of stars like a herd of camels (Arab. *kûmatu*[*n*]), but in 38.31 'Do you bind the bonds of *kîmāh*?' Dhorme proposes to see a word-play between 'bind' and the root *kâmu*, known in Ass. in the meaning ' to tie'; cf. *kimtu* ('family'). The Pleiades herald the season of cold weather and the vital winter rains in Palestine, and hence are a manifestation of God's positive Order.

10. In view of the limitations of humans vis-à-vis the might and method of the Creator (vv. 10f.) the worthy sufferer complains that he cannot expect vindication by the canons of human justice (vv. 11-22, 25-32). It seems to Job in his cumulative and unmitigated suffering that God is susceptible neither to justice or mercy (v. 15), and in mocking the sufferings of the innocent, encourages the abuse of human rights (v. 24), and sets a precedent for the rule of might over right. The wrath of God, from whom one might expect mercy if not justice (5.17ff.), is significantly emphasized in v. 13, being instanced in the vast destruction by God in his own Creation in what we regard as the obverse of the Hymn of Praise in vv. 8-10 and 5-7 in that order. The conclusion of Job's vehement statement of the indifference of God to good or evil in society (vv. 22-24) is tantamount to blasphemy, to which Job commits himself in full knowledge that it is a capital offence (v. 21).

12. The verb *ḥāṯap̄* occurs in the OT only here and in the nominal form *ḥeṯep̄* in Prov. 23.28, where it describes the objective of the lurking adulteress. Hence it is taken to mean 'prey', but that seems to assume a connection with Arab. *ḫaṭafa* ('to snatch'), which actually has a Heb. cognate *ḥāṭap̄* (Judg. 21.21; Ps. 10.9). In Job, however, the verb is not *ḥāṭap̄* but *ḥāṯap̄*. This suggests the Syr. cognate *ḥattēp̄* ('to break in pieces'); cf. Arab. *ḥatfu(n)* ('death, or 'dissolution'), and hence our translation 'he shatters. Who can then restore?' If the ending *-ennû* in MT *yᵉšîḇennû* is the pronominal suffix rather than the energic ending the sense would be 'Who could turn God back (from his purpose)?'

13. Verse 13b is a citation from the mythology of the conflict of Cosmos and Chaos from the liturgy of the autumn festival. The Mesopotamian myth relating to the spring New Year festival at Babylon celebrated the triumph of Marduk over Tiamat, the monster of the lower deep and its allies (*rêṣu*). *rahaḇ* is one of the monsters which menace God's Cosmos in the Psalms and Prophets in the OT, for example, Ps. 89.10f. (EVV 9f.), where, as in Job 26.12, it is parallel to Sea (*yām*), Isa. 51.9, where it is parallel to *tannîn* in the same connection, and Isa. 30.7, where it is used figuratively for Babylon and Egypt respectively, the historical expression of the forces of Chaos. The fact that among the other enemies of Cosmos in the Ras Shamra texts *rahaḇ* is not named may indicate that it was an appellation of Sea, the arch-enemy of Order in Canaanite and Hebrew, meaning 'the Agitated One'; cf. Aram. *rᵉhaḇ* ('to be agitated'), with Syr. and Arab. cognates meaning 'to tremble', usually through fear, and Akk. *ra'ābu* ('to be irritated'). 'The allies of Rahab' indicates familiarity with the Mesopotamian myth *Enuma elish* from the liturgy of the Babylonian New Year festival, where Tiamat created as allies the hydra, the red dragon, the *laḫamu*, the great lion, the wolf with the foaming mouth, the scorpion man, raging tempests, the fish man, the horned goat and others.

15. On the readings *'ē'āneh* and *ba'al mišpāṭ*, with forensic connotations like vv. 2-4, see textual note.

16. Job declares that if God did deign to answer He would do so on his own terms without particular reference to his questions. This is what actually happens in the Divine Declaration in 38.2–40.14. Note again the technical terms of a law-suit, *qārā'* ('to cite') and *'ānāh* ('to respond').

17. The root *šûp̄* is well attested in Heb. (e.g. Gen. 3.5) and in Aram., meaning 'to beat, bruise'. *śe'ārāh*, if correct, must be an orthographic variant of *se'ārāh*; cf. Nah. 1.3, where 'the way of Yahweh is in the whirlwind (*sûp̄āh*) and storm (*śe'ārāh*)', the demonstration of the wrath of God in natural catastrophes. In the present passage there may be an allusion to Bildad's reference to Job's vehement protest as 'a great bluster', 'mighty wind' (8.2). NEB renders *biśe'ārāh* as 'for a trifle' (lit. 'for a single hair') which might be supported by 'without cause' (*ḥinnām*) in the parallel colon.

19. On the reading *yô'îḏennû* see textual note. The verb means 'hold him to an appointment', or 'confrontation'; cf. 24.1.

20. 'My mouth' (*pî*) means 'my speech', or 'whatever I said', and is the subject of *yaršî'ēnî* ('would convict me'), though probably not of *wayya'qešēnî* ('would make me out perverse') in v. 20b. Job's statement in v. 3b 'though innocent He would make me out perverse' is his retort to Bildad's rhetorical question, 'Does the Almighty pervert the right (*ṣeḏeq*)?' (8.3).

21. MT *tām-'anî* may be repeated from v. 20b by scribal error; the second colon, moreover, is short of a beat, so Hölscher and Horst propose to insert *ṣādaqtî* or *ṣaddîq 'anî* ('I am right'). We propose that *kî* with the adversative sense is omitted by haplography after *-šî* in *nap̄šî* in the Old Heb. script, restoring the text:

lō' 'ēḏa' nap̄šî	I care not for myself;
kî 'em'as ḥayyāy	Nay, I despise my existence.

yāḏa' meaning 'to care for, to take special note of' is attested in Gen. 39.6; Deut. 33.9; Amos 3.2; Ps. 31.8 (EVV 7).

22. *'al-kēn* indicates that in his desperate case, with nothing to lose, Job will dare to assert that God deals indiscriminately with the good and the bad. The phrase is omitted by Duhm as a gloss (so also Stevenson).

23. *šôṭ* means 'lash'; cf. Arab. *śawṭu(n)*, hence Latin 'plague'. Beer suspected this reading and suggested *šiḇṭô* ('his rod') after S, denoting the ruler's sceptre, which signalled life or death; cf. Est. 5.2.

massat̲ may be derived from *nāsāh* ('to try') or from *māsas* ('to melt' or 'be destroyed'). The parallelism indicates the latter. The Niphal of *māsas* is used with the subject 'heart' denoting despair (e.g. Josh. 2.11).

24. On the text of v. 24c, *s*ᵉ*b̲îr*, see textual note.

26. *'im*, 'with' or, as regularly in Ugaritic and occasionally in Heb. 'against', is used of comparison occasionally in Ugaritic (e.g. Gordon *UT* 49.I.23) and in Classical Heb. (e.g. 37.18; 40.15; Pss. 73.5; 106.6).

'ēb̲eh, *hapax legomenon* in the OT, has an Ass. cognate *abu*, denoting 'papyrus', which is supported by *k*ᵉ*lê gōme'* ('vessels of papyrus') in Isa. 18.2. The speed of the craft suggests skiffs in the Nile current rather than 'ships', though sailing ships of bundles of papyrus reeds are attested in Egyptian sculpture and painting and by Thor Heyerdahl's experiment with the Ra.

nešer is either the vulture or the eagle, like Arab. *niśru*(*n*).

ṭûš is a *hapax legomenon* in the OT, but is found in Late Heb., Aram. and Syr. *ṭûs* ('to fly'), of which it may be a dialectic variant. The reference may be either to the deceptively swift gliding flight of the eagle or vulture, or its coming immediately from the incredible distance from which it spies carrion.

27. On the reading *'āmartî*, here 'I think', see textual note.

If *'e'ez*ᵉ*b̲āh pānay* formally might mean 'will leave (off) my (sad) face', the reference would be to scowling; cf. Cain's scowling brows in Gen. 4.6. But the verb may be a homonym, meaning 'to prepare', here in the sense 'compose', e.g. Neh. 3.8, with a cognate in Ugaritic *'db* (so Dahood 1959: 303-309). It may alternatively be an unknown Classical Heb. word meaning 'to sweeten' cognate with Arab. *'ad̲uba*, used in this sense in the IV form, the phrase thus meaning 'I put on a cheerful countenance' (so G.R. Driver 1955: 76), which would also be feasible in the context.

bālaḡ (cf. 10.20) is cognate with Arab. *balaja*, of faces 'beaming' on acquittal in the Qu'ran; cf. Ps. 39.14.

28. *gûr* is a strong verb meaning 'to fear, be in terror of' (transitive); cf. 3.25.

29. On the reading *hēn 'ānôk̲î* see textual note.

'eršā' is used in the forensic sense, 'I am guilty', and not in the moral sense, 'I am wicked'.

30. *šeleḡ*, which normally means 'snow', so understood by S and T, cf. Qere *b*ᵉ*mê šeleḡ* ('in snow water'), probably means rather 'soap-weed', Akk. *aslaku*, Mishnaic Heb. *'ešlaḡ* (Preuss 1923: 431; Löw 1924: I, 648f.). *bôr*, from the root *bārar* ('to be pure') is here a substance known as cleansel in Isa. 1.25 (cf. *bôrît̲* in Jer. 2.22), which was made from the ashes of certain plants, possibly mixed with olive oil, which was known in Mesopotamia c. 2000 BCE

(so Dhorme [1910: 111], citing Thureau-Dangin). Mowinckel (1955: 311) proposes that there is a reference to a rite of exculpation; cf. Deut. 21.6; Ps. 26.6; 73.13; MT 27.24; but in such a context as the present the language is figurative.

31. On the reading *b^eśuḥôṯ*, preferred to MT *baššaḥaṯ* ('in the pit') by Hoffmann, Beer, Duhm, Ehrlich, Dhorme, Hölscher, Stevenson, Horst and Fohrer after LXX, see textual note. The word may be an orthographic variant of *sûḥāh* ('offal') in Isa. 5.25.

33. MT *lō' yēš* is suspect, 'there is not' being normally expressed by *'ayin*; hence with LXX, S and many Heb. MSS and most commentators. *lû* ('would that') may be read. MT, however, is retained by V, T, Dhorme, Hölscher, Weiser, Horst and Fohrer.

môḵîaḥ denotes normally a judge, who gives an impartial verdict strictly according to the norm of justice, with the implication of reproof and punishment of the guilty party. Here it denotes an arbiter. Strahan (1914: 102) sees here 'an unconscious prophecy of incarnation and atonement', where he does well to qualify his statement by 'unconscious'.

35. MT *kî lō'-ḵēn 'ānōḵî 'immāḏî* has never been satisfactory to commentators, though it was evidently unquestioned in the ancient versions. Dhorme proposed to transpose the two cola, reading,

> Since it is not thus (sc. since there is no arbiter)
> I will reason with myself and not fear,

transposing *'ānōḵî 'immāḏî* from the end of v. 35b to the beginning of v. 35a, which upsets the meter. Fohrer retains MT, but assumes that *'ānōḵî* is a doctrinal adjustment of an original *hû'* (1989: 200), 'For he does not deal rightly with me'. A simple explanation would be to assume the scribal omission of an original interrogative *h* after *y* in *kî* in the Old Heb. script, and to take *kēn*, as Fohrer does, as an adjective 'true'; cf. Gen. 42.11, 19, 31, 33, 34; Exod. 10.29; 2 Kgs 7.9; etc.; thus we should read *kî h^alō' ḵēn 'ānōḵî 'immāḏî* ('For am I not true with myself?', i.e. 'Have I not a clear conscience?').

Chapter 10
Job's Second Rejoinder (Continued)

In utmost desperation, 'taking his life into his hand' in Heb. idiom (cf. 9.21), Job, confident of his innocence (10.7), presses his plea directly to God in 9.28-31, demanding the specific charges against him (v. 2b) though, before God transcendent he has no hope of an adequate hearing (9.3f.) as in human court guaranteed by an arbiter (9.33). Job's affliction before regular condemnation after a fair hearing is surely an abuse of God's marvellous, superhuman power

(10.16f.). Beyond human limitations (vv. 4f.), God might be expected to transcend justice in mercy, it may be implied, rather than acting like an over-zealous inquisitor (vv. 4-6), like the *śāṭān* of the Prologue, to which the passage may obliquely refer.

The detailed passage on the conception and birth of a mortal as a manifestation of God's creative activity (vv. 8-12), the object of God's 'visitation' (*pequḏāh*), here in the sense of God's special beneficence, may be taken as the application to the individual of the theme of the Hymn of Praise to the Creator of inanimate nature in 9.8-10, while His unrelenting and intensified affliction of a man like Job (10.8, 17) seems a similar application of the same theme in its negative aspect (9.5-7)—which might justify the view that the citation of the Hymn of Praise in 9.5-7 and 8-10 may be indeed from the author of the Book of Job adapted to suit his theme. The sufferings of the innocent in fact seem for Job to negate any positive purpose in God's creation of humanity (v. 3), while the withholding of mercy to the limited extent to which the worthy sufferer seeks it (v. 20) only sharpens his argument. In view of the limited prospect of the after-life in the Book of Job (vv. 21f.), beyond the interest or influence of God, the suffering of the blameless without relief or vindication seems to make nonsense of an honest person as 'the noblest work of God' (cf. vv. 18-22). If this is the end of the life of humans with their potential and will for good, like Job in happier times (ch. 29), Job may well re-echo the curse of the day of his birth (vv. 18f.; cf. ch. 3).

Chapter 10
Job's Second Rejoinder (Continued)

1. 'My inmost being loathes[1] my life;
I shall give free scope to my complaint,
2. I shall speak in my bitterness of soul,
I will say to God, "Do not condemn me".
Inform me of your case against me.

3. Do you like to oppress me,
that you spurn your own hands' labour?
(And shine on the purpose of the ungodly.)[2]
4. Have you eyes of flesh,
Do you see as man sees?
5. Are your days as the days of mankind?
Are your years as the years of a man,
6. That you subject my iniquity to your inquisition
And seek out my sin,
7. Though you know that I am not guilty,
and that there is none to deliver (me) from your hand?

8. Your hands have knit me together and finished me,
And after that[3] you have turned[4] and overwhelmed me.
9. Remember that it was of[5] clay you made me,

And back to dust you will return me.
10. Did you not pour me out like milk,
Curdling me like cheese,[6]
11. Clothing me with skin and flesh,
With a framework of bones and sinews?
12. You have invested me with life,[7]
And your special visitation has preserved the spirit within me.

13. But these things you laid up in your heart,
I know that this was your intention,
14. If I defaulted you would have me in custody,
And would not clear me of my sin;
15. If I were guilty, woe betide me!
Or if innocent, I may not lift my head,
[8](Sated with humiliation and filled[9] with affliction,
16. And if [my head] were raised up proudly you would hunt me like a lion
And renew your prodigious exploits against me.)[8]
17. Your renew your attack[10] against me,
And intensify your anger against me;
And you send in fresh forces[11] against me.

18. So why did you bring me forth from the womb?
Would that I had expired and eye had not seen me!
19. I should have been as if I had not existed,
Should have been carried from the womb to the grave.
20. Are not the days of my life[12] few?
Desist[13] from me that I may have a little cheer
21. Before I go, never to return,
To a land of darkness and gloom
22. A land of thick darkness [ ],[14]
The shining of which is as blackness.'

Textual Notes to Chapter 10

1. Reading *nāqaṭṭāh* for MT *nāqᵉṭāh*, from *qāṭaṭ*, possibly a byform of *qûṭ*.
2. Though an occasional tricolon is used in a predominant arrangement of bicola in Heb. and Ugaritic poetry, this is probably a later gloss.
3. Reading *'aḥar* with LXX and S for MT *yaḥaḏ*, *'* being corrupted to *y* in the Old Hebraic script and *r* to *d* at this or a later stage.
4. Reading *sabbôṯā* or the infinitive absolute *sāḇōḇ* for MT *sāḇîḇ*.
5. Reading *mēḥōmer* for MT *kaḥōmer* ('like clay'), assuming the corruption of *m* to *k* in the Old Hebraic script.
6. Reading *gᵉḇînāh* for MT *gᵉḇinnāh*.
7. Reading *ḥayyîm šattā 'immāḏî* for MT *ḥayyîm wāḥeseḏ 'āśîṯā 'immāḏî*, *metri causa*. See Commentary *ad loc*.
8. Probably to be omitted as a secondary expansion which impairs the argument.
9. MT *ûrᵉ'ēh* may be genuine, *rā'āh* being a byform of *rāwāh* ('to be sated'). See Commentary *ad loc*.
10. Reading *'eḏyᵉḵā* for MT *'ēḏeyḵā* ('your witnesses'). See Commentary *ad loc*.

11. Reading *wᵉtaḥᵃlîp̄ ṣᵉḇā'ōṯ 'immî* for MT *ḥᵃlîp̄ôṯ wᵉṣāḇā' 'immî*. See Commentary *ad loc.*
12. Reading *yᵉmê ḥeldî* for MT *yāmay yeḥdāl*. See Commentary *ad loc.*
13. Reading *šᵉḇōṯ* for MT *yᵉšîṯ*. See Commentary *ad loc.*
14. Omitting *kᵉmô 'ōpel ṣalmāweṯ* as a secondary expansion.

Commentary on Chapter 10

1. On the reading *nāqaṭṭāh* see textual note.

nep̄eš means 'life' or, as in Arab. 'very self', which is the meaning demanded here since 'my life' (*ḥayyay*) is the object.

'āzaḇ in the sense 'let go free', recurring in 20.13, recalls Exod. 23.5 (E) and the original ritual or legal phrase *'āṣûr wᵉ 'āzûḇ* ('restricted and free') in Deut. 32.36; 1 Kgs 14.20f.; 2 Kgs 9.18; 14.26. The Ugaritic cognate *'db* is used of releasing a hawk in the Ras Shamra Legend of Aqht (Gordon *UT* 3 Aqht 22f.).

3. *'āšaq*, which means commonly in the OT 'to oppress', gave offence to Jewish scribes as a divine activity, and the MT *kî-ṯa 'ᵃšōq* was read as 'that I am wicked' by Aq. and LXX in the texts they translated. The verb means also 'to act violently'. As the predicate of 'river' in 40.23, it is cited by Dhorme, assuming that it refers to the river in flood, *yᵉḡîa' kappeyḵā* (lit. 'toil of your hands') implies achievement with labour and pains as distinct from *ma 'ᵃśeh*, which signifies 'achievement'; cf. Isa. 41.4, *mî-p̄ā 'al wᵉ 'āśāh* ('Who wrought and achieved?'); cf. *'āśāh* used of creation in Ps. 95.6 and specifically of the creation of humanity in Ps. 119.73 and Genesis 1.

hôp̄îa' with God as subject describes His epiphany (Deut. 33.2) as effective ruler (*šōp̄ēṭ*) in Ps. 94.1; cf. Pss. 50.7; 80.2 (EVV 1). With the traditional implication of the vindication of God's people and the imposition of his Order it has peculiar point here in the case of Job, who thus rebukes God for intervening in support of those whom he should particularly have condemned. Here the noun *'ēṣāh* is ambiguous, meaning 'plan' or 'purpose' or, as in the Qumran Manual of Discipline, 'party'.

6. *biqqēš*, which usually means in Classical Heb. 'to seek', has here the meaning rather 'to examine' or 'inspect', with the nuance of inquisition.

lᵉ in *la 'ᵃwōnî* is probably the *nota accusativa*, as in Aram.

7. *'al* in this context means 'although, despite'.

Commentators have found no parallelism in this bicolon, and so Beer and Duhm propose to emend MT *wᵉ 'ên miyyāḏᵉḵā maṣṣîl* ('there is none to rescue me from your hand') to *wᵉ 'ên bᵉyāḏî mā 'al* ('there is no perfidy in my hand'), which is just graphically feasible though doubtful. Ehrlich sought to restore the parallelism he assumed by emending *'erša'* in v. 7a to *'ewwāšēa'*, which is graphically more feasible, reading *'al da'tᵉkā kî-lō' 'ewwāšēa'* ('Though you know that I cannot save myself'). But with Fohrer we should retain MT, taking the bicolon, admittedly and exceptionally not in the usual parallelism, in the whole context of Job's argument in the first strophe, particularly vv. 3ff., the point of which is that God was not bound to act as a human, punishing sin automatically, but had scope for mercy, even when persons might not be able to prove their innocence to his satisfaction. Job suggests that the mere fact that God had created humanity suggests a more positive purpose, which is belied by summary visitation. This is implied in v. 7b, which hints at the mercy of God since the sufferer has no other help.

8. *'āṣaḇ*, the preliminary of *'āśāh*, the finished work of creation of humanity (see above on v. 3), suggests a connection with *'ᵃṣabbîm* ('graven images'), and an Arab. cognate *'aḏaba* has been suggested (BDB); but Heb. *ṣ* does not correspond phonetically to Arab. *ḏ*, and so this etymology must be rejected. The correspondence is with Arab. *'aṣaba* and Syr. *'ᵉṣaḇ*, both used of a surgeon binding up a limb (so Ball and Koehler–Baumgartner). Hence we agree with Fohrer in his rendering 'you have knit me together', at which he arrived by the analogy of the creation of humans in v. 11 clothed with flesh in a (binding) framework of bones and sinews.

On the reading *'aḥar sabbôṯā* (or *sāḇôḇ*), see textual notes. Dhorme's suggestion, however, should be noted, that *sāḇîḇ* means 'utterly', citing 19.10.

9. On the reading *mēḥōmer* ('of clay') see textual note. For the conception of humans as moulded from clay, cf. 33.6; for *ḥōmer* ('clay') parallel to *'āp̄ār* in the constitution of humans, cf. 4.19, and for their return to the dust, cf. Gen. 3.19.

10. *gᵉḇinnāh* ('cheese') is not elsewhere attested in Classical Heb., but its cognates Aram. *guḇnā'* and Arab. *jubnu(n)* are well known.

The narrative imperfect in *tattîḵēnî* and *taqpî'ēnî*, with the force of the Greek aorist and the force and form of the Akk. preterite, is regularly used in the Ugaritic myths and legends.

11. *sōḵēḵ* ('constructing a framework') is used in the same connection in the Qal in Ps. 139.13.

12. The phrase *'āśāh ḥeseḏ 'im* ('to deal kindly with') is familiar, but *'āśāh ḥayyîm* is strange, and *ḥayyîm* is suspect; cf. the various proposals to emend. Beer's proposal, followed by G.B. Gray, to read *ḥēn* ('grace') for MT *ḥayyîm*, is the most feasible and is supported by the collocation of *ḥēn* and *ḥeseḏ* in Est. 2.17. MT is read by Dhorme, Stevenson, Hölscher and Horst. The meter demands one word fewer, however, and LXX 'you set' for MT *'āśîṯā* suggests the reading *šattā*, which would take *ḥayyîm* as the object. *ḥeseḏ* may then be

secondary, perhaps suggested by *'immāḏî*, involving the change of *šattā* to *'āśîṯā* (so Lindblom). Alternatively it is suggested that the compound phrase *ḥeseḏ 'āśîṯā 'immāḏî* should be retained and *ḥayyîm* taken in apposition to *ḥeseḏ* (so Dhorme and others). This leaves the difficulty of the overloaded colon.

p^e^quddāh means a visitation or special note taken here in kindness, though often in wrath and retribution.

The spirit in humans, preserved by God's special visitation (*p^e^quddāh*), is God's special gift which peculiarly gives humans affinity with God; cf. Isa. 31.5. See on 6.4.

13. *'im* denotes intimacy; cf. *'im l^e^ḇaḇ dāwiḏ* 'the purpose of David' (1 Kgs 8.17).

14. *šāmar* here is used not in the sense of protection, but of marking or detaining in custody.

15. *'al^e^lay* is probably interjectional, derived from a root *'ālal*, probably onomatopoeic, with an Arab. cognate, 'to moan' (in sickness). It occurs only here and at Mic. 7.1. The raising of the head may signify defiance (Judg. 8.28; Ps. 83.3), pardon (11.15) or relief, as here; cf. the Baal myth of Ras Shamra (Gordon *UT* 137.23, 27), where the gods lower their heads on their knees in discomfiture and raise them in relief. *r^e^'ēh '^o^nî* (cf. MT *'onyî*, with dittography of *y*) recalls Ben Sira 34.28, *yayin ništeh bā'ēṯ ûr^e^'î* ('wine drunk at the right time and to satiety'), in Prov. 23.31, *'al-tēre' yayin kî yiṯ'addām* ('do not drink wine to satiety when it is red'), and probably Prov. 31.4, where *r^e^'ēh* is parallel to *ś^e^ṯô* ('drinking') (Thomas 1962: 499f.); cf. Gordon *UT* 'nt I.12-15: *bk rb 'ẓm r'i*, 'a large goblet of mighty draught'. In the light of this evidence *r^e^'ēh* may well be genuine rather than *r^e^wēh* with the same meaning, which has been proposed.

16. 'And if my head exalted itself' is a paraphrase of MT *w^e^yiḡ'eh*, which the ancient versions read and paraphrased thus. Ball after S read *w^e^'eḡ'eh* ('and if I exalt myself'), assuming the scribal error of *y* for ', feasible in the Old Heb. script. *tiṯpallē'* is used ironically. The word implies the immediate effect of God's power without recourse to secondary causes for His own purpose and glory and beyond natural processes and human understanding. Terrien has well observed that this is an ironical reference to God's exploits as the theme of Hymns of Praise, as in Exod. 15.11 (cf. Ps. 77.15, and, with particular reference to the present passage, Isa. 29.14). The verb expresses the shocking effect of such activity.

17. *'eḏy^e^ḵā* ('your attack'), cognate with Arab. *'adiya* in the II and IV forms ('to be hostile'), is obviously to be read for MT *'ēḏeyḵā*, 'your witnesses' (so

Ehrlich, Dhorme, Stevenson, Steinmann, Pope). LXX reads a singular noun, but renders 'examination', thus seeming to support MT 'witnesses'. We read *w*^{e}*ṯaḥlîp̄ ṣ*^{e}*ḇā'ôṯ 'immî* for MT *ḥ*^{a}*lîp̄ôṯ w*^{e}*ṣāḇā' 'immî*, which, however, is possible assuming the omission of *w* before *ṣāḇā'* and understanding *ḥ*^{a}*lîp̄ôṯ* ('relays of forces') as the predicate of *t*^{e}*ḥaddēš* ('you renew'). *ḥ*^{a}*lîp̄āh* means a change of clothes (Judg. 14.12) or relief from duty (14.14). The emended text refers to the sending in successive waves of fresh troops; cf. Arab. *ḫalîfatu*(*n*) ('Khalif', 'successor'). Note the adversative sense of *'im*; cf. *nilḥam 'im* ('fight against').

18. *'egwa'*, like *'ehyeh* and *'ûbal* in v. 19, expresses a wish which should have been fulfilled at a fixed point of time in the past (GKC, §107n).

20. In v. 20a LXX, S and Jerome read 'the time of my life' which suggests the reading *y*^{e}*mê ḥeldî* to Wright, Bickell, Beer, Budde, Duhm, Ehrlich, G.B. Gray, Dhorme, Hölscher, D.W. Thomas and Fohrer for MT *yāmay yeḥdāl*. In v. 20b *yāšîṯ* is doubtful and various emendations have been proposed, e.g. *š*^{e} *'ēh* ('look away'), as Graetz, Beer, Ball, G.B. Gray, Hölscher, Fohrer, which has the support of LXX, 7.19 and Ps. 39.14, *hāša' mimmennî w*^{e} *'aḇlîḡāh*. Admirable as that may seem, we find it unlikely that such a distinctive letter as ' could have been corrupted to *y* in MT *yāšîṯ* at any stage of the development of the Heb. alphabet. Hence we prefer Lagarde's *š*^{e}*boṯ*, which is graphically feasible in the Old Heb. script.

22. This verse has been regarded as a series of glosses on 'a land of darkness and deepest gloom' (*'ereṣ ḥōšeḵ w*^{e}*ṣalmāweṯ*) in v. 21b (so Bickell, Beer, Duhm, Hölscher, Fohrer, who limits the glosses to MT *k*^{e}*mô 'ōp̄el ṣalmāwet*) (so Budde, Oort, Dhorme, Stevenson, Horst), reducing the couplet to the following:

> *'ereṣ 'êp̄āṯāh w*^{e}*lō' s*^{e}*ḏārîm*
> *wattōp̄a' k*^{e}*mô-'ōp̄el.*

'êp̄āṯāh may be noted as a rare form; cf. *'êp̄āh* (Amos 4.13).

s^{e}*ḏārîm*, if it is the plural of *sēḏer* in its usual sense of 'order', might indicate the ordered succession of day and night regulated by the sun; cf. Gen. 1.16-18 (P). LXX has suggested the reading *nāhār* (so Peters) or *s*^{e}*hārîm* ('celestial globes' [Beer]), which, however, is only attested in post-biblical Heb. G.R. Driver (1955: 76f.) is nearer the truth, following the clue of LXX, in suggesting that *s*^{e}*ḏārîm* is cognate with Arab. *sadira* ('to be dazzled'), taking *s*^{e}*ḏārîm* as 'beams of light'.

Job 11

ZOPHAR'S FIRST ADDRESS

Zophar's expostulation is arranged in six strophes which may be arranged according to their sense as vv. 2-4, Zophar's rebuke to Job's eloquence and moral confidence; vv. 5-6, 7-9, 10-12, the assertion of God's higher wisdom and human inadequacy; and vv. 13-16, 17-20, the assurance of God's grace on repentance.

In the first strophe the literary affinity is with the sapiential controversy; the second uses the diction of the controversy at law; the third states the transcendent wisdom of God in the style and diction of the Hymn of Praise; and the fourth is cast in the literary convention of the Wisdom Psalm on the theme of God's cognizance of human sin. In the second part of Zophar's address the fifth strophe directs an admonition particularly to Job, the literary affinity of which is the prophetic admonition and promise of blessing. The theme of blessing is sustained and elaborated in the last two strophes and, as a foil, the sapiential theme of the theodicy is asserted in the statement of the discomfiture of the wicked.

In asserting the transcendence of God (vv. 7-9), Zophar agrees with Job 9.11-16, 32; but, while Job deplores the inaccessibility of God in his desire for justice, Zophar urges that the same divine transcendence does not entitle one to dispute the sapiential doctrine of sin and retribution. Evil cannot escape God's notice though humans may not sufficiently consider their sin (v. 11), thus animadverting obliquely on Job's refusal to admit sin as the cause of his suffering. For the obtuseness of humanity in general and the mindless persons who ignore and dispute the tenets of Hebrew Wisdom he quotes what is possibly a proverb:

> An inane man will get sense
> As soon as a wild ass of the steppe may be trained as a donkey. (v. 12)

Thus Zophar urges the sapiential doctrine of retributive justice like Eliphaz and Bildad, but more brusquely and impersonally. Like them he asserts the positive as well as the negative aspect of the belief, with the prospect of blessing, which like Eliphaz he holds out to Job (vv. 16-19) conditional upon his ordering his mind (v. 13a), that is to display the traditional patience of the wise man who controls his passion (cf. *per contra* 5.2) and supplicate the mercy of God (13b; cf. 5.8ff. and 8.5-7). Characteristic of the more rigid Bildad and Zophar, the obverse of the blessing thus promised is the condign punishment of the wicked (20; cf. 8.22). The encouragement of all three friends is significantly lacking in the rest of the dialogue except, characteristically, in the last appeal of the more mature Eliphaz (22.21-28).

Chapter 11

1. Then Zophar the Naamathite answered and said:

2. 'Must the voluble talker[1] be answered?
Is a man right because he is glib?
3. Shall your babbling silence men,
And you scoff[2] and none reproach you?
4. "Yea", you say,[3] "my doctrine is pure",
And you are[4] clean in our eyes.

5. But would that God would speak,[5]
Might open His lips against you!
6. Yea, declare to you secrets of wisdom—
For his immediate activity[6] is related to its effect—
But be certain that God will question you[7] about your sins.

7. Can you find out the ultimate truth of God?
Can you reach the confines of the Almighty?
8. It is higher than the heavens.[8] What can you do?
Deeper than Sheol. What can you know?
9. Longer than the earth in measure,
And broader than the sea.

10. If He arrests and confines
And arraigns who shall answer Him?
11. For He knows false men
And sees evil, though men do not consider that.
12. For an inane man will get sense
As soon as a wild ass of the steppe be trained as a donkey.[9]

13. If you settled your mind
And spread out your hands to Him,
14. If evil be in your hand remove it,
Nor let wrong abide in your tent,[10]
15. Then you would lift up your face stainless,
And you would be firmly established with no fear.
16. In that case[11] you would forget trouble,
As water which has flowed away you will remember it.

17. Darkness[12] shall become as noontide,[13]
Thick gloom shall be as morning;
18. And you will be confident because there is hope,
And you will be protected,[14] lying down in security;
19. (And you shall lie down and none shall make you afraid;)[15]

And many shall court your favour;
But the eyes of the wicked shall fail;
20. They will lose the means of flight,
And their hope will be the expiration of breath.'

Textual Notes to Chapter 11

1. Reading *raḇ* for MT *rōḇ* with LXX, Sym., V and T. See Commentary *ad loc.*
2. Reading *w*^{e}*ṯil'aḡ* for MT *wattil'aḡ*.
3. Reading *w*^{e}*ṯō'mar* for MT *wattō'mer*.
4. Reading *hayîṯā* for MT *hayîṯî*, according to the sequel. See Commentary *ad loc.*
5. Reading *y*^{e}*ḏabbēr* for MT *dabbēr*, which is nevertheless possible.
6. Reading *p̄*^{e}*lā'āyw* for MT *kip̄layim*. See Commentary *ad loc.*
7. Reading *yiš'āl*^{e}*ḵā* for MT *yaššeh l*^{e}*ḵā*. See Commentary *ad loc.*
8. Reading *g*^{e}*ḇōhāh miššāmayim* with V for MT *gāḇ*^{e}*hê šāmayim*. See Commentary *ad loc.*
9. Taking *'ayir* as displaced from after *pere' 'āḏām* and reading *yillāmēḏ* for MT *yiwwālēḏ*.
10. Reading singular with several Heb. MSS for MT plural, but see Commentary *ad loc.*
11. Reading *'attāh* with S for MT *'attāh*.
12. Reading *hāleḵ* (pausal) for MT *hāleḏ*, as suggested by the parallelism. See Commentary *ad loc.*
13. Reading *k*^{e}*ṣoh*^{o}*rayim* for MT *miṣṣoh*^{o}*rayim*, assuming corruption of *k* to *m* in the Old Heb. script.
14. Reading *w*^{e}*ḥuppartā* for MT *w*^{e}*ḥāp̄artā*.
15. This colon is probably a secondary expansion after Isa. 17.2 and Zeph. 3.13.

Commentary on Chapter 11

2. On the reading *raḇ d*^{e}*ḇārim* for MT *rōḇ d*^{e}*ḇārîm* ('volubility') see textual note. The parallel *'îš ś*^{e}*p̄āṯayim* ('the glib one') (so Pope) indicates a personal subject.

3. *baddîm* means 'babbling', possibly signifying disarticulated or incoherent speech, if derived from Heb. *bāḏāḏ*, with an Arab. cognate meaning 'to be divided'; cf. 'babbling' in Isa. 16.6; Jer. 49.30.

4. For *liqḥî* S reads *leḵtî* ('my conduct'). *leqaḥ* is found outside Proverbs and Job only in Deut. 32.2 and Isa. 29.24, in both cases with associations of instruction in the formation of intelligence. In the present passage the sage projects his own person into the character of Job, and *leqaḥ* may therefore be admitted, probably contrasting with *baddîm*.

bar, lit. 'bright' (cf. Song 6.10), is now well illustrated from deeds of emancipation from the palace of Ras Shamra, which declare 'as the sun is clear (*br*) so shall X be clear'. Since Job's constant complaint is that God treats him as a condemned sinner, the sense cannot be as MT implies, that Job declares that he is right in God's eyes. Hence, as the sequel indicates, the text must be emended to read either *hāyîṯā ḇe'ênéyḵā* ('you were in your own eyes'), so Tur-Sinai, Pope, or, in direct speech like v. 4a, *hāyîṯî ḇe'ênay* ('I have been in my own eyes'), so Siegfried, Duhm, or *hāyîṯî ḇe'ênāwy* ('I have been in his eyes'), so Merx, Hölscher, Fohrer after LXX.

5. Though MT *dabbēr* might be admitted as the infin. constr., or verbal noun, as direct object of *yittēn*, *yedabbēr* should be read on the analogy of 6.8 and 14.13. The meter would demand perhaps the omission of *'elôah* or *we'ûlām*.

6. MT *kî-kip̄layim leṯûšiyyāh* was read by LXX and V and defended by Dhorme, who renders the colon, which he takes as parenthetical, 'For they are ambiguous to be understood'. *kip̄layim* means 'double' in Isa. 40.2, but this is quantitative, and the sense of 'ambiguous' is not attested. *tûšiyyāh* is parallel to 'wisdom' (*ḥoḵmāh*) and 'counsel' (*'eṣāh*) in Wisdom literature, and is so understood by Hölscher. But *ḥoḵmāh* and *'eṣāh* also denote respectively the foresight which envisages the implications and end of an action and the effective realization of one's plan; hence Fohrer renders *tûšiyyāh* ('Erfolg' and our 'effect' have the same implications). For MT *kip̄layim* Merx, Bickell, Hölscher, Horst and Fohrer suggest *kip̄elā'îm* ('as wonders'); cf. Budde, G.B. Gray, Buttenwieser and Stevenson, who omit *k* as a dittograph after *kî*, which we accept. We should press the significance of *pelā'îm* as manifestation of God's immediate activity to the realization of His purposes, discarding the complexity of secondary causes which enable humans to understand His activity. It is thus that God's wonders are secrets (*ta'alumôṯ*), and require the special revelation and explanation, which this verse promises.

What is stressed is that humans should not prejudge any case; it is the final effect (*tûšiyyāh*) that is really significant in God's immediate activity (*pelā'îm*). The imperative *da'* emphasizes the certainty of the following statement (GKC, §110i). MT of v. 6c, 'And know that God will make you forget part of your sins', is not in accord with the context, which emphasizes the automatic connection between sin and retribution and God's inexorable justice by the most censorious of Job's friends. Hence the following emendations should be seriously considered: *yešawweh leḵā ka'awōneḵā* ('adjusts [your punishment] to your fault'), so Budde, Bickell and Loisy after LXX, or *yiš'aleḵā mā'awōneḵā* ('will question you about your sin'), so Ehrlich, Dhorme, Sutcliffe (1949: 67), for which Dhorme cites Arab. *śa'ala 'an* ('to question about', lit. 'to question from').

7. Lévêque has well observed (p. 622) that *ḥēqer*, significantly occurring five times in the rest of the OT and seven times in Job, is a word of exceptional theological intensity, denoting not only search (Job 8.8), investigation (Job 5.9; 9.10), enquiry (Job 34.24) but also the inaccessible object of search (Isa. 40.28; Ps. 141.3), e.g. the bottom of the abyss (Job 38.16), the secrets of a king's heart (Prov. 25.3) and the ultimate motive of the Creator (Job 11.7).

The usage of the word in Isa. 40.28, Ps. 145.3 and Prov. 25.3 indicates the salutary sense of limitations acknowledged by Hebrew wisdom despite its earnest belief that the fulfilment of life depended upon the recognition of a Divine Order in nature and society of which it was possible to discern evidences and to which it was possible to adapt oneself.

māṣā' might mean, as usually, 'find', but as in Josh. 2.22, 1 Kgs 14.14, etc., it may also mean 'to reach' in the sense of 'overtake' or 'arrive at', as the Aram. cognate *m^eṭā'* (Dan. 7.13). The fondness of the author of Job for word-play indicates that in v. 7a it means 'find' and in v. 7b 'reach' as the locative preposition *'ad* indicates; cf. Arab. *maḍa(y)*, 'to pass right on', hence 'to penetrate to'.

taḵlîṯ from *kālāh* ('to be complete'), may mean 'perfection' (e.g. Ps. 139.22) or 'limit', as in 26.10; 28.3, where the verb *ḥāqar* governs *taḵlîṯ*.

8. For MT *goḇ^ehê šāmayim* LXX 'the heavens are high' indicates a reading *g^eḇōhîm šāmayim*, which may be a corruption of *g^eḇōhāh miššamayim* through the corruption of *h* to *y* in the Old Heb. script and the wrong division of consonants. This reading is supported by the comparison in the parallel colon.

9. *middāṯāh* should possibly be read for MT *middāh*.

10. In this verse MT *'im-yaḥ^alōp̄ w^eyasgîr w^eyaqhîl ûmî y^ešîḇennû* recalls 9.11b-12a, *w^eyaḥ^alōp̄ w^elō'-'āḇîn lô hēn yaḥṭōp̄ mî y^ešiḇennû*, and has been taken as a gloss after this passage (so Bickell, Beer, Duhm, Hölscher). We suggest that it is indeed an echo, but mindful of the fondness of the author for word-plays, we consider that he exploits certain homonyms, *ḥālap̄* as a synonym of *'āḇar*, as in 9.11, and *ḥālap̄* as the cognate of Arab. *ḫalafa*, the VIII form of which means 'to seize from behind', i.e. 'to arrest'. In *yaqhîl* the verb may be cognate with a Syr. root from which *qahlanayā'* ('litigious') is derived, and so may mean 'arraign'. Guillaume cites Arab. *qahala* ('to administer a severe reprimand').

In *y^ešîḇennû* the Hiphil of *šûḇ* ('to return') understands the object 'word', but as this is tantamount to the transitive verb 'to answer' it takes a personal direct object.

11. If MT *w^elō yiṯbônān* is accepted it has been suggested that the sense is that God knows the evil of humans immediately without having to consider the evidence narrowly (so G.B. Gray). Alternatively for the negative *lō'*, *lô* is suggested (cf. S), which omits the negative (so Reuss, Duhm, Dhorme, Hölscher, Kissane). Hölscher objects that *hiṯbônān* (reflexive) never takes *l^e* before the object, but this objection is invalid if *lô* is taken as an ethic dative, which seems to be implied in S. On the other hand the reference to 'an inane man' (*'îš nāḇûḇ*) in v. 12a suggests a word-play with *yiṯbônān* so that *lō' yiṯbônān* may mean 'one does not consider it', or, if the subject is *m^eṯê-šāw'* in

v. 11a, final *w* of an original *yiṯbônᵉnû* may be omitted by haplography before the initial *w* of the next word (so substantially Lindblom, Hertzberg, Szcygiel and Horst), 'they do not consider it'. Alternatively the meaning may be that God sees evil but permits no scrutiny of himself.

12. In *'îš nāḇûḇ yillāḇēḇ* Guillaume (1963: 111) has correctly noticed a word-play on *lēḇ*, meaning 'heart' and 'intelligence' in Heb. (cf. Arab. *'albāb* and *lubbu*[*n*], 'pith'), while *nāḇûḇ* has an Arab. cognate *'unbûb*, 'a hollow tube'; cf. *'inbb* used in the Baal myth of Ras Shamra of the shaft communicating between the earth and the remote home of the gods in Gordon *UT* 'nt IV.178 and 'nt pl. ix.II.4.

The phrase *pere' 'āḏām* must be taken as a compound phrase. Dhorme suggests that *'āḏām pere'* signifies that the subject has all the attributes of the species, and translates 'a proper onager'. Unfortunately he cannot cite evidence for this use of *'āḏām*. A more likely explanation is that of Dahood (1963a: 124f.) that *'āḏām* here and in *pere' 'āḏām* (the desert-dwelling Ishmael) in Gen. 16.12 means 'steppe'; cf. the better known Arab. *'adîmu*(*n*), which has this meaning, and cf. 36.28 *yir'ᵃpû 'ᵃlê 'āḏām rāḇ* (perhaps *rāḇîḇ*, 'They drip as showers on the steppe').

MT *yiwwālēḏ* is explained by Dhorme as 'becomes, assumes the nature of', citing Prov. 17.17, *bᵉḵol-'ēṯ 'ōhēḇ hārēa' wᵉ'āḥ lᵉṣārāh* (perhaps *lᵉṣār*) *yiwwālēḏ*, which he understands as 'A friend loves in every emergency but a brother becomes a rival' (cf. *ṣārāh*, 'a rival wife' in 1 Sam. 1.6, Arab. *ḍarratu*(*n*), but the meaning may rather be 'a brother is a born rival' (NEB). Fohrer reads *yillāmēḏ* for MT *yiwwālēḏ*, rendering 'and an onager stallion be trained'.

Though *'ayir* is masc., certainly in Gen. 32.16, there is no positive evidence that it meant specifically stallion, though that is likely. It denotes a mature riding animal, cf. Judg. 10.4; 12.14; Zech. 9.9 and the Ras Shamra texts Gordon *UT* 51.IV.4, 9, 1 Aqht 52, 57. The point is that the word signifies a domestic animal in contrast to the wild ass of the steppe. The original text of v. 12b may have read *kᵉ'ayir pere' 'āḏām yillāmēḏ*, assuming corruption of *k* to *w* in the Old Heb. script.

13. For MT *hᵃḵînôṯā* LXX reads *hᵃzîḵôṯā* ('you purified'). Dhorme retains MT, citing *hēḵîn lēḇ* in Ps. 78.8 and Ass. *kûn libbî*, 'faithfulness of heart'. The parallel in Ps. 78.8 suggests 'stability', hence our translation 'settle your mind'.

The spreading out of the hands (*kappîm*, lit. 'palms') denotes the conventional attitude of prayer in ancient Israel (Exod. 9.29, 33; 1 Kgs 8.22, 38).

15. The raising of the head signifies confidence as well as defiance (see above on 10.15) and also acquittal.

min in *mimmûm* is privative, thus 'stainless'.

mûsāq, lit. 'molten', e.g. of metal smelted from ore (28.2) and also 'set' (37.18), hence here 'firmly established'.

16. *'attāh* should probably be read for MT *'attāh*. See textual note (so Reiske, Merx, Siegfried, Hölscher, Weiser, Fohrer after S).

17. The parallel colon suggests that the initial *m* in *miṣṣohorayim* is scribal corruption of *k* in the Heb. script.

MT *ḥāleḏ* (pausal) has been thought to demand the pronominal suffix, so *ḥeldekā* is proposed (Duhm, Budde, G.B. Gray, Beer, Kissane after T). The parallelism supports Ehrlich's proposal that *ḥāleḵ* ('darkness') is to be read; cf. Arab. *ḥalika* ('to be very black').

MT *tā'upāh*, a verbal form from the root *'ûp̄* or *'îp̄* ('to be dark'), is rather to be pointed *te'upāh*, a verbal noun with preformative *t* (so S and T).

The usage of *qûm* meaning 'to become' is paralleled in Arab. *qāma yāqūm* ('to stand in place of').

18. For Ehrlich's reading *weḥuppartā* for MT *weḥāp̄artā* (so also Dhorme, Hölscher, Steinmann), cf. Arab. *ḥafara* ('to protect'). See textual note.

19. *weḥillû pāneyḵā* (lit. 'and they will sweeten your face') is borrowed from religious usage, where it may have originally denoted the anointing of some symbol of the divine presence (*pānîm*).

20. *mappaḥ-nep̄eš* means lit. 'the breathing out (root *nāp̄aḥ*) of the breath', i.e. expiring.

Job 12–14

Job's Statement

The first part of Job's statement (12.2–13.12), which is directed against his friends, consists of six strophes in the literary convention and idiom of sapiential controversy (12.2-3, 4-6; 13.1-3, 4-6, 7-9, 10-12). Into this direct argument of Job the passage 12.7-25 is inserted, probably the citation of a Wisdom poem[1] on the subject of natural knowledge of God's sovereignty in nature and history, where the cumulative activities of God are introduced by participles in vv. 17ff., a feature of the Hymn of Praise. The sapiential poet has adapted the Hymn, the subject being introduced in 12.7-8, 11-12, which, following Dhorme's arrangement, we take as the first strophe of the Wisdom psalm. In the context of the Book of Job the passage 12.7-25 serves to indicate Job's familiarity with the orthodox faith and morality which he criticizes. It has been suggested that it was a later interpolation (so Siegfried, Tur-Sinai, Gordis, Fohrer). But, whatever its origin, the emphasis on the negative aspect of the omnipotence of God reflects the mood of Job throughout the Dialogue and seems to us a strong argument for the adaptation of the poem, if not indeed the actual composition, by the author of the Book.

In the second part of his address (13.13-27) Job prepares to address his case directly to God (vv. 13-19), which he does in vv. 20-28. The figure and the dialectic of the contention at law characterizes this section, which may be divided into five strophes (vv. 13-15, 16-19, 20-22, 23-25, 26-27 + 14.5c).

In the third part (ch. 14) in eight strophes (14.1-2 + 13.28 + 14.3; 14.4-6, 7-9, 10-12, 13-14, 15-17, 18-19 + 14a, 20-22) Job deplores the brevity and misery of human life (14.1-2; 13.28) which he contrasts with a tree (14.7-9, 10-12) and in the second half he appeals to God to set a term to his suffering and eventually admit his appeal, but ends in a statement of despair. Here there is a mixture of juristic phraseology and figure and the arguments of the sapiential controversy, with analogies from natural phenomena reminiscent of Proverbs. In any case it is well adapted to Job's argument and is a striking elaboration of his statement in 7.6-10. Chapter 14 fittingly ends the first part of

1. Fohrer regards this passage as two Wisdom poems separate or in fusion, dividing the passage 12.7-11 and 12-25. Since both parts concern the sovereignty of God, even if with Dhorme we were to regard vv. 9-10 as displaced from before v. 13, it is not difficult to accept the unity of the passage.

the Dialogue, anticipating Job's direct appeal to God for vindication (cf. 16.13-22; 17.3), the statement of his sufferings, elaborated as in the Plaint of the Sufferer (16.7-17; 17.1-3, 4-16; 30.1-19, 26-31), with his final appeal in his great oath of purgation (31.5-32).

There is possibly some displacement of the text in chs. 13 and 14 as well as in 12.7-12.

Chapter 12

1. And Job answered and said:

2. 'Indeed you are the community,
And with you wisdom will die;
3. But I also have sense as you,
(I am not inferior to you)[1]
And who has not his share of the like?

4. I am one who is a laughing-stock to his neighbour,
As one who appealed to God and he tormented him.[2]
(The innocent and perfect man is a laughing-stock.)[3]
5. "We may despise calamity" is the thought of him who is at ease;
But[4] it is an urgent certainty for him whose foot slips.
6. The tents of brigands are at ease,
And those who trouble God enjoy security.
(Regarding him who had brought God into his power.)[5]

7. But ask the beasts[6]
And the birds of the sky that they may tell you,
8. Or the reptiles of the ground[7] that they may instruct you,[8]
Or the fish of the sea that they may tell you.
11. Does not the ear test words,
And the palate taste food?
12. Decrepitude is not the repository of wisdom,
Old age is not identical with understanding.

9. Who among all these does not know
That this is the effect of the power of Yahweh,
10. In whose hand is the life of all that lives,
And whose gift[10] is the spirit of all flesh?
13. With him is wisdom and might;
He has both purpose and insight.
14. If he destroys nothing can be rebuilt;
If he closes (the door) on a man it may not be opened;
15. If he restrains the waters they dry up;
And if he lets them go they overwhelm the land.

16. With him is strength and effective purpose;
To him relate the deluder and the deluded.
17. He makes delusions of the plans of counselors,[11]
Makes fools of rulers.

18. He unfastens the belt[12] of kings,
And fastens a loin-cloth on their loins;
19. He makes priests walk away barefoot,
And overturns established persons.

20. He deprives spokesmen of speech,
And takes away the discrimination of elders.
21. He pours contempt on princes,
And loosens the belt of the strong,
22. Revealing deep things from the darkness,
And bringing forth deepest gloom to light.

23. He makes peoples great and then destroys[13] them;
He spreads peoples[14] abroad and abandons them.[15]
24. He takes away the sense of the leaders of a people,[16]
And causes them to wander[17] in pathless deserts;
25. They grope in darkness with no light,
And stagger[18] like a drunkard.

Textual Notes to Chapter 12

1. This, which is not in LXX, is probably a gloss from 12.2.
2. Reading *way^{e}'annēhû* for MT *way'^{a}nēhû* ('and he answered him').
3. This also is wanting in LXX, and is probably a secondary expansion.
4. Assuming the omission of *w* after *m* and before *nāḵôn* in the Old Heb. script.
5. Probably to be omitted as a gloss.
6. Omitting MT *w^{e}ṯōrekkā* as a dittograph of *w^{e}ṯōrekkā* in v. 8a.
7. Reading *zōḥ^{a}lê 'āreṣ* for MT *śîaḥ lā'āreṣ*. See Commentary *ad loc.*
8. Reading *w^{e}yōrûḵā* for MT *w^{e}ṯōrekkā* in agreement with the plur. subject *zōḥ^{a}lê 'āreṣ*.
9. Reading *lō'*, emended from *lô*, the last word in v. 11, which must be transposed to v. 12 *metri causa*
10. Reading *'ôš* for MT *'îš*, assuming corruption of *w* to *y* in the stage of the development of the script represented by the Qumran MSS. See Commentary *ad loc.*
11. Reading *mil^{e}ḵê yô'^{a}ṣîm m^{e}šôlēl* for MT *môliḵ yô'^{a}ṣîm šôlāl*. See Commentary *ad loc.*
12. Reading *môsēr* for MT *mûsār*.
13. Reading *wî'abb^{e}ḏēm* for MT *way^{e}'abb^{e}ḏēm*.
14. Reading *l^{e}'ummîm* for MT *laggôyim*.
15. Reading *w^{e}yānîḥēm* for MT *wayyanḥēm*.
16. Omitting MT *hā'āreṣ*.
17. Reading *w^{e}yāṯ'ēm* for MT *wayyaṯ'ēm*.
18. Reading *w^{e}yittā'û* for MT *wayyaṯ'ēm*, taking *m* as dittograph of following *k* in the Old Heb. script.

Commentary on Chapter 12

2. In MT *'omnām kî 'attem-'ām* commentators have suspected the indefinite *'ām* and have suggested various emendations, e.g. *hā'ām* (Duhm, Weiser), 'with him', i.e. 'for him' (Loisy), *'^{a}rumîm*, 'cunning' (Beer), *yōḏ^{e}'îm*,

'knowing ones' (Steinmann, Horst), *hayyōḏᵉʻîm*, 'the knowing ones' (Klostermann, G.B. Gray, Ball, Hölscher, Stevenson) and *ʻam-ṭaʻam*, 'discriminating people' (Reiske, Horst). The ancient versions support *ʻām* or *hāʻām*, and the alliteration *ʻam…ʻimmāḵem* is probably intentional. If *ʻām* or *hāʻām* is to be read (so Dhorme, Tur-Sinai, Fohrer) the sense may be 'you comprise the tribe, or community, and its inherited traditions and experience', understanding *ʻam* in its Arabic sense. There is thus an emphasis laid on the traditional generalizing doctrine of the community against which Job cites his personal experience. The passage introduced by *ʼomnām* is keenly ironic.

In v. 2b Aq. and Sym. translate 'with you is perfection of wisdom', indicating a reading *tummaṯ*, or *tummôṯ*, *ḥoḵmāh* (so Tur-Sinai and J. Reider). This is feasible and deserves serious consideration.

3. *lēḇaḇ* denotes the heart as the seat of cognition (cf. 11.12), v. 2a probably alluding to Zophar's remark on the lack of sense in 'the inane man' in his reply to Job in 11.12.

Verse 2b is probably to be omitted as an inadvertent scribal repetition of 13.2b (so Merx, Siegfried, Beer, Duhm, G.B. Gray, Ball, Dhorme, Hölscher, Stevenson, Fohrer).

For the use of *nāp̄al* ('to abase onself'), cf. Est. 6.13.

4. Job's whole complaint is that he appeals to God and is not answered, so MT *wayyaʻᵃnēhû* ('and he answered him') may be pointed either *wᵉyaʻᵃnēhû*, 'that he might answer him' (so Reiske, Hoffmann, Oort, Hölscher, Stevenson, Horst) or *wayyᵉʻannēhû*, 'and he tormented him'. We would see a probable word-play between the expected answer (*ʻānāh*) and the actual response, torment (*ʻinnāh*). Fohrer retains MT.

5. *lappîḏ bûz* ('for calamity contempt') is probably a citation of the attitude, or thought (*ʻaštûṯ*) of 'him who is at ease' (*šaʼᵃnān*). *lᵉ* before *ʻaštûṯ* is explicable as the emphatic enclitic found before predicates in Arab. and Ugaritic.

nāḵôn, the Niphal participle of *kûn*, means 'certain' in Deut. 13.15; cf. 'fixed and prepared' (Prov. 19.29; 2 Chron. 8.16). The verb *māʻaḏ* ('to slip, totter') is attested only in Heb. poetry, e.g. 2 Sam. 22.37 // Pss. 18.37; 26.1; 37.31.

6. In MT as it stands v. 6c has a general reference to v. 6ab but the sing. verb and pronominal suffix in v. 6c indicates a different subject. Hölscher takes v. 6c as the second colon of a deficient bicolon 'Woe to him…whom God has brought into his hand'. Bickell, Siegfried, Beer, Ball, Fohrer regard it as a gloss on v. 6ab, meaning 'regarding him who has brought God into his power' either by magic (so Fohrer) or, as we prefer, having enlisted God secondarily to his material power, in agreement with Hab. 1.11: *zû ḵōḥô lēʼlōhô* ('whose own strength is his god').

8. For MT *śîaḥ lā'āreṣ* ('shrubs of the earth'), where *l^e* is questionable. *zōḥ^alê 'ereṣ* is proposed (Duhm, Beer, Dhorme, Stevenson, G.B. Gray, Mowinckel, Terrien), which is graphically more feasible than *ḥayyaṯ hā'āreṣ* (BH^3, adopted by Fohrer) or *š^elaḥ lā'āreṣ*, 'send to the earth' (Horst; cf. Pope's reading of MT 'speak to the earth'). In the context of the reference to beasts, birds and fish 'reptiles' (*zōḥ^alê 'ereṣ*) is most natural.

11-12. This passage, probably displaced in MT, concludes the sapiential introduction to the passage on the natural knowledge of the Sovereignty of God. The introductory strophe vv. 7-8, 11-12 emphasizes the significance of natural knowledge; each person has the ability to assess, reason and discriminate (v. 11), and this is not the monopoly of age (v. 12). On the transposition of *lô* from the end of v. 11 to the beginning of v. 12 and the emendation to *lō'*, see textual note. Alternatively Dhorme retains *lô* in v. 11 as an ethic dative and assumes the omission of *h^alō'* at the beginning of v. 12 by haplography after *h^alō'* at the beginning of v. 11. But this contradicts the sense of the strophe.

12. *yāšîš* ('old man') is well attested (2 Chron. 35.17; Ben Sira 8.6; and particularly Job 15.10; 29.8; 32.6). Here it has the nuance of its Arab. cognate *waṯwaṯa* ('to be decrepit'). The allusion is to Bildad's emphasis on the wisdom of the fathers (8.8).

9f. This passage is more apt as the introduction to the sapiential adaptation of the Hymn of Praise in vv. 13-25 in supplying in 'Yahweh' the required antecedent to the pronominal suffix in *'immô* in v. 13.

9. The significance of *zō'ṯ* is problematic. It has been referred to Zophar's statement of the providence of God, culminating in his statement after his assurance to Job of rehabilitation after supplication that 'the eyes of the wicked shall fail...' (11.20) or that God is omnipotent. We would refer it to a single proposition already expressed. This we find in Job's animadversion on the security of the wicked with impunity (v. 6), the survival of the strongest independent of moral considerations being characteristic of the beasts.

Here exceptionally in the Book of Job the divine name Yahweh is used in the poetic portion of the Book, and it is to be noted that the more regular term *'^elôah* appears here in five Heb. MSS. The name Yahweh, however, may be explained on the assumption that the writer has the citation of the Hymn of Praise (vv. 13-25) in mind, which recalls particularly hymns of praise in Deutero-Isaiah, and Dhorme has proposed that an original *'^elôah* was altered to MT 'Yahweh' by a writer who recognized the affinity of the passage in Job with Isa. 41.20.

10. In reading *'ôš* for MT *'îš* and rendering 'gift' we follow Dahood; cf. Arab. *'awśu(n)* ('gift'), the Nabataean-Aram. name 'aws al-Ba'ali (Cooke 1903: no.

104, 1.2; cf. 103) and the Heb. name Joash. This restores the chiastic parallelism in the colon, the pronominal suffix in *b^{e}yāḏô* doing double duty for the pronominal suffix wanting in the parallel *'ôš*, as regularly in Ugaritic.

ḥay may denote 'living creatures' and *bāśār* specifically humankind in the physical aspect, as in Gen. 6.12, 13; Num. 16.22; 27.16 (all P); Deut. 5.23; Pss. 45.21; 65.31; Isa. 40.5, 6; 49.26; 66.16, 23, 24; etc., though *kol-bāśār* also includes animals in Gen. 6.17, 19; 7.21; 9.11, 15ff.; Lev. 17.14; etc. If *kol-bāśār* in the present passage denotes specifically humankind, *rûaḥ* may denote the divine afflatus which gives humans affinity with God as distinct from physical animation (*nep̄eš*). See above on 6.4.

13. *ḥoḵmāh* here in conjunction with *g^{e}ḇûrāh*, means 'know-how', the phrase corresponding to 'brains and brawn' in English idiom; *'ēṣāh* is the firmly conceived purpose as well as the plans for carrying it out (see above on 5.12f.), and *t^{e}ḇûnāh* here denotes the divine intelligence and discrimination in the relation of his plan to the total situation, which is so often impugned by Job. Note also the association of *'ēṣāh* and *tûšiyyāh* in the function of Wisdom in Prov. 8.14. The element of discrimination is probably dominant in the verbal root *bîn* from which *t^{e}ḇûnāh* is derived; cf. *bên* ('between' and Arab. *bâna*[*y*], 'to be separated, conspicuous').

14. Here *hēn* means as in Aram. 'if'; cf. Arab. *'in*.

hāras is a strong word meaning 'to bring down in ruins', e.g. pagan altars (Judg. 6.25; 2 Sam. 11.25; 1 Kgs 18.30; 19.10, 14; 2 Kgs 3.25), strongholds (Ezek. 26.4; Lam. 2.2), walls (Ezek. 13.14: 28.12), and the house destroyed by a foolish woman (Prov. 14.1).

15. The same conception of divine 'constraint' (here *ya'ṣōr*) on the waters in drought, but with a different verb (*ṣrk*), occurs in the Ras Shamra legend of Aqht (Gordon *UT* 1 Aqht 42). In God's control of the waters it is to be noted that it is not His beneficence in restraining the floods and sending the necessary rain that is emphasized in v. 15, but his destructive potential in drought and flood, where the same verb (*hāp̄aḵ*) is used as in the overwhelming of Sodom and Gomorrah (Amos 4.11).

16. On *tûšiyyāh* meaning, 'effective purpose', see above on 5.12.

Duhm proposed to emend MT *šōḡēḡ* to *šōḡēh*, the more familiar form, which is actually found in certain Heb. MSS (cf. 6.24; 19.4), but *šōḡēḡ* may well be a byform; cf. Lev. 5.18, Num. 15.28 and Ps. 119.67, which are all late like the Dialogue in Job.

17. In MT the repetition of *môlîḵ*, the first word, and *šôlāl* (pausal), the third word, in vv. 17 and 19 is suspect, and may be the inadvertency of a copyist.

LXX^A reads 'the counsellors of the earth', which is adopted by Duhm, who further emends MT *šôlāl* ('barefoot') to *śikkēl* ('has made fools of'); cf. in a similar context *śikkēl* in Isa. 44.25, which is supported by Sym. (so also Beer). Hölscher and Mowinckel also read *śikkēl*, but for *môlîḵ* Hölscher reads *m^e laḵ*, thus *m^e laḵ yô ʿaṣîm śikkēl* ('he brings to nothing the counsel of counsellors'). Horst also reads *m^e laḵ* in its Aram. sense of 'counsel', but for MT *šôlāl* understands 'plunders', which does not suit the predicate 'counsel'. The verb *śikkēl* would be an apt parallel to *ye hôlēl*, though graphically not a likely original of the corrupt *šôlāl*. Accordingly we adopt Horst's reading *mil^e ḵê yô ʿaṣîm* ('the plans of counsellors'), but read *m^e šôlēl* for MT *šôlāl* from a verb, admittedly not attested in the OT, but cognate with Arab. *śâla, yaśûl* meaning in the II form 'to delude', following G.R. Driver (1936: 160).

18. For MT *mûsar* ('chastisement, correction') the general sense and the parallelism indicate the reading *môsēr* ('belt', lit. 'bond'); so V and T.

pāṯaḥ ('to open out', here a knot) is the opposite of *ḥāḡar* ('to put a girdle on, or, to gird on armour'; cf. 1 Sam. 17.39; 1 Kgs 20.11; Isa. 45.1). Dhorme takes this to mean that God sets kings free (looses their bonds); so too Fohrer, taking the noun to mean 'fetters'; and so also T possibly thinking of Manasseh (2 Chron. 33.13) and 'he binds fetters on them at will' (v. 18b); so too Hölscher. But *môsēr* is more likely to be a girdle of honour or uniform of a warrior and *ʾēzôr* in v. 13b a loincloth; cf. Arab. *ʾīzār* ('waist-sash'). This sustains the antithetic parallelism and may be supported by Isa. 45.1, *moṯ^e nê m^e lāḵîm ʾapattēaḥ*.

19. It is perhaps significant that *kōhēn* ('priest') occurs nowhere else in Job, which may indicate that the passage vv. 17-21 refers specifically to the Exile, when all the dignitaries mentioned were deported. MT *šôlāl* is found in the OT only here and in Mic. 1.6 (Qere) associated with *ʿārôm* ('naked'). It may be the corruption of the participle *m^e šullālîm* with haplography of *m* preformative and afformative respectively after *m* and before *w* in the Old Heb. script. The verb may be cognate with Arab. *śalla* ('to draw out', e.g. a sword from the sheath).

ʾēṯānîm is used in the singular in Amos 5.24 of a perennial wadi, and in the plural of the regular 'former rains' of early winter in Palestine, whence the name of the month Ethanim. As here it denotes persons 'firmly established' in Num. 24.21, *môšāḇ ʾēṯān* ('a firm seat'); cf. Arab. *watana* ('to remain long in a place').

sālap̄ in the Piel is used meaning 'to subvert' in Exod. 23.8 and Prov. 23.6.

20. As is demanded by *mēsîr* ('turning away') *l* here denotes 'from', as in Ugaritic; cf. T *minne ʾ^e mānîm*. Dhorme took *ne ʾ^e mānîm* to mean 'sincere', i.e. trustworthy. The ancient Jewish commentators connected the word with *n^e ʾum*

('oracle, prophetic declaration'), which the attribute *śāpāh* might support. In any case it denotes the accredited leaders of society; cf. *kōhēn ne'^{e}mān* in 1 Sam. 2.35, custodians of the traditions and interests of the community, as Fohrer suggests, and so, we consider, as indicated by *śāpāh*, its spokesmen. The parallel 'elders' supports this interpretation.

21. The parallelism and the general sense indicates that *'^{a}pîqîm* cannot have the usual meaning 'streams', and this is appreciated by T and S in rendering 'strong' (*t^{e}qîpîm*), and Beer so emends MT. But an Assyrian root *epêqu* ('to be strong') may be adduced, thus making emendation of MT unnecessary (so Dillmann, Friedrich Delitzsch, Dhorme, Perles, Hölscher, Stevenson, Horst, Fohrer); cf. Arab. *'afîqu*(*n*) ('excelling in noble qualities').

m^{e}zîaḥ is the same as *mezaḥ* of Ps. 109.18. Dhorme cites Ass. *mezaḫ*, a synonym of *mezirru* ('belt').

22. This verse is obviously a secondary expansion from some hymn, as maintained by Budde, Dhorme, Steinmann, Fohrer, Pope. *'^{a}muqôṯ*, 'deep things', with the nuance of 'wise', as in English, recalls Akk. *nemegu* ('wisdom').

23. *šāṭaḥ* means 'to spread out', with an Arab. cognate *śaṭaḥa* which, like the Hebrew verb, means either 'to spread out' or 'extend', like dough rolled out, or 'prostrate', for example, of a camel made to couch. So v. 23b could mean either 'He spreads people abroad and abandons them', reading *w^{e}yannîḥēm* for MT *wayyanḥēm* (see textual note) or 'He prostrates them and brings them into abeyance' (lit. 'causes them to rest', i.e. abandons them). The ancient versions and later commentators differ in reading MT *maśgî'* ('makes great' or 'numerous'), as V, T, Delitzsch, G.B. Gray, Dhorme, Mowinckel, Hölscher, Horst, Fohrer, Pope, Terrien, and *mašgēh* ('misleads'), as Theod., LXX, S and certain Heb. MSS, Merx, Graetz, Siegfried, Tur-Sinai, Stevenson. The problem is not conclusively solved by the complementary verb *wî'abb^{e}ḏēm* (see textual note), which means either 'He causes them to perish', which would support MT, or 'He causes them to be lost' (cf. 1 Sam. 9.3, 20), which would support *mašēh*. The parallel colon, reading *w^{e}yannîḥēm*, indicates the meaning 'destroys'.

24. In v. 24a LXX omits *'am* from MT *rā'šê 'am-hā'āreṣ*, which Jerome questioned. In v. 24b *wayyaṯ'ēm b^{e}ṯōhû lō'-ḏārek* ('and he caused them to go astray in a pathless desert') corresponds verbally to Ps. 107.40b, by which it may be directly influenced. In *lō'-ḏārek* and in *lō'-'ôr* in v. 25a the compound phrase is tantamount to a negative adjective.

25. *māšaš* ('to grope') in the Piel is attested in 5.14. The direct accusative 'darkness' is noteworthy, indicating the nuance of 'feeling' or 'touching' as in the Arab. cognate, cf. Exod. 10.21 ('darkness that can be felt'), alluding perhaps to the dullness of the dust-laden sirocco.

For MT *wayyaṯ'ēm* LXX, followed by Bickell, Beer, Duhm, G.B. Gray, Dhorme, Peters, Hölscher, Horst, reads *wayyittā'û* ('and they staggered'), which is supported by Isa. 19.14; 28.7, here also associated with *kaššikkôr* ('like a drunkard').

Chapter 13

Job's Argument (continued)

Verse 28 is obviously incongruous with its context in ch. 13, and is displaced from after 14.2, and 14.5c is probably displaced from after v. 27c.

1. 'Lo, my eye has seen all these things,[1]
My ear has heard and understood.
2. I know as well as you,
I am not inferior to you.
3. But I would speak to the Almighty,
Yea, I am determined to argue my case with God.

4. But you[2] plaster up a façade of delusion,
Quack doctors all of you.
5. Would that you would keep silent;
It would pass for wisdom with you.
6. Hear now the argument of my mouth,[3]
And pay attention to the contention[4] of my lips.

7. Will you speak what is wrong on God's behalf,
And chant[5] deceit for his sake?
8. Will you patronize the Almighty?[6]
Will you plead for God?
9. Would it be well if He were to examine you?
Do you trifle with him as you would trifle[7] with a human?

10. He will remonstrate severely with you
If dishonestly you show partiality to him.[8]
11. Will not his majesty appal you,
All his terror fall upon you?
12. Your maxims are ashes raked out,
Your answers[9] are silted-up cisterns.[10]

13. Be silent before me that I may speak,
Come upon me what may.
14. [11]I shall take my own flesh in my teeth,
And shall lay my life in my hand.
15. If he kill me, I am (in any case) without hope;
I will defend my conduct in argument to his face.

16. Yea, this[12] might be my salvation,
That no hypocrite might face Him.

17. [13]Now hear out what I have to say,
Yea, what I have to declare in your ears.
18. See, I set out my case,
I am sure that I am innocent.
19. Who could sustain his contention against me?
(If any could) I should hold my peace and (be content to) die.

20. Only do two things for me,
Then will I not hide myself from your face;
21. Remove your hand from upon me,
And let not terror of you overwhelm me;
22. Then call and I will answer,
Or let me make a statement, and do you answer.

23. How many are my iniquities and faults?
Inform me of my transgressions and sin.
24. Why do you hide your face,
And consider me as your enemy?
25. Will you harry a driven leaf?
Yea, will you[14] chase dry chaff?

26. Nay, but you debit me with things past
And entail upon me the iniquities of my youth;
27. And set my feet in the stocks,
And keep watch on all my paths.
You limit my roots,[15]
14.5c. You have set their bounds[16] that they may not pass.[17]

Textual Notes to Chapter 13

1. Reading with a certain minuscule of LXX, S, V and certain Heb. MSS. *kol-'ēlleh* for MT *kōl*.
2. Omitting *wᵉ'ûlām metri causa* as a dittograph of *'ûlām* in v. 3.
3. Reading *tôḵaḥaṯ pî* with LXX, as the parallel *riḇaṯ śᵉp̄āṯay* demands.
4. Reading *rîḇaṯ* with LXX, S, V and T for MT *rîḇôṯ*.
5. Reading *tᵉḇaddû* for MT *tᵉḏabbᵉrû*. See Commentary *ad loc.*
6. Reading *pᵉnê šadday*.
7. Reading *hattēl* in both instances.
8. Reading *pānāyw* for MT *pānîm* with Sym., S, T and V.
9. Reading *gāḇēḵem* for MT *gabbêḵem*. See Commentary *ad loc.*
10. Reading *gubbê* for *gabbê*. See Commentary *ad loc.*
11. Omitting MT *'al-māh* as a marginal correction of *'ālay māh* at the end of v. 13, which has crept into the text at the beginning of 14.
12. Reading *hî'* with LXX for MT *hû'*.
13. This verse is probably a secondary interpolation. See Commentary *ad loc.*
14. Reading *wᵉ'im* (interrogative) for MT *wᵉ'eṯ*.
15. Omitting *rag̱lay*, inserted after the displacement of 14.5c. See Commentary *ad loc.*
16. Reading *ḥuqqām* for MT *ḥuqqô* (Qere),
17. Reading *ya'ᵃḇōrû* for MT *ya'ᵃḇōr*.

Commentary on Chapter 13

1. 'Seeing' and 'hearing' refer to personal experience, which may both substantiate or modify accepted doctrine, supplemented by 'understanding' implying discrimination of what one hears. On the reading *kol-'ēlleh* for MT *kōl* see textual note. This may refer to the friends' statement of current doctrine or, we prefer, the theme of the Hymn of Praise just cited (12.13-25).

3. On *hôḵēaḥ*, here 'to argue', see above on 9.33.

The verb *ḥāp̄aṣ*, usually meaning 'to take pleasure', 'be willing', has here rather the nuance of the Syr. cognate 'to be eager, zealous', hence our rendering 'I am determined'.

4. *ṭōp̄ᵉlê šāqer*, lit. 'plasterers of falsehood', recalls the same verb and object in Ps. 119.69a, and is compared by Dhorme to the Ass. expression *tašqirtu ṭapiltu* ('a false imputation', or 'smear'); cf. Arab. *ṭafila* ('to be soiled by dirt'). This is the sense of Ps. 119.69a, but in the present passage the parallel *rōp̄ᵉ'ê 'ᵉlil* ('quack doctors') indicates not deliberate malice, but patching up or disguising unpalatable truth, as we should say, 'whitewashing', covering defects of building by plaster. Job's interlocutors are blinking awkward truths by reiterating orthodox statements uncritically. This interpretation is borne out by Job's imputation of partiality to God (vv. 8, 10), their acquiescence in justice in the theodicy (v. 7), and, in fact, their trifling with God (v. 10).

6. *tôḵaḥaṯ*, as the parallel *rîḇaṯ śᵉpāṯay*, 'contention of my mouth' (see textual note) indicates 'argument'. See on 9.33.

7. In v. 7b LXX varies the verb 'to declare' (MT *tᵉḏabbᵉrû*), rendering *phthengesthe* ('you speak out loud and clear'). As an emendation with the minimal disturbance of MT we may suggest *tᵉḇaddû* with its double meaning of 'talk wildly', 'babble', or 'sing out; cf. *bdd* in the Ras Shamra text, Gordon *UT* 'nt I.19, where *ybd* is parallel to *yšr* ('he sang'). Though the *double entendre* of the verb cannot be so neatly expressed in English, a not unapt translation might be 'chant', which might be supported by LXX.

halᵉ'ēl in v. 7a is by position emphatic, with emphasis on God.

8. The metre demands an extra beat in v. 8a, which suggests that for MT *hᵃp̄ānāyw* we should read *hᵃp̄ᵉnê šadday*.

9. In v. 9b the Piel of *hāṯal* ('to trifle with') should be read in both instances, as in 1 Kgs 18.24.

10. *hôḵîaḥ* has the sense both of 'to argue' and 'chastise' (see on 9.33), which we may express by 'remonstrate severely'.

bassēṯer (lit. 'in secret') means here 'dishonestly', i.e. willfully glossing over unpleasant truths and entrenching oneself in a false position, disguising conviction under the façade of orthodox declarations.

nāśā' pānîm (read *pānāyw*, see textual note), lit. 'lift the face', is a familiar phrase in the OT meaning 'to pardon', hence 'to show partiality', of which *prosōpon lambanein* in the LXX and the NT is a literal rendering, meaning 'to show partiality'. The phrase refers originally to the gesture of a potentate stretching forth his sceptre and raising the face of the prostrate suppliant, e.g. Est. 8.33ff.

11. *śᵉ'ēṯô* ('his elevation', so 'his majesty'), the infinitive construct, or verbal noun of *nāsā'* with the pronominal suffix, is deliberate word-play on the verb after *nāśā' pānāyw* in v. 10b.

On *bā'aṯ* ('to come suddenly upon', so 'to overwhelm') see above on 3.5; cf. 2 Sam. 22.5 = Ps. 18.5, where the physical sense of the verb is indicated by the parallel *'ᵃpāpûnî* ('whirled me', 'caught me up in their maelstrom'); cf. Arab. *baġata* ('to fall suddenly upon'). The verb, whether in this sense or meaning 'to terrify', is more common in Job than elsewhere in the OT, e.g. 3.5; 7.14; 9.34; 13.11, 21; 15.24; 18.11; 33.7. Here the parallel colon indicates the meaning is 'appal'.

12. *ziḵrōnêḵem* means 'your memorabilia', here either sayings worthy of record, i.e. maxims, or, as Rowley suggests, 'your memorized sayings, which you repeat parrot-like'.

In *mišᵉlê 'ēper* we would see a *double entendre* ('proverb of ashes' and 'ashes raked out', lit. 'extractions of ashes'), from a verb *šālāh*, admittedly not certainly attested in the OT, but a possible cognate of Syr. *šᵉlā'* with this sense. The figure would then be of dead embers extracted from the baking oven after their heat was gone, no unapt figure for the spent force of the arguments of orthodoxy which had outlived their usefulness and were irrelevant to Job's actual experience.

In v. 12b *gabbê* (lit. 'backs', or 'bosses for shields', cf. 15.26), is taken as synecdoche for 'shields', which, of clay, would be useless (so Duhm, Budde, G.B. Gray, Fohrer). The view which was first propounded by Beer is that *gāḇêḵem* should be read for MT *gabbêḵem*, the word being cognate with Syr. and Arab. *jūbatu*(*n*), plur. *jawāb* 'answers' (so Dhorme, Hölscher, Mowinckel, Larcher [JB], Horst, Lévêque). Seeing a word-play, we take MT *gabbê-ḥōmer* as *gubbê-ḥōmer* ('silted-up cisterns', lit. 'wells of mud'); cf. Aram. *gubbā'* and Arab. *jubbu*(*n*) ('a well').

The enclitic *lᵉ* introducing the predicate of a nominal sentence, as in Ugaritic and Arab, may be noted.

13. The indefinite *māh* ('whatsoever') with the ellipse of a second verb, in the sense here of 'come upon me whatsoever may', is paralleled in 2 Sam. 18.22f.

14. LXX omits *'al-māh*, which is probably a dittograph of the last two words *'ālay māh* in v. 13. Dahood's proposal to retain it as *'ôlāmāh* ('for ever') (1965b: 16) is to be rejected. Horst and Fohrer propose more feasibly that *'al-māh* should be taken with v. 13, reading *māh 'al-māh*.

The meaning of the figure of taking one's flesh in one's teeth, not elsewhere attested in the OT, is clear from the parallel 'taking one's life in one's hand' (lit. 'setting one's life in the palm of one's hand'), which has passed into English idiom; cf. Judg. 12.3; 1 Sam. 19.5; 28.21; Ps. 119.109). For the expression 'taking one's life in one's teeth' Buttenwieser has adduced an Arab. parallel from Hudheil *an-nafšu minhu bišidkihi* ('his life is in his jaws'), meaning 'he is in deadly jeopardy'. The general conception of the couplet is that confrontation with God endangers one's life (cf. Exod. 3.6; 33.20; Judg. 6.22; 13.22; Isa. 6.5). The significance of taking one's flesh in one's teeth may indicate that the subject is prepared for the ultimate emergency, as in the rigours of a siege, when people might resort to cannibalism (Deut. 28.56ff.; 2 Kgs 6.28ff.; Lam. 2.20; Ezek. 5.10; etc.; Josephus, *War* 4.3-4).

15. For MT *lō'* in v. 15a *lô* is read by the Masoretes (Qere), LXX, Aq., S, T and V, which is the basis of the familiar, though inaccurate, 'Though he slay me yet will I trust him' (AV). But MT may be retained, meaning '(in any case) I am without hope'; cf. Graetz's proposal 'I shall not be afraid' (*lō' 'āḥîl*); cf. *ḥîl* (lit. 'writhe, sometimes in anguish') // *yārē'* in Jer. 5.22 (so Ehrlich, Dhorme). Formally *yāḥal* is ambiguous, meaning 'to wait' (Gen. 8.12; 1 Sam. 13.8; etc.) or 'to hope' (6.11; 29.21, 23; Ps. 71.14; etc.), which seems to us best to suit the context. The verb *qāṭal* is rare, poetic and late in Heb., occurring only here, in 24.14 and Ps. 138.19, but it is regular in Aram. The regular verb 'to kill' in Arab. is *qatala*, where the dialectal variant in the second radical is to be noted.

Since the recognition of the significance of the root *drk* in Ugaritic and Heb. as 'rule, ordered regimen' (see on 24.4), *d^erāḵay* here and in other passages relating to conduct or way of life may be derived not from *dereḵ* ('road') but from a homonym cognate with Ugaritic *drkt* and Arab. *darakatu(n)*.

16. *y^ešû'āh* is not to be confused with *tûšiyyāh* ('success'), but means 'deliverance', 'relief', from a root cognate with Arab. *waśi'a* ('to be wide'). Here the sense is rather 'hope of deliverance'. We take *ḥānēp̄* here as in Aram. and Late Heb. to mean 'hypocrite', Job's animadversion or the 'dishonest partiality' of his friends to God (v. 10b).

17. *millāh* ('word') is Aram. and is a regular element in Job.

'aḥ^awāṯî ('my explanation'; cf. 15.17) recalls *'aḥ^awāyaṯ '^aḥîḏān* ('explanation of riddles') in Dan. 5.12, where it is definitely Aram. The verbal root occurs in the OT only at Job 15.17; 32.6, 10, 17; 36.2 and at Ps. 19.3 and regularly in the Aram. parts of Daniel.

18. The language is forensic. *'ārak̲* means 'to set out, arrange', e.g. a table (Ps. 23.5), a battle-line (Judg. 20.22, 1 Sam. 17.8; etc.) or, as here, a case.

19. The rhetorical question in v. 19a suggests 'If any could' as the protasis of a conditional sentence of which v. 19b is the apodosis.

20. *'al* taken as a negative particle contradicts the sense of the passage. It must be recognized as a positive particle also, as in Ugaritic, cf. Gordon *UT* 51.VIII.1, *'al ttn pnm* ('set your face', sc. 'direct yourself').

22. In *hᵃšîb̲ēnî*, the Hiphil *šûb̲* ('to return'), 'word' is understood, so that it is tantamount to 'answer', and so takes a direct object.

25. *'āraṣ* is cognate with Arab. *'araṣa* ('to be restless', of a beast).

'et̲ could possibly be (GKC, §117c) the *nota accusativa* before an indeterminative noun, where something particular is envisaged, but *'et̲* is not used even with definite objects in Job, so the emendation of *'et̲* to *'im* must be made.

qaš is used regularly for light brushwood or chaff, meaning 'that which is scaled off', and is figurative of that which is at the mercy of the wind or is of light account (cf. 41.20ff.).

26. *kāt̲ab̲* indicates either a recorded decision or charge or is a figure from commerce, as so often in the Qur'an. *kāt̲ab̲ 'al* means 'to debit', as in an administrative text from the palace of Ras Shamra (*PRU* II, p. 212), (*ḥm*) *šm ksp 'l gd* ('50 pieces of silver debited to God'), cited by Dahood (1965: 60).

The parallel with 'the iniquities of my youth' (*'ᵃwōnôt̲ nᵉ'ûrāy*) supports Guillaume's suggestion that *mᵉrōrôt*, generally taken as 'bitter things', means rather 'things past'; cf. Arab. *marra* ('to pass by').

27. *sad̲* here and at 33.11, which closely re-echoes the present passage, is for the confinement of the feet; cf. Acts 16.24, where S translates *sᵉd̲ā'*, indicating a block of wood for this purpose. The confinement of the hands in wooden blocks is known an ancient Egypt (cf. *ANET*, pl. 326). Noting that the sequel envisages Job at liberty, ibn Ezra took *sad̲* as a corruption of *sîd̲* ('chalk, gypsum'), taking the meaning to be the marking of the feet with chalk to have traces of where the subject had been. Fohrer follows this interpretation, taking MT *wᵉt̲āśēm* to mean 'and you marked' from a root *śāmam*, which he would recognize in Jezebel's painting her eyes with *kuḥl* (2 Kgs 9.30). No such root is attested elsewhere in the OT, but a cognate might be Syr. *samsam* ('to treat medically'). Taking *sad̲* to mean 'stocks' or the like, it has been suggested that the reference to close observance of Job's straying feet in v. 27bc indicates that *sad̲* was not an immobile block but an encumbrance to the free movement of the feet, as the wooden blocks on the teams of men in the Egyptian

sculpture already mentioned. Alternatively v. 27a may envisage a slave detained in an immobile block while v. 27bc might refer to him released for work when he is under observation.

In v. 27c *'al-šorᵉšê ragᵉlay tiṯḥaqqeh* has been taken variously. *ḥāqāh*, a byform of the more regular *ḥāqaq* ('to inscribe'), is taken by Dhorme to mean engraving on the mind, which is not attested in the OT and is therefore doubtful. *šorᵉšê*, meaning 'roots' and taken by Dhorme to mean 'where a man plants his feet', is also doubtful. Alternatively *tiṯḥaqqeh* is taken to signify 'prescribe bounds', which is well attested, but *šorᵉšê ragᵉlay* ('the soles of my feet') is very doubtful. Just at this point there is some disturbance of text, 13.28 being displaced from its original position after 14.2 (see below *ad loc.*). Tricola in the predominant arrangement of bicola in Job, while often intentional, must always be considered on their merits and are occasionally indications of disturbed text. Accordingly Duhm attached v. 27c to one of the cola in the next tricolon, viz. 14.5c, restoring:

13.27c *'al-šorᵉšay tiṯḥaqqeh*
14.5c *ḥuqqām 'āśiṯā lō' ya'ᵃḇōrû*

> You have imposed limits on (or 'made incisions') on my roots,
> You have set their bounds that they may not surpass.

The figure is thus that of root-pruning, *ragᵉlay* being added after *šorᵉšay* after the displacement according to the general sense of v. 27ab.

Chapter 14

This continues Job's direct address to God in 13.20-27, perhaps combined with a wisdom poem on the evanescence of humans (vv. 1f., 7-12, 15-22) in contrast to the revival of a tree when pruned or severely cut back (vv. 1f., 7-10) and like land-slides, water-worn stones and soil-erosion (vv. 18f.). The theme is the brief life of humans, full of trouble, his hard service (v. 14bc, cf. 7.1f.) and his ultimate death with no further prospect (vv. 1, 18-22, cf. 7.9bf.). The mortality of man entitles the sufferer to hope that God would condone man's limitations and grant him some relief (vv. 5f.). Here v. 14a, 'if a man die shall he live again?', is not a gleam of hope of the survival of death, of Sheol as a temporary refuge (v. 13a). Like 'Sheol' in v. 13a, it is probably a secondary insertion, but, whatever the belief of the late scribe who may have been responsible, in its context it has all the appearance of a rhetorical question which invites a negation, of which the chapter leaves us in no doubt.

Chapter 14
Job's Argument (Continued)

1. 'Man born of woman
Is brief of days with fill of trouble.

2. Like a flower he comes forth and wilts,
Fleeing and unstable as a shadow.
13.28. He wears out as a water-skin,[1]
Like a moth-eaten garment.
3. Is it then on such as this that you open your eyes,
Bringing him[2] into judgment with you?

4. [3](Who can separate the clean from the unclean? None can.)
5. Since his days are determined,
And you control the number of his months,
[4](His bounds you have set which he may not overstep),
6. Look away from him and forbear[5]
Until he discharges as a hireling his term.

7. For a tree has still hope
Though cut down; it may yet renew itself,
And its young shoots not cease.
8. Though its roots grow old in the ground,
And its stump is dying in the dust.
9. At the scent of water it will sprout,
And will develop shoots like a sapling,

10. But man dies and departs,[6]
Yea, mankind perishes and where is he?
11. Water from the sea may be exhausted,
And the river may be dried up and drained.
12. But man once he has lain down shall never arise,
Until the heavens wear out[7] he shall not awake,[8]
Nor be roused[9] from his sleep.[10]

13. Would that you would hide me (in Sheol),[11]
Conceal me till your anger abated,
Set a limit and remember me.
14 […][12]
All the days of my service would I hold out
Until my relief should come.

15. You would call and I should answer you;
You would care for the work of your hands.
16. But as it is you number my steps,
You keep watch[13] over my transgression;[14]
17. My sin is sealed up in a bundle,
And you put sealing clay on my iniquity.

18. A mountain falls in ruin,[15]
And a rock shifts from its place;
19. Water reduces stone to dust;
The flood[16] sweeps away the soil of the earth.
And you destroy the hope of man;
14a. If a man die shall he live?

20. You overpower him utterly and he passes away,
You change his appearance and send him away.
21. His sons attain honour, but he never knows;
They are reduced, but he does not perceive it.
22. But on his own account is his body pained,
And on his own account his life-breath laments.'

Textual Notes to Chapter 14

1. Reading *rōqeḇ* with LXX for MT *rāqāḇ*.
2. Reading *w*^{e}*'ōṯô* with LXX, S and V for MT *w*^{e}*'ōṯî*.
3. This passage, which is omitted in one Heb. MS, is probably a secondary interpolation.
4. Taking v. 5c (emended) as the second colon parallel to 13.27c (see above).
5. Reading *waḥ*^{a}*ḏal* with one Heb. MS for MT *w*^{e}*yeḥdāl* (pausal form).
6. Reading *w*^{e}*yah*^{a}*lōḵ* after LXX for MT *wayyeḥ*^{e}*lāš* (pausal form). See Commentary *ad loc*.
7. Reading *b*^{e}*lōṯ* with Aq., Theod., Sym. and V for MT *biltî*.
8. Reading *yāqîṣ* for MT *yāqîṣû* with LXX^{A} and V.
9. Reading *yē'ōr* with LXX^{A} and V for MT *yē'ōrû*.
10. Reading *miššenāṯô* with LXX^{A} and V for MT *mišš*^{e}*nāṯām*.
11. Probably a gloss as the metre indicates.
12. Omitting v. 14a as a gloss and displaced from after v. 19c (so Dhorme) or after v. 10 (so Fohrer).
13. Reading *l*^{e}*ṯišmôr* (with *l*^{e} enclitic) for MT *lō'-ṯišmôr*. See Commentary *ad loc*.
14. The parallelism with *ṣ*^{e}*'āḏay* ('my footsteps') suggests MT *ḥaṭṭā'ṯî* might be a word-play with Arab. *ḫuṭwatu(n)*, plur. *ḫuṭṭān* ('footstep').
15. Reading *nāpōl yippôl* with Theod. and S for MT *nôp̄ēl yibbôl*.
16. The verb *tišṭōp̄* demands the sing. subject, either *s*^{e}*p̄îḥāh* or *s*^{e}*ḥîp̄āh*, the latter of which, suggested by Budde, we prefer on the evidence of Prov. 28.3. See Commentary.

Commentary on Chapter 14

1. On *rōḡez* ('agitation, trouble'), here in the passive sense, see above on 3.17. The phrase *ś*^{e}*ḇa'-rōḡez* ('with his fill of trouble') is probably a conscious parody of the description of a happy life achieved as *ś*^{e}*ḇa' yāmîm* ('full of days', in 42.17; Gen. 25.8).

2. On the figure of humans as ephemeral as a flower (*ṣîṣ*); cf. Isa. 40.6-8; Ps. 103.15; and as a shadow; cf. 8.9; Pss. 102.12 (EVV 11); 109.23; 144.4.

yāṣā' ('to come forth') naturally expresses the emergence of flowers or vegetation (*ṣe'*^{e}*ṣā'*; cf. Gen. 1.12; 1 Kgs 5.1; etc.), and requires no emendation; cf. Beer's suggestion *yiṣmaḥ* ('sprouts').

mālal may mean 'wilt' (so Hölscher, Weiser, Gordis); cf. 18.16 and probably also 24.24 and Ps. 37.2, where it is parallel to *nāḇal* ('to wither'), and

Ps. 90.6. Alternatively it is suggested that it is a byform of *mûl* ('to be cut, circumcised'), as in Gen. 17.10; Josh. 5.2 (so G.B. Gray, Fohrer, Pope).

bāraḥ means 'to flee' in Hebrew but this is a secondary meaning. The primary meaning is rather 'to shift' from one position to another; cf. the bolt (*bārîaḥ*), and Arab. *'al-bāriḥ* ('yesterday'), and so also in Ugaritic of 'the primaeval serpent' (*bṯn brḥ*) of Chaos with its Hebrew counterpart *nāḥāš bārîaḥ* (26.13; Isa. 27.1).

13.28. After 13.27 in the first person sing. the pronoun *hû'* has been an embarrassment to commentators in its position in MT. Displacement is therefore suggested, after 14.1 according to Stevenson and Peters; after 14.2 according to Siegfried, Dhorme, Steinmann and Pope; or after 14.5 according to Bickell, Beer, Wright and Lévêque. The figure of wearing out as a wine-skin (*rōqeḇ*, MT *rāqāḇ*) or moth-eaten garment certainly demands ephemeral humanity as its antecedent and so must be transposed (*pace* Fohrer) to ch. 14, probably after the figures of the flower or shadow in 14.2. *rōqeḇ* for *rāqāḇ* ('rottenness') is suggested by LXX and S and is to be preferred as the concrete figure, like its parallel, the moth-eaten garment (*beḡeḏ 'ᵃḵālô 'āš*).

3. On the reading *'ōṯô* for MT *'ōṯî* see textual note.

4. The meaning of *mî yittēn* here is literal, 'Who can produce?' or perhaps 'separate?', and does not, as often, introduce a wish. The defective metre indicates a gloss (so Bickell, Beer, Dhorme, G.B. Gray, Hölscher, Horst). The preposition *min* does not necessarily denote derivation here, implying, as Rowley suggests, the ritual impurity of childbirth (cf. 'man born of woman') or the doctrine of original sin. The statement may rather indicate the impossibility of separating the clean from the unclean, humans being the victim of their environment rather than hereditary sinners. But the subject of the context, the natural limitations of humans, suggests that they are therefore excusable as the victims of their heredity. Dhorme, who retains the verse as original (so also Fohrer), explains the short colon v. 4b as deliberate for the sake of emphasis. The verse, however, may well be a theological gloss suggested by the conception of 'man born of woman' (*yᵉlûḏ 'iššāh*) in v. 1, who was first tempted and brought about the fall of humankind and who in childbirth is subject to ritual impurity.

5. *ḥᵃrûṣîm*, means literally 'cut sharp', e.g. the sharp-edged studs of the threshing sledge in Amos 1.3. Here it means 'defined' or 'decreed'; cf. 1 Kgs 20.40; Isa. 10.22.

On v. 5c, displaced here from after 13.27c, see on 13.27.

6. On the reading *waḥᵃḏal* see textual note. *šā'āh* ('to look') in the sense of 'look away from' is paralleled in 7.19. *rāṣāh*, meaning regularly in Classical

Hebrew 'to be pleased', means here 'to discharge an obligation'; cf. the keeping of the Sabbath in Lev. 26.34, 41, 43 (P). Confined to late passages in the OT, it is regularly used in this sense in Aramaic.

In Job's unremitted suffering it could hardly be said that he could 'enjoy his day' (RSV) any more than a hard-worked hireling. The reference is rather to discharging his term and what is involved to the satisfaction of the one who imposed it; cf. Isa. 40.2 (*nirṣāh ʿ*^{a}*wōnāh*). On *śāḵîr* ('mercenary, hired worker') see on 7.1f.

7. This is obviously not a regular bicolon, which is expected in the context, hence it has been suggested that the original text may have contained two bicola, a colon having dropped out after *tiqwāh* in v. 7a (Tur-Sinai), or between *yikkārēṯ* and *w*^{e}*ʿôḏ*, or between *w*^{e} and *ʿôḏ* (Duhm, Bell, Hölscher). Stevenson regarded v. 7c as a gloss, but this colon agrees with the sequel, which emphasizes the survival of the tree in its shoots (*yōnaqtô*) and goes on to explode the popular fallacy of a man's survival in his sons (v. 21f.). Bicola, however, may be relieved by an occasional tricolon in Hebrew and Ugaritic poetry, and so we should retain the text as it stands. Wetzstein reports such a means of renewing old fruit trees in Syria (cf. Dalman 1942: VII, 174f.). Cf. the branch from the stump (*gezaʿ*) of Jesse (Isa. 11.1). For the Hiphil of *ḥālap̄* ('to renew') cf. 29.20 and possibly Isa. 9.9; 40.31; Ben Sira 46.12.

8. Note *ʿāp̄ār* (lit. 'dust') as parallel to *ʾereṣ*, 'the ground', in view of the doctrinal implications which have been assumed by some commentators for *ʿāp̄ār* as reflecting the 'dust' of the grave; cf. on 19.25.

9. *mērêaḥ mayim* (lit. 'from the scent of the water') recalls *bah*^{a}*rîḥô ʾēš*, 'when it has a touch of fire' (Judg. 16.9). *yap̄rîaḥ* is to be retained in the Hiphil; cf. *yazkîn*, denominational Hiphil.

qāṣîr is a collective sing. ('branches'); cf. 18.16; 29.19.

10. *ḥālaš* describes the reduction of the oppressor in Isa. 14.12 and Exod. 17.13 (probably to be emended to Hiphil). The meaning 'to be weak' is hardly strong enough for the present passage, and the parallel with *ʾayyô*, 'where is he?', or as has been suggested, *ʾayin* or *ʾênennû* ('he is not'), indicates that LXX 'and he departed' (*wayyah*^{a}*lōḵ*) represents the original verb.

11. If the reference is to the natural drying up of waters *yām* would mean 'lake' or extensive rain-pond rather than 'sea' (G.B. Gray), there being practically no tide in the Near East. While this is possible, however, the reference to the river drying up is not. *nāhār* is a perennial river, not a seasonal wadi (*naḥal*), so that this is a case of proverbial exaggeration. Earlier Jewish commentators referred it to drink-offerings, thought in Near Eastern popular religion partially to revive the dead. Such offerings are attested in the Assyrian

records of Ashurbanipal and in grave installations at Ras Shamra (Schaeffer 1939: pl. XXIX, fig. 3.1) and actually at Samaria in the Israelite monarchy (Sukenik 1945: 42-58) and from a Jewish community in the Hellenistic age in Tob. 4.17; cf. Lk. 16.19-24 (Parrot 1937). On this explanation the sense would be 'you may exhaust all the water in sea and rivers but you will not revive the dead'. Dhorme interprets the passage as 'the sea and rivers will dry up sooner than a dead man will rise' (so also Horst, Larcher, Terrien, Lévêque).

12. The more graphic *bᵉlōṯ* is to be preferred to the negative *biltî* of MT as in the same figure in Isa. 51.6 and Ps. 102.27 (EVV 26). For support from ancient versions see textual note. The sky, as God's seat, and the heavenly bodies are proverbial for permanence (Pss. 72.7; 89.36f.), the implication in the divine oath on the permanence of his favour. For sleep as a figure of death, cf. Isa. 26.19; Dan. 12.2.

13. God's provision of a temporary refuge (*histîr*) till the passing of a crisis recalls the language of Pss. 27.5 and 32.7. Those suggest that *bišᵉ'ôl* may be a late addition and indeed it is superfluous to the metre. Throughout the OT Sheol is regularly represented as beyond the influence of God himself (e.g. Ps. 88.6, 11f. [EVV 5, 10f.]; Isa. 33.18), and as a place from which there is no return (7.9). Verses 13-17 have the character of an interjection with direct address to God intervening between the strophes vv. 10-12 and 18-19 on the evanescence of humanity with their vivid imagery.

14. In view of the unequivocal assertion throughout the chapter on human mortality without survival it is extremely questionable if the doctrine of personal survival after death had emerged at all in Judaism at the time of the definitive edition of the Book of Job. Hence 14a has been taken as a gloss; so Hölscher, Stevenson, Baumgärtel, Lindblom, Horst, and Fohrer, who regards it a misplaced from after v. 10a. Verse 14a possibly owes its present position to a revision of the Book, when the doctrine of resurrection was emerging in Judaism, but was contested, and may reflect the notion of compensation after death for the trials (*ṣābā'*) of life (cf. Lk. 17.17-25), as in Daniel (12.2) and 2 Maccabees (7.9, 14; 112.43-45). *ṣāḇā'*, however, need not refer to the whole of life, but simply to the long period of misery within life, nor need 'relief' refer to the absolute relief from life in death, which was small comfort to the sufferer, *pace* Job's sentiment in 3.11-22. The question in v. 14a, whatever its actual provenance, does not open a ray of hope, which at one stroke would deprive the Book of its problem; it is a rhetorical question tantamount to a negation, and may well emphasize the negation in v. 19c, after which Dhorme would read it. In v. 14, while disposed to admit occasional tricola in the general structure of bicola in Job, we must consider each tricolon on its own merits, with the constant possibility of displaced cola, and here we agree with Dhorme. On the military metaphor of service (*ṣāḇā'*) and relief (*ḥālîp̄*), see

above on 7.1, where, however, *ṣāḇā'* refers to the service of a day-labourer, and 10.17, where both words refer to relays of troops.

15. God's care for 'the work of (His) own hands' in temporary relief of Job's sufferings until a fair hearing is granted reflects the language of 10.8ff., where the suffering which God permits is out of accord with what humans might expect as the handiwork of the Creator.

The verb *kāsap̄*, from which the noun *kesep̄* (silver) is derived, means primarily 'to be pale', as with anxiety, hence the meaning here 'to yearn', or 'care for'.

16. *kî-'attāh* has been taken as stating the fact after the hypothesis implied in the wish in v. 13 and continued in vv. 14bcf. and rendered 'For then you would number my steps, you would not keep watch over my sin', so preserving MT *lō'-ṯišmôr* if indicative would contradict the sense of the context. This is the view expressed in RSV after Budde, Hölscher, Weiser, Horst. In agreement with Job's general complaint, however, and particularly with what we understand as the keeping account of Job's sins in v. 17, we consider this doubtful. We would take *kî* in the adversative sense, rendering *kî-'attāh*, 'but as it is'. In this case MT *lō'-ṯišmôr* would seem to contradict the sense of the context unless it is taken as a question (so G.R. Driver, Fohrer). We suggest that the phrase is affirmative, MT *lō'* being a scribal misunderstanding of the asseverative enclitic *lᵉ* as in Ugaritic and Arab. (cf. vv. 29, 24a). In view of the parallelism with *ṣᵉ'āḏay* ('my steps') there may be a word-play between *ḥaṭṭā'ṯî* ('my sin') and a possible Heb. homonym of Arab. *ḫaṭwātu*(*n*), 'footsteps', which might, at least in some degree, be reproduced in English by 'transgression'.

17. The reference here may be to the recording of charges on a papyrus document, which was then folded and sealed, instances of which have been found at Elephantine (*ANEP*, pl. 265). Pope envisages sins stored up with tokens in bags as commercial tallies mentioned in the Nuzu texts (Oppenheim 1959). *wattiṭpōl*, from *ṭāp̄al* ('to smear with clay or plaster'), parallel to *ḥāṯûm* and particularly *ṣᵉrôr*, suggests the sealing up of a bag of money or goods with wax or some such substance. In this connection it is interesting that a clay sealing in South Arabian characters was found in ninth-century debris at Bethel (Van Beek and Jamme 1958), doubtless a relic of the trade in incense, a precious commodity, which would demand sealing.

16ff. The general sentiment is that humans and their hopes are no more permanent than inanimate nature, even 'the eternal hills' (Gen. 49.26; Deut. 33.15), which are subject to landslide, detritus and soil-erosion.

18. MT *nôp̄ēl yibbôl* (lit. 'falling, withers'), if correct, may imply the various modes of ruin sudden and gradual (so Lévêque). But Theod. and S suggest the

reading *nāp̄ōl yippôl*, accepted by Lagarde, Graetz, Siegfried, Beer, Budde, Dhorme, Larcher, Hölscher, Horst, Fohrer and Lévêque. On *'āṯaq* ('to be removed') see on 9.5, also referring to the removal of mountains.

19. *šāḥaq* usually means 'to pulverize'; cf. *šaḥaq*, the fine dust on the scales in Isa. 40.15. The poet infers the action of water on rock in the fine detritus in the bed of the wadi.

MT *sᵉp̄îḥeyhā*, for which the verb *tišṭōp̄* demands the singular, suggests a common root with *sāp̄îaḥ*, grain accidentally 'spilled' in harvesting (Lev. 25.5) and what grows from it (Lev. 25.11; 2 Kgs 19.29; Isa. 37.30) and *misp̄āḥ* ('bloodshed') in Isa. 5.7. Thus it is possible that the word means here 'outpouring'. But *sᵉḥîp̄āh* has also been proposed by Budde, citing *māṭār sōḥēp̄* in Prov. 28.3 ('a driving rain'), so here 'flood'.

Fohrer suggests that v. 19c is the first colon of a bicolon, of which the second has been lost; cf. Dhorme's suggestion that v. 14a is the required colon, which we have accepted.

20. *tāqēp̄* here means obviously 'overpower'. It is found in late sources; cf. 15.24; Eccl. 4.12 and *tōqēp̄* in Est. 9.29; 10.2; Dan. 11.17. Hence it is probably Aram.; cf. *tqp* ('authority') in Nabataean inscriptions; it is well attested in Aram. *lāneṣaḥ*, usually meaning 'for ever', may here, as occasionally, indicate the superlative 'utterly' (Thomas 1956). *yahᵃlōḵ* might mean 'to go one's way', i.e. 'to die'; cf. Ps. 39.14 (EVV 13) and Akk. *ana šimtu alâku* ('he went to his fate'), cited by Horst; Duhm cites the Nabataean usage of the same verb. In the present passage, however, the form *yahᵃlōḵ* instead of the normal Classical Heb. *yēlēḵ*, usually taken as late poetic, may possibly be a homonym, cognate with Arab. *halaka* ('to perish, pass away').

21. The adjective *ṣā'îr* in the sense both of 'young' and 'little' (cf. Arab. *saġīr*, 'young, small, insignificant') is well attested in Classical Heb. The verbal root is found only in comparatively late sources (e.g. Jer. 30.19; Zech. 13.7) and here in Job.

22. 'His flesh upon him' (*bᵉśārô 'ālāyw*) is intelligible; 'his life upon him' (*nap̄šô 'ālāyw*) unusual. Obviously *'ālāyw*, repeated, must be emphasized, and that in contrast to the feeling one cannot have for the vicissitudes of one's family after one's death. Thus *'al* with the prepositional suffix emphasizes the intimate and personal nature of the experience. The experience and interest of the subject is concentrated in his present life, indicated by the conjunction of his flesh (*bᵉśārô*) and his animation (*nap̄šô*), and does not extend beyond it.

Job 15

Eliphaz's Second Reply: A Remonstration to Job's Obstinacy in Questioning the Theodicy

The address falls into two parts, vv. 2-16 in four strophes (vv. 2-6, 7-10, 11-13, 14-16), where Eliphaz remonstrates with Job, and six strophes (vv. 17-19, 20-22, 23-25, 26-28, 29-32 and 32-35), where God's providence in the moral order in the retribution of the wicked is asserted.

The literary affinity of the first half is with the controversial pieces in Wisdom literature where an opponent's personal authority and his doctrine is challenged, often by a succession of questions, but also by direct statements. The second part is cast in the form of the instruction of the sage ('I shall declare to you. Hear me…', vv. 15-17), the substance of his instruction being the traditional view borne out by personal experience that sin brought its own retribution.

From this point the debate sharpens, and Job turns progressively from his friends to God, while they no longer temper their admonitions with encouragement, except, briefly, the more mature Eliphaz (22.21-30). If the friends do not 'keep silence' as Job suggests (13.5), their statements are less direct arguments related to Job's case than sharp invective motivated by professional pique (15.9-10; 18.3; 20.3) at Job's critical attitude to traditional Wisdom to which they served themselves heirs (15.2-13; 18.1-4), and seek to overwhelm him with the weight of garnered wisdom that 'has been handed down by wise men' (15.18-19) on the theme of sin and retribution in the colourful, indeed often lurid, language of Proverbs (15.20-35; 18.5-21; 20.4-29), many aphorisms of which are cited. Besides, Eliphaz but reiterates the argument that God is beyond the imputation of injustice by frail humans in a passage (15.11-16) which, from its allusion to a word spoken in consolation (15.11), obviously refers to his statement in 4.15-21. In their introductory invective Eliphaz and Bildad both charge Job with arrogating to himself special knowledge of the mind of God (15.8), as though he was the first of humankind (15.7), whose case transcended Cosmic Order (18.4).

Chapter 15

1. And Eliphaz the Temanite answered and said:

2. 'Does a wise man answer with knowledge that is mere wind,
And fill his belly with the hot blast,
3. Argue with unprofitable argument,
And with words which are useless?
4. You annul reverence for God,
You detract from serious thought vis-à-vis God,
5. For your sin prompts your speech,
And you choose a crafty tongue.
6. Your own mouth condemns you and not I,
And your (own) lips testify against you.

7. Were you born the first of men,
Or were you brought forth in travail before the hills?
8. Are you admitted to listen in on the intimate counsel of God?
And do you assert a monopoly of wisdom?
9. What do you know that we do not know,
Or perceive that is unfamiliar to us?
10. The grey-haired and the aged are among us,
Older than your father.

11. Are the consolations of God too little for you,
(Our) word spoken[1] in gentleness to you?
12. How your heart prompts you to behave shamelessly,[2]
And how haughty[3] are your eyes,
13. That you let your anger recoil on[4] God
And spout words from your mouth!

14. What is man that he may be pure,
One born of woman that he may be innocent?
15. Lo, even his holy ones[5] he does not trust,
And the heavens are not pure in his sight,
16. How much less one who is abhorrent and corrupt,
A man who drinks up wrong like water!

17. I will enlighten you, listen to me,
And of what I have seen I will tell[6] you,
18. What the sages declare,
And their fathers did not conceal,[7]
19. To whom alone the land was given,
No stranger having come in to settle among them.

20. The wicked man is anxious all his days,
The years laid up for the wicked are few.[8]
21. The sound of flocks is in his ears;
Even when he is secure the spoiler shall come upon him.
22. He cannot rely on getting free of darkness
And he is marked off[9] for destruction.[10]

23. He is apportioned[11] as food[12] for the vultures,[13]
He knows that his collapse[14] is certain.
24. The dark day overwhelms him,[15]
Distress and anguish overpower him
Like the striding warrior[16] ready to attack,
25. Because he lifted his hand against God,[17]
Defied[18] the Almighty.

26. He charges him[19] with a horde,
With the mass of his shield-bosses;
27. Yea, he covered his face with fat,[20]
And put fat on his loins;
28. And he occupied ruined cities,
Houses which are uninhabited,
Which threaten to fall into ruin-heaps.

29. He will not be rich, nor will his wealth endure,
Nor will his possessions[21] reach the underworld.
30. ( )[22] His shoot the flame shall parch,
And his blossom[23] shall be blasted[24] by the wind.
31. Let one not trust in its generosity[25]
For its dates shall come to naught;
32. It will wilt[26] before its maturity,
And its frond will not grow green.

33. His unripe grapes will remain sour[27] on the vine;[28]
And cast its blossom like an olive tree.
34. For the company of the godless is barren,
And fire will devour the tents of corruption.
35. He is pregnant with trouble and gives birth to evil,
His belly[29] gestates delusion.’

Textual Notes to Chapter 15

1. Reading with T the verbal noun *dabbēr* for MT *dāḇār*, which is nevertheless intelligible.
2. Reading *mah-yyōḵîḥ*^{a}*ḵā libb*^{e}*ḵā* for MT *mah-yyiqaḥ*^{a}*ḵā libb*^{e}*kā*. See Commentary *ad loc.*
3. Reading *t*^{e}*rûmeynā* for MT *yizr*^{e}*mûn*. See Commentary *ad loc.*
4. Reading *‘al* for MT *’el.*
5. Reading *q*^{e}*ḏôšāyw* with Qere for MT (Kethib) *qdšw.*
6. Reading *’*^{a}*sappērāh* (pausal) after LXX, S and V for MT *wa’*^{a}*sappērāh.*
7. Reading *w*^{e}*lō’ kiḥ*^{a}*ḏûm ’*^{a}*ḇôṯām* for MT *w*^{e}*lō’ kiḥ*^{a}*ḏû mē’*^{a}*ḇôṯām*. Another possibility is *w*^{e}*lō’ niḵḥ*^{a}*ḏû mē’*^{a}*ḇôṯām* (‘which were not concealed from their fathers’), assuming omission of *n* before *k* in the Old Heb. script.
8. Reading *mispār* for MT *mispar*. See Commentary *ad loc.*
9. Reading *w*^{e}*ṣāp̱ûy* for MT *w*^{e}*sāp̱û*, with omission of *y* before *h* in the Old Heb. script.
10. Reading *ḥōreḇ* for MT *ḥāreḇ* (pausal).
11. Reading *nāḏûḏ* for MT *nōḏēḏ*. See Commentary *ad loc.*
12. Reading *l*^{e}*leḥem* for MT *lalleḥem.*
13. Reading *’ayyāh* for *’ayyēh* (‘where’?) with LXX.

14. Reading *pîḏô* for MT *b^{e}yāḏô*.
15. Reading *y^{e}ḇa'^{a}ṯēhû* for MT *y^{e}ḇa'^{a}ṯuhû*.
16. Reading *m^{e}haklēḵ* for MT *meleḵ*. See Commentary *ad loc.*
17. Reading *'al* for MT *'el.*
18. Reading *'al* for MT *'el.*
19. Reading *'ālāyw* for MT *'ēlāyw.*
20. Reading *ḥēleḇ* for MT *ḥelbô*, assuming a dittograph of final *w* before the following *w* in the Old Heb. script.
21. Reading *m^{e}nōlô* for MT *minlām*. See Commentary *ad loc.*
22. Omitting *lō'-yāsûr minnî-ḥōšeḵ* as a gloss on v. 22a displaced to its present position. See Commentary *ad loc.*
23. Reading *pirḥô* with LXX for MT *pîw*.
24. Reading *wîsō'ar* for MT *w^{e}yāsûr*; cf. Hos. 13.3.
25. Reading *b^{e}šû'āṯô* for MT *b^{e}šāw niṯ'āh*. See Commentary *ad loc.*
26. Reading *timmōl* for MT *timmālē'*. See Commentary *ad loc.*
27. Reading *yaḥmōṣ* for MT *yaḥmōs*, assuming corruption of *ṣ* to *s* in the Old Heb. script.
28. Reading *baggep̄en* for MT *kaggep̄en*, assuming scribal corruption of *b* to *k* in the square script.
29. Reading *biṭnô* for *biṭnām*, with corruption of *w* to *m* in the Old Heb. script.

Commentary on Chapter 15

2. In *da'aṯ-rûaḥ* there is a *double entendre*. The word *rûaḥ*, as in 7.7 and 16.3, and, as the parallel with *qāḏîm* (the east wind or sirocco) suggests, indicates 'wind' in the sense here of emptiness. It might also mean 'inspiration'. In Job's reply to Eliphaz in 16.3 the word-play is more pronounced.

3. On *hôḵēaḥ* ('to argue, criticize') see above on 5.17. *sāḵan* ('to be helpful') is peculiar to Job; cf. 22.2 and 35.3, where, as here, it is parallel to *hô'îl*. This implies the allegation of inanity in Job's 'windy words'.

4. *tāp̄ēr*, from *pārar*, means 'to break', literally as in 16.12 (*way^{e}p̄arp^{e}rēnî*, 'and he has shattered me'), or 'to violate' (e.g. a covenant), or 'to frustrate' (e.g. ordered government or judgment, 40.8), or, as here, 'to annul'; cf. Ps. 89.34, *ḥasdî lō' 'āp̄îr mē'immô* ('I shall not annul my covenant love with him'). *yir^e'āh*, here used absolutely, means 'fear' or 'reverence' of God, expressed in practical piety; cf. Arab. *taqwā* ('fear of God, piety'). It is the comprehensive Heb. term for 'religion'. *gāra'* means 'to withdraw', either in the sense of 'subtract', hence 'diminish' as in the tally of bricks in Exod. 5.8, 19, or 'remove', as at 36.7. It may denote removing to oneself, as, for example, in 36.27 (drawing drops of water), or monopolizing (15.8).

śîaḥ or *śîḥāh* is 'meditation' or 'serious thought'; cf. Ps. 119.97, 99. Job is here criticized for his extreme humanist approach to the problems of life and the divine involvement, having of his own initiative and insight 'chosen' the language of the worldly 'astute' (*'^{a}rûmîm*, v. 5). NEB renders v. 4b 'usurping the sole right to speak in the divine presence'. But *śîaḥ*, though meaning 'to talk about' in Judg. 5.10 (possibly), and Prov. 6.22, with direct object, means more often 'to meditate, think seriously' (Pss. 77.7, 13; 119.15, 23, 27, 48, 78, 97, 99); cf. Amos 4.13: *maggîḏ lā'āḏām mah-śîḥô* ('who declared to humanity what are its thoughts'). We take *lip̄ᵉnê* to mean 'about' or 'vis-à-vis'.

5. 'Your sin prompts your speech' (lit. 'your sin teaches your mouth') is an accusation of casuistic self-exculpation.

6. *'ānāh bᵉ* (lit. 'to answer against') is a common expression for 'to testify against', attested, as here, with 'mouth' or 'speech' as subject in 2 Sam. 1.16.

7. Whether or not this passage presupposes the conception of God's wisdom as the agent of his creation, the theme of Proverbs 8, esp. vv. 22-31, as Dhorme supposes (1926: 191), the language recalls that passage (cf. Ps. 90.2). Insofar as this verse signifies anything beyond the mere age of humans, it may animadvert upon the plan of God in creation ('before the hills') as a manifestation of his wisdom, to which humanity as the last stage of his creation was not admitted. This emphasis on the transcendent nature of God's wisdom recurs in the address of Zophar in 11.7-9 and particularity in the speeches of Elihu (36.24ff.; 37.24), and in the Divine Declaration in 38.2ff. On the other hand it may reflect the myth of the primaeval man to which Ezekiel refers (28.1-2, 12ff.), which has a counterpart in Mesopotamian mythology in the myth of the primaeval humans created not only before the animals but before plants and physical features after the earth.

8. *sôḏ* denotes either the intimate counsel of God, as in Amos 3.7, or intimate company, as in Job 19.19; Pss. 55.15 (EVV 14); 64.3 (EVV 2); Ezek. 13.9. It also denotes God's privy council (Jer. 23.18). Job 15.8 could refer to God's counsel or council, but the passage recalls Jer. 23.18 in his taunting question regarding the false prophets, which Eliphaz may consciously re-echo.

10. *yāšîš* means 'aged' without the sense of decrepitude as in 12.12. *kabbîr* in the sense of 'old' is regular in the Arab. cognate. The verbal and adjectival forms of the root are practically confined to Job in the OT, where Aramaism is likely. The word occurs in Phoenician inscriptions meaning 'great', but is more common in Aram. inscriptions from the eighth century BCE and later literary sources.

11. *tanḥumôṯ 'ēl* ('the consolations of God') means the consolations of Job's friends in their first addresses, which they considered inspired by God and were designed to turn Job in faith to God for assurance, like the milder tone of Eliphaz's first address with his counsel of supplication and hope of rehabilitation (5.8ff.). There may also be a reference to the inspired words of Eliphaz in

4.12ff. *dabbēr lā'aṭ* (MT *dāḇār*) ('our word spoken in gentleness') refers particularly to Eliphaz's first address to Job.

12. MT *yiqqāḥᵃḵā* is pointed as if from *lāqaḥ* ('to take'), which is generally accepted. G.R. Driver (1948: 235) associated the word with Arab. *waqiḥa* ('to behave shamelessly, be bold'), which suggests a reading *mah-yyōqîḥᵃkā*, lit. 'what has made you shameless?', being the regular form of exclamation in Arab., 'how shameless you are!' *rzm* is generally taken as a metathetic cognate of *rᵉmaz* found in Aram., Syr. and Late Heb., meaning 'to make signs, wink'. This is not very apt in the present context. In view of Driver's interpretation of the parallel verb we may seriously consider the variant in one Heb. MS—*yᵉrûmû*, cf. 'haughty eyes'. In the localization of moral qualities or propensities in parts of the body, arrogance is specifically associated with the eyes; cf. Prov. 6.17; 30.13. See further textual note.

13. *rûaḥ* here may mean rather 'anger' as in Judg. 8.3 and Prov. 16.32 (so LXX). Dhorme emphasizes 'from your mouth', i.e. hasty words instead of considered utterance from the heart. 'Words' (*millîn* again with the Aram. ending if the text is sound) may have the same emphasis. Here Pope translates 'Spouting words from your mouth', which with slight modification we have adopted. Duhm proposed *mᵉrî* ('rebellion'), which would be a much more colourful expression, but the ancient versions are unanimous in support of MT.

14. The synonyms *'ᵉnôš* and *yᵉlûḏ 'iššāh* recall *'āḏām* and *yᵉlûḏ 'iššāh* in 14.1, emphasizing the frailty of humanity.

15. The transcendence of God and his plans even beyond the angels, here 'holy ones' as in 5.1, is expressed already in 4.18, where 'his servants' is parallel to 'his angels'.

šāmayim is not a circumlocution for 'angels' (T and Rashi), but denotes the sky in its purity; cf. Exod. 24.10 (Driver and Gray 1921: 135). So 'pure' (*zakkû*) is used in its physical sense. The sentiment recalls the formula of emancipation in administrative tablets from the palace of Ras Shamra which declares an emancipated slave 'clear (*br*) as the sun is clear (*brt*)'.

16. On *'ap̄ kî* ('how much less') as a formula of *a fortiori* reasoning, see on 4.19.

ne'ᵉlāḥ is a rare word, found only here and in Pss. 14.3 and 53.4. It is a moral term in the OT without any trace of physical connotation, but the Arab. cognate *'alaḥa* in the VIIIth form is used of milk turning sour.

'A man who drinks up wrong like water', i.e. lives by it as a daily necessity, or with the same natural ease, recalls Elihu's charge that Job 'drinks up scoffing like water' (34.7).

17. On the verb *ḥiwwāh* ('to explain, reveal') see on 13.17.

On the reading *'ᵃsappērā* (pausal form), see textual note. *zeh* is the relative particle, Ugaritic and Aram. *dᵉ*; cf. Arab. *maḏa*; and see 19.19 and Ps. 68.9.

In citing the insights of the older sages he does not exclude his personal experience ('what I have seen', 4.7). In our reading *kiḥᵃḏû-m 'ᵃḇôṯām* for MT *kiḥᵃdû mē'ᵃḇôṯām* the enclitic *m* with the verb is to be noted as in Ugaritic (N.M. Sarna, 'Some Instances of the Enclitic *m* in Job', *JSS* 6 [1955], p. 110).

19. This relative clause with the relative particle omitted, as often in poetry. The Jewish author momentarily forgets the origin of Eliphaz beyond Israel. The golden age of tradition from the viewpoint of the writer of Job after the Exile was the days of the settlement in Palestine before the traditional faith were corrupted by extraneous humanistic philosophy. The passage recalls Joel's conception of Jerusalem and the Temple uncontaminated by foreign influences as the repository of the heritage of Israel (Joel 3.17; cf. Isa. 52.1). In support of the meaning 'to settle' for *'āḇar* Fohrer cites as a cognate Arab. *ġabara* with this meaning.

20. It is characteristic of the more mature Eliphaz that in contrast to the others he does not elaborate on the temporary success of the wicked before their downfall (cf. Pss. 10.2-11; 73.4-12), but assumes their success, haunted by constant fear, under 'the sword of Damocles', and their inevitable end. Where he does expatiate on the career of the arrogant tyrant in the flush of his power (Job 15.26-28) he is probably animadverting on Job's challenge to God, though in justice to Job his challenge is for a fair hearing and not aggressive defiance. *miṯḥôlēl* means 'to be tormented', the Hithpolel of *ḥûl* or *ḥîl* ('to writhe in pain or anxiety') as here; cf. *hiṯḥalḥal* (Est. 4.4). This suits the context better than the reading *miṯhôlēl*, 'shows his folly' (so Theod., Margolis) or 'boasts' (so S, V, Beer). MT *mispar šānîm* may mean 'a certain number of years', which in Heb. idiom would rather be *šᵉnê mispār*. *niṣpᵉnû* indicates a plur. subject. While *mispar šānîm* might be taken as a plural, we should take the verb in a relative clause of which *šānîm* is the antecedent, and *mispar*, read as *mispār*, being the predicate, and as being emphasized by its position.

21. We should notice a conscious word-play here between the homonyms *paḥaḏ* ('terror') and a cognate of Arab. *faḥad*(*u*) ('flock'); cf. Gordon *UT* Aqht V.17, 22f. *'imr bpḥd* ('a lamb from the flock'), and Akk. *puḫâdu* (Gordon *UT* 1628). The picture of the rich man in apparent security (*baššālôm*) is particularized by his hearing the bleating of his flocks, soon to be the prey of the spoiler (*šôḏēḏ*).

22. MT *lō' ya'ᵃmîn šûḇ minni-ḥošeḵ* ('he does not believe that he will come back from darkness'), though the anxiety of the wicked man is emphasized in

the passage, does not accord with the general emphasis on the confidence of such. Hence we should render the verb as 'rely' rather than 'believe'. For *šûḇ* NEB renders 'escape'; cf. Fohrer *entkommt*. This is obviously the sense, and we suggest that the verb is cognate with Arab. *śāba*, imperf. *yaśību*, which is used of beasts let free on the range. This would also be most apt at 33.30, *l^ehāšîb napšô minnî-šaḥaṯ* ('to deliver his life from the pit') and Ps. 35.17.

MT *ṣāp̄û* emended to *ṣāp̄ûy* (Qere) is preferable. G.R. Driver (1955: 78) takes the verb *ṣāp̄āh* in the sense of 'to mark down', after Ps. 37.32, where the verb is parallel to *biqqēš*; he cites the Ass. *ṣipû* ('to surround, enclose, delimit, mark off, survey'). Alternatively, the verb might be *ṣāp̄āh*, familiar in the Talmud, meaning 'to choose' (so Tur-Sinai); cf. Arab. *ṣafa(y)* with this meaning in the VIII form. We take the verb as *ṣāp̄āh* ('to spy out'). The passage may reflect the continual dread of the inhabitants of the border lands of being spied upon and marked down for a raid by Bedouin.

23-24. MT may be arranged as follows:

nōḏēḏ hû' lalleḥem 'ayyeh
yāḏa' kî-nāḵôn b^eyāḏô
yôm-ḥōšeḵ y^eba'^atuhû
ṣar ûm^eṣûqāh tiṯq^epēhû
k^emeleḵ 'āṯîḏ lakkîḏôr

In this passage LXX reads 'He has been appointed as food for the vultures', suggesting the reading *nāḏûḏ hû' l^eleḥem 'ayyāh*. The LXX rendering 'he is appointed' has suggested the emendation *nô'āḏ* (so Duhm, Buttenwieser, Hölscher, Kissane), *mû'āḏ* (Beer), *nôḏā'*, 'is known' (Dhorme). Fohrer and Pope retain MT *nôḏēḏ* ('wandering'), reading *l^eleḥem 'ayyāh* ('as food for vultures'), envisaging one who has lost his way and perished in the desert. MT is retained by G.B. Gray, Weiser and Horst meaning 'he wanders about for bread (saying), "Where is it?"' We would read *nāḏûḏ* for MT *nōḏēḏ*, taking the verb as cognate with Ugaritic *ndd* ('to apportion'); cf. Gordon *UT* 'nt I.8: *qṣ mr'i ndd* ('he apportioned slices of fatlings'), which accords with the rendering of LXX. Horst's objection that *'oḵlāh* and not *leḥem* would have been used for 'food' is invalid in view of the general meaning 'food' in the Ras Shamra texts and often in poetry in the OT and of the verb *lḥm* ('to eat') in the Ras Shamra texts; cf. Arab. *laḥmu(n)* ('meat'). *'ayyāh* is mentioned as a keen-sighted bird in 28.7 and listed among the unclean birds in Lev. 11.14 and Deut. 14.13. Hence 'vulture' would be most apt. In the second colon LXX reads 'he knows in himself that he is ready for a fall'. A 'fall' has suggested the emendation of MT *b^eyāḏô*, e.g. to *l^e'ēḏ* ('he is ready [*nāḵôn*] for calamity'), or *pîḏô* ('his collapse', so Wright, Ball, Dhorme, Hölscher, Tur-Sinai, Stevenson, Kissane, Horst, Fohrer, Pope). In the third colon in the above arrangement the verb should be singular in agreement with the subject *yôm ḥōšeḵ*.

24. On *tāqap̄* in the sense 'to overpower', see on 14.20. In v. 24a the agreement of the singular verb is with the nearer subject *m*ᵉ*ṣûqāh*. The necessary connection between the 'king' (*melek̠*) and 'ready to attack' (*'āṯîḏ lakkîḏôr*) is most unlikely in this context, and Hoffman's conjecture (1931: 144), *m*ᵉ*hallēk̠* for MT *melek̠*, is feasible, especially in the light of Prov. 6.11:

*ûḇā'-kim*ᵉ*hallēk̠ rē'šek̠ā*
*ûmaḥsōr*ᵉ*k̠ā k*ᵉ*'îš māḡēn*

Here *m*ᵉ*hallēk̠* is taken variously as 'highwayman' and 'vagabond'. On the evidence of the Ras Shamra texts *māḡēn* could mean either 'shield' or 'petition'. The more striking figure would be that of a warrior, probably reflecting the all too familiar experience of soldiers living off the country through which they passed. On the other hand, the 'man with the shield' would describe the figurine of Reshef, the god who slew men in mass in war or plague, who was conventionally depicted as an armed warrior striding out (*m*ᵉ*hallēk̠*) in a short kilt with a shield (*k*ᵉ*'îš māḡēn*) in bronzes from Palestine and Syria in the Late Bronze Age and Egyptian sculpture from the same period. Alternatively the word may mean 'destroyer', cognate with Arab. *halaka* ('to destroy'). This may be envisaged in Job 15.24. *kîḏôr* is not attested elsewhere in the OT, but in the context it is obviously cognate with Arab. *kedara* (VIIIth form), meaning 'to dart upon' (as a hawk on its prey); cf. Syr. *qadrā'* ('hawk').

25. *hiṯgabbēr* is used in a good sense of God in Isa. 42.13 ('to show himself mighty'), or, as here, 'to act defiantly'. The latter is the nuance of the Arab. cognate *jabbāru*(*n*) ('bully, giant').

26. MT *b*ᵉ*ṣawwā'r* has suggested the literal translation 'with a neck'. This, in view of the English slang 'hard neck' and German *Hartnäckigkeit*, is deceptively intelligible; cf. NEB 'with the head down' and V 'with neck erect'. Tur-Sinai's 'hauberk', i.e. 'neck-armour', German *Halsberge*, is not attested in Heb. The ancient versions do not help. Aq., Sym. and Theod. attest MT, but 'arrogantly' in LXX and Jerome's commentary, if they indicate MT, seems a paraphrase. If Dhorme is right in taking MT *gabbê māḡinnāyw* ('bosses of his shields') as interlocked shields like like the Roman *testudo* ('tortoise'), which the plural would seem to suggest, then *ṣawwā'r* may be cognate with Arab. *ṣawāru*(*n*) ('a herd of oxen'), hence 'horde'. This, rather than the reference to the neck of a single warrior, is suggested by the plural *gabbê māḡinnāyw*.

27. The fat of the prosperous wicked and oppressor was proverbial in the OT; cf. Jer. 5.28; Ps. 73.7. Fat characterizes the materialist, clogging humanity, spiritual susceptibility and intelligence (Ps. 119.70).

28. The Niphal of *kāḥaḏ* in the sense of 'to be effaced' or 'to be deserted' (of land, probably signifying the effacing of landmarks) is attested in Zech. 11.9, 16, and in the Hiphil meaning 'to wipe out, destroy' in Exod. 23.23 (of the Amorites in Canaan) and 1 Kgs 13.34 (of the House of Jeroboam). MT *lāmô*, which it is proposed to emend, may be retained as an ethic dative. *hiṯ'attᵉḏû* is attested only here, the Piel being attested in Prov. 24.27 in the sense of 'to prepare'; cf. *'āṯîḏ* in v. 23 and 3.8, 'ready, prepared to'. It expresses what is urgent or imminent, hence in reference to houses 'which threaten to fall into ruin-heaps' (*gallîm*); cf. Jer. 9.10; 51.37; 2 Kgs 19.25 = Isa. 37.26. The colon is suspected as a gloss (so Fohrer).

29. *yāqûm* means here 'to be established'. *minlām* is the problem in v. 29b. LXX renders the Heb. original at this point as 'shadow', which has suggested the emendation *ṣillām* ('their shadow'), perhaps *ṣillô* ('his shadow'), not a drastic emendation in the Old Heb. script. The conception may be that he will not live till sunset. Alternatively, the figure might be that of a wide-spreading tree or the spreading vine in Ps. 80.9-11 (EVV 8-10), cited by Dhorme. V, in rendering 'their root', indicates the reading *'eṣlām*, of which MT *minlām* is a feasible corruption in the Old Heb. script. T reads *min lām* ('of that which belongs to them', their possessions), which the parallelism suggests. Dahood is probably right in seeing what was probably originally *mānōl* from a root *nûl* cognate with Arab. *nāla, yanūl* ('to give'), hence 'that which is given', 'possessions'. The final *m* of *minlām* is probably a scribal corruption of *w* in the Old Heb. script, and we propose *mᵉnôlô* in *scriptio defectiva*. We propose that *'ereṣ* here as often in the OT and the Ras Shamra texts denotes the underworld. The figure envisages the burial of a king or notable with his wealth or goods, as in the tombs of pharaohs in what was for the writer of the Book of Job the vain hope of their use in the afterlife. This meaning of *mᵉnôlô* is supported by *ye'ᵉšar* ('be rich') and *ḥēylô* ('his wealth').

30. In v. 30a, *lō'-yāsûr minnî-ḥōšek*, which does not have any obvious connection with the context, is probably a gloss on v. 22a on the assumption that *šûḇ* means 'to return' (see on v. 22a) (so Bickell, Budde, Siegfried, Duhm, G.B. Gray, Dhorme, Hölscher, Holst, Fohrer). This eliminates an odd colon from the prevailing arrangement in bicola. *šalheḇeṯ* ('flame', or the scorching sirocco), is found in the OT only here and at Ezek. 21.3. It is one of the rare instances of the formation of a noun from a verbal root with preformative *š*, which is known as the preformative of the causative variation of the root in Akk., Ugaritic and vestigially in Aram.; cf. *šabblûl* ('snail', 'that which makes wet') in Ps. 58.9. For *wᵉyāsûr*, which is unintelligible in the context, the emendation *wᵉyissā'ēr* ('and it will be blasted') has been proposed by Beer, Budde *et al.*; cf. Perles, Duhm, Oort, Fohrer, who propose *wîsô'ar* (Pual). This sustains the figure, and suggests the emendation of MT *pîw* to *pirḥô* ('its

blossom'), which is read by Beer, Budde, Ball, Dhorme, Hölscher, Stevenson and Fohrer.

31. MT *'al-ya'ᵃmēn baššāw niṯ'āh* is a notorious crux. LXX paraphrases and ignores the main difficulty. S 'he does not believe in the falsehood which leads astray', and T 'he does not believe in a son of man who errs in falsehood', confirm MT without translating it accurately, and the ancient versions are also vague and confused about v. 30c, nor is there any more agreement among commentators. G.B. Gray accepts MT, rendering:

> Let him trust not in emptiness, deceiving himself,
> For emptiness will be his return for what he does.

While this is a feasible rendering of MT, it interrupts the figure in the passage, and so the verse has been taken as a gloss (so Hölscher, Horst, Fohrer). Alternatively, accepting the original of the passage, it is proposed to find a reference to the unreliability of the wealth of the wicked (reading *'ᵃšîrāṯô*, 'wealth', for MT *šāw niṯ'āh*), 'and what it might buy them' (*tᵉmûrāṯô*), lit. 'his exchanging', i.e. trade; cf. Ruth 4.7; Job 20.18; so T. In view of the figure of a fruit-tree in what precedes and follows, however, this is unlikely. The complex *šāw niṯ'āh* may be a corruption of *šû'āṯô*, the feminine form of a verbal noun either from the root *yāša'* cognate with Arab. *waśa'a* ('to enrich', used of God's favours) or from a verb *šā'āh* unattested in the OT, but cognate with Ugaritic *ṯ'y*, 'to give' (Gordon *UT* 62.56; 127.59), or perhaps a byform *šûa'*. In this assumption we offer the suggestion *'al-ya'ᵃmēn bᵉšû'āṯô* ('let one not trust in its generosity'). Houbigant suggested the reading *tᵉmôrāṯô* ('his palm-tree') for MT *tᵉmûrāṯô*. Certainly *kippāṯô* in v. 32b indicates a palm-tree, meaning generally 'branch', but specifically 'palm-frond' in Ass.; cf. Isa. 9.13 and 19.15, where in contrast to the reed it may denote the frond of the lofty palm. The reference to 'shoot' (*yōnaqtô*) and 'blossom' (*pirḥô*) is to the fruit of the palm-tree, dates (Arab. *tamru*[*n*]) rather than to the tree, to which the pronominal suffix may rather refer. *tāmār* is well-attested in Heb. but not *tamar* or *tamrāh* meaning 'date', though such a word is not unlikely. Hence we propose that MT *tᵉmûrāh* is a corruption of *tamrāh* with dittography of *w* after *m* in the Old Heb. script. We propose the reading:

> *'al-ya'ᵃmēn bᵉšû'āṯô*
> *kî šāw' tihyeh tamrāṯô.*

Alternatively, for MT *šāw niṯ'āh*, we might suggest *šô'āṯōh* ('its nobility [of stature]'); cf. the palm-tree (*tāmār*) with the cedar as a symbol of stature and flourishing in Ps. 92.12 (EVV 11).

32. Continuing the figure of the fruit-tree or date-palm we read after LXX, V, S and Graetz, Hoffmann, Perles, Budde, G.B. Gray, Dhorme, Beer, Hölscher, Stevenson and Fohrer:

bᵉlō'-yômô timmōl
wᵉḵippāṯô lō' ra'ᵃnānāh

It will wilt before its time,
And its palm-frond will not grow green.

33. The vine, it has been observed (Friedrich Delitzsch), does not cast its grapes before they are ripe (MT *bisrô*), but they may remain on the vine without ripening. In this case the vine that in apparently failing to supply the necessary nutriment to the fruit might be said to 'do it violence' (*yaḥmōs*), but this is not a natural expression. We would suggest that the original text read *yaḥmōṣ baggeṕen bosrô* ('his unripe grapes shall remain sour on the vine'), assuming scribal corruption of *ṣ* to *s* in the Old Heb. script. The vocalization *bōser* and not *bēser*, as assumed in MT, is attested in Isa. 18.5 and in the popular proverb in Jer. 31.29f. and Ezek. 18.2. The olive tree on the other hand does shed its blossom not only in its fruitful years, after pollination, but without fruition every year (Dalman 1928: I, 381; 1935: IV, 165, 300).

34. *'ᵃḏaṯ ḥānēp̄* ('the company of the godless') recalls *'ᵃḏaṯ ṣaddîqîm* in Ps. 1.5 and *'ᵃḏaṯ rᵉšā'îm* in Ps. 22.17, etc. The noun should not be pressed to mean an ideological society in view of the use of the word in *'ᵃḏaṯ dᵉḇôrîm* ('swarm of bees') in Judg. 14.8, though it does denote specifically the community at Qumran. On *ḥānēp̄* see above on 8.15.

35. On *galmûḏ* ('barren') see on 3.7. The infinitives absolute *hārōh* and *yālōḏ* emphasize the verbs and make them more graphic; cf. GKC, §113ff. On the general sentiment with slight variation, see on 5.6f. In v. 35b LXX and S read *tāḵîl* ('contain') for MT *tāḵîn*, which Dhorme would retain, seeing a reference to the 'preparation' of the embryo in the womb. This is now confirmed by the Ras Shamra texts, for example in Gordon *UT* 51 IV.48, 'nt V.44:

ṯr 'il 'abh	The Bull El her father,
'il mlk dyknnh	El the King who begot her.

Cf. the title of the mother-goddess Aṯirat in the Ras Shamra texts *knyt 'ilm* ('Procreatrix of the gods').

Job 16 and 17

JOB'S REJOINDER TO ELIPHAZ

The advance of the argument beyond the mere rebuttal of orthodox objections to Job's questioning of the situation of righteous sufferers in God's economy is marked by the summary reply of Job to his friends in the first part of his statement (16.2-4b, 4c-6) as compared with the more lengthy statement of his grievances against God (16.7-9b, 12-14, 15-17, 18-22) and the statement of his sufferings (17.1-4, 5-7, 11-13, 14-16).

In the first part of Job's reply (16.2-4b, 4c-6) the literary form is the sapiential controversy. The second part (vv. 7-9b, 12-14, 15-17, 18-22) is cast in the form of an appeal against an adversary in the law-court, including a protestation of innocence and appeal for vindication (vv. 18-22).This has much in common with the psalm of the type the Plaint of the Sufferer from which it borrows figures and phraseology, particularly in 13, 15-16. Job's statement of his cumulative griefs and his hopeless prospect follows this pattern.

Job 16.9c-11, where the sufferings of Job are at the hands of the wicked and not, as in the context, of God, are probably a secondary expansion cited from a plaint of the sufferer, v. 11 ('God delivers me up to wrong-doers') being possibly an adaptation of the insertion to the context, another sapiential gloss in the interests of orthodoxy in 17.8-10:

> The righteous are shocked at this,
> And the innocent is indignant at the impious;
> But let the righteous man hold to his way,
> And the pure of heart will gain strength.
> But come on again, all of you,
> I shall not find a wise man among you.

The incongruity of v. 8 with Job's attitude and argument has been noted, and the interruption of Job's lament between vv. 7 and 11. The passage has therefore been taken either as a gloss (so Hölscher, Fohrer; cf. Duhm, who takes it as a gloss on Bildad's statement at 18.3) or displaced. Stevenson suggested it followed 18.21 in Bildad's speech (cf. Kissane, who regards v. 10 in place, but reads v. 8 after 18.20 and v. 9 after 18.21).

Thus in his reply to Eliphaz's statement in ch. 15 Job indicates that he is as familiar with the inherent disability and jeopardy of the wicked and his miserable end as Eliphaz or any other sage (2.4a). He animadverts on 'troublesome comforters', referring, *argumentum ad hominem*, to their 'windy words' (16.3; cf. 15.2). Job seems to hint that sympathy rather than argument and indictment might have been more apt to this situation (3-5). His reply to Bildad is also summary and in the same vein (19.2-5, 21f.), while in his reply to Zophar he claims a patient and sympathetic hearing (21.2-6). The switch to Job's main theme of his plea to God for justice, prefaced by his statement of false accusation in the language of the Plaint of the Sufferer in such a case is indicated by *'aḵ-'attāh* (v. 7). This occupies the bulk of Job's reply to Eliphaz and a similar proportion of his reply to Bildad (19.6-20).

Chapter 16

1. Then Job answered and said:

2. 'I have heard many things like these;
Troublesome comforters are you all.
3. Is there a limit to windy words?
And[1] how aggravating is your retort!
4a. I too could talk like you.
Would that you yourselves were in my place!

Then[2] I could elaborate (the case) against you with words
And wag my head at you,
5. Or I could strengthen you[3] with what I had to say,
And sympathy would move my lips unceasingly.[4]
6. My sorrow, if spoken, would not be checked,
And if I would keep silent, how freely would it flow out!

7. But now malice[5] has worn me out;
Every one of my associates [8a] seized upon me.[6]
8. [7]One has testified against me and risen up in enmity against me,
A false accuser of me[8], testifying against me to my face.
9. His anger has made me a prey and persecuted me,
He has gnashed his teeth at me.

My enemies look daggers[9] at me.
10. They have gaped at me with their mouths,
They have buffeted my cheeks in insult,
Together they gang up against me.
11. God delivers me up to wrong-doers,
And throws me into the power of the wicked.[7]

12. I was at ease and he worried me,
He took me by the neck and shook me limb from limb.
Yea, he set me up as a target,
13. His archers[10] surrounded me;
He gashes my kidneys without pity
Pouring out my gall on the ground.
14. He breaks in on me breach upon breach,
He charges me like a warrior.

15. Sack-cloth have I sewn on my skin,
And I have abased my horn in the dust;
16. My face is reddened with weeping,
And on my eyes is darkness,
17. Though there is no violence on my hands,
And I may pray in all innocence.

18. O earth, cover not my blood,
Neither let there be a place for my flowing blood.[11]
19. Lo, I have a witness in heaven,
And one who will testify for me on high,
20. One who will interpret for me[12] my cry[13] to God,
One for whom[14] my eye is ever wakeful,
21. That he might argue with God for a man
As a man argues for another;
22. For a few years shall come
And I shall go on a road where I shall not return.

Textual Notes to Chapter 16

1. Reading *ûmah-yyamrîṣ^e^k̲ā* for MT *'ô mah-yyamrîṣ^e^k̲ā*. See Commentary *ad loc.*
2. 'Then' is not expressed in MT, but is inserted to introduce the apodosis after the hypothesis implied in the exclamation in b.
3. Reading *'ô ^a^'ammîṣ^e^k̲ā*, assuming haplography of *'*.
4. Reading *lō' yaḥśōk̲*; cf. LXX and S *lō' 'eḥśōk̲*.
5. Conjecturing *šimmût̲* for MT *h^a^šimmôt̲ā*. See Commentary *ad loc.*
6. Reading *tiqm^e^ṭēnî* for MT *wattiqm^e^ṭēnî* constructed with v. 7b.
7. Vv. 8-10 are taken as a secondary expansion, with v. 11 as an introduction to vv. 12ff.
8. Reading *k^e^ḥāšî* for MT *kaḥ^a^šî*. See Commentary *ad loc.*
9. Reading plur. throughout for MT sing. after S and Sym., which agrees with the plur. in the sequel.
10. Readinq *rôb̲āyw* for MT *rabbāyw*.
11. Reading *l^e^ze'āt̲î* for MT *l^e^za'^a^qāt̲î*. See Commentary *ad loc.*
12. Reading *m^e^lîṣ* for MT *m^e^lîṣay*.
13. Reading *rē'î* after LXX for MT *rē'āy* (pausal).
14. Reading *'ēlāyw*, assuming its omission by haplography after *'el-'^e^lôah*, with confusion of *y* in the Old Heb. script.

Commentary to Chapter 16.1-21

2. *m^e^naḥ^a^mê 'āmāl* may be a case of *double entendre*, 'troublesome comforters' according to the regular meaning of *niḥam* in the OT, and possibly a hitherto unrecognized cognate of Arab. *naḥama* ('to pant'), hence 'breathers out of trouble', as suggested by D.W. Thomas (1932–33: 192), which would accord with *dib̲^e^rê-rûaḥ* in the following colon.

3. *dib̲^e^rê-rûaḥ* ('windy words') is Job's pointed reply to the same allegation of Eliphaz (15.2) and Bildad (8.2). *mah-yyamrîṣ^e^k̲ā* (lit. 'what makes you sick?')

might signify that Eliphaz's urge to enter into altercation with Job was a disease. T renders 'what amuses you?', which suggests a reading *yamlîṣᵉḵā*, which might mean 'what makes you so agreeable?' (cf. Ps. 119.102). While this would be an apt ironic retort, it is not graphically a feasible original for corruption to *yamrîṣᵉkā*, and would seem to be influenced by Ps. 119.103, *mah-nnimlᵉṣû... 'imᵉrôṯeyḵā* ('how pleasant are your words!'; MT *'imᵉrāṯeḵā*). We would see in the expression in MT correspondence with the Arab. idiom used in interjection with *ma* with the causative and the direct object, hence our rendering 'How aggravating you are...'

4. *lû* might mean 'if' introducing the protasis, signifying remote possibility in a conditional sentence. We would regard the sequel in vv. 4c-6 as the apodosis, but take the alternative significance of *lû* introducing the optative, which nevertheless still implies a protasis.

taḥaṯ napšî (lit. 'in the place of me myself') is paralleled in the account of the succession of kings *taḥat 'aḇîw* ('in place of his father') in Kings. In v. 4c the verb in MT *'aḥbîrāh* is found in the sense of 'making (binding) spells' (Deut. 18.11; Ps. 58.6 [EVV 5]). It might signify 'to associate', that is, compose words or arguments (so Renan). Finkelstein (1956) proposes that the verb means 'to make a noise' as in the 'brawling household' (*bêṯ ḥeḇer*) with the nagging wife (Prov. 21.9; 25.24); so also O. Loretz (1961), who cites the Akk. verb *ḫuburu* ('to make a din'). The word might be a denominative Hiphil from *ḥāḇēr* ('friend, associate'), but *ʿᵃlêḵem* ('against you') is against this interpretation, as also *nûaʿ* ('to shake the head'), this not being, like *nûḏ*, an expression of sympathy, as in 2.11, but a gesture of mockery or gratification that the suffering of another confirms the conventional view of the theodicy (e.g. 2 Kgs 19.21 = Isa. 37.22; Pss. 22.8; 109.25; Lam. 2.15). It is suggested that the verb here is cognate with Arab. *ḥabara* ('to embellish', especially rhetoric [so Fohrer]), which we accept. In vv. 4-6, Job declares that if roles were reversed he *could*, rather than *would*, be as eloquent and censorious as his friends *or* (reading *'ô* before *'ᵃ'ammiṣᵉḵem*) encourage and console (*nûḏ*) them.

5. The positive sense of 5a seems to support the negative with the verb *yaḥᵃśōḵ* ('would not restrain', i.e. 'move unceasingly'), *nûḏ* or *nîḏ* ('nodding of the head', i.e. consolation, sympathy), being the subject and 'lips' (*śᵉpāṯay*), i.e. speech, the object. This we accept, though admitting that MT might still be retained in the sense that sympathy (*nûḏ*) would restrain (*yaḥᵃśōḵ*) or temper what Job had to say (*śᵉpāṯay*) (so Ehrlich, citing Prov. 10.19).

6. *'im 'ᵃḏabbᵉrāh* is a case of the cohortative in a hypothesis or contingent intention, as in Ps. 139.8-9, and, without *'im*, in Job 19.18 (GKC, §108e). Dhorme suggests that *mah* in *mah-mminnî yahᵃlōḵ* is negative (so V, also Hölscher), as in Arab. This is unnecessary as *mah-mminnî yahᵃlōḵ* may be an exclamation, describing Job's reaction to his friends' suffering if the occasion arose. *kᵉ'ēḇî* therefore is his sympathetic grief.

7. *'ak- 'attāh* signals the return to the actual case after the hypothesis. The verb *hel'ānî* requires a subject, which Dhorme finds in the otherwise awkward *hᵃšimmōṯā* pointed *haššimmôṯ*, which he takes as cognate with Arab. *šamita* ('to rejoice in another's misfortune') and renders 'the malicious one'. We would accept the association with the Arab. verb, but would take *šimmôṯ* as an abstract noun *šimmût* analogous in form to *šiqqûṣ*, omitting *h* as a dittograph of preceding *y* in the Old Heb. script, and rendering 'malice', taking it as belonging to v. 7a, and attaching *wattiqmᵉṭēnî* of v. 8a to v. 7b. *kol- 'ᵃḏāṯî* may be retained as meaning 'all my associates', the fem. sing. abstract having the force of a collective noun as in Heb. *yôšeḇeṯ* ('inhabitants'), *gôlāh*, ('exiles'), *'ôyeḇeṯ* ('enemies'), and in Ugaritic, for example, *t'dt ṯpṭ nhr* ('the witnesses of River the Ruler', Gordon *UT* 137.26) and *ṣrṭ* ('enemies', Gordon *UT* 68.9).

8. The verb *qāmaṭ* occurs in the OT only here and at 22.16, but it is well known in Aram. and Syr. meaning 'to seize, compress', with an Arab. cognate *qamaṭa* ('to bind together'). *bᵉ* is used, as regularly, to express hostility, and the present passage suggests *qāmû-ḇî 'ēḏê-šeqer* ('false witnesses have risen against me') in Ps. 27.12. The verb *kaḥaš* in Ps. 109.24 means 'to fall away' (subject 'flesh'), which suggests to Hölscher, Fohrer and Lévêque the rendering 'leanness' (so Rowley and RSV). But the root is better attested in Hos. 7.3; 10.13; 12.1; Nah. 3.1; Isa. 30.9, and possibly Ps. 59.12 (EVV 11) meaning 'falsehood'. So after Isa. 30.9, *bānîm kᵉḥāšîm*, we would read *kᵉḥāšî* ('my false accuser'; so Delitzsch, Dhorme, Peters, Kissane and Stevenson). *'ānāh bᵉ* (lit. 'to answer against', 'to testify against') is a regular usage in the OT. *bᵉp̄ānāy* could mean simply 'against me', but *pānay* should probably be emphasized, meaning 'to my face'.

9. For *'appô ṭārap̄* ('his wrath made [me] a prey'), cf. Amos 1.11, which is, however, generally emended after Jer. 3.5, S and V to *yiṭṭōr ... 'appô. śāṭam*, and particularly the MT of the present passage, is supported by *bᵉ'āp̄ yiśṭᵉmûnî* ('they persecute me in anger') in Ps. 55.4. *ḥāraq* is well known, 'to gnash the teeth' in the Plaint of the Sufferer in the Psalms (e.g. Pss. 35.16; 37.12), a gesture of mocking, anger (Acts 7.54) or of misery and regret (Mt. 8.12). For *yilṭōš 'ênāyw lî* ('he sharpens his eyes at me'; cf. whetting a sword in Ps. 7.13 [MT 12]), is a daring, but not unintelligible, figure (cf. English 'looking daggers').

9c, 10. The change to the plur. is abrupt, the subjects being indefinite, and the sufferings of Job elaborated in the convention, style and language of the Plaint of the Sufferer in the Psalms, as in vv. 8-9 as distinct from vv. 11ff., where the subject is God, suggesting that vv. 8-10, and certainly vv. 9c-10, is a secondary insertion (so G.B. Gray, Hölscher, Fohrer, Lévêque). *pa'ᵃrû bᵉp̄îhem* ('they gape...with their mouths') is repeated in 29.23, indicating a conventional figure from the Plaint of the Sufferer, like the buffeting of the cheeks in insult (*bᵉḥerpāh hikkû lᵉḥāyāy* [pausal]); cf. Lam. 3.30; Isa. 50.6; Mic. 4.14; Mt. 28.67f., where it was the supreme insult. *yiṯmallᵉ'û 'ālay* may mean 'they mass against me'; cf. the band (*mᵉlō'*) of shepherds who mass together when a lion attacks a herd (Isa. 31.4). Alternatively it might mean 'they support one another'; cf. Arab *tamāla'u 'alaya* ('they supported one another against me'). The phrase may be a military figure, referring to general mobilization, *millô'* (Thomas 1952: 47ff.).

11. For *'āwîl*, *'awwāl* is read in one Heb. MS, indicating a habitually bad man, which should probably be preferred. In MT *yirṭēnî*, the initial *y* should be taken as a radical, suggesting the emendation to the Piel perfect *yērᵉṭanî* from a root cognate with Arab. *waraṭa* ('to throw')—so an apt parallel to *wayyasgîrēnî* ('and he has delivered me up').

12. *wayyᵉp̄arpᵉrēnî* is the Pilpel of *pārar*, used in the Hithpalel in Isa. 24.19 of an earthquake and in the Polel in Ps. 74.13 of God's rough handling of the sea in parallelism with *šibbēr*. G.R. Driver (1955: 78) cites Arab. *farfara* ('shook'), as of a sheep mangled by a beast of prey, hence our translation 'worried'. In the parallel colon he took the verb *wayyᵉp̄aṣpᵉṣēnî* as cognate with Arab. *faṣfaṣa* ('to be dismembered'). The conception of the sufferer as a butt for God recalls 7.20, where *mip̄ga'* ('something to be hit when aimed at') is used for *maṭṭārāh* in the present passage, meaning literally 'something to be aimed at'. More specifically the whole passage recalls Lam. 3.12:

> *dāraḵ qaštô wayyaṣṣîḇēnî kammaṭṭārāh lāhēṣ*
>
> he bent his bow and set me up as a target for his arrow.

13. MT *rabbāyw*, where the context demands the meaning 'his archers', would be derived from the verb *rāḇaḇ* ('to be numerous'), and so should be emended to *rôḇîm*, from *rāḇāh* ('to shoot arrows'); cf. Gen. 21.20, *rōḇeh qešeṯ* ('archer').

The verb *pālaḥ* (Piel) is used in Prov. 7.23 of an arrow piercing the liver of an adulterer. 'Pouring out my gall (*mᵉrērāṯî*, lit. "my bitterness") on the ground' recalls Lam. 2.11, where *kᵉḇēḏî* ('my liver') is the object of the same verb *šāpaḵ*. This passage may have suggested v. 13c of the present passage as a secondary expansion.

14. The figure is now that of an assault upon a fortified city. *pāraṣ* is used of the breaching of a city wall in 2 Kgs 14.13; Isa. 5.5; Ps. 80.13; etc.; cf. Ass. *parâṣu*. *'al-pᵉnê* means 'over and above'. In the charge of the warrior (*gibbôr*), Job may be alluding to Eliphaz's figure of the wicked charging God in defiance (15.26).

15. The verb *tāp̄ar* ('to sew') is rare in the OT, occurring only here, and in Gen. 3.7 (J), Eccl. 3.7, and in the Piel in Ezek. 13.18. It probably does not mean here that the coarse, black cloth (*śaq*) was sewn on to the skin, but that it was stitched for permanent wear and worn next to the skin (*geleḏ*). This word is a *hapax legomenon* in the OT, where *'ôr* is regular, but it is the regular word for 'skin' in Ass., Aram. and Arab.

'ōlaltî ḇe'āp̄ār qarnî ('and I must lower my horn in the dust'), where the verb is a *hapax legomenon* in the OT, is now attested in the Ras Shamra text Gordon *UT* 137.23, where the gods in shame and humiliation 'lower their heads upon their knees' (*tġly 'ilm r'išthm lzr brktm*). The horn symbolizes strength as regularly in the OT.

16. *ḥomarmerû* means 'are reddened' (so Koehler–Baumgartner). The root is not attested in this sense in the OT, but is regular in Arab. (*'aḥmaru*, 'red'). *ḥamarmar* ('to be in a ferment') in Lam. 1.20; 2.11 (subject *mē'ay*, 'my bowels') is evidently a homonym. On *'ap̄'appayim* ('eyes' rather than 'eyelids'), see on 3.9.

17. *'al* here signifies 'though', the phrase recalling Isa. 53.9, *'al lō'-ḥāmās 'āś-āh* ('though he had done no violence').

18-21. Here the writer develops the accepted belief in the automatic claim of blood shed violently for vengeance, which was only allayed when covered with soil. This is well illustrated in Ezek. 24.8, 'to rouse up wrath to take vengeance I have set her blood on the bare surface of the rock so that it may not be covered'; cf. Isa. 26.21, 'and the earth will uncover the blood which is in it and will not cover any more those who are slain on it'. The conception of blood crying for vengeance from the ground after Cain's murder of Abel (Gen. 4.10f.) is another graphic illustration of that principle. The verbs *kissāh* ('cover') and *zā'aq* ('cry') here re-echo those passages, and, we believe, occasioned the corruption of *zē'āṯî* ('my flowing blood') to *za'aqāṯî* ('my cry') in v. 18b. The same conception might underlie 31.38a. See below *ad loc.*

18. *'al-yehî māqôm leza'aqāṯî* ('let there be no place for my cry') raises the difficulty of the interpretation of *māqôm*, which is taken variously as a place where the cry stops (so G.B. Gray, Hölscher, Horst, Guillaume, Fohrer, Lévêque) or where it is hidden (Dhorme) or stifled (Stevenson). Taking *za'aqāṯî* as a corruption of *zē'āṯî* ('my flowing blood'), cognate of Arab. *waḏa'a*, we should have the required parallel to *dāmî* ('my blood') with a more natural association with *māqôm* in its normal sense of 'place', or as meaning 'grave' or resting place, as in the Phoenician inscription of Esh-munazar (Cooke 1903: 159ff. ll. 3-4); cf. Ezek. 39.11, where *māqôm* is a synonym of *qeḇer* ('grave'), cited by Dahood (1962: 61f.). The theme is resumed in 19.25.

19. *gam-‘attāh* introduces a new, and here most significant proposition, that of a superhuman witness for Job. *bamm^{e}rômîm* is formally ambiguous, meaning possibly ‘among the exalted ones’, a meaning attested only twice in the OT in the late passages Isa. 24.4 and Eccl. 10.6, and ‘in the high places’, the usual meaning in the OT, which is supported here by the parallel *beššāmayim*. The Aram. *śāh^{a}ḏî*, the synonymous parallel of *‘ēḏî* (‘my witness’), is a regular feature in the language of the Book of Job; cf. *śah^{a}ḏûṯā’* in Gen. 31.47, where the Aram. is attested by the form and by the fact that a Heb. equivalent is given.

20. MT *m^{e}lîṣay rē‘āy* means either ‘my friends are those who mock me’ (from *lîṣ*) or, reading *mimm^{e}lîṣ rē‘āy* (‘from the scoffing of my friends’), which might possibly connect with v. 20b, if we include *’el-’^{e}lôah, ’el-’^{e}loah dal^{e}pāh ’ênî* (‘I look to God with wakeful eye’). But this breaks the sequence of thought between vv. 19 and 21, and might be suspected as a secondary intrusion, which the defective metre might suggest. The function of an intermediary between God and humans in vv. 19 and 21, however, suggests a mediator, the *mēlîṣ* in fact of 33.23f. In this case MT *m^{e}lîṣay rē‘āy* would require emendations such as *m^{e}lîṣ rē‘î* (‘one who may interpret my cry’), which would better accord with v. 21. If v. 20 is to be retained as part of the original text, the regularity of the metre might be restored by reading *’el-’^{e}lôah* (so Pope), reading the verse *m^{e}lîṣ rē‘î ’el-’^{e}lôah ’ēlāyw dal^{e}pāh ‘ênî* (‘one who will interpret my cry to God; to such a one my eye is ever wakeful’). LXX, however, reads ‘May my prayer come unto the Lord’, thus supporting the reading *rē‘î*, which is attested in Mic. 4.9 and Ps. 139.2. This suggested to Dhorme the reading *l^{e}māṣā’ rē‘î ’el-’^{e}lôah* (‘May my cry reach God!’) taking the verb as optative perfect, regular in Arab. and occurring in Ugaritic, introduced by the enclitic *l^{e}*. *māṣā’*, in this sense, as possibly in 11.7, is to be recognized as cognate of Aram. *m^{e}ṭā’*. On this view the asseverative enclitic *l^{e}* and *māṣā’* would have been displaced to give the reading *m^{e}lîṣî* (final *y* of MT being a dittograph of *’* in the Old Heb. script), perhaps under the influence of 33.23f. But *mēlîṣ* is well established with the nuance of ‘intercessor’ in the Elihu addendum, which was not much later than the main part of the Book of Job, so that there is nothing strange in the idea being familiar to the author of the Book. The word signifies an ‘interpreter’ of the language in Gen. 42.33 and in two Phoenician inscriptions (*CIS*, I, 44, 88), and the object *rē‘î* indicates that this is the sense of *mēlîṣ* if this reading is original in v. 20a. On the reading we have adopted an extra beat is required in v. 20b. Dhorme inserts *l^{e}pānāyw* after *dāl^{e}pāh*, after which he assumes that it has been omitted by haplography. But we find Pope's suggestion more acceptable, that *’ēlāyw*, occurring before *dāl^{e}pāh*, was omitted by haplography after *’el-’^{e}lôah*. The verb *dālap̄* is problematic. It occurs in Eccl. 10.16 referring to the collapse of a house, having an Ugaritic cognate. This is evidently the sense of the verb in Ps. 119.28, *dāl^{e}pāh nap̄šî*, as suggested by the antithetic parallel *qayy^{e}mēnî*. In

Prov. 19.13; 27.15, *delep̄* denotes the dripping of rain, which has suggested the translation of v. 20b as 'my eye drops (tears)'; but this rendering breaks the sequence of thought in the context. The phrase in v. 20b recalls Isa. 38.14f. from the Plaint of the Sufferer in Hezekiah's lamentation, where the verb is *dālal*, possibly a corruption of *dālap̄*, which would suit the context better, since the sufferer is orientated 'to on high', like Job in v. 19, and calls on God to stand surety for him (*'orᵉḇēnî*, Isa. 38.14b; cf. Job 17.3a). A fresh approach is opened by Fohrer, who adduces Akk. *dalâpu* ('to be sleepless') as a possible cognate of a homonym of Heb. *dālap̄* in its two known senses, which gives more meaning in the context of vv. 19 and 20.

21. The sing. *wᵉyôḵaḥ* ('that he might argue') would indicate that the 'witness' and the 'interpreter' were one and the same, and *'im-'ᵉlôah* would seem to preclude the notion of God as the heavenly witness testifying against himself, as Dhorme suggests (so G.B. Gray, Fohrer, Lévêque). In *ûḇen-'āḏām*, *w* is probably a corruption of *k* in the Old Heb. script, as T and V indicate, hence our reading *kᵉḇen-'āḏām lᵉrē'ēhû*. Here we would take *ben-'āḏām* as 'a human being' and *rē'ēhû* not as 'his friend', but as 'another'; cf. *'îš lᵉrē'ēhû* ('one to another'), a regular phrase in the Old 'Testament. We should further stress the meaning of *lᵉ*, 'in the interest of', supporting the role of Job's witness and interpreter in contention with (*'im*) God in the rôle of accuser.

22. Job, as the psalmist cited in the lament of Hezekiah in Isa. 38.14f., alleges the brevity of his life and the negative prospect of death and decline on the journey of no return, *'ōraḥ lō'-'āšûḇ* (cf. Akk. *uruḫu la taru*, cited by Dhorme). *mispār* qualifying a noun means 'few', that is, so few that may be counted; cf. *mᵉṯê mispār* (Gen. 34.30; Ps. 105.12; etc.) and Arab. *darāhimu ma'dūdatu(n)*, the few dirhams for which Joseph was sold. *'ᵃtā'* ('to come') is the regular Aram. and Arab. verb 'to come', which is also used in Classical Heb., though less extensively. In this part of Job's reply to Eliphaz he significantly passes from mourning in sackcloth (vv. 15-16) to the confident assertion of his innocence. Indeed, he makes a dramatic appeal for justice in the figure of the well-known convention of vengeance for blood spilt (v. 18) which cries for vengeance and the vindication of the victim, like the blood of innocent Abel shed by Cain (Gen. 4.11). The implication of Job's appeal could not be plainer. God must admit justice. The question is: Who should call him to account?

Orthodox theology, regarding God as final authority and as the final cause of suffering as retribution for sin, could not admit investigation of Job's case beyond the temporal experience. But confident of his innocence and of God's moral order, Job raises his case to a new dimension in referring it to a heavenly court, reminiscent of the court in the Prologue, a member of which, unlike the *śāṭān*, would be a natural upholder of the Order of the Divine Sovereign. Such a one might testify on his behalf and present his case intelligibly and sympathetically to God. Job further invites, one might almost say challenges, God to assume a pledge or guarantee for him (17.3). This declaration signifies Job's absolute confidence in his innocence and in the ultimate recognition of it by God, who would not be asked, nor would he be expected, to risk his credit by going bail in a dubious case. It is at once a daring challenge by Job and an expression of his confidence in God's justice. If we were disposed, like Dhorme and others, to see in Job's appeal to God to confront Himself in the sufferer's interest, we might admit the proposition to the extent that it is an appeal in confidence to the living God to vindicate His nature and economy against what orthodox theology in its inherent limitation had systematized.

Chapter 17
Job's Rejoinder to Eliphaz (continued)

Job's lamentation for his suffering (7, 11f.) permitted, if not actually inflicted, by God (6) and his hopeless prospect of a short remaining life and the oblivion of death (12-16) is the theme of this chapter. The gloom, however, is relieved by Job's reference of his case to God in calling on him to undertake the responsibility of bail in complete confidence of his innocence.

1. 'My spirit is broken!
My days are extinguished!
Only burial for me!
2. Surely I am the butt of mockers,[1]
And my eye is weary[2] with their contention.
3. Lay down a pledge[3] for me,
(For) who will take it upon himself to give surety for me?
4. Since you have closed their minds to understanding,
You will not let them prevail.[4]

5. "One who makes a lavish party[5] for others
While his own children faint."
6. But you have set me up[6] as a byword[7] to the peoples.
One in whose face men spit;
7. And my eye has grown dim through vexation,
And my limbs are spent[8] like a shadow.

8. [9]The righteous are shocked by this,
And the innocent is indignant at the impious.
9. But let the righteous man hold to his way
And the pure of hands will gain strength.
10. But come on again, all of you,[10]
I shall not find a wise man among you.[9]

11. My days have passed away without (the realization of) my plans,[11]
My heart's desires[12] are torn away;
12. Night is appointed[13] for a day,
And light[14] is near to darkness.

13. Surely I have no hope! Sheol is my home!
I spread[15] my bed in darkness.

14. I call the Pit my father,
Worms my mother and sister.
15. Where then is my hope,
And as for my piety, who will observe it?
16. Will they go down to Sheol with me?[16]
Shall we all together go down[17] to the dust?'

Textual Notes to Chapter 17

1. Reading *hôṯelîm* for the *hapax legomenon hᵃṯōlîm* as the personal antecedent to the pronominal suffix in *hamrôtām* (see also Commentary).
2. Reading *til'ennā* (energic form of the imperfect), assuming corruption of *'* to *y* in the Old Heb. script.
3. Reading *'erbōnî* with S and T for MT *'orᵉbēnî.*
4. Reading *tᵉrōmᵉmēm* or *tᵉrîmēm* for MT *tᵉrōmēm.*
5. Conjecturing *yāḡîḏ* for MT *yaggîḏ*. See Commentary *ad loc.*
6. Reading *wattaṣṣiḡēnî* for MT *wᵉhiṣṣiḡanî.*
7. Reading *limᵉšal* with LXX, Aq., Theod., T, Sym., and V for MT *limᵉšōl.*
8. Reading *kālû* for MT *kullām*, assuming corruption of *w* to *m* in the Old Hebrew script.
9. Probably a secondary expansion. See Introduction to Chapters 16–17.
10. Reading *wᵉkullᵉḵem* with S, V and certain Heb. MSS for MT *kullām* and omitting *wᵉ'ûlām* as a dittograph before *kullam.*
11. Reading *mizzimôṯay* for MT *zimmôṯay*, prepositional *m* (privative) being omitted by haplography after *w* in the Old Hebrew script.
12. Reading *ma'arᵉšê* for MT *mōrāšê*. See Commentary *ad loc.*
13. Reading *hûśām* for MT *yāśîmû*, reading final *w* of *yāśîmû* with the following word, *y* being a corruption of *h* in the Old Heb. script.
14. Reading *wᵉ'ôr* for MT *'ôr*. See textual note 13.
15. Reading *raḇaḏtî* or *ribbaḏtî* for MT *rippaḏtî.*
16. Reading *bᵉyāḏî* (perhaps spelt *bᵉḏî*, as in Phoenician inscriptions) as suggested by LXX (*hᵃ'immāḏî*), for MT *baddê.*
17. Reading *nēḥaṯ* as suggested by Sʰ for MT *nāhat.*

Commentary on Chapter 17

1. Proposed emendations of MT *yāmay* and *niz'āḵû* are designed to secure a 3:3 rhythm, for example *rûḥî hubbālāh 'immî ne'ezᵉḇû qᵉḇārîm lî* ('My spirit is destroyed within me, the grave remains for me'; so Fohrer after Duhm). For this meaning of *'āzaḇ*, Duhm cited Isa. 18.6, where, however the sense is 'abandoned'. If those proposals were accepted we should prefer the sense 'prepared', taking the verb as cognate with Ugaritic *'db*. In Job's anguish, however, the 2:2:2 metre is not unapt, and we find no reason to emend MT. *ḥāḇal* is cognate with Ass. *ḥabâlu*, Aram. and Syr. *ḥabbēl* and Arab. *ḫabala* ('to ruin, destroy'). *za'aḵ*, a *hapax legomenon* in the OT, is possibly a byform

of the more familiar *dā'aḵ* ('to be extinguished'), which would be quite appropriate to 'my day', sc. 'daylight'. The plural *qeḇārîm* may be abstract 'burial' or a case of *pluralis excellentiae* for emphasis.

2. *'im* here, as in 30.25 and 31.36, may be interrogative, but, with the negative, we prefer to take it as the introduction to a strong asseverative with ellipse of an oath. After the ancient versions, later commentators have taken *haṯulîm* as an abstract plural ('mockery') from the known verbal root *hāṯal*, and have emended MT *hammerôṯām* to *tamrûrîm* ('bitterness'); so Duhm and Dhorme after V and S. We would read the participle *hōṯelîm* as antecedent to the pronominal suffix in *hamrôṯām* (for MT *hammerôṯām*), the Hiphil infinitive construct of a root *mārāh* cognate with Syr. *mrā'* and Arab. *mara*(*y*) ('to dispute'). Here we may note Dahood's ingenious suggestion that the couplet reflects Canaanite mythology, where Baal sends his emissaries to *Mt* (Death) in his city *Hmry* ('Ruin'), on the way to which they come to 'the two mounts which hem in the earth' (*'im tlm ġṣr 'arṣ*), on the basis of which Dahood suggests the reading of Job 17.2:

> *'im lō' hattillayim 'immādî ûḇahamîrôṯayim tālîn 'ênî*
>
> Surely the twin mounts are before me, and in the two miry depths my eyes will sleep.

While this would amplify v. 1c, it does not accord with the sequel, with the reference to the third parties in v. 4, which demands an antecedent, which we would find in *hōṯelîm*.

3. *śimāh* requires an object, which suggests the emendation of MT *'oreḇēnî* to the noun *'erbônî* ('my pledge', i.e. 'a pledge for me'). Dhorme regards the pledge as given by Job, consisting of his sufferings. But the pledge was given by another, a guarantor that one under disability would not default, hence, as there is no other who may 'strike hands' with Job, that is, go bail for hire (cf. Prov. 6.1; 17.18; 22.26), God is appealed to deposit a pledge with himself. Horst avoids, or evades, the difficulty of God entering a pledge with himself by taking *śîmāh*, as is possible, as 'set' or 'fix', but the reflexive *yittāqēa'* in the parallel colon ('take upon himself to strike hands') indicates that it is God himself who is asked to go bail as in Hezekiah's prayer (Isa. 38.14).

4. *ṣāp̄an*, as well as meaning 'to hide', means 'to take into storage', that is, into safe keeping, hence the sense here 'to close up', the preposition in *miśśāḵel* being privative.

5. We propose that MT *ḥēleq* here is a cognate of Arab. *ḥalqu*(*n*) ('circle'), so 'a party' (cf. Arab. *ḥalaqa* in the II form ('to meet round a table') and that *yaggîḏ* is a corruption of an original *yaḡîḏ* cognate with Arab. *jāda*, *yajūdu* ('to be excellent') (cf. *jaudu*[*n*], 'generosity', and the verb in the V form, 'to vie in generosity'). The couplet is probably a popular proverb meaning

'Charity begins at home'. Fohrer takes it to apply to God, whose beneficence, frequently instanced in Hymns of Praise, contrasts with his treatment of Job. But in view of Job's animadversions on the alienation of his friends (v. 2) we regard the proverb as referring to the prodigality of their admonitions and perhaps the lavish scattering of their pearls of wisdom and their disproportionate sympathy for their worthy friend in his spiritual need. We would take *rē'îm*, without the pronominal suffix, not as 'friends' but as 'others', in contrast to *bānāyw* in v. 5b (cf. 16.21 and the phrase *'îš lᵉrē'ēhû*, 'one among others'). For the 'wasting' of the eyes, that is, fainting, cf. 11.20; Lam. 2.11; 4.17; Ps. 69.4 (EVV 3).

6. *hiṣṣîḡ*, from *yāṣaḡ*, is used of setting up firmly and deliberately, for example, a cult-object on its base, like Gideon's ephod at Ophrah (Judg. 8.27), or the Ark in the temple of Dagan (1 Sam. 5.2) and at Jerusalem (2 Sam. 6.17). Thus it is aptly used of setting up as an example (*māšāl*) or warning. The phrase *limᵉšal 'ammîm* recalls *wᵉhāyîṯā...lᵉmāšāl... lᵉḵol hā'ammîm* in the context of infidelity to the Covenant obligations in Deut. 28.37; cf. Ps. 44.15 (EVV 14). For MT *tōpeṯ lᵉpānîm* V reads *lip̄ᵉnêhem* and Perles proposed to read *mōp̄ēṯ* ('a portent') (so Beer, Budde, Klostermann, Ball, Stevenson). But MT may be retained and translated 'one in whose face men spit' (so Gray, Hölscher, Horst, Lévêque, Fohrer); cf. 30.9, where spitting is expressed by *rîq*, as in Isa. 50.6. *tōpeṯ*, found only here in the OT, is derived from *tûp̄* ('to spit').

7. *kāhāh* ('to be dim, extinguished') is used of the eyes in Gen. 27.1 and 1 Sam. 3.2 and of the wick of a lamp in Isa. 42.3. Vexation (*ka'as*) is said to impair the sight, as after weeping, in Ps. 6.8 (EVV 7). *yᵉṣurîm* (lit. 'the things that are fashioned') is taken by Rashi after T to mean 'limbs' which are 'spent' (*kālû* for MT *kullām*); so Houbigant, Reiske, Ehrlich, Duhm, Hölscher, Fohrer. 'Like a shadow' may denote either emaciation or rapid failing like a passing shadow.

9-10. Possibly a secondary expansion. See Introduction to Chapters 16–17.

8. *yiṯ'ōrār* (pausal) means 'grows excited', here in indignation. Indignation (*hiṯhārāh*) against the wicked, flourishing with apparent impunity, is the theme of Ps. 37.1, 7, 8. On *ḥānēp̄*, see above on 8.15.

10. Omitting *'ûlām metri causa*, *wᵉ* of itself in the context having adversative force.

In view of the second person plur. of the verbs, *kullᵉḵem* should probably with read with some Heb. MSS, S and V (so Dhorme, G.B. Gray and others).

11. *zimmāh*, from *zāmam*, means 'plan, device', usually in a sinister sense, but it is also used of God's gracious 'purpose' for Jerusalem in Zech. 8.15 and in a

neutral sense in Prov. 2.11; 3.21; 5.2. *ma'arešê* ('wish, desire'), which we read for MT *mōrāšê* (see Textual Note), supplies the parallel to *zimmāh*. It is known in the form *'arešeṯ* in Ps. 21.3, and in the verbal form in Ugartic *'arš* and Akk. *erešu*.

12. If MT *yāśîmû*, with the subject indefinite, is read in its usual sense 'they make (night day)', the verse would contradict the general sense of the passage. The versions give no help, nor are the interpretations of later commentators unanimous or convincing. Hence we suggest the reading:

> *layelāh leyôm hûśām*
> *we'ôr qārôḇ minnî-ḥōšeḵ*
>
> Night is appointed for day,
> And light is near to darkness.

The verse now agrees with the context.

13. On the emendation *ribbaḏtî*, lit. 'I have laid down the blankets (*marbaddîm*)' for MT *rippaḏtî* see Textual Note. The perfect here and in v. 14 may be understood as a declaratory perfect. The making of one's bed in Sheol recalls Ps. 139.8, where the verb is *yāṣa'* (cf. *yeṣûa'* 'bed').

14. The personification of 'the Pit' (*haššaḥaṯ*) as 'my father' and 'Corruption' or 'the worm' (*rimmāh*) as 'my sister' recalls the personification of Wisdom as 'my sister' in Prov. 7.4 and is an old literary figure in Canaanite poetry, as for example the Ras Shamra Legend of Krt, Gordon *UT* 127.35f.: *km 'aḫt 'rš mdw 'anšt 'rš zbln* ('Sickness is thy bedfellow, infirmity thy concubine').

15. The apparent repetition of *tiqwāṯî* in the couplet is almost inconceivable in a work with the range of vocabulary of Job, hence the second incidence of the word has been emended to *tôḇāṯî* ('my prosperity') after LXX by Merx, Bickell, Siegfried, Duhm, Hölscher, Stevenson, Horst). Guillaume (*Promise and Fulfilment*, ed. F.F. Bruce, 1963, p. 113) proposed to see in the second *tiqwāṯî* Arab. *taqway* ('piety, fear of God'), reflecting his view of the provenance of the Book of Job in the Hejaz. See Introduction, pp. 35-36.

16. MT *baddê* ('bars', cf. 18.3; 41.4, lit. 'limbs'; cf. the 'staves' on which the ark was carried, Exod. 25.13, 14, 15 etc.) is doubtful. LXX renders the colon 'or with me will they go down?', which may suggest *haḇeyāḏî* (so Dhorme, citing Ass. *ina idi*, lit. 'by my hand', i.e. 'beside me'). This is supported by the parallel *yaḥaḏ*. MT, pointed in *scriptio defectiva bîḏî*, as regularly in Phoenician inscriptions, may be preferred. *nāḥaṯ* must be pointed *nēḥaṯ* ('shall we descend?'); so LXX, as the parallel *tēraḏnā* indicates. The verb is Aram. *neḥaṯ*, but has a Ugaritic cognate.

Job 18

The Reply of Bildad

Like Eliphaz, Bildad abandons the attempt to bring Job to confess sin and seek God's grace. In an introductory strophe (18.2-4) he upbraids Job for presuming that he was wiser than his friends and for adducing his case to call the theodicy in question. From this point he goes on in six strophes of three bicola each, except the last, which is of two bicola (18.5-7, 8-10, 11-13, 14-16, 17-19, 20-21), to assert the theodicy in stating the fate of the wicked, whose sin brings its own nemesis, in a series of vivid figures.

The literary affinity of the opening strophe is with the contention at law and the sapiential controversy, and that of the sequel is the sapiential discourse or the subject of sin and retribution. The statement begins with what is probably the citation of a proverb, 'the light of the wicked is put out' (cf. Prov. 13.9, with 'lamp' for 'light'), which is cited again in 21.17, to be exploded by Job. The theme is then sustained in figures familiar in the assertion of faith in providence or the imprecation of the sufferer in poems of the type of the Plaint of the Sufferer, many of which reflect the empiric observations of the sage.

1. And Bildad the Shuhite answered and said:

2. 'How long until you stop speaking?[1]
Consider[2] and *we*[3] shall speak.
3. Why are we considered as beasts,
Accounted dull[4] in your sight?
4. You, who are one who rends himself in his anger,
Shall the earth be foresaken for your sake,
And the rock be shifted from its place?

5. Yea, the light of the wicked[5] is quenched,
And the flame of his fire does not shine.
6. The light in his tent is darkened,
And his lamp above him goes out.
7. His mighty strides are restricted,[6]
And his own plan makes him stumble.[7]

8. For he goes unrestrained into the net with his own feet
And he walks on to the hurdle;
9. The trap catches hold of his heel,
The noose closes tight on him;

10. The snare for him is hidden in the ground,
Yea, his trap on the path.

11. All around terrors overwhelm him
And they surround[8] him right to his feet.
12. His strength will become cowardice,
With disaster ready by his side.
13. [9]His skin is eaten away by disease,[9]
The first-born of Death devours his limbs.

14. He is torn from his secure tent[10]
And marched[11] before the king of terrors;
15. Flame[12] settles on his tent,
[13]Brimstone is scattered[13] on his homestead.
16. His roots dry up below
And his branch withers above.

17. His memory perishes from the earth,
And he has no name abroad.
18. He is thrust out from the light into darkness;
He is chased from the world,
19. Without kith and kin among his own people,
And without survival where he has lived in asylum.

20. At his fate folk of the West are appalled,
And folk in the East are seized[14] with horror.
21. Surely these are the dwellings of the wrong-doer,
And this is the place of the man who would not acknowledge God.'

Textual Notes to Chapter 18

1. Reading sing. *t^{e}śîmennā* (energic) for MT *t^{e}śîmûn* and *qēṣ* for MT *qinṣê* after 11QtargJob and LXX, and taking *y* of *qinṣê* as a corruption of *'* in the Old Heb. script and reading *'el-millîn* for MT *l^{e}millîn.*
2. Reading the singular *t^{e}ḇînennā* (energic) for MT *tāḇînû.*
3. Reading *'^{a}naḥnû* for MT *'aḥar* after LXX.
4. Reading *n^{e}ṭammōnû* for MT *niṭmînû.*
5. Reading *rāšā'* for MT *r^{e}šā'îm*, agreeing with the sing. pronom. suffix in v. 5b.
6. Reading *yēṣārû* for MT *yēṣ^{e}rû.*
7. Reading *w^{e}ṯakšîlēhû* with LXX for MT *w^{e}tašlîḵēhû.*
8. Reading *w^{e}hiqqîp̄uhû* for MT *weh^{e}p̄îṣuhû.*
9. Reading *yē'āḵēl biḏ^{e}way 'ôrô* for MT *yō'ḵēl baddê 'ôrô.*
10. Reading *mē' ōhel miḇtaḥô* for MT *mē'oh^{o}lô miḇtaḥô.*
11. Reading *w^{e}yaṣ'iḏēhû* for MT *w^{e}ṯaṣ'iḏēhû.*
12. Reading *mabbēl* for MT *mibb^{e}lî* (*lô y^{e}zōreh*).
13. Reading *lîzôrah* (Pual with enclitic *l^{e}* introducing imperfect) for MT *lô y^{e}zōreh.* See Commentary *ad loc.*
14. Reading *'āḥaz* for MT *'āḥ^{a}zû*, final *w* being a dittograph after *z* in the last development of the Heb. script. Alternatively the passive *'uḥ^{a}zû* may be read, taking *šā'ar* (MT *śā'ar*) adverbially, as proposed by Dahood (1962: 63).

Commentary on Chapter 18

2. In view of Bildad's address to Job in vv. 4ff., the singular of the verbs in vv. 2f. should be read, with energic ending and corruption of final *w* of the verbs from energic *n*. On our proposed reading, *teśîmennā qēṣ 'ēl-millîn*, based on 11QtargJob and LXX, see above, p. 80.

3. An original *be'ênekā* was probably corrupted to MT *be'enêkem* after the corruption of the verbs in v. 2 to the plural following the failure to recognize the energic ending of the imperfect sing. On the corruption of an original *neṭammōnû* ('we are dull') from *ṭāmam* with a Syr. cognate, see above, p. 81.

4. Bildad, having accused Job of treating his interlocutors as brute beasts, accuses Job of intensifying his sufferings by agonizing over the moral problem and scorning the comfort of orthodoxy, thus preying upon himself. He also animadverts on Job's accusation of God as rending him like a wild beast (16.9). In v. 4a Bildad objects that Job's claim to exception from the consequences of sin that he and his friends had accepted as the moral order of suffering is tantamount to his questioning God's Order in Creation (cf. Pss. 90.2; 93.2). In the sequel he cites instances of the moral order he assumes, while pressing his indictment of Job. *ṭōrēp̄ nap̄šô be'appô*, though the participle is in the vocative and the two following nouns are with the 3rd sing. pronom. suffix, is no problem, since the reference is to a category; cf. 2 Kgs 9.31, cited by G.B. Gray (*zimrî hōrēḡ 'adōnāyw*, 'Thou Zimri who slew his master').

5. *šeḇîḇ* ('flame'), attested in MT only here and in the Aram. part of Dan. (3.22; 7.9), is found in Ben Sira 8.10; 45.19. It is not to be taken forthwith as an Aramaism, being possibly attested in Ugaritic as *žbb* in Gordon *UT* 'nt III.43. The statement of the light of the wicked being quenched (vv. 5f.) possibly cites a regular proverb, and is explicitly contradicted by Job in 21.17.

7. MT *yēṣerû* should be emended to *yēṣārû* from *ṣārar*, a stative verb meaning 'to be restricted'. *'ôn* is parallel to *kōaḥ* ('strength') at 40.16. The restriction of the strong footsteps is characteristic of age or weakness; the length of the steps expresses strength, confidence and prosperity; see, for example, Ps. 18.37 (EVV 36): 'You lengthen (*tarḥîḇ*) my steps (*ṣa'aḏay*) under me, and my ankles do not totter', and cf. in the Mesopotamian myth of Atraḫasis, 'their long legs have become quite short' (Labat 1970: 133). On the reading *weṯakšîlēhu*, see Textual Note. In *'aṣāṯô* and in *beraḡlāyw* (v. 8a) we suggest that the pronominal suffixes should be emphasized: 'his own counsel' and 'with his own feet'.

8. The passive (Pu'al) *šullaḥ* is found again in Judg. 5.15, where the emphasis is on free and spontaneous, and indeed, impetuous movement; cf. Prov. 29.15,

na'ar m^ešullāḥ mēḇîš 'immô ('an unrestrained boy brings shame to his mother'). The figure of the wicked caught in a trap probably reflects the theme of the wicked caught in his own trap in the Plaint of the Sufferer in Pss. 9.11; 35.7; 140.6 (EVV 5). *ś^eḇāḵāh* means 'lattice-work', such as is on the top of the pillars Yakin and Boaz in the Temple (1 Kgs 7.17ff.) and in the window of a palace (2 Kgs 1.2). The conception of walking on lattice-work is found again in Ben Sira, where the word is *rešeṯ* (usually a 'net'). What is envisaged is obviously a light hurdle concealed by grass and earth covering a pit.

9. *paḥ* is a spring trap such as closes up and takes hold (*yō'ḥēz*) of its victim, like that which springs up from the ground and grips (*lāḵaḏ*) its victim (Isa. 24.18; Jer. 48.44; Eccl. 7.26). *ṣammîm*, derived from *ṣāmam*, cognate either with Arab. *ḍamma* ('to draw tight') or with Arab. *ṣamma* ('to enwrap', as with a bandage) probably denotes the noose of a snare.

10. *ḥaḇlô* ('his line'), if it does not denote a snare, may mean a rope stretched over a path to trip the unwary; cf. Ps. 140.6 (EVV 5), which refers to *ḥ^aḇālîm*. *malkuḏtô*, derived from *lāḵaḏ* (cf. Amos 3.5), is indeterminate. The various kinds of trap, *rešeṯ*, *paḥ* and *ḥeḇel* are mentioned in the Plaint of the Sufferer in Ps. 140.6.

11. MT *weh^ep̄îṣēhû* ('and they scatter him') is suspect. Ezekiel 34.21, cited by Dhorme in support of MT, is doubtful evidence. G.R. Driver (1953b: 256ff.) proposes that the verb is cognate of Arab. *fāṣa*, which in the IV form means 'to micturate', hence the consequence of extreme fear, which would suit the context. But in view of *sāḇîḇ* in v. 11a, *w^ehiqqîp̄uhû* seems a more likely reading, assuming the scribal error of metathesis of *p* and *q* with corruption of *q* to *ṣ* in the Old Heb. script.

12. MT *rā'ēḇ* in its usual sense of 'hungry' has been accepted by most commentators (so Duhm, Dhorme, Szczygiel, Ball, Kissane, Pope, Fohrer), though there has been difference of opinion as to the precise meaning of the colon. The matter is complicated by the meaning *'ôn* in the context, which in Heb. means variously 'strength' (Job 18.7; cf. Gen. 49.3; Deut. 21.17; Isa. 40.26; Hos. 12.4; Ps. 105.36; Job 40.16) and 'wealth' (Job 20.16; Hos. 12.9). Thus *rā'ēḇ* must have some natural relation to *'ôn*, probably in the sense of 'strength'. G.R. Driver (1953b: 259f.) suggests that the verb (here a participle) is cognate of Arab. *ra'iba* ('to fear, be cowardly'), which does suit the context, especially v. 11a, which mentions the terrors which overwhelm the sinner. Dhorme takes *l^eṣal'ô* (lit. 'to his rib, side') to mean 'by his side', citing the Ass. use of *ṣêlu* with the same force, but taking *nāḵôn* as 'standing up'. We prefer the translation 'disaster (*'êḏ*) is ready by his side'; cf. *nāḵôn* in this sense in 12.5 expressing the imminence of disaster.

13. The apparent repetition of *baddê*/*baddāyw* in MT is suspect, as usual in such cases. Wright, Budde, G.B. Gray, Tur-Sinai, Dhorme, Perles, Kissane, Hölscher, Fohrer and Pope read *yē'āḵēl biḏᵉway 'ôrô* ('his skin', sc. body, 'is eaten away by disease'). Stevenson's objection that *dᵉway* ('disease') is doubtful is hypercritical in view of the phrase *'ereś dᵉway* in Ps. 41.4 (EVV 3) and the occurrence of *dᵉway* with this meaning in 6.7 and the incidence in Aram., Syr. and Arab., cf. *mdw* in Ugaritic. 'Skin' (*'ôr*) here, as parallel to *baddāw* ('his limbs'), if it does not mean simply 'body', may denote the skin as the part of the body where the disease makes its first visible ravages. Death is personified on the precedent of the highly anthropomorphic Canaanite mythology in the Ras Shamra texts. On 'the first-born of Death' (*bᵉḵôr māweṯ*), Dhorme aptly cites the Mesopotamian conception that the plague-god Namtaru is termed 'the Grand Vizier of the Queen of the Underworld', an office which is also expressed in the idiom of Mesopotamian mythology by the designation of this figure as 'the first-born', as Mummu was 'the first-born of Apsu' (the Lower Deep) in the myth of the conquest of Chaos by Cosmos in the Babylonian New Year festival. For the Heb. usage of 'first-born' to express 'conspicuous' or 'foremost', cf. Isa. 14.30, 'the first-born of the poor', that is, the poorest, and Exod. 4.22, Israel as 'the first-born among the nations', that is, the foremost.

14. *nāṯaq* ('to tear away') is already attested at 15.11 and Jer. 6.20, and at Josh. 8.16, where it means 'withdraw'.

15. In MT *tiškôn bᵉ'ohᵒlô mibbᵉlî-lô*, *tiškōn* requires a suitable subject. Just possible, but, we think, unlikely, is *mibbᵉlî-lô*, 'none of what belongs to him', taking *min* as partitive. A noun feasibly suggested is the feminine *lîlîṯ*, 'the Night-hag', read by Voigt, Beer, Ball, Houtsma and Fohrer. Those suggestions, however, ignore the parallelism demanded by the reference to sulphur (*goprîṯ*) in v. 15b. Dhorme has suggested that sulphur may be used as a disinfectant or in a rite of separation, sc. from previous ownership or occupation, in which case the former suggestion is of itself just possible. But sulphur was also a means of destruction, as in the case of Sodom and Gomorrah, where it is associated with fire. Thus in v. 15a *mibbᵉlî* may be a corruption of 'fire'. Here Dahood (1957: 312ff.) happily adduces the Ugaritic noun *nbl* ('flame'); cf. Akk. *nablu*, as the original of which *mibbᵉlî* is the corruption. Thus he proposes to read *mabbēl* and to take MT *lô* as the corruption of emphatic enclitic *lᵉ* before the imperfect as in Ugaritic and Arab., thus restoring the couplet as:

> *tiškôn hᵉ'ohᵒlēhû mabbēl lîzōrāh 'al-nāwēhû goprîṯ*
>
> Flame settles on his tent, brimstone is scattered on his homestead.

nāweh is the abode of shepherds (Jer. 33.12), and is used of a house (Prov. 3.33) and even of the city of Jerusalem (Isa. 27.10; Ps. 79.7) and of the Temple (Exod. 15.13). In 5.24, as in the present passage, it is parallel to *'ōhel*, with its original pastoral nuance.

16. Here the fate of the wicked is described again in the figure of the tree, with its roots drying up and its branches wilting; cf. 15.30.

17. *zikrô* means 'mention of him' or 'his reputation', which preserves a man in some semblance of existence even after death according to popular belief in ancient Israel. *šēm* (lit. 'name') indicates also 'reputation' and also a man's actual name, which is perpetuated in his sons. *ḥûṣ* ('outside') is found in plural parallelism with *'ereṣ* in 5.10 as here. Dhorme assumes that it means 'desert' in contrast to the cultivated and inhabited land *'ereṣ*. This may be so in Prov. 8.26 and Ps. 144.13; cf. the Aram. rendering *bar*, which means both 'outside' and, as in the Arab. cognate, 'desert', but in Job the two terms may be synonymous.

18. In *yehdᵉpuhû* ('they thrust him out') and *yᵉnidduhû*, from *nāḏaḏ* ('to flee'), the 3rd plur. expresses the indefinite subject, which is tantamount to the passive of the sing. *nāḏaḏ* found in the Hophal in 20.8.

19. *nîn* and *nēḵeḏ* are used together in Gen. 21.23, Isa. 14.22 and Ben Sira 47.22 to denote a comprehensive number of one's people. *nîn* is not attested except here and in the passages cited. It may be connected with a verb *nûn*, which is possibly, but doubtfully, attested at Ps. 72.17. Since *nēḵeḏ* is not attested beyond these passages its derivation and precise significance are uncertain. The meaning may be rendered with similar alliteration in English 'kith and kin'. *śārîḏ* means 'survivor' of a great danger or calamity (cf. 20.21; 27.15). Note the contrast between *'ammô* ('his own people'), basically kinsmen, who derived their origin, like an Arab tribe, from a common ancestor *'amm*, and *mᵉgûrāyw*, to the place where he lives only as a sojourner or protected alien (*gēr*).

20. *yômô* in the sense of 'the day of his destiny' is attested in 1 Sam. 26.10 (*'im*) *yômô yāḇô' wāmēṯ* ('[if] his day come that he die'). Here, therefore, it signifies 'his fate'. The antithetic parallelism of 'the folk of the West' (*'aḥᵃrōnîm*) and 'the folk of the East' (*qaḏmōnîm*) to give a comprehensive picture recalls the passage in the Ugaritic Baal myth (Gordon *UT* 'nt II.7-8) where the goddess

> Smites the princes by the sea-shore (sc. West),
> Annihilates the folk in the direction of the sunrise.

ša'ar ('horror') is attested in the reduplicated forms in Jer. 5.30; 18.13 and Hos. 6.10. See Textual Note.

21. *yāḏa'-'ēl* is not limited to knowledge about God, but here denotes knowledge of God involving personal reaction to Him, acknowledgment rather than knowledge.

Job 19

Job's Rejoinder to Bildad

This speech is constructed of eight strophes (19.2-4, 5-8, 9-12, 13-16, 17-20, 21-24, 25-27, 28-29), each of three or four bicola, except the last, which consists of a bicolon and a tricolon. It is introduced by the first strophe (vv. 2-4) in the convention of a legal controversy. In the address proper, Job complains in the first two strophes (vv. 5-8, 9-12) in the convention of a plea at law, holding that God wronged him (esp. v. 6), and he elaborates on his sufferings at the hand of God in the hyperbolic and figurative language of the Plaint of the Sufferer, where the sufferer describes the alienation of his friends and associates who see his sufferings as a token of his sin and alienation from God. This serves Job to describe his own sufferings and to animadvert on the popular view of suffering as the consequence of sin as evidenced in the reaction of his friends. In the highly individualistic character of the Book of Job, it is not possible to limit the passages strictly to one literary type or another. Thus there is often a mixture of the characteristic motifs, phraseology and figures of the Plaint of the Sufferer and the legal controversy, while the conventional language and sequence of ideas in the legal controversy are often used in sapiential dispute. Thus the sixth strophe (vv. 21-24) opens with a plea for mercy in a legal context (vv. 21-22) and continues with the wish that the evidence for the accused were recorded for future reference, and in the seventh strophe (vv. 25-27) Job resumes the theme of his ultimate appeal before God, supported by a celestial witness and interpreter and possibly advocate, before his death (cf. 16.18-22). Now he declares his conviction (*yāḏa'tî*, v. 25) that he will live to see his vindication (vv. 25f.) despite his physical extremity (v. 26) and, the final contingency, before God himself (v. 26).

Chapter 19

1. Then Job answered and said:

2. 'How long will you torment me
And crush me with words?
3. These ten times now you approach me,
You are not ashamed to seem shocked at me.
4. And if indeed I have gone astray,
My error remains my own.

5. Would you indeed assume superiority to me,
And make reproach of me an argument?
6. Then know that it is God who has wronged me,
And cast his net about me.
7. If I cry out "Violence!" I am not answered,
If I cry for help there is no justice.
8. He has walled up my path and I may not pass,
He has set thorns on my path.

9. He has stripped me of my prestige,
And has taken away the crown from my head.
10. He breaks me down utterly and I am gone,
And he has uprooted my hope like a tree;
11. And he has kindled His anger against me,
And has counted me as His enemy.[1]
12. His troops come massed against me,
Yea, they raise up[2] their ramp against me,
They camp[3] around my tent.

13. My brothers have held aloof,[4]
My acquaintances are mere strangers to me;
14. My kinsmen and close friends have failed me.
The sojourners in my house have forgotten me,
15 Yea, my slave-girls treat me as an outsider,
I am a stranger in their eyes.
16. I have called to my slave and he does not answer me,
I have to entreat him with my own mouth.

17. My breath is repugnant to my wife,
And I am putrid to my own children.
18. Even children spurn me,
If I rise they turn their back on me.
19. All my intimates abhor me,
And those whom I loved have turned against me.
20. [5]My bones cleave to my skin,[5]
And I have escaped on the forfeiture of my flesh.[6]

21. But you, my friends, pity me, pity me,
For it is the hand of God that has touched me!
22. Why do you pursue me like God,
Never sated with my flesh?
23. Would that my words were written down,
Would that they were engraved in an inscription[7]
24. With an iron pen and leaded,
Were inscribed on the rock forever.

25. But I myself am sure: the One who will vindicate me is vital,
And the One who is the final authority will prove himself effective on this earth,
26. [8]And though my skin is stripped from my flesh
Even after that I shall come face to face with God,

27. Whom I myself shall see,
Whom I shall see with my own eyes,[9] himself and no stranger.
My reins grow faint within me…

28. If you say "How shall we prosecute him,
And find in him a pretext for a case?",
29. Fear the sword for yourselves,
For excessive zeal in wrong courses spells ruin.[10]
That you may know that there is a judge.'[11]

Textual Notes to Chapter 19

1. Reading *ṣārô* with LXX, S and T for MT *ṣārāyw.*
2. Reading *w^eyāsōllû* for MT *wayyāsōllû.*
3. Reading *w^eyaḥ^anû* for MT *wayyaḥ^anû.*
4. Reading *hirḥîqû* with LXX, Aq, Sym and S and one Heb. MS for MT *hirḥîq*, which is supported by 11QtargJob.
5. Reading *b^e'ôrî dāḇ^eqāh 'aṣmî*, omitting *ûḇiḇ^eśārî* in v. 20a. See n. 6.
6. Reading *b^eśārî* for MT *šinnāy*, assuming displacement from 20a. See Commentary *ad loc.*
7. Reading *b^esēp̄er* for MT *bassēp̄er.*
8. Reading *w^e'ôrî niqq^ep̄û mibb^eśārî // w^e'aḥar zō'ṯ 'eḥ^ezeh '^elôah.* See Commentary *ad loc.*
9. Reading *'ênay rā'ōh* for MT *'ênay rā'û.* See Commentary *ad loc.*
10. Reading *ḥōreḇ* for MT *ḥereḇ.*
11. Reading *šeyyēš dayyān* for MT *šaddîn.*

Commentary on Chapter 19

2. *tôḡyûn* is the Hiphil imperfect retaining the original final *y* of *yāḡāh*, cognate of Arab. *wajiya* ('to have a pain'). It occurs in rather late passages in the OT, the earliest being Zeph. 3.18, where the text is doubtful. Otherwise the incidences are postexilic, for example, Lam. 1.4, 5, 12; 3.32, 35 and Isa. 51.23. LXX read *tôḡî'ûn* ('do you weary?'), but MT better suits the parallelism. Here *nep̄eš* with the pronominal suffix has the force of the personal pronoun.

3. *tahk^erû* is a *hapax legomenon* on which T and the early Jewish commentators show no unanimity. The verb may be a cognate of Arab. *hakara* ('to be astonished'). On this assumption we would see a reference to Job's annoyance at his friends' affected astonishment at his protestation of innocence in the face of the conventional inference of sin from suffering. This describes the reaction of outraged orthodoxy to Job's embarrassing questions. 'Ten times' means simply repeatedly.

4. As appreciated by S, *w^e'ap̄-'omnām* means 'and if indeed…', the protasis of a conditional sentence without the conditional particle (GKC, §159b, h).

m^e^šûḡāh means not deliberate or heinous sin, but rather error or sin of inadvertency (cf. Lev. 4.10; Num. 15.22) or ignorance (Ezek. 20.25); cf. Job's admission of juvenile delinquency (13.26).

5. If, as Dhorme maintains, *'im-'omnām* introduces a question expressing indignant astonishment, it is nevertheless tantamount to the protasis of a conditional sentence. This is supported by the enclitic *'ēp̄ô* with the imperative *d^e^'û* in v. 6a; cf. Arab. *fa*, which introduces the apodosis when the verb is imperative. *tagdîlû* (lit. probably 'affect greatness') expresses the sense of moral superiority of the self-righteous in face of the suffering of Job believed to be retributory, an attitude which is described in similar language in Pss. 35.17 (EVV 16) and 55.13 (EVV 12).

6. *m^e^ṣûḏô* denotes a hunting implement, from the verb *ṣûḏ* ('to hunt'), which we may conjecture from the preposition *'al* to be a net. The noun is found complementary to *ḥerem* ('net') in Eccl. 7.26 and of a net for fish in Eccl. 9.12. From this point Job desists from his address to his friends and pointedly ascribes his afflictions to the inveterate enmity of God in striking figures and tone familiar in the fast-liturgy in Lam. 3.1-18.

8. The parallel with 'he has walled up my way' (*'orḥî gāḏar*)—cf. Lam. 3.8—leads us to question the meaning 'darkness' for *ḥōšeḵ* in v. 8b, and supports Guillaume's suggestion (1963: 114) that the word, perhaps differently pointed as *ḥāšāḵ*, is cognate with Arab. *ḥaśaku(n)* ('thorns'), which are used for an obstruction to cattle.

9. *k^e^ḇôḏî*, here, especially in parallelism with *'^a^ṭereṯ* ('crown'), might be rendered 'glory', though understood figuratively. This, however, is a secondary development of the primary sense 'weight, substance', hence 'honour', the opposite of *q^e^lālāh* ('lightness'), the result of the curse, or of *rîq* ('emptiness') of natural significance. Again, this may be the figure and motif of the Plaint of the Sufferer; cf. Lam. 5.16, 'Fallen is the crown of our head'. The conception of humanity as the acme of God's creation, crowned with glory and honour (Ps. 8.6 [EVV 5]), is suggested here, but the language may derive generally from the Plaint of the Sufferer, and perhaps specifically from the liturgy of the fast relating to the king as the representative of the community.

10. Note the use of *hālaḵ* ('to pass away, be gone'); cf. 14.20. The figure of a building ruined, if this is indeed the meaning of *yitt^e^ṣēnî*, as it normally would be in Heb., is not quite what is expected with a personal object, though it is not unintelligible (e.g. Ps. 52.7 [EVV 6]), and the military figure of the assault of a person as the breach of a besieged city. Here, as in 10.8 and 18.11, *sāḇîḇ* tips the adverbial sense of 'utterly'. *nāsa'* is used for the transplanting (after 'uprooting') of a vine in Ps. 80.9 (EVV 8).

11. For *wayyaḥar 'ālay 'appô* S and V read 'and His anger was kindled' (*wayyiḥar... 'appô*), which is a familiar Heb. expression. Here, however, the Hiphil may be retained with respect to God who is not swayed by passion, but deliberately rouses his anger. In view of LXX, S and T, 'his enemy' (*ṣārô*) may be read for MT *ṣārāyw* ('his enemies').

12. If MT *wᵉyāḇō'û* is read, *wᵉyāsōllû* must be read for MT *wayyāsōllu*. The military metaphor of preparing a ramp or siege-mound for a battering-ram and camping round the besieged city recalls the figures in 15.25f. and 16.14; cf. God's 'bands' (*gᵉḏûḏāyw*) in 25.3. The siege-ramp (*sōlᵉlāh*) (cf. 2 Sam. 20.15; 2 Kgs 19.32 = Isa. 37.33; Jer. 6.6; Ezek. 4.2; 26.8; etc.) is well illustrated in the siege of Lachish in the reliefs from Sennacherib's palace at Nineveh (*ANEP*, pls. 372, 373). 'My tent' is hardly congruous with the figure of a siege with ramps (v. 12b), and may cast doubts on the originality of v. 12c. But the tricolon may mark the end of the strophe as occasionally in the poems from Ras Shamra. In this case *'ōhel* may mean simply 'seat', reflecting, as not infrequently in Heb., the desert origin of the Semitic penetration of the settled land, for example 'to your tents, O Israel'.

13. The versions support the reading of MT *'aḵ-zārû* ('they have simply been strangers') as against the arrangement of the consonants in LXX, *'aḵzārû* ('they have been cruel'), which is attested as a verb in Aram. and as an adjective *'aḵzār* in Heb. (cf. 30.21; 41.2; Deut. 32.23). But *mimmenî* ('from me') militates against this reading. The verb as in MT must denote conduct unnatural to brothers, relatives and friends; hence *zāru* is a denominative verb 'to behave as strangers'. This interpretation is supported by v. 15.

14-15. The text should be arranged: *ḥāḏᵉlû qᵉrôḇāy ûmᵉyuddā'ay šᵉḵēḥûnî gārê bêṯî* ('My kinsmen and close friends have failed me, the sojourners in my house have forgotten me'). The sojourner (*gēr*) was one who had been admitted to the protection of the god of the community and to its social conventions. Such a person might be a travelling merchant, or one of those who came for seasonal grazing to a locality, a person staying abroad in a time of local famine or drought, for example, Naomi and her family in the plains of Moab (Ruth 1.1), or a refugee from blood-revenge who had been given the right of sanctuary and whom his hosts, for purposes of pride or policy, cared to maintain beyond a conventional limited period. Such a person among the Arab tribes, where there are many such, is called *jāru 'llāhi* ('protected alien of God'). Their rights in the community of Israel were recognized, but they were exempted from the strict ritual taboo that applied to Israel (e.g. in food, Deut. 14.21), and, as recognizing the God of Israel and enjoying his protection, they were admitted to the Passover provided they were circumcised (Exod. 12.48). Such alienation of a sufferer's friends and even relatives on the assumption that he lay under the Divine wrath is well known in the Plaint of the Sufferer, either in fact or figure, for example, in Pss. 27.10; 31; 31.12 (EVV 11); 38.12 (EVV 11); 88.9 (EVV 8); etc. The nadir of the sufferer's affliction is the revulsion or contempt of his slaves and young people (vv. 15f.).

17. *zārāh* is taken by Dhorme as derived from *zûr* ('to be strange'), but he adduces also *zûr* ('to be repugnant'), citing Haupt for this specific meaning of the Ass. *zîru*, of a wife feeling revulsion for her husband. *rēḥî* ('my smell') would be as apt as MT *rûḥî* ('my breath'). The MT pointing of *w^eḥannōṯî* indicates *ḥānan*, which is known in the Hithpael meaning 'to entreat', and is taken to mean this in the versions and most commentaries. But the Qal of this verb is not certainly attested, and in the context is certainly a homonym, with a Syr. cognate *ḥanînâ'* ('putrid'). Commentators have not failed to notice that Job's children according to the Prologue had all perished, and have explained 'sons of my belly' as uterine brothers, which is unlikely after the reference to brothers in v. 13 and in parallelism with 'wife' in v. 17. Others again (e.g. Wetzstein and W.R. Smith) take *baṭnî* as 'my clan' (cf. Arab. *baṭnu*[*n*]), but this is open to the same objection. The writer is simply using the language and imagery of the Plaint of the Sufferer to express the extremity of Job's misery—total excommunication—without any literal application.

18. The contempt of the young boys (*'^awîlîm*, derived from *'ûl*, 'to suck', Gen. 33.13; 1 Sam. 6.7, 19; Isa. 40.11; Ps. 78.71) contrasts with the respect of the young and even the old in the presence of Job in public before his disaster (29.8). *'āqûmāh* is the case of the cohortative introducing the protasis in a conditional sentence, without the conditional particle. The parallelism indicates that *dibbēr* is a denominative verb 'to turn the back' (so Eitan 1924: 33; G.R. Driver 1934: 55f.).

19. *m^eṯê sôḏî*, 'men who share my counsel', that is, intimates; cf. 15.8. *zeh* is the relative particle (GKC, §138h), *d* in Aram. and Ugaritic and related to Arab. *ḏû* (see above on 15.17). Here it refers to the plur. subject of the verb in the main clause; cf. Gordon *UT* 1024.7f.: *'št 'sr ḥršmmdtb'ln b'ugrt* ('eleven artisans who work in Ugarit'). This passage incidentally attests features which we have noted throughout this work, the 3rd plur. masc. of the imperfect in *t*, the energic ending of the imperfect, the relative particle *d* and the phonetic variant *b* for *p*.

20. In v. 20a there is one word too many for the metre. LXX reads 'In my skin my flesh rots, my bones were ripped in my teeth'. This indicates the reading *b^e'ôrî b^eśārî rāqaḇ*, which was read by Merx and Dhorme. In support of MT *dāḇ^eqāh*, which Merx would emend to *rāqaḇ*, cf. Ps. 102.6: *dāḇ^eqāh 'aṣmî liḇ^eśārî* ('my bones cleave to my flesh'). The familiarity of the writer may account for the inclusion of *ûḇ^eśārî* in 20. Hence we would read *b^e'ôrî dāḇ^eqāh 'aṣmî* ('my bones cleave to my skin'), and suggest that the text has been upset

by the failure to note a word-play in *'ôr* ('skin') in v. 20a, but 'pledge' in v. 20b; cf. Arab. *'i'āratu(n)* ('loan') from the root *'āra, ya'ūr*, which may suggest the translation of Isa. 53.12, *he'erāh lammāwet̠ nap̄šô* (with slight emendation of the verb) as 'he gave himself a pledge to death'. *b^eśārî*, superfluous in v. 20a, seems to have been displaced from after v. 20b, where it was misunderstood after *'ôr*, taken as 'skin' and corrupted to *šinnay*. Hence in v. 20b we propose the reading *wā'et̠mall^eṭāh b^e'ôr b^eśārî* ('and I have escaped on the forfeiture of my flesh'). This means that in his emaciated condition the sufferer has just survived, leaving his flesh a pledge in the hands of death.

21. Job claims not censure but pity since his suffering is the touch of 'the hand of God', which was not to be assessed or judged by human reason; cf. the reference to 'the hand of God' in the plagues of Egypt, which left the local magicians incompetent (Exod. 8.15). The Arabs have a delicate reaction to illness or abnormality as 'the touch of Allah'.

22. After the reference to 'the hand of God', which ought to have spared Job the censure of his friends, the MT reading *k̠^emô 'ēl* would be readily intelligible, though Fohrer, presumably discriminating between *'ēl* and *'^elôah*, takes *'ēl* in the sense of 'demon'. We might agree with Fohrer so far as to render 'like a god'. In accordance with the inveterate opposition of Job's adversaries in v. 22a, it is likely that the 'eating of a person's flesh' in v. 22b is the idiom familiar in Ass., Aram. and Syr. 'to slander'; cf. Dan. 3.8; 6.26 and Syr. *'akalqarṣâ'* ('the Devil', lit. 'slanderer'). Sexual abuse suggested by Tur-Sinai and adopted by Pope here and at 31.31 is, in our opinion, quite gratuitous.

23. LXX reads v. 24b immediately after v. 23b, v. 23a being inserted in LXX from Theodot., which would give the reading:

> 23a. *mî-yittēn 'ēp̄ô w^eyikkāt̠^eb̠û millāy*
> 24a. *b^e'ēṭ-barzel w^e'ôp̄āret̠*
> 23b. *mî-yittēn bassēp̄er w^eyuḥāqû*
> 24b. *lā'ad̠ baṣṣûr yēḥāṣ^eb̠ûn*

In v. 23b *sēp̄er* does not mean 'book', as the verb *ḥāqaq* ('to engrave') indicates, but 'inscription' (so Gehman 1944: 303ff., citing the word in Phoenician). An inscription on a copper plaque (Akk. *siparru*, Arab. *sifru*[*n*]) has been suggested (so Hölscher, Mowinckel, Terrien, Pope); cf. the copper scroll from Qumran. This, however, does not accord with the reference to lead. But there is a notable instance of an inscription engraved in rock with vestiges of lead filling possibly to preserve it against weather, but probably to make it more conspicuous and legible. This is the inscription of Darius I on the rock of Behistun (Weidner 1945–51: 146f.). This monument was doubtless well known through Jewish settlers in Persia after the Exile and to travelling merchants and other Jews with wide-spread business interests like Murashu Sons (Clay 1898).

25. The passage contained in vv. 25-27 is to be understood in the context of vv. 23-24, Job's wish that a memorial of his integrity should be inscribed on a rock as a permanent record of the justice of his case. In vv. 25ff. he goes further, declaring his certainty of actual vindication by a living vindicator (*gō'ēl ḥay*). Therefore we should take *kî* in the adversative sense—'But'. We agree with Fohrer that grammar demands that v. 25a should be rendered 'I know the One who will vindicate me is vital'. No mere memorial would satisfy Job, but vindication by a living vindicator, we might fairly infer 'the living God'. Besides the contrast to vv. 25-24, the adjective might signify the living God in contrast to the God of the orthodox dogma in the statements of Job's friends. There may also be the nuance of 'effective', as Fohrer claims, cf. *'ᵉlōhîm ḥay* in Hezekiah's prayer (Isa. 37.15-20 = 2 Kgs 18.29-33) with reference to the Assyrian's questioning of the efficacy of Yahweh. This convinces us that Job's *gō'ēl* is God and not an intermediary, which seems to us to be corroborated by *'ᵉlôah* in emphatic final position in v. 26b in what we regard as a striking *inclusio* in vv. 25-26. The connotation of *gō'ēl* in the OT, as distinct from *pōḏeh* (one who redeems by paying the price of redemption), one who rehabilitates or vindicates, with social connotation, militates against the interpretation of the word here in the Christian sense of 'Redeemer' *pace* Handel and RV. Job's longing throughout the Book is not for redemption from sin and its consequences, but for the vindication of his moral right, which he consistently avers until his great oath of purgation (ch. 31). Job's vindication is cast in the figure of the *gō'ēl*, the kinsman who has the duty of rehabilitating one of his family in his rightful possession, like Boaz in Ruth, or who avenged the blood of his kinsman (*gō'ēl haddām*). It extended to Yahweh's rehabilitation of his people, especially in Deutero-Isaiah; for example, in Isa. 44.6, where the Divine Vindicator is also entitled *rî'šôn wᵉ'aḥᵃrôn*, which we consider to afford a clue to the significance of *'aḥᵃrôn* in v. 25b.

We seriously question whether *'aḥᵃrôn* here means 'afterwards' (T), 'at the end' (S), or 'at the last day' (V with Christian implications). The word is formally an adjective or noun. Mowinckel (1925: 211) after Siegfried (1893) took *'aḥᵃrôn* as the synonymous, or rather complementary, parallel of *gō'ēl*, both referring to a celestial intermediary, and rendered *'aḥᵃrôn* as *Bürger* ('Guarantor' or 'Sponsor', so NEB). This sense of *'aḥᵃrôn* is not attested in the OT, but may be supported by *'aḥᵃrāyā'* in Aram. and Late Heb., and might refer to Job's celestial supporter in 16.19. But we consider this doubtful, and on the grounds that we have already cited we are still more doubtful of Mowinckel's view that *gō'ēl* is an intermediary like Job's 'witness' in 16.19 rather than God himself.

It has been proposed that *'aḥᵃrôn* signifies the party in a lawsuit who has the final argument and therefore the advantage over his opponent (so G.R. Driver 1950a: 46); cf. Prov. 18.17:

> He who speaks in his case (seems) right;
> but his colleague comes forward and gives him a grilling.

On the other hand, if *'aḥarôn* has the same sense as in the Divine title *rî'šôn wᵉ'aḥarôn* (Isa. 44.6) it would refer to God as final authority, who ultimately consummates what He has initiated, who disposes as He has proposed; hence our rendering 'final authority'.

It has been held that Job declares his confidence that he would be vindicated after death. This begs the question of the significance of *'āp̄ār* in v. 25b, which admittedly signifies occasionally the 'dust' of the grave (17.16; 20.11; 21.26; Isa. 26.19; Ps. 22.30 [EVV 29]; Dan. 12.2), but may also mean 'earth', as in 5.4; 10.9; 14.1; 41.25 (EVV 33). Again Job's appeal that his blood should remain where it has been shed, uncovered until it is avenged (16.18f.), might be cited in support of the vindication of his just cause after death. But this may be too literal an interpretation of a striking figure of speech. Any view of Job's hope of vindication after death seems emphatically contradicted by the wholly negative prospect of death in 14.22 and elsewhere throughout the Book, for instance, in 3.13-19; 7.8-10, 21 and particularly 14.13-21, where any gleam of hope of justification after death (14.13-15) is categorically dismissed in the immediate sequel (14.14-21). We consider the question to be settled by Job's declaration that he will see God (19.27) and, we suggest, be admitted to the confrontation (*'eḥᵉzeh*, 19.26b) he so ardently desires. This suggests to us that the formally ambiguous *'āp̄ār* means '(this) earth'. In this context we would note the pregnant sense of *yāqûm* connoting the decisive and powerful intervention of God in human affairs (as in Num. 10.27; Isa. 2.19-21; Jer. 2.27; cf. Job 31.14) rather than physical stance.

26. In v. 26a MT bristles with problems. *'aḥar* ('after') followed by the indicative of the verb MT *niqqᵉp̄û* without the relative particle *'ᵃšer* is anomalous, and has suggested the reading Aram. *'āḥûr* ('I shall see'; cf. the critical apparatus of BH³), which might give a synonymous parallel to *'eḥᵉzeh* in v. 26b. On this reading *'āḥûr* would require an object, which might be the original of MT *'ôrî*, such as *'ēḏî* (so BH³, *apparatus criticus*) or, nearer to MT *'ōzᵉrî* ('my helper'); cf. Job's celestial supporter in 16.19, which might support Mowinckel's understanding of *'aḥᵃrôn* as a celestial intermediary in chiastic parallelism. MT *niqqᵉp̄û zō'ṯ* is attested in LXX, the verb being rendered variously 'exhausted' and 'accomplished', cf. V 'enwrapped', as from *qûp̄*—the other ancient versions either ignore or offer a reading which does not reflect MT or anything resembling it. The *apparatus criticus* in BH³ suggests the reading *yizqôp̄ 'ōṯî*, which we consider doubtful since *'eṯ* as *nota accusativa* in Job is practically limited to the prose Prologue and Epilogue. On this reading ('who will raise me up?'), the verb would demand the original of MT *'ôrî*, for example *'ēḏî*, as suggested in BH³; cf. 16.19, or, we might suggest, *'ōzᵉrî* ('my helper'), and *mᵉšārî* ('my liberator'), both intermediaries. MT *'ôrî* and *mibbᵉśārî*, however, are unanimously attested in the ancient versions. Thus we find that the only viable alternative is the reading of the awkward MT after E.F. Sutcliffe (1950: 377), followed by R. Tournay (1962: 492ff.; 1967: 129) and Lévêque (1970: *ad loc.*):

w^e 'ôrî niqqap̄ mibb^eśārî
w^e 'aḥar zō'ṯ 'eḥ^ezeh '^elôah

which we would render

And though my skin is stripped from my flesh,
Even after that I shall come face to face with God.

Taking the verb *nāqap̄* in the sense it has in Isa. 10.34 (forests stripped by storm) and Isa. 24.13 (olive berries struck off), this reading has the merit of simplicity and retaining the elements of MT with rearrangement. Reflecting the skin disease in the Prologue as evidence of the alienation of the sufferer from God, Job declares that though his sufferings are intensified to the ultimate degree he will be accorded the confrontation for which he longed with God as He really is (*w^elō' zār*, v. 27b), sympathetic, who will vindicate the right of his faithful 'servant' (1.8).

In vv. 26b and 27a *'eḥ^ezeh* is used twice, which is exceptional in Job. If in both cases the verb means 'see', as in v. 27ab, the reference may be to the intensity of the subject's vision beyond the superficial, as in Amos 1.1f.; Isa. 1.1; 2.1; Mic. 1.1; Ezek. 24.4, 16; cf. the repetition of the verb in the infinitive absolute and the indicative. But, according to the word-play favoured by the author of Job, *'eḥ^ezeh* in v. 26b might be a homonym of *ḥāzāh*, 'to see', meaning 'to confront', the experience Job consistently desires; cf. *ḥāzeh*, 'the breast' of a sacrificial animal (Exod. 29.6; Lev. 7.30; 8.29; Num. 6.20; 19.19—all P); cf. Arab. *ḥiḏā(n)*, 'opposite', and the verb *ḥaḏā* meaning in the VIIth Form 'to sit opposite one another', which we prefer on stylistic grounds.

27. The last word in v. 27b, *zār*, is patient of various interpretations in the context. It may mean 'strange' in the sense of 'other' or 'estranged' and might refer to Job or to God. Baumgärtel, G.B. Gray, Weiser, Lindblom, Pope and G.R. Driver take it to refer to God as estranged from Job. Driver supports this interpretation by the assumption that *lî* after *'eḥ^ezeh* in the parallel colon means 'on my side'. The hyphen in MT, however, indicates that *lî* is the ethic dative emphasizing the personal pronouns in *'^anî* and *'ênay* (so Terrien and Fohrer). This suggests that *w^elō'-zār* means 'and no other' (cf. Prov. 27.2; Ben Sira 40.29) referring to Job (so Dhorme, Ehrlich, Hölscher, Gordis, Fohrer after LXX). In view of Job's complaint that he is treated by his own household as *zār* (v. 15), we should note the suggestion of L.A. Snijders (1954) that *zār* refers to Job as 'estranged'. Whether the word refers to God or to Job, the phrase might form an apt *inclusio* with *gō'^alî* in v. 25a. We consider *zār* in its normal sense in the OT too strong a term for 'other', but in its normal sense of 'stranger' it is an excellent antithetic parallel to *gō'ēl*, with the traditional implications of a kinsman as vindicator, in *inclusio*. An additional implication may be the contrast between 'the living God' as Job's vindicator and that other 'God' of orthodox dogma represented by the three friends.

In the context of the imperfect *'eḥ^{e}zeh* we would understand the imperfect sense of *rā'āh* in v. 27b, which consequently we read as the infinitive absolute *rā'ōh* for MT *rā'û*. In vv. 25-27, in accordance with our view that the survival of death is alien to the thought of the Book of Job those verbs cannot be taken in the physical sense, but as meaning that Job will come to see his relationship with God as it truly is, as in his declaration in 42.5 and the experience of Isaiah in the moment of revelation (Isa. 6.5). By the same token, *yāqûm* in v. 25b is, we consider, to be taken not in a literal sense, but of decisive Divine intervention in human affairs; see above on 25b.

If v. 27c belongs with vv. 25-27b, it expresses the ardent desire of the sufferer for the deliverance expressed in that passage; cf. Ps. 119.123, *'ênay kālû lîšû'āṯ^{e}ḵā* ('my eyes fail [looking] for Thy deliverance'). *kilyōṯay* (lit. my kidneys') is the seat of emotion for the ancient Hebrews. 'Within my bosom' (*b^{e}ḥēqî*) seems strange anatomy, but *ḥēq* means generally 'inside', and the phrase indicates 'intimate being'; cf. *napšî* in a similar context in Ps. 84.3. On the analogy of those passages in the Psalms, v. 27b is best taken as the first colon of an incomplete bicolon.

28. *lō'* is best taken as the Aram. *nota accusativa* with the pronominal suffix, the object of the verb. We take *māh* as the interrogative pronoun, here signifying 'How?'; cf. 9.2 *mah-yyiṣdaq* ('how will he prove his innocence?', 'what will he cite to prove his innocence?'). English 'the root of the matter is found in him' is misleading. The language is forensic. In the context *dāḇār* means 'a case' (cf. Exod. 8.16; 24.14). Hence *šōreš dāḇār* means 'pretext for a case' (so Dhorme). In the introduction *kî* may best be taken as 'But'.

29. This verse has caused much perplexity among commentators, among whom there is no agreement nor, we believe, any satisfactory solution through the rendering of *ḥ^{a}māh* as 'wrath' and assenting that in both instances MT *ḥoreḇ* means 'sword'. We propose that MT *ḥ^{a}māh*, an Aram. form, is cognate with Arab. *ḥamyatu(n)* ('excess of zeal'). Throughout Job the apparently identical word in parallel cola indicates a word-play. Thus we would take *ḥereḇ* in v. 29a as 'sword', 'the sword of God', as in Ezekiel 21, as Fohrer has well noted, and propose that in v. 29b the abstract noun from *ḥāraḇ* ('to destroy') should be read *ḥōreḇ* ('ruin, destruction'), v. 29b then meaning 'excessive zeal in wrong courses spells ruin'. Thus, we believe Job passes judgment on the excessive zeal of his friends to represent him as a sinner meriting his afflictions, and as defenders of the current doctrine of the theodicy despite the hard facts of experience.

In MT *šaddîn* ('[know] that there is a judgment'), the reading *šeyyēš dîn* or possibly *šeyyēš dayyān* ('that there is a judge') seems more suitable. The relative particle *še*—cf. Phoenician *'š* and Akk. *ša*—though common in Late Heb., is attested as early as the Song of Deborah (Judg. 5.7). This would nevertheless be the only instance in the Book of Job, and the odd colon always leaves a doubt as to whether it is the member of an incomplete colon, where for want of a parallel the text is doubtful, or is a late gloss. It is alternatively suggested that MT *šaddîn* is a scribal error for *šadday* ('the Almighty') (so Fischer 1961: 342ff.) and Pope. In this case, if the text is complete, the verb would mean not 'know' in the intellectual sense but 'acknowledge'.

Job 20

The Reply of Zophar

If Zophar's reply to Job's statement in ch. 19 is not simply a restatement of his former assertion of the theodicy with an accumulation of proverbs and figures from Wisdom literature in the manner of Oriental argument, it is still a direct reply to Job's declaration that he knows for certain the One who will vindicate him (19.25). His reply is introduced by the rhetorical question 'Do you not know?' (20.4), which introduces the time-honoured dicta of the sages on the social Order, repeatedly borne out by experience 'from the time that humans were put upon the earth'. In reply to the embarrassment to faith of the prosperity of the wicked so frequently felt and expressed in the Plaint of the Sufferer and in Wisdom poems (e.g. Ps. 73.3-11) as the prelude to their sure and often sudden fall (Pss. 73.18-20; 34.9-20), Zophar amplifies this theme with very striking imagery redolent of life in Palestine and its natural environment. Besides the sudden downfall of the wicked (vv. 4-7), their temporary prosperity, fleeting as a dream (vv. 8-9), the inherent weakness of wickedness is emphasized. Zophar adduces a series of figures, sickness through overindulgence in rich food (vv. 13-16), insatiable appetite (v. 17), anxiety (vv. 20-22), the vain efforts to escape retribution (vv. 24-25; cf. Amos 5.19f.), and final destruction by fire 'which needs no fanning' and flood and 'downpours on the day of (God's) wrath'. Finally in confirmation of this assertion of Order in society, Zophar sets this in Cosmic dimension in citing the testimony of heaven and earth (v. 27).

After a short introductory strophe of two bicola (vv. 2-3) in the style of sapiential controversy, Zophar's reply takes the form of a wisdom poem on the fate of the wicked in support of the theodicy. This is divided according to aspects of the subject and figures of speech into seven strophes (vv. 4-7, 8-9 + 11, 12-16, 17-19 + 10, 20-23, 24-26, 27-29). These are composed of a number of figures emphasizing aphorisms on the general theme of the retribution of the wicked, whose sin is his own undoing, and on the evanescence of his ill-gotten advantages. Those figures related to this theme are reminiscent of the couplets in Proverbs, but are here treated at greater length, not in couplets, but in strophes of three or four couplets.

The text is slightly disarranged. A double word-play indicates that v. 10 belonged originally after v. 19.

Chapter 20

1. Then Zophar the Naamathite answered and said:

2. 'On this my racking thoughts prompt an answer
On account of[1] my own deep-felt shame,
3. Hearing myself shamefully rebuked.
So after full consideration the spirit (within me) replies:[2]

4. Do you not[3] know this from of old,
From the time that humanity was put on the earth,
5. That the jubilation of the wicked is but for a short time,
That the joy of the impious is but for a moment?
6. Though his exaltation rises to the skies
And his head touches the clouds,
7. In proportion to his pre-eminence he perishes for ever;
Those who saw him will say, "Where is he?"

8. As a dream he flies away, and none will find him,
Dispelled like a vision of the night;
9. The eye that noticed him will do so no more,
And the place where he was will see him no longer.
11. His bones are full of lustiness,[4]
But his prime[5] shall lie in the dust,

12. Though wickedness is sweet in his mouth
And he lets it melt away under his tongue,
13. Though he cherishes it and will not let it go,
Holding it back on his palate,
14. His food in his bowels will be changed
To venom of asps within him.
15. The wealth he gorges will be spewed up;
God will expel it from his belly.
16. [6]He shall suck the poison of asps,
The tongue of the viper shall slay him.[6]

17. He will not be satisfied with streams of olive-oil,[7]
Nor torrents running with honey and curds;
18. The reward of his toil[8] he will not swallow,
None of the wealth[9] gained from his trade will he enjoy.
19. Since he has crushed the poor with force,[10]
Plundered a house that he has not built,[11]
10. His sons will make restitution to the poor,
And his children[12] pay back[13] his wealth.

20. Since he has never been at ease[14] in his belly,
Allowing none to escape his greed,[15]
21. None escaping from his devouring,
Therefore his goods shall not abide.
22. For all his full abundance he will be anxious,
All the force of trouble[16] shall come upon him.

23. [17]If his belly is full,[17]
(God) shall hurl the vehemence of his anger at him,
And shall shower upon him the flame of his wrath.[18]

24. He may flee from the iron weapon,
The bronzed bow shall transfix him;
25. The shaft shall[19] come clean through his body,[20]
And the gleaming blade go out from his liver.
[21]For him terrors are in store,
26. Total darkness is reserved.
A fire that needs no fanning[22] will consume him,[23]
He who survives in his tent shall be crushed.

27. The heavens will reveal his guilt,
And the earth shall rise up against him;
28. A flood[24] shall roll away[25] his house,
Downpours on the day of (God's) wrath.
29. This is the portion of the wicked[26] from God,
And the heritage of the rebel[27] from God.'

Textual Notes to Chapter 20

1. Reading *ba'*^{a}*ḇûr* for MT *ûḇa'*^{a}*ḇûr*, assuming dittography of *w* after *y* in the script used as in the Qumran texts.
2. Reading *ta'*^{a}*nēnî* for MT *ya'*^{a}*nēnî* in agreement with the fem. subject *ruaḥ*.
3. Reading *h*^{a}*lō' zō'ṯ* with LXX and one Heb. MS.
4. Reading *'*^{a}*lûmîm* for MT *'alûmāyw*, assuming corruption of final *m* to *w* in the Old Heb. script, perhaps after *scriptio defective* in *'*^{a}*lûmîm*.
5. Reading *'ammô* for MT *'immô*. See Commentary *ad loc.*
6. This verse is probably a gloss.
7. Reading *pal*^{e}*gê yiṣhār* for MT *p*^{e}*lagôṯ nah*^{a}*rê*, assuming corruption of *y* and *t* to *ṣ* and *n* in the Old Heb. script.
8. Reading *y*^{e}*gî'ô lō'* for MT *yāgā' w*^{e}*lō'* after one Heb. MS.
9. Reading *mēḥêl* for MT *k*^{e}*ḥêl*, *m* being corrupted to *k* in the Old Heb. script.
10. Conjecturing adverbial *'ōzām* for MT *'āzaḇ*. See Commentary *ad loc.*
11. Reading *bānāhû* for MT *yiḇenēhû* with V, and *lō'* for MT *w*^{e}*lō'*, understanding a relative clause without the relative particle as often as in Hebrew and Ugaritic poetry.
12. Reading *wîlāḏāyw* for MT *yāḏāyw* suggested by the parallelism.
13. Reading *y*^{e}*šîḇû-nā'* for MT *tāšēḇnā*, a corruption after the corruption of *wîlāḏāyw* to *yāḏāyw*. See Commentary *ad loc.*
14. Omitting *šālēw* as a gloss *metri causa*. See Commentary *ad loc.*
15. Reading *b*^{e}*ḥom*^{e}*ḏô* for MT *baḥ*^{a}*mûḏô*.
16. Reading *'āmāl* with LXX and V for MT *'āmēl*.
17. This colon is probably to be omitted as a gloss, as indicated by the original LXX.
18. Reading *'ālāyw mabbēl ḥummô* for MT *'ālêmô bil*^{e}*ḥûmô*. See Commentary *ad loc.*
19. Reading *šelaḥ* for MT *šālap̄* as suggested by LXX.
20. Reading *miggēwōh* for MT *miggēwāh* as suggested by LXX.
21. Reading *'ālāyw 'ēmîm liṣ*^{e}*pûnîm / kol-ḥōšeḵ ṭāmûn*. See Commentary *ad loc.*
22. Reading *nuppāḥāh* for MT *nuppāḥ* in agreement with the gender of *'ēš*.
23. Reading *tō'ḵ*^{e}*lēhû* for MT *t*^{e}*'āḵ*^{e}*lēhû*.

24. Reading *yāḇāl* for MT *yᵉḇûl* with one Heb. MS. See Commentary *ad loc.*
25. Reading *yāḡōl* with LXX for MT *yiḡel.*
26. *'āḏām* should probably be omitted.
27. Reading *mōreh* for MT *'imrô*. See Commentary *ad loc.*

Commentary on Chapter 20

2. *śᵉ'ippîm* here as in 4.13 denotes the movement this way and that of thoughts in the embarrassment to orthodoxy involved in Job's attitude. The Hiphil of *šûḇ*, with *dāḇār* understood, means 'answer' with the direct object of the person. Here it may mean 'make an answer' without the direct object. LXX reads *lō' ḵēn* for MT *lāḵēn*. Hence Stevenson reads 'untrue are the thoughts you address to us', reading *śᵉ'ippîm tᵉšîḇēnû*. The reading of LXX, 'this is not the answer my thoughts suggest to me', would be nearer MT. But the emendation of MT *lāḵēn* is in our opinion gratuitous. In MT *ûḇa'ᵃḇûr ḥûšî ḇî*, for which V offers only a paraphrase which has no relevance to MT, various emendations have assumed that v. 2b is the direct parallel of v. 2a. We regard the parallelism as extending to the whole strophe. Verses 2-3 are chiastic, v. 2a being parallel to v. 3b and v. 2b to v. 3a. Thus we propose that *ḥûšî ḇî* is parallel to *mûsar kᵉlimmāṯî* ('my shameful rebuke'), and take *ḥûšî* as cognate of Arab. *ḥāša*, Akk. *yaḥūšu* ('to feel shame'). In *ḥûšî ḇî* (lit. 'my shame is in me'), *ḇî* denotes the personal sense of shame; cf. *'ālāy* in Ps. 42.6, 12. In *kᵉlimmāṯî* the pronominal suffix is objective. In the middle members of the chiasmus Zophar declares that his orthodoxy, which Job has endeavoured to put to shame, prompts a reply. In v. 2a and v. 3b discriminating assessment (*bînāh*) between (*bên*) this proposition and that (*śᵉ'ippîm*) indicates that Job has succeeded in disturbing the conventional moral philosophy of the friends, which is now thrown sharply on the defensive.

3. In support of his rendering of MT *mûsar kᵉlimmāṯî* ('lesson which outrages me') after V, Dhorme cites *mûsar šᵉlômēnû* ('the chastisement which is our wholeness') in Isa. 53.5. The phrase *rûaḥ mibbînāṯî* in v. 3b may signify that, though roused and embarrassed by Job, he is nevertheless moved to retort by the spirit, here probably the special insight claimed by the sage but controlled by his intellect. If he goes on to cite what seems to be based on aphorisms of former sages, he emphasizes his own discrimination.

4. The confident expectation of an affirmative answer demands the reading *hᵃlō'* either with or without *zō'ṯ*. *śîm* may either be perfect passive with *'āḏām* as subject or infinitive construct with 'God' understood as subject; cf. 'God set humanity upon the earth' (Gen. 2.8f.) and 'God created humanity on the earth' (Dan. 4.32).

5. *r^e^nānāh* (cf. 3.7; Pss. 53.6; 100.2) derived from *rānan* ('to give a ringing, exultant cry', *rinnāh*), means 'jubilation', both joy and the cry of joy. *miqqārōḇ* ('of short duration') is a prepositional phrase usually spatial but here temporal, denoting a near objective. The parallel *'ᵃḏê-rāḡa'* (pausal) means 'for the flicker of an eyelid', *ad momentum*. On *ḥānēp̄* see on 8.13.

6. MT *śî'ô*, in the sense 'his elevation', a verbal noun from *nāśā*, for the more usual *śē'ṯô*, is read by all versions but LXX, which translates 'gift', obviously wrongly. The sense 'arrogance' (Aq., Sym., Theod.; so Hölscher, Pope) is possible as in Ps. 89.10, where the form is *śô'*, but here the parallel 'his head reaches the clouds' indicates that the word means either 'stature' or 'exaltation'.

7. MT *kᵉḡelᵃlô* has been taken by various commentators as 'dung'; cf. Arab. *jallatu*(*n*) and Ezek. 4.12, 15 (so V and Le Hir, Loisy, Renan, G.B. Gray, Hölscher, Pope, thinking of dung to be swept up as refuse; cf. 1 Kgs 14.10). Duhm and Fohrer after Wetzstein propose 'his dung-fire', sc. fire of dried dung, as in the desert, where fuel is scarce. Dhorme proposes as translation 'phantom', citing Ass. *gallu* ('evil demon' or 'ghost'). Cheyne proposed to emend to *kᵉḇôḏô* ('his glory') which is supported by LXX. This may indicate that the word is cognate of Arab. *jalla* ('to be illustrious'; e.g. *jallālatuhu*, 'His Majesty'). This is the meaning accepted by Gordis. We propose that since there is nothing in the parallelism to suggest 'dung', the meaning is 'pre-eminence', though a word-play with 'dung' was possibly intended. *kᵉ* may denote 'in proportion to', but, introducing the last couplet of the strophe, it may possibly be not a preposition but an enclitic clinching the argument as in Ugaritic, for example, in Gordon *UT* § 9.13; § 13.46; on *k* emphasizing the final verb, cf. Deut. 32.9. The vanishing of the wicked without trace is a common theme of Wisdom poetry; cf. 14.10; Ps. 37.36.

8. MT *yimṣā'ûhû* may be retained, the subject being indefinite and the form tantamount to a passive, which is read in LXX, S and V *yuddaḏ* ('is put to flight') may be retained (so Hitzig, Beer, Budde, Ball, G.B. Gray, Hölscher, Fohrer, Pope, Gordis).

9. *šāzap̄* ('to notice') occurs in the OT only here and at 28.7 and Song 1.6, where it is probably a corruption. It has been suggested that *tᵉšûrennû* should be emended to *yᵉšûrennû* in agreement with *mᵉqômô*. *māqôm*, however, though generally masc., is occasionally fem., as for example in Gen. 18.24; 1 Sam. 17.12. The verb, meaning 'to observe, notice, see', is rather poetic, and is used more frequently in Job (e.g. 7.8; 17.15; 20.9; 24.15; 33.14, 27; 34.29; 35.14) than in the rest of the OT.

10. The disappearance of the wicked having been noted, it is not unnatural to mention the fate of his sons. But, since v. 12 deals with the end of the wicked, v. 10 is either a gloss (so Duhm) or displaced from after v. 19 (so Dhorme), where it would be most apt. See below after note on v. 19.

11. Reading *ʿᵃlûmîm* in *scriptio defectiva* for MT *ʿᵃlûmāyw*, the word being an abstract plur., cf. *zᵉqûnîm* ('old age'), *nᵉʿûrîm* ('youth'). Thus *ʾᵃlûmîm* may mean youth; cf. Ugaritic *ġlm*, Arab. *ġulāmu*(*n*) ('young man'), perhaps with the nuance of sexual maturity. Note Arab. *ġalima* ('to be sexually excited') and Heb. *ʿalmah* (Isa. 7.14), where the word denotes not 'virgin', but a virgin bride, as in the Ras Shamra poems, hence a young woman sexually mature, bearing her first child. *tiškab̲* presents a problem of agreement if, as MT suggests, the subject is *ʿᵃlûmîm* (MT *ʿᵃlûmāyw*). Dhorme's citation of Ps. 103.5 *tit̲ḥaddēš kannešer nᵉʿûrāyᵉk̲î* may possibly warrant such an agreement, assuming that the abstract plur. is tantamount to a fem. abstract. But in the psalm *tit̲ḥaddēš* may be written defectively for *tit̲ḥaddᵉšî* as the predicate of the fem. *nap̄šî*, with *nᵉʿûrayk̲î* as an accusative of respect. We suggest that the subject of the fem. singular *tiškāb̲* is *ʿammô* ('his prime'), cognate with Arab. *ʿumumu*(*n*) ('completeness'), which we read for MT *ʿimmô*, and propose as an excellent correspondent to *ʿᵃlûmîm* ('lustiness'). On *ʿāp̄ār* ('dust') meaning either the earth, ground or true dust of the grave, see above on 19.25b.

12. *kāḥad̲* means 'to hide', the Hiphil meaning 'to make to disappear', hence Fohrer's proposal 'to make melt away', gradually to prolong the savour, as the context suggests.

13. *ḥāmal ʿal* means 'to spare', that is, 'he cherishes'. *ʿāzab̲* means 'to free' or 'let go' as 'to leave, abandon'; cf. 10.1, as in the legal phrase *ʿāṣûr wᵉʿāzûb* ('restrained, left free', cf. Exod. 23.5). The Ugaritic cognate *ʿdb* is used of the release of a hunting falcon, Gordon *UT* 3 Aqht 7.33.

14. *neḥpak̲* is the declaratory perfect.

15. *hôrîš*, lit. 'to make to inherit', or 'possess', means also 'to dispossess' as here and regularly in the accounts of occupation of the land which involved dispossession of the inhabitants.

16. *rōʾš* generally signifies the bitter juice of a poisonous herb; cf. Amos 6.12; Jer. 8.14; 9.14; 23.15 (*mê rōʾš*). It is parallel to *mᵉrôrāh* (cf. v. 14), in Deut. 32.32, which, as here, describes the venom of the serpent (*pet̲en*; cf. *btn* in the Ras Shamra texts) in Deut. 32.33.

17. MT *ʾal-yēreʾ* would be an optative usage of the jussive. But *ʾal* is used as a negative particle with the indicative in the Ras Shamra texts, so that the verb

may be emended to *yir'eh* in *scriptio defectiva*. We take the verb as a byform of the more familiar *rāwāh* ('to be satisfied, drink one's fill') (so too Tur-Sinai), which is attested in Prov. 23.31; Ben Sira 34.28 and probably Prov. 31.4, where *'ēw šēḵār* is probably a corruption of *rā'ô šēḵār* (Thomas 1962: 499-500). We find the root also attested in Ugaritic, Gordon *UT* 'nt I, 12-13, *bk rb 'ẓm r'i* ('a large goblet mighty of draught'). The parallel with *naḥalê debaš weḥem'āh* suggests the emendation of *nahărê* to *yiṣhār*, as proposed by Klostermann; cf. Gordon *UT* 49 III, 6-7: *šmm šmn tmṭrn nḫlm tlk nbtm* ('The skies rain [olive] oil, The wadis run with honey'), describing El's vision of the revival of nature with the revival of Baal.

18. For MT *yāgā'*, *yegî'ô* should probably be read with one Heb. MS, meaning lit. 'that which he laboured for', or 'his toil'. For MT *mēšîḇ* LXX read *laššāw'* ('for nothing'). The parallel *ḥêl temûrāṯô* ('the wealth from his trade') suggests that *mēšîḇ* is a noun cognate with Arab. *ṯawbu(u)* ('reward') from the verb *ṯāba yaṯūbu*. In *welō'*, in v. 18a and b, *w* should be attached respectively to *yegî'* and taken as a dittograph of *w* in *temûrāṯô*. The verb *'ālas* in the sense 'to enjoy' is attested besides the present passage only once, in Prov. 7.18, of sexual enjoyment.

19, 10. By reading v. 10 after v. 19 the sense is restored in a more natural context and two cases of word-play are recovered:

19. *kî rāṣaṣ* (for MT *riṣṣaṣ*) *'ōzām* (for MT *'āzaḇ*) *dallîm*
bayiṯ gāzal lō' (for MT *welō'*) *bānāhû* (for MT *yibenēhû*)
10. *bānāyw yeraṣṣû dallîm*
wîlāḏāyw (for MT *weyāḏāyw*) *yāšîḇû* (for MT *tāšēḇnāh*) *'ônô*

Since he has crushed the poor with force,
Plundered a house that he had not built,
His sons will make restitution to the poor,
And his children pay back his wealth.

We assume the reading *lō' ḇānāhû* as a relative clause without the relative particle. The phrase recalls Mic. 2.2. The condemnation is of the oppressor who plunders a house or family (both *bayiṯ*), which, in virtue of his status, he ought rather to have rehabilitated (*bānāh*; cf. Ruth 4.10-12) as a social duty. Here the word-play must be noticed between *rāṣaṣ* as in v. 10a ('to crush') and *rāṣāh* (Piel), 'to make restitution'; cf. Lev. 26.34, 41, 43 and Isa. 40.2, where the Niphal is used, and between *bānāh* and *bānāyw*.

20. MT *šālēw* is suspect for two reasons. It makes the metre in v. 20a too long, and, if it were admitted, the noun *šalwāh* rather than the participle *šālēw* is demanded if *yāḏa'* means 'he knew'. Both difficulties are obviated if we admit the proposal of D.W. Thomas (1935: 409-12) that *yāḏa'* here is cognate with Arab. *wada'a* ('to be at ease'), in which case *šālēw* may be dismissed as a gloss on the ambiguous *yāḏa'*. For MT *baḥămûḏô* we read *beḥomeḏô*, the verbal

noun for the passive participle. Here *b*[e] means 'from' as the verb demands, which is regularly the use of the preposition in Ugaritic, which has no preposition *min*.

21. In *l*[e] *'ok̲*[e]*lô* after *śārîḏ* ('survivor'), *l*[e], here 'from', has a similar force to *b*[e], as also in Ugaritic. *ḥîl* is used here as also in Ps. 10.5, if the text is sound, in the sense 'to be strong, firm'. These are the only two incidences of the verb in this sense in the OT, which is probably Aram., being well known in the intensive meaning 'to make firm'.

22. The sentiment recalls *semper avarus eget* ('the miser is ever in want' [Horace, *Ep*. 1.2.5b]). The plur. *m*[e]*lō'ôṯ* is a case of fem. plur. with the force of an abstract noun, 'abundance'; cf. *t*[e]*ḇûnôṯ*, 'understanding' (Isa. 40.14), *dē'ôṯ*, 'knowledge' (1 Sam. 2.3), *hawwôṯ*, 'fall' (Ps. 5.10), *m*[e]*nuḥôṯ*, 'rest' (Ps. 23.2), etc. (see GKC, §124e). *śēp̄eq* is better known in the verbal root *śāp̄aq*, meaning 'plenty'; cf. 36.18. If v. 22a were considered in isolation, *yēṣer lô* might mean 'he is in want', but the parallelism in v. 22b indicates the meaning 'he is anxious'; cf. 15.21; 18.12. With LXX and V, *'āmāl* ('trouble') may be read for MT *'āmēl* ('maker of trouble'), which is also possible. *yāḏ* on the reading we adopt means not literally 'hand' but 'power'.

23. *y*[e]*hî* is jussive introducing a protasis without the conditional particle in a hypothesis—cf. 22.28 (GKC, §109b)—but the whole phrase *y*[e]*hî l*[e]*mallē' biṭnô* is probably a later gloss on v. 22, as indicated by its omission in LXX. In view of the mention of missiles in the sequel, Dhorme suggests the reading *w*[e]*yamṭēr 'olmāyw bil*[e]*ḥûmô* ('and he shall shower his shafts on his body') for MT *w*[e]*yamṭēr 'ālêmô bil*[e]*ḥûmô*. This reading and rendering of *'olāmyw* and *l*[e]*ḥûmô* is based respectively on Ass. *ulmu* ('an arrow' or 'dart') and *l*[e]*ḥûmām* parallel to *dāmām* in Zeph. 1.17. The parallelism, however, with *ḥ*[a]*rôn 'appô* supports the reading after Dahood (1957: 314ff.).

w[e]*yamṭēr 'ālāyw mabbēl ḥummô* ('and he shall shower upon him the flame of his wrath'). On *mabbēl*, cf. Ugaritic *nbl* and see above on 18.15. The language recalls God's shower of fire and brimstone on Sodom and Gemorrah (Gen. 19.24; cf. Ps. 11.6).

24. *nēšeq* is usually collective, meaning 'arms'. *ḥālap̄* ('to pass from one point of place or time to another'; cf. 9.11) is found in the sense 'to pass through, pierce' in Judg. 5.26.

qešeṯ n[e]*ḥûšāh*—cf. Ps. 18.35 (EVV 34)—means not 'bronze bow' or 'bronze arrow' from the bow, but 'bronzed bow', that is, a composite bow of laminations of wood and strips of horn and animal sinew as described in the Ugaritic Legend of Aqht (Gordon *UT* 2 Aqht VI, 20-23), and probably bound at intervals, 'whipped' like a split cane fishing rod, with bronze wire.

25. For *šālap̄* ('to be unsheathed'), *šelaḥ* ('shaft, dart'; cf. Joel 2.8) should probably be read with LXX, *yēṣē'* for MT *wayyēṣē'*, and *miggēwōh* ('from his back') for MT *miggēwāh* with LXX, V and T. In v. 25b, *ûḇārāq mimmᵉrōrāṯô yahᵃlōḵ*, *mᵉrōrāh*, which means 'venom' or 'gall' in v. 14, means here the organ thought to secrete the gall, the liver. *bārāq*, lit. 'lightning', may denote 'gleaming blade'; cf. Deut. 32.41; Hab. 3.11. LXX and V read *yahᵃlōḵ* in the plur., taking it as the predicate of *'ēmîm* ('terrors') being *ṣᵉp̄ûnîm* ('stored up') in v. 26a (for MT *ṣᵉp̄ûnāyw*), *lᵉ* being the asseverative enclitic before the predicate in a nominal sentence as in Arab. The rearranged text in vv. 25-26 reads:

šelaḥ yēṣē' miggēwōh
ûḇārāq mimmᵉrōrāṯô yahᵃlōḵ
'ālāyw 'ēmîm liṣᵉp̄ûnîm
kol-ḥōšeḵ ṭāmûn

This arrangement obviates the metric irregularity in MT v. 26a.

26. For MT *nuppaḥ* either *nuppāḥāh* or *nᵉpuḥāh* must be read in agreement with the fem. *'ēš*. We have preferred the perfect Pual in a relative clause where the relative particle is omitted as often in poetry; cf. the relative in Arab. after an indefinite antecedent. Note the further emendation of MT *tᵉ'āḵᵉlēhû* to *tō'ḵᵉlēhû* after LXX, S, V and T. We take *yēra'* as the Niphal imperf. of *ra'a'*, an Aramaism (Heb. *rāṣaṣ*).

27. The general statement about heaven and earth revealing a person's sin and earth rising up as an enemy against that person is more natural after the particular calamities, such as flood (v. 28) and fire (v. 26). *miṯqômēm* is found as parallel to *'ōyēḇ* in 27.7. S apparently read *miṯnaqqᵉmāh* ('avenger'), which would reflect more specifically the earth calling for vengeance for blood shed (cf. the figure in 16.18f. and Gen. 4.10). If MT is read, however, the passage may reflect the convention expressed in treaties of calling to witness the various gods of the parties and heaven and earth and other natural features, as illustrated in Hittite vassal-treaties from the fourteenth and thirteenth centuries BCE; cf. Deut. 30.19.

28. For MT *yiḡel*, pointed as if from *gālāh* ('to be deported'), read *yāḡōl* from *gālal* ('to roll', transitive); cf. Gen. 29.3, 8 (to roll a stone from the well-mouth), which is suggested by LXX ('drag away') and T ('be removed'). *yᵉḇûl*, which regularly means 'produce' or 'increase', may be a variation of *yāḇāl*; cf. *yiḇᵉlê mayim*, 30.25; 44.4, cognate with Arab. *wablu*(*n*) ('heavy rain'); cf. also Akk. *bubbulu* ('flood'), cited by Dhorme (so Beer, Ehrlich, Stevenson, Fohrer and Pope). Only T has appreciated the meaning of *niggarôṯ*, rendering, though paraphrasing, 'flow'. The root *nāḡar* in the Niphal here is known from 2 Sam. 14.4, *mayim niggārîm* ('flowing water'), and Lam. 3.49, *'ênî niggārāh* ('my eye has flowed'), and in the Hiphil in Ps. 75.9, of the pouring out of the Lord's

fury, and in the Hophal in Mic. 1.4, of water poured down a declivity; cf. *ngr*, 'water-pourer' in a rite of imitative magic in the Ras Shamra Legend of Krt, Gordon *UH* 126, III, 4, 7, 8, 11, 12.

29. The superfluous *'āḏām* has crept into the text, being originally perhaps a scribal note, to indicate that the personal *rāšā'* should be read and not *reša'* (so Duhm). We expect a parallel to *rāšā'* in the position of MT *'imrô*, and the simplest solution is to read *mōrē'* ('rebel'). Dhorme retains *'imrô*, which he understands on the analogy of *mêmrāh* ('the word') for the person of God in the Targum, as 'himself' (so T at 7.8; 19.18; 27.3). While this is far from deciding the case, it deserves consideration. Stevenson read *'ªmārāyw*, translating 'his appointed share', sc. his 'ordered' share, associating the word with Arab. *'amara* ('to command'), but, while Heb. has occasionally this nuance, *'ªmārāyw* ('his appointed share') is extremely unlikely. In accordance with his theory, that Job was the Heb. translation of an Aram. original, Tur-Sinai makes the interesting suggestion that an original *mmrh*, to be pointed *mᵉmāreh* ('rebel'), was mistaken by a Heb. translator for Aram. *mēmrēh* ('his word'), which was then rendered into *'imrô*, as in MT. In the case of translation, however, it is unlikely that a comparatively rare word like *'ēmer* would have been preferred to the more usual *dāḇār*. We consider that the original was *mōreh* ('rebel').

Job 21

Job's Rejoinder to Zophar

This chapter falls into nine strophes (vv. 2-5, 6-9, 10-13, 14-16, 17-18, 19-21, 22-26, 27-30, 31-34), the last of which, we propose, has suffered disturbance reading originally vv. 31, 32a, 33a, 33b, 33c, 32b, 34; see Commentary *ad loc.*

The literary affinity is with the sapiential disputation. In the first strophe (vv. 2-5) Job states his claim to voice his complaint. The second strophe (vv. 6-9) poses the problem of the orthodox belief in the theodicy in face of the empiric fact of the prosperity of the wicked. The third (vv. 10-13), ending with the statement of the peaceful demise of the wicked, cites concrete and colourful instances of their prosperity. The fourth strophe (vv. 14-16) describes the defiant attitude of the wicked to God in a series of bold statements. The fifth strophe (vv. 17-18) questions the validity of certain aphorisms concerning the theodicy which are cited from proverb-collections such as the Book of Proverbs. The sixth strophe (vv. 19-22) cites from another of these 'God stores up iniquity for their sons' (v. 19a), to which the defenders of the conventional belief in the theodicy against the embarrassing facts cited by Job would resort, and states that this would not impress the sinner himself. The seventh strophe (vv. 22-25) opens with a statement concerning the transcendence of God and the inscrutability of his wisdom. This is a recurrent argument of the friends. Indeed it is the last resort of embarrassed orthodoxy, and it may be a citation on the part of Job, who cites as evidence of the aloofness and apparent moral indifference of God the common end of saint and sinner. In the eighth strophe (vv. 27-30) Job states that he knows the orthodox premises and arguments (v. 27), which so far he has been citing from the fourth strophe to the seventh, and which he continues to cite in v. 28. In confutation of the platitude of the inexorable end of the wicked Job cites the testimony of wayfarers, by which the writer may mean inscriptions or graffiti where they thank their pagan gods for safe guiding and preservation in their hazardous journeys. The ninth and final strophe (vv. 31, 32a, 33a, 33b, 33c, 32b, 34) in the conventional tradition of Hebrew wisdom, clinches the argument by the colourful description of the honourable burial of the wicked.

Job's reply in ch. 21 opens with an appeal for a hearing, animadverting on the consolation which his friends first intended (2.21), and in the statement 'you may mock' (3b) addresses himself to Zophar and the others who, with a wealth of striking images, had mocked the delusions and discomfiture of the wicked after their prosperity. Job proceeds; he re-echoes the problem of the sage in the Wisdom Psalm 73.2-12 (Job 21.6-16, 23-26), but whereas the sage in the psalm, like Zophar, advances to a positive solution of the moral problem in the not uncommon experience of the rascal's sudden downfall and the evanescence of his delusions (Ps. 73.18-20), Job uses the statement of the sage's dilemma as a contradiction to Zophar's statement of the theodicy (20.5ff.) and continues to elaborate his case by citing popular proverbs that support the Wisdom teaching on the theodicy (vv. 17, 18, 19a, 22, 28), which he immediately explodes (vv. 17, 18). To the proverb 'The trouble he incurs God keeps in store for his sons' (v. 19a), Job replies that this is not an adequate defence of the doctrine of the theodicy so long as the wicked live out their days in impunity (vv. 7-13). Job's final dismissal of Zophar's case is to remark upon the common mortality of both wicked and righteous (vv. 23-26), with the added mockery of the splendid funeral of the ungodly (vv. 32-33). So much, Job concludes, for the consolation of his friends which would convince him of the justice of God despite the personal agony of the innocent sufferer, whom they encourage to patient endurance and hope (5.8-26; 11.13-19) on the strength of the doctrine of the theodicy which they support by citation of the teaching of the sages and proverbs, while, blinking off unwelcome facts, they simply deceive themselves and lead their friends into delusion (v. 34). By his realistic citation of the prosperity of the wicked and his explosion of well-known proverbs in his trenchant criticism of the traditional doctrine of sin and retribution Job may well claim that his statement based on grim experience should induce shocked silence in his hearers (v. 5). It is Job's embarrassing realism, which exhibits nothing of the faith under duress that Wisdom recommended, that provokes the extreme condemnation of Eliphaz in ch. 22.

Chapter 21

1. Then Job answered and said:

2. 'Listen carefully to my words,
And let this be your consolation of me.
3. Bear with me and I will speak
Then after I have spoken you may mock.[1]
4. Is *my* complaint such that I should keep silence[2]
Why then should I not be impatient?
5. Turn to me and be appalled,[3]
And lay your hand on your mouth.

6. When I think of it I am confounded,
And shuddering seizes my flesh.
7. Why do the wicked live,
Prosper and grow mighty in power?

8. Their seed is established in their presence,
And their offspring stands fast[4] before their eyes.
9. Their houses are safe from fear;
No rod of God is upon them.

10. Their bull[5] engenders without fail,
Their cow[6] calves, and does not cast her calf.
11. They send forth their little ones like a flock
And their children skip about;
12. They sing[7] to the timbrel and the lyre,
And make merry to the sound of the pipe.
13. They finish[8] their days in prosperity,
And go down[9] to Sheol in peace.[10]

14. Though they say to God, "Away from us!
We care not to know your ways!
15. What is the Almighty that we should serve him?
And what is the good of praying to him?"
16. [11]See, their prosperity is not through their own power
The purpose of the wicked is far removed from God's.[12]

17. How often is "the lamp of the wicked put out"?
How often does "their calamity come upon them"?
(He destroys malefactors in his wrath.)
18. (How often) are they "as straw before the wind"?
Or "as chaff snatched away by a storm"?

19. "The trouble one incurs God keeps in store for his sons."
Let him (I say) requite the man himself, that he may feel it;
20. Let him himself[13] drink his fill[14] of his flagon,[15]
Let him drink of the wrath of the Almighty!
21. For what does he care for his house after him,
Seeing that his own tale of months is allotted to him?

22. Will anyone teach God knowledge,
Seeing that he governs the exalted ones?
23. One dies, having quite fulfilled himself,
Quite at ease[16] and in security,
24. His thighs[17] are full of fat,[18]
And the marrow of his bones fresh.
25. Another dies embittered,
With not a taste of good.
26. In the dust they lie down together,
And worms cover them both.

27. Indeed I know your thoughts
And the violence you do to reasoning to bear me down.
28. For you say, "Where is the house of the notable?",
"Where is the tent in which the wicked dwelt?"
29. Have you not asked those who travel the road?
Do you not accept their evidence

30. That the wicked is kept in the day of disaster,
Is guaranteed[19] in the day of wrath?

31. Who declares his way to his face,
Or requites him for what he has done?
32a. [20]But he is borne to the tombs,
33a. Having provided his own elegy, with flute and pipe,[21]
33b. And after him all men will walk in long procession,
33c. And all who go before him are innumerable,
32b. And watch is kept over his tomb.
34. How then will you offer me vain comfort?
And your answers amount to nothing but deceit?'

Textual Notes to Chapter 21

1. MT sing. *tal'îḡ*, if correct, would indicate that Job turns from the friends who are addressed before and after the verb to Zophar, the last speaker; but after LXX, Sym., S and V the plural should probably be read.
2. Conjecturing *lᵉ'eddōm* for MT *lᵉ'āḏām.*
3. Reading Niphal *hiššammû* for the Hiphil MT *hāšammû.*
4. Reading *'ōmᵉḏîm* for MT *'immām*, and taking it with 8b *metri causa.*
5. Reading *šôrām* with LXX and V for MT *šôrô* in agreement with the plurals in the context, *m* being corrupted to *w* in the Old Heb. script.
6. Reading *pārāṯām* with LXX and V for MT *pārāṯô*, assuming the same scribal error as in MT *šôrô.*
7. Reading *yāšîrû* for MT *yiśᵉ'û*. As the parallel *yiśmᵉḥû* indicates, *yāśîśû* ('rejoice') would also be apt, but the corruption of *yāšîrû* to *yiśᵉ'û* is graphically more natural.
8. Reading *yᵉḵallû* with the versions and Qere for MT *yᵉḇallû.*
9. Reading with Sym., S, T and V *yēḥāṯû*, from Aram. *nᵉhaṯ* for MT *yēḥāttû.*
10. Reading *ûḇirᵉḡôa'* for MT *ûḇᵉreḡa'.*
11. The couplet is possibly a later addendum.
12. Reading *mimmennû* ('from him', sc. God) with LXX for MT *mennî*, assuming haplography of *m* and the corruption of final *w* to *y* at the stage of development of the script represented by the Qumran MSS.
13. Reading *'ênô* for MT *'ênāyw* (conjecture). See Commentary *ad loc.*
14. Conjecturing *yir'eh* (variant of *yirweh*) for MT *yir'û*. See Commentary *ad loc.*
15. Conjecturing *kaddô* for MT *kîḏô*. See Commentary *ad loc.*
16. Reading with one Heb. MS *ša'ᵃnān* for MT *šal'ᵃnan*, a scribal error, introducing *l* in anticipation of the following *šālēw.*
17. Reading *'ᵃṭāmāyw* after S for MT *'ᵃṭînāyw* assuming corruption of *m* to *n* in the Old Heb. script.
18. Reading *ḥēleḇ* with LXX, S and V for MT *ḥālāḇ.*
19. Reading *yûḵal* for MT *yûḇālû*, final *w* being perhaps a dittograph of following *m* in the Old Heb. script, or to be attached as conjunction to the following *mî*. See Commentary *ad loc.*
20. On the arrangement of the text of vv. 32-33 see Commentary *ad loc.*
21. Conjecturing *miṯqōnēn-lô bᵉ'ûḡāḇ waḥᵃlîl* for MT *māṯᵉqû-lô rigᵉḇê nāḥal.* See Commentary *ad loc.*

Commentary on Chapter 21

2. In *tanḥûmōṯêḵem* the pronominal suffix is subjective.

3. MT *tal'îg̃* would refer specifically to Job's reply to Zophar's speech in ch. 20. But his citation of instances of the downfall of the ungodly from their prosperity and power is also the theme of the categorical statements of Eliphaz (15.20ff.) and Bildad (18.5ff.). With reference to their facile dismissal of him as a windbag full of foolish notions (8.2; 11.3; 15.2), the plur. of the verb must have been the original reading (so LXX, Sym., S and V), in agreement with the verbs in the rest of the strophe.

4. *'ānōḵî* is used proleptically with the pronominal suffix in *śîḥî* ('my complaint') for emphasis (GKC, §143a). MT *'āḏām*, meaning that Job's complaint is not to humans, implies that it is to God and is therefore beyond the scope of the limited wisdom of his friends, which is exposed in the sequel. But in the context of v. 4b MT *l^{e}'āḏām* is probably a Masoretic misunderstanding of *l^{e}'eddōm* from *dāmām* ('Am I to be silent in respect of my complaint?'), where *l^{e}* would be the asseverative enclitic, or it might rather introduce the imperfect after *śîḥî* ('is *my* complaint such that I may keep silence?'), which we prefer. In any case this reading best suits the context of v. 4b.

tiqṣar rûḥî (lit. 'my spirit is short') expresses impatience; cf. *wattiqṣar nep̄eš hā'ām*, of Israel in the wilderness (Num. 21.4) and of Samson nagged by Delilah (Judg. 16.6). The phrase describes destitution in the Ugaritic Legend of Keret (Gordon *UT* 127, 34, 47), where it denotes persons at the limit of their endurance.

5. In MT *hašammû* the Hiphil of *šāmam* might denote the entering into a certain condition (GKC, §53d). But we prefer to read the Niphal reflexive (so Hölscher, Fohrer). The laying of the hand on the mouth symbolized silence (cf. 29.9; 40.4; Judg. 18.19; Mic. 7.16; Prov. 30.32), or deference. In Egyptian legal convention it signified that a litigant desisted from his case; cf. Ball on 29.9. Dahood (1962: 64) suggests that the gesture may express astonishment, citing the seal with one marvelling at the flight of Etana on the eagle (*ANEP*, pl. 695).

7. *'āṯ^{e}qû* has an Arab. cognate meaning, as in Heb. 'to grow old', but a homonym means 'to thrive'. The verb is probably used here in the latter sense but with a *double entendre*, the former being suggested by *yiḥyû* in v. 7a and the latter in the complementary *gāḇ^{e}rû ḥayil* in v. 7b.

8. Our reading *'ōm^{e}ḏîm* for MT *'immām* ('with them') is supported by the parallel *nāḵôn* ('established') in v. 8a (so Ball, Dhorme).

9. In *battêhem šālôm*, *šālôm* may be used adverbially as in 5.24, *šālôm 'ohºleḵā*. LXX and V render it as a verb, and S as a participle, which might indicate a reading *šālᵉmû* (so Siegfried, Duhm) or perhaps *šᵉlēwîm* (from *šālēw*), 'secure' (so Houbigant).

10. In MT *šôrô 'ibbar wᵉlō yāḡ'îl*, T, Rashi and Qimchi understand *'ibbar* to refer to the passing of the semen properly without mishap ('soiling', *yāḡ'îl*, in the sense the verb has in Aram.). Alternatively, with this sense of *ibbar* in view, the word may be translated more broadly as 'engender, impregnate', as in Aram. and Late Heb. and *gā'al* may mean, as generally in Heb., 'to show aversion'. Perhaps *'āḇar* should be read and *gu'al* meaning respectively 'mount' and 'be rejected'. In the sense of 'giving birth' *pillēṭ* is used in the OT only here and at 39.3, where it is used in the Aram. Targum from Qumran. In 23.7b it means 'to bring off a case'. For the Piel of *šāḵōl* ('to be bereaved' or 'barren') meaning 'to abort', cf. Gen. 31.18; Exod. 23.26.

11. On *'āwîl* ('child') and its possible derivation, see on 19.18. The comparison of the skipping children to lambs, using the same verb *rāqaḏ*, recalls Ps. 29.6, where the quaking of mountains is compared to the skipping of calves. The same verb describes the motion of locusts in Joel 2.5, presumably when the young insects hop on the ground before taking flight.

12. On the reading *yāšîrû* ('they sing') for MT *yiśᵉ'û* ('they raise'), see Textual Note. If MT is correct, 'voice' must be understood, which is actually possible (cf. Isa. 42.11), but somewhat colourless in the context. For *kᵉṯōp̄*, LXX, V, S and T seem to have read *bᵉṯōp̄*, but MT may be retained in the sense of 'according to', that is 'to the accompaniment of'. The mention of the timbrel (*tōp̄*) and the stringed lyre (*kinnôr*) indicates that *'ûgāḇ* denotes a wind instrument, a kind of flute according to T.

13. On the reading *yᵉḵallû* (Qere), *yēḥāṯû* and *ûḇirᵉgôa'* ('and in peace'), see Textual Notes. The verb *rāga'* is found in the Niphal of a sword returned to its sheath (Jer. 47.6) and in the Hiphil meaning 'to give rest' (Jer. 31.2; 50.34; Isa. 51.4; Deut. 28.15; etc.); cf. Arab. *raja'a*, 'to return', sc. to rest after action. Again the Book of Job is emphatic. Death closes all accounts, without reward or punishment.

14. In *lō' ḥāp̄āṣnû*, the verb, which means usually in Heb. 'to take pleasure in', means rather 'to care about'; cf. Sym. *ḥāp̄îṭ* ('zealous') and Arab. *ḥafiẓa* meaning in the IIIrd Form 'to observe carefully'.

15. *mah-ššadday kî-na'aḇᵉḏennû* recalls the passage in the Ugaritic text Gordon *UT* Krt, 39: *m'at krt kybky* ('Who is Krt that he weeps?'), cited by Dahood (1963c: 60).

16-19. This passage in MT, asserting the traditional doctrine of the theodicy, has been taken, either wholly or partly, as an orthodox gloss. Siegfried so regarded vv. 16-18; cf. Budde, Hölscher, Stevenson. Stevenson suggested that v. 16 may continue the defiant words of the wicked in 15 and proposed the emendation *hᵃlō' ḇᵉyāḏēnû ṭûḇēnû.*

16. *rᵉšā'îm* supports the 3rd person pronominal suffixes in MT. Stevenson proposed to omit *rᵉšā'îm* and read *'ᵃṣāṯēnû*, giving the meshing of v. 16b 'our purpose is far beyond him'. *rᵉšā'îm* may in this case have been a dittograph of the same word in v. 17a, but we would retain MT as an orthodox gloss, introduced by *hēn* ('See'). Verses 17-19 then follow as Job's questioning of the conventional belief in retribution, if not of the sinner (vv. 17-18), then of his sons (v. 19).

17. Job's indignant question, 'How often is the lamp of the wicked put out?', is a citation of Bildad's assertion in 18.5, which in turn recalls the figurative statement in Prov. 13.9; 24.20. In v. 17c, *ḥᵃḇālîm yᵉḥallēq bᵉ'appô* (LXX 'pains shall seize them because of his anger') suggests a reading *yaḥᵃzîqûm* for MT *yᵉḥallēq*. LXX probably misunderstood *ḥᵃḇālîm*, which, Friedrich Delitzsch suggested, was a cognate of Akk. *ḫabâlu* ('to destroy') with cognates in Aram., Syr. and Late Hebrew (so Hölscher, Stevenson), giving the sense 'he metes out destruction in his wrath'. Alternatively Dhorme regards *ḥᵉḇālîm* as 'malefactors' as in Ass. and *yᵉḥallēq* as meaning 'he destroys' (cf. Ass. *ḫalêqu*), giving the translation 'He destroys malefactors in his wrath'. The odd colon with the change of subject indicates a gloss.

18. Both *teḇen* ('chopped straw') and *mōṣ* ('chaff') are winnowed from the heavier grain on the threshing-floor, when the peasant in Palestine took the advantage of the evening breeze. *teḇen*, lighter than grain but heavier than *môṣ*, falls at some distance from the grain and is used as fodder; *mōṣ* being carried clean away. The figure is a common one in the OT describing the total discomfiture of an enemy (Isa. 29.5) and specifically, as here, of the wicked; cf. Ps. 1.4; 35.5. In v. 18b *gᵉnāḇattû sûp̄āh* is a relative clause with the relative particle omitted as often in poetry. *gānaḇ*, regularly 'to steal', means also 'to snatch away surreptitiously'; cf. 27.20, also with *sûp̄āh* as subject, and also the eighth commandment (Exod. 20.15; Deut. 5.19; Gen. 40.15; Deut. 24.7), where the verb means 'to kidnap' (Alt 1953).

19. Rashi and Jewish exegesis take v. 19a as Job's citation of the argument of current orthodoxy. Verse 19b is Job's reply to the argument of orthodoxy which he has just cited. In v. 19a there may be a *double entendre*. Without *'ᵉlôah* as subject, *'ônô* might be understood as 'substance' which a man stores up for his sons; with *'ᵉlôah* as subject it means that God stores up the trouble a wicked man incurs for his sons.

20. In MT *kîḏô* may be a *hapax legomenon*, which none of the versions or commentators recognizes. The original may be *'êḏô*, as Rashi supposed, or possibly, and more likely, *pîḏô*, a corruption having occurred in the square script. *pîḏ* ('disaster') is well attested in Job (e.g. 12.5; 15.23). Dahood (1957: 316) has proposed that *kaddô* ('his flagon') should be read for MT *kîḏô*. *kāḏ* in Gen. 24.14ff. and Judg. 7.16 denotes a water-jar and in 1 Kgs 17.13f. a container for meal, but in the Ras Shamra texts it denotes a large liquid measure or container, like a flagon. The parallel colon indicates that drinking is involved, which suggests that MT *yir'û* might be a corruption, or perhaps a byform, of *yirweh* ('let him drink his fill'). The conception of 'drinking the wrath of the Almighty' reflects the image of 'the cup of the Lord's fury' from which the nations must drink in his judgment (e.g. Isa. 51.17, 22; Jer. 23.15). MT *'enāw*, read as singular *'ênô* (lit. 'his eye') in the context, means 'the man himself'; cf. Arab. *hūwa 'aynuhu* ('the very man'), which obviates any reference in the verb to 'seeing' rather than 'drinking one's fill'. Job's argument is that the doctrine of the theodicy would be more convincing if the malefactor *himself* were liable to retribution.

21. The verb *ḥāpēṣ* here means 'interest, concern' rather than 'take pleasure in', reflecting the nuance of the Syr. cognate and particularly Arab. *ḥafiẓa*, meaning in the IIIrd Form 'to observe carefully'. The reading *ḥuṣṣāṣû* is well attested in the ancient versions except S, being restored in Origen's recension of LXX from Theod. Aq. with his usual literalism renders 'was halved'. Theod. and V read 'was cut short', for which Dhorme cites the support of Ass. *ḫaṣâṣu* (so Hölscher). T and S on the other hand read 'have been assigned', which perhaps indicates a reading *ḥōraṣû*, proposed by Ewald; cf. 14.5a *'im ḥ^{a}rûṣîm yāmāyw*, 'since his days are determined'. The sequel to this passage might rather suggest *ḥuqqāqû* 'have been appointed, decreed', which would be closer to MT in the Old Heb. script. But there is no need to emend since the verb may be cognate with Arab. *ḫaṣṣa*, 'to assign exclusively to' (so G.R. Driver 1955: 83).

22. This verse is taken as a gloss by G.B. Gray, Stevenson, Tur-Sinai; cf. Pope, who observes that it is more appropriate to Job's friends. He treats it as the end of the citation of the orthodox opinions in vv. 19-21. Fohrer, who pays great attention to strophic arrangement, takes it as the conclusion of this strophe, where it serves as rebuke to those who would circumscribe God by a strict law of retribution. This is of course the final answer of the Book, but Job does not reach it so easily and certainly not at this stage. It may rather be another citation expressing Job's criticism of his friends' limitation of God's justice to the convention of human society, which he goes on further to criticize in the light of empirical experience in vv. 23-26, to which verses we regard it as the introduction. This couplet in its original context outside the Book of Job may reflect the sapiential tradition which aimed at adapting

humanity to the situation as it was under the divine economy, in which humans may impose their own conditions and moral judgment. *y^e^lammēḏ* is in the 3rd person of the indefinite subject.

rāmîm is formally ambiguous. It is taken in T to mean 'heavens' (cf. Ps. 78.69), but the verb *yišpōṭ* indicates a personal object 'exalted ones', the celestial ministers of God, who are subject to his correction (cf. 4.18; 15.15; Ps. 82.1). Here the significance of the verb is in its primary sense 'to rule, govern', as in the Ras Shamra texts, where the participle *ṯpṭ* is parallel to *mlk* ('king', Gordon *UT* 51, IV, 44; *'nt*, V, 40) and to *zbl* 'prince' (Gordon *UT* 68.15, 16f.; 22, 25). Judgment, which consisted in assessing a person's conduct in conformity with established government and bringing it into conformity, is a secondary meaning.

23. *'eṣem*, lit. 'bone', means here 'the essence'; cf. *'eṣem* with pronominal suffixes signifying 'oneself', etc.

MT *šal'ᵃnan* is a scribal error for *ša'ᵃnān* under the influence of MT *šālᵉwû* in v. 23b, which is a scribal error for the sing. *šālēw* through dittography at the stage of the development of the alphabet illustrated in the Qumran MSS.

24. For the *hapax legomenon* *'ᵃṭînāyw* Dillman conjectured the meaning 'pails', citing Heb. *ma'ᵃṭān* ('oil-vat') (so Budde, Duhm, G.B. Gray). The versions render the word as parts of the body parallel to his 'bones' in v. 24b, for example, 'entrails' (LXX, V), 'breasts' (T), 'sides' (S). The word is probably a corruption in the Old Heb. script of *'ᵃṭāmāyw* ('his thighs'), known in Aram. and Syr. (so Bochart, Klostermann, Ehrlich, Tur-Sinai, Hölscher, Stevenson, Fohrer, Pope, Terrien). Agreeable with this reading and the parallel in v. 24b, *ḥēleḇ* ('fat') must be read for MT *ḥālāḇ* ('milk'). *mōaḥ* is a *hapax legomenon* in the OT, but *mēḥîm* is found parallel and complementary to *šᵉmēnîm* ('fat') in Isa. 25.6, of fat burnt-offerings in Ps. 66.15 and 'fatlings' in Isa. 5.17. *ḥēleḇ* is supported by LXX, V and S. *šāqāh* is attested in the OT only in the Hiphil ('to give to drink') and here in the Pual. The specific sense of moisture, or freshness, to the marrow of the bones reveals *šiqqûy lᵉ 'aṣᵉmôṯêḵā* (Prov. 3.8).

25. *bᵉ* in *'āḵal baṭṭôḇāh* has a partitive significance; cf. *b* with the sense of Heb. *min* in Ugaritic.

26. It is not easy, if indeed possible, to determine whether *rimmāh* here means 'worms' (collective sing.) as the parallel *tôlēa'* in Isa. 14.11 and Job 25.6 indicates, or 'decay', 'corruption'; cf. Arab. *rimmatu(n)*.

27. *mᵉzimmôṯ* is ambiguous, meaning either 'reason, discrimination' (Prov. 1.4) or, more often, 'sinister thoughts' or 'devices' (Pss. 10.2; 21.12; 37.1; Jer. 11.15; Prov. 12.2; 24.8), in many cases, as here, parallel to *maḥšᵉḇôṯ*.

29. It has been assumed that *'ôbᵉrê ḏereḵ* were travelling merchants in caravans, and that their 'signs' (*'ōṯōṯ*) were not arguments or proofs, as Dillmann, Budde, Duhm, S.R. Driver and G.B. Gray assume, nor reminiscences of deliverance in straits (so Hölscher), but graffiti such as are known in Sinai and the Hejaz (so Dhorme), recalling deliverance from the hazards of the way. Fohrer, on the other hand, would see a reference to the reminiscences of any who had any breadth of experience in the world or even 'any passerby', as in Pss. 80.13 (EVV 12); 89.42 (EVV 41); Lam. 1.12; Prov. 9.13. The association with 'the day of wrath' (v. 30a) might seem inconsistent with the hazards of wayfarers, though they too were in peril of natural disasters (cf. 20.28).

30. For MT *yûḇālû*, for which in any case the masc. sing. should be read, the general sense and the parallel in v. 30a suggested the emendation to *yuṣṣal* ('rescued') to Dillman, Graetz, Beer and Hölscher, while Fohrer reads *yûḵal* nearer MT in the square script, citing the verb used of Jacob coming through his encounter at the Jabbok and 'prevailing' (Gen. 32.31). This verb, however, which we find acceptable, may rather be cognate with Arab. *wakala* ('to appoint a trustee', *wakīlu[n]*), of the Arab. invocation *'allāhu wakīlī*.

31. The implication of *'al-pānāyw* may be that no one can dare to convict the prosperous sinner 'in his despite'; cf. *'al-pānay* in the first commandment in the Decalogue (Exod. 20.3; Deut. 5.7); so E. König.

32-33. The sequence of the action indicates that the text of MT is disarranged. The meaning of the various cola apposite to the theme is in no doubt, with the notable exception of v. 33a, *māṯᵉqû-lô riḡᵉḇê naḥal* ('sweet to him are the clods of the valley'), which we find meaningless and incongruous with the context. After much consideration our first attempt to recover the sense of the colon was to take the verb in its literal sense, the only possible one in Heb., and read *māṯᵉqû-lô zûḇê nāḥal* ('sweet to him are the honey-flows', lit. 'secretions of bees'), involving no emendation but the assumption of the corruption of *z* to *r* (doubtful) and *w* to *g* in the square script. If this were the original it would refer to grave-offerings of food, actually attested in Israel in Samaria in the Israelite period (Sukenik 1945: 42-58). If this were accepted it would indicate a displacement from after the actual burial in v. 33bc. But we doubt this meaning of *naḥal*, which is certainly Arabic, but not attested in Heb., Aram. or Syr. We would therefore suggest that the colon should read:

> *miṯqōnēn-lô bᵉ'ûḡāḇ wᵉḥālîl*
>
> Having provided for his own elegy, with flute and pipe.

Admittedly, this is further from MT, with the graphic difficulty of the assumption of the omission of such a distinctive letter as ' in any Heb. script. In an obviously corrupt text, however, after initial corruption the text is liable to more extensive damage. We would therefore suggest that v. 32a notes the taking of the corpse for burial, v. 33a the elegy (*qînāh*) for the defunct, with musical accompaniment, v. 33bc describes the cortege, naturally preceded by the professional mourners, while v. 32b refers to the watch posted over the grave. We take *miṯqōnēn* as the Hithpael of *qōnēn* ('to declare an elegy', *qînāh*) in the reflexive sense, and would emphasize *lô'*; the rich sinner has had his own elegy prepared for him. The classical example of such an elegy, introduced by both noun (*qînāh*) and verb (*wayᵉqōnēn*), is David's elegy for Saul and Jonathan (2 Sam. 1.19ff.), which is both elegy and eulogy (vv. 22-24). We may be sure that, in the elegy which the flourishing sinner had had prepared for himself and duly edited, the element of panegyric was not lacking. The elegy in regular meter and sung or chanted may well have been accompanied by music, the plaintive wind-instruments, *'ûgāḇ*, used on a happier occasion in v. 12, and the pipe (*ḥālîl*), which could easily be handled in processions, as in the procession from Gihon after Solomon's anointing (1 Kgs 1.40).

32a. The plural *qᵉḇārôṯ* may denote a family burial-ground or it may be a *pluralis excellentiae* signifying conspicuous tombs of notables, as the rock-hewn tombs of the family of Tobiah (Neh. 6.1) at Iraq al-Amir east of the Jordan and northeast of Jericho in the Persian period, when the Book of Job was produced. The verb *yûḇal* is used with *qeḇer* in 10.19.

33bc. Buttenwieser cites a late Egyptian text which contrasts the cortege of a rich man with the burial of a poor man carried out on a reed mat 'with not a man on earth walking after him'.

33b. *māšak̲*, here intransitive, recalls the intransitive verb *māšak̲* in Judg. 4.6, describing the march of the men of Zebulun and Naphtali to Tabor in Barak's campaign, meaning, however, in that case, we believe, in small staggered parties (so 'long drawn-out') to evade suspicion.

32b. *gāḏîš* is found in the OT meaning a 'heap of sheaves' (5.26; Exod. 22.5; Judg. 15.5). Here, reading possibly *gaḏšô* from *geḏeš*, it signifies grave-mound, cf. Aram. *gᵉḏaš* ('to heap up') and more specifically Arab. *jadaṯu(n)* ('grave-mound'). In the verb *šāqaḏ* ('to be wakeful', hence 'watchful'), Dhorme suggests a reference to the statue or symbol of the presence of the defunct, like the obelisks above the rock-hewn tombs of Petra, watching over his tomb (so Merx, Budde and Duhm, who read the plural, and Hölscher, who reads *yiššāqēḏ*). But we prefer to retain *yišqōḏ*, the subject being indefinite, the implication being that there are grave-goods worth plundering. Hölscher and Fohrer think rather of the service to the dead, for example, drink-offerings and the like, citing *šᵉqēḏāh* in caring for (cattle) in Ben Sira 38.26, where, however, the parallel with 'attention' indicates that the meaning is rather 'alertness' in providing the fodder.

34. *hebel* means 'breath', 'vapour', as, for example, in Isa. 57.13 and Eccl. 1.14; 2.15; etc. where it is parallel to *rûaḥ* in the sense of 'wind'. Figuratively it means that which is insubstantial and elusive as, for example, in Jer. 10.15; 51.18, where it is parallel to *šeqer* ('deceit'). In the present passage it is used adverbially. *ma'al* usually denotes 'treachery' or 'deceit'. It refers to the friends' deluding *themselves* by blinking off facts and setting Job in a false light.

Job 22

Eliphaz's Statement

On our rejection of a third round of debate involving Job's intensified appeals for a legal confrontation with God (ch. 23; 26.1-4; 27.1-6, 11-12) in response to Eliphaz's indictment (22.6-9) and culminating in Job's *apologia pro vita sua* (ch. 29), the statement of his ruin (ch. 30) and his great oath of purgation (ch. 31), see above, pp. 59-61. This direct personal matter in the forensic idiom we distinguish on grounds of matter and form from secondary intrusions of sapiential poems (ch. 24; 26.5-14; 27.7-10, 11-15; ch. 28). Chapter 25, attributed, possibly secondarily, to Bildad, falls into the hymnal category.

Eliphaz's statement falls into two parts: vv. 3-20, which asserts the orthodox belief in the theodicy, and vv. 21-30, where Job is exhorted to humility and repentance, and consequent blessing is promised. The address is divided into six strophes (vv. 2-5, 6-9, 10-14, 15-20, 21-26, 27-30). The literary affinity of the first strophe (vv. 2-5), where Eliphaz takes up the debate by citing Job's statement (21.15) that a person's goodness or wickedness can neither profit nor harm God, is with a sapiential controversy. The statement that virtue profits the good person (v. 2b) is characteristic of the wisdom of Proverbs, and from the standpoint that Job's suffering implies sin (v. 4) the second strophe (vv. 6-9) arraigns the sinner. Here Job seems to be accused of the most blatant sins, which could not possibly have escaped notice, and were certainly not suspected by Eliphaz in his first speech, where it is recalled that Job had been a pillar of society (4.3ff.). That such an indictment was made, and especially by the most sympathetic and mature of Job's friends, is surely designed to afford Job the opportunity to answer the charges, anticipating his *apologia* (ch. 29) and his oath of purgation (ch. 31). The alleged sins are significantly against the poor and weak, of which a man of Job's status and prosperity may have been guilty, albeit by omission. Formally, the cumulative indictment of sin followed by the announcement of doom in vv. 10-11 introduced by *'al-kēn* ('therefore') is familiar in Hebrew tradition in prophetic address. Actually the passage on sin and retribution (vv. 5-11) and that on obedience to God and consequent prosperity (vv. 21-26), which is introduced by an imperative (with conditional significance), are expanded in conditional sentences. In the third strophe (vv. 10-14), v. 12, on God's exaltation is probably a gloss on v. 13 since it breaks the argument between vv. 11 and 14 and is pointless to the argument of Eliphaz here and is not included in the citation of Job's argument in vv. 13-14. Eliphaz follows the prophetic line of argument from sin in vv. 6-9 to retribution in vv. 10-11, facts of experience which refute Job's argument in vv. 13-14. This theme and the citation of the view which is to be refuted is familiar in sapiential dialectic and is paralleled in wisdom psalms (e.g. 73.11; 94.7). In the fourth strophe (vv. 15-20), in the form of a question, a warning is given, based on the downfall of the ungodly, with an assurance to the righteous. In the sapiential tradition that is familiar in the exhortation of a sage to his disciples.

In the second part of Eliphaz's address the bulk of the first strophe, the fifth in the chapter (vv. 21-26), is occupied with exhortation to return and reach agreement with God, and the second, the sixth in the chapter (vv. 27-30), with the assurance of consequent blessings. This had its literary counterpart in pre-exilic prophecy (e.g. Amos 5.14-15; Isa. 1.18-20; Hos. 6.1-3), and was also at home in the wisdom tradition in the exhortation of the sages. The passage ends with two couplets, vv. 29 and 30, assuring the innocent one who is humbly dependent on God and thereby asserting faith in the theodicy.

The text is almost certainly extended by later glosses, for example in v. 12 (see above) and vv. 17-18, which is probably prompted by 21.14-16. Verses 24-25, which exhort people to count their gold as pebbles of the wadis and accept the Almighty as their treasure, is a strange figure which interrupts the sapiential argument in the fifth strophe and is probably a later gloss; its removal reduces the strophe to more regular proportions and strengthens the argument.

Eliphaz's opening question makes God independent of any advantage from humans (v. 21), whose good conduct as the wisdom tradition insists, benefits himself (v. 2b), just, as we may infer, the sin of the wicked bears the seeds of their own destruction (15.20ff.; 18.6-14). Or, we may say, a good person has the responsibility, if not also the potential, to fulfil oneself. Eliphaz emphasizes God's independence of the best a human can offer by a figure from commerce. The blameless conduct of humans is not 'gratefully received' as a profit to God (v. 3). Asking the rhetorical question, which is tantamount to a strong denial, 'Would he reprove you for your piety towards him?', Eliphaz concludes, as in his opening address (4.8f.; 5.6), that suffering betokens sin, with which he now charges Job directly and specifically (v. 5). His particular indictment (vv. 6-9) is significantly limited to treatment of the underprivileged and contains mainly sins of omission. They relate therefore to Job's status and wealth, which have certain social obligations, *noblesse oblige*, as Job recognizes in his *apologia* (v. 29) in the prelude to his great oath of purgation. In Eliphaz's indictment there is the recognition that such prestige and affluence as Job had enjoyed has its peculiar dangers. The subject, himself free from poverty and not understanding its stresses, may be less than sympathetic to those in need (vv. 7, 9a). In certain cases his sins seem to be sins of commission rather than sins of omission, such as 'stripping the poor of clothing'

(v. 6a) and 'breaking the arms of orphans' (v. 9b). But this may simply mean neglecting to give an orphan a chance to maintain himself, while 'stripping the poor of clothing' and 'taking pledges (cf. Amos 2.8) where there was no actual need' (v. 6b), both probably refer to taking pledges, which was a legal right indeed but might well have been waived by Job. The imputation of God's transcendence and consequent aloofness to human conduct (vv. 13f.) is a more serious charge, where the argument of Job in 9.4-10 is cited (vv. 13f.). This, Eliphaz concludes, would explain Job's calamity, which he figuratively describes as 'snares', 'sudden terrors', 'darkening of his light' and 'flood' (vv. 10-11), citing the language and aphorisms that colour the depiction of the fate of the wicked in the addresses of Bildad and Zophar (18.5, 6, 8-10; 19.28), with particular reference to Job's demolition of their case (ch. 21).

Eliphaz's indictment concludes with the sapiential warning of the danger of pursuing the way of the wicked, sudden death and overwhelming flood (15f.) again reflecting the admonitions of Job's friends. This consideration of the social order which faith and wisdom upheld is confirmed, as in the Plaint of the Sufferer and Wisdom Psalms (e.g. Ps. 58.11ff. [EVV 10f.]), by the recognition of retribution by the righteous, not without manifest satisfaction and indeed 'unholy glee' (vv. 19-20).

Eliphaz's final word to Job (vv. 21-26) ends, as his first address (5.8-26), with encouragement to reconciliation with God and humble obedience (v. 25; cf. 5.8 and hope of rehabilitation (v. 26; cf. 5.16a, 18-26).

Chapter 22

1. Then answered Eliphaz the Temanite:

2. 'Can a man bring profit to God?
Nay, but the wise man simply profits himself.
3. If you are right does the Almighty "receive it with pleasure"?
Or is there any gain to him in your blameless conduct?
4. Is it for your piety towards him that he reproves you?
Could he come into court with you?
5. Is not your wickedness great,
And your iniquities endless?

6. For you have exacted pledges of your brothers where there was no need,
And stripped the naked of their clothing.
7. You have not given a drink of water to the weary,
And from the weary you have withheld bread.
8. The land was for the man of strong arm,
And the favoured man was settled in it.
9. You have sent widows away empty-handed,
And have broken[1] the arm of orphans.

10. Therefore snares are round about you,
And sudden terror confounds you.

11. Your light[2] is darkened so that you cannot see,
And a flood of waters covers you.
12. [3]Is not God the height of the heavens themselves?
See the highest stars, how exalted they are!
13. Yet you say, "What does God know?
Can He exercise judgment through the deep darkness?
14. The clouds hide Him so that he does not see,
And the vault of heaven is His beat."

15. Will you keep to the way of the wicked,[4]
Which men of sin have trodden,
16. Who were snatched away untimely,
Their foundations dissolved in a flood?
17. [5]They said to God, "Away from us!
Yea, what can the Almighty do to us?"[6]
18. Yet it was he who had filled their houses with good things,
But the purpose of the wicked is remote from Him.[7]
19. The righteous see it and are glad,
And the innocent laughs at them.
20. Is not their substance[8] wiped out,
And their abundance consumed by fire?

21. Be accommodating with Him and in accord,
Thereby is the way to happiness.
22. Accept direction from His mouth,
And lay up His words in your heart.
23. If you humbly[9] turn to the Almighty,
If you remove iniquity from your tent,
24. [10]And rate[11] your fine gold as[12] dust,
And gold of Ophir as the pebbles of the wadis,
25. And the Almighty becomes your gold ingots,
And your silver in heaps,
26. Then you will find your confidence in the Almighty,
And shall lift up your face to God.

27. You will make petition to him and he will hear you,
And you shall have reason to pay your vows.
28. And you will decide on a matter and it will be established for you,
And light will shine on your ways,
29. For he humbles[13] him[14] whose look is haughty,[14]
But the man whose eyes are lowly he delivers.
30. He even[15] scours an unclean man,
And he will be delivered with his hands clean.'[16]

Textual Notes Chapter 22

1. Reading *t*^{e}*ḏakkē'* with LXX, V, S, T for MT *y*^{e}*ḏukke'*, which lacks agreement.
2. Reading *'ôr*^{e}*ḵā ḥāšaḵ* with LXX for MT *'ô-ḥōšeḵ*.
3. The whole verse is probably a gloss. See Introduction to ch. 22.
4. Reading *'*^{a}*wîlîm*, possibly written originally in *scriptio defectiva*, for MT *'ôlām*.
5. Verses 17-18 are probably a gloss. See Introduction to ch. 22.

6. Reading *lānû* with LXX and S for MT *lāmô*, *n* being corrupted to *m* in the Old Heb. script.
7. Reading *mimmennû* for MT *mennî*. See on Textual Note 12 to ch. 21.
8. Reading *yᵉqûmām* with Theod. for MT *qîmānû*, assuming corruption of final *m* for *n* in the Old Heb. script, and the metathesis of *y* and *q*. See Commentary *ad loc.*
9. Reading *tēʿāneh* with LXX for MT *tibbāneh*.
10. Verses 24-25 are probably. See introduction to ch. 22.
11. Reading *wᵉšattā* or *tāšîṯ* for MT *šîṯ*, which, however, may possibly be retained as a perfect passive.
12. Reading *ʿim* (of comparison) for MT *ʿal*.
13. Reading *hišpîl* for MT *hišpîlû*, taking final *w* as a dittograph.
14. Reading *hāʾōmēr gaʾᵃwāh*. See Commentary *ad loc.*
15. Reading *gam yᵉmallēṭ metri causa*, *gam* having been omitted by haplography before *ym* of *yᵉmallēṭ* in the script at the stage of the Qumran MSS.
16. Reading *kappāyw* with S and V for MT *kappêḵā*, *w* being corrupted to *k* in the old Heb. script.

Commentary on Chapter 22

2. *sāḵan* ('to care for, do a service to'; cf. 15.3) is attested as a synonym of *šēreṯ* ('to serve') in 1 Kgs 1.2, 4. *kî* has the adversative sense 'Nay but'. *ʿalêmô* signifies 'on his own account'.

3. *ḥāp̄ēṣ* must be understood as parallel to *beṣaʿ* ('profit', lit. something broken off; cf. Gen. 27.26; Ps. 30.10; Mic. 3.14), and if, as seems likely, a figure from commerce is indicated (so Fohrer), *ḥēp̄eṣ* would correspond to a merchant's 'Gratefully received!' or 'My pleasure!'.

4f. On the significance of vv. 1-5, see above, p. 301.

6. 'Brothers' must be understood to refer to kinsmen, who merited more responsible patronage. The sins are introduced by *kî* ('because') in v. 6 and retribution by *ʿal-kēn* in v. 10 reflecting prophetic declaration. Dereliction of social duty is aggravated by the neglect of the obligation that when someone's outer garment is taken as pledge (cf. Amos 2.8) it must be retained before nightfall (Exod. 22.25-28; Deut. 24.10ff.). Consideration for the poor (v. 6) and hungry (v. 7), the widow and orphan (v. 9), while a charge on the community, is peculiarly the responsibility of a man of status and substance. Hence the condemnation of the abuse of power to grab land (v. 8).

8. This colon, not directly addressed to Job, may be an intrusion, perhaps the citation of a declaration, possibly prophetic, on the monopoly of land, which ought to have been a communal asset, by force (*zᵉrôaʿ*, lit. 'arm') or by political favour; cf. the animadversion of the prophets on such acquisition and monopoly of land (Isa. 5.8).

n^e^śû' pānîm (lit. 'he who has been lifted up in respect of face') refers originally to prostration before a superior, who then extended his sceptre and lifted the face of the one he favoured from the ground.

9. The care of the widow and orphan is frequently recommended in the OT (Deut. 10.18; 14.29; 16.11, 14; 24.19; 26.12; Isa. 1.17) and the neglect of this duty duly condemned (Exod. 22.22; Deut. 27.19; Jer. 7.6; Zech. 7.10). This is cited as the normal duty of a king in the Canaanite legends of Aqht and Krt (Gordon *UT* 127, 46-50):

ltdn dn 'almnt	Thou dost not judge the case of the widow,
lttpṭ ṭpṭ qṣr npš	Nor uphold the suit of the distressed;
ltdy tšm 'l dl	Thou dost not drive away the oppressor of the poor;
lpnk ltšlḥm ytm	Before thee thou dost not feed the fatherless;
b'd kslk 'almnt	The widow is behind thy back.

'Breaking the orphan's arm' may have been hindrance to his efforts to support himself and his mother.

10. As in Isa. 24.18, *paḥ* or *paḥaṯ* ('trap') is used in juxtaposition with *paḥaḏ*, which means 'pack (of hunting dogs)' as well as 'terror'. Here the emphasis is on 'terror', though there may be *double entendre*, the *net* being set for the quarry, which is *startled* by the pack as in Isa. 24.18. See further on 15.21 and 18.8-10.

11. On the reading *'ôr^e^ḵā ḥāšaḵ* for MT *'ô-ḥōšeḵ*, see Textual Note.

šip̄'āh ('flood') is found again at 38.34. The root *šapa'*, with an Aram. and Syr. cognate meaning 'to overflow, abound', is attested as *šepa'* in Deut. 33.19 and *šip'āh*, meaning a crowd of men (2 Kgs 9.17), horses (Ezek. 26.10), camels (Isa. 60.6) and, as here, waters.

12. The fact of God's exaltation, which is cited in Isa. 40.26-27 to encourage faith in his providential care, may suggest to the sinner that he is transcendent and beyond all care for human order. For *gōḇah*, T reads *b^e^ḡōḇah* and S reads *hiḡbîah* ('he has made high'). The abstract 'the height of the heavens' may be intentional, in apposition to 'God', but the verse is probably a gloss on v. 13.

14. 'The circle of the heavens' (*ḥûḡ šāmayim*) is the horizon where land and sea according to the ancient conception met in the surrounding sky, which was depicted as a vault; cf. 26.10, 'he has described a circle upon the face of the waters', and Prov. 8.27 and Isa. 40.22, 'the circle of the earth'.

15. In defending MT *'ōraḥ 'ôlām* ('the old way') against the proposed emendation *'ōraḥ '^a^wîlîm* (Ball, Tur-Sinai), which has no support in the ancient versions, Dhorme thought of the ancient sinners 'the sons of God of old' (*'^a^šer*

mē'ôlām), who mated with the daughters of men (Gen. 6.4) and the generation of the flood. Dahood (1962: 65ff.) makes the more feasible suggestion that the phrase, reading the abstract *'ôlām*, means 'dark path' (cf. 42.3 *ma'ᵃlîm 'ēṣāh*, 'obscuring the purpose'), but the parallelism supports the reading *'ᵃwîlîm* in *scriptio defectiva.*

16. *qummᵉṭû* ('were snatched away') is Aram. rather than Heb., being attested only here and 16.8. Eliphaz again cites Bildad's description of the fate of the wicked.

After the passive *yûṣaq* ('is poured over'), *yᵉṣôdām* may be taken as the accusative of the objective of the action (GKC, §121d).

17-18. This passage, which interrupts the sequence of thought in vv. 15-16, 19-20, is generally regarded as secondary, possibly inspired by v. 12, which also is possibly an intrusion; both passages are influenced by Job's citation of the statement of the wicked who flourish (21.14f.).

17. On the reading *lānû* with LXX and S for MT *lāmô*, see Textual Note.

18. Reading *mimmennû* with LXX for MT *mennî.*

20. This verse was not in the original LXX, and was restored by Origen from Theod. With a slight adjustment, *qāmênû* and *yiṯrām* might be read in the sense of 'our enemies' and 'their remnant' (so Olshausen, Siegfried, Ball, Duhm, Stevenson). The versions indicate the sing. of a noun in the former with the 3rd plur. masc. pronominal suffix in the latter. Theod.'s rendering, 'their substance' (*yᵉqûmām*; cf. Gen. 7.4, 23; Deut. 11.6—so Merx, Graetz, G.B. Gray, Dhorme, Hölscher, Weiser, Pope, Fohrer), suggests the meaning 'abundance' for *yiṯrām*, which may also mean 'their remainder' (so Fohrer, Rowley). If this were so, the passage would recall the destruction of the sinner's family without survivor in 20.26.

21. *hasken-nā' 'immô* is a rare expression. The Qal of the verb, meaning 'to benefit', is attested in v. 2 and 15.3, and the Hiphil, meaning 'to be accustomed', in Num. 22.30 (JE). This may support V 'to agree with', which is also implied in S, *'ešṭᵉwî* ('correspond to'). *šᵉlām* has its primary meaning 'to be whole, at one', that is 'in accord'. MT *tᵉḇô'āṯᵉḵā* is evidently a verbal noun, 'your coming', with preformative *t* analogous to verbal nouns such as *tᵉmûrāh*, *tᵉḇûnāh*, etc. The ancient versions, however, and some Heb. MSS, attest the reading *teḇû'āṯᵉḵā* ('your produce') (so Dhorme), but 'produce' in v. 21b seems out of context. Dillmann, Budde, Hölscher, Stevenson and most modern commentators read MT ('you shall reach').

22. *qaḥ* ('receive') from *lāqah*, is used of receiving the traditional wisdom of the sages, *leqaḥ*, a regular technical term in Proverbs and wisdom psalms.

tôrāh is used here in the general sense of 'revealed direction' and not in its specific sense of 'law', still less of the Pentateuchal Law.

23. MT *tibbāneh*, 'you will be rehabilitated', lit. 'built up (again)', would suggest the apodosis of a conditional sentence, after the protasis *'im-tašûḇ 'ad-šadday*. The apodosis, however, is introduced after an accumulation of protasis by *kî-'az* in v. 26. Thus *tibbāneh*, or more probably its original, is an imperfect of attendant circumstances like *tarḥîq* in v. 22b. For MT *tibbāneh* LXX read 'humble yourself', which suggests either *tikkāna'* (so Merx, Graetz, Siegfried) or more probably *tē'āneh* (so Ewald, Dillmann, Beer, Duhm, Oort, Ehrlich, Dhorme, Fohrer, Terrien). Hölscher notes both, but, while citing *tē'āneh'* first in his note, evidently preferred *tikkāna'* in his translation 'beugest dich' (so too Weiser).

24-25. This passage is taken as secondary, interrupting the sequence of thought in 23.26 (so Fohrer). The abrupt introduction of the striking metaphor of the Almighty as gold is strange, as is also the imperative *šîṯ* in the protasis of a conditional sentence, though that usage is attested in Heb. (GKC, §11o) and in Arab. Alternatively *w^{e}šattā* may be read. As *šîṯ*... is an abrupt usage of the imperative in the protasis after *'im-tāšûḇ* in vv. 23a, it probably indicates the intrusion of an aphorism from Wisdom.

24. *beṣer* (here pausal form *bāṣer*), parallel to *'ôp̄îr*, sc. 'gold of Ophir', is parallel in its plural form to *kesep̄* ('silver') in v. 25; cf. Ps. 68.31. It is a cognate of Arab. *baṣara* ('to examine', sc. after testing). Dhorme aptly cites *miḇṣār* in connection with *bāḥôn* ('testing') in Jer. 6.27. On Ophir, the source of the gold, see on 28.16. In v. 25b it is proposed to emend MT *ûḇ^{e}ṣûr* to *'uḵ^{e}ṣûr*, as in certain Heb. MSS. This, however, is to miss a deliberate word-play between *b^{e}ṣûr* ('in the category of pebbles', *b^{e}* being *beth essentiae*) and *beṣer* ('fine gold'). There is a similar word-play between *'āp̄ār* ('dust') and *'ôp̄îr* ('gold of Ophir'). Besides the word-play, the chiastic parallelism may be noted, giving the passage all the appearance of an intrusive aphorism.

25. Dhorme justly emphasizes the plural in *b^{e}ṣārêḵā* and *kesep̄ tô'āp̄ôṯ* in the sense of 'ingots of gold' and 'silver in heaps'. *tô'āp̄ôṯ* means literally 'heights' or 'protuberances' (Num. 23.22; 24.8). Bochart proposed that the word, from the root *yā'ap̄*, is a metathetic cognate of Arab. *yafi'a* ('to be high').

26. *kî-'āz* at length introduces the apodosis. *'āz* is used exactly as Arab. *'idan* ('in that case'). *tiṯ'annāḡ* here and in the similar colon in 27.10 is rendered by LXX *secheis parrēsian* ('you will have confidence'); cf. the usual meaning in Heb., 'to have pleasure'. In 27.10, S renders *t^{e}kal* ('trusted'). G.R. Driver (1955: 84) therefore, taking the verb as a metathetic cognate of Arab. *'ajana* ('to tie on a rope, support'), translated 'depend'.

28. *gāzar* means 'to decree', here 'to decide', and is probably an Aramaism. *'ômer* here has the nuance of Arab. *'amru*(*n*) ('a matter'). The verb *qûm* (lit. 'to stand'), means 'to be established' as the Hiphil means commonly 'to establish'.

29. MT is corrupt. The subject of the main verbs in v. 29a, b must be God, and so the sing. must be read for the plural. *gēwāh* ('back') is meaningless and has no parallel. *šaḥ 'ênayim* ('the man whose eyes are lowly', lit. 'the downcast of eyes') must have a parallel in the original of *wattō'mer gēwāh*. The solution is suggested by the verb *'amâru* in the Canaanite dialect of the local glosses in the Amarna tablets and in the Ras Shamra texts. In the latter it is found with the infixed *t* and the reflexive form of the causative meaning 'to see' (Gordon *UT* 137.32; 'nt I, 22). Instances in the OT are noted by Dahood in Pss. 11.1; 29.9; 71.10; 77.9; 94.4; 105.29 (1963b: 295ff.). So, in the present passage, for MT *hišpîlû wattō'mer gēwāh* we propose *hišpîl hā'ōmēr gē'eh* ('he humbles him whose look is haughty', lit. 'who looks haughtily'), which gives the desired parallel to 'but the man whose eyes are lowly he delivers' (v. 29b). Hebrew commonly localizes different emotions in particular organs, for instance, pride in the eyes (Isa. 2.11; 5.15; 10.12; Pss. 18.28 [EVV 27]; 101.5; 131.1; Prov. 6.17; 30.7).

In Classical Hebrew, *'î* is negative (e.g. *'ikābôd*, 'inglorious'). Theod., S and V either ignore MT *'î* or read *'îš*. MT *'î* may mean 'any' (cf. Prov. 31.4 and Arab. *'ayyu*), hence *'î nāqî* may mean 'any innocent man'. But in the context we prefer to read *'î* as a negative. The recurrence of the verb *mālaṭ* in the couplet is suspicious and surely indicates a word-play. We accordingly take the first *yemallēṭ* as cognate with Arab. *malaṭa* ('to scour'), which suggests that *'î nāqî* means 'unclean'. The assertion that God will scour the unclean man who turns humbly to him directly contradicts Job's assertion that even if he has been at pains to cleanse himself, God will resume him into filth (9.30-31). In agreement with the 3rd sing. masc. *nimlaṭ*, MT *kappêkā* may be emended to *kappāyw*, which involves only the reading *w* for *k*, which are easily confused in the Old Hebraic script.

Job 23

Job's Response to Eliphaz: His Ardent Desire for Confrontation with God

Chapter 23 consists of three strophes: vv. 2-7, 8-12, 13-17. The first (vv. 2-7) is in the forensic form of an appeal for a confrontation with one's opponent in open court; the second (vv. 8-12) elaborates the theme of the inaccessibility of God for such a confrontation and is otherwise cast in the legal form of an assertion of innocence; the last strophe (vv. 13-17) is in the form of a hymn praising God's sovereignty, omnipotence and awful majesty, but is adapted to the theme of the second strophe, the inaccessibility of God, whose will is arbitrary and whose majesty simply confounds humanity.

Here the drama moves near to its climax. Job is confident that, if confronted by God, he would be able to put his case with such confidence in his ability (vv. 4f.) and assurance of his innocence (v. 7) that God would have to take it seriously (v. 6b) and by the divine response Job might know the charge to answer (v. 5b). He is all too conscious of the transcendence of God (vv. 8-9), but he has also faith that God who is transcendent is also omniscient and indeed knows the intimate way of life of his obedient servant (v. 10), which Job specifies in the wisdom tradition expressed in Ps. 119.3, 13, 15, 19, 72, 88, 101, as the faithful keeping of God's commandments and 'storing up the words of his mouth' (v. 8). But despite his confidence in the justice of his case, which he questions if divine justice could gainsay, a confrontation with God is still a wish rather than a certainty. Job's statement significantly begins with his resentment at the heavy hand of God on the innocent (v. 2) and the consciousness of the inaccessibility of God (v. 3), which recurs at vv. 6-9, expresses his appalment at God's awful determinism (vv. 13-16), but ends with the subject's determination not to be silenced before the dark mystery which veils God (v. 17).

Chapter 23

1. Then Job answered and said:

2. 'Still is my complaint resentful;[1]
His hand[2] is heavy despite my groaning.
3. Oh that I knew where I might find Him,
That I might come to His seat!

4. I should state my case[3] before Him,
And fill my mouth with arguments.
5. I should know with what words He would answer me,
And understand what He should say to me.
6. Would His great power be (sufficient) in his contention with me?
No! He himself would have to give heed to me.
7. In that case He would have an upright man to reason with,
And I should bring off my case[4] completely.

8. If I go east, He is not there,
And west, I cannot perceive Him.
9. When I turn[5] north, I do not see him,[6]
I turn[7] south, but do not behold Him.[8]
10. But he knows my intimate way,
Were he to test me I should come forth as gold.
11. My foot has held fast to his steps,[9]
I have kept to course without swerving;
12. I have not departed[10] from the commandments[11] of His lips,
I have stored up the words of His mouth in my bosom.[12]

13. But if He chooses[13] who can turn Him?
What He himself desires that He does,
14. For He will complete what He has decreed,[14]
And many such things are in His mind.
15. Therefore His presence confounds me,
When I consider Him I am terrified of Him.
16. Yea, God has unmanned me,
And the Almighty has confounded me.
17. Yet I am not silenced by His obscurity,[15]
And by his presence[16] covered by thick darkness.

Textual Notes to Chapter 23

1. Reading *mār* with S, T and V for MT *m*^{e}*rî* (‘rebellion’).
2. Reading *yāḏô* with LXX and S for MT *yāḏî*.
3. Reading *mišpāṭî* with LXX for MT *mišpāṭ*, *y* being omitted by haplography before following *w* in the script at the stage of its development in the Qumran MSS.
4. Reading *mišpāṭî* with LXX, S, V and many Heb. MSS for MT *miššôp̄*^{e}*ṭî*.
5. Reading *ba‘*^{a}*śōṯî* for MT *ba‘*^{a}*śōṯô*, assuming corruption to *y* to *w* in the square script as at Qumran.
6. Reading *’eḥ*^{e}*zēhû* for MT *’āḥaz*.
7. Reading *’e‘*^{e}*ṭōp̄* for MT *ya‘*^{a}*ṭōp̄*. See Commentary *ad loc.*
8. Reading *’er’ēhû* for MT *’er’eh* assuming *scriptio defectiva.*
9. Reading *ba’*^{a}*šurāyw* with LXX and S for MT *ba’*^{a}*šurô.*
10. Reading *lō’ ’āmîš* with LXX, V and many Heb. MSS for MT *w*^{e}*lō’ ’āmîš.*
11. Reading *mimmiṣwōṯ* with LXX and V for MT *miṣwaṯ.*
12. Reading *b*^{e}*ḥêqî* with LXX and V for MT *mēḥuqqî.*
13. Reading *bāḥar* for MT *b*^{e}*’eḥāḏ.*
14. Reading *ḥuqqô* with S and V for MT *ḥuqqî*, *w* being corrupted to *y* in the script as in the Qumran MSS.
15. Reading *ḥoškô* for MT *ḥōšeḵ*, assuming omission of *w* after *k* in the Old Heb. script.

16. Reading *ûmippānāyw* for MT *ûmippānay*, assuming omission of *w* by haplography after *y* in the script represented by the Qumran MSS.

Commentary on Chapter 23

2. See Textual Note. In support of the reading *śîḥî* cf. 7.11, *'āśîḥāh bᵉmar napšî*, and 10.1, *śîḥî 'ᵃdabbᵉrāh bᵉmar napšî*. MT *mᵉrî*, if correct, would mean 'rebellion' in the sense of 'resentment', which may also be conveyed by *mar*.

3. As indicated by *mî-yittēn*, *yāḏa'tî* is an optative perfect, regular in Arab. *tᵉkûnāh* (lit. 'emplacement') denotes 'seat'; cf. *hēḵîn môšāḇ* in 29.7; Ps. 103.19 (so Jerome, Sym., T and S).

4. On *'āraḵ* (lit. 'to arrange in order', and specifically 'to draw up a case' [*mišpāṭ*]), see on 13.18. On *tôḵāḥôṯ*, here 'arguments', see on 5.17. The cohortatives without conjunctions in vv. 4 and 5a are tantamount to protasis in a conditional sentence to which v. 6a is the apodosis (GKC, §108a, f).

6. None of the ancient versions supports MT *yāśim*, for which Dhorme and Graetz read *yišma'* ('would hear') and Duhm *yāśîm lēḇ* ('would heed'). But *śîm* is used in this sense with *lēḇ* understood in Isa. 41.20, so MT may be retained. Tur-Sinai suggests that *raḇ-kōaḥ* means 'attorney' or 'plenipotentiary'. But Job is surely pressing that God cannot evade his argument, however remote he may be, but should answer him personally.

7. *šām*, most familiar in Classical Heb. as meaning 'there', is used here to mark the next stage of the argument, like Arab. *ṯumma*. Ugaritic *tm*, though occasionally meaning 'there', has possibly also the significance 'then' (e.g. Gordon *UT* 124, 4, 6, 8). See further on 35.12. Thus there is no need to assume an original *yišmōr* with Dhorme. The Piel *pillēṭ*, with no apparent object, is apparently a difficulty. It has been suggested that it is intransitive with a reflexive force, *napšî* possibly being understood. But this is not otherwise attested except possibly at 20.20. In both cases, if the sense is reflexive the emendation to the Hiphil could be more natural. In this case, MT *miššōpᵉṭî* ('from my judge') would be better emended to *mimmišpāṭî* after several Heb. MSS and LXX, S and V. Alternatively *mišpāṭî* ('my case') may be read as the object of the Piel *pillēṭ* in its usual transitive sense. This is the more probable since God is cited by Job as his adversary at law and not as his judge.

8. *hēn*, meaning 'if', is an Aramaism.

9. On this meaning of *'āśāh* ('turn'), cf. 1 Sam. 14.32 as understood by LXX (*ekklithē*) and probably 1 Kgs 20.40 and Ruth 2.19 and possibly Ugaritic *'šy* (Gordon *UT* 2 Aqht I.30; G.R. Driver 1950b: 53-55). Tur-Sinai, after D. Yellin

and I. Eitan, proposes that *'ᵃśōṯô* is cognate with Arab. *ġašwatu*(*n*) ('covering'), omitting *wᵉ* before the following *wᵉlō'* as a dittograph, which might have support in *'āṭap̄* in its usual meaning 'to cover', as Pss. 65.14 (EVV 13) and 73.6; but the context demands the finite verb in v. 9a, with *'e'ᵉṭōp̄* ('I turn') as parallel. *'āṭap̄* in this sense, so understood by S and V, is not attested elsewhere in Classical Heb., but has cognates in Syr. and Arab., adduced by G.R. Driver (1950b: 54) and Guillaume (1963: 115ff.). Verses 8f. have been regarded as secondary intrusion (so Budde, Duhm, G.B. Gray, Ball, Fohrer), but Dhorme retains the passage, which may be a parody of Ps. 139.7ff., where the psalmist declares that wherever he turns he finds God and is found by him.

10. For *dereḵ 'immāḏî* (lit. 'my way with me'), LXX and V have simply 'my way'. S reads 'my way and my standing', suggesting the reading *darkî wᵉ'omᵉḏî,* which Dhorme accepts, citing Ps. 139.2ff. (so too Hölscher). *'immāḏî* (lit. 'with me') means something intimate to one, something of which one is conscious; hence Friedrich Delitzsch proposed that *dereḵ 'immāḏî* meant 'the way of which I am conscious' (cf. Renan 'my conscience'), while Ewald and Dillmann proposed 'my usual, characteristic way'. The figure of assaying is familiar in Hebrew Wisdom literature (e.g. Prov. 17.1), Psalms (e.g. 66.10) and postexilic prophecy (e.g. Isa. 48.10). The 'way' or 'proper conduct' reflects the idiom of Wisdom literature (e.g. Prov. 2.8; Pss. 1.6; 37.34). The specific way of God's commandments (v. 12) reflects the phrase in the Wisdom Psalm 119.15, 31f.

11-12. See Textual Notes.

13. For MT *wᵉhû ḇᵉ'eḥāḏ,* T and V offer 'and (even) if he is alone', taking *bᵉ* as *beth essentiae*. But in this rendering *yāḥîḏ* would be expected. Alternatively, *bᵉ'eḥāḏ* might be defended by assuming the hostile sense of *bᵉ*, 'if he is against a certain one'; cf. Gen. 16.12, *yāḏô bakkōl wᵉyaḏ kōl bô* ('his hand is against all and the hand of all is against him'). But the parallel indicates that MT is a corruption of *bāḥar* ('he chooses'); so Beer, Duhm, Budde, Oort, G.B. Gray, Dhorme, Hölscher, Mowinckel, Fohrer, Pope after LXX.

14. On the reading *ḥuqqô* for MT *ḥuqqî* with S and V, see Textual Note.

16. *hēraḵ libbî* (lit. 'has made my heart tender') means 'unmanned', the heart being the seat of courage or resolution as well as cognition; cf. *nāmas lēḇ* ('courage melted away', Josh. 2.11). The phrase is used parallel to 'fear' in Deut. 20.3; Isa. 7.4; Jer. 51.46.

17. MT *niṣmattî* recalls *ṣāmaṯ*, also used in Aram., Syr. and Arab. meaning 'to be quiet', which is understood by S. In this case, MT *lō'* may be retained with *kî* used conversatively, 'yet I am not put to silence'.

Job 24

Job's Response to Eliphaz (continued, vv. 1-12), with Two Citations from Wisdom Poetry (vv. 13-18, 19-25)

Commentators have differed widely on this chapter. It is generally agreed that the assertion of the condign punishment of the oppressor (vv. 19-25) is not part of Job's statement in the intention of the author (so Dhorme and G.B. Gray). It expresses the theme of Job's friends, and has been claimed for Bildad (so Hoffmann, including vv. 13-17, and Barton, who would include vv. 5-8, but would limit 17ff. to 17-22, 24), and it must be said that the exceptionally short statement of Bildad in the following ch. 25 seems to demand a supplementation, either from this passage or from what follows ch. 25. As for the rest, Siegfried regarded vv. 17-24 as a later interpolation asserted to modify one statement of oppression without redress in vv. 1-12. The unity of vv. 1-18 has been further disputed. Certainly vv. 13-18 seems a self-contained unit, and has been regarded as an importation (so G.B. Gray and Westermann, who included in this category vv. 5-8, 10f.). The same view is taken by Duhm and Fohrer, who would resolve the whole chapter into a number of independent poems from sapiential circles. Considerations of form-criticism would certainly suggest some such solution. Verses 1-12 have their prototype in Egyptian Wisdom literature in the Complaint of the Eloquent Peasant (*ANET*, 407-10) and similar works; the formal prototype of vv. 13-18 is the listing of subjects with common characteristics, as in Prov. 30.15f. (things never satisfied), 30.18f. (progressive forces which are imperceptible), 30.21-23 (things intolerable), 30.24-28 (things small but effective), 30.29f. (things stately). On the same formal grounds we may distinguish a sapiential poem on the theodicy in vv. 19-25, which was probably inserted as a corrective to the satire in vv. 1-12. From this point until Job's *apologia pro vita sua*, culminating in his oath of purgation (vv. 29-31), we are confronted by the disruption of the former regularity of sequel of addresses and by a substantial amount of poetic interpolation, culminating in the poem on Wisdom (ch. 28), so that it is fair to discern in ch. 24 the beginning of this process. Of the secondary nature of vv. 13-18 and 19-25 we are in no doubt but we regard the case as different in 1-12.

Granted the poetic matter cited in vv. 1-12, which Fohrer would resolve into series of independent poems (vv. 1-4, 10-12, 22-23, 5-8, in that order, with

v. 9 a gloss on v. 3), this is held together by the introduction 'Why are set times (of judgment) not fixed by the Almighty...?' (v. 1) and the conclusion 'The life-breath of the injured cries out, yet God pays no heed to their prayer'. This is the theme of Job's complaint so that we have no hesitation in regarding it as a citation by the author himself to form the conclusion of Job's statement in the short ch. 23. We see no compelling reason to differ from the order in MT except to admit Fohrer's view that v. 9 is a secondary elaboration of injustice to the widow and the destitute in v. 3. The tricolon in v. 12 thematically concludes the opening question of God's neglect of redress for the injustice described in vv. 2-11.

The order in MT of the above sections seems to us to raise no question. The statement that 'the needy of the land are all made to hide themselves' (v. 4) is naturally developed in the passage on their furtive nightly depredations from their refuge in the wilds (vv. 5-6), where their exposure (vv. 7-8) leads to the statement that, keeping the flocks of others as landless paupers, they are insufficiently clad (v. 10a), hungry while as day-labourers in another's harvest (v. 10b), with festering sores, they manipulate the heavy stone oil-press (v. 11a), and thirsty, they tread another's wine-vats (v. 11b).

Admitting Fohrer's bracketing of v. 9 as a gloss or variation on v. 3, we follow Dhorme's arrangement of text between vv. 14 and 17, viz. vv. 14ab, 15ab, 14c, 15c, 16abc, 17ab, but read v. 18acb as the tricolon ending the passage.

Chapter 24

Job's Response to Eliphaz (continued, vv. 1-12), with Two Citations from Wisdom Poetry (vv. 13-18, 19-25).

1. 'Why are set times (of judgment) not fixed by the Almighty,
And those who acknowledge Him[1] never see his days of reckoning?
2. The wicked[2] remove boundary marks;
They lift flock and shepherd.[3]
3. They drive off the ass of the fatherless;
They take the widow's ox in pledge;
9. [4]They snatch the orphan from the breast,
They take the suckling[5] of the poor in pledge.
4. They divert the poor from the administration,
And the needy of the land are all made to hide themselves.

5. As[6] wild asses in the wilderness
They go forth at dusk,[7]
Anxiously seeking what they may snatch in the evening
Since there is no food[8] for their children.
6. In fields by night[9] they reap,
They hastily gather the grapes of the vineyard of the wicked;

7. They lie naked[10] all night without clothing,
Without covering from the cold.

8. They are wet with the downpour of the mountains,
And cling to the rocks for want of shelter;
10. Keeping the flocks,[11] they go about without clothing,
And themselves hungry, they carry the sheaves;
11. With festering sores[12] they press olive-oil;
They tread the wine-vats, though they (themselves) are thirsty.
12. The bowels[13] of the dying[14] groan,
And the life-breath of the injured cries out,
Yet God pays no heed[15] to their prayer.[16]

13. There are those who rebel against God,[17]
They do not recognize his ways,
And will not abide in his paths.
14. When it is not yet light[18] the murderer rises,
To slay the poor and needy;
15. The eye of the adulterer watches for the twilight,
Saying, "No eye will mark me".
14c. And at night the thief ranges,[19]
15c Yea, he puts a veil on his face.
16. In the dark he breaks into houses;
Day is a terror to all of them,[20]
They are all alike[21] strangers to the light,
17. For the morning is the shadow of death to them,
But they are familiar[22] with the destructive works of deep darkness.
18a. Headlong they rush[23] from the daylight,[24]
c. (Such a one) dare not take the road on the heights,[25]
b. His allotted portion[26] in the land is cursed.

19. The drought and the heat snatch away[27] snow,
So for the wicked,[28] Sheol snatches them away.[29]
20. The mother who suckled (such a one) shall forget him,
His eminence[30] shall no longer be remembered.
So wickedness is broken like a stick!
21. He mates with a barren woman who has no child,
And with a widow and it does not benefit him.
22. But God shall grip the mighty in his strength,
He shall rise up and (the wicked) may not rely on his security.[31]
23. (God) shall put him down flat on his face, and he will be spread-eagled,
Yea, the eyes of Yahweh[32] are upon his ways.[33]
24. His exaltation[34] is for a little while and it is gone;
Yea, he droops[35] like dog-tooth,[36] shrivelling up,
Cut down[37] like the top ears of corn.
25. And if it is not so who will give me the lie,
And reduce my statement to nothing?'[38]

Textual Notes to Chapter 24

1. Reading the plur. *yōḏᵉʿāyw* with Qere.
2. Inserting *rāʿîm* or *rᵉšāʿîm* with LXX *metri causa.*
3. Reading *wᵉrōʿô* with LXX for MT *wayyirʿû.* See Commentary *ad loc.*
4. The verse is probably a secondary expansion of or variant on v. 3.
5. Reading *ʿāl*, the participle of an *ʿ/w* verb for the preposition *ʿal* in MT. See Commentary *ad loc.*
6. Reading *hēḵ* or *ʾēḵ* after LXX, V and S for MT *hēn.*
7. Reading *kᵉp̄î ṣillîm* for MT *bᵉp̄oʿᵒlām* (conjecture).
8. Reading *bᵉlōʾ leḥem* for MT *lōʾ leḥem.* See Commentary *ad loc.*
9. Reading *bᵉlayl* for MT *bᵉlîlô*, taking final *w* as a dittograph of following *y* in the script at the stage of the Qumran MSS.
10. Reading *ʿᵃrûmîm* for MT *ʿārôm*, as suggested by the number of the verb.
11. Reading *rōʿîm* for MT *ʿārôm.* See Commentary *ad loc.*
12. Reading *binᵉšûrōṯām* for MT *bên šûrōṯām.* See Commentary *ad loc.*
13. Reading *mēʿê* for *mēʿîr.*
14. Reading *mēṯîm* for MT *mᵉṯîm.*
15. Reading *yišmaʿ* for MT *yaśîm.*
16. Reading *tᵉp̄illāṯām* after S for MT *tip̄lāh*, the pronominal suffix having been lost through similarity to the following *hēmmāh.*
17. Reading *ʾēl* for MT *ʾôr*, as indicated by the pronominal suffixes in the sequel.
18. Reading *lōʾ ʾôr* for MT *lᵉʾôr.* See Commentary *ad loc.*
19. Reading *yᵉhallēḵ gannāḇ* for MT *yᵉhî ḵᵉgannāḇ.* See Commentary *ad loc.*
20. Reading *yôm mᵉḥittām kullāmô* for MT *yômām ḥittᵉmû-lāmô.* See Commentary *ad loc.*
21. Reading *yaḥdāw* after MT *wᵉlōʾ-yāḏᵉʿû ʾôr* in parallelism with *kullāmo* (ʻall of them'), restored in v. 16b. *yaḥdāw* has been displaced in MT to v. 17a, where it is superfluous to the metre.
22. Reading *yakkîrû* for MT *yakkîr*, the final *w* being omitted by haplography after *r* in the square script.
23. Reading *qallû ʿal-pānîm* (conjecture) for MT *qal-hûʾ ʿal-pᵉnê.* See Commentary *ad loc.*
24. Reading *miyyôm* for MT *mayim.* See Commentary *ad loc.*
25. Reading *mᵉrāmîm* for MT *kᵉrāmîm*, with corruption of *m* to *k* in the Heb. script and transposing v. 18b and c. See Commentary *ad loc.*
26. Reading *ḥelqāṯô* for MT *ḥelqāṯām* in agreement with the context.
27. Regarding MT *mayim* as displaced from v. 19b after corruption. See following Textual Note.
28. Reading *mûmāyîm* corrupted to MT *mayim* and displaced before *šeleḡ* in v. 19a.
29. Reading *ḥᵃṭāp̄ām* for MT *ḥāṭṭāʾû* (pausal).
30. Reading *rûmōh* for MT *rimmāh.*
31. Reading *bᵉḥayyāyw* for MT *bᵉḥayyîn.* See Commentary *ad loc.*
32. Reading *ʿênê yhwh* for MT *ʿênêhû.* See Commentary *ad loc.*
33. Reading *dᵉrāḵāyw* for MT *darᵉḵêhem*, with V.
34. Reading *rûmô* for MT *rômmû.*
35. Reading *wᵉhummaḵ* for MT *wᵉhummᵉḵû.*
36. Reading *kîḇālāʾ* after 11QtargJob for MT *kakkōl.*
37. Reading *yimmal* for MT *yimmālû.*
38. Reading *lᵉʾayin* for MT *lᵉʾal.*

Commentary on Chapter 24

1. The versions give no clear idea of the meaning of the text, owing mainly to their assumption that the verb *ṣāpan* means 'to hide' as in many passages in the OT, and this has occasioned certain assumptions on their part as to the state of the Heb. text. But the verb means also 'to store up' or 'preserve' (e.g. 15.20; Hos. 13.12; Ps. 31.20; Prov. 2.7; Song 7.14), and may also have a homonym cognate with Arab. *ṣafana* ('to set the feet evenly'), hence conceivably 'to fix regularly', which the context of the present passage demands best suiting the object *'ittîm* ('[set]) times'), parallel to 'his days', sc. of reckoning; cf. the 'day of Yahweh' in Amos 5.18ff.; Zeph. 1.7ff.; Isa. 2.12ff.; and particularly Joel 4.1ff. (EVV 3.1ff.), where 'that day' is parallel to 'that time' (*'ēṯ*) in the present passage and is associated with judgment.

2. *śûḡ* is an orthographic variant of the more regular *sûḡ* ('to be removed'). The metre demands one more beat, hence *rā'îm* or *rᵉšā'îm* should be added after LXX. Perhaps *rā'îm* was omitted by error owing to its resemblance to *wᵉrō'ô* ('and its shepherd', for MT *wayyir'û*) in v. 2b. The shepherd was taken with the sheep, so that he could not be a witness to the crime. Thus to the crime of theft the malefactor adds that of kidnapping, which is a capital offence in the Israelite apodeictic codes (Exod. 20.15; 21.16ff.; Deut. 5.9; 24.7). Alternatively the meaning may be that wicked creditors are not merely content with foreclosing a mortgage on the flock but they take also a mortgage on the shepherd's person and foreclose it remorselessly, distraining him as a slave. See further on v. 9.

3. The taking of the ass or the ox of the poor in pledge deprived them of the necessary means of livelihood, like the distraining of millstones which was forbidden in Deut. 24.6, 'One must not take the nether or upper millstone in pledge (*yaḥbōl*), for (he who does so) takes a man's life in pledge'. The offence was the more heinous since the victim was a widow, who was a special charge upon the charity of the community in Israel as in Ugarit; cf. Deut. 24.17-22, where it is forbidden to take a widow's cloak in pledge (Deut. 24.17).

9. This verse, with specific reference to inhumane treatment of orphans, presumably the children of widows, belongs here (so Dhorme), rather than in the list of deprivations between vv. 8 and 10 in MT, where it has been taken as a marginal gloss on vv. 2-3 (so Siegfried, Budde, Duhm, Hölscher, Stevenson, Fohrer). G.B. Gray admits the possibility that, if not a gloss, it belongs after vv. 2-3. In any case it seems best taken as a gloss, or variant on v. 3. *gāzal* means 'to plunder' or 'snatch forcibly'. The latter is the sense here; cf. 20.19; Gen. 31.31; Judg. 21.23; 2 Sam. 23.21. MT *šôd*, where the sense of the context indicates 'breast', is attested in Isa. 60.16, 66. Elsewhere in the OT the word means 'plunder', and *šôḏ* has been suspected as a scribal error for *šēḏ*

('breast'), but the recurrence of *šôḏ* in Isaiah indicates that, as Fohrer suggests, it may be a byform of the more regular noun. For MT *'al-'ānî yaḥbōlû* ('they take pledges to the disadvantage of the poor') which is tautological and colourful in the context, Klostermann proposed *'āl* for MT *'al* ('the suckling'), the participle of *'ûl*, cognate with Arab. *ġāla, yaġīl* ('to suckle'). The context indicates the taking of children for the debt of parents; cf. Exod. 21.7; 2 Kgs 4.1; Neh. 5.5; Isa. 50.1; and, in Mesopotamia, the Code of Hammurabi §117.

4. *dereḵ* usually means 'way' in Classical Heb., which in this context has no particular point. Here and in other contexts which imply ordered government of humans or God the noun is cognate with Arab. *daraku(n)* ('administration'), a usage well attested in the the Ras Shamra texts (e.g. Gordon *UT* Krt, 41f.), where *drk(t)* is parallel to *mlk* ('kingship'). Thus in Amos 2.7 *weḏereḵ 'anāwîm yaṭṭû* may be read *ûmiddereḵ 'anāwîm yaṭṭû* ('and divert the poor from the administration').

5. *hēḵ* or *'ēḵ* should be read for MT *hēn*, an Aram. particle meaning 'as'. In v. 5b the metre demands another beat. Besides, MT *bepo 'olām* (var. *kepo 'olām*, cf. S, T and V *lepo 'olām*), meaning 'on their business' does not suit the figure of wild asses in v. 5a. Hence we propose that this is the corruption of an original text *bepî* or *kepî ṣillîm* ('at dusk', lit. 'in proportion to shadows'), assuming corruption of *ṣ* to *'* in the square script. *šiḥar* denotes anxious search as in 7.21. *'arāḇāh* is probably an adverbial accusative, common in Arabic, meaning 'in the evening', rather than *'ereḇ* with *h locale*, meaning 'until evening' as suggested by Dahood (*UHP*, p. 16). In view of nightly depredation by wild asses on border lands, the former meaning is to be preferred. Weiser, Fohrer, Gordis and Pope take the word as indicating the desert, where like wild asses the destitute seek food. But the following verse referring to nightly pilfering of cornfields and vineyards supports our interpretation. The familiar meaning of *ṭerep* in Classical Heb. is 'prey', but it also means 'food' in general (e.g. Ps. 111.5, *ṭerep̄ nāṯan lîrē'āyw*; Mal. 3.10; and possibly Prov. 31.15). Here we propose that the word is taken in the Aramaic sense of *ṭerap̄*, used of a creditor snatching his debts, hence our translation 'what they may snatch'. Oppression and destitution breed theft.

In MT *lô leḥem lanne'ārîm* Wright read *lō'*... (so Budde, Beer, Duhm, Dhorme, Stevenson; Guillaume proposed *lû*... '(to see) if there be food...', while Hölscher read *lalleḥem* ('for the food...'; so too Fohrer). Perhaps we may rather read *belō' leḥem*... ('since there is no food...').

6. MT *belîlô* ('his mixed fodder') might possibly be read *belî lō'* ('which does not belong to him'), or better, *belî lāmô* ('which does not belong to them'), with the omission of *m* before *w* in the Old Heb. script, after LXX, S, V and T, the plur. being demanded by the verb *yiqṣōrû*. One Heb. MS reads *belayelāh* ('by night') and is evidently supported by 'before daylight' (so LXX). In view

of our interpretation of v. 5 this is feasible (so Merx, Bickell, Beer, Budde, Duhm, Oort, G.B. Gray, Dhorme, Peake, Hölscher, Fohrer). According to the former reading the reference would be to the poor who are hired or forced to do work in the fields of others, and would agree with vv. 10bff.; according to the latter it would agree with v. 5 according to the interpretation we have adopted, stealing at night by the destitute. In v. 6b it is proposed to emend *rāšā'* to *'āšîr* (so Budde, Beer, Duhm, Oort, Peake, G.B. Gray, Fohrer, *op.cit.*, p. 369, though translating 'Frevler' in p. 367), but without the support of the versions. *rāšā'* may well stand, denoting the prosperous wicked, as often in the Psalms. *lāqaš* at first sight suggests *leqeš* and *malqôš*, respectively the 'late aftergrowth' and 'rains at the end of winter', which coincide with the first mowings of spring pasture. Here the verb may be the Heb. cognate of Arab. *laqaṯa* ('to gather up hurriedly', as thieves in a vineyard).

8. *zerem* ('rainstorm') and *maḥseh* ('shelter') are found together as here in Isa. 25.4, where God is a shelter from the storm. *rāṭaḇ* is found in the OT only in Job, in 8.16 of a fresh, sappy plant; cf. Arab. *raṭdu*(*n*) ('fresh', as distinct from clotted dates). Here it means 'wet', as the cognate in Ass., Aram. and Syr.

10. Though 'naked' (MT *'ārôm*, which in any case should be plur. in agreement with the verb) would agree with 'without clothing' in v. 10a, we prefer to regard it as a corruption of *rō'îm* ('shepherding'). Since vv. 10f. refers to men harvesting, though themselves hungry, pressing olive-oil, though themselves blistered (see below), and treading out grapes, though themselves thirsty, it is natural to find reference to shepherds of the wool-bearing flocks, themselves without clothing.

11. *yaṣhîrû*, 'they press out olive-oil' (*yiṣhār*), a denominative verb, has suggested that *šûrōṯ* or *šûrōṯâm*, which may be a dual, refers to 'rows' of olive trees (so Dahood 1962: 68, 'between the rows they pass the noonday', *ṣohorayim*), or possibly, as Hölscher suggested, the dry stone terrace-walls of the hillsides, where olive-trees are grown (so also Mowinckel). Larcher's translation in JB, 'they have no stones for pressing oil', evidently envisages the reading *be'ên šûrāṯayim* and assumes that the noun means an olive-press of two stones like two courses of masonry, the usual meaning of the noun. In agreement with the rest of vv. 10f., where the particular privation of the destitute is mentioned with relation to their particular labour, we suggest that the text behind MT *bên šûrōṯām* contains a reference to a particular hardship of those who press out the olive-oil which the produce for which they labour was meant to relieve. Hence we propose that MT is a corruption of *bineśûrōṯām* (lit. 'with their abrasions'), taking *neśûrōṯ* as cognate with Arab. *naśara* ('to rub off') the V form meaning 'to break out, suppurate'; cf. Syr. *neṯar*, to suppurate'. In this case the noun would refer to blisters and suppuration from open sores of those who manipulated the heavy stone olive-press.

12. MT *mē'îr m^{e}ṯîm* is suspect, having no parallel. This, however, is partially restored if we emend to *mē'^{a}ḇōḏāṯām* ('by reason of their bondage', as Fohrer, Lévêque after Steuernagel). Closer to MT, and completely restoring the parallelism, is the emendation *mê'ê mēṯîm* (*yin'āqû*) ('the bowels of dying men [groan]'). *nā'aq* is known in the OT only here and in Ezek. 30.24 and in the noun form in Exod. 2.24; 6.5; Judg. 2.18. The groaning of the bowels of dying men is no more strange than 'the life-breath of the injured crying out'. Isaiah 63.15 refers to 'trouble of the bowels', which does not exclude sound. S supports the reading *mēṯîm*, the desired parallel to *ḥ^{a}lālîm*. The enormity of such oppression is appreciated in view of the law in the Book of the Covenant which awards compensation even to injured slaves (Exod. 21.26f.). The sudden tricolon after the predominant bicola throws the emphasis on to the third and final statement, which alleges the indifference of God. MT *yāśîm tip̄lāh* ('considers it a moral obtuseness'; cf. 1.22) if not impossible, is at least suspect, and two Heb. MSS read *t^{e}p̄illāh* ('prayer'), which was also read by S. This would indicate the reading *yišma'* ('hears') for MT *yāśîm* (so Graetz, Budde, Ehrlich, Ball, Dhorme, Hölscher), though *yāśîm*, with *lēḇ* understood, meaning 'pays heed to', is possible (so Mowinckel, Fohrer, Pope, and evidently NEB).

13. Dhorme suggested that this verse, introduced by the pronoun *hēmmāh*, is displaced from after v. 16, with which indeed the general sense would agree. Hölscher regards the verse as in position. He notes that vv. 14-18 was lacking in the original LXX, and argues that after the addition of vv. 14-18 the original v. 13 was adapted by the substitution of *'ôr* ('light') for an original *'ēl* ('God') and then introduced by *hēmmāh*, which referred to nocturnal miscreants mentioned in vv. 14-18. In support of this view it must be admitted that MT *mōr^{e}ḏê* ('those who rebel against') more naturally indicates a personal object than the impersonal *'ôr*, and that *'ēl* is the more natural antecedent of the pronominal suffix in *d^{e}rāḵāyw* ('his ways') and *n^{e}ṯîḇōṯāyw* ('his paths'). *b^{e}* in *b^{e}mōr^{e}ḏê* is probably *beth essentiae*, signifying 'in the category of', being analogous to *bi* introducing the predicate in a nominal sentence in Arab.

14. For MT *lā'ôr*, which is contradicted by the main point of this passage, *lō' 'ōr* ('while it is not yet light') has been read generally since it was suggested by Wright. Hölscher suggested *b^{e}lō' 'ôr* with the same meaning. The verb *rāṣaḥ*, used in the commandment in the Decalogue (Exod. 20.13; Deut. 5.17), though used for unpremeditated manslaughter in the case of an accident (Deut. 4.42; 19.3, 4, 6), usually denotes premeditated killing, whether murder or in discharge of blood-revenge (Num. 35.27, 30). *qāṭal* ('to kill') is certainly an indication of Late Hebrew, probably under Aram. influence. The only instances in the OT are here and 13.15 as well as Ps. 139.19 and in the verbal noun *qeṭel* in Obad. 9. Verse 14c, on the thief, goes naturally with vv. 15c and 16a, which refers to burglary, and has been displaced in MT.

15. *nō'ēp̄* is the adulterer, the participle of *nā'ap̄*, being used in the Piel in the seventh commandment (Exod. 20.14; Deut. 5.18). *nešep̄* is the twilight (cf. 7.4ff.). The adulterer in Ben Sira 23.25f. remarks 'the darkness is about me'. The twilight is also noted in Prov. 7.9 as the time when the prostitute spies out her clients. *sēṯer* has the connotation of Arab. *śatara* ('to veil').

16. The verb for house-breaking, *ḥāṯar*, lit. 'to dig', recalls *maḥtereṯ* in the Book of the Covenant (Exod. 22.1 [EVV 2]) and Gk. *toichōruchos* (lit. 'one who digs through a wall'), a relatively simple operation in mud-brick building or even stone building without mortar. In MT *yômām ḥittᵉmû-lāmô* (lit. 'by day they seal up for themselves') the transitive verb lacks an object. Dhorme reads the sing. with S and takes the clause as a relative clause without the relative particle and with 'houses' as antecedent ('[houses] which he has sealed during the day'), that is, on which he has set an identification mark. According to the arrangement of the text which we adopt v. 16b is parallel to v. 16c ('they are all strangers to the light'); so we read *yôm mᵉḥittām kullāmô* ('day is a terror to all of them') after Stevenson. The couplet v. 16bc categorized the nocturnal miscreants introduced as 'those who rebel against God' in v. 13a. In v. 16c, for the sake of metre, *yaḥaḏ* ('all together') should be transposed from v. 17a to before *lō' yāḏᵉ'û*, thus giving a parallel to *kullāmô* ('all of them') in v. 16b. The transposition also relieves the overloaded v. 17a.

17. *ṣēl māweṯ* ('the shadow of death') should probably be read for MT *ṣalmāweṯ* in v. 17a, and *ṣalmûṯ* ('darkness') for MT *ṣalmāweṯ* in v. 17b. *ballᵉhôt* occurring in 18.11, 14; 27.30; 30.15, meaning 'terrors', means rather 'calamity' or 'destruction' in Isa. 17.14 (sing.) and Ps. 73.19; Ezek. 26.21; 27.36; 28.19. Here the plur. means 'destructive works'. LXX *tarachos* ('confusion') suggests the reading *bᵉhālôṯ*.

18. Dhorme retains MT *qal-hû' 'al-pᵉnê-mayîm* ('he is a light thing on the surface of the water'); so also Pope, who regards it as displaced from the end of ch. 27, which he assigns to Zophar. Certainly it connects obviously with nothing in the strophe vv. 19-24. Budde and Beer emend, reading *qal hû' 'al-pᵉnê šāmāyîm* ('he is accursed in the sight of Heaven'), which has the merit of agreeing with v. 18b. But since v. 18c refers to the wicked avoiding the exposed ground to evade detection, Larcher's rendering in JB, 'Headlong he flees from the daylight', evidently reading *qal-hû' 'al-pānāyw miyyôm* has much to recommend it, and we adopt it with the modification of the reading *qallû* (so Fohrer) and *pānāyw* for MT *pᵉnê* proposed by Larcher. The avoidance of the heights by the miscreant to escape detection reflects the highways of ancient Palestine which often kept to the height of a ridge, which was dry in all weathers and, once the ridge was attained, more level. Movement along wadis under the general surface of the land is also a well-known stratagem of raiding and smuggling parties in the desert. We propose to see a word-play

between *qallû* ('flee hastily') in v. 18a and *t^equllal* ('will be accursed'). On this reading and interpretation we would see v. 18acb as the conclusion of vv. 13ff. See further, Textual Notes.

19. *mêmê* may be omitted from v. 19a *metri causa*. It has probably been transposed from v. 19b, where it has suffered corruption from an original *mûmāyîm* ('miscreants'); cf. Syr. *mûmāyā'*). This would certainly be an Aramaism in Job, not occurring elsewhere in the OT. *mûm* is used in the OT to denote 'blemish', physical (Lev. 21.17ff.; Song 4.7 etc.) and moral (Job 11.15; Prov. 9.7). This indicates the reading *ḥ^aṭāp̄ām* ('snatches them') for MT *ḥāṭā'û* (pausal) in v. 19b, *mûmāyîm* being used proleptically. The verb is a gnomic perfect.

20. The abrupt change to the sing., if the passage is a unity, may be explained through the mention of the sing. *reḥem* ('womb'). Alternatively the sing. pronominal suffix may refer to the indefinite subject 'one'. For MT *reḥem m^eṯāqô*, Beer (followed by Duhm, Hölscher, Mowinckel and Fohrer) read *r^eḥōḇ m^eqōmô* ('the public place of his town'), and Dhorme read *reḥem p^eṯāqô* ('the womb that formed him'); cf. Akk. *patâqu* ('to form'). But MT may be retained, *m^eṯāqô* meaning 'which gave him suck'; cf. Syr. *m^eṯaq*. An apparent difficulty is the use of *reḥem* (lit. 'womb'), when 'breast' might rather be expected. By synecdoche, however, the noun may mean 'young woman' or 'potential mother'; cf. Judg. 5.30 and the Moabite Stone. In the context *rimmāh* is likely to be a corruption of *rûmōh* ('his eminence'; so Michaelis, Bickell, Budde, Beer, Duhm, Peake, Kissane) rather than *š^emōh* ('his name'; so G.B. Gray, Dhorme, Mowinckel, Fohrer).

21. The transitive usage of *rā'āh* ('to keep company with') may be attested in Prov. 29.3, *rō'ēh zônôṯ*, cited by Tur-Sinai, though here the word may be a noun rather than the participle. Verse 21b refers to the convention of levirate marriage with the childless widow of a deceased brother. In this case the property of the dead man is secured not for the husband and his family, but for the offspring of the widow. The embarrassment of this situation is indicated in the reluctance of Naomi's kinsman to marry Ruth, lest he impair his own property in redeeming his kinsmen's property with his own capital when it would not be an asset to himself or his own family but to Ruth and her children (Ruth 4.6).

22. As noticed by Dhorme, MT *māšaḵ* is cognate with Arab. *maśaka* ('to grasp'), as in Pss. 10.9; 28.3. Dhorme further reads the participle *mōšēḵ*, the subject being God. *yāqûm* would then have the pregnant sense of rising in hostility, as in Exod. 15.7; Deut. 22.26; Amos 7.9; etc.; cf. Arab. *qawmu(n)* ('enemies'). For MT *b^eḥayyîn* read *b^eḥayyāyw* with LXX, Sym., V and three Heb. MSS. The word may be taken as in Prov. 27.27; cf. *miḥyeh* (Judg. 6.4; 17.10) as signifying 'his means'. Or there may be the nuance of the verbal

noun in the IInd Form of the Arab. verb *taḥiyatu(n)* ('security'), being a word-play with *ḥayyāyw* in this sense, which is usually expressed in Heb. by *bāṭaḥ*, and continuing with *lābeṭaḥ* in v. 23a, but with the Arab. sense of 'flat on his face', from Arab. *baṭaḥa*, 'to spread out, flatten' (so Guillaume).

23. *lô* seems a clear case of Aram. *l*ᵉ as *nota accusativa* with the pronominal suffix. In the context in MT *yiššā'ēn* is feasibly taken by Guillaume as cognate with Arab. *ša'ana* ('to be dishevelled'), hence our rendering 'he will be spread-eagled'. On this interpretation v. 23b would refer to the eyes of God upon the wicked with hostile intent. Taking *ḥayyāyw lābeṭaḥ* and *yiššā'ēn* in their usual Heb. sense, Fohrer sees a reference to God's support of the wicked oppressors even when their own confidence fails (v. 22b) and to his looking protectively on them (v. 23b); accordingly he regards vv. 22-23 as displaced from after v. 12. The objection to the otherwise feasible reading *'ênê yhwh* for MT *'ênêhû* is that the divine name Yahweh is practically never used in the poetic dialogue in Job except in citation of a well-known phrase. If the emendation is accepted it may support the view that 24.19-25 is such a citation and is secondary.

For MT *darᵉkêhem* V reads *dᵉrākāyw*, which agrees with the sing. subjects in vv. 22b and 23a.

24. Suddenly in MT, as often in this passage, the number changes to the plur. In this particular verse, the number changes in a single colon (v. 24a). Preference for the sing. *'ênennû* involves less disturbance to MT, where MT *rômmû* ('they have been exalted') may be the corruption of *rûmô* ('his exaltation'; so, after LXX, Bickell, Duhm, Beer, G.B. Gray, Dhorme, Hölscher, and Mowinckel, who renders 'his arrogance'). This would involve the reading *wᵉhummak* after LXX, involving dittography in MT of *w* between final *k* of *wᵉhummak* and initial *k* in *kakkōl* in the Old Heb. script. *mākak* is a rare verb in the OT, being attested in Eccl. 10.18 of a roof-tree subsiding and in Ps. 106.43 of the wicked drooping. The verb is used in the Baal myth in the Ras Shamra texts of Sea 'subsiding' in his conflict with Baal (Gordon *UT* 68.17). For MT *kakkōl* 11QtargJob reads *kybl*, which van der Ploeg and van der Woude (1971: 28) render as 'dog-tooth' after I. Löw (1881: 183). MT *yiqqāpᵉṣûn* (lit. 'they are drawn together', sc. 'shrivelled up'), is confirmed by 11QtargJob. For MT *yimmālû* the sing. may be read, the final *w* being a dittograph before initial *w* of the following word. The verbal *mālal* is found in a similar figure in 14.2; 18.16; Pss. 37.2; 90.6. 'Cut down like the top ears of corn' refers to the corn cut not by scythe near the ground, but nearer the top of the stalk with the sickle. The tricolon marks the end of the citation, and v. 25 marks the author's personal assertion.

25. Here, as in 19.6, 23, *'ēpô* is simply an enclitic, like Arab. *fa*. Parallelism demands the reading in v. 25b *wᵉyāśēm lᵉ'ayin millāṯî* ('and reduce my statement to nothing').

Job 25 and 26

The Introduction of Bildad's Third Address: Introduced by 26.2-4, Continued by 25.2-6 and Concluded by 26.5-15*

The ascription of the short ch. 25 to Bildad and the lack of the usual dialectic introduction suggests that 26.2-4, ascribed to Job in MT, is really the introduction to Bildad's third address in the same tone as Eliphaz's opening address (4.3ff.), which may indicate a secondary attempt to construct a third round of debate. A secondary hand is indicated by the introduction of a Hymn of Praise in 25.2-6, completed, probably secondarily, by another hand responsible for 26.5-14. The dread of the imperial power of God by the powers 'in the heights' (25.2) is balanced by the dread of 'the shades beneath' of the majesty of the Creator. But the first part of the hymn from 25.3 is interpreted by the sapiential argument *a majore ad minus* to assert the futility of the claim of a mere human being to state the justice of his case to God.

The passage so arranged (26.2-4; 25.2-6; 26.5-14) falls into three parts: the introduction in the style of sapiential dialectic (26.2-4); a hymn of praise to divine power and righteousness (25.2-6), which by its adaptation to the sapiential statement of the significance of man recalls the sapiential adaptation of the Hymn of Praise in Psalm 8; and finally the continuation of the hymn of praise to the power and providence of God (26.5-14), without sapiential adaptation. 25.2-6 is a single strophe; 26.5-14 falls into two strophes, each consisting, like 25.2-6, of five couplets (26.5-9, 10-14), supporting the view that structurally as well as thematically 25.2-6 and 26.5-14 comprise a unity.

The ascription of 26.2-4 to Bildad rather than, as in MT, to Job is significantly supported by 11QtargJob.

Chapters 25 and 26 (25.1; 26.2-4; 25.2-6; 26.5-14)

25.1. Then answered Bildad the Shuhite and said:
( )[1]
26.2. 'How you have supported the weak!
How you have saved the arm of the powerless!
3. How you have counselled the disingenuous,
And shown sound wisdom to the simple![2]

* See General Introduction, p. 57.

4. From whom[3] do you declare such words?
Whose spirit is it that has come forth from you?

25.2. Dominion and awe rest with Him;
He maintains peace in His heights.
3. Is there any counting of His troops?
Whom does his ambush[4] not surprise?
4. How can a man be innocent before God?
And how can one born of women be guiltless?
5. If even[5] the moon does not continue to shine,[6]
And the stars are not pure in His sight,
6. How much less a human—a maggot?
And a son of a human—a worm?

26.5. The shades writhe beneath,
The waters and their inhabitants.
6. Sheol is naked before Him;
Uncovered is Perdition.
7. He it is that stretches out a firmament over the void,
That suspends the earth over nothing,
8. That binds up the water in His clouds,
Yet the clouds are not burst under their weight.
9. He covers the face of the full moon,[7]
Spreading his cloud over it.

10. He traces a circle[8] on the face of the waters
At the very limit of light and darkness.
11. The pillars of the sky rock,
Astounded at His rebuke.
12. By His power he stilled the sea,
And by His wisdom[9] he struck down Rahab.
13. By the winds of heaven[10] He broke him in pieces;[11]
His was the hand that pierced the primeval serpent.
14. These indeed are but the outskirts of His government.[12]
And what but a whisper of His purpose do we hear therein?
And His powerful thunder[13] who can understand?'

Textual Notes to Chapters 25–26

1. Omitting 26.1 after the rearrangement of the text as Bildad's speech.
2. Reading *labbûr* for MT *lārōḇ*. See Commentary *ad loc.*
3. Reading *mē'eṯ-mî* for MT *'eṯ-mî.*
4. Reading *'ōreḇô* with LXX for MT *'ôrēhû*. See Commentary *ad loc.*
5. Reading *'ôḏ* for MT *'aḏ.*
6. Understanding *yāhēl* with LXX, Aq., T, V and one Heb. MS.
7. Reading *kese'* for MT *kissēh*. See Commentary *ad loc.*
8. Reading *ḥōqēq-ḥûg̱* with S and T for MT *ḥōq-ḥāg̱*. See Commentary *ad loc.*
9. Reading *ûḇiṯeḇûnāṯô* (Qere) for MT *ûḇiṯeḇûnāṯô.*
10. Reading *berûḥôṯ šāmayim* for MT *berûḥô šāmayim*. See Commentary *ad loc.*
11. Reading *šibbērô* for MT *šip̄erāh*. See Commentary *ad loc.*
12. Reading *derāḵô* or *darkô* for MT *derāḵāyw*. See Commentary *ad loc.*
13. Reading *ra'am geḇûrāṯô* (Qere).

Commentary on Chapters 25–26

2. *l^e^lō'-ḵōaḥ* is another instance of the Aram. *nota accusativa l^e^*.

3. For MT *w^e^ṯûšiyyāh lārōḇ hôḏā'tā* ('and you have given abundant evidence of sound wisdom') a reading is demanded which observes the parallelism with 'How you have counseled the disingenuous?'. Here one Heb. MS reads *lbr* for MT *lārōḇ*, which suggests either *labbā'ēr* ('the brutish', so Graetz) or *labbûr* ('the simple'); cf. Syr. *b^e^rîrā'* and late Heb. *bûr* ('simple, rude'). On the meaning of *tûšiyyāh* as 'plan', which includes both counsel and successful effect of counsel, see above on 5.12. The parallelism *'ēṣāḥ // tûšiyyāh* occurs again in Isa. 28.29 and Prov. 8.14; cf. *tûšiyyāh* as parallel to *m^e^zimmāh* in Prov. 3.21.

4. MT *'eṯ-mî* is taken by Hölscher as 'by whose help' (lit. 'with whom?'). Alternatively *mē'eṯ-mî* ('from whom?', i.e. 'By whose authority?') may be read. In v. 4b 'Whose breath comes forth from you?' animadverts on Job as a mouthpiece. The sense is 'Who inspired you?' where *rûaḥ* might be expected; but Bildad may prefer a more derogatory term *n^e^šāmāh* ('breath'), though the word is found in parallelism with *rûaḥ* and qualified by 'of the Almighty' in 32.8, so that we may translate 'spirit'.

25.2. The association of *hamšēl* with *paḥaḏ* ('fear' in the sense of inspiring awe) indicates that the verb is infinitive absolute of *māšal* ('to rule') used as a verbal noun. It emphasizes the theme of divine government or Kingship. The Hiphil may imply God's imposition of his rule, and in consequence his 'peace', like that of an imperial sovereign over powers that would contest it, for example, *yām* and *tannîn*, which God holds in check (7.12) and 'the champions of Rahab' (9.13), a theme developed in postexilic eschatology, God's final punishment of 'the host of heaven, in heaven' (Isa. 24.21) and rebellious angels in Dan. 10.13.

3. *'ōr^e^ḇô* ('his ambush') sustains the military figure in v. 3a. The verb *qûm* for rising from an ambush (*ma'^a^rāḇ*) is used in Josh. 8.19. The sing. participle is collective, denoting the actual party in ambush.

4. The language is forensic. *zāḵāh* means 'to be clean', i.e., innocent, in parallelism with *ṣāḏaq*, as in Ps. 51.6 (cf. Mic. 6.11). There is a word-play between *zāḵāh* in this sense in v. 4 and as meaning 'pure' or 'bright' in v. 5.

5. In MT *'aḏ-yārēaḥ w^e^lō' yā'hîl* the ancient versions indicate that *'* in *ya'hîl* is a *mater lectionis*, the verb being *yāhēl* from *hālal* as in 31.26. This suggests the reading *'ôḏ yārēaḥ lō' yāhēl* ('even the moon does not continue to shine'). The *w* is omitted before *lō'* in certain Heb. MSS and S and T.

6. *tôlēʿāh* ('worm'), parallel to *rimmāh* ('worm') as in Isa. 14.11, means literally 'gnawer'.

26.5-11. This passage is omitted in the original version of the LXX. It is included in its present position in Theod., but that does not exclude the possibility that it is part of Bildad's speech. It may have been included in Bildad's speech in MT as part of the orthodox adjustment which the text apparently suffered in chs. 24–27 to soften the arguments of Job against the divine economy.

5. In view of the well-known motif of the conflict of God and the powers of Chaos, typified as in the Babylonian New Year liturgy and its Canaanite counterpart by the unruly waters and monsters of the deep, we take *mayim* with *šōḵᵉnêhem* as the subject of *yᵉḥôlᵉlû* (pausal form *yᵉḥôlālû*) which involves the reading of the colon:

> *hārᵉpāʾîm yᵉḥôlᵉlû mittaḥaṯ*
> *mayim wᵉšōḵᵉnêhem*

rᵉpāʾîm are primarily the shades in the underworld known to be consigned to the underworld with the various enemies of Cosmos including 'the Many-headed One', that is, *ltn*, or Leviathan (cf. 26.13) in a hymn to the sun included in the Baal myth of Ras Shamra (Gordon *UT* 62 rev., 38-52). Among these enemies of Baal who also menace his kingship and are put in subjection are *tnn* and *ltn*, *tannin* and Leviathan, who menace the kingship of Yahweh and are overthrown in the OT (e.g. Isa. 27.1; 51.9; Ps. 74.13-14). In his argument for the theodicy, Bildad is citing a Hymn of Praise from the liturgy of the New Year festival, the major theme of which was familiar in Israel.

From meaning the shades of the departed *rᵉpāʾîm* came to mean the vanished races who to the Israelites were invested with gigantic proportions, hence the rendering 'giants' in Theod., Jerome (commentary and Vulgate), S and T. Symmachus's rendering *theomachoi* obviously has in mind the Titan-myth, while Aq. merely transliterates.

6. The parallelism 'naked' (*ʿārôm*) // 'without covering' (*ʾên kᵉsûṯ*) is found again in 24.7, where the words are used literally. The omniscience of God penetrates even to Sheol, where Job had wished for refuge and oblivion (14.13). The parallelism Sheol // Abaddon ('Perdition') is found again in 28.22 and Prov. 15.11; 27.20. Abaddon is derived from *ʾābad* ('to perish'), but there is no certain derivation of Sheol. It may be a noun derived from *šōʾāh*, found in 30.14 meaning 'ruin' and in Isa. 10.3; 47.11; Zeph. 1.15 meaning 'ruin', or 'destruction' and compounded with *ʾēl* in the elative sense, meaning 'vast', or 'prodigious ruin'; cf. *harᵉrê ʾēl*, Pss. 36.7; 50.10; *ʾarᵉzê ʾēl*, Ps. 80.11.

7. *ṣāp̄ôn* in the OT designates generally the North, but this is a secondary meaning, derived from Mt Saphon, *jebel 'al-'aqrā* on the northern horizon of Ras Shamra, and the seat of Baal as King in the Ras Shamra texts after his victory over the forces of Chaos. *ṣāp̄ôn* in such a context symbolized the divine rule and order, like 'the mountain of the Lord's house' at Jerusalem (Isa. 2.2). It is doubtful if this is the sigificance of the word in the present passage. It derives rather from *ṣāp̄āh* ('to spread out'); cf. *ṣāppîṯ* ('carpet'). The Piel of the verb is used of overlaying with sheet or molten metal (1 Kgs 6.20, 32, 35) or laying a floor (1 Kgs 6.15); cf. *rāqa'*, with the same semantic range and the significance of 'firmament' or ceiling (*rāqîa'*) in Gen. 1.6ff.; cf. NEB 'spread the canopy of the sky over Chaos'. The establishment of the firmament over the void (*tōhû*) and the earth over 'nothing' (*b^e^lî-māh*) reflects the initial stage of creation from *tōhû wāḇōhû* in Gen. 1.2 (P). In vv. 7ff. note the introduction of the various exploits of God by participles, a regular feature of the Hymn of Praise in Israel and in Mesopotamia.

8. The conception of God 'who binds up the waters in his clouds' recalls Prov. 30.4, again in a rhetorical question, *mî ṣārar-mayîm baśśimlāh*. The figure in Job may envisage the water-seller's skin, which conserves the shape of the animal, with the apertures for the legs 'tied up'. The conception of the clouds as celestial water-skins (*niḇ^e^lê šāmayim*) is found again at 38.37. The verb *bāqa'* describes the colossal cloudburst in the Flood (Gen. 7.11) and the bursting of wineskins in 32.19.

9. Several Heb. MSS, Theod., S and V read *kissē'* ('throne'), seeing a reference to the veiling of the throne (cf. Isa. 66.1, 'the sky is my throne'). Duhm proposed to emend MT *p^e^nê* to *pinnê*, reading *m^e^'aḥēz kiss^e^'ô* ('establishing firmly the pillars of his throne'). Besides the fact that *pinnāh* is found in the masc. only once in a doubtful passage (Zech. 4.10), and means not 'pillar' but 'corner' or 'corner-stone', this would be the only instance of the Piel of *'āḥaz*, which has this meaning in the Qal. In this case *m^e^'aḥēz*, attested in the sense 'to close up' at Neh. 7.3, might be taken as cognate with Aram. and Syr. *'^a^ḥaḏ* ('to close up'); cf. Akk. *uḫuzzu* ('to overlay with gold or silver'; so Dhorme, Hölscher and G.R. Driver), a meaning which the verb has in the Hophal in 2 Chron. 9.18.

paršēz is a peculiar form, apparently a mixed form of *pāraš*, or rather *pāraś* ('to spread out') and *pāraz* ('to separate'). The form may have arisen from a scribal note of a variant reading, *ś* of the original *pāraś* being corrupted to *š* for the sake of pronunciation before final *z* in MT. At any rate, the verb is treated as *pāraś* ('to spread out') in Theod., S, T and V. The parallelism with *m^e^'aḥēz* in the sense 'overlays' supports this and may indicate the participle *pōrēś*.

10. The conception is that of God tracing a circle on the waters which surround the earth according to the Mesopotamian conception of the world, East and West being boundaries of light and dark. We should read the participle *ḥōqēq* in agreement with the style of this Hymn of Praise, but this refers to the unrepeated act of God in creation, hence the perfect may be read, *ḥaq-ḥûḡ*. The phrase recurs in the reference to creation in Prov. 8.27, *beḥûqô ḥûḡ 'al-penê tehôm*. We should take *ḥāqaq* here in the sense not of drawing or engraving, which it often has, but of defining, or prescribing, a boundary, as in 38.10; Jer. 5.22; Prov. 8.29; Ps. 148.6; Mic. 7.11, and in the phrase *belî ḥōq* ('without limit') in Isa. 5.14.

'im has here the sense 'to' as regularly in Ugaritic and occasionally in Heb., especially in comparison, meaning 'over against'.

11. 'The pillars of the sky' (*'ammûḏê šāmayîm*) recalls the Mesopotamian conception of the 'pillars of heaven' (*išid šamê*) laid at the horizon, which was also a Greek conception; cf. Pindar, *Pythian Odes* I, 39, 20 *kiōn ourania* ('the pillar of heaven').

The verb *rāp̄ap̄*, not attested elsewhere in the OT, is taken by Aq. and Jerome as 'rock, quake', probably cognate with Arab. *raffu* ('to throb, quake'). *rap̄* in Syr. means 'to be removed'.

The verb *yiṯmehû* is pointed as the imperfect Qal of *tāmah*, well known in Heb. as 'to be astounded'. This may seem odd of pillars, but no more so than pillars as the object of God's rebuke, *ga'arāṯô* ('his thunder'; cf. Pss. 18.6; 104.7; Isa. 50.2); that refers to the convulsions of nature such as the effect of thunder as the sign of the power of God (so, also of Baal in the Baal myths of Ras Shamra).

12. The verb *rāḡa'* poses a problem. The parallel *māḥaṣ rāhaḇ* suggests violent motion, as in Isa. 51.15 and Jer. 31.35, *rōḡa' hayyām wayyeḥemû gallāyw*. The verbal correspondence between those two passages indicates an origin in the liturgy. With the same relevance to God's control of the sea the verb *ḡā'ar* is used in Ps. 104.7, with which the reading of the verb in the present passage in S *gā'ar* would agree. This reading is not proposed by any of the versions in Isa. 51.15 and Jer. 31.35, so it is likely that the verb means 'to trouble', perhaps a metathetic cognate of Arab. *ra'aja* with this meaning in the IVth Form. The association with *yām* and *rahaḇ* in the present passage recalls the reference to *rahaḇ hammešubbāt* (MT *hēm šāḇeṯ*) in Isa. 30.7. For that reason we find it likely that *rāḡa'* is a homonym of the verb in Isa. 51.15 and Jer. 31.35, meaning 'to be at rest'; cf. Arab. *raja'a* ('to return', sc. to where one belongs, sc. to rest) and Jer. 47.6, *hērāḡ'î wāḏōmmî* ('be at rest and silent'), of a sword returned to its sheath. The parallel with *maḥaṣ* suggests that the verb may be transitive, perhaps Piel, though the Niphal in Jer. 47.14 indicates that the verb in the Qal has this sense.

māḥaṣ occurs in the same context of the establishment of Order against the menace of Chaos in the Baal myth of Ras Shamra; cf. Gordon *UT* 67 I, 1, 12: *ktmḫṣ ltn bṯn brḥ* ('though thou didst smite Lotan the primeval serpent'). On *rahaḇ*, possibly 'the agitated one', an appellative of Sea as the adversary of God in his establishment of Order, see above on 9.13. *kōaḥ* and *tᵉḇûnāh* ('power' and 'wisdom') are the instruments of God's ordered creation in Jer. 10.12, which like the present passage reflects the liturgy of the New Year festival.

13. It is proposed to read *rûḥô* for MT *bᵉrûḥô* as a fem. sing. subject to the verb in v. 13a. Dhorme understands MT *šip̄ᵉrāh* to refer to the wind dispelling the clouds, citing the use of the Arab. verb *śafara* with this sense. We prefer the suggestion of Lyon (1895: 134-35), *bᵉrûḥê šāmayim šibbērô* ('he broke him in pieces with the winds of heaven'). Dhorme surprisingly questions how winds could be said to break the monster in pieces. In fact in the Babylonian creation myth Marduk first distended the belly of Tiamat the monster of the Lower Deep with the storm-wind, which forced her mouth open; through her mouth he then shot an arrow which 'pierced her stomach, clave through her bowels, tore into her womb...' (Wilson 1858: 10). *bārēaḥ* (cf. *brḥ* the epithet of Lotan, the serpent in the Ras Shamra texts), does not mean 'fleeing', but 'belonging to the past'; cf. Arab. *bariḥa* ('to pass from one point to another', e.g. *'al-bāriḥu*, 'yesterday')

14. *hen* is the equivalent of Arab. *'innā* ('Verily!').

qᵉṣôṯ, if associated with Heb. *qēṣ* ('end'), from *qāṣaṣ* ('to break off'), means not the 'consummation' but the 'outskirts' of God's works, perhaps even 'fragments'. In view of the main theme of the passage, the ordered government of God, *dᵉrāḵô* (for MT *dᵉrāḵāyw*) must surely be taken as 'government', as *drkt* in the Ras Shamra texts in parallelism with *mlk* ('kingship') (Gordon *UT* Krt, 42), and *daraku*(*n*) in Arab. (so Dahood 1964a: 404).

In *mah-ššēmeṣ* Dhorme takes *mah* as exclamatory and *šēmeṣ* ('whisper') as derogatory. See above on 4.12.

In *dāḇār* in v. 14b the close connections between God's word or purpose and the event which he effects is well illustrated. In Heb. *dāḇār* signifies now the spoken word, and now the matter in purpose or effect, that is to say the event. Here perhaps the nuance is 'purpose' as in Arab. *dabbara*, for example the proverb *'al-'inśānu yudabbiru wallāhu yuqaddiru* ('Man proposes, God disposes').

gᵉḇûrōṯāyw (for MT *gᵉḇûrōṯāw*) is either a plural of excellence or an abstract plural.

The thunder (*ra'am*) is the voice of God which proclaims his power and heralds the rain, which was anticipated at the New Year festival, where the theme was God's triumph over the menace of Chaos and his establishment as

King. In the Baal myth of Ras Shamra, which was related to the same occasion and celebrating the same theme, Baal, in announcing a new phase of creative activity, boasts of his new weapon, lightning, the secret of which he declares (Gordon *UT* ʻnt III, 17-28):

rgm ltdʻ nšm	A word which men do not know,
wltbn hmlt ʼarṣ	Nor the multitudes of earth understand.

Lévêque (1970: I, 306f.) does well to note that apart from in the Book of Job, *raʻam* ('thunder') occurs only four times in the OT: in Ps. 77.19 (EVV 18), where the Great Deliverance at the Reed Sea is a specific instance of the assertion of God's order, the theme of the great Autumn Festival, where his triumph over Chaos was celebrated; in Ps. 81.8 (EVV 7) in connection with the same theme on the same cultic occasion; in Ps. 104.7, in connection with God's triumph over the chaotic waters as a prelude to creation, so feasibly in the same cultic context; and in Isa. 29.6, with reference to the theophany and reassertion of the order of God in the political situation.

Job 27

JOB'S FINAL RESPONSE TO HIS FRIENDS

Ascribed to Job (v. 1), there is general agreement that 27.2-6 truly expresses his ardent assertion of his innocence and his determination to maintain his integrity. But beyond this point the majority of scholars judge the matter of this chapter quite uncharacteristic of Job. The condemnation of the ungodly man and his hopeless prospect (vv. 7-10), with the poem on his miserable end (vv. 13-23), has been assigned to Zophar, whose sentiments it certainly expresses, despite the fact that there is no customary ascription to him (so Bickell, Duhm, Peake, Strahan, Stevenson, Ball, G.B. Gray, Hertzberg, Barton, Lefèvre, Tournay, Pope). Dhorme and Hölscher regard vv. 7-12 as Job's statement, confining Zophar's address to vv. 13-23. According to Dhorme, Zophar's statement begins at v. 13 and continues with 24.18-24; 27.14-23, which would correspond more closely to the proportions of the various rounds of debate. Hölscher is also conscious of the deficiency of 27.13-23 as a speech of Zophar, and conjectures the loss of the first part of his statement. Fohrer assigns vv. 11-12 to Job as the end of his statement in 26.1-4; 27.2-6, and regards 27.7-10, 13-23 as a separate poem on the end of the wicked. In view of Zophar's known sentiments on that subject, it may be, if Fohrer is right, that this was a separate poem intended to be at some stage of the redaction of the Book Zophar's third statement, but never actually assigned to him. On Fohrer's view vv. 11-12,

> I will teach you concerning the hand of God,
> What is with the Almighty I will not conceal.
> You have all seen it for yourselves.
> Why then this empty vapouring?

is Job's statement, though he finds difficulty in believing that what Job had to communicate is anything new. Thus he concludes that vv. 13-23 are no part of Job's statement, and conjectures that Job's communication here promised has been lost. On our analysis of ch. 27 we would assign the whole to Job.

We would resolve the chapter, Job's final reply to his friends, into three strophes (vv. 2-6, 7-10, 11-23). In vv. 2-6, introduced by an oath, Job protests his integrity and refuses to accept his friends' assumption that his suffering betokens sin. In vv. 7-10 he invokes the convention of curse in the Plaint of the Sufferer on those who alienate themselves from him ('his enemy' or 'antagonist') on the assumption that such as sinners are alienated from God. In

vv. 8-10 the consequences of the curse are elaborated. Here we would see the implication that Job expresses his awareness of the consequences if his assertion of innocence under oath were unfounded. In vv. 11-12, in didactic style, Job introduces his elaboration of the fate of the wicked in vv. 13-23, with whom he has associated his antagonists in v. 7, citing their own theme in their arguments against him, 'all of which they have seen for themselves', well-worn dicta assimilated superficially and repeated parrot-fashion, hence 'empty vapouring' (v. 12). This may well be the citation of a poem from the Plaint of the Sufferer in its application in the Wisdom tradition.

We suggest that the new element of which Job proposes to convince his friends (v. 11), who have recurrently but objectively expatiated upon divine retribution, was his subjective appreciation of the consequences if he were as guilty as they allege. After Job's initial oath, therefore, we would assign vv. 13ff. to Job as having the same force as the imprecation in his oath of purgation in ch. 31. This character of Job's final statement to his friends, with oath (vv. 2-6) and imprecation expressed (v. 7) and implied (vv. 8ff.) explains the heading to the chapter as Job's *māšāl*; cf. Balaam's curses and imprecations in colourful figures (Num. 23.6ff., 18f.; 24.3ff., 15ff., 20, 21f., 23f.)

Chapter 27

1. And Job added his sworn declaration and said:

2. 'As God lives who has put aside my right,
As the Almighty lives who has embittered my life!
3. As long as all my breath is within me,
And the God-given breath is in my nostrils,
4. My lips shall speak no falsehood,
Nor my tongue patter deceit!
5. God forbid that I should admit that you were right!
Till I die I will not give up my integrity.
6. I hold fast to my innocence and will not let it go;
None of my days is a reproach[1] to my heart.

7. Let my enemy be as the wicked,
My antagonist as the unrighteous!
8. For what is the hope of the godless[2]
When he lifts up his soul to God?[3]
9. Will God listen to his cry
When distress comes upon him?
10. Will he have confidence in the Almighty?
If he calls to God, will his entreaty be admitted?[4]

11. I will teach you concerning the power of God,
The purpose of the Almighty I will not hide.
12. You have all seen it for yourselves;
Why then this empty vapouring?
13. This is the portion[5] of the wicked from God,
And the lot of the tyrant[6] which he will receive from the Almighty.

14. If his sons grow up it is for the sword,
And his offspring have not enough to eat;
15. Those of his sons who have survived are gathered up[7] by the plague,
And he will have no widows to weep.
16. Though he heap up silver like dust,
And lay up dress in piles,
17. He may provide himself, but the just shall wear it,
And the innocent shall divide the silver;
18. His house which he builds is like a bird's nest,
Even like the hut which a crop-watcher makes.
19. He lies down rich for he has a store;[8]
He opens his eyes and it is gone.
20. Terrors overtake him by day,[9]
In the night he is snatched away by a tempest.
21. The east wind lifts him up and he is gone,
Yea, it sweeps him from his place;

22. Men bombard him without mercy,
He strives hard to flee from their power.
23. Men clap their hands at him,[10]
And hiss him away from wherever he may be.'

Textual Notes to Chapter 27

1. Reading *yeḥārep̄* for MT *yeḥerap̄*.
2. Omitting MT *kî yiḇṣā'* after the corruption of v. 8b. See following note.
3. Reading *yiśśā' le'elôah nap̄šô* after LXX and S for MT *yēšel 'elôah nap̄šô* in agreement with the following verse.
4. Reading *yē'āṯēr-lô* with LXX and S for MT *bekol-'ēṯ*.
5. Omitting the superfluous *'āḏām*, *metri causa*.
6. Reading *'ārîṣ* for MT *'ārîṣîm*, omitting final *m* as a dittograph before the following *m*.
7. Reading *yiqqaḇēṣû* for MT *yiqqaḇērû*. See Commentary *ad loc.*
8. Reading *welô 'āsôp̄* for MT *welō' yē'āsēp̄*.
9. Reading kayyôm for mt kammayim. See Commentary ad loc.
10. Reading *yiśpōq 'ālāyw kappayim* with Theod. and V, assuming dittography of *m* before *w* in the Old Heb. script. For MT *kappêmô* S and LXX[A] and [L] read 'his hand'.

Commentary on Chapter 27

1. In MT *māšāl* (lit. 'likeness'), insofar as it applies to Job's declaration, might be rendered as 'reflection', denoting the statement of truths *corresponding* to experience, like Proverbs (*mišelê šelōmōh*) and, like them, couched in figurative language and often simile. But in view of Job's curse upon his estranged friends as 'the wicked', elaborated in graphic detail in vv. 4ff., *māšāl* may have the same significance as *māšāl* introducing Baalam's pronouncements in Num. 23.6ff., 18ff; 24.3ff., 15ff., 20, 21f., 25f. The curse, with consequences graphically elaborated thus becoming a by-word or admonitory example (*māšāl*), is well exemplified in the Twelve Adjurations and the sequel in Deut.

27.15-26; 28.16ff.; cf. esp. v. 37. This well exemplifies Job's oath (vv. 2-4) and its amplification (vv. 8, 14-23), with his awareness of the like consequences to himself of guilt and hypocrisy, like his self-imprecation in his great oath of purgation (ch. 31). This suitably ends his dialogue with his friends. Though we may understand this specific sense of Job's *māšāl* in ch. 27, we do not find it possible to express its full connotation in a single word, certainly not 'discourse' of EVV, but hope that 'sworn declaration' may convey the sense.

2. The clauses *hēsîr mišpāṭî* and *hēmar napšî* are relative clauses, the relative particle being omitted as often in poetry.

3. *kî* is the asseverative particle introducing the vow after the oath. The apparent tmesis between *kol* and *nišmāṯî* (cf. *kol-'ôd napšî bî* in 2 Sam. 1.9) is explained in GKC (§128e) as not tmesis at all, but, 'on the assumption of the adverbial sense of *kol*, 'wholly''. According to the punctuation of MT, however, *'ôd* is regarded as a noun, which is apparent in the phrases *bᵉ'ôḏî* and *mē'ôḏî*, *kol-'ôḏî* meaning thus 'the whole while' (so Dillmann, Budde, Ehrlich, whom we follow). *nᵉšāmāh* is here the life-breath, and *rûaḥ*, which may denote inspiration, has here the same significance, though the physical breath is visible evidence of the invasive divine influence (*rûaḥ*); cf. Gen. 2.7.

4. *hāḡāh* means 'to con over' inaudibly or audibly, as for instance the Law (Ps. 1.2). In the present passage, by our translation 'patter' we have tried to convey the manner of the recital of conventional moral platitudes, which Job spurns. Specifically Job may be disowning acquiescence in his friends' indictment and their exhortation to seek pardon for guilt that he will not admit, the substance of his declaration in v. 5.

5. *ḥālîlāh llî* ('*ad profanum!*') is part of the oath formula, indicating that which was not to be tolerated with relation to God. The acuteness of Job's dilemma is underlined in this passage in his oath by the life of God who, he claimed, had wronged him (v. 2) and by his assertion that to admit the guilt that his friends allege against his own clear conscience would be sacrilege in the sight of God.

6. The verb *ḥārap̄* is attested as transitive in the Qal (e.g. Pss. 69.10; 119.42; Prov. 27.11), but is generally used transitively in the Piel, which we adopt here. The objection to MT *lō'-yeḥᵉrap̄ lᵉḇāḇî miyyāmāy* is that the verb seems to want an object. It is proposed to find that in *miyyāmāy*, *min* being taken in the partitive sense, 'None of my days is a reproach to my heart', sc. conscience (so Dillmann and the older commentators), which we adopt. Duhm and Dhorme emended *yeḥᵉrap̄* to *yeḥpar* ('my heart is not ashamed of my days').

7. The colon, assigning Job's adversaries (his 'enemy', *'ōyēḇ*, and 'antagonist', *miṯqômēm*), that is, those who, in inferring his guilt from his suffering, alienate themselves from him, to the category of those who are foredoomed to the

punishment described in vv. 8-10, 14ff., is to be understood in the formal category of the curse of the innocent sufferer in the Plaint of the Sufferer, esp. Pss. 58.7-10 (EVV 6-9); 69.23-29 (EVV 22-28); 139.19-22.

8. According to MT of vv. 8ff., the sense is 'What hope has a man of a hearing when he is cut off (*yibbāṣēa'* being read by Oort) when God withdraws (*yēšel*) his life?' But Hölscher feasibly proposes that *kî yibbāṣēa'* is a gloss on *yēšel 'ᵉlôah napšô* after the corruption of an original *yiśśa' le'ᵉloah napšô* ('lifts his soul to God'), read by Ball, Dhorme, Tur-Sinai, Hölscher and Peake after S. For the phrase *nāśā' nepeš*, meaning 'to appeal', cf. Deut. 24.15; Pss. 25.1; 86.4; 143.8; Jer. 22.27. This reading and interpretation is supported by the following verse. This sense of *yiśśa' napšô* suggested to Mandelkern that MT *kî yibṣa'* should be emended to *kî yipga'* ('when he entreats', so also Dhorme). This, however, in our opinion, overloads the colon, though it is admitted by Mowinckel, Pope and Terrien.

10. On *yiṯ'annāḡ* ('puts his confidence in'), see on 22.6. Taking the parallelism in vv. 9-10 as chiastic, we accept the reading *yē'āṯēr-lô* ('will his entreaty be accepted?') for MT *bᵉkol-'ēṯ* ('at all times'), which has no parallel in the context (so Beer, Hölscher, Stevenson after LXX and S). *yiqrā'* is a case of the jussive in the protasis of a conditional sentence without a conditional particle (GKC, §159b).

11. *yāḏ* (lit. 'hand'), means here 'power' or even 'management' as parallel to 'purpose'.

'ᵃšer 'im-šadday (lit. 'what is with the Almighty') denotes God's intimate thought and purpose; cf. *'immāḵ* in parallelism with *bilᵉḇaḇᵉḵā* in 10.13; cf. 9.35; 23.14; 1 Kgs 11.11 and Arab. *'andī kaḏā* (lit. 'with me like this', i.e. 'it is my opinion').

12. *heḇel* is used here as in 7.16; 9.29; 21.34, and the refrain in Eccl. 1.2; 2.1, 14, 15; 6.4, 12; 7.15; 9.9; etc. to mean vapour or what is insubstantial.

13. As the verse stands in MT it consists of two cola, each of four beats. This is supported by the ancient versions, but it may well have consisted originally of two cola, each of three beats. MT may be reduced by the omission of *'āḏām*, which seems superfluous in v. 13a and by *yiqqāḥû* in v. 13b, which seems pleonastic.

' in MT *'im-'ēl sh*ould probably be omitted as a dittograph of ' in *rāšā'* notwithstanding *'im* meaning 'from' in Ugaritic, which Dahood considers (*UHP*, p. 32; Pope).

In v. 13b the versions attest MT *'ᵃrîṣîm*, which we suspect after the sing. *rāšā'* in the parallel colon, and we assume a dittograph of final *m* before *miššadday*.

14. In v. 14a *lᵉmô-ḥāreḇ* (pausal), where the archaic form of the preposition may be noted, is a truncated form of the nominal sentence as the apodosis of a conditional sentence.

15. MT *śᵉrîḏāyw* (Qere) *bammāweṯ yiqqāḇērû* ('his survivors shall be buried by the death') is highly suspect and various conjectures have been made. Stevenson's conjecture *šōḏᵉḏim yāmîṯû qᵉrōḇāyw* is not so far from MT as it seems and, if correct, would imply a man would have no kinsman to bury him, nor widows to mourn him (v. 15b) in his community since they too would be captured by raiders. The sword and famine having been listed as taking off a man's family, it is natural to look for a third cause of death. This Dhorme found in pestilence, in which sense he took *hammāweṯ* of MT, where the definite article excludes 'death'. Dhorme cites this specific meaning of *mûtu* in the Tell el-Amarna Tablets (Knudtzon 1908–15: 244, 31f.), and *mûtânu* as the appellative of the plague in Ass. (so Buttenwieser and Mowinckel). Still, the statement 'his survivors will be buried by the plague' is strange, and we propose the emendation *yiqqāḇēṣû* for MT *yiqqāḇērû* ('[his survivors] will be gathered by the plague'), which recalls the passage in the Ugaritic Legend of Krt, 18 *mḫmšt y'itṣp ršp* ('at five years old Rešef gathered them to himself'); cf. Arab. *qubiḍa* (lit. 'he was gathered', i.e. he died). The implication is that his wives will also be taken so that he will have no widows to mourn him nor, if he die childless, will his name and estate be perpetuated by levirate marriage. In support of this interpretation is the alternative of *māweṯ* and *ḥereḇ* in Jer. 15.2; 43.11, where also, significantly, *māweṯ* has the definite article.

16. For MT *malbûš* ('clothing') LXX read 'gold', which the parallelism would lead us to expect. But the sequel in v. 17 supports MT. Clothes, implying the wardrobe of a rich man, with which he is at pains to provide himself (*yāḵîn*) contrast the meagre shift of the poor. The equation wicked/rich, poor/righteous (*ṣaddîq*) reflects the sentiment of the Plaint of the Sufferer in the Psalms, and the conception of the 'righteous, falling heir to the possessions of the wicked' recalls Prov. 13.22. *hēḵîn* (lit. 'cause to be') in the sense of 'providing beforehand' is attested in 1 Chron. 22.8, 14 (materials for the Temple), and in Job 39.41 (food for the ravens).We take *ḥōmer* as a homonym of *ḥōmer* ('mud'), attested in the 'piles' (*ḥᵒmārîm*) of dead frogs in the plague in Egypt (Exod. 8.10); cf. the wordplay between the word in this sense and *ḥᵃmōr* ('ass') in Samson's exploit with the jaw-bone of an ass (Judg. 15.10).

18. On v. 18a LXX has a conflation of two readings, MT *'āš* ('moth') and *'ᵃḵāḇîš* ('spider'); cf. 8.14, where 'the house of the spider' is the symbol of impermanence. The latter reading is supported by S (so Mowinckel, Fohrer, Terrien). It is suggested on the other hand that MT *'āš* is cognate with Arab *'aššu(n)* ('a bird's nest'; so Schultens, Ehrlich, Dhorme); cf. Akk. *asasu*, which gives a better parallel with the hut of the watcher of the crops in v. 18b (*sukkāh 'āśāh nōṣēr*, cf. Arab. *nāṭiru[n]*).

19. For MT *yē'āsēp̄* ('he will [not] be gathered') LXX and S read *yôsip̄* ('he will not do so again'). Taking the pronominal suffix in *'ênennû* to refer to the man's wealth (RSV) rather than to himself, we would find an antecedent in *'āsōp̄* ('store'), and for MT *welō' yē'āsēp̄* we suggest *welô 'āsōp̄* ('he has a store'); cf. Neh. 12.25; 1 Chron. 26.15.

20. The parallel 'by night' in v. 20b indicates *yômām* ('by day') for MT *kammayim* (Wright, Budde, Ehrlich, Ball, Dhorme, Hölscher) or *kayyôm*.

The feminine singular of the verb with the feminine plur., here *ballāhôṯ* (cf. *še'al-nā' behēmôṯ weṯōrekkā*, 12.7), is the regular agreement in Arab. when the verb precedes the subject.

gānaḇ here has not so much the sense of removing stealthily as summarily, as in kidnapping in the Book of the Covenant (Exod. 21.16) and Deut. 24.7; cf. Gen. 40.15 (of Joseph being kidnapped and sent away summarily to Egypt). The verb has probably the same sense in the Decalogue (Exod. 20.15; Deut. 5.19) (Alt 1953).

21. *qāḏîm* ('the East wind') is the sirocco, the blasting hot wind from the desert, and is so understood by Theod, and V, where it is rendered as 'the burning wild'; cf. the sudden ruin of Job's family (1.18).

The Piel of *śā'ar* is a denominative verb from *śa'ar*, an orthographic variant of the more common *sa'ar* ('whirlwind').

The driving forth of the miscreant in vv. 20ff., every man's hand against him (vv. 22-23), recalls the fate of Cain (Gen. 4.12-15) and of the murderer of Dn'il's son in the Ras Shamra text (Gordon *UT* 'Aqht 152ff.), on whom Dn'il invokes a curse that he should be

> *'amd gr bt 'il* Ever seeking sanctuary at the shrine of El,
> *'nt brḥ p'lmh* A fugitive now and for ever.

22. *hišlîḵ 'al* ('to throw a missile at') without the direct object is found in Num. 35.20. The pronominal suffix in *yāḏô* refers to the indefinite subject of *hišlîk* ('one', i.e. persons).

23. The clapping of the hands, perhaps with a glancing blow of palm from palm, as in the Arab gesture to indicate that an affair is finished, is like whistling (cf. Lam. 2.15; Jer. 49.17; Zeph. 2.15), a gesture of mockery.

Job 28

An Independent Poem on the Transcendence of Wisdom

This is an independent poem on the transcendence of Wisdom. It is of uncertain authorship, possibly composed by one of the circle of the author. It may an independent composition by the author of the Book of Job himself, justly valued by his circle and included in the Book in appreciation of the master. Its insertion at this point was determined by the fact that the Dialogue with the friends ends with Job's declaration in ch. 27 before his direct challenge to God in his *apologia pro vita sua* (ch. 29), culminating in his oath of purgation (ch. 31). As anticipating the theme of the Divine Declaration (38.1–40.14), the poem was probably not included by the author of the Book. As a sapiential poem on the transcendence of Wisdom it has a general literary affinity with the self-laudation of Wisdom in Proverbs 8 or the short hymn on Wisdom and its benefits in Prov. 3.13-18.

The poem is divided into three parts, possibly strophes, by the refrain 'Where shall Wisdom be found…?' (v. 12) and 'Whence comes Wisdom?' (v. 20). The omission of the question from the beginning of the poem indicates that it is a conclusion to vv. 1-11 and vv. 13-19, but as such it serves also as an introduction to vv. 13-19 and vv. 21-27 (v. 28 being an appendix), with a certain analogy to question and answer in the sapiential tradition (e.g. Prov. 23.29ff.; Eccl. 8.1ff.; so Westermann 1977: 104-107). Fohrer after Duhm divides the poem into four strophes: vv. 1-6, 7-11 + 24, 12-18 (19?), 20-27. Besides the interrogatory introduction at vv. 12 and 20, he conjectures its inclusion before vv. 1 and 7 (so also Lefèvre). This, however, has no support either in MT or any of the ancient versions. The subject-matter of vv. 1-11, the inaccessibility of Wisdom to humans who determinedly penetrate the furthest regions and 'move mountains'(v. 9) in persistent prospecting for precious metals and gems, does not readily fall into two strophes. Nor does vv. 12-19, on the inestimable value of Wisdom, present such a strophe as Fohrer claims, opening as it does with the same theme as vv. 1-11, while vv. 21-27, where, after deliberate suspense, the answer is reached, is certainly a definite strophe, as Fohrer recognizes. On such considerations we propose to treat the poem as falling into three parts distinguished by the interrogatory refrain in vv. 12 and 20.

The subject matter indicates that vv. 7-8 in have been displaced from between vv. 12 and 13, and v. 28 is probably an editorial gloss (see Commentary *ad loc.*). In admitting that wisdom is accessible to humans, except by the fear of God, v. 28 apparently contradicts, or at least modifies, the main part of the poem on the transcendence of Wisdom. Another indication of the editorial gloss is the divine title *ʾaḏōnay*, which is unique in the Book.

Chapter 28

1. Surely there is a mine for silver,
And a place for gold which humans refine.
2. Iron is taken from the earth;
And humans make stone to exude[1] copper.
3. Humanity[2] has put an end to the darkness,
Searching its furthest bounds
For stones in gloom and darkness.
4. They have opened shafts[3] where no one lives;
Let down[4] without foothold,
They have hung far from others; they have swayed to and fro.
5. The earth from which food should come
Is turned[5] underneath[6] into something like a fire,
6. A place the stones of which are lapis lazuli
With its specks[7] of gold.
9. (Humanity) has put forth its hand on the flinty rock,
And overturned mountains by the roots.
10. In the rocks they have cut channels,
And their eyes have seen every precious thing.
11. They have searched[8] the sources[9] of rivers,
And brought hidden resources[10] to light.
12. But Wisdom—whence comes she?[11]
And where is the abode of understanding?

7. The pathway the vulture knows not,
Nor has the eye of the hawk descried it.
8. Big game has not trodden it,
Nor the lion passed over it.
13. Humanity does not know the way to it,[12]
Nor is she found in the land of the living.
14. The deep says, 'She is not in me',
And the sea says, 'She is not with me'.
15. No fine gold may be given for her,
Nor silver weighed out as her price.
16. Not in gold of Ophir can she be valued,
In precious onyx and lapis lazuli.
17. Gold and glass are not to be valued with her,
Jewels of fine gold cannot be exchanged for her.
18. Speak not of coral or crystal;
The possession of Wisdom is above rubies.

19. The topaz of Cush cannot compare with her,
In pure gold she cannot be valued.
20. But Wisdom—whence comes she?
And where is the abode of understanding?

21. She is hidden from the eyes of all living,
She is concealed from the birds of the heavens.
22. Perdition and Death declare,
'With our ears have we heard a rumour of her'.
23. God understands the way to her,
And He knows her abode;
24. For He looks to the ends of the earth;
He sees all that is under the heavens.[13]
25. He who settled[14] the force of the wind,
And meted out the waters by measure,
26. When he made a decree for the rain,
And a course for the rumble of the thunder;
27. Then did he consider and assess her,
He studied her[15] and explored her potentialities.
28. And he said to humanity, "Behold!
The fear of the Lord is Wisdom,
And turning from wrong is understanding".'

Textual Notes to Chapter 28

1. Reading *yāṣîq* or *yaṣṣîq* for MT *yāṣûq*. See Commentary *ad loc.*
2. Inserting *'āḏām* after *śam* as an antecedent to *hû'* in v. 3b.
3. Reading *pārᵉṣû* for MT *pāraṣ* assuming omission of *w* by haplography before *n* of *nᵉḥālîm* and assuming haplography of *m* in MT *naḥal.*
4. Assuming MT *hanniškāḥîm* to be a corruption of *hannišpāḥîm* ('let down'). See Commentary *ad loc.*
5. Reading *nehpᵉḵāh* in agreement with *'ereṣ.*
6. Reading *taḥtêhā* for MT *wᵉṯaḥtêhā*, *w* being a dittograph of *m* in preceding word in the Old Heb. script.
7. Understanding the plur. as 'dust particles'.
8. Reading *ḥippēš* with LXX, Aq., Theod. and V for MT *ḥibbēš*. See Commentary *ad loc.*
9. Reading *mibbᵉḵê* for *mibbᵉḵî*. See Commentary *ad loc.*
10. Reading fem. sing. ending for MT possessive suffix.
11. Reading *tāḇô'* with one Heb. MS, cf. v. 20, for MT *timmāṣē'*. Alternatively *tēṣē'* may be read.
12. Reading *darkāh* with LXX for MT *'erkāh* ('comparison'), which is probably a secondary variant.
13. Reading *kol-taḥaṯ-haššāmayim metri causa* with LXX and V for MT *taḥaṯ kol-haššāmayim.*
14. Reading *ha'ōśeh* after LXX, A and V, where a perfect or a participle is suggested.
15. Reading *hᵉḇînāh* for MT *hᵉḵînāh* with five Heb. MSS.

Commentary on Chapter 28

1. *kî* may be formally a conjunction, in which case it would indicate that the poem was introduced by the interrogative refrain (so Duhm, Fohrer). But, rejecting such an assumption, we regard it as the asseverative enclitic, as in Ugaritic, where it emphasizes the final verb (e.g. Gordon, *UT* 51, II, 13f., *hlk b'l 'ṯtrt kt'n*, 'Atharat indeed eyed the going of Baal'), and in Heb. poetry introducing the final verb (e.g. Ps. 118.10-12) or a final statement (e.g. Deut. 32.9). The parallelism with *lazzāhāḇ yāzōqqû* ('for gold which they refine') suggested to Dahood (1963c: 52) that *môṣā'*, from *yāṣā'*, is cognate with Arab. *waḍu'a* ('to be pure', hence, 'to refine'), or, as he suggested, 'to smelt'. The parallelism with *māqôm*, however, indicates the meaning 'source' or 'mine'. The verb *zāqaq*, used of refined metal in 1 Chron. 28.18; 29.4; Ps. 12.7 and parallel to *ṭihar* ('to purify') in Mal. 3.3, may be a cognate of Ass. *zaqâqu* ('to blow violently') as in the refining process. The verb describes distillation from the clouds in 36.27 and purified wine in Isa. 25.6, so that it may be no more than an incidental homonym of Ass. *zaqâqu*.

2. *'eḇen*, being fem., must be the object of the verb, the subject being indefinite ('one makes to exude...'). The verb may be either the Hiphil of *ṣûq* (cf. 29.6, *ṣûr yāṣûq...šāmen*, 'the rock used to exude...olive oil'), in which case *yāṣîq* or *yaṣṣîq* should be read for MT *yāṣaq*, with the same meaning. Terrestrial iron as distinct from meteoric iron came into use in Palestine in the thirteenth century BCE, having been already worked by the Hittites in Asia Minor in the middle of the second millennium BCE, when it was still a precious metal in Egypt. In the first millennium BCE it was mined in the Ajlun district of Transjordan (Glueck 1945–49: 336-50) and worked at Khirbet Deir Alla, possibly Sukkoth, in the Jordan Valley.

3. *taḵlîṯ*, as in 26.10, means the 'limit' or 'outmost boundary'. In v. 3c *'eḇen 'ōp̄el w^eṣalmûṯ* (MT *ṣalmāweṯ*) is taken by Hölscher as a gloss (so Fohrer). We have taken *'eḇen* as a collective sing., the object of the search, precious stones and ores which were set in gloom and darkness. Pope and Terrien apparently take it in opposition to *taḵlîṯ* as the 'rock' which is searched. The final colon of a tricolon is always suspect to Hölscher, but an occasional tricolon was used to relieve the monotony of the prevailing bicola. If the colon v. 3c is original, *'eḇen* as the object of *ḥôqēr* in v. 3b is suspended until the final colon, a literary convention quite common in Heb. and Ugaritic poetry; see, for example, Gordon *UT* 127, 54f.:

yṯbr ḥrn ybn	May Horon break, my son,
yṯbr ḥrn r'išk	May Horon break thy head,
'ṯtrt šm b'l qdqdk	Athterat-name-of-Baal thy skull.

A glossator would surely have used a much less poetic figure and form. It may be noted that v. 3c is omitted in LXX, which also omits vv. 4a, 5-9a, 14-19, 21b-22a, 26b-27a. This, however, indicates compassion in LXX rather than glosses to the original text, such compassion being a marked literary tendency in LXX.

4. In view of the 3rd plur. verbs *dallû* and *nāʿû*, we would read MT *pāraṣ* in v. 4c as plur., either in *scriptio defectiva* or with the omission of final *w* by haplography before the following *n* in the Old Heb. script. For MT *naḥal* the plur. should possibly be read. The word in Heb. and Arab. normally means 'valley' or 'torrent', but in Late Heb. it denotes the shaft or gallery of a mine, comparable possibly to a narrow valley. In MT *hanniškāḥîm minnî-reḡel* ('forgotten from/without foot') is practically unintelligible. We would suggest that the verb is a scribal corruption of the verb *śāp̄aḥ* in the square script. This verb, meaning 'to pour', may be understood in the context as 'paying out' a rope on which workers are 'let down' 'without a foothold' (*minnî-reḡel*). Heb. *śāp̄aḥ* has an Arab. cognate *śafaḥa* with the same meaning, and the noun *śafaḥu*(*n*) ('foot of mountain') may derive from a homonym meaning 'to lower', but this we cannot attest. MT *dallû* is assumed to be from *dālal*, which has an Arab. cognate, *dalla*, used in the form *tadaldala* ('to dangle'), the obvious sense of the verb in v. 4c. *dālal* seems a byform of the more usual *dālāh*, which has this sense in Prov. 29.7. In v. 4a, reading *pāraṣ nᵉḥālîm ʿam gēr* (pausal *gār*) for MT *pāraṣ naḥal mēʿim-gār*, Graetz renders 'a strange people has bored galleries' (so Giesebrecht, Dhorme, Hölscher, Fohrer), after V and S. This may be supported by the remoteness of the mining operations from where the Book of Job was written or to specialized industry of a miners' and smiths' caste, such as the Kenites, who might fairly be called *ʿam gār* as federates of Israel. Dhorme notes besides that Semitic foreigners were employed by the Egyptians in the mines of Sinai, as their graffiti show. Similarly, condemned Christians were employed by the Romans in the copper mines of Punon (modern Feinān) and other mines in the escarpment east and west of the Arabah. *gēr* may have already acquired the connotation of 'slave', as apparently in 1 Chron. 22.2 and 2 Chron. 2.16ff., where *gērîm* ('resident and protected aliens') were conscripted by Solomon for public works (so Buttenwieser). *mēʾᵉnôš* ('far from men'), however, in v. 4c indicates that MT *mēʿim gār* is parallel, and means 'where no one lives', *min* in both cases indicating remoteness or an uninhabited region. The operation, and indeed the whole verse, is reminiscent of Bedouin ventures in the quest for scroll fragments in the Dead Sea escarpments and the Wadi Murabbaʿat.

5. The colon seems to point to the contrast, the natural production of food on the earth's surface in cooperation with nature and the unnatural 'rifling the bowels of their mother earth' which in consequence glows either with the miners' torches or by reason of the breaking of rocks with fire, a technique of mining known in ancient and modern times (so Hölscher after Löhr in 173ff.).

6. *māqôm sappîr 'ᵃḇānêhā* (ignoring the hyphen in MT) and taken in the sense 'a place the stones of which are lapis lazuli' may be suggested by the familiar description of the Promised Land in Deut. 8.9, 'a land of stones of which are iron'. This may have occasioned the use of the fem. pronominal suffix in *'ᵃḇānêhā*, which is incongruous with the masc. pronominal suffix in *lô* and after the antecedent *māqôm*. *'ap̄ᵉrōṯ zāhāḇ* (lit. 'dust-grains of gold') may refer to the shining specks of iron pyrites in lapis lazuli.

9. The poet selects the hardest stone 'flint' (*ḥallāmîš*), Akk. *elmešu*, as the object of human effort, and the largest mass, 'he has overturned mountains by the roots'.

10. *yᵉ'ōr* with the definite article or defined as *yᵉ'ōr miṣrayim* (Amos 8.8; cf. 9.5), is an Egyptian loanword, 'the Nile', and is taken here to denote figuratively mine-galleries. We question if the meaning is not rather drainage channels near the source of a river ('in the rocks') for diverting the streams in search for folds in their beds, which seems to agree with a kindred operation in v. 11, the damming up of rivers to bring hidden treasures to light.

11. *mibbᵉḵê*, or better *mabbᵉḵê*, *nᵉhārôṯ* may be preserved; cf. *mbk nhrm* ('the sources of the rivers'), the seat of El in the Ras Shamra texts (Gordon *UT* 49.I, 5; 51, IV, 21; 2 Aqht VI, 47), where the variation *nbk* also occurs.

For MT *ḥibbēš* ('he has bound up') LXX, Aq., Theod. and V render 'he has searched', which suggests *ḥippēš*, but the interchange of *b* and *p* might indicate an orthographic variant as frequently in Semitic languages. If *ḥibbēš* is read meaning 'binds up', the reference might be to the diversion of a river to search its bed for alluvial gold by damming up ('binding') its source (so Weiser, Gordis and Fohrer). But the 'searching' of the sources gives a more natural parallel to the bringing of the secrets to light in v. 11b, and should be accepted (so Mowinckel, Pope). The sources of rivers may refer to subterranean depths, whence the rivers rose from the lower deep of Semitic cosmology, but it may also refer to the depth of the sea or 'ocean currents' (*nᵉhārîm*), specifically referring to pearl fishing, as in the Persian Gulf. In MT *'ôr* we understand the locative sense, the locative ending being omitted in *scriptio defectiva*.

7. *'ayiṭ* (pausal *'āyiṭ*) is an unspecified bird of prey, such as those Abraham drove away from his sacrifice (Gen. 15.11), probably the vulture, selected because of its strong flight and far sight, and ready location of prey from an apparently impossible distance. The word is probably an appellative, 'screamer', from a verb known in 1 Sam. 25.14 (of Nabal scolding David), with Syr. and Arab. cognates.

'ayyāh may be cognate with Arab. *yu'yu'u*(*n*), a kind of hawk, possibly another onomatopoeic word 'screecher'.

The verb *šāzap̄* ('to look upon') is known only here and at 20.9 and in Song 1.6, *šeššᵉzāp̄aṯnî haššemeš* ('because the sun has looked upon me').

8. This is another pair of relative clauses qualifying *nāṯîḇ* ('a path'). *bᵉnê-šaḥaṣ*, a phrase used in the OT only here and in 41.26 possibly, is of uncertain significance. In Job 28.8 it is parallel to *šaḥal*, which is usually taken as a lion (see on 4.10). We should probably take *bᵉnê-šaḥaṣ* in its general sense 'great beasts' after the Arab. cognate cited by BDB, *šaḫiṣu(n)* ('bulky' or 'a man of great rank'), so 'big game'. The usual phonetic correspondence of Heb. *š* to Arab. *ś* or *t* is here contravened because of the final *ṣ*.

'āḏāh ('to pass') is known only here in the Qal in the OT. It is very common in Aram., Syr. and Arab. in the sense of 'passing on, away'.

This passage, describing the remoteness and inaccessibility of the place where Wisdom is to be found, insofar as it interrupts the account of mining in vv. 1-6, 9-11, is probably displaced from between vv. 12 and 13, where it effects a bridge between the passages on the inaccessibility of Wisdom and its rare value.

13. The verb *timmāṣē'* ('it is [not] attained'), in v. 13b supports the LXX reading *darkāh* ('the way to it') for MT *'erkāh*, which is probably a secondary variant which supplanted *darkāh* after association with vv. 15ff.

14. *tᵉhôm* is the subterranean water, Akk. *tiamtu*, the primordial power of Chaos subdued by Marduk; *yām* again denotes, as well as the sea confined to its proper place, the primordial power of chaos which menaced the power of Baal in the Canaanite myth of the New Year festival. In view of this association of the lower deep and the sea with the primordial conflict at which ordered creation emerged, there may be a double reference to Wisdom as beyond human attainment now and as being with God 'in the beginning' and above Chaos; cf. Prov. 8.22-31, particularly v. 24, 'when there were no depths (*tᵉhōmôṯ*) I was brought forth', and v. 29, 'When he assigned to the sea its limit (...then I was beside him)', also John 1.1, 'In the beginning was the Word, and the Word was with God...'

15. The incomparable value of Wisdom beyond that of precious stones, the theme of vv. 15-19, is the theme also of Prov. 8.10-11, 19.

sāḡûr for MT *sᵉḡôr*, in full *zāhāb sāḡûr*, found in 1 Kgs 6.20, is taken by Dhorme as 'massive gold', citing Ass. *huraṣû sagru*, and suggesting that the root of Heb. *sāḡûr* is *sāḡar* ('to close'). The term, however, may be connected with Arab. *śajara* ('to heat in an oven or crucible'), so meaning 'to refine'.

taḥtêhā means lit. 'in its place', as in the succession of kings in the Books of Kings.

16. *lō'-tᵉsulleh* means literally 'it will not be balanced', that is, weighed. The verb is found only here and at v. 19, again in the Pual, and as a variant form in Lam. 4.2. BDB connects it with *sal* ('a basket', Gen. 40.16, 17, 18; Exod. 29.3, 23, 32; Lev. 8.2, 26, 31; Num. 6.15, 17, 19; Judg. 6.19), in which grain was probably weighed, hence the meaning 'to weigh'.

keṯem is understood by all the ancient versions through its association with Ophir as 'gold'. The word is possibly cognate with Ass. *katâmu* ('to cover, or close up'); cf. Arab. *katama* ('to conceal'). The term may have arisen through the careful concealment of gold in store or transit. A more probable explanation is given by Pope on the basis of Egyptian references to *nb-n-ktm* ('gold of *ktm*'), *ktm* denoting the deserts of Upper Egypt and the Sudan from which gold (*nb*) was drawn, making Egypt the great source, or entrepot, of gold in the ancient Near East, as is indicated in the Tell el-Amarna tablets. The locality of Ophir is uncertain. In Gen. 10.29 it is located between Sheba and Havilah, thus in southern Arabia. The mention of apes and baboons among Solomon's cargoes from Ophir (1 Kgs 9.28f.), however, suggests remoter regions, which have been sought in Africa and India. Since Solomon's trading voyages lasted three years (1 Kgs 10.22) it has been suggested that Ophir must have been much further away than southern Arabia or Somaliland (Punt), which is known from Egyptian inscriptions as a source of gold. In favour of East Africa is the known Phoenician contact with the region between the Zambesi and the Limpopo. The Sanskrit word for 'apes', however, in 1 Kgs 10.22 suggests contacts with India. In view of the biblical tradition that Ophir was in Arabia, known to the Phoenicians as auriferous (Ezek. 27.22), Ophir may denote southern Arabia as an entrepot for merchandise from the farther East and also from east Africa. LXX renders Ophir with an initial S, which has suggested Sofala some 200 miles from the famous ruins of Zimbabwe in East Africa, and Supara on the Malabar coast. This spelling, however, has no basis in MT, and probably reflects the seaborne trade with India in Ptolemaic times, when LXX was produced. *šōham*, noted with gold as a product of Havilah in Gen. 2.12, is mentioned as one of the semi-precious stones, usually taken as onyx, in the high priest's pectoral (Exod. 25.7; 28.9; 20).

17. zᵉḵôḵîṯ is *hapax legomenon* in the OT, but is better known in Aram. *zᵉḡôḡîṯ* and Arab. *zajājatu(n)*, which had a scarcity value in antiquity. Blown glass was unknown until Roman times, where already Akka was famous for this industry by the middle of the first century CE (Josephus, *War* 2.10.2). But it had been made in ancient Egypt since the second millennium BCE of a fusion of quartz sand containing calcium carbonate with natron or plant ashes and colouring, material such as manganese, copper, cobalt and iron compounds. Strips of this were built up round a sandy clay core, or, in the case of beads, around wire, which was later extracted, and the article was then re-fused and

polished (Engelbach 1942: 133f.). Such glass was used largely for inlay, as on the throne of Tutankhamen. From the sixth century BCE until the Roman era it was sufficient of a rarity to be valued highly like gold

t^e^mûrāh, as in 20.18, is 'exchange', from *hēmîr*.

paz is known as the finest of gold, as indicated by LXX at 1 Kgs 10.18, where *zāhāḇ mûpāz* (from *pāzaz*) is rendered *chrusos dokimos*, 'well-approved gold'.

18. *rā'môṯ*, a substance in which the Edomites trafficked (Ezek. 27.16), hence reasonably associated with the Red Sea, is probably coral, and *gāḇîš*, which is a *hapax legomenon* in the OT, suggests Ass. *algameš*, or rock-crystal.

The context suggests that MT *mešeḵ* may be emended to *meḵeś* ('price'; cf. *miḵsaṯ hā'erk^e^ḵā*, 'the price of your assessment' in Lev. 27.23), but the consonants of MT may be retained and read *m^e^śōḵ*, cognate with Arab. *maśaka* ('to grasp, hold, contain'); cf. *mešeḵ zera'* (Ps. 126.6), which L. Köhler (1945: 59-61) explains as 'a bag of seed' (so Tur-Sinai).

p^e^nînîm are not pearls, as Rashi thought, since in Lam. 4.7 they are red; they are either 'red coral', the word possibly alluding to Arab. coral's 'branching' growth (cf. Arab. *fananu*[*n*], 'branch') or 'rubies'.

19. *piṭ^e^ḏaṯ* is always rendered 'topaz' in LXX.

21. The parallelism with *'ôp̄* indicates that MT *ḥāy* should possibly be emended to *ḥayyāh* ('beasts'); cf. 37.8 and the more common *ḥayyaṯ haśśādeh* ('the wild beasts').

22. Note the personification of *'^a^ḇaddôn* and *māweṯ*. The latter is personified, and indeed deified, as the inveterate enemy of Baal in the highly dramatic Baal myth of Ras Shamra.

23. *darkāh* (lit. 'its way') means here 'the way to it'.

24. On text of v. 24b see Textual Note.

25. *tikkēn* ('he measured, adjusted') and *middāh* ('measurement'), from *māḏaḏ*, recalls the famous passage on creation in Isa. 40.12:

> *mî-māḏaḏ b^e^šo '^a^lô mênyām* (so 4QIsa)
> *w^e^šāmayim bazzereṯ tikkēn*
>
> Who meted out the waters of the sea in the hollow of his hand,
> And measured out the heavens with a span?

26. The association of Wisdom with the divine control of the seasons in vv. 26-27 recalls the association of Wisdom with God's ordering of the elements in Prov. 8.27-30.

A decree for the rain may refer to the seasonal rains, the heavy rains of early winter ('the former rain' of the OT) and the light rain of late winter and early spring ('the latter rain'). This has been taken to indicate the Palestinian origin of the Book of Job, but the high country of Edom also enjoys those rains and the Hejaz has at least the expectancy of rain at the same season as Palestine though it does not always materialize.

In v. 26b *derek̲*, in parallelism with *ḥōq* ('decree, prescription'), may denote a fixed or regular course (cf. on 24.4), but in the same phrase *wᵉd̲erek̲ laḥᵃzîz qōlôt̲* in 38.25, *derek̲* means 'way'. In 28.26 the ambiguous term 'course' may be preferred, with the implication of 'regulation'.

The meaning of *ḥᵃzîz* is uncertain. Here and at 35.25; Zech. 10.1; Ben Sira 35.26 it is associated with rain, but also with thunder (*qōlôt̲*). A connection with forked lightning (cf. Arab. *ḥazza*, 'to notch') has been suggested (G.B. Gray 1921: I, 243; II, 197-98). If this were correct the association with rain would recall the saying of the modern Arab peasant *al-baraq 'alāmatu 'l-maṭar* ('the lightning is the announcement of the rain'). But *ḥazza* in Arab. also means 'to speak roughly', hence *ḥᵃzîz qōlôt̲* may mean 'the rumble of thunder' (so Dhorme, Hölscher, Mowinckel).

27. *rā'āh* recalls God's consideration of his creation at its various stages in Gen. 1.1–2.4. The Arab. nuance of considering as well as seeing in the Arab. cognate is present also here.

sippar may have here the literal meaning 'to count' or 'assess'.

ḥᵃqārāh (lit. 'searched her out') means probably 'examined her potentialities', as one would do with a new instrument, which in effect Wisdom was in God's creation (Prov. 8.23ff.).

The parallelism with *rā'āh* indicates the emendation of MT *hᵉk̲înāh* to *hᵉb̲înāh* (so Dhorme, Mowinckel, Pope).

28. This verse, which is markedly prosaic after the sublime poem on Wisdom, and incorporates a quotation, though not quite verbatim, from the sapiential tradition (Ps. 111.10; Prov. 1.7; 3.7; 16.6), has been taken as an editorial gloss. Actually the conception of *ḥok̲māh* is quite different from that in the poem, connoting not the intelligent master-plan of the Creator, but, as is indicated by *yir'at̲ 'ᵃd̲ōnay* circumspect conduct, the objective of the *ḥᵃk̲āmîm* in their practical task of education and the due response of all to God as *nôrā'* ('one to be dreaded' or 'revered'). The verse may be an addition by a sage (*ḥāk̲ām*), conscious of the significance of his profession, to counter any discouragement which the poem on the inaccessibility of God's Wisdom might have caused, by stating that there was nevertheless a wisdom attainable by humans through reverential and conscientious response (*yir'āh*) to God as *nôrā'*. Lévêque in his excellent study of wisdom in all its connotations (1920: 607ff.) finds the connection between the two orders of wisdom in the poem and the addendum in v. 28 in that degree of the wisdom of the Creator that he reveals

particularized in the Law as the definition of a practical response to God (pp. 648f.). The explicit identification of Wisdom with the Law, to be sure, is not made until Ben Sira (c. 190 BCE), after which it is familiar in Jewish Wisdom, but it is clearly implied in the postexilic Wisdom Psalms 19.8 (EVV 7) and 119.97ff. *'ᵃḏōnāy* for Yahweh, exceptional in the poetic part of Job, has been taken as evidence of a redactional addendum. This is possible, but it may well be by the author of the poem himself, rounding out his poem on Divine Wisdom by a sapiential citation expressing the conception of practical wisdom which the sages represented in their effort to commend social order. We would see also in the relation of social wisdom and conduct to cosmic Wisdom in vv. 24-27 reflection of the culmination of creation in humanity and what is expected of it before its presumption in exceeding the limit of reverent response (*yir'aṯ 'ᵉlōhîm*, 'fear of God') in seeking to match God in 'knowledge' (to which we would relate *bînāh* in v. 28b).

Job 29

Job's Review of his Former Prosperity

Job's challenge to God in his oath of purgation (ch. 31), preceded by his account of his enjoyment of the divine favour and the benefits which his community had shared (ch. 29), which serves to emphasize by contrast his ruin (ch. 30), are to be taken as a unity. Chapters 29–30 particularly recall the picture of past prosperity in Ps. 44.2-9 (EVV 1-8) as a foil to the Plaint of the Community in vv. 10-20 (EVV 9-19) and the favour to the Davidic king in Ps. 89.20-38 (EVV 19-37) followed by the Plaint of the royal sufferer in vv. 39-52 (EVV 38-51). In the context of the forensic aspect of this appeal to God in vv. 29–31 the account of his great social potential (v. 29) nullified by his ruin (v. 30) is tantamount to an accusation of his divine adversary. Further, in the convention of the Plaint of the Sufferer an important element is the call for, or expectation of, a reassuring divine response in oracle or intervention (e.g. Ps. 44.24-26 [EVV 23-25]). To be sure, this is not voiced in Job's plaint in ch. 30, though his wish for a restoration of his prosperity in 29.1-8 might amount to as much, and particularly his statement, 'This is my ardent desire; let the Almighty answer me' (31.35). Be this as it may, his oath of purgation invites, indeed demands, divine response, which in fact materializes in the Divine Declaration (38.1ff.), though in rebuke rather than in reassurance.

The chapter may be divided according to its subject matter into six strophes of unequal length: vv. 1-6, 7-10, 21-25, 14-17, 11-13, 18-20. The first, introduced as a wish, depicts the material and family blessings Job had enjoyed, the second (vv. 7-10) and the third (vv. 21-25) amplifying this by describing the social prestige he enjoyed and shared. The fourth strophe (vv. 14-17) sustains the figure of the king in v. 25 by the theme of righteousness (*ṣeḏeq*), and justice (*mišpāṭ*) as Job's distinctive roles (cf. the Royal Psalm 72.1ff.; see Caquot 1961) and describes how Job discharged responsibility to society. The fifth strophe (vv. 11-13) continues this theme and depicts the popular approval of Job's use of his influence, and the chapter ends (vv. 18-20) with the hope Job had had of a continuance of God's blessings.

Other arrangements of the text have been proposed (e.g. vv. 1-10, 21-25, 11-20; so Dhorme, Mowinckel, Fohrer, Pope). But we submit that this fails to do justice to the significance of the robe and turban of righteousness (v. 14) as reflecting the technical language and imagery of the ideology of kingship (vv. 21-25), which seems to demand that vv. 14-17 should be read immediately after vv. 21-25, where Stevenson places them, though apparently not under this consideration.

Chapter 29

1. And Job represented his case afresh and said:

2. 'Oh to be as in the months of old!
As in the days when God watched over me,
3. When he made his lamp shine[1] over my head,
And by his light I walked through the darkness,
4. As I was in my autumn days,
When God set a screen[2] about my tent,
5. When as yet the Almighty was with me,
And my children stood[3] around about me.
6. Then my nomads had abundance of curds,[4]
And the rock (press) exuded rivers of oil.

7. When I went out to the gate in honour,
Or took my seat in the public place,
8. The young men saw me and withdrew,
The aged rose up and stood;
9. Notables refrained from speaking,
And laid their hand on their mouth.
10. The voice of the nobles was tied up,[5]
And their tongue clave to the roof of their mouth.

21. They listened to me and were in suspense,
And kept silent for my counsel.
22. After I spoke they did not speak again.
My word fell upon them like raindrops,
23. And they waited for me as for the rain,
Open-mouthed as for the latter rain.
24. If I smiled upon them then indeed[6] they gained confidence,
If my face was bright[7] they beamed.[8]
25. I chose their government and sat as chief,
I lived like a king in prestige.
[9]Where I led them they let themselves be led.[9]
14. I put on righteousness and it clothed me,
Justice[10] like a robe and turban.
15. I was eyes to the blind,
And feet to the lame;
16. I was a father to the poor,
And I searched out the case[11] of the stranger.
17. But I shattered the fangs of the wicked,
And rescued[12] the prey from his teeth.

11. Whenever the ear heard it blessed me,
And when the eye saw it testified its approval of me,
12. For I rescued the poor when he cried,
Even the orphan and the helpless.

13. The blessing of him who was about to perish came upon me,
And I made the widow's heart to sing.

18. So I thought, like a reed-cane[13] will I thrive,[14]
Like a palm-tree[15] multiply my days,
19. My root spreading free to the water,
And the dew settling at night on my branches.
20. My dignity fresh within me,
And my strength[16] renewed in my hand.

Textual Notes on Chapter 29

1. Reading *bahillô* with T for MT *b*^{e}*hillô*. See Commentary *ad loc.*
2. Reading *b*^{e}*sōḵ* (cf. 1.10), with LXX, Sym. and S for *b*^{e}*sōḏ*, final *k* being corrupted to *d* in the square script. MT *soḏ*, however, may possibly be cognate with Arab. *ṣadda* ('to protect'). See Commentary *ad loc.*
3. Reading *'ām*^{e}*ḏû metri causa*, assuming displacement of *'mdw* to v. 6b, where it is superfluous to the metre, with subsequent corruption to *'immāḏî*.
4. Reading *b*^{e}*ḥem'āh* with certain Heb. MSS, LXX, T and V for MT *b*^{e}*ḥēmāh*.
5. Reading *neḥkā'* for MT *neḥbā'û* and omitting *w* as a dittograph. See Commentary *ad loc.*
6. Reading the asseverative enclitic *l*^{e} for MT *lō'*. See Commentary *ad loc.*
7. Reading *w*^{e}*'ārû pānay* for MT *w*^{e}*'ôr pānay*, assuming metathesis of *r* and *w*.
8. Reading *l*^{e}*yaḇlîḡû* for MT *lō' yappîlû*, assuming scribal misunderstanding of *l*^{e} enclitic, metathesis of *l* and *y*, and the corruption of *g* to *w*, *w* to *n* and *b* to *p* in the square script.
9. Reading *ba'*^{a}*šer 'ôḇîlēm yinnāḥû*, proposed by Herz, for MT *ka'*^{a}*šer '*^{a}*ḇēlîm y*^{e}*naḥēm*. See Commentary *ad loc.*
10. Reading *mišpāṭ* with LXX and S for *mišpāṭî*.
11. Conjecturing *rîḇ* for MT *rāḇ*.
12. Conjecturing *'ešlōp̄* for MT *'ašlîḵ*. See Commentary *ad loc.*
13. Reading *qāneh* for MT *qinnî*, assuming corruption of *h* to *y* in the Old Heb. script. See Commentary *ad loc.*
14. Reading *'eggōa'*, from *naga'*, for MT *'eḡwā'*. See Commentary *ad loc.*
15. Reading *k*^{e}*naḥal* with LXX and V for MT *w*^{e}*kāḥôl*, assuming corruption of *k* to *w* and *n* to *k* in the Old Heb. script. See Commentary *ad loc.*
16. Reading *ûq*^{e}*šûṯî* for MT *w*^{e}*qaštî*.

Commentary on Chapter 29

1. It has been suggested (e.g. Hölscher) that the reading *wayyōsep̄ 'iyyôb ś*^{e}*'ēṯ m*^{e}*šālô* ('and Job represented his case afresh') instead of the customary 'and Job answered', or 'spoke up and said' is secondary, occasioned by misplacement of text in chs. 25–27, Job being the last speaker before the insertion of the poem on Wisdom (ch. 28). In chs. 29–31, however, Job, having finished his debate with his friends, makes a fresh statement of his situation, to which we refer the heading in MT. *māšāl* means lit. 'likeness', hence generally an 'example', good or bad, which sets people talking and affords an illustration of

moral principles. It is thus used of a parable, which reflects reality, of a proverb, which by simile, metaphor or antithesis emphasizes certain features of the actual situation. In Job's concluding monologue it is the *representation* of his actual situation brought into sharp focus.

2. *kᵉ* is used pregnantly as a particle of comparison, but with reference to time attached to *yarᵉḥê-qeḏem* and *yᵉmê*... (GKC, §118u). The use of a construct before an adjectival clause in *kîymê ʾᵉlôah yišmᵉrēnî* should be noted (cf. GKC, §130d). *mî yittᵉnēnî* is tantamount to *mî yittᵉnēnî ʾehyeh* ('would that I were').

3. For MT *bᵉhillô* we should probably read *bahillô*, contraction of *bᵉhahillô*, the infinitive construct of the Hiphil of *hālal* ('to shine') with the preposition and pronominal suffix (so T, Beer, Duhm, Dhorme). The conception of the lamp as symbolizing the presence of God is known in the cult at Shiloh (1 Sam. 3.3) and possibly also in the Temple of Solomon, the free-standing pillars Jachin and Boaz supporting fire-cressets (1 Kgs 7.15) according to W.R. Smith (1889: 287-89), W.F. Albright (1942: 18ff.), and H.G. May (*ibidem*: 88; 1942: 19ff.); cf. Isa. 60.2; Ps. 50.2 (EVV 1). It is used figuratively for God's abiding favour in the quotation of a proverb in 18.5 and in 2 Sam. 22.29 = Ps. 18.29 (EVV 28).

ḥōšeḵ may be a circumstantial, or adverbial, accusative or a direct accusative of that through which one walks, which is unusual but attested; cf. Deut. 1.19, *wannēleḵ ʾēṯ kol-hammiḏbār*, and Deut. 2.7; 2 Sam. 2.9.

4. S in rendering MT *ḥorpî* ('my shame') gives quite the opposite sense from that demanded by the context, obviously thinking of the more familiar *ḥerpāh* ('reproach'). Theod., Sym. and V render 'my youth', which has suggested the emendation *pirḥî* ('my bloom', so Volz, Budde, Hölscher). Fohrer translates 'Frühzeit' not, however, in the sense of 'youth', which does not accord with Job's family all about him. He recognizes *ḥōrep̄*, well attested in the OT meaning 'harvest' or 'harvest-time', but takes it as a homonym, but without attesting the meaning he adopts (1963: 402). 'Harvest-time', figuratively 'maturity', seems the obvious sense in view of Job's family, his prosperity and his standing which even the notables respect. In v. 4b *ʿᵃlê ʾohᵒlî* supports the emendation *sōḵ* for MT *sôḏ* ('intimate council'). The reading *sōḵ* in 1.10 and 3.23 further supports the emendation, which makes D.W. Thomas's view that *sōḏ* is a homonym of *sôḏ* ('council') from a root *sāḏad* cognate with Arab. *ṣadda* meaning in the IVth Form 'to avert' and in the VIIIth Form 'to veil oneself' unnecessary, though it remains interesting.

6. If *hᵃlîḵay* means 'goings' or 'steps' (cf. Nah. 2.6; Ps. 68.25; Prov. 31.27; Hab. 3.6), and *rāḥaṣ* means 'to wash', the expression is very strange, though perhaps reminiscent of the Blessing of Asher in Deut. 33.24, who would 'dip his foot in oil'. Dahood (*UHP*, p. 60) suggests that it may refer to a footsore traveller, and, reading

birᵉḥōṣ hᵃlîḵay bᵉḥemʼāh wᵉsōrî
ṣōq ʽᵃmûḏay palᵉḡê šāman,

he translates

When my feet were bathed in cream and balsam,
And rivers of oil flowed over my legs.

We suggest that both *rāḥaṣ* and *hᵃlîḵay* have been misunderstood, and take *rāḥas* as cognate with Akk. *raḫâṣu* ('to overflow') or Arab. *raḫaṣa* ('to be cheap' and so 'plentiful'). *hᵃlîḵāh* is used of a 'caravan' or 'travelling company' of merchants in 6.19. We suggest that it denotes Job's nomad herdsmen wandering in search of pasture. In v. 6b we would see in *ʽomᵉḏî* (for MT *ʽimmāḏî*) a complementary parallel to *hᵃlîḵay*, the noun denoting the chief's headquarters as distinct from the scattered gratings of his herds during the season of pasture. This was envisaged as a settled land where the hills were terraced for olive trees and other fruits. *ḥemʼāh* is the butter and buttermilk churned by the Bedouin women, whose constant occupation is rocking their skin containers. The conception of the rock pouring forth or exuding oil (see above on the verb *ṣûq* on 28.2) recalls Deut. 32.13, 'and he gave him to suck honey out of the rock and oil out of the flinty rock', but *ṣûr* may rather denote the heavy stone olive press (see above on 24.11).

7. *qereṯ* is used in the OT denoting city only in Prov. 8.3; 9.3, 14; 11.11, and possibly here, but is regularly used in the Ras Shamra texts. The gate above the city is dubious, notwithstanding Dhorme's explanation of the main gate as a high fortification dominating the city, which would certainly be out of place in the home envisaged for Job. We would see *ʽᵃlê-qereṯ* as parallel to *môšāḇî*, the latter denoting the place or posture of honour recognized by the old men, who stand up deferentially. Thus we take *qereṯ* as the infinitive construct of *yāqar* ('to be honourable'), as probably in the Ras Shamra text Gordon *UT* 52.3, *ytnm qrt lʽlyn(m)* ('let them give honour to the exalted ones'). *rᵉḥôḇ* is the broad, relatively empty space about the main gate, still the place of business and gossip and occasional markets in the Arab towns.

8. *neḥbāʼû* might mean 'hid themselves', but here means 'made themselves inconspicuous, withdrew'; cf. Isa. 26.20 where the Qal of the verb is used parallel to *bōʼ baḥᵃḏārêḵā* ('go into your chambers').

On *yāšîš* see on 12.12.

9. *śārîm* is used of local notables; cf. those of the Israelite town of Succoth in Transjordan in the time of Gideon (Judg. 8.6, 14).

ʽāṣᵉrû bᵉmillîm, lit. 'they set restraint upon words', with *bᵉ* of the object restrained, is analogous to the expression *ʽāṣar bᵉʽaḏ kol-reḥem* ('he set a restraint on all wombs') in Gen. 20.18.

In v. 9b the putting of the hand to the mouth (cf. 21.5; 40.4; Judg. 18.19; Mic. 7.16; Prov. 30.32) might denote silence, but it might also be a gesture of deference; cf. the attitude of the worshipper, or listener, before the god, for example in the Hammurabi stele, or of a person at court; cf. a passage in the Ras Shamra Legend of King Krt (Gordon *UT* 125, 41-42): *qḥ 'apk byd* ('Hold thy hand over thy nose', lit. 'take thy nose in thy hand'); *(b)r(l)tk bm ymn* ('Thy right hand over thy throat', lit. thy throat in thy right hand). It also indicated in Egyptian legal convention that one had no further argument (Couroyer 1960).

10. MT *neḥbā'û* in *qôl-nᵉgîḏîm neḥbā'û* is suspect, partly because the verb in its known sense of 'hide' or 'withdraw' does not suit the subject *qôl*, and partly because a poet with the wealth of diction of the author of Job would not have repeated the verb so soon after v. 3. Hence we propose the emendation *neḥkā'*, with a word-play with *ḥikkāh* ('palate) in v. 10b. *ḥāḵā'* is not attested in Heb., but it is well known in Arab. (*ḥaka'a*) meaning 'to tie', or 'tighten a knot'.

21-25. Verses 21-25, continuing the theme of the deference of even the notables to Job, is displaced in MT.

21. In *wᵉyiḥēllû* the verb is *yāḥal* ('to wait'), being used in the Piel; the *daghesh* in *l* is *daghesh forte affectuosum*, to preserve and emphasize the quantity of the vowel in the principal pause (GKC, §20i).

22. For MT *dᵉḇārî* some commentators (e.g. Merx, Budde, Duhm, Hölscher), read *dabbᵉrî*, as in 21.3, but this is not necessary.

šānāh is a denominative verb from *šᵉnayim*, and means 'to double, repeat, do again'; cf. Mishnah, the re-application of the Law.

nāṭap̄ signifies the dropping of rain (cf. 36.27), introducing the figure of the expectancy of rain in v. 23.

23. This apt figure reflects the intense expectancy of the early rains (Deut. 11.14; Jer. 5.24) about October or November after the long summer drought, which refill the cisterns and soften the hard crust of the dry earth and make cultivation possible again. Verse 23b refers to the light rains (*malqôš*), 'the latter rains' at the end of winter and early spring, which fall when the corn is forming the ear. It is important that the latter rains come at this stage of the growth before the siroccos of late April and May finally check the growth.

The opening (*pā'ar*) of the mouth denotes eager expectancy; cf. Ps. 119.131.

24. Verse 24a and b are conditional sentences, introduced respectively by the imperfect and perfect without the conditional particle in the protasis. In MT the negative *lō' ya'ᵃmînû* has excited the suspicion of some commentators (e.g.

Budde, Bickell, Beer, Duhm, Peake, Hölscher, Stevenson, Mowinckel). Retaining the negative, others translate 'If I smiled on them they would not believe it', that is, they were transported beyond belief; cf. 9.16 (so Ball, Dhorme, Peters, Pope, Terrien). But Stevenson rightly observes that this would imply that Job's favour was something unusual, which is quite the opposite of what the context conveys. G.B. Gray takes *lō' ya'ᵃmînû* as the imperfect of attendant circumstances, rendering 'I laughed at them when they believed not', and goes on to interpret v. 24b as meaning that general despondency never affected Job's cheerfulness; though grammatically possible, this interpretation is somewhat forced, especially in v. 24a. Kissane takes v. 24a to mean that Job laughed the people out of false counsel and false confidence, while he interprets v. 24b to mean that they did not fail to respond to his cheerfulness, which is again possible if even more forced. Duhm, Budde, Steuernagel, Mowinckel and Fohrer omit *lō'* in v. 24a as a dittograph of the negative in v. 24b, with a similar interpretation to Kissane's in v. 24b.

Those interpretations ignore the phenomenon of the proclitic *lᵉ* with asseverative force, which has also escaped the notice of the Masoretes, by whose time it had fallen obsolete. It is, however, well known in Ugarit, and commonly introduced the apodosis of a conditional sentence, as here. Regularly the Masoretes, expecting Classical Hebrew, assume that *l* with the finite verb in the consonantal text is the negative *lō'*, possibly because the Canaanite enclitic was vocalized *lo*. Thus in v. 24a we would read *'eśḥaq 'ᵉlêhem lᵉya'ᵃmînû* ('If I smiled to them then indeed they gained confidence'). We take *'ôr* in v. 24b, emending to *wᵉ'ārû*, as the verb in the protasis of a conditional sentence without the conditional particle. But MT might be retained as the infinitive absolute with the force of the perfect. *yappîlû* may be a corruption of *yaḇlîḡû*, resulting in the reading *wᵉ'ārû pānay lᵉyaḇlîḡû* ('and if my face shone they fairly beamed'); cf. 9.27; 10.10. G.R. Driver (1955: 88) would preserve the consonants of MT *lō' yappîlû*, taking the latter word as a scribal misunderstanding of a *hapax legomenon ya'ᵃpîlû* ('grow dark'), rendering 'their darkness was dispelled', hence NEB 'lost their gloomy looks'. *lō'* he would understand as introducing a rhetorical question without the interrogative particle. For the conception of the light of the face signifying favour; cf. Num. 6.2, 5; Ps. 4.7 and particularly Prov. 16.15a, 'For the light of a king's face is life'.

25. In v. 25a *darkām* means 'their government' as in Ugaritic (see on 26.14). On the Ben Asher pointing of *'eḇḥar*, with *hateph pathah* under *b* before the guttural, see GKC, §10g. In this particular context we have taken *sāḵan* in the familiar sense 'to dwell', but understanding the pregnant sense of being firmly established; we admit that it may reflect the status of Ass. *zukanu*, a provincial governor, familiar in Palestine in the Babylonian and Persian periods. 'Among the troop' (MT *baggᵉḏûḏ*) in conjunction with the 'swelling' or 'abiding' of a king is suspect, and we propose that *gᵉḏûḏ* is cognate with Arab. *jaddu*(*n*) ('excellence' or 'prestige'). A third colon, like v. 25c, is always suspect as a

gloss or a displacement unless it obviously ends a passage and may readily be connected in sense with the preceding two cola. So in v. 25c MT *'ᵃbēlîm yᵉnaḥēm* was taken to have been displaced from after *wᵉ'ôr pānay* in v. 24b, which was then translated 'and the light of my face comforted mourners'(so Budde, Bickell, Beer, Duhm, Peake, Richter, Stevenson). G.B. Gray, Mowinckel and Fohrer omit v. 25c as a gloss. But we submit that it is the last colon of a tricolon which ends the passage on Job's status among the elders and notables (vv. 8-10, 21-25) before the passage on his protection of the destitute (vv. 14-17, 11-13), thus punctuating the strophe, which it ends as it does often in the Ras Shamra myths. The agreement of v. 25c and v. 25a and b is secured by Herz's plausible emendation of MT *ka'ᵃšer 'ᵃḇēlîm yᵉnaḥēm* to *ka'ᵃšer 'ōḇîlēm yinnāḥû* (1900: 163), or, we consider, better, *ba'ᵃšer 'ōḇîlēm yinnāḥû*, which the reading of Sym. supports (so Dhorme).

14-17, 11-13. These two strophes follow the reference to Job's kingly prestige in v. 25, and reflect the Israelite tradition of the responsibilities of royalty; cf. Ps. 72.1-4; Isa. 11.3-5 (see Introduction to ch. 29).

14. *ṣeḏeq* is 'right', with here a moral connotation, which is properly secondary to the word, which means primarily that which is 'proper', 'right' rather than 'righteousness'. *mišpāṭ* is also primarily a neutral word, the regular 'government' or 'rule' which is imposed and upheld by a *šôpēṭ*, the Ugaritic cognate of which, *ṯpṭ*, in the Ras Shamra texts is parallel to *mlk* ('king'). Hence *mišpāṭ* denotes primarily 'order' and secondarily 'judgment'. The meaning of such words is to be determined from the context, though in Israel, which admitted the rule of Yahweh, whose nature and will was revealed in the Covenant and its religious and social obligations, the words had usually a moral connotation. In the present context, which after the prototype of the royal ideology emphasizes the responsibility of Job in society, both words have certainly the moral connotation.

The conception of being 'clothed in right' is familiar in Ps. 132.9. 'Clothing' and 'clothed' may denote being in uniform, as Ahab and Jehoshaphat at the gate of Samaria on the eve of their expedition to Ramoth-Gilead (1 Kgs 22.10), or it may denote the clothes of men of standing as distinct from the stripped workman or half-clad pauper. In any case it denotes the characteristic of Job, from which he was known plainly to the people and which he proud to exhibit; cf. Arab. *mā'aẓhara 'inśānu(n)* ('what a man shows undisguisedly', lit. 'what a man has on his back', as distinct from 'what he has in his belly', i.e. conceals, *mā'abṭana*).

mᵉ'îl is the overcloak (Arab. *'abbāyatu[n]*) that is worn by men of status or in leisure.

ṣānîp̄ is the headdress of a king (Isa. 62.3) or of the high priest (Zech. 3.5); cf. *miṣnep̄eṯ* of the priest's turban in Exod. 28.4ff., where the insignia proper was a golden flower fastened on it (Exod. 28.36-38). The nature of *ṣānîp̄* as a turban is clear from its derivation from the verb *ṣānap̄* ('to wind', or 'wrap'; Lev. 16.4; Isa. 22.18). Again the turban carefully wound is a status symbol, as in Islam today.

15. *pissēaḥ* denotes 'limping', as of the lame Mephibosheth (2 Sam. 19.27). The association of the verb with the Arab. cognate *fasaḥa* ('to be dislocated') expresses the use of the verb to describe the jerky ritual dance of the prophets of Baal round the altar on Carmel (1 Kgs 18.21), perhaps on half-bent knees (*'al-šᵉtê hassᵉ'ippîm*) (de Vaux 1941: 9). The association of this verb with *pesaḥ* ('Passover') is doubtful.

16. The description or Job as 'father to the poor' recalls the claim of Hammurabi in the epilogue to his famous Code (*ANET*, 178).

The usage of *lō'-yāḏa'tî*, which is properly a relative clause with the antecedent and the relative particle omitted, describes either a *gēr*, or resident alien in the community, who depended upon such as Job for his rights, or one who was not a kinsman (cf. *môḏa'* [Qere], 'kinsman', in Ruth 2.1). In this case Job's sense of justice was not confined to those whom convention strictly bound him to vindicate.

17. *mᵉtallᵉ'ôṯ*, from *tāla'* ('to gnaw'), denotes the incisor teeth, particularly of an animal (Joel 1.6; Ps. 58.7), and, as here, is parallel to *šinnayim* ('teeth') in Joel 1.6 and Prov. 30.14. The conception of the wicked devouring persons as prey (*ṭerep̄*) is familiar in the Psalms; cf. Ps. 124.6 and Job 4.10. The figure of the breaking of the teeth of the oppressor is peculiarly at home in the declaration of faith in the Plaint of the Sufferer (e.g. Ps. 3.8).

If MT of v. 17b is correct this would be the one instance in the OT of *hišlîḵ* in the sense of 'to deliver', hence *'ešlōp̄* is suggested, the verb meaning 'to draw out', as of a sword from its sheath. G.R. Driver, however (1955: 35) defends MT, citing Arab. *śalaka* ('to save oneself', which also in the IInd Form means 'to draw a sword from the sheath'). The verb has possibly a Phoenician cognate.

11. *kî* has a temporal significance, here 'whenever', as in 1.5; it also introduces v. 11b.

In v. 11b the verb *hē'îḏ* ('to attest call to witness') with the direct object is rare, but intelligible, the person being the object of testimony. The verb is so used of evidence against in 1 Kgs 21.10, 13, where the more common usage would be *hē'îḏ bᵉ*.

12. The succour of the widow and orphan was the peculiar concern of the king in the legends of the Canaanite kings Dn'il and Krt in the Ras Shamra texts Gordon *UT* 1 Aqht 31, 160, and *UT*, 127, 46-49:

ltdn dn 'almnt	Thou dost not judge the case of the widow,
ltṯpṭ qṣr npš	Nor decide the suit of the oppressed.
ltdy ṯšm 'l dl	Thou dost not drive away those who prey upon the poor,
lpnk ltšlḥm ytm	Before thee thou dost not feed the fatherless;
b'd kslk 'almnt	The widow is behind thy back.

LXX has an interesting reading of v. 12a: 'For I delivered the poor man from the potentate', reading *miššôa'*. This word means generally 'noble' (cf. 34.19), with the nuance of 'generous', which may be connected with Ugaritic *ṯ'y* ('to give'); cf. Isa. 32.5, where *šôa'* is parallel to *nāḏîḇ* with the same connotation. In the Royal Psalm 72.12 in a bicolon of the same purport and with close verbal correspondence LXX, S and Jerome read *miššôa'* for MT *m^ešawwēa'*. MT in both cases, however, is to be preferred, with the familiar motif of hearing the cry (*ša'wāh*) of the oppressed.

18. The rendering of MT might be: 'And I said, "I will expire with my nest and my days will be as numerous as the sand"'. *'im-qinnî* in the first colon has been taken to mean 'with my nestlings', a somewhat unlikely expression, which is not attested of a human family elsewhere in the OT. LXX renders v. 18a as 'But I said, My life will reach old age', which suggests that MT *qinnî* is the end of *z^eqûnay* ('my old age'). Dhorme read *'immî*, which he construed with *wā'ōmer* ('I said to myself'; cf. this use of *'im* with the pronominal suffix in 10.13, where *'imm^ekā* is parallel to *bill^eḇāḇ^ekā*), reading *wā'ōmer 'immî zāqēn 'eḡwa'* (so Saydon 1961: 252; Pope). It must be admitted that this gives an excellent parallel to v. 18b (MT), 'And my days will be as numerous as the sand', though in view of the figure of a growing plant in the following verse we have some reserve. Herz (1913: 345) proposed that *qn* was an Egyptian loanword meaning 'strength', which was accepted by G.R. Driver (1955: 85) and Terrien (1963). Actually if this is the meaning of 18a there is no need to invoke Egyptian, since *qn* is attested in the Ras Shamra texts (e.g. Gordon *UT* 62, 4 and 67 VI, 20), where it signifies, as has been recognized in Job 31.22, the shoulder socket which might well, like 'arm' (*z^erôa'*), signify 'strength'. *'im-qānî* might then be read, meaning 'with my strength unimpaired'. If MT of v. 18b is correct then Dhorme's reading of 18a or our proposed modification of Herz's interpretation would be acceptable. This, however, depends on the connection of v. 18 with the figure in v. 19, and on the reliability of the MT reading *kaḥôl* in v. 18b. There was a Rabbinic reading *kaḥûl*, 'like the phoenix', *b. Sanh.* 108b), with an allusion to the legendary phoenix, which has been adopted by certain later commentators (e.g. Hitzig, Ewald, Dillmann, Friedrich Delitzsch, Budde, Duhm, Peake, Hölscher, Stevenson, Mowinckel, Terrien, Fohrer). This would, if genuine, support MT *'im-qinnî*. But it is suspiciously like a secondary tradition derived from the LXX translation of v. 18b, 'like a palm-stem (*phoinix*) I shall live a long time'. This indicates a Heb. original *k^enaḥal* ('like a palm-tree'; cf. Arab. *naḫlu*[*n*]). This reading was known to Jerome, as is evident from his commentary and the Vulgate and is

adopted by Ball and Kissane. We consider that it may represent a genuine pre-Masoretic variant and perhaps even the original text. The fact that *naẖlu(n)* is the regular Arab. word for 'palm-tree', which is regularly *tāmār* in Heb., is no objection, since it is actually attested in the OT, though only once more (Num. 24.6). We consider this reading, which is not far from MT, more natural in view of the sequel, which refers to the roots and branches of a tree, which has so far not been mentioned in MT.

In v. 18a S retains a double reading, translating 'I will deliver the poor people', implying a reading *'am 'ānî 'ôšîa'* for MT *'im-qinnî 'eḡwa'* ('and will finish as a reed'), rendering a Hebrew text *we'im qāneh 'eḡwa'*, and this affords a clue to the restoration of the couplet. If we read *kenaḥal* ('like a palm-tree') in v. 18b, *'im* in v. 18a would naturally be the comparative preposition, a sense which is attested for *'im* in Proverbs. The standard of comparison would naturally be a plant, like a palm-tree, and from v. 19a, one which throve in water. This would suggest the reading *qāneh* for MT *qinnî*, with which S was familiar. The problem then remains is MT *'eḡwa'*. As a pure conjecture we might suggest *qāneh gōmē'* ('a reed which sucks up water'; cf. Gen. 24.17, *haḡmi'înî nā' me'aṭ-mayim*, 'let me drink a little water'), but there is nothing in this reading to correspond to the distinctive letter ' in MT *'eḡwa'*. On the hint of the first variant of S we might read *'iwwēšēa'* ('will spread myself'), the verb *yāša'* being cognate with Arab. *waśi'a* ('to be wide'), but *š* is too distinctive to be readily corrupted to *w* or *g*. Our conclusion is that for MT *'eḡwa'* we should retain the consonants, but read *'eggôa'* from *nāga'*, a cognate of Arab. *naja'a* ('to thrive' as beasts on pasture, *manja'u[n]*). So in v. 18a we read *'im-qāneh 'eggôa'* ('I shall thrive like the reed-cane').

19. The use of the passive Qal *pāṯûaḥ* is interesting, meaning 'let go free'; cf. Gen. 24.32 (Piel) of camels loosed at the end of a journey.

yālîn (lit. 'shall spend the night') is very apt in the case of dew.

20. This bicolon is full of ambiguity. *qaštî* in v. 20b immediately suggests 'my bow', which has suggested the emendation of MT *kebôḏî* in v. 20a to *kîḏônî* ('my javelin', so Hoffmann). The sense of *ḥāḏaš* as parallel to *taḥalîp̄* ('to be renewed', or 'ever fresh'), does not suit *kîḏōn*, nor yet *keḇēḏî* ('my bow handle'), which was proposed by G.R. Driver (1955: 85-86), citing Arab. *kabidu(n)* ('the centre-piece, or handle of a bow'). The Hiphil of *ḥālap̄* is found in 14.7 of a tree renewing itself in fresh shoots, but while it would be expected that the figure of the tree should be continued from v. 19, this does not seem possible in the text. We claim that after the figure of the reed cane and the palm-tree the poet returns to the actual subject of his dignity (*keḇôḏî*) and his strength (reading *qešûṯî* for MT *qaštî*, lit. 'hardness'). There is probably a similar misunderstanding of *qšt* in Gen. 49.24:

wattēšeḇ be'ēṯān qaštô
wayyāp̄ōzzû zerō'ê yāḏāyw

Here *qešûṯî* ('my strength') is a better parallel to *zerō'ê yāḏāy*. Though the poet has returned to literalism in *keḇôḏî*, he bridges the gulf of the figures by using *ḥāḏaš* and *taḥalîp̄*, which might refer either to renewal of dignity and strength or of vegetation.

Job 30

Job's Plaint

With various components of the Plaint of the Sufferer Job voices his lamentation. The distinctive elements of the prototype, however, are scrambled because of the contrast with the prosperity and status he had enjoyed by God's favour. Thus in the first strophe (vv. 1-2, 9-10) Job's contempt for those who are alienated by his suffering (vv. 1-2, 9-10), probably secondarily amplified by an independent poem in vv. 3-8 (so Fohrer, who includes v. 2), points the contrast to Job's status among the notables in 29.7-11, which the sufferer felt so keenly. Having struck this note, Job continues in the second strophe (vv. 11-14) with the theme of the alienation of those who too readily conclude that his suffering betokens sin. Their estrangement is described in the figure of military assault (vv. 12-14; cf. Ps. 62.4f. [EVV 3f.]). In the third strophe (vv. 15-19) Job laments his fall from high standing, *n^e^d̠îḇāh* (v. 15b) to dust and ashes (v. 19), noting his bodily affliction (vv. 17f. in the language of the Plaint of the Sufferer with particular reference to his own actual affliction; cf. 2.7f.). The fourth strophe (vv. 20-23) opens with the cry of the sufferer to God (v. 20), but only to elaborate on his sufferings and his hopeless end, which he imputes to God (vv. 21-23) in contrast to his free acknowledgment of the divine favour in 29.2-5. In the context of Job's oath of purgation, to which chs. 29 and 30 are the prelude, this is an accusation.

In the second part of Job's statement (vv. 24-31), the first strophe (vv. 24-27) emphasizes his unmerited suffering in language that reflects Pss. 35.13f. and 7.5f. (EVV 4f.), where it is the declaration of the innocent sufferer. In its present context in the forensic convention it anticipates Job's oath of purgation (ch. 31). The final strophe (vv. 28-31) is in the convention and figure of the Plaint of the Sufferer.

Verses 3-8, which with Fohrer we take to be a secondary poetic insertion with the same antecedents as 24.5ff., describes miscreants who, for some reason, have been scourged out of the land (vv. 5-8) and must live as pariahs beyond the settled land on which they prey stealthily as brigands (vv. 5-7). This seems obviously a digression in Job's statement in vv. 1, 9-10, which justifies Fohrer's opinion that it is a citation, with v. 2 also possibly secondary.

Chapter 30

1. 'But now I am mocked by men
Younger in years than myself,
Whose fathers I should have disdained
To set with the dogs of my flocks.
2. Of what significance to *me* would the strength of their hands have been,
Men whose strength even for their own sakes had perished?
3 . . .
Through want and hard hunger.
They gnaw the roots[1] of the dry ground,
The land of the wastes[2] of the wilderness.
4. They pick the salt-wort and the leaves[3] of bushes,
And roots of wild broom to warm themselves.[4]
5. They are driven out from the body of the community;[5]
Men shout at them as at a thief.
6. On the slopes[6] of the wadis they live,
Among the caves of the earth and rocks;
7. Among bushes they bray,
Where thistles grow they are banded together,
8. Sons of a churl, without repute,
Who have been scourged out of the land.
9. But now I have become something for them to sing about,
Even a byword[7] for them.
10. They abhor me; they withdraw far from me;
And do not refrain from spitting in my face.

11. Since God has loosened my tent-cord[8] and humbled me,
They have cast off restraint even in my presence.
12. They raise[9] places for battering-rams[10] against me,[11]
They raise[12] their destructive siege-causeways.
13. They break up my path to make me fall;[13]
They attack;[14] no one restrains them.[15]
14. As through a wide breach they come;
At the place they make the rain they roll on.

15. Terrors are turned[16] upon me,
My honour is driven away[17] as by the wind,
And my wellbeing has passed away like a cloud.
16. [18]My life within me is poured out;
Days of affliction have taken hold of me.
17. At night my bones are hotter[19] than a cauldron;[20]
And my veins[21] have no rest.
18. With great violence affliction grips me as[22] my garment,
Constricting me about like the collar of my tunic.
19. It has sent me down[23] into the mire and confusion,[24]
And I am made like dust and ashes.

20. I cry to you but you answer me not;
I stand, and you do not heed[25] me.

21. You turn cruel to me,
With all your strength you wreak your animosity against me,
22. You lift me up and make me ride the wind,
And you dissolve me in a rainstorm.[26]
23. For I know certainly that you will bring me to death,
Even to the place certainly appointed for all living.

24. But to any who made a request[27] I would put out my hand,[28]
If one cried in his calamity to me.[29]
25. Did I not weep for him whose day was hard?
Did not my soul grieve for the needy?
26. [30]If I looked for good evil came,
And if I expected light darkness came.
27. My inside is made to boil without remission,
Days of affliction confront me.

28. I have gone about black, but not with the sun,
I have stood up in the assembly, calling for help.
29. I have been brother to the jackals,
And the companion of ostriches.
30. My skin is black with scorching,[31]
And my bones are burnt with fever.
31. So my lyre is turned to mourning,
And my pipe to the voice of mourners.

Textual Notes to Chapter 30

1. Inserting *‘iqq^{e}rê*, possibly omitted after *‘ōr^{e}qîm*. See Commentary *ad loc.*
2. Reading *’ēm šô’āh* for MT *’emeš šô’āh*. See Commentary *ad loc.*
3. Reading *‘^{a}lê* as plural of *‘āleh*.
4. Reading *l^{e}ḥummām* for MT *laḥmām*.
5. Adding *’^{a}nāšîm metri causa*, omitted through haplography before *y^{e}ḡōrāšû* (pausal) in the Old Heb. script. See Commentary *ad loc.*
6. Reading *ba‘^{a}rûṣê* for MT *b^{e}‘ārûṣ*. See Commentary *ad loc.*
7. Reading *l^{e}māšāl* for MT *l^{e}millāh*.
8. Reading *yiṯrî* (Qere) with S and T for MT *yiṯrô*.
9. Reading *yāqîmû* for MT *yāqûmû*, *y* being corrupted to *w* in the stage of the script represented by the Qumran MSS.
10. Reading *mip̄dāḥōṯ* for MT *pirḥāḥ*. See Commentary *ad loc.*
11. Reading *‘ālay* for MT *‘al-yāmîn*. See Commentary *ad loc.*
12. Omitting MT *raḡlay šillēḥû*. See Commentary *ad loc.*
13. Reading *l^{e}hawwōṯî* for MT *l^{e}hawwāṯî*. See Commentary *ad loc.*
14. Reading *ya‘^{a}lû* for MT *yō‘îlû*.
15. Reading *‘ōṣēr* for MT *‘ōzēr*.
16. Reading *hohp^{e}ḵû* for MT *hohpaḵ*.
17. Reading *tinnāḏēp̄* after LXX for MT *tirdōp̄*, with corruption of *n* to *r* in the Old Heb. script.
18. Omitting *w^{e}‘attāh* as a dittograph after *y^{e}šu‘āṯî*.
19. Reading *niqq^{e}ḏû* for MT *niqqar*, with corruption of *d* to *r* in the square script and omission of final *w* by haplography before *m* in the Old Heb. script.

20. Reading *mē ʿ*^{a}*lî*, for MT *mē ʿālāy*. See Commentary *ad loc.*
21. Reading *ʿ*^{a}*qāray* with LXX for MT *ʿōr*^{e}*qay*.
22. Reading *yitpōś kil*^{e}*ḇûšî* with LXX for MT *yiṯḥappēś l*^{e}*ḇûšî*, understanding the object as the pronominal suffix of the parallel verb in v. 18b doing double duty, as regularly in Ugaritic poetry, with omission of *k* after *s* in the Old Heb. script.
23. Reading *hōrîḏānî* for MT *hōrānî*.
24. Reading *l*^{e}*ḥōmer ûl*^{e}*homrî metri causa*. See Commentary *ad loc.*
25. Reading *w*^{e}*lō' tiṯbōnēn* with one Heb. MSS and V for MT *wattiṯbōnen*.
26. Reading *t*^{e}*šû'āh* for MT *tûšiyyāh* (Qere).
27. Reading *l*^{e}*'ay bō'eh* for MT *lō'-ḇ*^{e}*'î*. See Commentary *ad loc.*
28. Reading *'ešlaḥ* for MT *yišlaḥ*, *'* being corrupted to *y* in the Old Heb. script.
29. Reading *lî y*^{e}*sawwēa'* for MT *lāhen šûa'*, *y* of *lî* being corrupted to *h* in the Old Heb. script, and *y* to *n* in the last stage of the script.
30. Omitting MT *kî* with LXX, S and V *metri causa*.
31. Reading *mē ʿ*^{a}*lî* for MT *mē ʿālāy*. See Commentary *ad loc.*

Commentary on Chapter 30

1-8. It has been maintained that vv. 2-8 (introduced by v. 1, which, it is claimed, is editorial) is part of another passage in Job, perhaps really belonging to Job's speech in ch. 24, which is fragmentary (so Duhm, Bickell, Tur-Sinai). Fohrer treats vv. 2-8 as a later insertion which breaks the sequence of thought between vv. 1 and 9ff. The passage is indeed an embarrassing interruption of the argument, and may well be part of a citation of part of a Plaint of the Sufferer, from which such adaptations are regularly made in the Book of Job, often at greater length than is strictly necessary for the argument. We would admit v. 2, and take vv. 3-8 as one of those extended quotations, perhaps secondary to the Book of Job.

1. The reference in v. 1c and d may be to the order of preference at a Bedouin guest-meal, where the honoured guests and as many male adults as can sit at meat are first served, then poorer tribesmen and juniors, then servants and women, the remains being gnawed by the dogs.

2. Dhorme rightly in our opinion defends MT *lāmmāh llî*, emphasizing *lî* which refers to Job at the height of his prestige when he was independent of the support of such people, even if they had been strong, to say nothing of them in such an enfeebled state. This suggests that the pronominal suffix in *'ālêmô* is also emphatic, in antithesis to *lî*, 'their strength, even for their own sakes (*'ālêmô*) is perished'. For this use of *'al* with the pronominal suffix, cf. v. 16; 10.1; Pss. 42.6, 12; 43.5.

On *kelaḥ*, Syr. *kelaḥ*, see on 5.26.

3. *kāp̄ān* is Aram., 'hunger, famine'.

galmûḏ, which means 'sterile' in 3.7 and 15.34, is best taken here in its Arab. nuance as 'hard'.

b^eḥeser w^ekāpān galmûd may be the first colon of a tricolon, but is probably the second colon of a bicolon, of which the first colon has dropped out (so Hölscher, Mowinckel).

LXX takes *ʿōr^eqîm* as the Aram. verb 'they flee', but it is cognate rather of the Syr. *ʿ^araq* ('to gnaw'). The colon is short of a beat, which may be restored by the inclusion of *ʿiqq^erê* ('roots', so Dhorme, Ball, Hölscher, Mowinckel, Fohrer), which may well have been omitted by haplography after *hāʿōr^eqîm*. Alternatively the missing object of *ʿōr^eqîm* may be *ṣeʾ^eṣāʾê* ('growth'), which might be omitted by haplography before *ṣiyyāh*. We prefer the former solution, reading *ʿiqq^erê*, a conscious word-play with *ʿōr^eqîm*.

In *ʾemeš šôʾāh ûm^ešōʾāh* ('Evening' [or 'yesterday'], 'ruin and desolation') the simplest solution is to assume a dittograph of *š* and read *ʾēm šôʾāh ûm^ešōʾāh* (lit. 'mother of the waste and wilderness'), a description of *ṣiyyāh*. For a similar description of localities, cf. Umm Lakîś ('Mother of Itch') near Gaza and Umm Faḥm ('Mother of Charcoal') near Megiddo.

4. The verb *qāṭap* ('to pluck') is found again in 8.12 and 24.24.

mallûaḥ, rendered *halima* in LXX, Aq. and Theod., is 'salt-wort' (so Bochart, Dhorme, Fohrer, Pope).

If v. 4b is taken in strict parallelism with v. 4a, *laḥmām* might denote 'their food' (so G.B. Gray, Dhorme, Kissane, Weiser, Terrien). There is no evidence, however, that the roots of desert broom (*reṯem*) were edible, but they were known to be used to produce charcoal (Ps. 120.4), so for *laḥmām* we should read *l^eḥummām* ('to warm themselves'; so Köhler, Hölscher, Tur-Sinai, Mowinckel, Fohrer, Gordis, Pope, Lindblom).

5. Dahood's suggestion that *min-gēw* is a corruption of *gm*, known in Ugaritic as 'with a shout', that is, 'aloud' (1957: 318ff.), certainly gives a parallel to *yārîʿû* in v. 5b, but it would be more convincing in an archaic passage in the Psalms than in a relatively late sapiential passage that shows Aramaic influence. It is in any case unnecessary. For the problematic *gēw* Bochart proposed *gōyî*, but there is no need to emend, since *gēw* is attested in Phoenician (Cooke 1903: 33.2), Aram. and Syr., meaning 'community' (so Hoffmann, Budde, G.B. Gray, Dhorme, Hölscher, Kissane, Dhorme, Mowinckel, Fohrer, Pope, Terrien). Another beat is required in this colon, and *ʿ^anāšîm* may be read, having been omitted by haplography before *y^egōrāšû* in the Old Heb. script.

6. The parallelism with *ḥōrê ʿāpār* ('holes of the earth') supports the meaning 'slopes of the wadis' (*ʿ^arûṣê n^eḥālîm*; cf. Arab. *ʿirḍu*[*n*], 'the slope of a hill'; so Michaelis, Wetzstein, Dhorme, Hölscher, Mowinckel, Fohrer, Pope, Terrien).

kēpîm ('rocks') is found in Jer. 14.29 and in Ass. *kapû*, and is familiar in Aram.

7. On *nāhaq* ('to bray') see on 6.5. The people utter their cries to keep in touch with one another.

ḥārûl denotes not 'nettles', but rather 'thistles', which grow over three feet high (Dalman 1932: II, 318). The reference is possibly to the outcasts stalking up to the settlement under cover of the thistles and bushes of the waste, where they keep in touch by animal noises, preparatory to making a petty raid.

8. On *nāḇāl* see above on 2.10.

nāḵā' is an Aram. form of Heb. *nāḵāh* (Hiphil and Hophal), found only here and in Isa. 16.7; Prov. 15.13; 17.22; 18.14; cf. Tur-Sinai, who proposes to emend to *niḵr*^{e}*ṯû* ('they are cut off', so Dhorme).

9. *n*^{e}*ḡînāh* is primarily the accompaniment of psalms on a stringed instrument and secondarily music or singing in general. Here, as in Lam. 3.14, where *n*^{e}*ḡînāh* is parallel to *ś*^{e}*ḥōq* ('laughingstock'), it means the theme of a song, possibly improvised in jest in idle entertainment, as in the Plaint of the Sufferer in Ps. 69.13 (EVV 12), where the word denotes drinking songs, in which, as here, the innocent sufferer is mocked. As a parallel to *n*^{e}*ḡînōṯ* in this context *millāh* ('word') should probably be emended to *māšāl* ('byword'); cf. 17.6.

10. Note the assonance *rāḥ*^{a}*qû* and *rōq*. On the spitting in the face in the familiar imagery of the Plaint of the Sufferer, cf. Isa. 50.6 and Job 17.6.

11. This is another ambiguous verse. Kethib *yiṯrô* ('his cord') is read by LXX and V, while Qere *yiṯrî* ('my cord') is the reading followed by S and T, which we adopt. *yeṯer* is taken by Dhorme as a tether, which would be a fitting parallel to *resen* ('halter'), but the sense is rather 'bowstring' (cf. Judg. 16.7-9) or 'tent-cord' (cf. Jer. 10.20, where the form is *mêṯār*). We prefer the latter.

pāṯaḥ (here intensive) is used of loosening (the knots of) bonds (12.18; 38.31; 39.5) or of the thongs of armour (1 Kgs 20.11). The passage might possibly refer to the loosening of the bowstring, that is, the disarming of a defeated enemy (so G.B. Gray, Terrien, Fohrer). The verb militates against Mowinckel's interpretation of God unloosing his bowstring to shoot at the victim and against Kissane's view that the phrase means 'he stripped off my excellency', a meaning which *yiṯrî* has in other contexts. We regard the reference to the loosening of the tent-peg to denote the condition of a homeless castaway. This interpretation is possibly supported by the cliché in the Ras Shamra Baal myth referring to the discomfiture of a party as the up-rooting of his tent-pegs (Gordon *UT* 129.17; 49.VI, 27-28). Here in the phrase *lys' 'alt ṯbtk* it is doubtful whether *'alt* is *'ahl* ('tent') with the *h* elided or a cognate of Arab. *'ālatu*(*n*) ('a spear', as the symbol of royalty).

In v. 11b *resen* ('bridle'; cf. Ps. 32.9; Isa. 30.28), signifies 'restraint'. We should emphasize *mippānay* in this context as meaning 'even in my presence'.

12. This verse is greatly overloaded in MT, and should probably be reduced to a bicolon of three beats in each colon rather than treated as a defective tricolon. *'al-yāmîn* ('on the right hand') is suspect in the absence of 'on the left hand' in v. 12b, unless it means that Job's enemies dared to attack him on the right hand, the sword hand, hence the side not protected by the shield. In view of the military figure in the parallel colon it is unlikely that v. 12a refers to the right hand as the place where the accuser stood (so Dhorme, citing Zech. 3.1 and Ps. 109.6), as in the Shari'a courts in Saudi Arabia today, where plaintiff and defendant stand side by side before the judge to symbolize the impartiality of justice. Hence with Budde, Beer, Peake, Duhm, G.B. Gray, Hölscher, Stevenson and Fohrer we read *'ālay* for MT *'al-yāmîn*. To account for *m* and *n* in MT *yāmîn* we conjecture *m* as the preformative of the following word. Hence we propose to get rid of the embarrassing *pirḥaḥ*, which, even if it meant 'brood', is quite out of place in a military metaphor, by emending it to *mip̄dāḥ*, the instrument for making a fracture (Arab. *fadaḫa*), a battering-ram, or the ramp for its use; cf. the reference to the breach of a wall (*pereṣ*) in v. 14a. MT *yāqûmû* must then be emended to *yāqîmû* ('they mount a battering ram against me', or 'they raise places for battering-rams against me'). The second *ḥ* in *pirḥaḥ* is a simple dittograph, or perhaps the corruption of final *t* in an original *mip̄dāḥôṯ* to *ḥ*.

If MT *raḡlay šilléḥû* is not the remnant of a defective colon referring to the sending in of infantry (reading *raḡlî*), the phrase may be eliminated as a dittograph of *šilléḥû* in v. 11b.

'ālay in v. 12b should almost certainly be eliminated, leaving the couplet to read:

> *'ālay mip̄dāḥôṯ yāqîmû*
> *wᵉyāsōllû 'orᵉḥôṯ 'êḏām*
>
> They raise places for battering-rams against me,
> They raise their destructive siege-causeways.

Here we follow Hölscher and Fohrer. *sōlᵉlāh* is used literally as a siege-mound in 2 Sam. 20.15; 2 Kgs 19.32 = Isa. 37.33; Jer. 6.8; Ezek. 4.2; 17.17; etc., and the verb from which it is derived is used figuratively in the imagery of the Plaint of the Sufferer in 19.12. It must be admitted *'orᵉḥôṯ* in the sense of siege-causeways is strange, unprecedented to our knowledge and even suspect, but nevertheless intelligible.

13. *nāṯᵉsû*, a *hapax legomenon*, is a late orthographic variant for *nāṯᵉṣû*. Dhorme has, in our opinion, rightly interpreted 'the breaking up of the path' as destruction of the escape route. Such a way out of a city under siege is depicted in the exit from a postern through which people escape with what they can salvage down the steep glaçis of Lachish on the reliefs of Sennacherib's siege from his palace at Nineveh (*ANEP*, pl. 373). The sing. in MT *lᵉhawwāṯî* ('for my ruin') is attested only once, at Job 6.2 (Qere); cf. Pss. 5.10;

38.13; 52.4; 55.12; 57.2; 91.3; Prov. 19.13; etc., where the plural is used. Here we may read *l^ehawwōṯî* ('to cause me to fall'), from *hāwāh* cognate with Arab. *hawa(y)* ('to fall'). The military metaphor is sustained in *yā ʿ^alû* ('they attack'; cf. Num. 13.31; Judg. 1.1; 12.3; etc.), for MT *yō ʿîlû* ('they profit'), which yields no feasible sense in the context. For MT *ʿōzēr* (elsewhere in the OT 'helper') *ʿōṣēr* ('one who refrains') is generally read after Dillmann, which is supported by the direct object *lāmô*, with *l* as the *nota accusativa*. G.R. Driver would defend MT, citing Arab. *ʿazara* ('to rebuke') and, with the preposition *ʿan* ('from'), 'to hinder' (1936: 163); cf. Akk. *ezeru* ('to scold'). This is not supported by *ʿāzar* in any other passage in the OT and in the present passage there is no word-play to occasion the citation of a less familiar homonym.

14. *ʾāṯāh* in the OT is poetic and generally late, with regular Aram. and Arab. cognates, but it is the regular verb 'to come' in Ugaritic. For *taḥat* ('the place of') cf. Gordon, *UT* 1 Aqht 21; 2 Aqht V,6-9:

ytšʾû yṯb bʾap ṯġr	He rose to take his seat at the entrance of the gate
tḥt ʾadrm dbgrn	In the place of the notables who are in the public place.

15. A tricolon is more usual among prevailing bicola at the end of a strophe rather than the beginning, and v. 16a may well be a late addition.

If MT *hohpaḵ* is correct it would be a case of the passive of the suppressed agent. But it is probably a case of simple haplography, final *w* being omitted after *k* in the Old Heb. script.

For MT *tirdōp̄* we may read *tērāḏēp̄* (so Siegfried, Beer, Hontheim, Peters, Hölscher, Fohrer) or *tinnādēp̄* (so Graetz, Duhm, Budde, Tur-Sinai, G.B. Gray). We prefer the latter, the same verb being used of chaff driven away by the wind in Ps. 1.4 or of smoke blown away by the wind in Ps. 68.3, and of a driven leaf in Job 13.25.

y^ešuʿātî is used here in its primary sense of freedom from cramping circumstances; cf. Arab. *waśiʿa* ('to be wide'). *wāśiʿ* (generous') as an epithet of Allah in the Qur'an suggests that in Job's complaint of the impairing of his social potential *y^ešuʿāṯî* may mean 'my largesse'.

16. *w^eʿattāh* gives an extra beat in the first colon, and is probably to be omitted as a dittograph after the end of *y^ešuʿāṯî*.

ʿālay ('on my account') indicates the object of Job's lament; cf. 10.1; Ps. 42.6, 12; 43.5.

17. Dahood (1966: 230) has, in our opinion, solved the problem of this difficult text in seeing that MT *ʿālay* is *ʿ^alî*, a cognate of Arab. *ġala(y)* ('to boil'; cf. *ġalayatu*[*n*], 'cooking-pot'), but we consider that he is wrong in assuming without evidence a root *qrr* or *qrh*. We propose rather the emendation of MT *niqqar* to *niqq^eḏû* in *scriptio defectiva*, from *yāqaḏ* ('to be kindled,

burn'; cf. Arab. *waqada*, 'to be hot, glow'). Dahood has noticed that *m* in MT *mē'ālay* is the comparative *min* with *mē'ᵃlî* ('than a cauldron').

For MT *'ōrᵉqay* in v. 17b LXX read 'my nerves' (*'ᵃrāqay*), rightly apprehending that a part of the body was denoted, parallel to *'ᵃṣāmay* ('my bones'). Actually Saadya, Ibn Ezra, Qimḥi and Rashi took the word as cognate with Arab. *'urūq* ('veins'). This is a good description of the symptoms of fever; cf. Mowinckel, who translates 'feverish pulse'.

18. For MT *yiṯḥappēś* ('it is sought out' or 'it is disguised') we read *yiṯpōś* ('it seizes') (so LXX, Houbigant, Siegfried, Beer, Dhorme, Hölscher, Mowinckel, Fohrer, Terrien, Pope). The subject in the 3rd person cannot be God, as Dhorme asserts, since Job appeals to God in vv. 20ff. in the 2nd person. We take the subject therefore as *'ōnî* ('my affliction') in v. 16.

19. For MT *hōrānî* ('it shot me') Duhm proposed the emendation *hōrîḏānî* ('it brought me down'). The colon is still short and an introductory *hēn* may have been omitted through haplography. Alternatively we might propose a similar assonance to *kᵉ'āp̄ār wā'ēp̄er* in v. 19b in *lᵉḥōmer ûlᵉhomrî* ('to mire and confusion'). This is suggested by the reference to the city of Mot the god of death in the Ras Shamra texts as *hmry* ('Ruin, Dissolution'), cognate with the Arab. *hamratu*(*n*) ('confusion'). The texts in question are Gordon *UT* 51 VII,12 and 67 II,15, on which see J. Gray 1965: 55 n. 56f., where we find a cognate of Ugaritic *mhmrt* with the same significance in Ps. 140.11 (cf. Gordon *UT* 67 I,7-8).

20. *'āmaḏtî* ('I stand', or 'have taken my stand') is possibly a forensic term, indicating that Job has come to the bar and expects God to do likewise (e.g. Deut. 19.17; Ps. 109.6; Zech. 3.1). But it may also denote the attitude of prayer (Jer. 15.1); cf. Solomon's prayer at the dedication of the temple, standing before the altar with his open hands stretched out (1 Kgs 8.22). For MT *wattiṯbōnen* one Heb. MS and V read *wᵉlō' tiṯbōnen* ('and you do not heed') which is read by Bickell, Siegfried, Beer, Duhm, Peters, Hölscher, Dhorme, Mowinckel, G.E. Gray, Fohrer, Terrien. Stevenson retains MT, rendering the verb 'you stare' (so Pope).

21. *hāp̄aḵ* in the Niphal with the adjective introduced by *lᵉ* in *tēhāp̄ēḵ lᵉ'azkār lî* ('you turn cruel to me') has an excellent parallel in Isa. 63.10, *wayyēhāp̄ēḵ lāhem lᵉ'ôyēḇ* ('and he turned their enemy'). MT *bᵉ'ōṣem yāḏᵉḵā* ('with the strength of your hand') is readily intelligible, but perhaps *'eṣem-yāḏᵉḵā* was intended (lit. 'bone of your hand', i.e. the full strength of your hand); cf. *'eṣem-haššāmayim* (Exod. 24.10), *bᵉ'eṣem tummô* ('having quite fulfilled himself', Job 21.23), etc., and the same use of Aram. *gerem* (lit. 'bone'). Here, as in Deut. 8.17, *'eṣem yāḏᵉḵā* may mean 'all your strength'. *tiśṭᵉmēnî* would mean 'wreak your animosity against me'; cf. Gen. 16.9; 27.41; 49.23; 50.15;

Ps. 55.4 (EVV 3). The reading has a variant reflected in LXX 'you scourge me', implying *t*ᵉ*šōṭ*ᵉ*ṭēnî*.

22. In view of the conception of God as 'He who Mounts the Clouds' (Pss. 18.11 [EVV 10]; 68.5, 34 [EVV 4, 33]; 104.3; Deut. 33.26), like Baal in the Ras Shamra texts (Gordon *UT* 51 III, 11, 18; V, 122; 67 II, 7; 68,8, 29; 76 I,7; III, 22, 37; etc.), v. 22a may have a *double entendre*, referring to the sufferer caught up (*tiśśā'ēnî*) and made to ride the wind or raised to the status of God, from which he is reduced to ruin. However this may be, the ruin of Job is described in v. 22b, where he is 'liquidated' as a cloud. The verb *mûḡ* is found meaning 'to dissolve' (Ps. 65.11), expressing the dissolution of a solid substance; cf. Muhammad's description of the fate of the wicked fusing together in the sea of fire, *yamūjūna ba'ḍu fī ba'ḍihim* ('they welter one on the top of another').

The Qere *tûšiyyā* ('sound counsel, success') is quite unsuitable in this context. The Kethib *tušiwwāh* is a relic of the correct reading *t*ᵉ*šu'āh* ('storm'), which is attested in the plural in 39.7; Isa. 22.2; Zech. 4.7 in the sense of 'tumult'. *t*ᵉ*su'āh* is a formation from the root *šā'āh*, from which the noun is usually *šô'āh*, which means generally 'ruin' or 'dissolution', but specifically 'storm' in Ezek. 38.9 and Prov. 1.27. *t*ᵉ*šu'āh* may be the subject of *t*ᵉ*mōḡ*ᵉ*ḡēnî*, or, as we prefer, the adverbial accusative, which is common in Arab.

23. Job's return (*t*ᵉ*šîḇēnî*) to death reflects the conception that humans are from the dust and will return to the dust (Gen. 3.19, J).

There is probably a word-play between *yāḏa'tî* ('I know certainly', 'I am sure') and *mô'ēḏ* ('certainly appointed'). Alternatively *bêṯ mô'ēḏ l*ᵉ*ḵol-ḥāy* might be rendered 'the meeting place for all living' (so Dhorme, Hölscher, Mowinckel, Kissane, Fohrer, Terrien, Pope). This conception is expressed in 3.17ff., and this sense of *mô'ēd* is supported by the compound nouns *har mô'ēḏ* ('mount of assembly') and *'ōhel mô'ēd* ('the Tent of Meeting') in the Exodus tradition (Exod. 33.7-13; etc.). If this interpretation is accepted it might explain the etymology of *r*ᵉ*p̄ā'îm* ('the defunct') as 'those joined together' in the underworld, the verb *rāp̄ā'* being possibly a byform of a verb cognate with Arab. *rafa*(*y*) ('to darn, join') as H.L. Ginsberg proposed (1946: 23, 41). But *r*ᵉ*p̄ā'îm* may have originally signified the dead in their influence over fertility (lit. 'healers'), from the well-known Heb. verb *rāp̄ā'* ('to heal or restore fertility'), which we have proposed on the basis of the Ras Shamra texts (J. Gray 1949; 1965: 120 nn. 129-31).

24. MT in v. 24a means 'But he did not stretch out a hand against a ruin-heap', which makes no sense in the context, even figuratively. *'aḵ*, which inaugurates a train of thought contrary to what precedes, generally introduces the statement of faith against apparent alienation from God (e.g. Pss. 49.16; 62.2, 3, 5, 6, 7; 73.1), but may also introduce the protestation of innocence (e.g. Ps.

73.13). The second instance illustrates the force of *'aḵ* in the present passage, where it turns the train of thought from what precedes and introduces Job's protestation of innocence. This rules out the proposal that MT *b*^{e}*'î* is the corruption of *ṭôḇēa'* ('sinking'), giving the meaning 'Does not a drowning man stretch out a hand?' (so Dillmann, Fohrer). But there is nothing in the text that makes a corruption of *ṭ* graphically feasible, nor does *šālaḥ yāḏ* mean 'to stretch out a hand for help', but rather to give help, and in fact more often in the OT denotes 'attack'. Nor does it afford a parallel to v. 24b. Job's protestation of innocent conduct introduced by *'aḵ* demands the reading *'ešlaḥ* for MT *yišlaḥ* (so LXX), giving the meaning 'I would stretch out (my) hand'. The connection with the sequel expressing Job's concern for the destitute (*q*^{e}*šēh-yôm* and *'eḇyôn*) has suggested the emendation of MT *b*^{e}*'î* to *b*^{e}*'ānî*, 'I did not stretch out my hand against the poor', as proposed by Wright (so Dhorme, Kissane, Pope). Beer also reads *b*^{e}*'ānî* as stretching out a hand to help the poor, assuming either the omission of MT *lō'* or the interrogative sense without the interrogative particle, which is possible. In the text as understood by Dhorme and others the denial of aggression towards the poor would contrast oddly with Job's positive charity in vv. 24b-25, and we find such a claim singularly weak. Under these circumstances NEB comes nearer the truth with 'Yet no beggar held out his hand but...', though we would follow LXX in reading *'ešlaḥ*. This follows G.R. Driver's suggestion that the original of MT *b*^{e}*'î* was the participle *bō'eh*, lit. 'asking' (1936: 164f.). The verb, which denotes a question in Isa. 21.12, also signifies a request in Gen. 19.2 (cf. Syr. *b*^{e}*'ā'* in Jn 14.16), and is found in both senses in the Aram. sections of Dan. Cf. Arab. *bāġāy* ('to ask', used in the IVth Form meaning 'to help to attain'). Accordingly we would read *bō'eh* for MT *b*^{e}*'î*, assuming scribal corruption of *h* to *y* in the Old Heb. script. We would resolve the problem of *lō'* in v. 24a by assuming a scribal corruption of an original *l*^{e}*'ay* with dittography of *'* and corruption of the second *'* from *y* in the Old Heb. script. *'ay* in this case might mean 'any'; cf. Arab. *'ayyu*(*n*), which is attested, though doubtfully, in Prov. 31.4. The sense, 'But to any who made a request I would stretch out my hand', thus agrees with the context and particularly with the parallel colon, especially if we follow LXX in reading a form of *šiwwēa'* for MT *šûwa'*. We would further suggest that MT *lāhen šûwa'* is a corruption of *lî y*^{e}*šawwēa'* ('cried to me'), assuming the corruption of *y* to *h* in the Old Heb. script and *y* to final *n* in the stage of the development of the script in the second and first centuries BCE.

25. *'āḡam* ('to be grieved') is a *hapax legomenon* in the OT, but is well attested in Aram. and Syr.

26. In v. 26a MT *kî* is disregarded by LXX, S and V, and the usual causative sense of *kî* is inappropriate in the context. Hence we take it as the enclitic which is found in Ugaritic introducing the final verb, which is thus emphasized (Gordon *UT*, §9.13; cf. Pss. 49.16; 118.10-11). A final sentence may be so

introduced with the same effect; for example, Deut. 32.9, and possibly Isa. 5.7. The antithesis of light and well-being and darkness and calamity is very familiar in Israel, for example, Amos 5.18 and in the Qumran theology; for instance in 'The War of the Sons of Light against the Sons of Darkness'.

27. The verb *rāṯaḥ*, found also in 41.23 (Hiphil), is used in Ezek. 24.5, meaning 'to boil'; cf. Ben Sira 43.3. Turmoil or fermentation may be denoted, as here in the bowels (*mēʿay*) of the sufferer.

dāmam may express either stillness or silence.

qidd^{e}*munî* ('confront me') has also the temporal implication of 'prematurely'. The Piel of the verb is used in the locative sense in 3.12 and probably also in the Song of Deborah (Judg. 5.21), where the reference may be not to the 'ancient' (MT *qāḏîm*) River Qishon, but to the river 'heading off' (*qiddēm*) the fugitives from the battle.

28. To 'go about black' (*qōḏēr hillēḵ*), that is, in mourning, is a conventional figure from the Plaint of the Sufferer (cf. Pss. 38.7; 43.2, where the verb is in the Hithpael). The reference may be either to the black sack-cloth worn by mourners, or to the unwashed or blackened face, which was one of the rites indicating suspension of normal activities designed to frustrate the supernatural powers to which the primitive community considered itself particularly vulnerable at such social crises as death.

In MT *b*^{e}*lōʾ ḥammāh* Dahood (1966: 93) suggests that the first word was originally *b*^{e}*luʾ* ('scorched'), citing the Ugaritic root *blʾa*. This root is indeed attested in the Ugaritic texts, but the appreciation of the present passage as of the literary type the Plaint of the Sufferer indicates the real significance of *qōḏēr hillaḵtî* as in the guise of a mourner as against the literalism of Dahood's interpretation.

ḥammāh from the root *ḥāmam* ('to be hot') is known as 'sun' (Isa. 24.23; 30.26; Song 6.10). On the other hand Duhm proposed the reading *b*^{e}*lōʾ n*^{e}*ḥāmāh* ('uncomforted'; so Budde, Tur-Sinai, G.B. Gray, Hölscher, Mowinckel, Fohrer), but MT is unanimously attested, either as *ḥammāh* ('sun', LXX, T, Sym., S and V) or *ḥēmāh* ('wrath'). We prefer the interpretation 'and not by the sun' as giving stronger emphasis to the significance of *qōḏēr hillaḵtî*.

In v. 28b we take *ʾ*^{a}*šawwēaʿ* as the imperfect of attendant circumstances, more common in Arab. than in Heb. The significance of this colon as parallel to v. 28a is that the sufferer has duly performed his mourning rites of separation, dictated by his apparent alienation from God, and has appealed for reinstatement in the community (*haqqāhāl*).

29. *tan*, not to be confused with *tannîn*, which in certain passages denotes one of the monsters associated with the primaeval waters of Chaos (*tnn* of the Ras Shamra mythology; see on 7.12), means 'jackal', Arab. *tînānu*(*n*). Job's affinity with the jackals may be his wailing, which one always associates with

night-fall in Palestine; cf. Arab. *wāwiyāt*, the expressive onomatopoeic word for jackals, but the main point of comparison is the association with the country beyond human settlement, or the desert, as the mention of *bᵉnôṯ ya'ᵃnāh* in the parallel colon indicates, especially if 'ostriches' are denoted, which, it must be admitted, is not certain. The two are paired again in Mic. 1.8; Isa. 43.20, and the former is explicitly associated with the desert (Mal. 1.3) and with ruins (Jer. 9.10; 10.22; 49.33; 51.37; Isa. 34.13; 35.7; Ps. 44.20). The latter is known as an unclean bird in Deut. 14.15 and Lev. 11.16, where its association with the raven may indicate the owl rather than the ostrich. In Mic. 1.8, like the Job passage, reproducing the imagery of the Plaint of the Sufferer, the reference is to mourning like the jackals and *bᵉnôṯ ya'ᵃneh'*, which again rather indicates owls.

30. Here as in v. 17 *mē'ᵃlî* (for MT *mē'ālāy*) may mean '...than a cauldron', but in view of the parallel *minnî-ḥōreḇ*, where *min* denotes the cause of the effect, *'ᵃlî* is better taken here as a verbal noun 'scorching'.

31. On *kinnōr* and *'ugāḇ* see on 21.12.

Job 31

Job's Great Oath of Purgation

Job's negative confession, though peculiar to his Jewish milieu, has formal affinity with the detailed ancient Near Eastern lists of delinquencies, social and, unlike Job's confession except 31.26f., religious and ritual. Such a declaration, for example, marked the conclusion of the king's humiliation in the ritual of the Babylonian New Year festival (*ANET*, 334) and were a part of Assyrian fast liturgies, where the king represented the community. It is found again in the clearance of a private individual from sin alleged to be the source of suffering (Jastrow 1898, cited by G.B. Gray), where the subject raises the possibility of certain sins, religious and social, which invite exculpation, probably under oath, with the consciousness of the fearful consequences of perjury. The enumeration of twelve offences from which Job exculpates himself has a certain analogy in the statement of the Eloquent Peasant in Egypt (*ANET*, 408-10, nine times before a noble and the tenth time before the king). However, with the enumeration and certain particular social grievances of the Peasant the analogy with Job 31 stops. It is not an exculpation nor is it part of an Oath of Purgation.

Job's negative confession, despite the analogies we have cited from the Semitic milieu of Mesopotamia, is properly at home in Israelite tradition. Here declared innocence of specified social evils admits one to fellowship with worshippers in the sanctuary (Pss. 15; 24.3ff.). Again the specification of certain social evils with an adjuration (Ps. 7.4f.) may be associated with an individual's exculpation from false accusation, or it may precede a ritual act of purification (Ps. 26.4-6).

While Ps. 7.4f. affords analogy to Job's oath of purgation, the twelve specific sins he disowns indicate the influence of the twelve adjurations of the covenant community in Deut. 27.15-26, though excluding the religious offences (v. 15) and the specific sexual offences within the forbidden degrees (vv. 20-23). A closer analogy to Job's negative confession is in the Decalogue (Exod. 20.3-17), though again excluding religious offences (Exod. 20.3-10), where, however, there is no commitment under adjuration as in Deut. 27.15-26. In the holiness code nearer the time when the Book of Job was written, though characteristically religious and ritual observances are enjoined, there are twelve social evils forbidden (Lev. 19.11-18). Thus, whether formulated originally as apodictic law in the covenant sacrament or the crystallization of instruction of local elders or heads of families, this became the norm of the social ethic of Israel, as is reflected in the prophets from Amos to Ezekiel, who lists five social evils (18.6b-13), all included in Job's Oath of Purgation. The numbers ten or twelve indicate a mnemonic expedient to impress the demands of the code upon the popular memory in transmission of the social demands in particular by local elders and heads of families. By the same token the professional instructors of young aspirants to administration may well have enumerated the virtues they commended and the vices they condemned. So much at any rate is suggested by the thirty wise sayings of Prov. 22.17-22, with its prototype in the thirty sayings of the Egyptian scribe Amenemope c. 1000 BCE (*ANET*, 421-25).

Thus in presenting Job's Oath of Purgation the author draws on a well-established tradition in Israel which informed daily life in the community in the law, the cult and in the instruction of the sages. In the element of adjuration, however, it is the forensic and the religious tradition which is reflected.

The chapter falls into two parts, Job's great oath of purgation (vv. 1-34 including vv. 38-40b) and his challenge to God to state and subscribe his indictment in order that there might be a concrete charge to answer in Job's defence of his innocence (vv. 35-37).

The first part consists of ten strophes (vv. 1-4, 5-8, 9-12, 13-15, 38-40b, 16-17+ 19 + 20 + 18 + 21-22, 24-28, 29-32, 33-34 + 23).

The first strophe is formally distinct from Job's oath of purgation in that it is not introduced by the protasis and concluded by the imprecation. Nor is it the disavowal of a concrete sin. It is a direct statement that Job had made a covenant with his eyes not to look upon a virgin. *kāraṯ b^{e}rîṯ*, well known in Heb. as the technical phrase for making a covenant, has a different significance here from what was usual in Israel. It is rather to be understood in the light of a vassal-treaty, such as those imposed by the Hittite kings upon their North Syrian vassals, including the king of Ugarit (Nougayrol 1956: 40-44). Here the suzerain secures his own interests, while firmly imposing control of the actions of his vassals, as in the covenant in Israel. Thus at the outset of his oath of purgation Job asserts that he has achieved complete self-control, the aim of the wise man. His eyes as the object of his control, and sexual lust, which at first sight seems tautological in view of the denial of adultery (v. 9) may be explained as synecdoche, signifying complete control of the senses. The statement prepares us for the suppression of the evil inclination implied in the denial of the actual sin, which is a feature of the chapter. Here Heb. Wisdom anticipates Jesus' radical teaching in the Sermon on the Mount (Mt. 5.21f., 28).

Thereafter the passage follows the literary form of the oath of purgation, as in Psalm 7. Innocence of particular sins is declared in a hypothesis positive or negative with the imprecation as apodosis, either expressed or understood (e.g. vv. 7-8, 9-12, 21-22, 38-40b, 33-34, 23). In such cases as a formal protasis is not followed by an imprecation in the apodosis, as in vv. 16, 17, 19, 20, 18,

24-28 and 29-32, the formal protasis of the incomplete conditional sentence is tantamount in Hebrew idiom to an emphatic assertion either positive or negative. It is significant, in connection with the twelve adjurations with which Israel endorsed the definitive obligations of the covenant, that Job in his oath of purgation declares his innocence of twelve sins, for example, lust or lack of self-control (vv. 1-4), deceit (vv. 5-6), covetousness (vv. 7-8), adultery (vv. 9-12), evasion of legal obligation to his slaves or tenants (vv. 13-15, 39a), neglect of charitable obligations (vv. 16-21), materialism (vv. 24-25), atavistic reverence for astral bodies (vv. 26-28), malicious gloating over an enemy's misfortune (vv. 29-30), inhospitality (vv. 31-32), fear of public opinion, occasioning either hypocrisy or failure to declare himself in a just but unpopular cause (vv. 33-34) and land-grabbing (vv. 38, 39b).

The second part of the chapter, the single strophe in vv. 35-37, is wholly in the legal convention, the citation of the accuser.

The arrangement of the text is in some doubt among scholars. The proper end of Job's oath of purgation and its grand climax in his appeal to the tribunal of God is at v. 37. The declarations of innocence and the adjurations in vv. 38-40b belong in form and content to vv. 5-34, 23. This is generally agreed, but there is no agreement as to where the passage actually belongs. G.B. Gray and Fohrer locate it after v. 24; Dhorme, Kissane and Mowinckel after 32; Hölscher and Pope after v. 8; and Stevenson after v. 20. We suggest that the reference to the treatment of peasant tenants indicates a grouping with the other dependants, slaves of both sexes in vv. 13-14, which leads to the final oath in v. 40ab. The final statement that 'the words of Job are ended' (v. 40c) is editorial. The position of v. 23 is also doubtful, though G.B. Gray, Kissane, Fohrer and Terrien retain MT. Hölscher omits it, evidently as a gloss, though he goes on to state that, however it may be interpreted, it does not fall after v. 22. The last proposition is generally admitted, but is variously explained. Stevenson, admitting its association with v. 24, suggests that the verse is displaced from 'after 24ff.', while Dhorme treats it as the heading to vv. 24ff. Pope reads it after v. 14 and Mowinckel after v. 27. In vv. 24-34 Job's various disavowals lack the adjuration or the equivalent. In this case, of course, we may still take his statements introduced by *'im* or *'im lō'* as emphatic denials or asseverations in which the adjuration is simply understood. But we should expect either an adjuration or at least a statement that Job has laid himself under divine sanctions. Thus we regard v. 23 as displaced from after v. 34, where Job's assertion that he feared God comes naturally after his reference to fear of public opinion.

Verse 18, if the text is correct, is pointless in its position in MT, and is probably displaced from after v. 20, where it may be read naturally as the blessing of the destitute on his benefactor.

We assume a lacuna before v. 35c, which, however, may be no more than the first colon of a bicolon ending in v. 35c.

Chapter 31

1. ‘I had made a covenant with my eves
Not to look[1] upon a virgin.
2. What then is the portion (allotted by) God above,
What requital from the Almighty from on high?
3. Is not disaster (the portion) of the wicked,
And calamity for the workers of iniquity?
4. Does *he* not mark my way,
And number all my steps?

5. If I have walked with falsehood,
Or my foot hastened to deceit,
6. Then may (God) weigh me with just balance,
And let him know my innocence.
7. If my steps ever swerve from the way,
And my heart stray after my eyes,
Or anything[2] stick to my hands,
8. Then may I sow and another eat,
And my produce be uprooted!

9. If my heart has been seduced by a woman,
And I have lurked at my neighbour’s door,
10. May my own wife grind to another,
And may others lie upon her.
11. That[3] were indeed a wanton crime,
A criminal wrong!—
12. [4]A fire that consumes even to Perdition,
Which would scorch up[5] all my crops.

13. Never did I spurn the case of my slave,
Or of my maidservant if they had a suit against me—
14. For what should I do if God rose up against me,
And if he held enquiry what should I answer him?
15. Did not he who made me in the womb make him,
Did not the same One fashion us[6] both in the womb?

38. If the land I occupied cried out because of me,
Its furrows all weeping with it,
39. If I consumed its strength without cost,
Drove its workers[7] to exhaustion,
40a. Instead of wheat may thorns come forth,
b. And instead of barley noxious weeds!

16. I never restrained the poor from what he wanted,
Nor disappointed the widow,
17. Nor ate my morsel alone,
And the fatherless ate not of it.
19. Never did I see one perishing for want of clothing,
The poor man without a covering.
20. Surely men’s loins[8] blessed me
When they were warmed by the fleece of my lambs,

18. (Saying) "Surely from my youth he brought me up[9] like a father,
And from my mother's womb he guided me".[10]

21. If ever I shook my fist against the innocent[11]
Because I saw my bullies in the gate,
22. May my shoulder-blade fall from its socket[12]
And my arm be broken off from its joint.[13]

24. If I made gold my confidence,
And called fine gold my trust,
25. If ever I was elated with my abundant wealth
Because my own power had got much,
26. If ever I marked the sun when it was bright
Or the moon in its cool course,[14]
27. My heart being secretly seduced,[15]
My hand throwing a kiss from my mouth,
28. He himself would mark my tricks,[16]
For I should have been false to God above.

29. I never rejoiced at my enemy's calamity,
Nor was glad[17] when evil befell him,
30. Nor suffered my mouth to sin,
Demanding his life in a curse.
31. The inmates of my tent will declare,
"Who could adduce one who has not been filled with his meat?"
32. The stranger never had to pass the night in the street,
I opened my door to the wayfarer.[18]

33. I never covered up my sins from others,[19]
Hiding my iniquity in my bosom,
34. Because I feared the rumour of the capital,
And because the contempt of the families scared me,
So that I kept silence and refrained from coming out of doors,
23, For the terror of God overwhelms[20]
And before his majesty I am powerless!

35. O that one might give me a hearing!
Behold, this is my ardent desire;[21] let the Almighty answer me!
(Would that I had) the indictment written by my adversary!
36. I would certainly shoulder the liability,
I would bind it on me like a turban.[22]
37. I would account to him for my every step,
As a notable should I would present it.'

40c. The end of Job's statement.

Textual Notes to Chapter 31

1. Reading *mēhiṯbônēn* for MT *ûmāh 'etbônēn*.
2. Reading *m^e'ûmāh* for MT *m^e'ûm*.
3. Reading *hî'* (Qere) for MT *hû'* (Kethib).

4. Omitting *kî*, *metri causa.*
5. Reading *t^erašśēš* for MT *t^ešārēš*. See Commentary *ad loc.*
6. Reading *way^ekōn^enēnû* for MT *way^ekunennû.*
7. Conjecturing *pō^{ʿa}lêhā* for MT *b^e ʿālêhā.*
8. Conjecturing *ḥ^alāṣām* for MT *ḥ^alāṣô.*
9. Reading *gidd^elanî* for MT *g^edēlanî.*
10. Reading *ʾanḥennî* for MT *ʾanḥennāh*, assuming corruption of *y* to *h* in the Old Heb. script.
11. Conjecturing *ʿ^alê tām* for MT *ʿal-yāṯôm.*
12. Reading *šikmāh*, with 3rd fem. sing. pronom. suffix.
13. Reading *miqqānāh* (with 3rd fem. sing. pronom. suffix).
14. Reading *yāqar* (Hiphil of *qārar*) for MT *yāqār*. See Commentary *ad loc.*
15. Reading *wayyippāṯ* for MT *wayyipt.*
16. Reading *gam-hûʾ ʿōyēn nipt^elōṯāy* or *p^e ʿālāy* (pausal forms) for MT *gam-hû ʿāwōn p^elîlî*. See Commentary *ad loc.*
17. Reading *w^ehiṯrō ʿaʿtî* with T for MT *w^ehiṯ ʿōrartî.*
18. Reading *lā ʾōrēaḥ* with LXX, Aq., S, T and V for MT *lā ʾōraḥ.*
19. Reading *mē ʾāḏām* for MT *k^e ʾāḏām*, *m* being corrupted to *k* in the Old Heb. script.
20. Reading *kî paḥaḏ ʾēl yā ʾîd ʿālāy* for MT *kî paḥaḏ ʾēlay ʾēḏ ʾēl* (v. 23). See Commentary *ad loc.*
21. Reading *taʾ^awî* for MT *tāwî.*
22. Reading *ʿ^aṭereṯ* for MT *ʿ^aṭārôṯ.*

Commentary on Chapter 31

1. On *kāraṯ b^eriṯ* in this context see introduction to ch. 31. In MT *ûmāh ʾeṯbônēn*, *māh* might introduce a rhetorical question, though this would be abrupt with no syntactical connection with the context. The text may be a corruption of *ʾim ʾeṯbônēn*, in the protasis of a conditional sentence with aposeopesis of the imprecation to express a strong denial, which would be in order after the mention of the covenant, implying oath, in v. 1a. Alternatively the original may have been *mēhiṯbônēn* ('not to consider'), as suggested by V, which, however, does not exclude the first suggestion. The reference to *b^eṯûlāh* ('a virgin') stands in peculiar isolation in the chapter, and might be doubted in view of the denial of adultery in v. 9. Hence Duhm conjectured *h^aṯûlāh* ('folly' or 'mockery'); cf. Peake's conjecture *n^eḇālāh* ('senselessness'), so Pope, which is much further from MT. But MT, which is attested in the ancient versions, recalls a similar phrase in Ben Sira 9.5ff. See further the Introduction to ch. 31.

3. *nēḵer* is found in Classical Heb. only here and in the form *nōḵer* in Obad. 12, where it means 'affliction'. It has the same nuance as Ass. *nakâru* and Arab. *nakura* ('to be harsh, hateful').

4. 'Way', 'steps', 'walking' (with falsehood); cf. 5, for 'conduct' is characteristic of sapiential idiom.

5. Here again 'walking with falsehood' (*šāw'*), 'the foot hastening to deceit' (*mirmāh*), 'steps swerving from the way' and 'the heart straying after the eyes' is in the sapiential idiom. In the propensity to deceit (v. 5) and covetousness leading to determination to acquire ('the heart straying after the eyes', v. 7b) Job recognizes the evil inclination as the prelude to the overt act of forcible appropriation ('or anything stick to my hands, v. 7c); cf. *ḥāmaḏ* in the Decalogue (Exod. 20.17; Deut. 5.18). It has been suggested that, with LXX, S and two Heb. MSS, we should read *'im-m^{e}ṯê šāw'* for MT *'im-šāw'* in v. 5, 'with men of vanity' (so Bickell, Grimme) or *'im-'an^{e}še šāw'* (so Ley), which is a more likely original, but the parallelism with the abstract *mirmāh* ('deceit') supports MT.

5-6. The form *wattāḥaš* seems to come from *ḥāšāh*, probably a byform of the regular *ḥuš*. The weighing visualized by Job may reflect the Egyptian conception of the weighing of the soul of the dead against the feather of Ma'at ('truth', 'order') and the recording of his account by Thoth, the ibis god; cf. the famous judgment scene in the book of the Dead (*ANEP*, pl. 639). Though there may be here the nuance of 'righteousness' in *ṣeḏeq*, the phrase *mô'z^{e}nê-ṣeḏeq* denotes primarily 'right balances', that is, properly adjusted.

7. After his confident protestation of innocence Job continues with his famous oath of purgation with its solemn adjurations. From this point onwards *'im* is the conditional particle in the oath formula. The adjuration 'Let me sow and another eat' (v. 8a) indicates that v. 7 visualizes the breach of the tenth commandment, *lō' taḥmōḏ*, both in its primary sense 'Thou shalt not appropriate rapaciously' and, as apparently taken from the Deuteronomic form of the Decalogue, 'Thou shalt not covet'. In v. 7c MT *ûḇ^{e}ḵappî dāḇaq m^{e}'ûm* the last word may be either a masc. form of the noun or *scriptio defectiva* for *m^{e}'ûmāh* (so Weiser) or simply a scribal error for *m^{e}'ûmāh*; cf. Deut. 13.18 (EVV 17), *w^{e}lō'-yiḏbaq b^{e}yaḏ^{e}ḵā m^{e}'ûmāh*. V evidently read *mûm* ('spot, blemish'), so also T, but alongside the reading *m^{e}'ûmāh*. In view of the passage in Deut. 13.18, *me'ûmāh* or MT *m^{e}'ûm* as a masc. variant may be read, but in view of the close verbal correspondence with this passage it may be an editorial expansion in Job (so Hölscher, Fohrer).

8. The intensive *šērēš* (here Pual 'to be uprooted') has both positive and privative senses, meaning both 'to root' (e.g. Isa. 40.24; Jer. 12.2) and 'to uproot' (e.g. Ps. 52.7; cf. Arab. *jaladda* ['to bind (a book)' or 'to skin (a beast)']).

The adjuration 'Let me sow and another reap' is reminiscent of the elaboration of the curse after the Twelve Adjurations in Deut. 27.15-26 in the Covenant-sacrament (Deut. 28.15ff., particularly Deut. 28.30, 33. This is the general context against which the social ethic implied in Job's oath of purgation is to be set.

There may be a *double entendre* in *ṣe'^{e}ṣā'ay*, which signifies both vegetable produce and offspring.

9-12. Verses 9-10, with vv. 11-12 probably a sapiential expansion, concern the breach of the commandment against adultery, and may have been introduced by v. 1 in MT. *'iššāh* undefined implies a wife, as the parallel colon indicates, with its vivid image of the adulterer lurking at his neighbour's door to see him leave the house.

9. *lēḇ* has here the sense of 'reason' or 'understanding', as generally in Heb.

pāṯah ('to be simple, to be seduced') is the regular word for the seduction of either sex (e.g. Exod. 22.16; Judg. 14.15; 16.5; Hos. 2.16 [Piel]), or in the general sense; cf. v. 27; Prov. 1.10; 16.29; etc.

Lurking, lit. lying in ambush (*'āraḇ*), at the door of one's neighbour is the tactic of the adulterer, as the context indicates.

After the disavowal of the crime the adjuration recalls the curse in Deut. 28.30. We cannot attest a sexual sense for *ṭāḥan* which would fit the context, as has been assumed by V and T here and in Lam. 5.13b (cf. Jerome in his commentary on Judg. 16.21), though this would be intelligible if the verb were passive; cf. Tur-Sinai, who reads the Niphal *tiṭṭāhēn* for MT *tiṭḥan*. Grinding denotes a menial task of the lowest class of female (cf. Exod. 11.5; Isa. 47.2) and was the first operation of the day while it was yet dark. The depth of the woman's degradation, or rather that of her husband, is indicated by the plural, *'aḥērîn*, of those who would lie with her. As adultery was regarded as an infringement of a man's honour, and indeed property, without regard to the humiliation or delinquency of the woman as such, so his wife is merely instrumental in the punishment of the adulterer as one of his goods and chattels quite apart from her own rights as an individual. The plural ending of *'aḥērîn*, if MT is correct and not simply a scribal error of *n* for *m* in the Old Heb. script, is one of the many Aramaisms in the Book of Job.

11. This may be the first gloss on vv. 9-10.

zimmāh, cognate with Arab. *damma* ('to be foul') or *ḏamma* ('to blame'), is used in the OT for various wanton acts such as murder (Hos. 6.9; Prov. 10.23; 21.27), but particularly of sexual wantonness (e.g. Lev. 18.17; 20.14; Jer. 13.27; Ezek. 23.21, 27, 29, 35).

MT *'āwōn pelîlîm* (cf. Exod. 21.22) would seem to mean 'a wrong for arbitration', that is, to be punished by the judges, or as we should say 'a criminal offence'. The note is repeated in v. 28a, where MT reads *pelîlî* as an adjective, which should probably be read also in v. 11b. V and T read the phrase respectively as 'a very great iniquity' and 'an extraordinary sin', suggesting the reading *pele'* for MT *pelîlî(m)*, which is orthographically feasible. *pele'* and its associate forms denotes something which implies the initiative and the immediate activity of God without the evidence of secondary causes. On this reading, the text, if original, might mean a sin which provoked God's immediate retribution. D.R. Ap-Thomas (1956: 253) proposed that *'āwōn pelîlî* means a wrong that excludes a man from the community, which might claim the support of Arab. *falla* ('to escape, be routed'). But the verse may be a gloss suggested by the corruption of *'ōyēn nip̄tᵉlōtay* in v. 28a, on which see.

12. This verse, possibly a sapiential expansion, cites a popular proverb (cf. Prov. 6.27-29). *kî* may indicate the gloss, or it may be an inadvertent repetition of *kî* in v. 11 or a dittograph of *k* after final *m* of the preceding word and of *y* before *'* of the following word in the Old Heb. script. But it may be a scribal error for the comparative preposition *kᵉ*.

'ad-'ᵃḇaddôn, which we have taken as 'even to Perdition', may mean 'for ever'; cf. Arab. *'abadan* with a negative 'never' and *'abadī* ('perpetual').

tᵉšārēš is not appropriate for fire, hence the reading *tiśrōp̄* is proposed (Wright, Duhm) and is generally accepted. The corruption of *p* to *ś*, however, is unlikely at any stage of the development of the script. More feasible graphically in the Old Heb. script would be *tᵉšārēḇ* ('parched'); cf. Isa. 49.10, *wᵉlō'-yakkēm šārāḇ wāšāmeš* ('And there shall not strike them scorching nor sun'), and *šārāḇ* in modern Hebrew for the sirocco. This would accord with *tᵉḇû'â* in the sense of 'crops'. G.R. Driver's suggestion (1955: 88f.), however, is much more likely, that *tᵉšārēš* is a corruption by metathesis of *tᵉraššēš*, a cognate of Akk. *rašâšu* ('to be red-hot').

13-15. Job clears himself of the charge of injustice to his slaves, whose legal rights (*rîḇām* in v. 13b), though less than those of a freeman, were nevertheless admitted in the Book of the Covenant (Exod. 21.1-11). In this case the adjuration is omitted, hence as in the truncated form of the oath in asseveration or denial we must translate 'Never did I spurn…', understanding the adjuration. Instead of the adjuration there is an interesting statement of the equality of persons in v. 15. In v. 14 it is implied that as the master had sovereign rights over the slave in the community, the slave has no vindicator but God, and to no other, and no less, is the master responsible.

14. *pāqaḏ* means 'to review' or 'take stock of', here 'to call to account' and so to note deficiency; cf. *nip̄qaḏ* ('to be lacking') and Arab. *faqada* ('to lose'). The Hiphil of *šûḇ* ('to return') with or without the object *dāḇār* ('word') means regularly 'to answer', and takes the direct object, since it is tantamount to a transitive verb.

15. *'ehaḏ* does not qualify *reḥem* ('womb') as LXX, Sym., S, T and Jerome in his commentary assume but, as V indicates, it is the subject of the verb in MT, which might better be read *wayyᵉḵônᵉnēnû*. This is the interpretation of most commentators except Delitzsch, Ehrlich and Stevenson. Hölscher takes it as a gloss.

38-40b. On the position of this passage after v. 15 suggested by the common theme of oppression of subordinates, see the Introduction to ch. 31. Job declares that the land he occupies (*'ad^e^māṯî*) is not acquired as Ahab had acquired Naboth's vineyard; there is consequently no entail of tears (cf. the blood of Abel 'crying out from the ground', Gen. 4.10) with the consequence of infertility (cf. v. 40ab). The conception of the land crying out for vengeance and refusing to yield because of blood shed violently on it is connected with the conception of the close connection between a man and his land; cf. the establishment of a dead man's name on his hand (Ruth 4.5).

38. Consuming the strength of the land without cost (*b^e^lî ḵesep̄*) and the sequel seems indicate exploiting the land and its workers (*pô ʿ^a^lêhā* for MT *b^e^ ʿālêhā*) through over-cropping in the precarious situation, where natural fertility was restored only by the release of the chemicals of the earth through rain and the heat of the sun or through the meagre dung of the working animals. In the circumstances a fallow year was necessary (Deut. 15.1ff.). Duhm in fact explains the passage as the failure to observe the year of release.

39. *kōaḥ*, generally 'strength', means here 'produce' as in Joel 2.22, where it is parallel to *p^e^rî* ('fruit'). MT *b^e^ ʿālêhā* ('its masters'), which Mowinckel takes to mean 'spirits of the field', could mean the owners of the land, the victims of ruthless exploitation, like Naboth (1 Kgs 21). Pope thinks of share-farmers, and Larcher of 'workers' (*pō ʿ^a^lîm*), which we prefer (so too Dahood). *hippāḥtî* means literally 'I caused to breathe out' (cf. *mappaḥ nāp̄eš* in 11.20), hence 'drove to exhaustion' rather than 'caused the death of…' (RSV).

40. The curse of weeds recalls the curse on the land after the fall (Gen. 3.17-18). *ḥôaḥ* is well attested in the OT as 'thorns', but *bā'šāh* is a *hapax legomenon*; cf. *b^e^'ušîm*, weeds or inferior grapes in Isaiah's Song of the Vineyard (Isa. 5.2, 4). We might cite Arab. *bi'ś* as a term of opprobrium ('harm') and hazard the translation 'noxious weeds'.

16-20, 18. In Job's statement of his philanthropy there is no adjuration explicitly expressed, hence the formula *'im…* must be translated as an emphatic denial.

16. This may refer to the withholding of justice from the poor or to grudging their relief or charity (cf. Deut. 15.7-8) or to deferring their daily wages (Deut. 24.14). The widow (*'almānāh*) and the orphan (*yāṯôm*) (v. 17) were peculiarly the responsibility of the leaders of the community (see above on 29.12-13).

The failing (*kālāh*) of the eyes describes disappointed expectation; cf. Deut. 28.32.

The eating of a piece (of bread) alone is a striking expression of antisocial conduct, of particular point in the ancient East and in a particularist community such as the village or tribal kinship.

18. This verse is lacking from LXX before Origen's recension, and is obscure and pointless in its context in MT. It is treated as a gloss (Hölscher, Fohrer) on MT *g^e^d̲ēlanî* emended to *'^a^ḡadd^e^lennû* ('I reared him'), which, after the final *y* in the preceding word is graphically feasible in the Old Heb. script. In this case *'anḥennāh* ('I led her') would refer to the widow in v. 16b (so Dhorme, Pope). On this we may remark that Job's guidance of the widow 'from the womb', that is, all her life, is rather strange. If the verse must be retained in its present position in MT a more feasible suggestion might be to emend MT *'anḥennāh* to *'^a^naḥ^e^mennah* ('I would comfort her') with haplography of *m* before *n* in the Old Heb. script, but even so the difficulty of the conception of Job assuming this responsibility 'from the womb' remains. It seems more natural to take 'from the womb' to refer to the beneficiary, hence we propose to read *'anḥennî*, assuming the corruption of *y* to *h* in the Hebraic script. We read *gidd^e^lanî* for MT *g^e^d̲ēlanî*, and transpose the verse to after v. 20, where it is the blessing of the destitute mentioned in vv. 19-20.

20. *gēz* is little attested in the OT, only in fact in Amos 7.1 and Ps. 72.6, where it is used of mowing, and in Deut.18.4, where, like the verb *gāzaz* in 2 Sam. 13.23, it signifies sheep-rearing as here.

21-22. This strophe, in the regular form of the oath of purgation, reflects the misuse of power by the influential who corrupted judgment by personal menace (v. 21a) or intimidation through the presence of 'strong-arm men' (v. 21b). After the case of the orphan has been dealt with in 17 it is unlikely that he should be again mentioned in isolation in v. 21. Hence with Duhm, Budde, G.B. Grey, Peters, Hölscher, Stevenson, Mowinckel and Fohrer we read *'^a^lê tām* ('against the innocent') for MT *'al-yāt̲ôm*, which Dhorme, Pope and Terrien retain. The verb *nûp̄* means 'to wave', here the hand, in menace, 'shaking the fist' (Ball), as in Isa. 10.32; 11.15; 19.16; Zech. 2.13. *'ezrāt̲î*, generally taken as 'my help', that is, support, may be a collective singular of a cognate of Ugaritic *ġzr* ('young henchman'); cf. Gordon, *UH* 'nt II,22, and in the OT Ezek. 12.14 and Ps. 89.20:

> *šiwwēt̲î 'ōzēr* (for MT *'ēzer*) *'al-gibbôr*
> *h^a^rîmōt̲î bāḥûr mē'ām* (possibly *mē'āṣûm*)
>
> I have set a youth above a mighty man,
> I have raised a young man above the people (possibly 'the mighty').

(See Albright 1949: 233, and, for other instances in the OT, with Ugaritic references, J. Gray 1965: 263f.) Analogies for the fem. collective sing. are *'ōr^e^ḥāh* ('travellers') and *gôlāh* ('exiles'), and in the Ras Shamra texts *t'dt* ('witnesses') and *ṣrt* ('enemies') (Gordon *UT* 137,22 and 68.9).

22. *qāneh* means the beam of a balance in Isa. 46.6. A *hapax legomenon* here as part of the body, the word is attested in the description of mourning rites in

the Baal myth of Ras Shamra; cf. Gordon *UH* 62.4; 67.VI, 20: *qn zrh yḥrṯ* ('he scores the humeral joint of his arm').

23. See below after v. 34.

44. The Psalms and sapiential literature of the OT are full of animadversions on those who place their confidence (*kesel*, *mibṭāḥ*) in material wealth rather than God (e.g. Pss. 49.7-8 [EVV 6-7]; 52.9 [EVV 7] etc.; cf. Job 22.25). The strophe vv. 24-28, introduced by the protasis of a conditional sentence as in the oath of purgation, lacks the final imprecation, having instead the assertion of God's notice of the faults. As in vv. 5-8 two delinquencies are denied, materialism and superstition, both possibly indicating misplaced trust.

25. *kabbîr* is familiar in Job in the sense of 'big', as in Arab. (e.g. 8.2, 'numerous', that is, in age; cf. 15.10); cf. *kabbîr yāmîm* in 34.7, which is also familiar in Arab., and 'mighty' in power or status (e.g. 34.24; 36.5), as in Phoenician, to judge from the Greek transliteration *kabiroi* describing the great gods. It is more familiar in Aram. The parallelism of *kabbîr* and *rāḇ* here recurs in Isa.16.14.

14. The incidence of *kabbîr* in Job indicates a late usage and possibly Aram. influence, though Isa. 16.14 indicates that the word in this sense was already known in Classical Heb. *māṣā'*, as well as meaning 'to find', means 'to light upon' or 'acquire'; cf. Prov. 18.22, *māṣā' 'iššāh māṣā' ṭôḇ wayyāp̄eq rāṣôn mēyhwh* ('He who gets a wife gets a good thing and acquires favour from Yahweh').

26. The astral cults were practised throughout the Near East and had been promoted in Israel, particularly under Assyrian domination during the reign of Manasseh (685–641 BCE), a situation reflected in Deut. 4.19; 2 Kgs 23.5; Jer. 8.1-2; Zeph. 1.5. The reference in Job is rather to long-established popular respect for the sun and moon, on the regular influence of which on the seasons the local peasant depended. Such local superstition is well attested by the figurines of the fertility-goddesses Astarte and Asherah in various archaeological sites in Syria and Palestine. *'ôr*, generally 'light' in Classical Heb., is rendered 'sun' in LXX, which is undoubtedly the meaning here. The sun was one of the deities, actually a goddess, in the pantheon of Canaan known from the Ras Shamra texts, among which there is a hymn to the sun (Gordon *UT* 62,42-52). There are specific allusions to the recrudescence of sun-worship at the end of the Davidic monarchy in 2 Kgs 23.5, 11, and in the exile (Ezek. 8.16). The worship of the moon is attested at Ugarit in texts referring to ritual at given phases of the moon and particularly in a text celebrating the marriage of the moon-god (*yrḥ*) and the moon-goddess (*nkl*), the centre of whose cult in antiquity was at Harran in northern Mesopotamia. In MT *yāqār hōlēḵ* the

pointing of *yāqār* indicates an adjective ('honourable') or the adverbial accusative, as the attachment to *hōlēḵ* may indicate, ('stately'). Even so, this is not an apt parallel to the brightness of the sun in v. 26a, which V and T obviously expected in rendering 'bright'. Ball's emendation of MT *yāqār* to *yārōq* is suggested by LXX 'the waning moon', *yrq* being possibly from the root *rāqaq* ('to be thin'). This hardly denotes an essential attribute of the moon comparable to the brightness of the sun. The parallelism is surely between the essential characteristics of each. Hence we propose that MT *yāqār* be pointed *yāqar*, the Hiphil of *qārar* ('to be cool'), the coolness of the moon being complementary to the brightness of the sun, and a welcome relief from its heat.

27. MT *wavyip̄t libbî* might be better read *wayyippaṯ...libbî*; cf. v. 9a. In the phrase *wattiššaq yāḏî lᵉp̄î* the first word means 'kiss' as it usually does in Classical Heb., but we should expect rather 'my mouth kisses my hand'. But if we take the verb as the Niphal in the passive sense, the meaning in normal Heb. idiom would be 'my hand is kissed by my mouth', as in 'throwing a kiss', doubtless a reference to a well-known superstitious rite.

28. Hölscher discards this verse from the original Book of Job as a gloss, but Stevenson seems nearer the truth in suggesting that it is the source of the gloss in v. 11 (see above *ad loc.*). The difficult text is possibly to be reconstructed from S, which reads 'he also sees all my misdeeds' (*gam-hû' 'ōyēn* [*kol-*] *'alîlōṯāy*) or, better, we suggest, *nip̄tᵉlōṯāy* ('my tricks').

29-32. This is another case where sin is denied without the formal adjuration. So the introductory *'im* signifies strong denial. As in vv. 5-8 and vv. 24-28 two sins are denied, vindictiveness (vv. 29f.) and inhospitality (vv. 31f.), which is stated positively. Job does not take pleasure in even his enemy's calamity (*pîḏ*), thereby observing the principle laid down in the Book of the Covenant that one must not let enmity hinder one from doing a good turn to one's neighbour (Exod. 23.4-5). Proverbs 24.17 is much nearer the present passage with its injunction, 'Do not rejoice when your enemy falls, and let not your heart be glad when he stumbles'. The intensive of the verb *śānē'* denotes habitual and intensive hatred, and perhaps malice in encouraging others to hate. MT *wᵉhiṯ'ōr'artî* would mean 'and I got excited', which has only the dubious analogy of 17.8. The parallel *'eśmaḥ* suggests that *wᵉhiṯrō'a'tî* ('shouted for joy') should be read (cf. Pss. 60.10; 65.14); cf. *tᵉrû'āh* ('shout of joy'). This is supported by T and also probably by LXX, S and V (so Tur-Sinai, G.B. Gray, Stevenson and most modern commentators).

30. The phrase *šā'al nep̄eš* ('to ask for the life of…') is actually used in 1 Kgs 5.11, where Solomon is commended for not asking for the life of his enemy in the famous theophany at Gibeon. Hölscher quotes also Ezek. 13.17-23, where

black magic towards this sinister end is condemned. Job's commendable restraint contrasts with the curse of the impassioned sufferer in the Plaint (Pss. 58.7-10 [EVV 6-9]; 59.12-14 [EVV 11-13]), an indication of the restraint of passion that wisdom teachers encouraged, indicative also of their independence of the cult.

31. Like an Arab sheikh Job fulfils the ideal of generosity (Arab. *karmu[n]*). 'The men of my tent' (*m*^{e}*ṯê 'oh*^{o}*lî*) may signify the people of the guest-tent but, in view of the mention of the 'stranger' and the 'wayfarer' in v. 32, it probably refers to the *habitués* of Job's tent, that is, his own people; cf. Arab. *'ahlu*(*n*). The allusion to homosexuality which Tur-Sinai and Pope have claimed is surely gratuitous in Job's oath of purgation, though philologically possible. 'My meat' contrasts with the 'piece of bread', the day to day diet of the poor. The guest is honoured with a special meal; cf. Abraham's entertainment of his guests at Mamre (Gen. 18.7f.), the fatted calf for the Prodigal Son, and the unique horse slaughtered by the Arab for a guest. *mî-yittēn* does not, as it usually does, introduce a wish, but here a rhetorical question, 'Who could adduce...?'

32. Job's hospitality to the stranger in the settlement is exactly paralleled by Lot's at Sodom (Gen. 19.1-3) or that of the old man of Gibeah to the Levite and his concubine from Bethlehem (Judg. 19.16-21) and may be suggested by those passages. It is difficult to determine the specific significance of *gēr* here. In sedentary communities in Israel it would denote a resident alien, not necessarily a refugee from justice seeking asylum in an alien community, whose rights depended upon men of status such as Job. In the border lands, however, *gēr* might be like *jāru 'llāhi*, the refugee from the avenger of blood to whom the right or sanctuary has been granted. But the parallelism with *'ōrēaḥ* ('wayfarer') may indicate the chance sojourner rather than the refugee.

33-34, 23. The final strophe in Job's oath of purgation conforms to the regular pattern provided that v. 23 with the imprecation is transposed from after v. 22, where it is superfluous.

33. Hypocrisy or dissemblance (*kissāh*) of sins is noted as a heinous offence in Ps. 32.5 and Prov. 28.13. *k*^{e}*'āḏām* is taken by T as 'like Adam', who sought to hide his sin from God (Gen. 3.8, so Strahan, Tur-Sinai, Gordis, Pope, Terrien). Dhorme cites van Hoonacker with approval for the interpretation 'like any man' (cf. Hos. 6.7; Ps. 82.7; so also Kissane, Weiser). The passage in Hosea however, is doubtful metrically, and a gloss 'like Adam' is to be suspected, while Ps. 82.7 refers to general mortality. Graetz's reading, *mē'āḏām* ('from humans'), may be preferred (so Budde, Ball, Hölscher, Stevenson, Mowinckel, Fohrer), *m* having been corrupted to *k* in the Old Heb. script. In v. 33b *ḥubbî*, which Fohrer takes as 'fold in the breast of a cloak', is probably Aram.

Logically this implies that Job had some sin to hide, which would not accord with his oath of purgation. Fohrer proposes to get over this difficulty by assuming that Job asserted that he would not have played the hypocrite if he *had* sinned.

34. For the comparatively rare use of *'āraṣ* ('to fear') in Classical Heb., cf. Deut. 1.29; 7.21; 20.3; 31.6; Josh. 1.9. The difficulty of the juxtaposition of masc. *hāmôn* and fem. *rabbāh* is probably to be solved by pointing the former noun as a construct before the absolute *rabbāh* in the sense of 'the capital' (so Dhorme, citing Chajes); cf. *rabbaṯ 'ammôn*. Verse 34c is probably a secondary expansion (so Volz, Jastrow, Hölscher, Mowinckel, Fohrer).

23. In MT *kî paḥaḏ 'ēl yā'îḏ 'ālā*, which LXX paraphrases 'for the fear of the Lord constrains me', we regard *'êd* as cognate of Arab. *'āda, ya'īd* ('to be strong'), *'aydu* (*n*) ('power, authority'), rendering 'For the fear of God overwhelms me'.

35-37. The second part of ch. 31, in forensic idiom, concludes with Job's final appeal for a hearing with the charges openly stated by his divine adversary, which, confident in his innocence asserted in his oath of purgation, he should appropriate together with the imprecation in his oath.

35. In MT *mî yittēn-lî*, the *lî* is probably a dittograph of the second *lî* at the end of the colon. E.F. Sutcliffe's proposal to take it as the remnant of an original *mî yittēn 'ēl yišma'* (so too Ball, G.B. Gray) would overload v. 35a and detract from the effect of the suspended mention of 'the Almighty' in v. 35b. *tāwî* is generally taken as 'my sign', that is, the cross, the last letter of the alphabet in the Old Heb. script, the signature of an illiterate (so Mowinckel, Richter, Rowley, Fohrer). Stevenson suggested that the mark was a cult-sign tattooed on the hand or arm of Job as a worshipper of Yahweh, to whom he now appeals for vindication. This is no less a conjecture than the interpretation of the cross as a signature, which, at the end of Job's statement has more point. Larcher in JB, on the other hand, emphasizes *taw* as the last letter of the alphabet and renders 'I have had my say, from A to Z'. V and T, however, suggest that *tāwî* means 'my desire', indicating a reading *ta'wî* from the verb *'āwāh* (so G.R. Driver 1936: 166; Sutcliffe 1949: 71f.; Saydon 1961: 252). This would accord with *mî yittēn* ('Would that I had…') in v. 35a.

We prefer to regard v. 36c as the second colon of a couplet where the first colon containing the verb was dropped out (so Driver–Gray, Hölscher, Mowinckel, Fohrer).

The figure is that of a bill of indictment drawn up by an opponent at law (*'îš rîḇî*). For *sēp̄er* as the technical term for such a document, cf. the deed of divorce in Deut. 24.1, 3 and Isa. 50.1, and of conveyance in Jer. 32.11f., 14, 16. Job desires to have the charge specified, confident that he can refute it.

36. 'I would take it upon my shoulder' may refer to a rite whereby liability was imputed and admitted, as the key of the house of David upon the shoulder of the royal chamberlain Eliakim (Isa. 22.22; cf. 9.5). The binding of the charge about the head like a turban may have had a like significance, symbolizing the appropriation of the curse involved in the charge if it could be sustained (so Fohrer). There may also be a reference to the keeping of legal documents in the turban, as the Scottish barons in the Isle of Arran kept their title deeds given by King Robert the Bruce in their bonnets. There is of course in *ʿaṭārāh* ('crown') the implication of dignity, not necessarily royal dignity, as in Prov. 4.9; 12.4; 14.24; 16.31; 17.6; Ben Sira 1.18; 25.6, though Job's appeal does reflect the tradition of the ordeal of the king as representative of his people.

37. *mispar ṣeʿāḏay*, lit. 'the number of my steps', emphasizes 'the number', that is, 'my every step'.

There is a word-play between *'aggîḏ* ('I will declare') and *nāḡîḏ*, which is generally taken in this passage to denote 'a leader' accustomed to authority and responsibility and not a suppliant. This is probably the sense, but *nāḡîḏ* may have the sense of 'directly' or 'without evasion'; cf. *neḡdô* ('straight in front of him', Josh. 6.5; Amos 4.3; Jer. 31.39; Neh. 12.37). Throughout this final appeal Job has assumed the role of a leader in the community, to which, like an Arab sheikh or ancient king, he has responsibilities and of which he is the representative; cf. ch. 29, especially v. 25. A. Caquot (1960) has well emphasized the role of the king, especially in the fast-liturgy, as the prototype of the sufferer in this section especially of Job. We consider it probable that many psalms of the type of the Plaint of the Sufferer, which are a Hebrew prototype of the Book of Job in general and of individual passages in the Book, were originally from fast-liturgies in which the king represented the community in rites of penance. Lévêque (1970: 492) would see in Job *kemô nāḡîḏ* ('as a leader') his conscious role as representative of all worthy sufferers.

Job 32–37

Interpolation

Chapters 32–37 of the book of Job are generally regarded as a later insertion. This is supported by the fact that Elihu is not named among Job's friends in the Prologue (2.11) or the Epilogue (42.7-9), where those are specifically named, and by the fact that the statements of Job in the Dialogue are cited and systematically countered in these speeches. The section, extending unbroken over six chapters, is a lecture rather than part of the dialectic argument between Job and his friends. It disrupts the literary structure of the book and barbarously impairs the dramatic effect of God's reply to Job (38.1–40.14) both by its insertion after Job's passionate appeal in his oath of purgation and by anticipating the substance of God's reply that the ultimate explanation and purpose of creation and human experience lies with God transcendent (chs. 35–37). Thus in the context of the debate in Job it makes no fresh contribution except to insist on the aspect of suffering such as Job's as a positive discipline under divine control (33.15-18) and that there are supernatural forces commending humans to God's mercy (35.19-20). The Elihu section is therefore best explained as the contribution of a later sage who feels uneasy at the possible effects of Job's trenchant criticism of the theodicy as expressed by the three friends and by their inability effectively to contradict him. But for all his embarrassment the sage can only support orthodox dogma by emphasizing what has been already stated.

By the criterion of his respective addresses to Job and his three friends the matter may be arranged after the prose introduction (32.1-5) and by his introductory statement to the four (32.6-22) thus: 33 (to Job); 34 (to the friends); 35.1–36.26 (to Job); 36.27–37.13 (a Hymn of Praise to the Creator, suggested by Elihu's statement on God's sovereignty (36.22-26, at the conclusion of his statement to Job); 37.14-24 (to Job, stressing human limitations vis-à-vis the Creator in hymnic style).

Job 32

Elihu's First Address (vv. 6-22) after the Prose Introduction (vv. 1-5)

This, in the form of the sage's introduction to the statement of his opinion, his title to be heard, the reason for his intromission, namely, the inadequacy or arguments hitherto adduced to counter Job's controversial statements, the compulsion of the truth he feels, and the assurance of his impartiality, is in the true style of sapiential dialectic. The speech may be divided into three strophes: vv. 6-9, 15-16 + 11-14, and 17-22.

The sudden switch to the 3rd person plur. in v. 15, after the 2nd plur. in vv. 11-14, and the reversion to the helplessness of Job's friends in the argument indicates that this passage is displaced. Duhm suggested that it stood originally after v. 9, which is certainly a much more appropriate place, and that v. 10 is a gloss, which is supported by the repetition of the verse at v. 17a. Hence the arrangement which we adopt: vv. 6-9 (10); 15-16 + 11-14; and 17-22.

Chapter 32

1. Now these three men gave up answering Job since he was convinced of his innocence. 2. Then the anger of Elihu the son of Barachel the Buzite of the family of Ram was kindled; and he was angry because he justified himself rather than God. 3. And he was angry with Job's three friends because they had found no answer (to him) and had made God[1] seem unjust. 4. But Elihu had waited while they spoke with Job[2] for they were older than he. 5. But seeing that there was no answer in the mouth of the three men, Elihu became angry.

6. Then up spoke Elihu the son of Barachel the Buzite and said:

'I am young in years,
And you are aged,
Hence I was timid and afraid
To declare my opinion in your presence.[3]

7. I said, "Let years speak,
and many years teach wisdom!"

8. But it is the spirit of Yahweh[4] in a human,
The breath of the Almighty, which gives him understanding.[5]

9. It is not merely the seniors who have wisdom,
Nor the elders who are discriminate in judgment.

10. Therefore I say, "Listen to me;
Let me also declare my opinion".

15. They have been confounded; they have had no more to say in answer,
Word passed beyond them.
16. Had I to wait[6] while they had nothing to say,
While they stood with nothing more to reply?
11. I waited indeed for what you had to say,
I listened[7] while you gave your reasons,
While you searched out what you had to say;
12. And I gave heed to you,
And see! none convicted Job,
None of you had any answer for what he said.
13. Take care not to say, "We have encountered (such) wisdom
That (only) God may refute him and not a human".
14. But I will not marshal[8] arguments like these,[9]
Nor will I answer him with your statements.

17. I too will give my share of the answer;
I too will declare my opinion.
18. For I am full[10] of words,
The spirit within me constrains me.
19. Indeed my belly is like wine unopened,
Like wine-skins which new wine bursts.[11]
20. I must speak that I may find relief;
I must open my lips that I may give an answer.
21. I would show partiality to none,
Nor give flattering titles to any one,
22. For I do not know how to conceal (the truth),
Else soon would my Maker take me off.

Textual Notes to Chapter 32

1. MT is a scribal adjustment (*tiqqûn sôp̄ᵉrîm*) for doctrinal reasons; understand 'God' for 'Job'.
2. Conjecturing *bᵉd̲abbᵉrām 'et̲-'iyyôb for* MT *'et̲-iyyôḇ bid̲ᵉḇārîm*.
3. Reading *'ittᵉk̲em* for MT *'et̲ᵉk̲em*. See Commentary *ad loc.*
4. Reading *yhwh* for MT *hî'*.
5. Reading *tᵉḇînennû* in agreement with the sing. *'ᵉnôš* for MT *tᵉḇînēm*.
6. Reading *hahôḥaltî* for MT *wᵉhôḥaltî*.
7. Reading *'a'ᵃzîn* with certain Heb. MSS for MT *'āzîn*.
8. Reading *'e'ᵉrōk̲* with S for MT *'ārak̲*, assuming haplography of initial ' after preceding *lō'*.
9. Reading *kᵉ'ēlleh* after LXX for MT *'ēlay*, *k* being omitted by haplography after initial *k* in the preceding word, and *h* being corrupted to *y* in the Old Heb. script.
10. Reading *mālē't̲î* with certain Heb. MSS for MT *mālēt̲î*.
11. Reading *kᵉnō d̲ôt̲ tîrôš yiḇqa'*. See Commentary *ad loc.*

Commentary on Chapter 32

1. For MT *bᵉ'ênāyw* one Heb. MS, LXX, Sym. and S read *bᵉ'ênêhem* ('in their eyes'), signifying that the friends had admitted Job's innocence and in so

doing 'had made God seem unjust' (v. 3), where MT 'Job' is a scribal adjustment (*tiqqûn sôpᵉrîm*) for doctrinal purposes. Since Elihu's argument, however, is directed against Job as well as his friends, we accept MT as referring to Job's stubborn stand on his innocence. Elihu does not upbraid the friends for their acquiescence in Job's case but for their failure to find adequate objections to it (vv. 3, 5; cf. v. 13).

2. Elihu's father's name Barachel may denote a sapiential school rather than an actual family affinity, but 'Buzi' may be artificial, borrowed from Gen. 22.21, where Buz is associated with Uz, being located by Jer. 25.23 with Teima and Dedan.

4. MT *ḥikkāh 'eṯ-'iyyôḇ biḏᵉḇārîm*, if not unintelligible, is awkward, and Wright's conjecture *ḥikkāh bᵉḏabbᵉrām 'eṯ-'iyyôḇ* ('waited while they spoke with Job') is followed by most modern commentators. Hölscher omits 'with Job' against the evidence of MT and the ancient versions.

6. *wayya'an* here as in the Ras Shamra texts means probably 'spoke up', not 'replied', though Elihu's speech is actually a reply to the case of Job and his friends.

yᵉšîšîm ('aged') is found in the sing. form *yāšēš* only once (2 Chron. 36.17) outside Job; cf. 12.12, where the word has a nuance of its primary sense 'decrepit', and in 15.10; 29.8. See on 12.12.

zāḥal, here the parallel of *yārē'*, suggests the late Aram. *dᵉḥal* ('to fear'), but the form *zᵉḥal* ('to fear') is actually attested in the Aram. inscription of Zakir (I,13) (Gibson 1975: 8). The verb *zāḥal* is attested in Classical Heb. describing the motion of reptiles (e.g. Deut. 32.24 and Mic. 7.17). Fohrer (*ad loc.*) takes the verb in Job 32.6 to be from this root, meaning 'to shrink'. This is questionable, and seems to be contradicted by S, which renders *daḥlēṭ* ('I feared'), though Syr. has another root from which *daḥlā'* ('locust') is derived. The connection of Heb. *zāḥal* describing the motion of reptiles and of *zāḥal* in Job 32.6 with Arab. *zaḥala* ('to withdraw, slip [of a landslide]') is possible, but not certain. We prefer to regard *zāḥal* in Job 32.6 as a homonym of Heb. *zāḥal* describing the motion of reptiles, cognate with Aram. and Syr. *dᵉḥal* and with the early Aram. *zᵉhal* of the Zakir inscription (c. 800 BCE).

ḥiwwāh, relatively frequent in the Elihu passages (e.g. vv. 10, 17; 36.2, 6), is the regular Aram. verb 'to declare', being found only twice in the OT (Pss. 19.3; 52.11) outside Job except in the Aram. part of Dan. It is unlikely that there is any connection with Arab. *waḥa(y)* ('to suggest, insinuate').

dēa' ('knowledge') for the more regular *da'aṯ* is a peculiarity of the Elihu passages and one of the linguistic features which sets it apart in the Book of Job. *ḥawwōṯ dē'î* might be taken as meaning 'to inform' so making possible a direct accusative *'eṯᵉḵem*, but the more normal reading would be *'ittᵉḵem* ('in your presence').

8. *nišᵉmaṯ šadday* in v. 8b demands a divine name after *rûaḥ* in the parallel position in v. 8a, where Sym. suggests *'ēl* or *'ᵉlôah* for MT, but *hî' yhwh* would be nearer MT. The divine proper name is avoided in the Book of Job as distinct from the prose Prologue and Epilogue except in 12.9, where it is the citation of a common compound expression. The use of *yhwh* in the compound expression *rûaḥ yhwh* would be analogous to *yaḏ yhwh* in 12.9. The argument here may be that only a special divine inspiration gives Elihu a right to speak in face of the empirical wisdom of the elders, but the parallelism of *rûaḥ* and *nᵉšāmāh* indicates that this was not a special revelation, but the common share of the spirit (*rûaḥ*) with which God animated humanity at creation. Elihu is then claiming that this spirit in any person may transcend the advantage of age and empirical wisdom. This general portion of the spirit in humans is taken by Dhorme in justification of MT. Even so, the *rûaḥ* is *rûaḥ yhwh*.

9. For *rabbîm*, *rōḇ yamîm* is proposed after S, which is the general sense also of LXX and V. The parallel *zᵉqēnîm* indicates that this is certainly the meaning. Dahood, however (*UHP*, p. 71) cites a passage in the Ras Shamra texts (Gordon, *UT* 51 V, 65-66), which supports MT in this sense:

rbt 'ilm lḥkmt	Thou art aged, O El, and truly wise,
šbt dqnk ltsrk	The grey hair of your beard indeed instructs you.

Cf. Gen. 25.23, *wᵉrab ya'ᵃḇōḏ ṣā'îr* ('and the elder shall serve the younger').

10. *'ᵃḥawweh dē'î 'ap̄-'ānî* is repeated in v. 17, and emphasizes the personal contribution of the writer to supplement the argument of the friends in the dialogue, though this verse is probably a later gloss on *dēa'* and *ḥiwwāh*; see on v. 6.

15-16. On the displacement of text, see Introduction to ch. 32.

15. *he'ᵉṯîq* ('to pass, go beyond') is attested in the narrative of the wandering of the patriarchs in Gen. 12.8; 26.22.

11. *'āzîn* is generally taken as an elision of *'a'ᵃzîn* (actually found in certain Heb. MSS), the Hiphil imperfect of the denominative verb from *'ōzen* ('ear'). Dahood has suggested (1963c: 38) that the verb may be a homonym ('to weigh, ponder'), found in Eccl. 12.9 as a parallel to *ḥiqqēr* and *tiqqēn*. Arab. *wazana* has also a mental sense; cf. *'awzana nafšahu 'alay šayyi(n)* ('he applied his mind to something'), where the use of the causative as in the present passage is interesting. The preference cannot be certainly decided. The plur. *teḇûnōṯ* suggests the meaning 'various reasons'. *millîn*, again the Aram. word and plur. ending, indicates here not the *mots justes*, but the substance of the words and arguments.

12. *ḥoḵîaḥ* means here 'to bring one's guilt home to him'. Sometimes this denotes the process of argument and criticism; at other times, as here, it denotes the end of the process, conviction.

13. This colon is ambiguous. According to NEB the meaning is 'Take care then not to claim that you have found wisdom; God will rebut him, not man'. It is not clear, however, whether 'God will rebut him…' is the conclusion of the wisdom the friends claim or is the independent statement of Elihu. Alternatively it may mean that in Job's statements the friends admit to have encountered (*māṣā'nû*) wisdom which only God can refute, and so are content to leave it to God to do so. On this interpretation Elihu implies that he has sufficient sapiential acumen to answer Job without invoking divine intervention. In this case, as Peake suggested, the Elihu addendum here might be an animadversion on the resort to the theophany and Divine Declaration in 38.1–40.14, which went beyond the strictly sapiential tradition. If so this would be a strong argument for the originality of that passage. However that may be, the sequel indicates that Elihu is confident in his own sapiential acumen to answer Job without invoking divine intervention. In this context *māṣā'* denotes not 'found' but 'lighted upon, encountered'.

nāḏap̄ means 'to drive' in Classical Heb., but rather in the sense of 'to disperse'; the Arab. cognate, however, means 'to drive a beast forcibly', and this may be the sense here, the reference being to God's relentless prosecution of his argument with Job, which could also be expressed by the verb *rāḏap̄* which one Heb. MS reads. The prosecution of the case thus left to God is actually carried on in 38.1–40.14. Alternatively the verb may be pointed *yᵉḏappennû*, a cognate of Arab. *daffa*, in the IInd Form 'to despatch a wounded man', hence meaning in the present passage 'to finish off'.

14. *wᵉlō'-'āraḵ-'ēlay millîn* ('but he has not directed his arguments against me') might be defended on the interpretation that Job has not had Elihu to contend with, who has arguments more effective than those of the friends, and are to be much more systematically arranged and presented. The same ultimate sense may be secured by reading *'eʿᵉrōḵ* with S for MT *'āraḵ*. LXX 'such things' indicates a reading *kᵉ'ēlleh* for MT *'ēlay*, indicating haplography of *k* after the preceding word. Arguments 'like these' may refer to the friends' dependence on God for a conviction of Job which they have not been able to secure.

17. On *ḥiwwāh* and *dēa'* see on v. 6.

18. *rûaḥ biṭnî* (lit. 'the spirit of my belly') may mean simply 'the spirit with me'; cf. Arab. *'abṭana* ('to keep within one') and *baṭanīyu*(*n*) ('esoteric').

19. In v. 19a *lō' yippātēaḥ* means 'wine which is not yet opened'. The real problem lies in v. 19b, MT *kᵉ'ōḇôṯ ḥᵃḏāšîm yibbāqēa'*. The only apparent

subject of the sing. verb is *biṭnî*, which is fem. The agreement *'ōḇôṯ-ḥ^{a}ḏāšîm* is also highly suspect. *'ôḇ* is known in the OT as 'familiar spirit' or 'revenant' and not as 'skin bottle', which is generally assumed here. Thus scribal corruption may be suspected. LXX 'like smiths' bellows' suggests the reading *k^{e}mappûaḥ ḥārāšîm yibbāqēa'* ('as smiths' bellows [sing.] are like to burst'). The parallel, however, indicates rather *k^{e}nō'ḏôṯ tîrôš yiḇqa'* ('like wineskins which new wine bursts'). For *nō'ḏôṯ* cf. Josh. 9.4, 13.

20. The impersonal verb *yirwaḥ* means 'to find relief'; cf. Arab. *rāḥa', yarūḥu* in the II Form.

21. *nāśā' pānîm* means 'to lift the face', that is, 'to show partiality'; see on 13.8. *kannāh* means 'to address by one's title' (Arab. *kunyatu*[*n*]), a title of honour or a byname, often 'son of a (famous) father' or 'father of a (distinguished or first-born) son'. The verb is attested of a worshipper being called by the name of his God in Isa. 44.5; 45.4, and of Baal called 'the son of Dagan', which means also 'corn' in Ps. 65.10, *tāḵîn d^{e}ḡānām kî ḵēn ṯ^{e}ḵînehā*, which we emend to read *tāḵîn d^{e}ḡānāh kî kēn ṯ^{e}ḵenneh* ('You prepare its corn according to your patronymic'). This is the Heb. adaptation of a Canaanite psalm with this among other features barely distinguished.

21-22. The two couplets are arranged in chiastic parallelism. Thus there is a word-play between *'eśśā' pānîm* in v. 21a and *yiśśā'ēnî* in v. 22b. Possibly there is also a word-play between *'^{a}kanneh* in v. 22b and *'^{a}ḵanneh* in v. 22a, where we suggest that the verb is cognate with Arab. *kanna* ('to conceal'). The statement of Elihu's inability to conceal the truth would thus accord with his statement that he is likely to burst with it (vv. 19-20).

Job 33

Elihu's First Statement

This statement is addressed to Job and falls into five strophes (vv. 1-7, 8-12, 13-18, 19-24, 25-30) according to the subject matter and stages of Elihu's argument. Verses 31-33 are probably displaced in MT. The literary form throughout is the sapiential disputation.

The first strophe (vv. 1-7) is the speaker's introduction of himself, with the characteristic statement of the Hebrew sage that he proposes to dispute the case not on the basis of revelation but of humanistic experience and argumentation (vv. 5, 6, 4, 7). In the second strophe (vv. 8-12) he cites Job's thesis and in fact his actual statements (vv. 8-11) in order to refute them (v. 12). In the third strophe (vv. 13-18) he again cites Job's words (v. 13) and develops his first antithesis that, far from persecuting the sufferer, God persists in his efforts to save humans from the fatal consequences of his own sin, warning them and stirring their conscience in the privacy of their own thoughts (vv. 14-18). In the fourth strophe (vv. 19-24) this theme is further developed, sickness being a token of God's persistence to warn humans to seek his grace, which is available through angelic intercession (vv. 23-24). The fifth strophe (vv. 25-30) emphasizes that the reaction of the sufferer should be penitence and prayer; God's grace is thus accessible and his ultimate purpose is the individual's good.

The arrangement of the text is in our opinion generally in good order, but v. 4 may be displaced in MT from after v. 6, where it better describes the animation of humans after their creation from the common clay (v. 6). Verse 23c was probably followed by a colon reading 'And to show him his sin', as read by LXX, and a verb is probably missing at the beginning of v. 24. The various addresses of Elihu do not normally end with a call to hear, as in vv. 31-33, and those verses are almost certainly displaced. Fohrer has noted that, exceptionally, ch. 35 lacks the customary introduction in this style, and proposes that 33.31-33 is displaced from the beginning of ch. 35. This is the more likely because ch. 34 is not addressed to Job, but to the wise men at large, whereas ch. 35 resumes the address to Job directly in the 2nd person sing., like 33.31-33, with a citation of Job's thesis followed by Elihu's antithesis.

With supreme self-confidence Elihu pronounces on the debate in the Dialogue, beginning first with Job's assertions. He questions Job's claim to innocence (v. 9) with the conclusion that his sufferings signify the wrath of God. On this assumption Job's contention with God according to the canon of human justice is berated on the grounds that 'God is greater than man' (v. 12).

He next objects to Job's complaint that his divine opponent does not answer him in response to his claims on legal grounds. God does indeed, Elihu asserts, respond to humans, for instance, in their disturbed conscience, when they with consternation ('terror', v. 16) become aware of the will of God with which their begetting propensity to sin is recognized to be at variance. The response of God to a person's spiritual need rather than to one's demand for justice is to arrest the development from evil propensity to overt sin, with its fatal consequences (vv. 17f.). Or again God may arrest a person's sinful propensity or actual sin by sickness (vv. 19-22). This, it is implied, need not drive one to complain of God's injustice, as if one had a legal claim on him, but should rather direct one to hope for God's mercy, encouraged by the interest of an angelic intermediary who may quicken the conscience and 'declare to a man his duty', which may be presented to God as ransom for one's life (vv. 23-24).

God is thus presented as no judge exulting in the death of a sinner, but as concerned to divert a person from the path to which one's evil propensity may lead one, and ready to admit a plea for mercy, even taking the initiative through an angelic intermediary. The one thus rescued will seek God's continued favour in prayer and find joy in his presence (v. 26), dwelling upon the deliverance from sin and its fatal consequences and, to use the convention in the Plaint of the Sufferer, giving public testimony to the grace of God (vv. 27-28).

Chapter 33

1. 'But listen, Job, to my words,
And give ear to what I say.
2 Behold, I have opened my mouth,
My tongue in my palate has spoken.
3. There are in my heart words of knowledge;[1]
My lips have spoken sincerely.
5 Answer me if you can;
Marshal your arguments; take your stand.
6. I am related to God in the same degree as yourself,
I too was nipped off from the clay.
4. It was the spirit of God that made me,
And the breath of the Almighty gave me life.
7. Indeed no terror of me need appal you,
Nor shall my hand[2] be heavy upon you.

8. But you have said in my hearing,
And I have heard you distinctly say,[3]
9. "I am pure, without sin,
I am clean, without iniquity.

10. In fact he finds occasions[4] against me,
He counts me as his enemy.
11. He sets[5] my feet in the stocks,
Watches all my paths."
12. See, in this you are not right. My answer is
That God is greater than humans.

13. Why do you object to him
That he gives no answer to (one's) words?
14. For in one way God speaks,
Yea in two he indicates (his will):[6]
15. In a dream, in a night-vision[7]
[When deep sleep falls on humans,][8]
In slumber on one's bed.
16. Then he uncovers the ear of humans,
And in their conscience[9] terrifies them,[10]
17 To turn them aside from what they would do,[11]
And to cut away[12] pride[13] from a person,
18. To keep back one's life from the Pit,
And one's vitality from passing through the stream (of death),

19. Or the person is chastened with pains on his bed,
And the quaking in his bones is perpetual,
20. And his life loathes[14] bread,
And his very being appetizing food.
21. His flesh is wasted[15] away so that it cannot be seen,[16]
And his bones are laid bare, lacking moisture.[17]
22. And his life draws nigh[18] to the pit,
And his vitality is dead.[19]
23. If there is an angel by him,
A mediator, one of a thousand,
To declare to a man his duty,
...
24. ...[20] and to seek mercy for him, saying,[21]
"Set him free[22] that he go not down to the pit.
I have found a ransom for his life."[23]

25. His flesh shall become plumper[24] than in his childhood,
And will be restored as in the days of his youth.
26. He will pray to God that he may show him favour,[25]
And he may see[26] his face with joy:
And he may restore[27] a man's innocence to him,
27. So that he may sing[28] before men, saying,[29]
"I sinned and perverted the right,
And he did not requite[30] me according to my sin.[31]
28 He redeemed my soul[32] so that it passed not to the Pit,
And my life[33] shall be illumined[34] by the light."
29. All these things indeed God does,
Twice, yea thrice with a man,
30. To bring back his soul from the Pit
To enjoy the light in the land[35] of life.'

Textual Notes to Chapter 33

1. Reading *yēš b^{e}libbî ’im^{e}rê da‘aṯ* for MT *yōšer-libbî ’^{a}mārāy w^{e}ḏa‘aṯ*, prepositional *b* in *b^{e}libbî* being corrupted to *r* and attached wrongly to *yēš*.
2. Reading *w^{e}ḵappî* with LXX for MT *w^{e}’aḵpî* and, in agreement, *tiḵbāḏ* for MT *yiḵbāḏ*. See Commentary *ad loc.*
3. Lit. ‘the sound of your words’, reading *millêḵā* for *millîn* after LXX$^{\aleph A}$ and S.
4. Reading *tô’^{a}nôṯ* for MT *t^{e}nû’ôṯ*.
5. Reading *yāśîm* for MT *yāśēm*.
6. Reading *lîšûrennû*, with emphatic *l^{e}*, for MT *lō’ yešûrennāh*. See Commentary *ad loc.*
7. Reading *b^{e}ḥezyôn* with S and certain Heb. MSS and MT *ḥezyôn*.
8. Omitting v. 15b (‘when deep sleep falls upon humans’) as a gloss after 4.13.
9. *ûḇ^{e}musārām* with Aq., S, T, and V for MT *ûḇ^{e}mōsāram*.
10. Reading *y^{e}ḥattēm* with LXX, Aq. and S for MT *yaḥtōm*.
11. Reading *mimma‘^{a}śēhû* with S, T, and V for MT *ma‘^{a}śeh*.
12. Reading *yiḵsāh* for MT *y^{e}ḵasseh*. See Commentary *ad loc.*
13. Reading *w^{e}ga’^{a}wāh* for MT *w^{e}gēwāh*.
14. Reading *w^{e}zih^{a}māh* for MT *w^{e}zih^{a}mattû*. See Commentary *ad loc.*
15. Reading *yiḵleh* for MT *yiḵel*.
16. Reading *mēr^{e}’î* for MT *mērō’î*.
17. Reading *rā’û* for MT *ru’û*. See Commentary *ad loc.*
18. Reading *w^{e}ṯiqraḇ* for MT *wattiqraḇ*.
19. Reading *l^{e}mô mēṯîm* for MT *lam^{e}miṯîm*. See Commentary *ad loc.*
20. Perhaps a word has dropped out here.
21. Reading *wîḥunnennû w^{e}yô’mar* for MT *wayy^{e}ḥunnennû wayyō’mer*.
22. Reading *pār^{e}‘ēhû* with two Heb. MSS for MT *p^{e}ḏā‘ēhû*. See Commentary *ad loc.*
23. Inserting *l^{e}napšô* after *kōp̄er*, *metri causa*, *napšô* being omitted by haplography before *rûṭ^{a}p̄aš*.
24. Reading *yiṭpaš* for MT *ruṭ^{a}p̄aš*. See Commentary *ad loc.*
25. Reading *w^{e}yiṣēhû* for MT *wayyirṣēhû*.
26. Reading *w^{e}yir’eh* for MT *wayyar’*.
27. Reading *w^{e}yāšîḇ* for MT *wayyāšeḇ*.
28. Reading *yāšîr* for MT *yāšōr*.
29. Reading *w^{e}yō’mar* for MT *wayyō’mer*.
30. Reading *šiwwāh* for MT *šāwāh*.
31. Reading *ka‘^{a}wōni* with LXX.
32. Reading *nap̄šî* with Kethib as against Qere.
33. Reading *ḥayyāṯî* with Kethib as against Qere.
34. Reading *tā’ôr* for MT *tir’eh*.
35. Reading *b^{e}’ûr* for MT *b^{e}’ôr*. See Commentary *ad loc.*

Commentary on Chapter 33

The length of v. 3a and that of v. 3b in the arrangement of MT in BH^{3} is respectively too short and too long. This is adjusted by pointing MT *’^{a}mārāy w^{e}ḏa‘aṯ* as *’im^{e}rê ḏa‘aṯ*, which belongs to v. 3a (so Wright, Duhm, Beer, Driver–Gray, Ball, Hölscher, Dhorme, Mowinckel, Fohrer, Terrien, Lévêque).

The verb is obtained by emending *yōšēr*. Dhorme reads *yāšûr*, for which he assumes the meaning 'repeats', citing vv. 14 and 17 and Hos. 14.9—all very doubtful evidence. Alternatively *yāšîr* ('sings') is proposed (Terrien), with nothing in the parallel colon to support it. The same remark applies to Duhm's proposal to read *yāšîq* ('overflows', as wine vats; cf. Joel 2.24), which Fohrer adopts, and to Beer's proposal *rāhaš* ('is stirred'), which is preferred by G.B. Gray; cf. Driver, who preferred *yāšîq*. The parallel, referring to a pure declaration, indicates that Hölscher is much nearer the truth in proposing *yāšēr*, the Hiphil of *šārar*; cf. Syr. *šᵉrar* ('to be firm, true'), which is accepted by Mowinckel. If this is the verb we suggest that it is better taken in the Qal with *'imᵉrê ḏa'aṯ* as adverbial accusative ('My heart is fortified with words of knowledge'). But the simplest and probably the most apt reading is that of Ball, *yēš bᵉlibbi 'imᵉrê ḏa'aṯ* ('There are in my heart words of knowledge'), which we adopt. This involves one of the most natural scribal errors, the corruption of *b* to *r*, probably in the Old Hebrew script.

4. This verse interrupts the sequence of thought between v. 3 and v. 5, and it has been taken as a gloss inspired by 32.8 (so Budde, Duhm, Hölscher). Dhorme, however, has perceived that it fits aptly between v. 6 and v. 7; cf. MacFadyen (1917: 82), and Steinmann (1955: 211), who transpose v. 4 to before v. 6. Dhorme's arrangement, where the order of physical creation followed by divine animation preserves the tradition of Genesis, is to be preferred.

5. Dhorme doubts if *'erᵉḵāh*, the imperative of *'āraḵ*, means 'marshal your arguments' here, as it does in 32.14 and 13.18 and 23.4. Certainly Job does not address Elihu, but Elihu nevertheless does summarize Job's answers. Dhorme takes the verb in the military sense (metaphorically) (cf. 6.4), and cites in support 38.3 and 40.7. The last two passages, however are not military metaphors perhaps, but rather a figure from the primitive practice of belt-wrestling as a trial by ordeal, known in Mesopotamian law in the fourteenth century BCE at Nuzi (Gordon 1950–51). *hiṯyaṣṣēḇ* may refer to this practice, but it may also be a legal term, 'to take one's stand at the bar or in the dock', to answer charges, as *hᵃšîḇēnî* in the parallel colon suggests.

6. *lā'ēl* is not 'for God' (so Dhorme, Hölscher, Mowinckel, Fohrer, Lévêque), nor 'like God' (Terrien), but rather 'vis-à-vis God' (so Dhorme, Weiser), i.e. as created and animated by him, as the context indicates.

MT *kᵉpîḵā* does not require emendation to *kāmôḵā* as is suggested in BH³. Dhorme cites Ass. *kî pî* ('like'), and *kᵉpî* ('in proportion to') as familiar in Classical Heb., for example, *'îš kᵉpî 'oḵᵉlô* (Exod. 16.21), *kᵉpi šānāyw* (Lev. 25.52), hence we render 'I am related to God in the same degree as yourself'.

mēḥōmer qōraṣtî ('I was nipped off from the clay') recalls the creation of the man Enkidu in the Mesopotamian Gilgamesh epic (I.ii.34), where the god 'pinched off clay and cast it in the steppe'. The same verb is used in the Ras Shamra text Gordon *UT* 127.27ff., where the god El moulds a figure in clay or dung for use in apotropaic magic.

4. For the order of the verse and its significance in the argument, see Introduction to ch. 33.

7. Elihu refers obliquely to Job's objection that God puts him out of countenance with terror (9.34; 13.21). *'ēmāh,* actually *'êmāh,* is a very strong word and poetic, usually expressing terror inspired by God hence it is appropriate here, where Elihu is insisting that he as a man like Job and, in the characteristic sapiential tradition, was confident in the adequacy of human reason to adjust Job to his circumstances.

For *'aḵpî* LXX indicates the reading *kappî* ('my hand'), which would involve the further emendation of *yiḵbāḏ* to *tiḵbāḏ*. V arranges the letters of MT *'aḵpî* to read *'aḵ pî* ('nay…my mouth'), and S and T also retain MT. S interprets the word as 'concern for me' after a root *'kp* in the Syr. dialect, and renders 'my burden', which suggests that MT *'aḵpî* is a noun *'eḵep̄* (a *hapax legomenon* in the OT) with the pronominal suffix. *'eḵep̄* might be derived from the verb *'āḵap̄* ('to compel', Prov. 16.26). This word is known in Late Heb., Aram., Syr, and Arab., as may be assumed from the Arab. *'akāfu*(*n*) ('pack-saddle'). The reading of LXX, however, is supported by the language of Job 13.21:

> *kappᵉḵā mē'ālay harḥaq*
> *wᵉ'ēmāṯᵉḵā 'al-tᵉḇa'ᵃṯannî.*

8. On the reading *millêḵā* for MT *millîn,* see Textual Note. The Aram. word is again used.

9. The meaning of the *hapax legomenon ḥap̄* is not in doubt in this context owing to the parallelism with *zaḵ* ('pure') and the antithesis with *wᵉlō' 'āwōn lî* ('nor have I sin'). It is well attested in Late Heb. in the root *ḥāp̄ap̄* ('to wash the head') and as *ḥûp̄* in Syr., into which the root probably came through Ass. from Akk., where Dhorme cites the root *ḫâpa* ('to clean').

10. *hēn* here means 'indeed, in fact'; cf. Arab. *'inna.*

MT *tᵉnû'ôṯ* would be derived from a verbal root *nû'*, which is attested in Akk. and Arab. meaning 'to oppose'. The verb *yimṣā'*, however, does not suggest this verbal noun 'opposition' as an object, since this would proceed from God, who would then have no need to discover it. Thus, following S and Rashi, we may read *tō'ᵃnôṯ* (from *'ānāh*, Arab. *'ana*[*y*], 'to be seasonable'), hence 'occasions'; cf. 'opportunities' for a quarrel (Judg. 14.4). In v. 10b Elihu quotes Job in 13.24b and, not so accurately, in 19.11b.

MT *yāśēm* should be pointed *yāśîm*. The verse cites 13.27, which see.

12. For MT *hēn-zô'ṯ lō' ṣāḏaqtā 'e'ᵉnekkā* LXX implies a reading *hēḵ tō'mar ṣaḏaqtî lō' 'ē'āneh* ('How say you, I am right, I get no answer'). But MT requires no emendation, and is the more natural introduction to *kî* and the rest of v. 12b.

In v. 12b LXX 'He who is above mortals is eternal' has suggested that MT *yirbeh* may have been a corruption of *kabbîr*. This is gratuitous. Even on this interpretation *yirbeh* may be a byform of *rāḇaḇ*, from which *raḇ* is derived meaning 'aged'; cf. 32.9. In any case, whether as meaning 'aged' or, as probably, 'great', *yirbeh* must be preserved in view of the word-play between it and *rîḇôṯā* ('contended') in v. 13.

13. For MT *dᵉḇārāyw* V read *dᵉḇārêḵā*, which is feasible but unnecessary, since the 3rd masc. suffix refers to *'ᵉnôš* in v. 12b.

rîḇ ('contend') in the sense 'to object' is attested at Judg. 21.22.

14. 'One time...two times' means 'repeatedly'; cf. Amos 1.3, 6, 9, 11, 13; 2.1, 4, 6 and other instances in the OT too numerous to mention. It is a convention also used in Ugaritic poetry.

In MT *ûḇištayim lō' yᵉšûrennāh, lō'*, if negative, is difficult. The verb *šûr* is known in Classical Heb., meaning 'to take note of', and is so taken here, with *lō'* as negative, by Jerome in his commentary, and by T, which paraphrases 'and he has no need to consider it'. V and S, however, translate the verb as 'repeat', evidently reading *yᵉšannennāh*, which is graphically feasible in the Old Heb. script for *yᵉšûrennāh* in *scriptio defectiva*. Dhorme adopts this reading, which would be expressive of God's peremptory and persistent declarations, citing 40.5, where *wᵉlō' 'ôsîp̄* would correspond to *lō' yᵉšannennāh* in 33.14b. We suggest that MT *yᵉšûrennāh* is the energic form of the imperfect of *šûr*, cognate here with Arab. *šāra, yašūru*, meaning in the IInd Form 'to point out'. We suggest further that the enclitic *lᵉ*, well known in Arab. and now also in Ugaritic, has been misunderstood by Heb. scribes as the negative. Omitting ' of MT *lō'*, we would read *ûḇištayim lîšûrennāh*, 'yea, in the two he indicates (his will)', the substance of which is given in the sequel. Fohrer's interpretation, which assumes the indefinite subject of the verb in the MT, is grammatically possible, but in the construction of the couplet it is very unlikely that the subject should change so abruptly without being explicitly noted.

15. Elihu, like Eliphaz in 4.12ff., cites a theophany, which is introduced in v. 15a and b by a citation of 4.13, but the substance is much more positive. Perhaps the verbal citation in v. 15b may be omitted as a gloss (so Hölscher, Mowinckel, Fohrer). Here the theophany is an audition in a dream. The dream has just such a significance in the ancient Near East, as evidenced by the plethora of omen texts from Mesopotamia, the reference to dreams and their interpretation by prophetic figures in affairs of state in the Mari texts and by the patriarchs in the early narratives of the Pentateuch (e.g. Gen. 20.3;

28.12-15; 31.11ff.; 37.5-10) and in traditions of the reigns of Saul (1 Sam. 28.6) and of Solomon (1 Kgs 3.5-14). The great prophets of Israel were more discriminating in their attitude to dreams as the medium of revelation, and did not regard dreams as automatically genuine revelation, which might be artificially induced or arbitrarily interpreted (Deut. 13.1-5; Jer. 23.25-32). Jeremiah, nevertheless, does admit the possibility of genuine revelation to a prophet in dreams, which is admitted by Joel as a function of prophecy and the consequence of the possession of the spirit (Joel 3.1f. [EVV 2.28f.]) and regularly in apocalypticism. Even in so late and sophisticated a sage as Ben Sira, who despised reliance on dreams as such (34.1-5) the possibility of a genuine dream-revelation is admitted (34.6).

16. MT *ûḇᵉmōsārām yaḥtōm* means lit. 'and by their bonds seals (them)', which is obscure. Aq., V, S and T read *ûḇᵉmusārām* ('and by their admonition'). The sense of *yaḥtōm* in this association is not clear, but the meaning of v. 16 may be 'he opens the ear of men and seals it up again with admonitions to them'. But the ancient versions show a great measure of agreement in variations from MT, especially Aq., LXX and S, in reading *yᵉḥattēm*, the Hiphil of *ḥāṯaṯ*, meaning 'he frightens them'. LXX, in reading 'with appearances of fear', seems to conflate two variants of MT *musārām*, namely, *mar'îm* ('appearances, visions') and *mōrā'îm* ('terrors'). Neither the one nor the other is what is expected as the medium of revelation mentioned in v. 16a, so we follow Aq., V, S, and T and with slight variation read *ûḇᵉmusārām*, which is identical with MT so far as consonants are concerned. But with Dahood (1963c: 35) we take *mûsār* as the seat of admonition from the verb *yāsar* ('to admonish, discipline'); cf. Ps. 16.7, *yissᵉrûnî kilyôṯāy* ('my reins have admonished me'), a vivid description of the action of conscience, which has a parallel in the Ugaritic legend of Krt, Gordon *UT* 127,26 *wywsrnn ggnh* ('and his inwards admonish him'). Hence, reading *ûḇᵉmusārām yeḥattēm*, we render 'and in their conscience he terrifies them'. This gives in conscience an organ of the divine revelation parallel to 'the ear of humans' in the parallel colon.

17. The purpose of the theophany is so that the evil purposes of humans may not be brought to effect. With S, T, V and most moderns we read *mimma'ᵃśēhû*.

In v. 17b *ga'ᵃwāṯô* ('his pride') should certainly be read for MT *gēwāh* ('body').

Dhorme reverses the order of *ma'ᵃśēhû* (MT *ma'ᵃśeh*) and *ga'ᵃwāh* (MT *gēwāh*), rendering 'turning man from pride, hiding his action from man'. This is not supported by any of the versions and Dhorme's second colon introduces a concept foreign to the purpose of the revelation. The verse is improved if, with the two emendations proposed, the Qal *yiḵsaḥ* is read (so Beer, Hölscher, Fohrer), a verb also attested in Aram. and Syr.; cf. Arab. *kasaḥa* ('to sweep away').

18. The parallel with *šaḥaṯ* ('pit') has suggested the emendation of MT *baššālaḥ* (pausal) to *biše'ôl* (so Duhm, Hölscher). Dhorme proposes that *šelaḥ* here means 'grave-shaft'; cf. *šelaḥ* in Neh. 3.15 and Isa. 8.6 (the Siloam tunnel) and Ass. *šiliḫtu* ('canal'). But in these cases the root meaning of the verb from which they are derived means 'to distribute', and they denote not a vertical shaft but a horizontal distribution of water. Hence our preference for 'the stream of death'; cf. NEB 'the river of death', recalling 'the waters of death' in the Gilgameš Epic (so Tsevat [1954: 43], and Rin [1963], who takes the word to refer, by synecdoche, generally to the underworld; see also Pope). The sage in the Elihu addendum is using the same poetic licence as the Christian hymnologist in speaking of 'death's cold, sullen stream'. The word may have this sense in the Ugaritic legend of Krt in the phrase *bšlḥ ttpl* describing deaths in the royal family by various means or by various expressions. There it has been taken to mean a weapon, a sword (Caquot, Sznycer and Herdner 1974: 506) or spear (Gibson 1978: 82), taking *šlḥ* as cognate of Arab. *śilāḥu(n)* ('sword'); cf. G.B. Gray and Fohrer on Job 33.18, where Fohrer translates *'aḇōr bešelaḥ* ('running on the spear'). But in the Ugaritic text *šlḥ* might equally well mean 'the stream of death'. In any case in the passage in Job the parallel with *šaḥaṯ* indicates the underworld, *šaḥaṯ* being parallel to *še'ôl* in Ps. 16.10.

19. For MT *werîḇ 'aṣāmāyw 'ēṯān* (Kethib) Dhorme cites the Akk. *rîbu* ('to quake') (so G.R. Driver 1955: 73); cf. 4.14. *'ēṯān* is used of 'abiding' or 'perpetual', for example, in Num. 24.21, Jer. 5.15.

20. For MT *wezihamattû* we may read *wezihamāh*. The verb, however, may take a double accusative with *ḥayyāṯô* as the subject, though in this case the translation 'his life makes him loathe his food' is awkward. The verb is found in the OT here and possibly, with restoration, in 6.7, on which see; but it also has cognates in Aram. meaning 'dirty' and in Syr. meaning 'putrid, stinking'.

21. MT *yiḵel* should probably be read *yiḵleh* ('wastes away'), the corruption having probably occurred through *scriptio defectiva*. *mērō'î* may mean 'so that it is not seen', a case of privative *min* with a form of the verbal noun of *rā'āh*. The suggestion of Duhm to emend *mērō'î* to *mērezî* ('by reason of emaciation') (cf. Budde's suggestion *mērāzôn*), while graphically feasible in the Old Heb. script, misses a probable word-play between *rā'āh* ('to see') and *rā'āh*, a byform of *rāwāh*, a verb which is probably used in Prov. 23.31 and Ben Sira 34.28 (1962: 499-500). To these instances we should probably add Ps. 36.10 (EVV 9), *'immeḵā meqôr ḥayyîm biḇe'ēreḵā' nir'eh* (for MT *be'ôreḵā nir'eh-'ôr*), 'For with thee is the source of life; from thy well we shall be satisfied'. *šuppû* is probably from *šāp̄āh*, which is known as meaning 'to be bare'; cf. *har-nišpeh* ('a bare mountain') in Isa. 13.2, and also Isa. 49.9; Jer. 3.2; 4.11; 7.29; and 12.12, where it describes desert.

22. *w* copula is to be read and not *w* consecutive. MT *lam^emiṯîm* is read *lamm^emōṯ^eṯîm* as in RSV, which translates 'to those who bring death' (so G.B Gray, Terrien); cf. MacFadyen, 'to the angels of death', after LXX; so Fohrer, translating 'the messengers of death' in Prov. 16.14, and citing the analogy of the seven evil demons, 'the slayers' (*mušitûti*) of Assyrian superstition (so also apparently Mowinckel), and of the *śāṭān* of the Prologue. But the parallelism in our opinion supports the reading *l^emô mēṯîm* 'to the dead', that is, 'to the place of the dead' (so Hoffmann, Perles).

23. In this passage LXX is much fuller than MT, possibly indicating paraphrase, and possibly a double translation of the Heb. text. It suggests that v. 23c may be the first colon of a couplet, the second of which read 'and to show him his folly', but the known tendency of LXX to paraphrase and occasionally to amplify must make this a matter of uncertainty. The Heb. text, however, has been disturbed at this point, a verb having certainly been lost at the beginning of v. 24, so that the loss of a colon after v. 23c is the more likely. In v. 23a *'ālāyw* may mean 'by (i.e. with) him'; cf. *'āl yāḏ* (so Dhorme, citing 1 Kgs 22.19, *'ōmēḏ 'ālāyw mîmînô ûmiśś^emō'lô*). *mal'āḵ* is well attested in the MT and versions. Rowley, admitting that *mal'āḵ* ('messenger') may be human or divine, opts for the former 'probably', with the function of interpreter (*mēliṣ* of God's will to humans and/or to express the case of a person to God, as the *m^elîṣîm* (NEB 'spokesmen') in Isa. 43.27, where, however, the parallelism indicates another reading and interpretation. But the figure of the *śāṭān* among the 'celestials' (*b^enê ^{'e}lōhîm*) and the 'celestials' in 5.1 supports the celestial rather than the human nature of the of *mal'āḵ* in the present passage. The figure of an intercessory angel emerges in the 'angel of Yahweh' who intercedes for Jerusalem and the cities of Judah in Zech. 1.12f. Here the angel is not the representative of the individual as in Job 33.23f., but his intercessory function is the same as in Job. The passages in Zechariah (late sixth century BCE) and the Elihu Addendum at least a century later are sufficiently close for the affinity to be significant and sufficiently removed to account for the individualization of the conception of the angelic intercessor in Job 33.23f., a sympathetic counterpart to the *śāṭān* among the celestials in the Prologue, a figure with a function like that of Michael in Dan. 12.1 and in Apocalyptic in the Apocrypha. Such a figure has a counterpart in the protecting gods of households and individuals in Mesopotamia (Mowinckel 1925: 208), a figure which also appears, significantly for the passage in Job, in Mesopotamian wisdom texts cited above (pp. 5-20), with its development in the conception of the protecting or intercessory angel in later Judaism and Christianity (e.g. Mt. 18.10). The function of such a figure in the context of the plaint and purification rites of the sufferer in ancient Mesopotamia was to make their significance with relation to the cause of them clear to the sufferer and also to help to communicate the emotions, confessions and prayers of the sufferer to God, hence the term *mēlîṣ* ('interpreter'); cf. 16.20, where, however, it may be a

corruption (see Commentary). In Elihu's statement the function of the *mēlîṣ* was to interpret a person's sufferings as a divine discipline, recalling one to one's duty, to point that person to the grace of God and to intercede for one and to 'offer ransom' for one, that is, possibly to represent to God the rites of expiation as tokens of genuine contrition which will make redemption effective (*pārᵉ'ēhû*). T renders *mēlîṣ paraqlîṭa'*, the *pareklētos* ('advocate') of Jn 14.16; cf. Richardson 1955: 169; Schedl 1942; Irwin 1962: 218.

As an angel (*mal'āḵ*) was the proper mediator of God's will to humans as here and in Gen. 31.11 (E), he mediates also the needs of mortals to God (v. 24). *mēlîṣ*, meaning here as in Gen. 42.23 'an interpreter', refers to the dual role of the mediator. This had been familiar in Israel in the role of the prophets, who mediated the will of God to the community and the wishes and disposition of the community to God. It was probably because of this institution in Israel that the conception of a supernatural intermediary did not develop in Judaism until after the prophetic era in the late sixth century and later. Though we compare the prophetic office to that of the supernatural *mēlîṣ* in Job 33.23 we do not subscribe to Dhorme's view that *mᵉlîṣêḵā* in Isa. 43.27 denotes prophets, since we believe that, as the parallel suggests, *mōlîḏêḵā* ('parents') should be read.

The significance of 'one of a thousand' is not clear. The preposition does not suggest that LXX is right in interpreting 'If ten thousand angels of death are there (cf. v. 22) not one of them will hurt him...' A more legitimate interpretation would be to understand in parenthesis 'and there are 999 besides'. The phrase, however, is found in Eccl. 7.28, where it denotes the exception, as in Ben Sira 6.6, 'The friends of your prosperity are many, but your intimate is one of a thousand' (*'ehāḏ mē'elep̄*). Assuming that this was a popular proverb, the qualification of the mediator as 'one of a thousand' may describe him as sharing a person's intimate secret (*sôḏ*) and as exceptionally loyal. In v. 23c *yošrô* would mean 'his uprightness', translated by Dhorme as 'his duty', that is, what is proper for him; cf. *yšr* in the sense of 'proper', parallel to *ṣdq* in the Ugaritic Legend of Krt (Gordon *UT* Krt, 12.13).

24. MT *pᵉḏā'ēhû*, if correct, would be a *hapax legomenon*. The general sense is quite clear, and *kōp̄er* in the parallel colon supports a translation 'redeem'. This would naturally suggest *pāḏāh* ('to set free by ransom'), as S, T and V understand. But this may be a coincidence. The letter ' is too distinctive to be lost to any other in the context, but *r* may easily have been corrupted to *d*, so *pᵉrā'ēhû* may be read ('free him'), from *pāra'* ('to break loose', Exod. 32.25) used in the Hiphil meaning 'to set free' in Exod. 5.4 (so Budde, Duhm, Wright, Hölscher, Beer, Graetz, Weiser, Fohrer, Lévêque). This is read by two Heb. MSS. To meet Dhorme's objection that the Qal of *pāra'* does not mean 'to set free' we may read the intensive (causative) *pārᵉ'ēhû*; cf. Arab. *faraġa* ('to free from work') meaning in the IVth Form 'to help in extremity'. *kōp̄er*, used of a bribe in 36.18; Amos 5.12; Prov. 6.35, means here rather 'a ransom'.

The word occurs in legal terminology, as in compensation for injury by a goring ox (Exod. 21.30) or as an offering of propitiation after a census (Exod. 30.12) or as the ransom of an individual (Prov. 13.8; 21.18; Ps. 49.8f.). It is not certain what ransom is envisaged in Job 33.24. The statement that this is something the angel might find for Job is equivocal since it is not stated that he would find it out of his own resources. The fact that the function of the angel would be to convince a person of one's duty, that is, his fitting relationship to the will of God, would indicate that Job's contrition evoked by the angel might be the ransom found by him, as Lévêque has suggested (1970: 55ff.).

25. MT *ruṭᵃp̄aš* might possibly be a metathetic cognate of Arab. *ṭarfaša* ('to be convalescent'), which would be quite apt in the context, though the imperfect is demanded and the comparative *min* with *nō'ar* precludes this. *yirṭaḇ* has been proposed, meaning 'he will be fresher'; cf. 8.16a, and Arab. *raṭaba* ('to be fresh, moist' of fruit; so Dhorme, Tur-Sinai, G.B. Gray, Terrien). In this case *ś* might have come in by dittography from *bś* in the following word *beśārô*. A more likely alternative to *yirṭaḇ* in our opinion is *yiṭpaš* ('is plump[er]'; so Siegfried, Budde, Duhm, Beer, Hölscher, Lévêque and evidently NEB), which occurs in Ps. 119.70 in the sense 'gross'.

26. *'āṯar* is generally used in the Niphal, but is found in the Qal here and in Gen. 25.21; Exod. 8.26; 10.18; Judg. 13.8. *rāṣāh* means 'granted favour' (*rāṣôn*); cf. Arab. *raḍa(y)*. To 'see the face of' a person means to be admitted to one's presence (Gen. 32.21) as a mark of favour (Gen. 43.3, 5; 44.23, 26; Exod. 23, 28; 2 Sam. 14.24, 28, 32; 2 Kgs 25.19; Est. 1.14). *tᵉrû'āh* means properly the shout of joy or triumph, hence generally 'joy'. The association here with 'seeing the face of God' may reflect the characteristic shout of acclaim at the New Year festival which greeted the assurance of God's presence as King; cf. Ps. 47.6 (EVV 5), 'Yahweh has gone up with acclamation' (*biṯᵉrû'āh*), where the verb corresponds to the more regular *mālaḵ* ('he is installed as King') in psalms which like Psalm 47 are from the liturgy of the New Year festival. In v. 26b the subject of the verb (reading *wᵉyāšîḇ* for MT *weyyāšeḇ*) is God, who restores a person's innocence and proper (*ṣaddîq*) status in the sacral community.

27. The experience just described is that often expressed in the Plaint of the Sufferer in the Psalms in a hymn of thanksgiving, which is the theme of vv. 26-27, where *yāšîr* must be read for MT *yāšōr*. The preposition *'al* meaning 'over against', hence 'before', may be attested in a similar context in the Ras Shamra texts, where one sings *'l b'l*, possibly 'before Baal' at a feast in his honour (Gordon *UT* 'nt I, 20-21), though in the context the phrase may mean 'about Baal'. Verse 27b is a good instance of the use of *yāšār* ('straight') and *'āwāh* ('to be crooked') in their primary sense, though here also, of course, with a moral significance. In MT *wᵉlō'-šāwāh*, if the text is correct, the verb

would be used impersonally (so Dhorme). But the metre demands an extra beat, which is secured by pointing the verb as *šiwwāh* and the addition of *k̲ᵉḥaṭṭā'ṯî* (so Bickell) or *ka'ᵃwōnî* (so Duhm) after LXX. The verb in the Qal means 'to be equal, comparable', and in the Intensive (Causative) is peculiarly fitting for the expression of retribution.

28. In the Qere of MT, where *nap̄šô* and *ḥayyāṯô* were read, it has not been understood that vv. 27-28 are a hymn of thanksgiving, and that hence the 1st person must be read, as in Kethib.

29. On 'two, yea, three times', denoting repetition and continual activity, see on v. 14; cf. Hos. 6.2:

> After two days he will revive us,
> On the third day he will raise us up.

The light symbolizes life in contrast to the darkness of death; cf. v. 28. MT *bᵉ'ôr* has been emended by Budde and Hölscher to *lirᵉ'ôṯ* after S, and Reiske read *bᵉ'ereṣ* (*haḥayyîm*) for MT *bᵉ'ôr*, 'the land of the living' being a familiar phrase; cf. Ps. 27.13, *he'ᵉmantî lirᵉ'ôṯ bᵉṭûḇ-yhwh bᵉ'ereṣ ḥayyîm*. Ehrlich reads *lirᵉ'ôṯ bᵉ'ôr bᵉ'ereṣ haḥayyîm*, which is metrically possible, if somewhat cumbersome. Dhorme preserves MT, treating *lē'ôr* as the elided form of the Niphal infin. constr. *lᵉhē'ôr*; cf. 2 Sam. 2.32, where the verb is used impersonally, and Ps. 76.5, where, if MT is correct, it means 'enveloped in light'. This, with *'ereṣ* for *'ôr*, is possibly the best reading. Dahood (1966: 222-23) has questioned if *'ôr haḥayyîm* in the Psalms should not be pointed as *'ûr haḥayyîm* ('the land of the living'); cf. Ps. 54.14, where S reads *'ereṣ* for *'ôr*. He adduces as evidence the phrase *'ûr kaśdîm*, where LXX reads *chōra* ('region') for *'ûr*, noting that Gen. 24.4, 7 specifically notes *North* Mesopotamia as Abraham's birthplace, whereas Ur is in the South. The reading *lē'ôr bᵉ'ûr haḥayyîm* would give a word-play very characteristic of the Book of Job.

In the final passage vv. 27f. reflect the public acknowledgment of deliverance in the Plaint of the Sufferer in the cult.

Job 34

Elihu's Second Statement

Having directed his first address to Job in order to demolish his case (ch. 33), Elihu now turns ostensibly to his friends, but really to all interested in the problem of the theodicy. His method and style are the same as in his first address, to state or explode Job's theses (e.g. vv. 5, 9, 31-32), and then to state and develop his own antitheses. This is done progressively and systematically in the convention of the sapiential disputation in five strophes after the introduction (vv. 2-4), viz. vv. 5-9; 10-15; 16-19, 29c-30, 20-22, 25; 23-24, 26-29b; 31-37.

In the first strophe of his argument (vv. 5-9) directed against Job's persistent refusal to be admonished either by mental or by physical distress, he cites Job's thesis (vv. 5-6) and condemns him for subscribing to the view of the godless (vv. 7-8) and for his cynical conclusion that conduct which ought to please God is a matter of indifference to him (v. 9). He berates Job's rejection of orthodox arguments, so often given in mockery (v. 7), as in his citation of the prosperity of the wicked (21.7-34), with his mockery of the proverbs of the wise in support of the theodicy (21.17f.). Such conduct associates Job with the wicked (v. 8; cf. Ps. 1.1), as does his statement 'a person has no profit from pleasing God' (v. 9), perhaps citing Job's questioning of God's countenancing the prosperity of the wicked in 21.14, a sentiment implied in his statement that God destroys both the innocent and the guilty (9.22f.). In the second strophe (vv. 10-15) Elihu asserts the doctrine of the theodicy; God, to whom justice is relevant, cannot be accused of injustice (vv. 10-12), perhaps recalling Gen. 18.25 ('Shall not the judge of all the earth do what is just?'); God, on whom all being depends, cannot be called to account by any of his creatures (vv. 13-15). In the third strophe (vv. 16-19, 29c-30, 20-22, 25) the idea of God as the upholder of Order, the theme of the Enthronement Psalms, is taken as axiomatic, in support of which an appeal is made to general experience in history with the rise and fall of dynasties, with possible reference to the dynastic turmoils in northern Israel, Assyria and Babylon. The reference to the removal of the strong one by 'no (human) hand' (v. 20c) and sudden death at midnight may refer to the destruction of Sennacherib's army (2 Kgs 19.35) or the tradition of the sudden death of the first-born of the Egyptians in the Passover legend. In the fourth strophe (vv. 23-24, 26-29b) Elihu animadverts on Job's appeal for God to set an appointment for a hearing and opportunity for justification, which is implied in the oath of purgation; and in the fifth strophe (vv. 31-37) he states that it is not for Job to make this demand—God alone may decide the moment of such an encounter and the extent of his retribution, independently of all extenuating circumstances one may adduce (vv. 31-33). Finally Job's wealth of argument against the theodicy, not without reduction to absurdity, no less than his sin, which Elihu like Job's friends deduce from his suffering, is roundly condemned (vv. 36-37).

The order of the text is generally well preserved, but in its place in MT vv. 23-24 on the subject of divine retribution, the theme of vv. 26ff., break the sequence of thought on the omniscience of God and the impossibility of evading detection, which is the theme of vv. 21-22 and v. 25, hence v. 25 is displaced from after v. 22. Verse 29c is suspect in its present position and in sense seems to belong to the odd colon at the end of v. 19. So far as subject matter is concerned, vv. 29c and 30a could be read as an apposite couplet:

> 29c. And over nations and persons alike he watches,
> 30. That there should rule no impious man to ensnare the people.

Verse 30, however, is too long for a single colon, and v. 30b is too short, so that the verse, though probably following the couplet vv. 19c + 29c, is either a gloss or a fragmentary piece of text. There is probably the lacuna of a colon before v. 10a, which after 34.34 may be restored:

> *lāḵēn ḥ^{a}ḵāmîm ha'^{a}zînû*
> *w^{e}'an^{e}šê lēḇāḇ šim^{e}'û lî.*

Chapter 34

1. And Elihu spoke:

2. 'Hear my words, you wise men,
   And, you who have knowledge, give ear to me.
3. For the ear tests words,
   As the palate tastes food.[1]
4. Let us test for ourselves what is right,
   Let us determine among ourselves what is good.

5. For Job has said, "I am innocent,
   But God has dismissed my case;
6. Despite my just case I am smitten with pain,[2]
   My wound[3] is sore though I have done no wrong".
7. What man is like Job,
   Who drinks up scoffing like water?
8. Who goes in company with workers of wrong,
   Walking with wicked men?
9. For he has said, "A man has no profit
   From discharging his obligations to God".

10. Therefore, [wise men, give ear],[4]
Men of understanding hear me.
Far be it from God to do evil,[5]
And from the Almighty[6] to pervert the right.[7]
11. But according to the work[8] of each man he requites him,
And according to a man's ways he makes him go through with it.
12. Assuredly God does no wrong,[9]
Nor does the Almighty pervert justice.
13. Who gave him orders over his own earth,[10]
And who has held him liable for the whole world?
14. If he should take back[11] his spirit[12] to himself,
And gather his breath to himself,
15. All flesh together would perish,
And humanity would return to dust.

16. So if you have understanding[13] listen to this,
Give ear to the sound of my words.
17. Shall one who hates government govern?
Do you convict of wickedness the Just and Mighty One?
18. He it is who says[14] to a king, "Worthless!",
To nobles, "Wicked!",
19. Who shows no partiality to nobles,
Nor regards the noble more than the poor,
For they are all the work of His hands;
29c. And over nations and men alike He watches,[15]
30. Lest an impious man rule,
One of those who would ensnare the people and wrong them.[16]

20. Suddenly they die at midnight,
The notables are shaken[17] and pass away;
The strong one is removed[18] by no (human) hand;
21. For his eyes are on the ways of a man,
And he marks all his steps.
22. There is no darkness or gloom
Where the workers of iniquity may be hidden,
25. But he notes their works,
He overwhelms them[19] in a night and they are crushed.

23. But not on any man's account is there an appointed time[20]
For one to go before God with a case.
24. He shatters the mighty without investigation,
Setting[21] others in their place.
26. On the scene of their crime[22] he strikes them,
Where others may gloat over them,[23]
27. Because they turned from following him,
And had no consideration for his ways,
28. To bring before him the cry of the poor,
So that he might hear the cry of the afflicted.
29. Then if he keep silent[25] who can move him?[26]
If he avert his face, who can make him turn again?[27]

31. If one were to say to God,[28]
“I have been seduced,[29] I am not liable;[30]
32. So that I may see[31] do thou instruct me.
If I have done wrong I will do so no longer.”
33. Is it on your initiative that he should requite you[32] seeing that you[33] have rejected him?
For the choice (of your course) was yours not his.[34]
[Say what you know.][35]
34. Men of understanding will admit to me,
Even a wise man, who will listen to me,
35. That Job does not speak with knowledge,
And his words are not with insight.
36. [36]May Job be tried to the end
For answering like wicked men;
37. Because he adds to his sin,
Denying sin in our midst,
And speaks volubly[37] his words against God.’

Textual Notes to Chapter 34

1. Reading yuḏā‘û (pausal) for mt yāḏā‘û (see Commentary ad loc.)
1. Reading *’ōḵel* with LXX, S, and V for MT *le’^{e}ḵōl.*
2. Reading *’eḵ’āḇ* for MT *’^{a}ḵazzēḇ*. See Commentary *ad loc.*
3. Reading *maḥ^{a}ṣî* for MT *ḥiṣṣî.*
4. Reading *lāḵēn ḥ^{a}ḵāmîm ḥa’^{a}zînû / w^{e}’an^{e}šê lēḇāḇ šim^{e}‘û lî.*
5. Reading *mēr^{e}šōa‘* for MT *mērešaʻ.*
6. Reading *ûl^{e}šadday* for MT *w^{e}šadday.*
7. Reading *mē‘awwēl ṣeḏeq* after LXX for MT *mē‘āwel*; cf. v. 12. See Commentary *ad loc.*
8. Reading *kî k^{e}pō‘al* with LXX and S for MT *kî pō‘al.*
9. Reading *yirša‘* for MT *yaršîa‘.*
10. Reading *’arṣôh*; cf. one Heb. MS (*’arṣô*) for MT *’arṣāh.*
11. Reading *yāšîḇ* with certain Heb. MSS, LXX, and S for MT *yāśîm.*
12. Omitting *libbô*, *metri causa.* See Commentary *ad loc.*
13. Reading *h^{a}ḇînōṯā* with LXX, Aq., Sym., S, T and V for MT *bînāḥ.*
14. Reading *hā’ōmēr* with LXX, S, V and one Heb. MS for MT *ha’^{a}mōr.*
15. Reading *yeḥ^{e}ḏeh*, an Aram. form of Heb. *yeḥ^{a}zeh*, for MT *yāḥaḏ* (pausal form).
16. If MT *mimmōq^{e}šê ‘ām* is not a gloss, the metre demands an extra word to complete the colon, such as *ûm^{e}‘aqq^{e}šām*, if we may suggest a word which might easily have been omitted by haplography after *mōq^{e}šê ‘am.* This would be such an assonance as the writer of Job favoured.
17. Reading *y^{e}ḡō‘^{a}šû šô‘îm* for MT *y^{e}ḡō‘^{a}šû ‘ām.* See Commentary *ad loc.*
18. Reading *w^{e}yāsûr* for MT *w^{e}yāsîrû.*
19. Reading *wah^{a}pāḵām* with S for MT *w^{e}hāpaḵ.*
20. Reading *kî lō’ ‘al-’îš mô‘ēḏ* for MT *kî lō’ ‘al-’îš yāśîm ‘ôḏ*, assuming dittography of *y* and *s* of *’îš* and erroneous grouping of *m* with *y* and *s* instead of with *‘ēḏ* corrupted to MT *‘ôḏ.*
21. Reading *w^{e}ya‘^{a}mîḏ* for MT *wayya‘^{a}mēḏ.*
22. Reading *riš‘ām* for MT *r^{e}šā‘îm.*

23. Adding *ʿalêhem* after *rō'îm, metri causa, ʿalêhem* possibly being omitted by dittography before *ʿal-'ašer* in v. 27. See Commentary *ad loc.* and Textual Note 24.
24. Reading *ʿal 'ašer* for MT *'ašer ʿal* and omitting *kēn*, *kn* being possibly a dittograph of *šr* of *'ašer* in the Old Heb. script.
25. Reading *yišqōṭ* with one Heb. MS for MT *yašqiṭ*.
26. Reading *yar'išennû* for MT *yaršia'...*, with omission of *n* by haplography before *w*.
27. Reading *yešîḇennû* for MT *yešûrennû* assuming corruption of *b* to *r* in the Old Heb. script and *y* to *w* in the script at the stage of development of the Qumran MSS.
28. Reading *kî 'el-'elôah 'āmar* for MT *kî-'el-'ēl he'āmar*. See Commentary *ad loc.*
29. Reading *niššē'ṯî* for MT *nāśā'ṯî*. See Commentary *ad loc.*
30. Reading *'ēḥāḇēl* for MT *'eḥbōl*. See Commentary *ad loc.*
31. *ʿaḏ 'eḥezeh* for MT *bilʿāḏê 'eḥezeh*, assuming haplography of *bl* after *'eḥbōl*.
32. Reading *yešallemekkā* for MT *yešallemennāh*, assuming corruption of *k* to *n* in the Old Heb. script.
33. Reading *me'astāw* for MT *mā'astî*.
34. Reading *hû'* for MT *'ānî*, assuming corruption of *h* to *w* and *'* to *n* in the Old Heb. script.
35. The colon is possibly to be omitted as a gloss.
36. Omitting MT *'aḇî* as a dittograph under the influence of *'iyyôḇ*. See Commentary *ad loc.*
37. Reading *weyarbeh* for MT *weyereḇ*.

Commentary on Chapter 34

3. *le* introducing *'ōḵel* (for MT *'eḵōl*) is a case of *nota accusativa*, another of the many Aramaisms in the Elihu passages.

4. The parallelism with *bāḥan* ('to assay') in the simile in vv. 3-4 indicates the meaning of *bāḥar* here, 'to test', as regularly in Aram. This is also implied in the regular meaning of the verb in Heb. 'to choose'; cf. Isa. 48.10, *beḥartîkā bekûr ʿōnî* ('I have tested you in the furnace of affliction'). *mišpāṭ* here is 'justice', 'what is right' in the abstract, as the parallel *mah-ṭṭôḇ* ('what is good') indicates. The lecturer touches on the particular case only to abstract general principles.

5. Citing Job's proposition that he is innocent (*ṣādaqtî*) and that confidence in God's justice is not justified (v. 9), Elihu goes on to argue for the efficiency of the theodicy.

'ēl hēsîr mišpāṭî ('God has dismissed my case') cites Job's words in 27.2.

6. For MT *'aḵazzēḇ* LXX reads *yeḵazzēḇ* ('he [i.e. God] makes me out a liar'). MT is a scribal adjustment (*tiqqun sōp̄erîm*) to avoid the association of God with wrong. Duhm retains the consonants of MT, pointing *'ekkāzēḇ* ('I am accounted a liar'). Ehrlich's emendation *'eḵ'āḇ* ('I suffer') is graphically feasible, and would give an excellent parallel to *'ānûš maḥaṣî* ('sick of my wound'), for MT *'ānûš ḥiṣṣî* ('sick of my arrow'), as proposed by Duhm; cf. Mic. 1.9, *'anûšāh makkôṯêhā* ('sick of her wounds') and Jer. 30.12.

7. *la'aḡ* ('mockery') refers to Job's embarrassing citation of empiric facts to upset conventional beliefs. In so doing he is said to have ranked himself with 'evil-doers' (*pō'ᵃlê 'āwen*) and 'wicked men' (*'anᵉšê reša'*) (v. 8), who are associated with scoffing in the Psalms (e.g. Ps. 1.1; 32.7; 35.15, 19, 25; 69.13 [EVV 12]).

9. This verse, which Hölscher after Budde would excise as anticipating Elihu's argument after 35.3, where the same question is introduced and discussed fully, is not out of place here, where it specifies wherein Job goes the way of the wicked, and summarizes the proposition to be refuted. Verse 10, which Budde also rejects as interrupting the argument, must also be retained as introducing Elihu's own argument after his citation of Job. On the verb *sāḵan* ('to care for', hence 'benefit, profit'), see on 15.3. *rāṣāh* here is better taken to mean 'to fulfil one's obligations', as in 14.6; cf. discharging the penalty for sin (Isa. 40.2) and keeping the Sabbath-obligation (Lev. 26.34, 43; 2 Chron. 36.21).

10. Again the appeal of the lecturer to his general audience, *'anᵉšê lēḇāḇ* ('men of intelligence', lit. 'heart'), and the general repudiation of the imputation of injustice to God mark the sapiential method so characteristic of Elihu's speeches. If v. 10a was indeed a couplet certain words have dropped out from the first colon, which we may restore from 34.34: *lāḵēn ḥᵃḵāmîm ha'ᵃzînû* ('Wherefore, ye wise men, give ear').

In v. 10b the metre demands an extra beat, hence with LXX we read *mē'awwēl ṣeḏeq* ('not to pervert the right'). This suggests that *mēreša'* in v. 10b, though intelligible, might be better emended to *mērᵉšōa'*. *šadday* governed by *ḥālîlāh*, like *'ēl*, should have the preposition *lᵉ*.

11. Here *māṣā'* has clearly the nuance of its Arab. cognate *mᵉṭā'* ('to arrive'). God causes a person to arrive, that is, brings him to the end of the path he has chosen for himself.

13. On the reading *'arṣōh* ('his earth') see Textual Note.

We understand *'ālāyw*, *'al* expressing liability after *śām* in v. 13b, where it would disrupt the metre. In the Ras Shamra texts the same preposition is often omitted before a second noun in the parallel colon.

14. On the reading of v. 14a, *'im-yāšîḇ 'ēlāyw rûaḥ*, see Textual Note. After the corruption of *yāšîḇ* to *yāśîm*, *libbô* was written alongside *rûaḥ*. The latter word is superfluous both to the first and second cola if *libbô* is preserved, and it belongs to the first colon as the natural parallel to *nᵉšāmāh* in the second, the two being frequently parallel, expressing God's animation of humanity (e.g. 32.8; 33.4). The sentiment of this couplet and the following recalls Ps. 104.29b, c:

tōsēp̄ rûḥām yiḡwā'ûn
wᵉ'el-'ᵃp̄ārām yᵉšûḇûn

You withdraw their spirit and they expire,
And return to their dust.

15. It is often doubted whether *'āp̄ār* ('dust') signifies the grave, or underworld, as it often does, or simply 'ground'. Here it probably refers to humanity created from dust and returning to dust (Gen. 3.9). So S, 'his dust'.

16. On the reading *hᵃḇînôṯā* see Textual Note.

17. *ḥāḇaš* means generally in Classical Heb. 'to bind', or 'harness'; cf. Arab. *ḥabaśa* ('to imprison'). *'āṣar* has the latter sense in Heb., and also means 'to restrain' in the sense of 'to govern' (1 Sam. 9.17). *ḥāḇaš* has evidently this meaning in Isa. 3.7.

The primary connotation of *mišpāṭ* and its verb *šāp̄aṭ* ('to rule') is clear from the Ras Shamra texts, where the participle *ṯpṭ* is found as the parallel of *mlk* ('king') (see, e.g., Gordon *UT* 49 VI, 29) and of *zbl* ('prince') (see, e.g. Gordon *UT* 68.15, 16-17, 22, 25). Judgment, which was an essential function of the ancient king, was a secondary meaning.

On *kabbîr*, here 'mighty', a divine epithet, see on 31.25.

18. The participle *hā'ōmēr* (for MT *ha'ᵃmōr*, see Textual Note) qualifies 'God', the antecedent of the relative particle in v. 19. There is an affinity here with the participle with the definite article which introduces the exploits of God as king in the Hymn of Praise.

19. The mention of *śārîm* ('notables', see on 29.9) after 'kings' and 'nobles' (*nᵉḏîḇîm*) in v. 18 indicates that the subject of *hā'ōmēr* and *nāśā' pānîm* in v. 19 is the same.

nikkar is used in the Piel only here and in 21.29, the usual form being Hiphil, and so is a linguistic peculiarity of Job. The meaning 'to show partiality', which is attested of the Niphal in Deut. 1.17; 16.19; Prov. 24.23; 28.21 is also comparatively rarely attested.

On *šôa'*, 'noble' in rank and 'generous', see on 29.11.

29c. We adopt Ehrlich's suggestion that *yaḥaḏ* is either a corruption of *yaḥaz*, an apocopated form of *ḥāzāh*, or a dialectic form reflecting the phonetic shift from *z* to *d* in Aram.

30. Verse 30b is short of a beat. If the passage is original and not a gloss we may suggest that *ûmᵉ'aqqᵉšām* ('and who wronged them') has been omitted by haplography after *mimmōqᵉšîm*. The assonance is characteristic of the style of the writer of Job and his circle.

20. The verb gā'aš, here in the Pual (cf. Jer. 25.16; 46.8 in Hithpoel) is attested besides only in Ps. 18.8 = 2 Sam. 22.8. The reading has been questioned here, and various plausible emendations, all conjectural, have been proposed. For MT yᵉḡō'ᵃšû 'ām Budde proposed yᵉḡō'ᵃšû šô'îm ('the nobles are shaken'); Hölscher yiḡwᵉ'û sô'îm, 'the nobles expire' (so Mowinckel, Fohrer, Larcher); Duhm yᵉḡō'ᵃšû mē'ām ('they are shaken out of the people'), for which a better translation might be 'they are shaken so that they are no longer a people'; Tur-Sinai suggested yānîa' sô'îm ('he drives forth the nobles') or, more close to MT, yigga' šô'îm ('he strikes the rich') (so Beer, Kissane, Stier, Lévêque). Dhorme's interpretation of the deposition of a ruler by a popular rising is not apt in the context, where the immediate agency of God ('without a hand') is emphasized. Pope reads MT, taking 'am as 'notables' or 'gentry', like 'am hā'āreṣ in 2 Kgs 21.24; 23.30, where they are politically significant, over against the feudal retainers of the king; cf. 2 Kgs 25.19, where, with the royal family and retinue, sixty of them are deported; see also Jer. 25.2. The limited number of these alone on this occasion indicates the status of the 'am hā'āreṣ, whom Alt (1959: 237) has compared to nišê mati ('men of the land'), local notables deported with unsatisfactory rulers according to Assyrian imperial inscriptions of the eighth century (Gilleschewski 1922: 137ff.; Galling 1929: 32; Gordis 1935: 242ff.; Würthwein 1936). 'am were probably so called because they represented the kinship units, also called 'am in Arab tribal society, and the ancestor (Arab. 'am) from whom those groups claimed descent. This may be the significance of the term in 34.20. While we prefer Budde's reading, we admit the feasibility of Pope's interpretation.

MT wᵉyāsîrû must be emended either to wᵉyāsîr, understanding God as subject, or, with 'abbîr as subject, wᵉyāsûr or, if 'abbîr is taken as a collective sing., wᵉyāsûrû.

lō' bᵉyāḏ is ambiguous. It may signify 'effortlessly' (so Dhorme, Kissane) or 'without human agency' (G.B. Gray, Mowinckel, Fohrer, Terrien, and apparently also Pope, to judge from his citation of Dan. 2.34 and 8.25). This is the meaning which we adopt as best suiting the context, though the phrase of itself is patient of the former interpretation and might even signify 'without memorial'; cf. yāḏ, the memorial set up by Absalom in Jerusalem to perpetuate his name (2 Sam. 18.18).

25. lāḵēn here has probably, as Dhorme suggests, a nuance of Arab. lākin ('but'). This adversative conjunction would link the verse excellently with v. 22, whereas in its present position it breaks the sense. See Introduction to ch. 34.

ma'bāḏ is an Aram. form, the Classical Heb. being ma'ᵃśeh.

Our reading waḥᵃpāḵām for MT wᵉhāpāḵ is suggested by S.

wᵉyiddakkā'û (pausal form) is a case of the Hithpael with the assimilation of t to the initial dental, as in 5.4.

23. On the reading *kî lō' 'al-'îš mô'ēḏ*, this probably refers to Job's claim for an appointed hearing; cf. 14.13; 24.1, where *'ittîm* denotes appointed times for a divine assize. *îš* denotes an individual as distinct from generic *'āḏām*.

26-27. The text is probably corrupt here, resulting in a short colon in v. 26b and an overlong colon in v. 27a. The uncertainty is increased by the fact that the ancient versions are not all complete at this point, and those which do contain this passage, or part of it, show variant readings. Of these LXX^A may suggest the completion of v. 26b, 'they are seen in the presence of their enemies', a reading which is supported by V. This may indicate the reading *bimᵉqôm rō'îm bāhem* (lit. 'in the place of those who look upon them'). This may be the idiom *rā'āh bᵉ* ('to see one's desire upon', e.g. Mic. 7.10; Ezek. 28.17; Obad. 12, 13; Pss. 22.18; 112.8; cf. the Mesha Inscription, l. 4). The phrase means 'to gloat over'. We take *rā'āh 'al* as a variant of this idiom in Job 34.26, which we read *bimᵉqôm rō'îm 'ᵃlêhem*. We suggest that v. 27a continued: *'al-'ᵃšer sārû mē'aḥᵃrāyw* ('because they turned from following him'), MT *kēn* having come in as a dittograph of the following *s* and *r* in the Old Hebraic script. On this view *'ᵃlêhem* in our restoration of v. 26b probably dropped out before *'al-'ᵃšer*, which it resembles in that script.

In v. 26a *taḥat* has its locative sense; cf. in the Ras Shamra texts, *tḥt 'adrm dbgrn* ('in the place of the notables who are in the public place'). There may be an allusion to the death of Jehoram in Naboth's town Jezreel (2 Kgs 9.26f.).

After S we adopt Houbigant's reading *riš'ām* for MT *rᵉšā'îm*.

sāpaq is probably an orthographic variant of *śāpaq* ('to slap'), that is, the thigh in sorrow or remorse, or the hands in mockery (e.g. 27.23; Lam. 2.15), hence here possibly, with the direct object, 'to strike', as in the Arab. cognate *śafaqa*.

28. The repetition of *ṣa'ᵃqaṯ* in two parallel cola is unusual, and Duhm proposed *ṣiwᵉḥat* ('the cry of') with the same meaning in the second place. Here, however, it may be observed that *dal* and *'ᵃniyyîm* and not *ṣa'ᵃqaṯ* are the items in parallelism. On the infinitive construct followed asyndetically by the imperfect expressing purpose with Ugaritic precedent, see on 33.17.

29. This verse, which is composed of two conditional sentences with the protases introduced by the jussive without a conditional particle and the apodosis rhetorical questions, animadverts on Job's claim that the operation of the theodicy was not immediate or evident. This anticipates Elihu's later statement of the transcendence of God. In v. 29b Budde proposed to emend MT *yᵉšûrennû* to *yᵉyassᵉrennû* ('who will upbraid him?'), which is certainly a more exact parallel to *yaršia'* in v. 29a. On the other hand MT *yaršia'* may be a corruption of *yar'îš* ('[who can] move him?'); cf. Isa. 14.16, where this verb is parallel to *rāḡaz* ('to trouble'). The sentiment is that God cannot be compelled at the will of a human to action in accordance with human expectation. If MT

of v. 29b is correct, *y^e^šûrennû* may indicate a reading *y^e^šîrennû* ('[who] will oblige him to investigate?'). For this possible sense of the verb, cf. Arab. *ṯāra, yaṯūru*. But we prefer to emend to *y^e^šîḇennû*, assuming corruption of *b* to *r* in the Old Heb. script and *y* to *w* at the stage of development as in the Qumran MSS. We take *w^e^yastēr* as the reflexive of *sûr* ('to turn away'), either as an Iphteal form, such as is attested in the Mesha Inscription and, with this verb, regularly in the Ras Shamra texts, or the regular Hithpael of Classical Heb. with the metathesis of *t* and the initial sibilant of the verb. This would support the reading of the parallel *y^e^šîḇennû*.

31-33. This is a notorious crux, and the ancient versions do not give much help, so that we must be guided by the general sense, taking into account Elihu's argument which he has already adduced and what is to follow. First, a new word division in v. 31a gives the reading *kî-'el-'^e^lôah 'āmar* ('if one were to say to God', so S). For MT *nāśā'ṯî* most modern commentators read *niššē'ṯî* ('I was seduced'); cf. Isa. 19.13. Dhorme proposed that MT *'eḥbōl* in v. 31b means 'I shall sin', as the verb means in 21.7 and Neh. 1.7, and that it was followed by *'ôḏ* ('again'). He treats *bl* of MT *bil'^a^ḏê* in v. 32a as a dittograph of the last two letters of the preceding word *'eḥbōl*, continuing *'^a^ḏê 'eḥ^e^zeh 'attāh hōrēnî* ('that I may see do thou instruct me'). Dhorme accepts MT in the sequel, but assumes a lacuna after *mā'astā* in v. 33a (so Hölscher). Fohrer and Pope take the text here as complete, which is supported by the natural parallelism *kî m^e^'astāw* (for MT *mā'astā*) and *kî-'attāh tiḇḥar*, especially if the latter verb is taken in the sense of 'choose'. Dhorme and Hölscher take the verb as meaning 'to examine, assess', a sense which it certainly has in Aram. and in the Elihu passages (e.g. 34.4).

Pope's emendation of MT *'ānî* to *hû'* is not so drastic as it seems at first sight, if it is assumed that the corruption took place in the Old Hebraic script.

Verse 33c is either an incomplete couplet or, as Fohrer proposes, a gloss, which we consider more probable. In v. 31b, which we take as part of the argument imputed to an imaginary sinner, which ends at v. 32, we suggest the pointing of MT *'eḥbōl* as *'ēḥāḇēl* ('I shall [not] be liable'). This is the most common meaning of the verb in Classical Heb., in the Qal 'to take a pledge' and in the Niphal 'to bind oneself by a pledge', that is, to admit liability. Here, the sinner is palliating his sin, alleging that he has been seduced (*niššē'ṯî*) and is therefore not liable (v. 31b); as a simpleton he is in need of instruction (v. 32a), after which he undertakes to sin no more (32b). Elihu's indignant question to the imaginary sinner questions if when a person has rejected God (*m^e^'astāw*, v. 33a) and chosen his own course (*tiḇḥar*, v. 33b), he can expect God to requite him on his own terms (MT *hamē'imm^e^ḵā yešall^e^mennāh*), which may mean rather 'at your own initiative' and, it is implied in the argument, 'on your own terms'. We might further propose that in the verb *y^e^šall^e^mennāh*, which we take as the energic form, the original may possibly have been *y^e^šall^e^mekkāh* in *scriptio plena* with the corruption of *k* to *n* in the Old Hebraic script.

Fohrer's suggestion should be noted, namely that v. 31 read originally *h^{a}yō'mar 'ēl 'ēlêḵā* (so Duhm, Beer), continuing with God's confession that he was wrong. According to this view MT represents the adjustment of the texts by orthodox scribes (*tiqqûn sōp̄^{e}rîm*) through motives of reverence. The view, in our opinion, is interesting, but gratuitous.

36. *'āḇî* has been connected with the precative particle *bî* ('Please!'), which is derived from *'āḇāh*, cognate with Arab. *'aba(y)* ('to consent, be willing'; see Honeyman 1944: 81ff.). Dhorme proposed to emend to *'^{a}ḇāl* ('but') after LXX, but the metre demands that it be omitted, having originally come into the text through a scribal inadvertency through the influence of *'iyyôḇ* in the same colon.

Job's general position has already been condemned (v. 35); Elihu now proposes to deal with his arguments in detail 'to the end' or possibly 'thoroughly', *'aḏ-neṣaḥ* (Thomas 1956: 106).

'al-t^{e}šuḇôṯ means 'in the matter of', or 'for answers (given)'.

b^e'an^{e}šê-'āwen means, if correct, 'in the category of men of iniquity', which is tantamount to 'like…'. Though *b^e*, as the *beth essentiae*, is grammatically possible, it may be a scribal error for *k^e*, in the last stage of the development of the script.

37. We follow Dhorme's arrangement of the text here into a final tricolon:

> *kî yōsîp̄ 'al-ḥaṭṭā'ṯô*
> *peša' bênênû yispôq*
> *w^{e}yarbeh '^{a}mārāyw lā'ēl.*

Dhorme takes *sāp̄aq* in its Aram. sense 'to doubt', that is, 'refuse to admit', which may possibly be pointed as the Hiphil as Dhorme proposes, meaning 'cast doubts upon'.

Job 35.1; 33.31-33; 35.2–36.25

Elihu's Third Address

In nine strophes (33.31-33 + 35.2-3; 35.4-8; 9-14; 35.15–36.4; 36.5-7a; 7b-10; 11-15; 16-21; 22-25) the sage continues to cite significant propositions in Job's argument (e.g. 35.2, 3, 14-15), and to demolish them and develop his antithesis in support of his belief in the theodicy. The address opens with the usual call to hear and answer (33.31-33; 35.2-3), continues in the style, not so such of sapiential discourse, but rather of a controversial lecture like most of the Elihu speeches, and culminates in the citation of a hymn of praise (36.22-25) to clinch the argument for the divine economy.

The first strophe (33.31-33 + 35.2-3) culminates in the citation of Job's assertion of his claim on God (35.2b-3). Here Job seems to be accused of inconsistency, of asserting in the one breath his claim on God in virtue of his alleged innocence (35.2b) and of declaring in the other that on the basis of his affliction his good or bad conduct has no bearing on what he may expect from God (v. 3). In reply in the second strophe (35.4-8) Elihu states that, as nature itself indicates, God is transcendent, beyond the effects of good or bad conduct of humans, which affects only society or the individual. In the third strophe (35.9-14) Elihu develops the theme of the sufferings of the oppressed who cry out and are apparently unanswered. He lays the responsibility for such afflictions on society and not on God as Job had maintained. People cannot cry inarticulately to God and expect immediate relief; they must rather look to him to give them fortitude, hope and faith in his purpose, which is beyond the immediate perception and reaction of the brutes. In the fourth strophe (35.15–36.4) Elihu cites Job's objection that social injustice seems to contradict the theodicy (35.15-16), and he prepares to contradict it and clear God of the charge of injustice (36.3). In the fifth strophe (36.5-7a) he asserts the validity of the theodicy. In the sixth strophe (36.7b-10) he appeals to the facts of history, kings raised by the grace of God and their fall, possibly animadverting on the experience of Manasseh of Judah (2 Chron. 33.10-13). This is God's opportunity to convince them of their sin. The seventh strophe (36.11-15) develops the theme of contrition in suffering as anticipating restoration to blessing (36.11); obduracy is fatal (36.13-14) but affliction may be a salutary discipline. In the eighth strophe (36.16-21), it is objected to Job that his long-accustomed prosperity and exemption from the divine discipline of affliction has moved him to question God's economy. The last strophe (36.22-25) asserts the orthodox belief in the theodicy, which suggests the fuller citation of a Hymn of Praise on the Sovereignty and Providence of God in the following section (36.27–37.13).

On the inclusion of 33.31-33 as the introduction to 35.2ff., see the Introduction to ch. 33. Job 36.1 is probably secondary and redactional. The text is probably defective in 36.16, and 36.19-20 are either defective or a secondary addition to the original.

Chapters 35.1; 33.31-33; 35.2–36.25

35.1. And Elihu spoke up and said:

33.31. 'Pay heed, Job, hearken to me,
Keep silence that I may speak.
32. If you have anything to say answer me,
Speak, for I desire to clear you.
33. But if not, listen to me,
Keep silence, and I will teach you wisdom.
35.2. Do you consider this right?
Do you say, "It is my right from God?"
3. That you say, "What good does it do you?"
"What the better am I that I have not sinned?"

4. I will give you an answer,
And your three[1] friends along with you.
5. Look at the heavens and see,
And observe the clouds which are higher than you.
6. If you sin, how will you affect him,
And if your sins are numerous, what do you do to him?
7. If you are righteous, what do you give him?
Or what does he receive from your hand?
8. It is a man like yourself that your sin affects,
And a son of man your righteousness.

9. Because of many oppressive acts people cry out[2]
They call (for help) from the arm of the great ones.
10. But they do not say,[3] "Where is God our Maker,[4]
Who gives courage in the night,
11. Who imparts to us more knowledge than the beasts,
And more wisdom than the birds of the sky?"
12. Then they cry, but he does not answer
Simply because of the shouting[5] of the wicked.
13. But vain is the statement, "God does not hear,
Nor does the Almighty pay any regard!"
14. Even though you do say, "He does not regard me!",[6]
Be still[7] before Him and wait patiently[8] for him.

15 But now, because "for all his anger he makes no visitation,[9]
And for all his might[10] he is indifferent to transgression",[11]

16. Job opens his mouth in vain talk,
And talks insolently without knowledge.
36.1. [12]...
2. Wait for a little that I may show you,
For I have yet something to say for God.
3. I will bring knowledge from afar,
And will justify my Creator.
4. For truly my words are no falsehood;
You have to contend with one who is perfect in knowledge.

5. See, God is great in might,[13]
He does not reject the pure[14] of heart;
6. He does not let the wicked thrive,
But admits the just case of the poor sufferer,
7. He does not withdraw his eyes from the innocent one.

He has set[15] kings on the throne
And lets them be enthroned in splendour, and they are exalted;
8. And if they are bound with fetters,
Held fast in bonds of affliction,

9. He declares[16] to them what they have done,
How they have sinned defiantly in their tyranny,
10. And he lets them clearly hear[17] reproof,
And orders[18] them to turn back from evil.

11. If they listen to him, so as to serve him,
They live out their days in prosperity,
And their years pleasantly;
12. But if they do not listen they pass away,[19]
And perish without taking notice,
13. But the impious nurse[20] wrath;
They do not cry to him when he has arrested them.
14. So their personality perishes in their prime,
Their vitality spent like sacral catamites.
15. He delivers the sufferer through his suffering,
And makes affliction a means of revelation.

16. But[21] superabundance[22] has moved you,
Plenty and no pinch where you are placed,[23]
And your table-top full of fatness,
17. And you are full of the food of the guilty
While they manipulate a case at law.
18. But beware[24] lest one entice you with satiety
And a large bribe warp your judgment.
19. Will all your wealth be comparable[25] to what you have lost,[26]
Or all the power you have accumulated?
20. You need not long for the night
For worries to be dislodged.[27]
21. Take care not to turn to mischief,
Seeing that is why you have preferred exultation[28] to affliction.

22. See, God is exalted in his might.
Who is a ruler[29] like him?
23. Who has prescribed his government for him?
Who has said, "You have done wrong"?
24. Remember to exalt his works,
Of which men have sung.
25. All humanity faces him from a distance,
Mere mortals look upon him from afar.

Textual Notes to Chapters 35.1; 33.31-33; 35.2–36.25

1. Reading *š^{e}lōšeṯ* with LXX for MT *'eṯ*.
2. Reading *yiz'^{a}qû* (pausal) for MT *yāz'îqû*.
3. Reading *'ām^{e}rû* for MT *'āmar* in agreement with v. 11.
4. Reading *'ōśēnû* for MT *'ōśāy* in agreement with v. 11.
5. On the meaning 'shouting', suggested by the parallelism, instead of 'arrogance' (*gā'ôn*), and the possible corruption in MT of a cognate of Ugaritic *ḡ* ('voice'), see Commentary *ad loc.*
6. Reading *t^{e}šûrennî*, a quotation of Job's words.
7. Reading *dôm* for MT *dîn*, as in Ps. 37.7, but for a possible defence of MT *dîn* see Commentary *ad loc.*
8. Reading *w^{e}hôḥēl*, from *yāḥal*, for MT *ûṯ^{e}ḥôlēl*.
9. Reading *pōqēḏ* for MT *pāqaḏ* after Theod. and Sym.
10. Reading *m^{e}ō'ḏô*, including *w* from the following word. See Commentary *ad loc.*
11. Reading *b^{e}p̄eša'* with Theod., Sym and LXX for *bappaš*.
12. Omitting 36.1 as a gloss.
13. Assuming displacement of *kōaḥ* from v. 5b.
14. Reading *b^{e}rê*, assuming dittography of *k* after *m* in Old Heb. script and metathesis of *y* and *r* in MT *kabbîr*.
15. Conjecturing *šāṯ* for MT *'eṯ*.
16. Reading *w^{e}yaggîḏ* for MT *wayyaggēḏ*.
17. Reading *w^{e}yō'mar* for MT *wayyō'mer*.
18. Reading *w^{e}yiḡleh* for MT *wayyiḡel*.
19. Omitting *b^{e}šelaḥ metri causa* as a gloss after 33.18.
20. Conjecturing *yišm^{e}rû* for MT *yāśîmû*.
21. Conjecturing *'aḵ* for MT *w^{e}'ap̄*.
22. Conjecturing *miprāṣ* for MT *mippî-ṣār*. See Commentary *ad loc.*
23. Reading *taḥtêḵā* for MT *taḥtêhā*.
24. Reading *ḥ^{e}mēh* for MT *ḥēmāh*. See Commentary *ad loc.*
25. Reading *yē'ārēḵ* for MT *ya'^{a}rōḵ*.
26. Reading *l^{e}ḇoṣr^{e}ḵā*. See Commentary *ad loc.*
27. Reading *mittaḥtām*, assuming haplography of prepositional *m* after *m* of preceding word. See Commentary *ad loc.*
28. Reading *'^{a}lîzāh* for MT *'al-zeh*.
29. Reading *mārē'* for MT *môreh*, after LXX.

Commentary on 35.1; 33.31-33; 35.2–36.25

33.33. Nothing could differentiate the Elihu passages from the Dialogue of the Book of Job more clearly than the statement *'a'allep̄ekā ḥokmāh* ('I shall teach you wisdom'), and his summons to the sages in 34.2ff. The verb *'ālap̄* ('to learn') with the causative intensive 'to teach' is peculiar to Wisdom literature in the OT, where it is comparatively rare (e.g. Prov. 22.25; Job. 33.33; 35.11).

35.3. If *sākan* means 'to profit' here as in 15.3, where, as here, it is parallel to *hô'îl*, it might seem as if MT *lekā* might be emended to *lî* (so Graetz, Duhm, Beer, Budde, Hölscher, Mowinckel, Fohrer, AV, RV, NEB). In the light of Elihu's direct reply to this quotation of Job, however, we consider that *lekā*, sc. God, should be retained. In consideration of v. 7 too we take *min* in *mēḥaṭṭā'tî* as privative, meaning 'my sinlessless'. Retaining *'ō'îl* in v. 3b, we take the couplet to mean that Job questions if his sinlessness is any advantage to God or to himself. The connection of this couplet with Elihu's reply in v. 7 also rules out Tur-Sinai's suggestion that *mēḥaṭṭā'tî* means 'because of my appeasement', a sense of the verb (Piel and Hithpael) which he adduces from the Talmud and Midrash Rabbah.

4. We assume the omission of *šelōšet* by homoeoteleuton after *'et-* in v. 4b.

5. *gābehû* is the verb in the relative clause, the relative particle being omitted as often in poetry.

6. Verse 6b is a conditional sentence with the perfect verb as the protasis, the conditional particle in the protasis in v. 6b doing double duty. For MT *bô* S and V read *lô*, but *bô* may be retained, the preposition denoting hostility; cf. *penê yhwh be'ōsê rā'* Ps. 34.16 [EVV 17]).

9. The Qal must be read for the Hiphil of the verb in v. 9a.

kabbîrîm ('the mighty') is proposed for MT *rabbîm*, but this is not necessary, since *rab* is used as a synonym of *'āṣûm* ('powerful') in Isa. 53.12.

10. In v. 10a S reads the plural *'āmerû* and *'ōśēnû*, which is suggested by the plural in the following verse, and is graphically feasible.

In v. 10b 'songs (*zemirôt*) in the night' is unparalleled in the OT and has been accepted too readily perhaps because of the recollection of the praises of Paul and Silas in the prison of Philippi (Acts 16.25). Noting the collocation of *nātan* with *qôl* in the sense of thunder, Dhorme so interprets the passage, but there seems no particular reason why thunder by night should be more impressive than during the day, and description of thunder as songs is doubtful.

Various emendations have been suggested, for example, *š^{e}mārôṯ*, 'watches' (Bickell), *m^{e}'ôrôṯ*, 'lights' (Ehrlich), *mazzārôṯ*, 'the Hyades' (Wright; cf. 38.32), which is graphically the most feasible of these suggestions. The matter is complicated by the uncertainty as to whether 'night' is used in a literal or a figurative sense. If the former, our preference is for Wright's suggestion, the allusion being to God's provision of the vital rain while the peasant slept. But in the context 'night' may rather signify a season of ordeal and doubt, as for instance in Ps. 46.6: 'God shall answer us as it turns to morning'. We would regard *z^{e}mirôṯ*, the feminine plural, as an abstract noun, 'might, courage' (so Tur-Sinai, Pope; cf. Kissane, 'succour', Habel , 'protection'), from a root *zmr*, recognized by Tur-Sinai in Exod. 15.2; Isa. 12.2; Ps. 118.14 in the statement *'ozzî w^{e}zim^{e}rāṯî* (MT *zim^{e}rāṯ*) *yāh* ('Yahweh is my strength and might'; cf. *z^{e}mîr '^{a}rîṣîm y^{e}'anneh* (MT *ya'^{a}neh*), 'he humbles the might of tyrants', Isa. 25.5). This, Pope suggests, may be the significance of the name Zimri. It may thus be cognate with Arab. *ḏamara* ('to be violent, mighty, courageous'; cf. *dmrn*, which U. Cassuto (*hā-'ēlāh 'anat*, 1951: 46) recognized as a title of Baal in the Ugaritic text Gordon, *UT* 51 VII, 38-39.

11. The preposition *min* in v. 11a is ambiguous. It has generally been taken as comparative. If this is so Elihu is implying that affliction should not result merely in a howl of pain as in the case of animals when they are hurt, but that humans should reason from effect to cause (cf. Amos 3.4-5, 6cd). This is just what the friends of Job had urged, that he accept his affliction as meaningful as coming from God who had regulated the natural and moral order, and address himself to God in penitence and patience. Those who take *min* as 'from' the beasts (so Dhorme, Pope) regard the animals and their regular habits as evidences of God's order in nature, which is part of the argument in the divine speech (chs. 38–41).

The elision of ' in *mall^{e}pēnû* (*m^{e}'all^{e}pēnû*) may be owing to a scribal inadvertency. Guillaume takes it to indicate the origin of the Book of Job and the Elihu addendum in the Hejaz, where, though at a much later date, C. Rabin (1951: 131ff.) notes the elision of initial ' as a dialectic peculiarity.

12. We find in *šām* the same force as in Arab. *ṯumma*, indicating the next stage in the narrative or argument; cf. Ps. 66.6 (see on 23.7). This seems a more probable explanation than that of Dahood (1957: 307), that this is Akk. *šumma* ('if'). Such a solitary survival in a late book is surely most unlikely.

This verse evidently resumes the thought of v. 9, and is to be understood as very pregnant, meaning that God does not hear mere animal cries of distress (v. 12a), nor is he, rather than the arrogance of the wicked, responsible for the sufferings which prompt the cries. Such a pregnant couplet, however, where v. 12b reads almost like a gloss, is still awkward, and as an alternative we might suggest that MT *g^{e}'ôn* is a form, or a corruption, of *ḡ*, known in the Ras Shamra texts as a loud voice; cf. *gm yṣḥ* ('he cried aloud'). The meaning would then be 'Simply because of the shouting of wicked men...' This might suggest that *gē'* and *ge'ôn* in Isa. 16.6, where the nouns are the objects of *šāma'* ('to hear'), may mean 'shouting'; cf. Jer. 48.29.

13. If T is accepted there are various interpretations: 'God does not listen to frivolity' (so Renan; cf. Le Hir, G.B. Gray, Kissane, Pope, Terrien, after LXX); 'It is in vain; God does not hear it' (Dhorme, Hölscher, Mowinckel, Fohrer). Connecting the verse with v. 14, we follow Ehrlich's interpretation, and take 'God does not hear' as a quotation of Job's allegation, which is dismissed as vain (*šāw'*).

The ending of *yešûrennāh* has occasioned difficulty, the ending being taken as the 3rd fem. sing. pronom. suffix. Those who take *šāw'* as the object of the verb (proleptic) emend to *yešûrennû* (so Budde, Oort, Duhm). We would retain MT as an example of the energic ending of the imperfect as in Ugaritic.

14. *'ap̄ kî* in the sense of 'how much less?' is already used in the dialectic of Job in 9.14 and 25.6, but it might have a concessive force, anticipating the exhortation to hope in Job.

In a passage which contains so many of Job's statements it is natural to expect Job's direct speech in v. 14 and, we suggest in v. 15, which indicates the emendation of MT *tešûrennû* ('you see him') to *tešûrennî* or *yešûrennî*, though this is a pure conjecture unsupported by the ancient versions. MT in v. 14b is generally taken to mean 'The case (*dîn*) is before him, so wait for him' (so Dhorme and most modern commentators). Perles, citing Ps. 37.7, suggested the reading *dom lepānāyw hôḥēl lô* ('Be still before and wait for him'; so Hölscher, cf. Kissane). Alternatively MT *dîn* may be the cognate of Arab. *dāna*, *yadīn* ('to submit') as Jacob suggested (1912: 191; accepted by Guillaume 1968).

15-16. Having thus argued his case against a hypothetical interlocutor, to whom he has attributed Job's statements, Elihu now states the case more generally, but still with the citation of Job's sentiments in v. 15. Here we accept MT in the main, literally rendered:

> But now because his anger makes no visitation
> And his might takes no note of transgression,

(see textual note) which we may paraphrase:

> But now, because for all his anger he makes no visitation,
> And for all his might he is indifferent to transgression.

For *'ap* as subject cf. Job 16.9 and for *me'ōḏ* as a noun cf. Deut. 6.5 *beḵol-me'ōḏeḵā*. See further textual note *ad loc.*

16. *yaḵbîr* may mean 'to make big' or 'to make numerous' according to the meaning of *kabbîr* noted above (see on 34.17). We take the verb here with the

meaning of the Arab. cognate in the Vth Form of the verb, 'to behave insolently'.

36.2. *kattēr* in Aram. and Syr. means regularly 'wait'.

'ᵃḥawwēh ('let me declare') is also an Aramaism, used frequently in the Elihu passages; cf. 32.6, 10, 17.

zᵉ'êr ('a little') is found probably in a quantitative sense in Isa. 28.10, 13, but here of time; cf. *'ôḏ mᵉ'aṭ miz'ār* ('Yet a little while') in Isa. 10.25; 29.17.

In v. 2b LXX 'in me' has suggested that MT *le'ᵉlôah* is to be emended to *le'ᵉlîhû* (Hoffman) or even to *lî* with *le'ᵉlîhû* as a gloss (so Duhm). Accepting MT Hölscher takes *le* in *le'ᵉlôah* as 'concerning' God, but 'for God' is more likely (so Dhorme and most modern commentators); cf. 13.7. This is supported by v. 3b ('I will justify my Creator').

3. Again *dēa'* is used in the Elihu passages (cf. 32.6, 10, 17) for the more common *da'aṯ*.

lᵉ in *lᵉmērāḥôq* is now explicable in the light of Ugaritic, where *lᵉ* means 'from', as reinforcing *min*. Perhaps in Heb., which, unlike Ugaritic, had the preposition *min*, *min* was inserted into the expression *lᵉrāḥôq* to obviate the ambiguity of *le* in Classical Heb.

4. *'im* has here the adversative sense, as with certain verbs in Classical Heb., for example, *nilḥam*, *rîḇ*, *nišpaṭ*, *ne'ᵉḇaq* ('to wrestle'), as regularly in Ugaritic, where it also denotes motion towards.

5. On the reading, supported by S, and first suggested by Nichols (1910–11: 162), who read the sing. *bar* (so Dhorme, Pope) see Textual Note.

7. *dîn* ('just case') has been suggested for MT *'ênāyw* ('his eyes'); so Bickell, Budde, Beer, Peake, Dhorme, Stevenson, Larcher. But in view of the regular mention of the eyes of God upon the just (e.g. Ps. 33.18; Prov. 22.12), there is no reason to doubt MT. In v. 7c *lāneṣaḥ* is ambiguous. Usually it means 'for ever', but it also means 'splendour', for instance, God as the Splendour (*neṣaḥ*) of Israel (1 Sam. 15.29). Either sense is possible here. If the former, it might be an ironical reference to a coronation formula; cf. Ps. 89.5, 29, 37 (EVV 4, 28, 36), where the formula is *'aḏ-'ôlām* or *lᵉ'ôlām*, but we prefer the latter.

9. *peša'* signifies deliberate sin in defiance of authority either human or divine. For the verb in v. 9b, a denominative verb from *gibbôr*, cf. Arab. *jabbār* ('bully, tyrant').

10. Literally 'Opens their ear in reproof', almost literally recalling Elihu's statement in 33.1.

11. *'āḇaḏ*, meaning 'to do, till, serve, worship' in Heb. means here probably 'serve (God)'; cf. J.E. MacFadyen's felicitous reading 'do him homage'. The reference is usually taken to be to the tradition of the detention of Manasseh in Assyria and of his later release by the grace of God upon his repentance. In spite of the unqualified condemnation of Manasseh by the Deuteronomistic historian in Kings, a legend developed of his restoration, probably associated with Esarhaddon's invasion of Egypt (A.L. Oppenheim, *ANET*, 291), after his contrition, which was established by the time of the Chronicler (2 Chron. 33.11-13) in the second half of the fourth century BCE. If, as seems likely, Job 36.7ff. refers to this tradition, it would suggest a period considerably later than the completion of the Deuteronomistic History, in its final recension about the middle of the sixth century BCE.

12. Colon a seems overloaded, and possibly *bᵉšelaḥ*, 'in the stream (of death)' should be omitted before *ya'ᵃbōr*, repeated from 33.18. *bᵉlî ḏa'aṯ* is ambiguous. It may mean that no one takes any notice or cares, the passing away of the subject without any memory, or, as we prefer in the context, 'without themselves paying heed' to what their conduct involves (NEB 'their lesson unlearned').

13. *ḥᵃnap̄-lēḇ* is found in the Ras Shamra Legend of Aqht in the promise of El that the miscreant (*ḥnp lb*) who has offended the goddess Anat should be trampled down (Gordon *UT* 3 Aqht rev., 17). On *ḥānēp̄*, see on 8.13. MT *yāśîmû 'āp̄* has been a notorious difficulty. Thus Lévêque proposes *yāššîmû 'āp̄* ('breathe forth wrath'). The verb may be cognate with Arab. *šāma, yašīmu* ('to hide', so Guillaume 1964b: 33). The usual phonetic correspondence is between Heb. *s* and Arab. *ś* or *ṯ*, but this is not invariable, as, for example, with Heb. *šemeš*, Arab. *šamśu*, Heb. *šāḇiḇ*, Arab, *šāba* ('to blaze up'). MT *yāśîmû 'āp̄* would mean 'assume the appearance of anger', perhaps 'scowl', but we have preferred Dhorme's suggestion to read *yišmᵉrû 'āp̄*, assuming omission of *r* before *w* by haplography in the Old Heb. script; cf. Amos 1.12.

14. *nep̄eš* is the whole person, animated body, what makes a person a whole individual as God intended (Gen. 2.7). *ḥayyāh* is here not 'life' per se, as distinct from *ḥayyîm*, but 'vitality'; cf. Isa. 57.10, 'vigour' (Exod. 1.19). In *baqqᵉḏēšîm*, *b* signifies 'in the category of'. *qᵉḏēšîm* means those with a sacral function, specifically sacral prostitutes; cf. the fertility goddess Qodsu and Assyrian *qadištu* ('sacral prostitute'). Such persons, both male and female, were known in Israel (Deut. 23.18; 1 Kgs 14.24). The reference is evidently to the castration of such males (Deut. 23.1), as understood by LXX *titrōskomenoi* ('wounded, impaired'). The reference may be either to their early failing health or death through abuse or their inability to perpetuate themselves through posterity, a pointed reference to the total extinction of the wicked.

15. As against most commentators Fohrer translates *yᵉḥallēṣ 'ānî bᵉ'onyô* as 'He delivers the unfortunate from his misery', which might be supported by the sense of the preposition *bᵉ* 'from', well attested in Ugaritic and Heb. poetry. But, as the parallel colon indicates, the reference is to the disciplinary effect of suffering. Here the writer of the Elihu passages shares the view of Ben Sira (2.4-5). The word-play between *yᵉḥallēṣ* ('he delivers') and *laḥaṣ* ('tribulation') is characteristic of Wisdom literature.

16. This passage, where MT is well attested in the ancient versions, is a notorious crux. The odd colon 16a poses a problem for the text and interpretation. If v. 16a is the first member of a deficient bicolon there is nothing to indicate certainly the actual meaning. If it is the last colon of a tricolon with v. 15ab, 16a might be read *wᵉ'āp̄ hᵃsîṯô mippî-ṣār*, 'and he has even withdrawn him from the enemy' (so Duhm, citing 2 Chron. 18.31, *wayyᵉsîṯēm 'ᵉlōhîm mimmennû*, viz. Jehoshaphat in the battle of Ramoth). In view of the usual sense of *hēsîṯ*, 'to incite to good' (Judg. 1.14) or 'evil' (2 Sam. 28.19; Jer. 43.2 etc.) in the same strophe at v. 18, however, we question this reading and interpretation. We take v. 16a as the first colon of a tricolon with v. 16bc, which, with what immediately follows, refers to the temptation of affluence, and the entertainment of rich miscreants to one in authority to pervert justice. This suggests to us the reading *'aḵ hᵃsîṯᵉḵā mip̄rāṣ* ('but prosperity has moved you') for MT *'ap̄ hᵃsîṯᵉḵā mippî-ṣār*; cf. *pāraṣ* ('to abound') in Gen. 30.43; Exod. 1.12; Isa. 54.3; Hos. 4.10; Job 1.10. In v. 16c we would retain *naḥaṯ* as a construct before *šulḥānᵉkā*, meaning 'a level place', here 'a level board'; cf. Arab. *nāḫa, yanūḫu* ('to level') and in the Baal myth from Ras Shamra, where as associated with 'throne' it might mean 'dais'. Gordon *UT* 'nt IV, 46f.:

> *grš lks'i mlkh*
> *lnḫt lkḥt drkth*
>
> Who would drive him from his royal throne,
> From the dais, the seat of his sovereignty.

17. *rāšā'* in the context may mean 'rich', cognate with Arab. *raśīġ* (Guillaume 1963: 116) or 'guilt'. In view of the sequel referring to bribery to divest justice (v. 18), we prefer the latter sense, but there may be a *double entendre*. The noun *dîn*, formally repeated in v. 17a and b, if a synonym, is a solecism which the writer would never have perpetrated. Tur-Sinai therefore divided the consonants of MT to read:

> *wᵉḏîn rᵉsā'îm lō' tāḏîn*
> *ûmišpaṭ yāṯôm kw-*(?)
>
> And you do not judge the case of the wicked
> And the justice of the orphan… (?).

Pope follows this reading, suggesting *k̲izzab̲tā* as the fragmentary last word. This, however, interrupts the reference to fat living in vv. 16 and 18. *din*, which we translate as 'food' in v. 17a, is unknown in this sense in Heb., though *māzôn* from the root *zûn* is attested with this meaning in Gen. 45.23 and 2 Chron. 11.23 and in Biblical Aramaic in Dan. 4.9, 18. We suggest that the writer availed himself of the known phonetic variation *z*/*d*; cf. Heb. *zeb̲aḥ*/Syr. *dbaḥ*, Heb. *zûb̲*/Syr. *dûb*, Heb. *z*^{e}*'ēb̲*/Syr. *d'bā'*, to secure a word-play with *dîn* ('judgment') in v. 17b. The verb *tāmak̲* ('to grasp, hold, handle'), may here have the nuance 'manipulate'.

18. In the context of bribery through lavish entertainment there seems no point in a reference to 'wrath' (MT *ḥēmāh*) and 'mockery', lit. 'handclapping' (*sēp̄eq*; so Fohrer), though there is more to be said for NEB 'lavish gifts of wine'. We find the emendation of MT *ḥēmāh* to Aram. *ḥ*^{e}*mēh* ('beware') more attractive, with *sep̄eq* meaning 'satiety' as in Syr. (so Dhorme, Kissane, Pope).

19. *kōaḥ* is ambiguous, perhaps deliberately so. It means generally 'power', the phrase *ma'*^{a}*maṣṣê kōaḥ* recalling *y*^{e}*'ammēṣ kōaḥ* in Amos 2.14, but also 'wealth' (6.23; Prov. 5.10). *šôa'* refers to one's noble standing or prestige; cf. *šôa'* parallel to *nād̲îb̲* in Isa. 11.32 and to *śārîm* in Job 34.19, but it may also refer here to the lavish entertainment by which the subject is bribed. The word is a form of *yāša'* in the sense of 'generosity', either social or material. Both senses are possible here, but the physical sense of the Arab. cognate *waśi'a* ('to be wide'), with a verbal noun *śa'atu*(*n*) ('wealth, amplitude of life'), indicates that *šôa'* here means 'wealth' or 'amplitude of life' which the ill-gotten wealth of the subject facilitates. This might best suit the following *b*^{e}*ṣor*, for which we read *boṣr*^{e}*k̲ā* ('what you have lost', lit. 'what you have had cut away'; cf. 42.2, *lō'-yibbāṣēr mimm*^{e}*k̲ā m*^{e}*zimmāh*). The verb *'ārak̲* ('to draw up, arrange') is used of comparison.

20. MT *'al-tiš'ap̄ hallāy*^{e}*lāh la'*^{a}*lôt̲ 'ammîm taḥtām* ('Do not long for the night for peoples to go up from their places') has been the despair of commentators. Duhm proposed the emendation *'al-taššî'*^{a}*k̲ā hōlēlôt̲ lē'ālôt̲ 'im mit̲ḥakkēn* ('Do not let folly deceive you into raising yourself up with those who aspire to wisdom'). Kissane proposed *'al-tiš'ap̄ hallō' l*^{e}*k̲ā la'*^{a}*lôt̲ 'amm*^{e}*k̲ā taḥtām* ('Do not trample on [cf. Amos 8.4] that do not belong to you so that your own kinsmen will be raised up in their place'). Either of these is graphically feasible, but rather abrupt in the context. Others translate v. 20b literally (e.g. NEB, Habel; cf. Fohrer, who omits it as 'unheilbar verderbt', 'corrupt beyond repair'). Tur-Sinai renders v. 20b 'to emerge from under them (reading *mittaḥtām*) in the dark', taking *'am* as cognate with Arab. *ġamma* ('to be overcast'). We would agree with Tur-Sinai in reading *mittaḥtām*, but in the sense 'from their place', sc. 'from where they have settled', but take *'ammîm*

as cognate with Arab. *ġammu(n)* ('grief, worry'), rendering 'You need not long for the night for worries to be dislodged'. Night brings no relief from the complications of a wicked life just described or from a bad conscience.

21. Taking *bāḥar* in the sense of Syriac *bḥar* ('to test'; cf. Isa. 48.10), Wright rendered 'this is why you have been tried by affliction' (so also Dhorme, and NEB), which would necessitate reading Pual for Qal of MT. This, to be sure, would accord with Elihu's view of the therapeutic value of suffering, but in the context of the strophe vv. 18-21 we take MT *bāḥartā* in the sense it usually has in the OT, 'to choose', which is supported by the comparative *m* in *mē'ōnî*. *'al-zeh* has been emended to *'awelāh*, which is graphically feasible in the square script, rendering 'Because you have preferred wickedness to humility' or 'affliction' (so Fohrer), but in the context of 'high living' to corrupt a poor man we prefer to emend MT *'al-zeh* to *'alîzāh* ('exultation'), a variant on the regular *'alîṣāh*; cf. *zā'aq/ṣā'aq*.

22. Elihu prepares to end his statement with a Hymn of Praise, vv. 26ff., to which vv. 22-25 serves as a prelude, as well as a conclusion to 36.2-25. God's exultation in power (v. 22a) supported the reading *mārē'* ('lord, ruler'), an Aram. word, in the parallel colon.

23. In the context of the sovereignty of God, 'government' seems a more apt translation than 'way' for *derek*; cf. *drk* parallel to *mlk* ('royal rule') in the Ras Shamra texts.

24. 'Remember to exalt his works of which men have sung' reflects the Plaint of the Sufferer, who, after having voiced his plaint and experienced the assurance of relief, gives public testimony, often expressed in the Hymn of Praise to the sovereignty and providence of God (e.g. Pss. 34; 35; 57.7ff.). There is no doubt that *šōrerû* means 'have sung', Polel of *šîr* with a transitive sense, as in Zeph. 2.14; 1 Chronicles 6; 2 Chron. 29.28; cf. *môṯēṯ* from *mûṯ* (Judg. 9.54; 1 Sam. 17.51; 2 Sam. 1.10; Jer. 20.17; Ps. 34.22).

25. In rendering *ḥāzû* 'stand back from' NEB evidently understood the verb as cognate with Arab. *ḥāḏā* ('to be opposite'); cf. Exod. 29.26ff.; Lev. 8.29; Num. 6.20, *maḥazeh*, the 'breast' of a sacrificial animal, Aram. and Syr. *ḥadyā'*. The verb may have this sense in Job 19.26. The rendering in NEB seems to understand *mērāḥôq* in v. 25b as qualifying *ḥāzû* in colon a as well as *yabbîṭ* in colon b, which is possible. In any case, the verb admirably expresses the compulsive attraction of mortals to God the Wholly Other.

Job 36.26–37.13

Elihu's Citation of a Hymn of Praise

God's impressive works in nature are adduced as evidence of his unsearchable greatness and wisdom, but also of his providential care. The thunder and accompanying rain is such a token. This was traditionally the token of the kingly power of Baal triumphant, the power of providence in nature in ancient Canaanite religion, liturgies of which on the same theme were adapted in Israel as hymns of praise to Yahweh on his epiphany as King in the New Year festival (Kapelrud 1940: 38-58; J. Gray 1956; 1961). The ideology of the triumph of Cosmos over Chaos is evoked by the hymn, which thus rounds out Elihu's argument for the theodicy.

The hymn may be arranged in 10 short strophes as follows: 36.26-28, 31; 29-30; 36.32–37.1; 37.2-3, 4, 5-6, 7-8, 9-10, 11-12c, 12d-13.

Here significantly the sage directs us for the ultimate understanding of life beyond the analysis of reason to the deeper experience of the joy of living and the wonder of the creation from which so much joy is to be derived by all but those who are wilfully obsessed by their own private problems. The ultimate truths are beyond cold reason, and are captured by the intuition and sympathy of the poet and those whom he may stimulate when the philosopher has failed. In this the author of the Elihu speeches emphasizes what the Divine Address signifies in adducing the wonders of creation beyond the comprehension or immediate convenience of humanity, not indeed to tease them with his omnipotence, but to lift them beyond the narrow sphere of their experience and vexation into the wonder and beauty of the larger sphere where the many tokens of the power, wisdom and love of God disclose infinite possibilities for humans, who are still near to God even in the depth of their suffering.

Chapters 36.26–37.13

36.26. 'Lo, God is great beyond our knowledge,
The number of his years is unsearchable.[1]
27. For he scoops up drops from the sea,[2]
Distils them[3] as rain for the abyss,
28. With which the clouds pour,
Dropping showers on the earth.
31. Yea, by these he feeds the peoples;
He gives food in abundance.

29. Can anyone understand how the clouds are spread out,
The crashing from his tabernacle?
30. Behold, the Most High[4] spreads out his light,
And covers the tops of the mountains.[5]

32. In his hands the lightning flashes,[6]
He discharges it[7] to a certain target.[8]
33. "Thunder" announces his coming,[9]
Showing zealous wrath against iniquity.[10]
37.1. At this moreover my heart trembles
And starts out of its place.

2. Hear, O hear, the turmoil of his thunder,
And the rumbling that comes forth from his mouth.
3. Under the whole sky is his flashing;[11]
And his light to the edges of the earth,

4. In the wake of it his voice roars,
He thunders with his majestic voice;
And he does not restrain the water,[12]
As peal upon peal is heard.[13]

5. God does[14] wondrous things,
He does great things beyond our ken,[15]
6. For he commands the snow, "Fall to the earth!",[16]
And the downpour and the rain,[17] "Be strong!"[18]

7. He seals up all human activity,
That every man may leave off his work,
8. And the wild beasts go to their lair,
And stay in their dens.

9. From the Chamber comes the whirlwind,
And from the Scatterers the cold.
10. By the breath of God ice is made,[19]
And the expanse of water is made solid.

11. Moreover, his bright (sun)[20] thrusts away the thick cloud,
Its light dispels the great cloud;
12. And it goes its course[21] in its circuits,
Turning at his guidance,
To do all the work[22] He commands it.[23]

On the face of the whole world,
13. Whether for chastisement or for favour,[24]
Or in token of steadfast grace, he makes it light on one.

Textual Notes to Chapters 36.26–37.13

1. Reading *lō'-ḥēqer* for MT *w*^{e}*lō'-ḥēqer*, *w* being a dittograph after the preceding word.
2. Reading *n*^{e}*ṭāp̄îm miyyām* for MT *niṭ*^{e}*p̄ê-māyim*.
3. Reading *y*^{e}*zuqqēm* for MT *yāzōqqû*, *m* being corrupted to *w* in the Old Heb. script.
4. Reading *'elyôn* for MT *'ālāyw*.

5. Reading *w^e^rā'šê hārîm* for MT *w^e^šor^e^šê hayyām*.
6. Reading *nās^e^sāh* for MT *kissāh*. See Commentary *ad loc.*
7. Reading *w^e^yaqlî'ehā* for MT *way^e^ṣaw 'ālêhā*, *q* being corrupted to *ṣ* in the Old Heb. script.
8. Reading *b^e^mip̄ga'* for MT *b^e^map̄gîa'*.
9. Reading *'elyô* for *'ālāyw*.
10. Reading *m^e^qannē' 'ap̄ 'al-'awlāh* for MT *miqneh 'ap̄ 'al-'ôlāh*. See Commentary *ad loc.*
11. Reading *š^e^rēhû* for MT *yišrēhû*. See Commentary *ad loc.*
12. Reading *y^e^'aqqēḇ mayim* for MT *y^e^'aqq^e^ḇēm*. See Commentary *ad loc.*
13. Reading *mippî* for MT *kî*. See Commentary *ad loc.*
14. Reading *yip̄'al* for MT *yar'ēm*, and omitting *b^e^qôlô metri causa*.
15. Reading perhaps *lō'*, omitting *w^e^* in a relative clause, for MT *w^e^lō'*.
16. Reading *h^e^wēh* for MT *h^e^wē'*.
17. Reading *w^e^laggešem ûmāṭār* for *w^e^g̅ešem māṭār* and omitting *w^e^g̅ešem miṭ^e^rōṯ* as a dittograph.
18. Reading *'uzzû* for MT *'uzzô*.
19. Reading *yuttan* with Sym., S and T for MT *yitten*. See Commentary *ad loc.*
20. Reading *bārô* for MT *b^e^rî*. See Commentary *ad loc.*
21. Reading *yiṯhallēḵ*, lost by haplography before *miṯhappēḵ*.
22. Reading *lip̄'ōl* for MT *l^e^p̄o'^o^lām*, *m* being a dittograph before *k* of the following *kōl* in the Old Heb. script.
23. Reading *y^e^ṣawwēhû* for MT *y^e^ṣawwēm*. See Commentary *ad loc.*
24. Reading *'arṣû* for MT *'arṣô*. See Commentary *ad loc.*

Commentary to Chapters 36.26–37.13

36.26. On the significance of the Hymn of Praise in relation to the liturgy of the New Year festival and the theme of the Kingship of God, see the General Introduction (pp. 49-50). As related to this theme the Hymn of Praise with its reminiscences of this great occasion in the religious year of Israel fittingly rounds out the argument of orthodoxy.

27. *gāra'* has already occurred in v. 7, meaning 'to withdraw'; here it means 'to withdraw something to oneself', 'to scoop up', and in 15.8 'to monopolize'.

For *niṭ^e^p̄ê-māyim* ('drops of water'), *n^e^ṭāp̄îm miyyām* ('drops from the sea') should almost certainly be read, though that is conjectural.

In v. 27b *zāqaq* is a transitive verb ('to purify'), used of gold in 28.1. Here the verb must clearly be emended to *y^e^zuqqēm*, 'which [i.e. drops from the sea] he distils' as rain.

In MT *l^e^'ēḏô*, *'ēḏ* occurs in the OT only once besides here, in Gen. 2.6. It is very doubtful if the sense is 'mist', as Albright has demonstrated (1939: 102ff. n. 25). *'ēḏ* in the OT is probably a loanword, Akk. *edû*, the reservoir of subterranean water from which the land was visualized as being watered before the rain. The final vowel of MT *'ēḏô* may be the last vowel of the Akk. word rather than the pronominal suffix. The conception seems to be that God draws up drops from the sea, refines them, purifying them of salt, and replenishes the fertilizing subterranean water with rain.

28. The antecedent of *'ašer* is *neṭāp̄îm*, the drops from the sea so distilled, some for the subterranean water and some to fall from the clouds as rain for the surface of the land.

nāzal in Classical Heb. means 'to flow'. The verb is intransitive, and we prefer to take *šeḥāqîm* ('clouds') as subject with *neṭāp̄îm*, or rather its relative pronoun, understood as internal accusative; cf. Isa. 45.8, *šeḥāqîm yizzelû-ṣeḏeq* ('the clouds pour righteousness').

rā'ap̄ is known as meaning 'to drip', for example, in Prov. 3.20, *šeḥāqîm yir'ap̄û-ṭāl* ('the clouds drip dew').

rāḇ has been taken as the participle of *rāḇaḇ*, *'alê 'āḏām rāḇ* being taken as 'upon many men'. S evidently took *rāḇ* as an adverb, 'greatly'. In view of Wright's conjecture that the word is a byform of the more familiar *reḇîḇîm*, 'showers' (so also Beer, Ball, Moffatt, Pope), it is surprising that it is retained as meaning 'upon many men' by G.B. Gray, Dhorme, Hölscher, Fohrer and Terrien; cf. Mowinckel, who proposes to read *'aḏāmāh rabbāh* ('the great earth'). The form *rb* ('showers') is now attested in the Ras Shamra texts as the name of one of Baal's 'girls', *ṭly bt rb* ('Dewy the girl of rain', Gordon *UT* 51 I, 18; IV, 56 etc.). *'āḏām* may mean here as in Prov. 30.14b; Jer. 32.20, 'the surface of the earth'; cf. Arab. *'adīmu*(*n*), as first suggested by Dahood (1963a: 123-24).

31. On the meaning of *yāḏîn* ('to feed'), here corroborated by the parallel *yitten-'ōḵel* ('he gives food'), see on v. 17.

29. MT *'im* has been taken as a corruption of *mî* by practically all modern commentators since Siegfried, Duhm and Budde, which we doubt, retaining *'im* as an interrogative particle and understanding the subject of *yāḇîn* as indefinite (so Pope).

We had thought seriously about the emendation of *tešu'ôṯ* to *maśśe'ôṯ* ('elevation'), an abstract fem. plur., regarding *maśśe'ôṯ sukkāṯô* ('the elevation of his tabernacle') as a reference to the building of the house (palace) of Baal in the Ras Shamra Baal myth, which was appropriate to the celebration of the triumph of Baal as king over the forces of Chaos and drought and sterility at the New Year festival, when the rains of the new season and their accompanying thunder were anticipated. This would be fitting in this passage, the theme of which is God's providence and government. We may cite the reference in Ps. 105.39, *pāraś 'ānān lemāsāḵ* ('he spread out the clouds as his screen'), and the parallelism between *sukkāṯô* and *'ānān* in Ps. 18.12 (EVV 11), as a figurative reference to the clouds as God's temporary pavilion (so Pope). Graetz suggested the emendation of MT *tešu'ôṯ* to *tešuyôṯ*, an Aram. word meaning 'carpet', with the emendation of MT *yāḇîn* to *yāḵîn* ('he sets'). But *tešu'ôṯ*, from *šā'āh* ('to make a din, crash') is probably to be read here, and at 30.22, where it means 'a rainstorm', on which see above. In 36.29 *tešu'ôṯ* would mean appropriately the din of thunder. Now in the Baal myth of Ras Shamra Baal announces his advent as king in thunder and lightning, which is the accompaniment of the heavy rains of winter, as, for example, in Gordon, *UT* ʻnt III, 17-28:

'abn brq dl td' šmm	I will create lightning, which the heavens do not know,
rgm ltd' nšm	A matter that men do not know,
'ultbn hmlt 'arṣ	Nor the multitudes of earth understand.

Many of the psalms relevant to the New Year festival were either adaptations of Canaanite liturgies of the same occasion or reflected their mythology and imagery. Thus we should retain MT *yāḇîn tᵉšu'ôṯ*, agreeing with G.B. Gray, Dhorme and most modern commentators. 'The crashing of his tabernacle' means of course 'the crashing from his tabernacle'.

30. With Pope, but independently, we take MT *'ālāyw* as the corruption of a title of Yahweh, as it had been of Baal (Gordon *UT* 126, III, 8), possibly *'elyôn*, possibly in the form *'ālî* (see also Dahood 1963c: 19).

In v. 30a MT *'ôrô* ('light') is read as *'ēḏô*, so transcribed in Theod. and T (so Duhm, Budde, Beer, Dhorme, G.B. Gray, Mowinckel, Kissane). This is then taken as 'mist', with which God overspread 'the tops of the mountains (reading *rā'šê hārîm*, with Duhm, for *šorᵉšê hayyām*, 'the roots of the sea'). But the meaning 'mist' for *'ēḏô*, understood apparently as 'rain' by T, is uncertain and improbable (see on v. 27); hence we take *'ôr* in the sense of lightning, as in v. 32 and 37.15.

We take v. 30b as describing a fresh manifestation of God's power in the storm, the storm-clouds as the concomitant of the lightning (*'ôrô*) in v. 30a. 'The roots of the sea' is a meaningless phrase, but MT *šorᵉšê hayyām* may be a corruption of *šorᵉšê hārîm* ('the roots of the mountains'; cf. 28.9). Dahood suggests that *kissāh* ('to cover') had here the privative sense 'to uncover'; cf. *šērēš* ('to root' and 'uproot') and Arab. *jallada* ('to skin a beast' and 'cover a book'). The uncovering of the roots of the mountains might be explained in the light of a passage in the Baal myth of Ras Shamra, where Baal, now in the ascendant and in his full kingly power, enrages his enemy Death, by drought and sterility of the summer, which had penetrated the forests and deep glens, the last refuge of the verdure in summer, as, for example, in Gordon *UT* 51 VII, 25ff.:

'ib b'l t'iḫd y'rm	The foes of Baal occupied the forests,
sn'u hd gpt ġr	The enemy of Hadad the inmost recesses of the mountains.

It might be thought proper that Baal in his triumphant lightning-flashes uncovers the roots of the mountains occupied by his enemies. We should nevertheless read *wᵉrā'šê hārîm kissāh* ('and he covers the tops of the mountains'), referring to the heavy rain-clouds, which with the thunder and lightning herald the heavy rains so vital to cultivation.

32-33. This passage is another notorious crux in the Book of Job, but it is possible that this may be owing to rare words and faulty word-divisions rather than to serious corruption of the text. The reading of MT *'al-kappayim kissāh-'ôr* ('he covered both hands with lightning') is suspect, and Dhorme's suggestion that this was the corruption of an original *nāśā'* ('he took up') first to *nissāh* through a scribal error in dictation and then to MT *kissāh*, if unlikely in the first stage of the corruption which he assumes, is certainly graphically feasible in the second. Pope's suggestion that the verb in the original text was *nasᵉsāh*, the 3rd fem. sing. perf. of a verb *nāsas*, which he cites in the Hithpolel in Zech. 9.16, and possibly in Isa. 10.18 in a passage dealing with burning, is acceptable. This meaning of this verb 'to flash' is supported by Akk. *nasâsu* ('to vibrate'), hence Pope renders 'on his palms the lightning prances'. 'Flickers' or 'flashes' is a more apt rendering in our opinion, and is evocative of Mesopotamian glyptic, where the lightning in the hand of Adad is represented by a jagged bolt (e.g. *ANEP*, pl. 533).

On this interpretation the fem. *'ôr* is to be noted, this being attested in Jer. 13.16 and in Akk., where the cognate *urrû* is fem.

Taking *'ālêhā* as meaning 'upon it', that is, the lightning, v. 32b is intelligible in the sense 'he gives it a charge concerning a target', reading *mip̄ga'* for MT *map̄gîa'* after Olshausen; cf. G.R. Driver's conjecture (1955: 90-91) of *wayyaṣlî'ōh*, citing Arab. *ṣala'a*, the II Form of which describes 'the sun emerging from the clouds'. We suggest rather *wᵉyaqlî'ehā* (lit. 'slings it'), assuming scribal corruption of *q* to *ṣ* in the Old Heb. script.

33. The ancient versions are discordant and vague about this verse, the MT of which they nevertheless in some form indicate. The confusion in interpretation is indicated by the fact that T has three different interpretations, and in 1905 Peake enumerated more than 30, which have since been generously amplified.

For MT

> *yaggîḏ 'ālāyw rē'ô*
> *miqneh 'ap̄ 'al-'ôlāh,*

Dhorme read

> *yaggîḏ 'ālāyw rô'ô miqneh š'ap̄ 'alᵉ'ôlāh*

> He warns his shepherd of it,
> the herd which sniffs the storm.

According to this interpretation there is an allusion to the well-known fact of animals' premonition of a storm. This interpretation is feasible, but is rather an abrupt change of subject. More recently Hölscher after Duhm proposed MT *rē'ô* indicated a noun derived from *rûa'* (to shout), as a war-cry or cry of triumph (cf. possibly Exod. 32.18, more commonly *tᵉrû'āh*), and he translates v. 33a: 'His triumph-shout gives notice of him'. He renders v. 33b: 'Stirring up wrath against iniquity', giving the reading of MT *miqneh*, as *mᵉqanneh* after

Böttcher, this being possibly an orthographic variant of *m^eqannē'*. This is substantially the interpretation of Kissane, Mowinckel, Fohrer and Terrien. In v. 33a, however, Kissane read *ra'am* ('the thunder') for MT *rē'ô*, which is graphically feasible in the Old Heb. script, and Fohrer and Terrien read *ra'ᵃmô* ('his thunder'), after Budde. Actually there is no need to emend the consonantal text to *ra'am* or *ra'ᵃmô* if *rē'ô* is taken as a cognate of Arab. *raġā* ('to rumble, as thunder'). In the mythological fragment RS 24.245 in the description of Baal seated on his holy mountain 'bundles of thunderbolts (*'isr r't*) are mentioned with a quantity of lightning bolts (Virolleaud 1968: 557-59), G.R. Driver (1955: 90-91) proposed that v. 33a and b have been transposed, reading, with emendations of MT, *qānāh 'appô 'alᵉ'ôlāh wᵉyaggîḏ 'elyô ra'ᵃmô* ('By his anger he creates the storm, and by his thunder he announces its coming'). This, it must be admitted, is intelligible as a description of the continuance of the storm. None of Driver's emendations is drastic or graphically unlikely, though one might take exception to the transposition of text. Making a laudable effort to read MT with the minimum of emendation, Pope proposes the graphically feasible reading *yaggîḏ 'ālî bᵉra'ᵃmô maqnî' 'appô 'al 'awlāh* ('*Ali* [the Most High] speaks with his thunder, venting his wrath against evil'). Here we note the substantial agreement with Kissane, Mowinckel, Fohrer and Terrien in the interpretation of v. 33b. The whole hymn, though describing God's order in nature, has the ultimate aim of demonstrating his order in society, so that the poem might be expected to culminate in just such a declaration. This, to be sure, is not the culmination of the hymn, which continues to 37.13, but it does mark a definite period in it.

Our own preference, which requires only vocalic modification of MT, is for the reading:

> *yaggîḏ 'elyô rē'ô*
> *mᵉqannē' 'ap̄ 'al-'awlāh,*
>
> His thunder announces his coming,
> Showing zealous wrath against iniquity.

The verbal noun *'ᵉlî* 'coming', which we postulate after Driver, recalls the use of *'ālāh* in Ps. 47.6, *'ālāh 'ᵉlōhîm bitᵉrû'āh*. This is an Enthronement Psalm referring to the Epiphany of God as King at the New Year festival, which, as we have indicated, contained in its liturgy many elements adapted from the festival in Canaanite nature-religion. *'ālāh* here refers symbolically to the great moment of God's assumption of his throne in the plenitude of his power, and in the Canaanite Baal myth appropriate to the same seasonal crisis Baal's power is signalized by thunder (cf. the thunder at the theophany at Sinai; Exod. 19.22-35). In the context of the Israelite adaptation of the liturgy of the New Year festival on the theme of the Kingship of God, his order in society is also emphasized, hence our preference for the reading *'awlāh* ('iniquity') in v. 33b rather than *'alᵉ'ôlāh* ('storm').

37.1. *yittar* may be from *nāṯar*, attested in 6.9, meaning 'to be untied', hence here 'is dislocated, starts', but Dhorme proposes a connection with Akk. *tarâru* ('to palpitate'), which is also possible. The general sense is not affected, especially as such a convenient translation as 'starts' is available.

2. *qōlô* (lit. 'his voice') is used absolutely for 'thunder' in the OT (e.g. 1 Sam. 12.17; Ps. 18.14 [EVV 13] etc.) and in the Ras Shamra texts (e.g. Gordon *UT* 51 VII, 29, 31).

rōḡez, which means generally in the OT 'agitation, anger' (e.g. Job 3.17, 26; 14.1), might mean 'thunder', as in the VIII Form of the Arab. cognate verb *rajaza*, a sense which was apparently familiar in Aram. in the first century CE from the rendering of *bᵉnê ruḡzā'* (Gk. *Boanerges*) as 'sons of thunder' (Gk. *huioi brontēs*) (Mk 3.17). In the present passage, however, in view of the association in 36.33 of thunder with the wrath of God, and the fact that in such a context *qôl* of itself means 'thunder', we prefer the usual Classical Heb. meaning of *rōḡez* in the present passage. This is supported by the association of thunder (*qôl*) and the verb *rāḡaz* ('to be agitated') in Ps. 78.17-18, which, like Job 36.26–37.13, is replete with the imagery of the Canaanite mythology from the liturgy of the New Year festival as adapted by Israel.

heḡeh denotes an inarticulate sound, as the growl of a lion (Isa. 31.4), the cooing of a pigeon (Isa. 38.14; 59.11). This is the only case where the word is used of thunder,

3. Tur-Sinai takes *yišrēhû* as 'his approval' (lit. 'what seems good to him') in antithetic parallelism with *'ôrô*, which he renders as 'his condemnation' (lit. 'his curse'). Alternatively *yišrēhû* has been taken as the imperf. of a verb *šārāh* cognate with Syr. *šᵉrā'* ('to let loose'). Dhorme supposes that the pronominal suffix refers proleptically to *'ôrô* in v. 3b, but as we have seen in 36.32 this noun is fem.; hence if *yišrēhû* is a verbal form the object would be more likely *rōḡez*. Moreover the fact that v. 4 states that the thunder follows indicates that v. 3 cannot refer to thunder. With H.L. Ginsberg (1943) we take *yišrēhû* as a corruption of *šᵉrēhû* ('his flashing'); cf. Arab. *šara(y)*, 'to flash repeatedly' of lightning. *šārāh* is attested in the verbal noun *šr* in a passage in the Baal myth of Ras Shamra, which corresponds very closely to the present passage; see Gordon *UT* 51 V, 70:

wytn qlh b'rpt	And he sends forth his thunder in the clouds,
šrh l'arṣ brqm	His flashing to the earth in lightning.

4. For MT *yar'ēm*, the Hiphil, the Qal *yir'am* should possibly be read.

In v. 4c the verb *'āqaḇ* has been taken in the sense 'to hold back'. Budde noted that v. 4c is defective couplet and proposed to read *wᵉlō' yᵉ'aqqēḇ bᵉrāqîm* ('And he does not restrain the lightnings') in the first half of v. 4c (so Beer, Dhorme, RSV, Hölscher, Driver–Gray, Fohrer, Terrien, Lévêque). Pope accepts this sense of the verb, but reads the final *m* in *yᵉ'aqqᵉḇēm* as the

Canaanite enclitic, taking the subject as indefinite and rendering 'Men stay not when his voice is heard', a four-beat line which is long and labouring, to say nothing of the fact that the verb is transitive. We suggest that the final *m* in *yᵉʿaqqᵉḇēm* is the remnant of an original *mayim*, omitted by haplography before *mippî*, which we read for MT *kî* in the last colon. Thus we restore MT v. 4c:

wᵉlōʾ yᵉʿaqqēḇ mayim	And he does not restrain the waters,
mippî yiššāmaʿ qôlô	As peal upon peal is heard.

We take *mippî* here as meaning 'in proportion as', which is usually expressed by *kᵉp̄î* (Exod. 16.3; Lev. 25.52; Num. 6.21; 7.5), *lᵉp̄î* (Exod. 12.4; Num. 26.54; Josh. 18.4; 1 Kgs 17.1) or *ʿal-pî* (Gen. 43.7; Lev. 27.8; Deut. 17.10, 11; 2 Sam. 13.32; Prov. 22.6). The rain is the natural concomitant of thunder and lightning, as in the proverb of the peasants of Palestine, *ʾal-baraq ʿalāmatu ʾl-maṭar* ('The lightning is the harbinger of the rain'). The Aram. sense of *ʿāqaḇ* ('to restrain') is to be noted here; cf. Arab. *ʿaqaba* in the VIII Form with the sense.

5. MT

yarʿēm ʾēl bᵉqôlô nip̄lāʾôṯ	God thunders with his voice wondrously,
ʿōśeh gᵉḏōlôṯ wᵉlōʾ nēḏāʿ	Doing great things and we do not know,

is regardless of parallelism, both cola being overloaded. Another reference to thunder would surely be tedious in this introduction to the other marvelous manifestations of God's power and providence in nature. So in v. 5ab *bᵉqôlô* may be excised, having perhaps been introduced inadvertently through familiarity with the enumeration of the works of God. *yarʿēm* may also be questioned. Duhm proposed *yarʾennû* ('he shows us', so Hölscher, Fohrer, Terrien) for which *ʿ* for *ʾ* would be an error of dictation and *m* a corruption of *n* in the Old Heb. script, with final *w* a dittograph in the same script. Dhorme proposed *yaʿᵃmōl* ('he does') for MT *yarʿēm*, which is nearer the sense, though *yip̄ʿal* would be more easily corrupted to *yarʿēm* in the Old Heb. script. The metre may be improved by omitting *wᵉ* before *lōʾ* in 5b, and reading:

ʿōśēh gᵉḏōlôṯ lōʾ-nēḏāʿ	He does great things beyond our ken.

6. For MT *hᵉwēʾ* we should probably read *hᵉwēh*. This is the one certain instance of the verb in the OT and may be an Arabism (cf. Arab. *hawa[y]*, 'to fall'), though Pope notes that the nouns *hawwāh* and *hawwôṯ* in the OT indicates that the verbal root was not unknown in Hebrew.

In this overloaded couplet, especially in v. 6b, either *wᵉḡešem māṭār* or *wᵉḡešem miṭᵉrōṯ* must be omitted as a dittograph, and as a parallel to the imperative *hᵉwēh* in v. 6a we should read *ʿuzzû* for *ʿuzzô* after Hoffmann. The plural here suggests that *wᵉḡešem ûmāṭār* should be read and *wᵉḡešem miṭᵉrōṯ* omitted, *w* in *ûmāṭār* being omitted by haplography before *m* in the Old Heb.

script. Further we suggest that the omission of *l^{e}* before *gešem* in v. 6b indicates that *'āmar* in v. 6a means not 'to say', but to 'command', as Arab. *'amara*. In this case *l^{e}* before *šeleḡ* may be the introduction to the direct object, as in Aram. The first colon is still rather long, perhaps because after *'āmar* direct speech is used.

7. MT *b^{e}yaḏ* may be emended to *b^{e} 'aḏ* as in 9.7 with the same verb *ḥāṯam* ('to seal up'; so Hitzig, Duhm, Graetz, Beer, Dhorme, Fohrer, Pope), but insofar as the passage probably denotes the suspension of activities, *b^{e}yaḏ* may be retained (so Hölscher, Mowinckel, Kissane, Terrien, Lévêque).

In MT *lāḏa'aṯ kol-'an^{e}šê ma'^{a}śēhû* D.W. Thomas (1954: 56ff.) proposes to read *lāḏa'aṯ kol-'^{a}nāšîm…*, or, better, *lāḏa'aṯ kol-'îš mimma'^{a}śēhû* ('that all men may be inactive from their work'), finding in the verb *yāḏa'* a cognate of Arab. *wada'a* ('to let go free from restriction') (see on 9.5). This would give a good parallel to v. 7a. Alternatively the reading may be *lāḏa'aṯ kol-'îš ma'^{a}śēhû* ('that every man may know what he does'). The sense in this case would be that a man's enforced inactivity gives him the opportunity to know how much he depends on God in the ordinary course of nature; cf. 'Be still and know that I am God' (Ps. 46.11 [EVV 10]). Thomas's interpretation, however, best suits the sequel in v. 8.

8. *'ereḇ*, usually 'ambush', hence 'lurking-place', is found in the OT in the sense of a wild beast's lair only once besides, in 38.40, whereas here it is parallel to *m^{e}'ônāh*.

9. The reference in MT *haḥeḏer* and MT *m^{e}zārîm* may refer to directions, taken from the sky. The former, 'the Chamber', is probably 'the Chambers of the South' (*ḥaḏ^{e}rê ṯêmān*), the constellation in 9.9 (so Friedrich Delitzsch, Dhorme; cf. Duhm, who actually read *ḥaḏ^{e}rê ṯêmān*). *sûp̄āh* is the whirlwind with its sandstorms and dust-devils, associated with the deserts in the South in Isa. 21.1. This would indicate that *m^{e}zārîm* signifies the North, which seems corroborated by the reference to *qārāh* ('cold'). The pointing of *m^{e}zārîm* indicates a fem. plur. participle (Piel) of the verb *zārāh* ('to scatter, fan or winnow'), cf. Arab. *ḏara(y)*. In fact the Qur'an (*Surah* 51.1) actually refers to *ḏāriyāt*, probably 'the winds that scatter', but what they scatter is not known. Dhorme is explicit when he states, followed by Hölscher, Fohrer and Pope, that the Qur'an here refers to the cold north winds as the scatterers of rain.

10. For MT *yitten* the passive *yuttan* may be read with Sym., S and T.

In MT *b^{e}mûṣāq*, *b^{e}*, if correct, would be a *beth essentiae*, meaning 'in solid condition'; cf. 38.38. *mûṣāq* is the Hophal participle of *yāṣaq* ('to melt' or 'mould' metal); cf. 1 Kgs 7.37. The word is found again in v. 18, describing a mirror of smooth polished metal.

11. *'ôr* in v. 11b evidently suggested to Beer that MT *b^erî* in v. 11a should be emended to *bārāq* (so Hontheim, Budde, G.B. Gray, Ball, Dhorme, Pope), which we consider rather drastic, assuming a scribal error of *y* for *q*, which at any stage of the development of the script is very unlikely. Nor is *bārāq* supported by the versions, which attest either *bar* (so Sym., V) or *b^erî*. S, rendering 'delicately' (*bar^eḵîḵā'îṯ*), seems to indicate a reading *reḵîḵ*, which might be a corruption of *bir^ewî* ('with moisture'), which is read by Hölscher, Kissane, Mowinckel, Weiser, Larcher (JB), Fohrer and Lévêque; cf. Terrien, who reads *bārāḏ* ('hail'). *r^ewî* would be a form of the infinitive construct, or verbal noun, from *rāwāh*, like *'^anî* from *'ānāh*, *'^aḏî* from *'āḏāh*, *š^eḇî* from *šāḇāh*, *ḥ^olî* from *ḥālāh*, and *'^alî* from *'ālāh*, which, with G.R. Driver, we find attested in 36.33. The parallelism with v. 11b, however, does not suggest this reading or interpretation. We take *'ôr* in v. 11b not as 'lightning', as in 36.30, 32 and 37.3, but as 'sun' as in v. 21; 31.26; 41.10 and Hab. 3.4, and so are not predisposed to read *bārāq* for MT *b^erî*. If *ṭāraḥ* has the sense it usually has in Classical Heb., 'to toil, labour, be burdened' (e.g. Deut. 1.12; Isa. 1.14 and the Targum on Num. 11.11; Deut. 6.11 and Eccl. 2.11; so G.B Gray, Hölscher, Weiser, Terrien, Larcher [JB], Gordis and Lévêque), it might suggest the translation 'he loads the thick cloud with moisture' (so also Mowinckel and Kissane); cf. the passage in the Qur'an noted à propos of 'the Scatterers', where 'the Burdened Ones' (*'al-ḥāmilāt*) are taken by the predominant Muslim tradition to refer to the clouds as burdened with rain. The parallelism suggests, however, that the original text behind MT *b^erî* is a synonym of *'ôr*, hence we suggest the reading *bārô* ('his bright sun'), of which MT *b^erî* is a corruption in the square Heb. script. We may add that *bārar* is used specifically of the sun in deeds of emancipation from the the palace at Ras Shamra. Thus in the text RS 15.125 (*PRU* II, 1957, 5), a deed of emancipation (*dt brrt*), the formula of emancipation is used, *km špš brrt kmt br ṣṭqšlm b'unš 'd 'lm* ('As the sun is clear so S. is clear of obligation for ever'). Taking *ṭāraḥ* in the sense of Arab. *taraḥa* ('to thrust away'), we may render the couplet 'Moreover his bright (sun) thrusts away the thick clouds; its light dispels the cloud'. This suits the sequel, which in our opinion concerns the sun.

12. In v. 12a the meter demands another beat; hence *yiṯhallēḵ* may be read, having been omitted by haplography before the similar *miṯhappēḵ*. *miṯhappēḵ* is used of the flaming sword brandished by the cherubim who guarded the way to the tree of life in the Garden of Eden (Gen. 3.24), but, referring to the sun, it refers rather to the current rising and setting, going the round of sky and underworld according to the ancient cosmology. The sense and metre demands that MT *l^ep̄o'^olām* (emended to *lip̄'ōl*) should be taken with the next colon, giving the reading:

> *w^ehû' m^esibbôṯ yiṯhallēḵ*
> *miṯhappēḵ b^eṯaḥbulôṯāyw*
> *lip̄'ōl kol-'^ašer y^eṣawwēhû* (for MT *y^eṣawwēm*)

The reference to the course 'in circuit' (*m^e^sibbôṯ*), turning over at God's guidance (taking *taḥbulôṯ* as an abstract plural), indicates that the subject *'ôr* is the sun, as distinct from *'ôr* meaning lightning in v. 32a, which is feminine. The 3rd masc. plur. pronom. suffixes in MT *l^e^pō ʿ^o^lām* and *y^e^ṣawwēm* reflect a misunderstanding that *bārô* and *'ôrô* refer to different phenomena. The reference to the sun in our opinion is supported by the sequel in v. 13, where the sun as the all-seeing is patron of justice, discovering mortals for chastisement (*šēḇeṭ*, lit. 'rod', LXX *paideia*) or favour (*'arṣû*).

MT *tēḇēl 'arṣōh* is found again in Prov. 8.31 (spelled *'arṣô*) in parallelism with *b^e^nê 'āḏām* with an obviously universal significance; hence the phrase may mean 'the whole habitable world'; cf. Ass. *taḇâlu* ('the whole round world').

13. The parallelism with *šēḇeṭ* suggests that *'arṣû* in v. 13a may be a Heb. or Aram. form of Arab. *raḍwu(n)* ('favour'). This occurs in an Aram. form *r^e^ṣû*, cf. the god *'arṣu* in a Palmyrene inscription, which is rendered *Monimos* (Arab. *munā 'imu[n]*, 'the Gracious') in the Latin translation Monimos (Ingholt 1928: 42ff.). *r^e^ṣû* or *'arṣû* would thus be a synonym of *ḥeseḏ*, which may have been used to make the somewhat rare Aram. word explicit. The subject of *yamṣi'ēhû* is God and the object the sun, the second object expressed in the pronom. suffix being indefinite. The verb may be used in the sense of 'to light upon'. The use of *šēḇeṭ* ('a rod') for 'chastisement' is attested in Lam. 3.1. The reference may be either to the sun as a medium of parching or fertility or as revealing the works of humans in their true light and according to their true merits, as in Mesopotamian thought, where the sun-god was the patron of justice, as explicitly noted in Hammurabi's law code.

Job 37.14-24

Conclusion of the Elihu Section: Address to Job

After the citation of the Hymn of Praise on the theme of God's inaccessible power and wisdom and his providence, Elihu directs Job to appropriate the signs in nature of God's transcendent power and wisdom, before which human limitation makes their questioning of the divine economy mere presumption. This is the substance of the Divine Address to Job in 38.2ff., and may be an appendix to the Hymn of Praise (36.26–37.13), which rounds out Elihu's arguments, thus adapting this addition to the Book of Job and indicating Elihu's agreement with the final answer of God, as he had noted his disagreement with the arguments of Job.

The literary form of this section is borrowed from the Divine Address to Job, which in turn is in the convention of the sapiential controversy where one sage challenges another with a series of questions. The best illustration of this is the famous altercation of the Egyptian scribe Hori with Amenope (Erman 1927: 227ff.).

The section may be divided into two strophes, vv. 14-18, which challenges Job's understanding of the forces and processes of nature, and vv. 19-24, the subject of which is the inaccessibility of God, a reflection of whose glory nevertheless, as a cloud shot through by sunlight, gives a hint of his majesty, if at the same time emphasizing his transcendence (vv. 21-24).

Chapter 37.14-24

14. 'Give ear to this, O Job,
Stand still and consider the wonderful works of God.
15. Do you know when God lays their functions upon them,[1]
And how his cloud flashes with light?
16. Do you know anything about the balancing of the clouds,
The wonders[2] of him who is perfect in knowledge,
17. You whose garments grow hot
When the land is becalmed from the South?
18. Would you beat out the sky like him,
Hard as a mirror of molten (metal)?

19. Teach us what we should say to him.
We shall not state our case; we shall keep silence.[3]

20. Is it said to him, "Nay, but I will speak?"
Has anyone ever said, "Nay, but he will be told?"
21. Now no one can see[4] the sun
When it is obscured in the clouds,
But the wind has passed over and cleared it.[5]
22. From concealment comes brightness.[6]
About God dreadful is the splendour.
23. The Almighty we cannot attain,
Great in power and justice;
He distorts[7] not the case of[8] innocence.
24. Wherefore let mortals fear him,[9]
He does not regard any who are wise in their own conceit.'

Textual Notes to Chapter 37.14-24

1. *ʿalêhen* for MT *ʿalêhem.*
2. Reading *nip̄leʾô̲t* for MT *mip̄leʾô̲t* with corruption of *n* to *m* in the Old Heb. script.
3. Reading *ḥōśek̲* for MT *ḥōšek̲*. See Commentary *ad loc.*
4. Reading *rāʾô* (infinitive absolute) for MT *rāʾû.*
5. Reading *watteṭahᵃrennû* for MT *watteṭahᵃrēm.*
6. Reading *zōhār* for MT *zāhāb̲*. See Commentary *ad loc.*
7. Reading *yeʿawwēh* for MT *yeʿanneh.*
8. Reading *rîb̲* for MT *rōb̲.*
9. Reading *yîrāʾûhû* with LXX for MT *yerēʾûhû.*

Commentary on Chapter 37.14-24

15. *śîm ʿal* is ambiguous, meaning 'to pay attention to' (understanding *lēb̲*) or 'to lay a task upon' (Exod. 5.8) or 'to set an appointment for' (34.23), with a specified object. Taking *nip̄leʾô̲t* to denote the wondrous agencies of God's immediate activity, we may render the MT of v. 15a as 'Do you know when God lays their functions upon them?'

16. *mip̄leśê-ʿāb̲* recalls *mip̄reśê-ʿāb̲* of 36.29, which is in fact read by Budde. The variation may be suggested by the parallel word *mip̄leʾô̲t*, itself an admissible variation of the usual *nip̄leʾô̲t*. In *mip̄leśô̲t* nevertheless we should see a formation from *pālaś*, a dialectic or orthographic variation of the usual root *pālas* ('to balance', Isa. 40.12; Prov. 16.11).

temîm dēʿîm ('perfect in knowledge') recalls *temîm dēʿô̲t*, by which Elihu designates himself (36.14). Both cases may be instances of the plur. signifying the abstract noun.

17. The reference to Job sweltering in his clothes in the sirocco might suggest some reference to the clouds as the garments of God in a line which may have dropped out. This may have happened through a close resemblance with v. 16 because of a word-play between *mip̄leśê-ʿāb̲* and something like *milbešê* or even *milpešê*, or possibly *melippô̲t* ('wrappings, robes') from a root cognate

with Arab. *laffa*. But this is a conjecture. Dhorme understands the reference to the helplessness and discomfort of humans in the sirocco in the light of what follows; they are not able to spread out clouds in the sky. Actually in the sirocco the shade is not particularly desirable since the sky is in any case dull. We take the reference in v. 18 to be to the appearance of the late autumn clouds, which herald the end of the season of siroccos, which are most grievous in September. If there is no reference to the clouds as the robes of God in such a lacuna as we have conjectured, we must take the reference to Job's garments in v. 17 as part of a pregnant clause, 'You who are so hot that you cannot bear your clothes'. The silence of the land because of the south wind in v. 17b aptly describes the lifelessness of nature under the sirocco. Pope felicitously renders 'When the land is becalmed from the South'. The effect of the sirocco, including the phenomenal stillness remarked upon, here and possibly in Isa. 25.5, is vividly described by W.M. Thomson (1860: 537):

> There is no living thing abroad to make a noise. The birds hide in thickest shades; the fowls pant under the walls with open mouths and drooping wings; the flocks and herds take shelter in caves and under great rocks; the labourers retire from the fields, and close the windows and doors of their houses; and travellers hasten, as I did, to take shelter in the first cool place they can find. No one has energy enough to make a noise, and the very air is too weak and languid to stir the pendent leaves even of the tall poplars. Such a south wind with the heat of a cloud does indeed bring down the noise and quiet the earth.

18. *'immô* implies contention or comparison, 'Can you vie with him in beating out the clouds?' Note Aram. *lᵉ* as *nota accusativa* in *lišᵉḥāqîm*. The Hiphil of *rāqa'*, as the parallel colon indicates, does not envisage the sky as a curtain, but as a solid ceiling beaten out, hence 'firmament' (*rāqîa'*) in Gen. 1.6, 7, 8; cf. Exod. 39.3; Num. 17.4; Jer. 10.9. *mûṣāq* means metal melted and set; cf. *mûṣāq* describing ice in v. 10. The ancient mirror (*rᵉ'î*), mostly known from tombs in Egypt, was of smooth, polished metal.

19. *na'ᵃrōḵ*, lit. 'to arrange', here one's case, is common in forensic idiom. For *mippᵉnê-ḥōšeḵ* ('by reason of darkness') Fohrer after Perles reads *mippᵉnê ḥōśeḵ* ('by reason of speechlessness'). *ḥāśaḵ* is found with *pî* ('my mouth') in 7.11 and with *śᵉp̄āṯayim* ('lips') in Prov. 10.19. Those passages suggest deliberate restraint rather than inability to find words, and under this consideration Lévêque's proposal (1970: 520) may be noted, *pînû naḥsōḵ* ('we shall keep silence').

20. The force of this couplet is emphasized by the conjunction *kî*, meaning here 'Nay but…', emphasizing a person's determination to command a hearing from God. In v. 20b, *yᵉbulla'* has been sadly misunderstood. As the parallel *yᵉsuppar*, this is the passive of the cognate Arab. *balaġa* ('to reach'), used in the phrase *balaġani* ('it has reached me', i.e. 'I am informed'; Jacob 1912: 287). The verb is attested, also in the passive, in this sense in 2 Sam. 17.16.

21. The 3rd masc. plur., appearing suddenly in v. 21, is suspect, and we prefer to read *rā'ô*, the infinitive absolute with the indefinite subject, 'people see', but admit the possibility of the corruption of an original passive participle *rā'ûy* with *'ôr* as subject. Here again we take *'ôr* as 'the sun'. In v. 21b *bāhîr*, which is a *hapax legomenon*, has been taken as 'fright' after the interpretation of *baharet̲* in Leviticus 13 as 'bright spot' and from Aram. *b^ehar* and Arab. *bahara*, which have this sense. But Friedrich Delitzsch cited Syr. *b^ehîrā'* ('dark'), which Dhorme accepts as the meaning here (so also G.B. Gray, Kissane, Terrien). In v. 21c there is probably a *double entendre* in *rûaḥ*, 'wind' and 'spirit'. The sense is that, not being able to see the sun, obscured as it is in the clouds, humans may despair, but the wind will clear the sky and they will see the sun again, so also while in perplexity one cannot compel an explanation, the spirit of God may make that possible.

22. This verse should probably be taken with v. 21c, with *ûmiṣṣāp̄ôn* the original reading, assuming haplography of *w* in MT before *m* in the Old Heb. script. The colon has been variously interpreted. Assuming MT *zāhāb̲*, AV and RSV render 'golden splendour' (cf. NEB 'golden glow'), and Guillaume (1968: 129) thinks of light rain gilded by the sun, citing Arab. *ḏihbatu(n)*. Pope would find a reference to the Baal myth of Ras Shamra, where the palace prepared for Baal as King on Mt Saphon is plated with gold. The context, however, indicates an atmospheric phenomenon, brightness after obscurity, which might support Tur-Sinai's suggestion that *ṣāp̄ôn* means 'concealment' (1957: 517ff.) He proposed that MT *zāhāb̲* is a scribal corruption of *zōhar* ('brightness'), which is graphically feasible. G.B. Gray adopts this view, seeing a reference to the Aurora Borealis, a highly unlikely phenomenon in the Near East. We consider it more likely that the poet has been influenced by Ezek. 1.4 which refers to the vision of the storm-wind 'coming from the North' with fire and radiance (*nōḡāh*). 'About God dreadful is the splendour' (v. 22b) may be a secondary expansion, expressing the belief that at the heart of mystery is God himself, not to be compelled to a hearing, yet nonetheless manifesting his power and concern for order in nature and society (v. 23b, c).

23. In *m^eṣā'nuhû* we suggest the nuance of the Aram. cognate *m^eṭā'* ('to attain to'); cf. *māṣā'* ('to catch up with', Josh. 2.22; 1 Kgs 13.14; 21.20).

24. The wordplay between *yārē'* ('to fear, reverence') and *rā'āh* ('to see') is to be noticed. Fohrer regards this verse as a gloss. However this may be, it signifies the sage's admission of the limitations of the humanistic tradition he represented, as is stated in Prov. 9.10 that 'the fear of the Lord is the beginning of wisdom' and as the scepticism of Ecclesiastes was corrected by the orthodox redactor who added (Eccl. 12.13) 'Fear God and keep his commandments, for this is the duty of all'. In view of the Heb. conception of *lēb̲* as the seat of cognition, *ḥak^emê-lēb̲* might signify 'the *intelligentsia*'.

Introduction to Job 38–41

Chapters 38–41 correspond to the theophany or reassuring oracle in the Plaint of the Sufferer and are demanded moreover as the response to Job's oath of purgation in the forensic tradition. The Divine Declaration had a two-fold significance. In response to Job's reiterated appeal to be personally confronted by God, the fact of the Divine Declaration emphasizes that God cares, and explodes the conventional view, already belied by the sufferings of the really worthy man, that suffering in all cases implies sin and alienation from God. But the author is still sufficient of a humanist not to exceed the evidence of experience by dogmatizing on how God cares. The personal confrontation with God which Job had sought is granted, but does not address his personal problem just as he had hoped. God does not condescend to an apology for his economy. His ultimate purpose in nature and society is at his own discretion. It is sufficient for humans that they may discern in the multitude and wonder of God's works tokens of the divine wisdom and providential care for his creatures and accept the situation in which they find themselves and be prepared to respond to the will of God in humble dependence (42.4-6).

Like the Egyptian scribe Hori, whose altercation with a rival scribe (*ANET*, 477-78) the divine reply to Job formally reproduces, God does not explain or defend himself; he challenges the understanding and agility of his opponent. This aims to engender in Job a proper sense of his limitations. It challenges Job's understanding of creation (38.4-11) and the elemental phenomena of nature (38.12-38), reminding him that the full significance of the plan and purpose of creation is the ultimate secret of the Creator. In his power and providence he is not to be called in question, but, as is hinted in the angelic hymn of praise (38.7), praised and adored. But in disclosing 'marvels beyond marvels'[1] God lifts Job's prospect—and his hope—beyond the narrow limits of individual human experience. Job was abased before the *mysterium tremendum*[2] (40.4-5; 42.2-6), as it was meant that he should be; but new hope was kindled by the *mysterium fascinans*. The very token of the 'otherness' of God and the evidences of his power and providence beyond the competence of humankind stimulate hope beyond human limitations.

1. 'Behind each of its marvels lies another great marvel, and not one of these does God allow to be taken out of his hand' (Von Rad 1962–65: I, 416).

2. R. Otto (1925: 80-83) has rightly apprehended the significance of the Divine Declaration in Job.

Thus in the Divine Declaration the passages on the rain in the desert (38.26-27), the wild creatures, the lion (38.39-40), the raven (38.41), the ibexes (39.1-4), the onager (39.5-8), the wild ox (39.9-12), the ostrich (39.13-18), the migrant hawk (39.26), the keen-eyed vulture (39.27-30) and the intractable crocodile (40.25-30 [EVV 41.1-6]) remind humans that they are not the sole object of God's providential care, which they call in question on the basis of their peculiar experience. So setting the problem of human suffering in this wider perspective in the Divine Declaration, the writer of the Book of Job has presented it not as an intellectually satisfying answer, but rather as a challenge to faith—not, however, without encouragement.

The passage on Leviathan (40.25-30 [EVV 41.1-6]) belongs stylistically to the passages on the animals in ch. 39, introduced as it is by the rhetorical question addressed personally to Job and emphasizing its characteristic, its intractability. It was probably displaced after the secondary description of the crocodile was developed (41.4-26 [EVV 41.12-34]), and situated after the similar descriptive and secondary passage on Behemoth, the hippopotamus (40.15-24, 31-32; 41.1-3 [EVV 40.15-24; 41.7-11]).

The Divine Declaration is carefully constructed and may be analysed according to literary form as follows:

Part I. *38.1–39.30 with 40.25-30 (EVV 41.1-6), Displaced*

A. *Introduction*
First strophe (38.2-3): God's challenge to his opponent in a reflection of the forensic tradition (vv. 2-3a). Job is then called upon to answer to a series of questions designed to emphasize the limitations to his knowledge, and thus invalidate his title to question the conduct and propositions of his adversary. The best example of this literary form is Hori's interrogation of a rival scribe, Amen-em-opet, in his satirical letter from the thirteenth century BCE.

B. Interrogation on the secrets of elemental and natural forces (38.4–39.30; 40.25-30 [EVV 41.1-6]):

a. in creation (vv. 4-21),
Second strophe (vv. 4-7): the control of the earth;
Third strophe (vv. 8-11): the control of the sea;
Fourth strophe (vv. 12-15): the control of day and, it is implied, night;
Fifth strophe (vv. 16-18): the bottom of the sea and the underworld;
Sixth strophe (vv. 19-21): the source of light;

b. the direction of creation (38.22-38),
Seventh strophe (vv. 22-30): the weather;
Eighth strophe (vv. 31-38): meteorology and related phenomena;

c. providential care for creatures beyond human experience (38.39–39.30)
i. in nourishment (38.39-41),
Ninth strophe (38.39-41): the lion and the raven;
ii. in breeding (39.1-4),

Tenth strophe (39.1-4): the ibex and the hind;

iii. in untameable spirit (vv. 5-12),

Eleventh strophe (vv. 5-8): the onager;

Twelfth strophe (vv. 9-12): the wild ox;

iv. in characteristic properties (vv. 13-30),

Thirteenth strophe (vv. 13-18): the speed of the ostrich;

Fourteenth strophe (vv. 19-25): the strength and spirit of the warhorse;

Fifteenth strophe (vv. 26-30): the flight and sense of direction of the migrant hawk and predatory vulture;

Sixteenth strophe, displaced (40.25-30 [EVV 41.1-6]): the crocodile ('Leviathan').

Part II. *40.2, 7-14, Conclusion*

A. *Introduction*

Seventeenth strophe (40.2, 7-9): in the same literary form as the introduction to Part I, but anticipating the limitation of Job's knowledge of God's economy in society.

B. *God's Challenge*

Eighteenth strophe (40.10-14): emphasizing human limitations in nature and particularly in society in comparison with God's power and ordered rule, so often the theme of the Hymn of Praise, the style of which is reflected here to evoke the same theme. Here the literary type of the forensic dispute in its adaptation to sapiential controversy introduces the two parts of the address (38.1-3 and 40.2, 7), which is cast in the form of interrogation of an opponent in sapiential controversy. The systematic grouping of categories, moreover, in the interrogation in 38.4–39.30 is also in the sapiential tradition, reproducing the classified lists of natural and social categories known in ancient Mesopotamian (Matous 1933; von Soden 1930) and Egyptian wisdom tradition (Gardiner 1947), which became familiar in Israel in the humanist culture of Solomon's[3] court and is most familiar in the classified lists in Prov. 30.15-16, 18-19, 21-23, 24-28, 29-31, being reflected elsewhere in Job (e.g. 24.13-17). But in spite of the style of the law-court and sapiential disputation in the introduction to the two parts of the Divine Declaration and the sapiential interrogation and the classified categories in the Declaration itself, the exaltation of God, which is the object of the Declaration, has elevated the literary medium occasionally to the style of the Hymn of Praise, as notably on the passage on creation in 39.4-21, with its rich imagery, where the writer even cites ancient Canaanite mythology (38.7, 8).

3. Alt 1953: 90-99; Scott 1955. This was probably the source of the tradition that Solomon 'spoke of trees from the cedar that is in Lebanon to the hyssop that grows out of the wall and of beasts and of birds and of reptiles and of fish' (1 Kgs 4.33).

In this section the passage on the stupidity of the ostrich and its callous disregard for its young (39.14-17), noting its phenomenal speed (v. 18) despite its weak wings (v. 13), disrupts the poem and may be a secondary expansion, perhaps the citation of a poem on the ostrich. On the other hand it might be original, the argument being that in spite of the proud plumage of the ostrich, it is stupid, risking the extinction of its brood by its callousness, yet God provides for its preservation by its fleetness of foot (so Weiser). In the present state of the text (see Commentary *ad loc.*) this is a hard question to decide, though we prefer the suggestion we made above. Job 40.1f. is probably secondary, the citation of sapiential poems on the beasts in chs. 38–39 suggesting this note in introduction to the dialectic conclusion to the Divine Declaration to 40.7-14. Job 40.3-5 in its present position renders God's continued censure of Job in 40.7-14 unapt, and is displaced from before 42.2-6, 42.1 being redactional after this displacement of text and the insertion of the matter on the hippopotamus (40.15-24, 31-32; 41.1-3) and the crocodile (41.4-26).

Job 38

THE DIVINE DECLARATION: PART I

Chapter 38

1. Then Yahweh answered Job out of the whirlwind and said:

2. 'Who is this that obscures (our) purpose
By words without knowledge?
3. Brace yourself like a man[1]
That I may question you and you may declare to me.

4. Where were you when I was laying the foundation of the earth?
Tell me, if you know how it was established.[2]
5. Who set its measures, if you know,
Or who stretched the line over it?
6. In what were its bases embedded?
Or who laid down its corner-stone,
7. When the morning stars cheered together,
And all the beings shouted acclaim?

8. Who shut in[3] the sea with doors,
When it burst forth, issuing from the womb,
9. When I gave it the cloud as its clothing,
And the dark cloud as its swaddling-band,
10. And I set the gauge of the bounds to which it might come up,[4]
And set a bar and doors,
11. And said, "Hither shall you come,[5]
And here shall the pride of your waves be broken"?[6]

12. In all your days did you ever order Morning to his post?
Or cause the Day-Star to know[7] its place,
13. Taking hold of the skirts of the earth
That the wicked might be shaken out of it,
14. It being changed as clay under the seal,
Taking colour[8] like a garment,
15. Their light being withheld from the wicked,
And the uplifted arm broken.

16. Have you penetrated to the springs of the sea,
Or walked in the sources of the deep?
17. Have the gates of death been disclosed to you,
Or have you seen[9] the frontiers of deepest darkness?
18. Has your comprehension extended to the breadth of the underworld?
Declare if you know its extent.[10]

19. Which way leads to the home of light,
And where is the abode of darkness,
20. That you may[11] take it to its territory,
Or bring it into its homeward paths?
21. You know it for you were born of old,
And the number of your days is many.

22. Have you entered the arsenals of the snow,
And seen the hoards[12] of the hail,
23. Which I have held for the time of distress,
For the day of assault and battle?
24. Which is the way by which the heat[13] is distributed,
Which the sirocco scatters over the earth?
25. Who cleft a channel for the flood,
And a way for the thunder-shower,
26. Sending rain on the land unpeopled,
The desert where no human is,
27. To satisfy the waste wilderness,
And to cause the thirsty land[14] to sprout with growth?
28. Has the rain a father?
Or who has begotten the dew-drops?
29. From whose womb has the ice come forth?
Or the hoar-frost from the sky—who has given it birth,
30. The waters being congealed[15] like a stone,
And the face of the deep solidified?

31. Do you fasten the bonds[16] of the Pleiades,
Or loose the bonds[17] of Orion?
32. Do you bring out the Hyades in their season,
Leading the Bear and its satellites?
33. Have you appointed[18] the laws of heaven,
Do you impose rules[19] on the earth?
34. Can you raise your voice to the clouds,
That a deluge of water may cover it?[20]
35. Can you send the lightnings that they go,
Saying, to you, "Here we are!"?
36. Who has given wisdom to the ibis?
And who has given wisdom to the cock?
37. Who can empty out the clouds by his wisdom?
Or who can tilt out the waterskins of the sky,
38. When the dust runs into a fused mass,
And the clods cohere?

39. Do you hunt his prey for the lion,
Or satisfy the appetite of the young lions,
40. When they crouch in their dens,
Lying in wait in the thicket?
41. Who provides its food for the raven,
When its young[21] cry to God,
Staggering[22] for want of food?

Textual Notes to Chapter 38

1. Cf. *k^e^ḡibbôr* in one Heb. MS, S and T for MT *ḵ^e^ḡeḇer*. See Commentary *ad loc.*
2. Conjecturing *kûnāh* for MT *bînāh*. See Commentary *ad loc.*
3. Reading *mî sāḵ* with T and V for MT *wayyāseḵ*.
4. Reading *wā'ĕsbōr ḥuqqê 'elyô* for MT *wā'ĕsbōr 'ālāyw ḥuqqî*. See Commentary *ad loc.*
5. Either MT *wā'ōmar* or *w^e^lō' tōsîp̄* must be omitted *metri causa.*
6. Reading *yištabbēr g^e^'ôn* after LXX and V for MT *yāšîṯ biḡ^e^'ôn*. See Commentary *ad loc.*
7. Taking *h* in MT *yidda'tāh* as a *mater lectionis* and not as the definite article with *šaḥar* as in Qere.
8. Reading *w^e^ṯiṣṣāḇa'* for MT *w^e^yiṯyaṣṣ^e^ḇû*.
9. Reading *rā'îṯā* for MT *tir'eh*. On the variant reading see Commentary *ad loc.*
10. Reading *kammāh* with LXX for MT *kullāh*.
11. Reading *t^e^ḇî'ennû* for MT *tāḇîn*, assuming the omission of *'* after *y* in the Old Heb. script by haplography and addition of *w* after *n* in the same script.
12. Reading *n^e^ṣurôṯ* for MT *'ōṣ^e^rôṯ*, the latter having been inadvertently repeated after its incidence in the preceding colon.
13. Conjecturing *'ûr* for MT *'ôr*. See Commentary *ad loc.*
14. Reading *miṣṣiyyāh* for MT *mōṣā'*, as the parallelism demands, *y* being corrupted to *'* in the Old Heb. script.
15. Reading *yiṯḥamm^e^'û* for MT *yiṯḥabbā'û*. See Commentary *ad loc.*
16. Reading *ma'^a^naddôṯ* with LXX for MT *ma'^a^ḏannôṯ*.
17. Reading *mōs^e^rôṯ* for MT *mōš^e^ḵôṯ*.
18. Reading *h^a^yā'aḏtā* for MT *h^a^yāḏa'tā*.
19. Reading *mišṭārîm* for MT *mišṭārô*.
20. Reading *t^e^ḵassennāh* for MT *t^e^ḵassekkā*, assuming corruption of *n* to *k* in the Old Heb. script.
21. Reading *y^e^lāḏāyw* (Qere).
22. Reading *yittā'û* for MT *yiṯ^e^'û*.

Commentary on Chapter 38

1. The divine name Yahweh is confined to the prose introduction to the Divine Declaration here, to 40.1 and 6, to Job's replies to God in 40.3 and 42.1, and to the prose narrative in the Prologue and Epilogue except for one case in the Dialogue (12.9) in the citation of a familiar formula. The response of God from the storm-wind (*s^e^'ārāh*) may be a secondary feature suggested by the passages on the activity of God in nature in 36.29–37.4 in the Elihu Addendum, or it may be suggested by Job's statement in 9.17 that God crushes him with a tempest (*s^e^'ārāh*), or it may reflect a well-established tradition of the theophany in Israel (e.g. Pss. 18.8-16; 50.3; Nah. 1.3; Ezek. 1.4; Zech. 9.14). The association of the *s^e^'ārāh* with fire (Pss. 18.8-16; 50.3), the cloud as dust under his feet (Nah. 1.3), and with the South (Zech. 9.14), suggests the sirocco from the southern deserts as the medium *par excellence* of the theophany of Yahweh as the God of Sinai; cf. the fiery manifestation of his presence in Deut. 33.2; Hab. 3.3-4; and the theophany so expected in 1 Kgs 12.11-12.

2. *maḥšîk* ('obscures' or in English idiom 'befogs') is paralleled by another meteorological figure *ma'alîm* ('obscures') in 42.3. On *'ēṣāh* as 'purpose' or 'plan', the end as well as the method of 'counsel', so correctly rendered here by Dhorme as 'Providence', see above on 5.12 and 12.13. *'ēṣāh* is the firmly conceived and strenuously executed policy of the ruler (Isa. 11.2), who is thus called *yô'ēṣ* in Isa. 9.5 (EVV 6). God's purpose (*'ēṣāh*) will stand firm despite the incidentals of history (Isa. 46.10; Ps. 35.11) and the 'little systems' (Tennyson) and designs of humans (Prov. 19.21) and, we may add, in the light of the present passage and 42.3 in spite of human doubts and the dialectics of scepticism. Again we note the Aram. form *millîn*.

3. One Heb. MS reads *gibbôr* for MT *geḇer*, which is evidently understood by S and T. *geḇer*, however, may be retained, since it gives the full range of the meaning of the root covered by *gibbôr*, a mature and active man, including a warrior (*gibbôr*) (Judg. 5.30; Isa. 22.9; 41.16, 20), the responsible head of a family (Exod. 10.11; 12.37; 1 Chron. 24.4; 26.12; Jer. 43.6; Mic. 2.2; Prov. 6.34), a man confident in his power and in fact an overconfident materialist (Ps. 52.9 [EVV 7]; Job 33.17). God is thus addressing Job as a mature, responsible person (perhaps with the nuance an individual in his special care; cf. the king in 2 Sam. 23.1), but there may also be the hint of a rebuke to one who in his confidence defied (cf. *hiṯgabbēr*, 15.25) God or to humans generally in their temporal limitations, which *geḇer* signifies in Job. 3.23; 4.17; 10.5; 14.10; 16.21; 22.2; 34.5, 17, 29. In view of the parallel colon, 'Gird up your loins' may be an idiom taken from belt-wrestling as an ordeal in ancient law, as attested in sculpture and painting from Mesopotamia and Egypt and in legal documents from Nuzu cited by C.H. Gordon (1950–51). In strict dialectic the divine reply is a shocking evasion of the issue. Job had appealed to God for a hearing, with a direct charge which he might rebut, or an opportunity to justify himself; instead God questions him not on his specific case, where he would have been at a disadvantage, but only to abash Job with the limitations of his knowledge and experience. Indeed God even retains the secret of the relevance of human conduct, and even of faith, to his ultimate purpose.

4-6. Sometimes the earth, and particularly the sky, is visualized as a Bedouin tent with curtains stretched out over poles (Isa. 48.13; 51.13, 16; Zech. 12.1), called in Arab. 'pillars' (*'awāmidu[n]*). At other times, as here, a solid building is visualized with foundations (v. 4a; Pss. 89.12 [EVV 11]; 102.26 [EVV 25]; 104.5; Prov. 3.19; Isa. 48.13; 51.13; Zech. 12.1), sunk, as in Babylonian cosmology, in the lower deep (cf. Ps. 24.2).

The phrase *yāḏa'tā bînāh* is difficult, and Dhorme hardly succeeds in his interpretation, 'Do you understand the truth?' MT *bînāh* may possibly be a scribal corruption of *kumāh* ('its establishment'), that is, how it is set on its base (*māḵôn*), which would give an excellent parallel to *'êpōh hāyîṯā beyosedî-'ereṣ*

('Where were you when I was laying the foundations of the earth?'). If MT *bînāh* is retained it might mean the master intelligence that the Divine Declaration inculcates throughout.

The figure of the builder's line (v. 5b) recurs in Zech. 1.16. It was a technique in ancient building to mark the wall for level dressing by a cord rubbed with vermilion or some other marking substance, stretched taut between two measured marks. The cord was then pulled out and snapped back against the wall. Some ancient buildings in the archaeological sites in the Near East still show signs of the vermilion.

6. The 'bases' (*'ᵃḏānîm*) on which pillars are set are mentioned in Song 5.15. They denote also the socketted framework of the Tabernacle (Exod. 26.19). For the conception that the foundations of the earth were laid in the lower deep, the primaeval chaos of mud and water, which according to Mesopotamian cosmology was overcome by the god Marduk, earlier by the Sumerian Enlil, prior to the ordered creation of nature, cf. Ps. 24.2. The question in v. 6a implies time, place and forces beyond the power and even the knowledge of humans. Mention of the bases of the earth suggests the capstone, or 'cornerstone' (*'eḇen-happinnāh*; cf. *hā'eḇen hārō'šāh*, Zech. 4.7) in antithetic parallelism.

The verb *yārāh* (lit. 'to throw down') is used of the setting up of a standing stone (*maṣṣēḇāh*) by Laban in Gen. 31.51.

The laying of the corner-stone was accompanied by auspicious acclamation, for example, *ḥēn ḥēn* ('Grace! Grace!', Zech. 4.7). Acclamations and fanfares of trumpets and clanging of cymbals are noted at the foundation of the Second Temple (Ezra 3.10). Thus a positive antidote was provided against the possible influence of the evil eye or the curse of an enemy.

7. *rōn*, the infinitive construct, verbal noun of *rānan*, indicates the *rinnāh*, or 'cheer', appropriate to this auspicious occasion, as *wayyārî'û* indicates the raising of the *tᵉrû'āh*, the shout of acclamation, or triumph. Humanity not yet being created, acclamation is voiced by the stars (v. 7a), the divine 'beings' (*bᵉnê 'ᵉlōhîm*) (v. 7b). The apparent equation of these two indicates the conception that the stars were divine. Israelite orthodoxy had relegated the stars as manifestations of gods to the status of the supernatural retinue of God, either in his court (e.g. 1 Kgs 22.19) or in his armies (*ṣᵉḇā' haššāmayim*) (Jer. 33.22). The conception of the stars as manifestations of gods is illustrated in the myth from Ras Shamra (Gordon *UT* 52) celebrating the birth to El of the senior god of the Canaanite pantheon of the Venus-star in its twin manifestations *šḥr* ('Dawn') and *šlm* ('Completion [of day]'). The acclamation of God by the heavenly bodies recurs in Pss. 19.2 and 148.2-3.

8. MT *wayyāseḵ* ('and he has closed in') should be emended with T and V *mî sāḵ* ('who closed in?').

Ball's proposal, citing 5.22, to read *b*[e]*ḥôl* ('with sand') for MT *biḏ*[e]*lāṯayim*, is metrically feasible, but in view of the wealth of colourful mythological imagery in this passage, and particularly v. 10, it is extremely prosaic. Actually *d*[e]*lāṯayim* ('double doors') suggests the bolts and bar with which the triumphant Marduk confined his adversary Tiamat ('the lower deep') in the Babylonian cosmic myth, which culminated in creation (*ANET*, 67, ll. 139-40), aptly cited by Pope. The control of the sea is the expression of God's control over primaeval chaos, the theme of the Babylonian New Year festival at the vernal equinox, and of the Canaanite myth of the conflict of Baal and the unruly waters (Gordon *UT* 129; 137; 68; see our translation and commentary in *The Legacy of Canaan* 1965: 21-38), which probably related to the Canaanite New Year festival at the autumnal equinox, to which the same theme related in the Enthronement Psalms in the OT.

gîaḥ means 'to gush forth', hence Gihon, one of the rivers of the Garden of Eden (Gen. 2.13, J) and Gihon ('the Gusher'), the intermittent spring in the Qidron Valley at Jerusalem.

9. If the reference to the birth of the sea (v. 8b) and its being swaddled in Darkness (v. 9b) is mythological, as the personification and the context suggest, the source is so far unknown, like the birth of the world after travails in Ps. 90.2.

10. MT *wā'ešbōr 'ālāy ḥuqqî* cannot mean, to yield any sense, 'and I broke my prescribed bound over him'. We take the verb as a homonym of *šāḇar* ('to break'), cognate with Arab. *śabara* ('to estimate'), as suggested by Guillaume (1963: 123), and suggest the transposition of MT *'ālāyw* and *ḥuqqî*, reading with emendation only of the vowels, *wā'ešbōr ḥuqqê 'elyô* ('and gauged the bounds to which he might come up'). On the form of the verbal noun from *'ālāh* and other *l/h* verbs, see on 36.33. For the general conception, cf. Isa. 40.12.

11. *w*[e]*lō' tōsîp̄* should probably be omitted *metri causa*.

In MT *yāšîṯ big*[e]*'ôn* a possible emendation is the transposition of *t* and *b*, thus *yišbōṯ g*[e]*'ôn* ('pride will be stayed'), which has some support in S. Actually LXX and V indicate a reading *yištabbēr*, or *yiššāḇēr*, *g*[e]*'ôn* ('pride will be broken'). We decide the matter in favour of one of the latter alternatives, since we see a word-play between *šāḇar* ('gauged') in v. 10a and *šāḇar* ('broke') in v. 11b.

12. Now that *šaḥar* ('Dawn') is known as a Canaanite god from Ras Shamra (see above on v. 7), *bōqer* in v. 12a also may be understood as a god ('Day-Star'), as the verb 'ordered' (*ṣiwwîṯā*) suggests.

13. The figure here is possibly that of the Bedouin who sleep in their cloaks on the ground and in the morning shake the dust and the vermin out of them. The association of night and wickedness is universally familiar, and is the subject of the very striking passage on criminals in 24.13-17. We attempt to reproduce the figure by rendering MT *rᵉšāʿîm* as 'pests'; cf. Isa. 22.17.

14. In MT *ḥōmer ḥôṯām* Dhorme understands red medicinal earth, which Pliny attests as exported with trade-seals from Lemnos. Dhorme takes v. 14a to refer to the colour that earth assumes after sunrise. In view of the lapse of about half a millennium between the Book of Job and the time of Pliny, this is a hazardous interpretation. It is more likely to denote the distinctive contours revealed after sunrise as clay after sealing (*ḥōmer ḥôṯām*). Clay sealings are familiar in excavations in the Near East, for example, a clay stamp with a South Arabian sealing from ninth-century debris at Bethel, a relic probably of the caravan-borne incense trade with South Arabia (Van Beek and Jamme 1958: 9-16).

MT *wᵉyiṯyaṣṣᵉḇû* ('and they stood up') in association with a garment is not intelligible, and is generally taken after Ehrlich and Beer as a corruption of *wᵉtiṣṣāba'* ('and assume colour', lit. 'are dyed'). The variegated colours of clothing are illustrated in the patterns and coloured robes of semi-nomadic tribespeople in the panel depicting the party under the chief Absha, who brought eye-salve to Egypt, in a mural from a nineteenth-century tomb at Beni Hasan (*ANEP*, pl. 3).

15. This couplet is possibly transposed from after v. 13, probably a gloss prompted by the recollection of the passage on nocturnal criminals in 24.13-17.

zᵉrôaʿ rāmāh is an instance of the tendency in Classical Heb. to particularize a sin in a bodily member, e.g. 'haughty eyes', 'lying lips', etc. The phrase recalls the 'high hand' of Exod. 14.8 and Num. 15.30; 33.3.

16. In MT *niḇᵉḵê-yām* it has been proposed to emend to *miḇᵉḵê-yām*, but *nbk* parallel to *mqr* ('source') is attested in the Ras Shamra Legend of King Krt (Gordon *UT*, 216). The passage is reminiscent of the vain quest of Gilgamesh for immortality through the gates guarded by the scorpion-man on his way over the waters of death. *ḥēqer*, from the verb *ḥāqar*, denotes search and the object of search, and the ultimate source.

17. The verb *gālāh* in the particular context of v. 17a recalls *gly* in the Ras Shamra texts, which is used of crossing the threshold in the stock phrase *gly šd*, which we render 'clear the threshold' (Arab. *śaddu*[*n*], 'barrier'). The Arab. verb *jala*(*y*) means 'to emigrate', Heb. *gālāh*, 'to go into captivity'. In v. 17a the verb has rather the sense of 'reveal' as the parallel *rā'îṯā* (for MT *tir'eh*) and *hiṯbōnantā* and *yāḏaʿtā* in v. 18b indicate. As in the case of apparent synonyms in the same couplet in Job, there may be a word-play

between *ša'ar* in Classical Heb. in v. 17a ('gate') and *ša'ar*, cognate with Arab. *ṯaġaru*(*n*) ('frontier') in v. 17b (so Guillaume 1963: 124). Alternatively, as LXX suggests, v. 17b may mean 'Do the gate-keepers of the darkness fear you?', reading *wešô'arê ṣalmāweṯ* (or *wešô'arê māweṯ*, 'the gate-keepers of Death') *rā'îṯā* for MT *weša'arê ṣalmāwet tir'eh*. This might reflect the keepers of the various gates of the underworld, the scorpion-man of the Gilgamesh Epic or those encountered by Ishtar in her descent to the underworld (so Larcher, JB). If MT is correct there may be a particular reference to the seven gates in this Mesopotamian myth (*ANET*, 107).

18. *raḥaḇê-'āreṣ* recalls *irṣitu rapištu* ('the broad land', i.e. the underworld; cf. Isa. 14.9, and also in Ugaritic, cf. *rp'i'arṣ*, defunct kings in the underworld). For MT *kullāh* in v. 18b we prefer Duhm's emendation *kammāh* ('its extent') after LXX; cf. Arab. *kam* ('how much'), *kamîyatu*(*n*) ('quantity'). This is a better parallel to *raḥebê-'āreṣ* in v. 18a.

20. The parallelism indicates that for MT *tāḇîn* we should read *teḇî'ennā*, assuming the omission of *'* by haplography after *y* in the Old Heb. script.

21. The tone is sarcastic; Job is ironically treated as Wisdom, God's assessor (Prov. 8.22ff.), and the repository of the secrets of his purpose in creation. T and S lose the point in the irony in treating the verse as a question.

'āz denotes a decisive juncture in the argument, narrative or historical record, being a regular formula in the Books of Kings, in which Montgomery (1934) has detected the feature of annalistic sources. It may also mean, particularly with the preposition *min*, remote antiquity; cf. Isa. 44.8; 45.21, where it is parallel to *qedem*, Isa. 48.3, 5, 7, 8; Ps. 93.2, where *mē'āz* is parallel to *mē'ôlām*, and probably Ps. 46.2 (reading *mē'āz* for MT *me'ōḏ*) and Prov. 8.22. The last passage, referring to God's creation of Wisdom as the first of his works, is particularly relevant to the significance of *'āz* in the present passage.

22. *'ōṣerôṯ*, if it means 'treasures' of the elements, recalls Deut. 28.18; Jer. 10.13; Pss. 33.7; 135.7. The conception of keeping such elements for a visitation is familiar, as for example in Ben Sira 39.23ff., in the plagues of Egypt (hail); Ezek. 13.13 and specifically, in view of the reference to war, in the hailstorm in Josh. 10.11. This reference and the reference to war in v. 23b indicates the specific meaning 'arsenals', as in Jer. 50.25. The incidence of apparently the same word in parallelism is suspect. This suggests that *'ōṣerôṯ* in v. 22b is either a scribal corruption or a homonym. If the former, we might suggest *neṣurôṯ* ('hoards'). If *'ōṣerôṯ* in v. 22b is a homonym we may recall Baal's panoply in his royal seat in the mythological fragment RS 24.245, 11.6-7 (Virolleaud 1968: 557), including lightning and thunder, *'iṣr r't* ('bundles of thunderbolts'); so in v. 22b *'ōṣerôṯ bārāḏ* might mean 'concentrations of hail'.

24. Hoffmann assumed that LXX 'mist', for MT *'ôr*, suggested an original *'ēḏ* (cf. the problematic *'ēḏ* in Gen. 2.6); so Bickell, Duhm, Hontheim, Dhorme, Terrien, Pope, who takes it as an Akkadian loanword 'flood'. With regard for the parallelism with *qeḏem* ('east, wind, sirocco'), Ewald emended to *rûaḥ* (so Merx, Wright, Budde, Hölscher, Mowinckel, Fohrer). The corruption of *'ôr* to *rûaḥ* is graphically most unlikely. G.R. Driver (1955: 91-92) proposes the pointing *'ûr*, meaning 'heat', citing its incidence in Isa. 31.9; 44.16; 47.14; 50.11; Ezek. 5.2; and probably Zech. 14.6. Particularly relevant to the present passage is Arab. *'ûru(n)*, cited by Freytag, for the heat of the sirocco. We admit the possibility of the meaning of *ḥālaq*, 'to create' (cognate with Arab. *ḫalaqa*), which was regularly used by Ben Sira, but the parallelism with *yāp̄îṣ* (for MT *yāp̄ēṣ*), indicates that the meaning is 'distributed', as *'ê-zeh hadderek̲* suggests.

25. *peleḡ* is an irrigation channel in Ps. 1.3.

t^e'ālāh, with an Arab. cognate, is known as the channel from the spring of Gihon in Jerusalem in 2 Kgs 18.17, and as Hezekiah's tunnel in 2 Kgs 20.20.

šeṭep̄ is a flood; cf. Ezek. 13.11; 28.22, *gešem šôṭēp̄* ('rain that floods away').

qōlôṯ means 'thunder-peals' (see on 37.2), which suggests that the rare word *ḥ^azîz* is a concomitant of the thunder. The word is attested only here and at 28.26 and in Zech. 10.1, where *ḥ^azîzîm* is in parallelism with 'rain'. The association with thunder might suggest that the lightning is thought of as a thunderbolt, if we may connect the word etymologically with Arab. *ḫazza* ('to pierce'). But the association with rain in vv. 25a and 26, and in 28.6 and Zech. 10.1, indicates that it may be the thundershower, perhaps so described as 'piercing' the clouds or the ground after the long summer drought; cf. Chaucer's Prologue to the *Canterbury Tales*:

> Whan that Aprille with his shoures sote
> The Droughte of Merche hath perced to the rote.

The word may occur in the Ugaritic Legend of King Krt (Gordon *UT* Krt, 92-93) where the march of an army is described:

> *hlk l'alpm ḫẓẓ*
> *wlrbt kmyr*

Having with reserve translated this couplet,

> Marching in thousands, clanking,
> Yea, in tens of thousands as a dust-storm (J. Gray 1966a: 13, 41),

we now relate *ḫzz* to *ḥ^azîz* in these OT passages, and translate:

> Marching in thousands like a deluge,
> Yea, in tens of thousands like the early rains.

26. The rain on the desert is more impressive evidence of divine power and grace than in the settled lands with their regular seasonal rains. Here it may serve to remind the sufferer that the Providence of God is wider in scope than his personal experience.

27. *šō'āh ûm^{e}šō'āh* is found, again denoting the desert, in 30.3 and Zeph. 1.15. For the collocation masc. and fem. with the same meaning is designed to convey the sense of completeness; cf. Jer. 48.46,

> *'ôy-l^{e}ḵā mô'āḇ*
> *'āḇaḏ 'am-k^{e}môš*
> *kî-luqq^{e}ḥû bānêkā bašš^{e}ḇî*
> *ûḇ^{e}nōṯeyḵā baššîb^{e}yāh*

MT *môṣā' deše'* may be emended either to *miṣṣāmê'* ('from the thirsty land', cf. Isa. 44.3; so Budde, Wright, Duhm, Driver–Gray, Kissane, Pope) or *miṣṣiyyāh* ('from the dry land', so Beer, Dhorme, Hölscher, Tur-Sinai, Fohrer).

28. In *'eḡ^{e}lê-ṭal* the first word is a *hapax legomenon*, meaning according to an Arab. etymology (*'ajale*, 'to concentrate') 'concentrations of dew globules'.

29. *k^{e}p̄ōr*, parallel to *qeraḥ* ('ice') is in little doubt, meaning hoarfrost, to which manna is compared (Exod. 16.14). It is mentioned with snow as being sprinkled on the ground in Ps. 147.16.

30. *yiṯḥabbā'û* in the description of freezing seems to defy direct etymology. It may be either a textual corruption of *yiṯḥamm^e'û* in the square script or a dialectic variant, as Hitzig proposed (cf. *ḥem'āh*, 'coagulated milk or butter'), and accepted by Dhorme, Hölscher, Kissane, Pope. The interchange of the labials *b*, *p* and *m* is not uncommon in the Semitic dialects, for example, Heb. *šemeš*, Ugaritic *špš*, and in Ugaritic *ybmy*/*ymmt* (female relative, sister-in-law); cf. Moscati, Spitaler, Ullendorff, von Soden (1964: 25-26). Fohrer retains MT, and understands MT *kā'eḇen* as *k^{e}ḇā'eben*; cf. GKC, §118w, rendering 'the waters are hidden as in a stone'. *yiṯlakkāḏû* is used of the scales of the crocodile interlocking in 41.9 (EVV 23), literally 'grasping one another'. The Arabic cognate *lakada* may be cited, which means in the Vth Form 'to be congealed'. This was understood by the Targum of Job from Qumran (*yiṯqar^{e}ḥû*, 'freeze').

31. *kîmāh* is rendered 'Pleiades' in LXX and V. It is found in parallelism with *k^{e}sîl* ('the Presumptuous Fool', Orion) in 9.9 and Amos 5.8. It is probably connected etymologically with Arab. *kumu*(*n*) ('a herd of camels'). AV 'the sweet influence of the Pleiades', which were associated with consequent vegetation, is an example of imaginative interpretation, which uncritical acceptance of MT often involves. The word rendered 'sweet influences' is MT

ma'ᵃdannôṯ, which is known besides only in the passage describing the death of Agag (1 Sam. 15.32), who went *ma'ᵃdannōṯ*, which AV renders 'delicately', obviously influenced by the noun *'ēḏen* ('delight'); cf. *ma'ᵃdannîm*, which means 'delicacies' in Gen. 49.20 and Lam. 4.5. Actually, as indicated by the verb *qāšar* ('to bind'), the word should be read *ma'ᵃnaddôṯ* ('bonds', so LXX and T), both here and probably also at 1 Sam. 15.32; cf. the verb *'ānaḏ*, which means certainly 'to bind' in 31.36 and in Prov. 6.21, where it is parallel to *qāšar*. The parallelism and the verb *pāṯāḥ* (lit. 'to open', hence 'unloose') indicates that the unknown *mōšᵉḵôṯ* of MT should be read *mōsᵉrôṯ* ('bonds') (so S), but LXX renders 'fence', reading *misᵉḵaṯ*, which is feasible but inferior to *mōsᵉrôṯ*. The reference is not to Orion as a fettered giant, which is unknown in the ancient Near East, but, as Fohrer has observed, to fixed constellations, as 'the bonds' of the Pleiades also indicate.

32. *mazzārôṯ* is identified, and confused, with *mazzālôṯ* (lit. 'stations') of Babylonian astronomy, by T. These are known as the planets or signs of the Zodiac. 'In its time', however, indicates that as in the rest of the passage a particular constellation is denoted, as S and V understood. Michaelis associated the word with *nēzer*, rendering 'Diadem'. Dahood (1963c: 33) derived the word from *zûr*, which would suggest the spelling *mᵉzārôṯ*, presumably with reference to the Hyades. But *zûr* and its cognates mean 'to squeeze, or 'twist', the connection with 'flowing' for which Dahood contends being limited to the matter being pressed out of a wound (*māzôr*, e.g. Isa. 1.6; Jer. 30.13; Hos. 5.13). *mazzārôṯ* may be a term indicating a vocation, from the verb *māzar*, cognate with Arab. *mazara* used in the II Form meaning 'to fill up waterskins', a task which was women's work in the East, hence the feminine form in Heb. With the significance of the association with the rainy season, we retain the meaning Hyades. On the significance of *'āš*, which should probably be read for MT *'ayiš*, see on 9.9. This may be the Great Bear, called by the Arabs 'the Bier', *'al-wa'śa(tu)*. *'al-bāneyhā* (lit. 'over and above her sons') suggests Arab. *banātu 'l-wa'śa(ti)* (lit. 'the daughters of the Bier'), denoting the three stars in the tail of the Great Bear.

33. The parallel *tāśîm mišṭārôṯ* (for MT *mišṭārô*) suggests that MT *yāḏa'tā* here may be the cognate of Arab. *wada'a* ('to lay down, deposit'), so here 'Have you imposed (the laws...)?' Duhm proposed that MT *yāḏa'tā* might be pointed *yidda'tā* and rendered 'Have you made known?' But that would demand another object, as in v. 12. We assume corruption of *yā'aḏtā* ('have you appointed').

Final *w* in MT *mišṭārô*, but with no immediate antecedent, as a pronominal suffix, may be the corruption of an original *m* in the Old Heb. script. The root *šāṭar* is known in Classical Heb. through the participle, which is used of 'officers' who see that rules are carried out (Exod. 5.14; Deut. 1.15; Josh. 1.10; 3.3; Prov. 6.7). Aram. *šᵉṭārā'* ('a document') is derived rather from Akk.

šaṭaru ('to write'). Arab. *miśṭaratu*(*n*) means a paper-ruler, hence our translation 'rules'.

34. As the association with a deluge (*šip̄ᵉ'at̲-mayim*) in v. 34b and the lightning in v. 35a indicates, there is *double entendre* in *qôlᵉk̲ā* meaning 'voice' and 'thunder'.

On *šip̄ᵉ'āh* ('abundance', 'overflowing'), see on 22.11.

In v. 34b, LXX alone of the ancient versions renders the verb 'that they may obey you', evidently reading *ta'ᵃnûk̲ā* for MT *tᵉk̲assekkā*. This is accepted by Duhm and Mowinckel; cf. Terrien ('respond to you'). Fohrer suggests the reading *tᵉk̲assehā* ('cover it', i.e. the earth). We accept this sense of the passage, but suggest that an original *tᵉk̲assehā* was corrupted in the Old Heb. script to *tᵉk̲assekkā*. Possibly, however, LXX has preserved the correct reading, MT being occasioned by scribal familiarity with 22.11b, with which this colon is verbally identical.

36. This couplet has caused great trouble to interpreters both ancient and modern. T and Jewish scholars were evidently familiar with a word *ṭuḥôt̲* meaning 'kidneys', since they so translate *ṭuḥôt̲* here and in Ps. 51.8, where it is parallel to *sāt̲ûm* ('secret'), the only other place where it is used in the OT. This would suggest that the couplet is an ironical rhetorical question in parenthesis to the context, hence RV:

> Who hath put wisdom in the inward parts,
> Or who hath given understanding to the mind?

It has been suggested that MT *śek̲wî* in v. 36b may be a corruption of *kᵉsîl* ('fool').

The bewildering variety of interpretations of *ṭuḥôt̲* and *śekwî* in the versions is notorious; for example, for *ṭûḥôt̲* 'skill in weaving', the word evidently being derived from *ṭāwāh* ('to spin') (LXX), 'kidneys' as the seat of reflection (T, V), 'secretly' (S); and, for *śek̲wî* 'variegated work', possibly influenced by the doubtful *śᵉk̲iyyôt̲* ('pictures') in Isa. 2.16 (LXX), 'heart'(1st T), 'cock' (2nd T, V), 'understanding' (S).

Commentators therefore found this very much an open question and there is no lack of conjectures. It must suffice to give only those which are most feasible.

ṭuḥôt̲ has been taken to refer to celestial phenomena, which the context might possibly suggest, signifying perhaps 'those that are overcast' (lit. 'smeared'), so clouds, in which case 'wisdom' could only refer to the clouds as presages of the weather. In this connection Arab. *ṭaḥā'u*(*n*) is cited (Hirzel). Another suggestion is that *ṭuḥôt̲* is a cognate of Arab. *ṭāḥa* ('to wander') and means 'meteors' (Schultens). For *śek̲wî*, the Aram. *śᵉk̲āh* is adduced to support the meaning 'consideration', the meaning given in S.

The explanation of this variety of interpretation in the versions is probably that both are foreign loanwords. The former is probably Egypt. *ḏḥwtj* ('the Ibis'), the bird of Thoth, the god of letters and wisdom (so Hoffmann, Dhorme, Steinmann, Larcher, Fohrer).

Pope adopts Hoffmann's suggestion that *śeḵwî* is connected with the Coptic name for the planet Mercury, and takes the reference of *ṭuḥôṯ* to be Thoth. Such a reference is unlikely in a sober work of Jewish philosophy, especially in the divine speech. Mowinckel also connects *ṭuḥôṯ* and *śeḵwî* respectively with the planets Mercury and Saturn; cf. *sakkûṯ*, for MT *sikkûṯ* in Amos 5.26. *śeḵwî* 'the cock' is familiar in Late Heb. and Aram., as the 2nd T suggests; being according to Dalman a foreign loanword. Both birds were accredited with prescience, the ibis of the Nile floods, and the cock of the rain (Jaussen 1924: 574ff.).

The wisdom of the cock in being able to distinguish between the night and day was respected among the Jews, and is explicitly mentioned in the statutory morning prayer. The domestic hen, bred from the Indian game fowl, was introduced to Western Asia via Persia at the end of the seventh century BCE. A fine figure of a fighting cock is known on the seal of Yaazaniah from Tell en-Nasbeh (Mizpah) at the end of the Jewish monarchy in 586 BCE (*ANEP*, pl. 277)

37. In v. 37b the reference to 'the waterskins of the sky' (*niḇᵉlê šāmayim*) supports the meaning 'tilts' for *yaškîḇ* (cf. Arab. *śakaba* and the name of the constellation Aquarius *śākibu 'lmā'i*). This indicates that *sippēr* in v. 37a has not its usual meaning in Classical Heb. 'to count' or 'tell', as G.B. Gray, Dhorme, Hölscher, Kissane, Mowinckel, Weiser, Fohrer, Pope and Terrien among modern commentators assume (cf. NEB 'to marshal the clouds'; and *hassōp̄ēr śar haṣṣāḇā' hammaṣbi' 'et-'am hā'āreṣ*, 2 Kgs 25.19). G.R. Driver (1955: 92) takes the word as a dialectical variant of Arab. *safara*, which is used of clearing the clouds from the sky or of women unveiling the face. Actually a close correspondence, and one which gives a more satisfactory meaning in the context, is with Arab. *safara*, which means in the IVth Form 'to empty out a vessel', which we accept. The reference to the decanting of the clouds 'with wisdom' refers to the regular rains in due season, the heavy 'early rains' (*yôreh*) and the 'latter rains' (*malqôš*).

38. *ṣeqeṯ* is the infinitive construct and *mûṣāq* the Hophal participle of *yāṣaq* ('to pour out'). The general meaning of *rᵉḡāḇîm* ('clods') is not in doubt, thanks to the parallel *'āp̄ār* ('dust'). We are more doubtful about its association with the only other instance of the word in the OT at 21.33, where we have emended MT *rigᵉḇê naḥal*; see Commentary *ad loc.*

39. *ṭerep̄* associated with *lāḇî'* ('lion') indicates that *tāṣûḏ* means 'to hunt', but read as *tᵉṣayyēḏ*, which is graphically feasible, it would mean 'provide food',

which *ṭerep̄* might mean (e.g. 24.5; Ps. 111.5; Prov. 31.15; Mal. 3.10) as well as its more usual meaning 'prey'. This might be supported by the parallel verb *t*ᵉ*mallē'* ('fill'). We prefer the former meaning, though admitting a *double entendre*.

In v. 39b *ḥayyāh*, probably 'appetite', is to be noted as the sole example of the word in this sense in the OT. There may be the nuance of 'sustenance', however; cf. Arab. *muḥāyātu*(*n*) ('nourishment given to young children').

41. *ṣayiḏ* denotes generally provision for a journey (e.g. Gen. 42.25; 45.21; Exod. 12.39; Josh. 1.11; 9.11; 1 Sam. 22.10), but is here used generally.

Observing that 'wandering' (*yiṯ'û*) suits the old beasts rather than the young, Hölscher assumes a lacuna of a colon before v. 41c (so also Fohrer). Pope takes the verb in a psychological sense, rendering 'frantic for lack of food', which is possible, though when used in a physical sense *tā'āh* has an ethical connotation. It means in the Niphal 'to stagger' in 12.25, as indicated in LXX, and in Isa. 19.14; 28.17, where it is used of the staggering of a drunken man. Though 'staggering' is not quite unsuitable for young birds, Hölscher and Fohrer may well be right in assuming a lacuna in this verse of three cola in a predominant arrangement of bicola.

In v. 41b the conception of the young ravens crying to God' (*'el-'ēl*) is strange. *'el-'ēl* may be intended to suggest the woeful cry *'al*ᵉ*lay* ('Woe is me!', Job 10.15), if indeed it is not a corruption of that interjection.

Job 39 and 40.25-30 (EVV 41.1-6)

THE DIVINE DECLARATION: PART II

Chapter 39

1. 'Have you appointed[1] the time for the ibexes to give birth,
Keeping watch over the calving of hinds?
2. Counting the months of their pregnancy,
Do you know when they shall bring forth,
3. Crouching down and bringing forth[2] their young,
Shooting out their foetus?[3]
4. Their young ones thrive and grow up;[4]
They go forth and do not come back.

5. Who let the wild ass go free?
Yea, who loosed the bands of the brayer,
6. Whose home I have made the steppe,
And the salt-land his haunts?
7. He laughs at the tumult of the city,
He does not listen to the shouts of the driver;
8. He spies out[5] the mountains as his pastures,
And searches after every green thing.

9. Will the wild ox be willing to serve you?
Or spend the night by your manger?
10. Will you bind a yoke on his massive bulk?
Will he draw your furrow straight in the plain?
11. Could you trust his great strength,
Or leave to him what you have toiled for?
12. Would you rely on him to come back,[7]
And gather your crop to the threshing floor?[8]

13. The wing of the ostrich is weak
In comparison with the wing of the stork or the hawk.[9]
14. Nay, she leaves her eggs on the ground,
And neglects them in the dust,
15. And forgets[10] that a foot may crush them,
And a wild beast trample on them.
16. Her young she treats harshly[11] as none of hers;[12]
Her toil is in vain, she has no chick.[13]
17. For God has made her forget wisdom
And has given her no share of understanding.[14]

18. When occasion arises in running[15] she spreads her tail-feathers,
Laughing at the horse and his rider.

19. Do you give the horse strength?
Do you clothe its neck with its mane?
20. Lo! you may send him hurtling[16] on his way like locusts,
His glorious snorting spelling terror.
21. He paws[17] in the plain, exulting;[18]
In strength he goes out to meet the weapons;
22. He laughs at fear and is not dismayed,
And he turns not back from the sword.
23. [19]The quiver may twang about him,
The flashing spear and javelin,
24. Quivering and excited he swallows the ground,
His whole trust in the sound[20] of the trumpet.
25. To the accompaniment[21] of the trumpets he neighs Aha!
And from afar he scents the battle,
The thunder of the captains and the war-cry.

26. Is it by your wisdom that the hawk takes wing,
That he spreads his wings to the Southwind?
27. Is it at your command that the vulture towers,
And that the falcon[22] makes his nest so high?
28. The rock is his habitation, and his night-roost
Is upon the crag of the rock and the fastness.
29. From there he spies out food,
His eyes scan afar.
30. His young[23] gulp up[24] blood,
And where the slain are, there is he.

40.25-30 (EVV 41.1-6)

25. Can you draw out[25] Leviathan with a hook?
[26]Or contend with him with a line in despite of his teeth?
26. Can you put a bridle[27] on his snout,
Or pierce his jaws with a hook?
27. Will he make many supplications to you?
Or speak softly to you?
28. Will he make a compact with you
That you should take him for a servant for ever?
29. Could you make a pet of him like a bird,
And put him on a string for your little girls?
30. Will the wholesale merchants haggle over him?
Will they divide him among the retailers?

Textual Notes to Chapter 39 and 40.25-30

1. Reading *yā'aḏtā* for MT *yāḏa'tā*. See Commentary *ad loc.*
2. Reading *tᵉp̄allēṭnā* for MT *tᵉp̄allaḥnā.*
3. Reading *ḥaḇᵉlêhen* for MT *ḥeḇᵉlêhem.*

4. Omitting *babbār* as a dittograph and corruption after *yirbû*, *metri causa*.
5. Reading *yāṯûr* for MT *y^eṯûr*.
6. Reading *h^aṯiqšōr nîr ba'^aḇōṯô / 'im-y^eśaddēḏ bā'ēmeq ḥ^arāṯêḵā*. See Commentary *ad loc*.
7. Reading *yāšûḇ* (Kethib) for MT *yāšîḇ* (Qere).
8. Reading *w^ezar'^aḵā ḡornāh* for MT *zar'eḵā w^egorn^eḵā*.
9. Reading *k^enap̄ y^e'ēnîm ne'^elāzāh / 'im-'eḇraṯ ḥ^asîḏāh w^enēṣāh*. See Commentary *ad loc*.
10. Reading *w^eṯiškaḥ* for MT *wattiškaḥ*.
11. Reading *taqšîaḥ* with two Heb. MSS for MT *hiqšîaḥ*.
12. Reading *k^elō'-lāh* for MT *l^elō-' lāh*.
13. Reading *peraḥ* for MT *pāḥaḏ*.
14. Verses 14-17 are possibly a secondary expansion. See Commentary *ad loc*.
15. Reading *b^emērôṣ* for MT *bammārôm*.
16. Reading *hēn tar'îšennû* for MT *h^aṯar'îšennû*.
17. Reading *yaḥpîr* with LXX, S and V for MT *yaḥp^erû*.
18. Reading *yāśîś* for MT *w^eyāśîś*.
19. Reading *tāronnāh 'ašpāh*. See Commentary *ad loc*.
20. Reading *b^eqôl* for MT *qôl*.
21. Reading *b^eyaḏ* for MT *b^eḏê*.
22. Reading *w^eḵî ḵîḏôr yārîm qinnô* after 11QtargJob. See Commentary *ad loc*.
23. Reading *'ep̄rōḥāyw* for MT *'ep̄rōḥāw*.
24. Reading *y^ela'l^e'û* for MT *y^e'al^e'û*. See Commentary *ad loc*.
25. Reading *h^aṯimšōḵ* with one Heb. MS for MT *timšōḵ*.
26. Reading *ûḇ^eḥeḇel tiškeh 'al šinnāy* for MT *ûḇ^eḥeḇel tašqîa' l^ešōnô*, assuming corruption of *h* to *y* in the Old Heb. script in MT *tašqîa'* and the omission of *y* in *šinnāyw*, resulting in MT *l^ešōnô* after the wrong division of *'al šinnāyw*. See Commentary on 40.25-30.
27. Reading *zāmām* with 11QtargJob for MT *'aḡmôn*.

Commentary on Chapter 39; 40.25-30 (EVV 41.1-6)

1. MT *yāḏa'tā*, as suggested by *tišmōr* in v. 1b, would, if correct, mean 'take note of' (cf. Amos 3.2), in which case *'ēṯ* might be a dittograph of the last two consonants of *yāḏa'tā*. But the reference to the control of the breeding of the ibex in v. 2b indicates that it is not a case of knowing when the beasts would cast their young, but of being able to arrange it as in the case of domestic cattle, hence *yā'aḏtā 'ēṯ* should be read 'have you appointed the time?' This having been arranged, the counting of the months of gestation and the knowing of the time of birth (v. 2) would naturally follow; hence in v. 2b we should retain MT *w^eyāḏa'tā*. The author probably exploits the opportunity of word-play, so congenial to him, between *yā'aḏ* and *yāḏa'*.

The ibex, *yā'ēl* (Arab. *wa'lu*[*n*]), mentioned besides only twice in the OT (1 Sam. 24.3; Ps. 104.18), where it is associated with the rocks in desert regions (1 Sam. 24.3), was apparently almost as rare in the time of the author of Job as at the present day, where Doughty notes it as known, but as a rarity, in the Hejaz.

3. *kāra'* (lit. 'to bow down') describes the posture of women in childbirth in the ancient East; cf. 1 Sam. 4.19 and in the Ras Shamra texts, e.g. Gordon *UT* 75.I, 26-27, where the root is not *kāra'* but a form of *brk*, a denominative verb from *brkm* ('knees').

t^epallēṭnā (for MT *t^epallaḥnā*), with the direct object *yal^edêhen*, is found of giving birth in 21.10, and is read by most modern commentators.

In v. 3b *ḥab^elêhem* should be read for MT *ḥeb^elêhem*. This word used to be taken as 'birth-pangs', but it is now recognized that it means 'their young', a fitting parallel to *yal^edêhen* in v. 3a and the object of the verb in v. 3b; cf. Arab. *ḥablu*(*n*) ('foetus') and *ḥibbēl* ('to conceive') cited by Dhorme in Ps. 7.15 and Song 8.5. Fohrer, however, retains MT, translating 'they are free from their birth-pangs'.

4. In v. 4a *babbār* ('in the open country') (cf. Arab. *bariyatu[n]*, ['desert']), is probably to be omitted, *metri causa*, as a dittograph after *yirbû*, though it is attested in all versions.

yaḥl^emû has an Arab. cognate ('to be healthy'), but in view of the meaning of this verb in the V form, 'to put on flesh', this may be the meaning here, especially in conjunction with *yirbû*. The English 'thrive' matches the ambiguity of the Heb. word in this respect.

5. *šillaḥ ḥopšî* is a legal phrase, used of release from domestic servitude (Deut. 15.12ff.). Dhorme sees an apt figure here of the wild ass, visualized as a tame ass set free.

'ārûḏ is an Aram. word, one of the many instances in Job of an Aram. word used as a synonym of a Heb. word in parallelism. It is an appellative, 'the brayer' (cf. Arab. *ġarada*, 'to bray'), and is actually used of the wild ass by the Arab poet Imru 'al-Qais. In the Babylonian Talmud, *Berakot* 9b, *'ārûḏ* is compared and contrasted with the ass (*ḥ^amôr*) as the wolf with the dog, in discussing the time to recite the Shema' when it is sufficiently light to distinguish the one from the other.

6. *m^elēḥāh* recalls *'ereṣ m^elēḥāh*, parallel with (*'ereṣ*...) *lō' ṯēšēḇ* ('the uninhabited land'), as the haunt of the wild ass in Jer. 17.6. Etymologically 'the salty land' as contrasted with the fruitful land; for example, Ps. 107.34 denotes the crust of chemical deposits drawn from the soil and deposited on the surface in evaporation. Such soil must be washed out, 'bleached', before agriculture is possible. This may be observed in the south part of Iraq, where Van Beek (1962: 13) compares the salty deposit to hoar-frost, and observes that '2½ per cent salt means no wheat, 1 per cent no barley and 2 per cent no dates'.

7. *hāmôn* signifies both the sound, as here, and the number of a crowd (e.g. Judg. 4.7; 1 Sam. 14.16; etc.). It describes the familiar turmoil of the city, as here, in Isa. 32.14.

t^esu'ôṯ, which means 'shouting' here, means the din of thunder in 36.29.

nôḡēś, which means 'task-master' in 3.18, here means the driver of a beast, the Arab. cognate of the Heb. verb being used to describe the beating of game.

8. *tûr* means perhaps 'scours'; cf. *'an^ešê tārîm*, 'travellers' or 'itinerant merchants' in 1 Kgs 10.15, but the parallel with *dāraš* indicates the meaning 'spies out', as in the reconnaissance of Palestine in Num. 10.32; 13.12, 16ff.; 14.6; cf. Judg. 1.23 (so Theod., T, V).

9. The verb *'āḇāh* is emphatic, expressing willing consent.

rêm is spelled *r^e'ēm* in Deut. 33.17, which is more usual. Aq, LXX and V render 'rhinoceros', hence AV 'unicorn'. Deuteronomy 33.17 indicates that a two-horned beast is indicated, the wild-ox, which, unlike the rhinoceros, was found in western Asia in historical times. The killing of one *rîmu* in Syria was considered sufficient of an exploit to be noted by Tiglath-pileser, an indication of the rarity and ferocity of the beast. A variant of the noun may be Ugaritic *r'im*. The strength and ferocity of the beast is proverbial in Num. 23.22; 24.8; Pss. 22.22 (EVV 21); 29.6. It is suggested that the conception of the unicorn arose from the representation of the animal with its horns in profile, as on the Ishtar Gate at Babylon (*ANEP*, pl. 760; Godbey 1939). *'āḇûs* ('manger') is comparatively rare in the OT; cf. Isa. 1.3; Prov. 14.4.

10. The repetition of *r^e'ēm* in v. 10a is doubtful and we follow LXX in reading *nîr* ('yoke'), assuming scribal corruption of *n* to *m* and *y* to *'* in the Old Heb. script and metathesis, reading *h^atiqšōr nîr*. We suspect also MT *^aḇōṯô*, which LXX understood as 'ropes' (cf. Isa. 5.18), also in association with 'yoke'. The pronominal suffix suggests rather that *'^aḇōṯ* is singular, the verbal noun of *'āḇāh* ('to be thick'), giving a reading *h^aṯiqšōr nîr ba'^aḇōṯô* ('Will you bind a yoke on his massive bulk?'). We would explain *b^e* as misplaced in MT after *ṭelem*, a gloss on an Aram. word for 'furrow' in v. 10b.

Both LXX and 11QtargJob understood *y^eśaddēd* not as 'harrowing', unknown until comparatively recently in Palestine (Dalman 1932: II, 189-91) but as 'ploughing'. The verb is found only here and in Isa. 28.24 and Hos. 10.11, being associated with ploughing in both passages. The verb may be cognate with Arab. *śadda* ('to be straight'), hence in the IInd Form 'to make straight', an apt predicate of an object 'furrows', which we would find in the Aram. *ḥ^arāṯêḵā*, of which we suggest that MT *'aḥ^arêḵā* ('after you'), quite the opposite of ploughing, was a scribal corruption. This word (cf. Syr. *ḥrat*, 'to spit', Ugar. *ḥrt*, 'to score'), we suggest, was that on which MT *ṭelem* in v. 10a, found here neither in LXX nor the Qumran targum, was a gloss. Thus for v. 10b we propose the reading *'im-y^eśaddēḏ bā'ēmeq ḥ^arāṯêḵā* ('Will he draw your furrows straight in the plain?').

11. In v. 11b *yᵉgîʿᵉḵā* is ambiguous, meaning primarily 'labour', and secondarily 'that for which one labours'. The former sense might be supported by the parallel colon v. 11a, the reliance of the farmer on his beast for the preparation of the crop being emphasized. The colon, on the other hand, might be taken with what follows, in which case *yᵉgîaʿ* would refer to the produce, the corn to be brought in to the threshing-floor and threshed by the beast.

12. In v. 12a we prefer the Kethib *yašûḇ* to Qere *yāšîḇ*, and in v. 12b we read the locative *gornāh* ('to the threshing-floor') for MT *wᵉgornᵉḵā*.

13. The passage vv. 13-18 is a *crux interpretum*, vv. 14-18 being noticed in Origen's Hexapla as lacking in the original LXX, which was then supplemented from the original of Theodotion's translation. The transliterations of *neʿᵉlāsāh*, *ḥᵃsîḏāh* and *wᵉnōṣāh* of MT in LXX, S and A, which probably also derived from Theodotion's translation, attest the Heb. text, but indicate a failure to understand it. The same may be said of the phrase *pteryx terpomenon* ('the wing of the joyful ones'), which is a literalism with no attempt to understand the meaning in the context, like the 'wing of those who praise' of Aq, S and T. None of the versions understands *neʿᵉlāsāh*, which is a Niphal participle. Aq, V and T, however, understand *ḥᵃsîḏāh* and *nōṣāh* as respectively 'stork' (cf. Lev. 11.19; Ps. 104.17; Jer. 8.7; Zech. 5.9) and 'hawk' (cf. *nēṣ*, Lev. 11.16). *'eḇrāh* caused some trouble to translators, and is omitted in Aq. Sym understands *ḥᵃsîḏāh* as 'stork', but takes *nōṣāh* as 'feathers', which is possible (cf. Ezek. 17.3 and Ass. *nāṣû*, cited by Dhorme), and renders *'im-'eḇrāh* as 'if (the stork hugs its) feathers' or possibly 'does (the stork hug its) feathers?', which is another unintelligible literalism. From the few reliable hints of the versions, translations and interpretation of modern commentators have been many and various, and none quite convincing. The sequel makes it certain that the ostrich is described (so V), which suggests the emendation of *rᵉnānîm* to *yᵉʿēnîm*. The speed of the ostrich on the ground (v. 18) contrasts with its inability to use its wings to fly. This has suggested that *'eḇrāh* means 'wing', which is possible, especially as *kᵉnap̄* stands in the parallel position in v. 13a; and it is so taken by Dhorme, whose translation may be cited as illustrative of the attempt to preserve the conventional meaning of MT, and as the basis of our reinterpretation:

> The wing of the ostrich is joyous,
> (The ostrich) is the possessor of a graceful wing and plumage.

Here Dhorme takes *ʿālas* in *neʿᵉlāsāh* as a byform of *ʿālaṣ* or *ʿālaz*, and points MT *'im* as *'ēm* (lit. 'mother'), which introduces a conspicuous feature in a nickname, as in Arabic. The rendering of *'eḇrāh ḥᵃsîḏāh* as 'graceful wing' is scarcely felicitous, since *ḥāsîḏ* denotes a moral and not a physical quality. If instead of Dhorme's 'graceful' we admit the meaning of *ḥᵃsîḏāh* as 'stork' with Aq, V and T, MT *nōṣāh* would have to be pointed *nēṣāh*, meaning 'hawk', as those versions understood. Verse 14, however, raises a difficulty, the conjunction *kî* introducing the theme of the callousness and stupidity of the ostrich in leaving her eggs to hatch in the sand at the mercy of the feet of wild beasts. This suggests either that a passage has dropped out or that v. 13 is corrupt. Van Hoonacker (1913: 420ff.) proposed to read for MT *'im 'eḇrāh ḥ^a^sîḏāh, 'ēm 'āḇ^e^rāh ḥ^a^sîḏāh* ('a mother who has lost all tenderness'), which would admirably introduce the sequel. In this case, however, MT *nōṣāh* would have to be explained either as an intrusion, perhaps a dittograph of *bēṣêhā* in v. 14 or rather a corruption of *lāneṣaḥ*.

Hence after van Hoonacker the following reconstruction is possible:

k^e^nap̄ y^e^'ēnāh ne'^e^lāzāh	The wing of the ostrich is weak—
'ēm 'āḇ^e^rāh ḥ^a^sîḏāh lāneṣaḥ	A mother who has quite lost all tenderness.

While agreeing with the sequel, however, this reconstruction of v. 13b has no relation to v. 13a. We suggest that the meaning of the passage has been bedevilled by the scribal error, through dictation, of *'im* for *'im* as the preposition of comparison, and of the misunderstanding of *ne'^e^lāsāh*, a corruption or the Heb. rendering of an Arab. *'alaza*, 'to be weak' (so Guillaume 1963: 125). Guillaume proposed the rendering:

Is the wing of the ostrich weak,
Or strong like the stork or the hawk?

Guillaume takes Heb. *'eḇrāh* as a verb *'āḇ^e^rāh*; cf. the adjective *'abbîr* ('the strong one', 24.22; 34.20; 1 Sam. 21.8; Judg. 5.22; Isa. 46.12; etc.). The great difficulty here is the want of a preposition of comparison before 'the stork and the hawk'. This suggests a modification, which is in our opinion more feasible:

k^e^nap̄ y^e^'ēnāh ne'^e^lāzāh	The wing of the ostrich is weak
'im-'eḇraṯ ḥ^a^sîḏāh w^e^nēṣāh	In comparison with the wing of the stork and the hawk.

In the various passages on the beasts the emphasis is laid on one characteristic. Here without doubt it is the speed of the ostrich that contrasts so strongly with the weakness of its wings. This suggests that v. 13 was originally followed by v. 18 and that vv. 14-17 was a later expansion, possibly from a passage which described the traditional characteristic of the ostrich abandoning her clutch and even her young. Fohrer (1989: 514f.) explains the source of the tradition as the habit of the ostrich of laying an egg every two days and covering the clutch with sand for protection against the strong sun until it is ready for normal incubation, while its abandoning of its young is through self-preservation and reliance on its speed, possibly to distract whatever threatens, as our native game birds which feign a broken wing. *r^e^nānîm* is a *hapax legomenon* in the OT, hence the emendation *y^e^'ēnîm* proposed by Hoffmann (so Budde, Duhm *et al.*); cf. Lam. 4.3; Job 30.29, *b^e^nôṯ ya'^a^nāh* (lit. 'daughters of greed'), referring to the voracious and rough feeding of the ostrich. Fohrer (1989), retaining MT *r^e^nānim*, refers to the raucous cries of the bird.

The hawk (*nēṣāh*) is attested in the masc. in v. 26, where the reference is probably to its migration. This would suit the reference to the stork, the endurance of both migrants of the wing contrasting very strongly with the weakness of the wing of the ostrich, which cannot even fly.

14. The parallelism with *ta'ᵃzōḇ* in v. 14a suggests that *tannîḥēm* ('leaves them') may be read for MT *tᵉḥammēm* ('incubates them'). Tur-Sinai may be near the truth in seeing in *tᵉḥammēm* the intensive form of an Aram. verb *ḥᵃmāh* ('to neglect').

15. *zûr* is used of wringing out fluid, for example water from a fleece (Judg. 6.3, 8), so here of breaking eggs. *dûš* is used of threshing in Amos 1.3, originally done by the trampling of animals.

16. *qāšāḥ* is used in the OT only here and at Isa. 63.17. Its meaning 'to be hard, harsh' is in no doubt; cf. Arab. *qaśaḥa* ('to be firm, hard, tough').

'Her toil' (*yᵉḡî'āh*) is the laying of the eggs.

'She has no fear' (MT *bᵉlî-pāḥaḏ*) is strange and unexpected, and is barely explicable in the sense 'without anxiety'; for which *paḥaḏ* ('terror') is too strong. In spite of the unanimous support of the versions we would question MT, proposing either *peraḥ* (cf. Arab. *farḫu[n]*) either as the verbal noun 'hatching' or as 'chick', or that *paḥaḏ* is used here in the sense of 'kin' (cf. Albright 1957: 248).

18. In MT *kā'ēṯ bammārôm tamrî'* the ancient versions attest MT, but differ in interpretation, largely owing to unfamiliarity with *tamrî'*. Dhorme attempts to support MT in assuming that the sense of 'to rise up' is the primary sense from which *mārāh* ('to rebel') was developed. But to argue back from *mārāh* ('to rebel') to the assumed sense of an unknown verb is questionable philology. The verb has been connected with Arab. *mara(y)* ('to beat'), either the air with the wings by the ostrich when running (so Hölscher, G.B. Gray, Kissane, Mowinckel, Fohrer), or the beating of the ground with the feet. In the latter case *bammārôm* would require emendation; hence Hitzig and Duhm proposed *kā'ēṯ bᵉmērôṣ tamrî'* ('when occasion arises in running she stamps the ground'), which implies only the scribal error of *m* for *s* in MT *bammarôm* in the Old Heb. script. Certainly the implication in v. 18b suggests some reference to running in v. 18a, though we may still doubt the meaning proposed for *tamrî'*. Tur-Sinai and Pope after Wetzstein read MT and assume a technical hunting term in *tamrî'*, referring to the spreading of the tail-feathers of the ostrich in running; they cite in support for Wetzstein a passage from the Arab poet Rashid (see Pope). In support of this interpretation, Tur-Sinai adduces the noun *mur'āh* in Lev. 1.16, which refers to the rump of a sacrificial pigeon, which is taken off with the tail-feathers and thrown away as refuse. The connection at the verb *tamrî'* with *mur'āh* would admirably explain the Hiphil

of the verb, which would thus be denominative. Another possible reading which may be admitted is that of Wright and Budde, *k*e *'ēṯ bō' mōrîm* for MT *kā'ēṯ bammārôm*, meaning 'when the archers come'. We should still prefer Tur-Sinai's interpretation of *tamrî'* with the emendation of *bammārôm* to *b*e*mērôṣ*. The merit of the reading of Wright and Budde is that it gives the occasion of the running of the ostrich, and offers a concrete picture in parallelism with 'the horse and his rider', which the running of the ostrich implies. The whole point of the passage, however, demands a more explicit reference to running, and so we prefer the reading of Hitzig and Duhm, with Tur-Sinai's interpretation of *tamrî'*. A propos of v. 18b, Xenophon (*Anabasis* 1.5.2) cites an actual case where ostriches outstripped horses. For this whole passage Pope has assembled interesting and informative data, both scientific and popular, on the habits of the ostrich.

19. The conception of the clothing of the horse's neck with thunder, MT *ra'am* (so AV), is highly poetical, but philologically absurd since *ra'am* denotes strictly the noise of the thunder. Theod., Jerome in his commentary and V, as well as certain modern commentators, take this as a reference to neighing, but in this case the verb 'clothe' is not appropriate.

The concealed word is obviously 'mane', for which LXX has *phobos* ('fear'), a corruption of an original *phobē* ('mane'). The word in this sense is a *hapax legomenon* in the OT, from which an analogy is adduced from Arab. *'umm ri'mi(n)* ('mother of a mane'), that is, a hyena (so Koehler and Baumgartner 1952).

20. The verb *rā'aš* means generally 'to quake' or 'quiver'; in v. 24 it describes the vibration of the hurtling javelin. In Nah. 3.2 it describes the violent motion of chariot-wheels; cf. Jer. 10.22; 47.3, where it evidently describes the rattling chariots, and Job 41.21, where it describes the hurtling of a spear. As expressing both motion and sound, we opt for the translation of *tar'îšennû* ('send him hurtling on his course'). The comparison of the chariot- or cavalry-charge to locusts (here probably collective singular) is probably an adaptation of the comparison of locusts to a chariot- or cavalry-charge in Joel 2.4ff., where the comparison is in respect of motion as well as sound. In the present passage the point of comparison may be the irresistible onward charge of the warhorse.

21. MT *yaḥp*e*rû* might be intelligible, meaning 'digs', but it is probably better emended to *yaḥpîr* and taken as a denominative Hiphil of a verb cognate with Arab. *ḥāfiru*(*n*) ('hoof'), cited by G.B. Gray.

bā'ēmeq is ambiguous. It might denote an open valley, or plain, most suitable for the movement of chariotry or cavalry; cf. Isa. 22.7, 'your choicest valleys were full of chariots'. But as in Akk. and Ugar. the word may also mean 'power', or 'violence'. Pope cites Jer. 47.5 as an instance of this meaning of *'ēmeq* in Heb., but this is doubtful evidence in view of the LXX reading

ʿanāqîm for MT *ʿimqām*, that is, the remnant of the Anakim associated with the Philistine country; cf. Josh. 11.22.

We would omit *wᵉ* in MT *wᵉyāśîś*, which we take as an imperfect of attendant circumstances, as in Arabic, arranging the text:

yaḥpîr bāʿēmeq yāśîś	He paws in the plain, exultant,
bᵉḵōaḥ yēṣēʾ liqraʾṯ-nāšeq	In strength he goes out to meet the weapons.

23. The spear and the javelin in v. 21b indicate that the quiver (*ʾašpāh*) denotes really the contents of the quiver. This is supported by the verb *tārōnnā* (MT *tirneh*), which is cognate with Arab. *ranna* ('to twang', e.g. of a bow-string). The spelling with final *h* suggests that the verb should be pointed *tārōnnāh*, with energic ending as in Prov. 1.20; 8.3 (so Dahood 1963c: 4).

lahaḇ in v. 23b denotes both flames and flashing of bright metal, as in the 'flaming sword' in Gen. 3.24 (AV). In a context similar to the present one, in Nah. 3.3 *lahaḇ ḥereḇ* denotes the flashing sword.

24. On *raʿaš*, here 'quivering', as suggested by the association with *rōḡez* ('agitation'), see on v. 20. The verb *gāmāʾ* is attested in the OT only here and in Gen. 24.17: *haḡmîʾînî-nāʾ mᵉʿaṭ-mayim* ('Let me swallow a little water'). The figure is illustrated by Bochart from Arab. poetry *ʾiltaḥama ʾlfaraśu ʾlʾarḍata* ('horse ate up the ground').

Verse 24b has been deemed unduly difficult through the failure to recognize the exceptive force of *kî*. LXX and V understood *yaʾᵃmîn* as 'believe' and took the verse to mean that so eager was the horse for battle that it could not believe its ears when the trumpet sounded. A way out was sought by Gesenius, Ewald and most moderns by taking the verb in the sense of 'standing firm', 'he stands still no longer at the sound of the trumpet' (so G.B. Gray, Mowinckel [with reserve], Fohrer, Pope, Guillaume). But in this case the verb would surely be Niphal and not Hiphil, as in Isa. 9.9; 22.23, 25. Duhm doubted the condition of the text and conjectured *lōʾ yêmîn wᵉlōʾ yaśmᵉʾîl* ('and he turns not right or left') (so Hölscher), which admittedly gives a better parallel, though graphically MT is not a likely corruption of this text, and the versions give no support. We should read *yaʾᵃmîn* and *bᵉqôl* for MT *qôl*, and, taking *kî* in the exceptive sense, render 'his whole trust is in the sound of the trumpet'.

25. According to his tendency in the case of an apparent tricolon, Hölscher assumes the loss of a colon from an original statement in bicola, here between vv. 24b and 25a, and Fohrer assumes the loss of a colon between v. 25a and b. The poet, like those in the Ras Shamra myths and legends, however, varies the monotony of bicola by an occasional tricolon, which has often the effect of punctuation, ending a subject or a period. Here we would retain the tricolon as ending the passage on the warhorse. In the passage on wild beasts beyond human control and convenience that on the warhorse is exceptional. It is suggested in its present position by the comparison of the ostrich with the

steed in v. 18. In accordance with the theme of the context, the poet, who obviously warms to his subject, cites the reckless courage of the warhorse as a phenomenon unexpected from a creature usually so docile. In the time of the author of the Book of Job, however, the horse was used almost solely in war.

b^e^ḏê is pointed as if it meant 'insufficiency', which would rather be *middê* ('in proportion to', 'as often as'). We propose to read *b^e^yaḏ* ('to the accompaniment of'); cf. *'al-y^e^ḏê k^e^lê dāwîḏ* ('to the accompaniment of David's instruments', 2 Chron. 29.27; cf. Amos 6.5). *hē'āḥ* is an exclamation of satisfaction (Isa. 44.16; Ezek. 25.3; 26.2; etc.). *t^e^rû'āh* is used of the triumphant and confident war-cry, as in Amos 1.14.

26. On the evidence of Thomson (1860: 326) this is taken as a reference to two migrant birds. *pāraś kānāp̄* is found parallel to *dā'āh* ('to fly') in Jer. 48.40 and 49.22.

27-30. MT in this passage refers to another bird, *nešer*, which meant both eagle and vulture, to the latter of which vv. 29-30 would be particularly appropriate. In v. 27 Duhm would excise *yagbîah nāšer w^e^ḵî* and in v. 28 *sela' yiškōn*, as suggested by LXX, and *ûm^e^ṣûḏāh* in v. 28b, as inserted by an editor who remembered the passage on the vulture (*nešer*) in Jer. 49.16. Duhm would arrange the remaining text thus:

> *'im 'al-pîḵā yārîm qinnô*
> *w^e^yiṯlônēn 'al-šēn sela'*
> *miššām ḥāp̄ar-'ōkel.*

The reference to carrion, which the vulture detects from an apparently impossible distance (vv. 29-30; cf. Mt. 24.28; Lk. 17.37) suggests the references in MT to the vulture, which, rather than the hawk, feeds on carrion. In MT *w^e^ḵî* is awkward, but the text may be restored thanks to 11QtargJob which read *'ûzā'*, a certain kind of eagle, for MT *w^e^ḵî*. This suggests to us *kîḏôr*, which denotes a falcon in 15.24; cf. Syr. *kawdrā'*. On this reading scribal corruption occurred through the omission of *dr* of *kîḏôr* before *yr* in *yārîm* and dittography of *w* after *r* in the Old Heb. script.

28. *šen-sela'* (lit. 'tooth of rock') is used of an isolated crag in 1 Sam. 14.4.

29. *ḥāp̄ar* is used of the reconnaissance of the land by the spies sent out by Moses from Sinai (Deut. 1.22; cf. Josh. 2.3).

30. *'ep̄rōḥāyw* (for MT *'ep̄rōḥāw*) is attested in this form in Deut. 22.6 and Ps. 84.4; cf. our proposed reading *peraḥ* in v. 16b. Formally MT *y^e^'al^e^'û* from *'āla'*, unattested in the OT, with no apparent cognate, may be suspected. Aq, Sym and S imply the reading *y^e^la'l^e^'û* from *lā'a'*, possibly an Aramaic form of *lāqaq* ('to lap' or 'gulp up', Judg. 7.5); cf. MT *šāṯû w^e^lā'û* in Obad. 16.

40.25-30 (EVV 41.1-6), displaced in MT to after 40.24. See the Introduction to chs. 33–41.

40.25ff. This section is defective in LXX, which omits 40.26a, 31a; 41.4, 8a, 15b, 18b, 21a, 24b. On the peculiarities of LXX see the General Introduction.

25. On Leviathan, primarily the mythical marine monster of primaeval chaos, *ltn* of the Ras Shamra texts, cf. Job 3.8; Isa. 27.1. Here the natural crocodile is denoted as a force defying the skill or power of humans; see on vv. 14ff. The verb *timšōḵ* is probably chosen to evoke the Egyptian word for crocodile, which survives in Coptic *temsaḥ*.

MT *bᵉḥeḇel tašqîa' lᵉšōnô* has caused commentators a good deal of trouble. The verb is familiar in Classical Heb. in the Qal, meaning 'to sink down'; see on v. 23. 'Press down his tongue with a line' (G.B. Gray, Hölscher, Kissane, Mowinckel, Fohrer, Pope) might refer to the effect of a hook in the throat, but is not a natural expression conjuring up any obvious image. Nor does it help to render 'will you bind his tongue with a line?' as Michaelis suggested following Aq, Theod. and V and citing *šāqa'* ('to bind') in a Samaritan text on Lev. 8.13 (so Dhorme, Terrien). This does not correspond to fishing technique, which the parallel colon seems to demand. The same might be said of Ball's rendering 'will you bind cords on his teeth?'. This, however, does suggest part of the solution, to get rid of the awkward reference to 'tongue' (*lᵉšōnô*) by reading *'al-šinnāyw*. Actually there is a verb *šaqa(y)* in Arab. ('to vie with'), the cognate of which may be read here, allowing *'* of MT *tašqîa'* to be attached to *l* so reading *'al-šinnāyw*; hence our reading *ûḇᵉḥeḇel tišqeh 'al-šinnāyw* ('or contend with him with a line despite his teeth?').

26. The reference in v. 26b to boring the beast's cheek with a hook (*ḥôaḥ*) is misleading. In the OT *ḥôaḥ* is never used of a fish-hook, but of a hook (cf. *ḫaḫû*) which Assyrian captors inserted in the cheeks of their captives (2 Chron. 33.11) (e.g. *ANEP*, pls. 296, 447; 2 Kgs 19.23; Isa. 37.29; Ezek. 19.4, 9; 29.4; 38.4). Ezekiel 29.4 refers to the treatment of Egypt figuratively described as the monster *tannîn* (MT *tannîm*), *tnn*, one of the primaeval monsters in the Baal myth of Ras Shamra, but here particularized as the crocodile of the Nile. Indeed this passage may well have suggested the equation of Leviathan in Job with the crocodile. In any case the figure has changed in v. 26 from that of angling to that of captivity.

'agmôn in the OT means 'rushes' or a 'marsh' (Isa. 9.12; 19.15; 58.5). The reference can hardly be to a rope or halter of rushes, poor material surely for holding so strong a creature. So we welcome the interpretation of 11QtargJob, which reads *zmm* for MT *'agmôn* (cf. Syr. and Arab. *zamām* ['bridle']), which would give excellent sense in the context. Assuming mythological overtones, Pope suggests a reflection of the muzzling of the primaeval monsters of Chaos, for example, Mummu in the Babylonian *Enuma Elish* (*ANET*, 6.72) and of *tnn*

in the Ras Shamra texts (Gordon, *UT* III, 37). See further, General Introduction, Text and Versions, p. 85.

28. The reference to covenant may indicate not vassal-treaties, as those of Hittite and Assyrian kings, which were imposed by the suzerain, but rather, as late as the time of the composition of the Book of Job and its addenda, the contract whereby an *'ibrî* slave who had mortgaged his freedom had the option of release in the seventh year or perpetual servitude (Exod. 21.2-6).

29. The conception of 'Leviathan' as a play-thing for children is a variant of that of God's making of Leviathan for sport (Ps. 104.26), the supreme assertion of confident monotheism in so relegating the traditional rival to God's Order (Kaiser 1962).

30. The verb *yiḵreh* here must mean 'seek to buy', hence 'haggle over'. The verb is attested in Dan. 2.6, and, possibly in the sense of 'hire', in Hos. 3.2; cf. Arab. *kara*(*y*) in the Vth Form ('to hire'). MT *ḥaḇērîm* seems more than 'associates', the regular meaning of the noun in Classical Heb. Tur-Sinai is surely right in connecting it with Akk. *bît ḫeber* ('warehouse'). In this case MT *ḥaḇērîm* may thus be pointed as a noun denoting a vocation, *ḥabbārîm* ('wholesale merchants'), who buy provisions in bulk and sell them to retailers (*kena'anîm*). The latter term, originally denoting traders in purple (*kinaḫḫu*), for which the Phoenician coast was famous and after which it was named *kinaḫna* (Canaan), dealers in cloth to dye (Prov. 31.24) came to have a generic significance as 'merchants'. The verb *ḥāṣāh* is used of dividing a carcass in Exod. 21.35.

Job 40.2, 7-14

The Divine Declaration: Conclusion

Job's declaration that he will say no more (vv. 3-5) is belied by his declaration in 42.2-6, to which it should be transposed after the poems on Behemoth (40.15-24) and Leviathan (40.25–41.26 [EVV ch. 41]), which are later insertions in the Book. Verse 6 ('And God answered Job from a tempest and said') is probably a gloss after 38.1 occasioned by the misplacement of vv. 3-5. Verse 1 ('And Yahweh answered Job and said') has no point in the present text, since Job has not yet spoken in reply to God's questions in chs. 38–39. It is thus a gloss reflecting 38.1, a conclusion supported by its omission from LXX and one Heb. MS. Verse 7, which has also been suspected as a gloss after 38.3, may simply resume the challenge of God after the long declaration on God's sovereignty in nature. Introducing God's questioning of Job's challenge of divine justice in vv. 8-14 in forensic idiom, it is particularly appropriate.

On the division into two strophes (vv. 2, 7-9 and 10-14) and their style and content see above, p. 453.

Chapter 40.2, 7-14

2. 'Will he who contends[1] with God yield?[2]
And he who argues with God? Let him answer.
7. Brace yourself like a man. I will ask and do you inform me.
8. Will you indeed disrupt my Order,
Convicting me to acquit you?
9. Have you an arm like God's?
And with a voice like his can you thunder?

10. Pray deck yourself with pride and exaltation,
And put on glory and splendour.
11. Pour forth the spate of your anger,
And lay low every haughty man[3] you see.
12. If you see any proud man abase him,
And pull down the wicked from their place;[4]
13. Hide them in the dust together,
Imprison their persons in the lowly ground.
14. And I will render *you* praise,
That your right hand has wrought deliverance for you.'

Textual Notes to Chapter 40.2, 7-14

1. Reading *hªrāḇ* for MT *hªrōḇ*. See Commentary *ad loc.*
2. Reading *yāsûr* with Theod. and V for MT *yissôr.*
3. Reading *wᵉgāḇōah* for MT *gē'eh.* See Commentary *ad loc.*
4. Reading *mittaḥtām* for MT *taḥtām*, *m* being omitted by haplography after the previous word.

Commentary on Chapter 40.2, 7-14

2. MT *rōb* has been taken as an infinitive absolute (so Fohrer), which is formally possible, but, we consider, unlikely. The whole couplet in MT is formally possible, *yissōr* being taken as a noun, 'a fault-finder' (so Merx, Dillmann, Siegfried, Budde, Duhm, G.B. Gray, Peake, Fohrer). The parallelism, however, indicates an imperfect, as Theod. and V indicate, reading evidently *yāsûr* ('turn aside, give way'). Sym., T and V read the participle *rāḇ* for MT *rōḇ*, which is more likely as a parallel to *môḵîaḥ* in v. 2b (so Michaelis, Hoffmann, Tur-Sinai, Ball, Dhorme, Hölscher, Kissane, Mowinckel, Pope, Terrien). We take *ya'ªnennāh* as jussive, with the energic ending, familiar in Ugar. and Arab.

7. On the figure, see on 38.3.

8-14. Having exposed the inadequacy of humans to divine God's ultimate purpose and to match his ordering of natural phenomena, God exposes the inadequacy of humans to maintain moral order in society, which is more immediately relevant to Job's case; so Eissfeldt (1965: 459) emphasized, finding that passage, with Job's reply in 42.1-6, more closely linked with the theme of the dialogue than with anything else in the Divine Declaration. The argument from the theme of God's Order (*mišpāṭ*) in nature to his sovereignty and Order in society, with dire consequences to all, even in Israel, who militated against God's Order, had been the dominating theme of Amos and Isaiah of Jerusalem.

8. *hª'ap̄* asks an indignant rhetorical question, usually on a preposterous proposition, as here. The verb *pārar* (lit. 'to speak, interrupt') in the Hiphil is used in the sense of 'frustrating' or 'nullifying', for example, the nullifying of Ahithophel's counsel (2 Sam. 15.34; 17.14), and it is regularly used of breaking the covenant, the expression of God's Order (*mišpāṭ*) in society. The forensic language of v. 8b might indicate, alternatively, the rendering 'thwart my just case'; cf. *taršî'ēnî* ('convict me', lit. 'make me wrong') and *tiṣdāq* ('acquit yourself' lit. 'be right').

9. As often in Heb., an abstract quality is symbolized by a particular bodily member. So 'arm' is used for 'power', as in Exod. 15.16; Isa. 40.10; 51.5; etc.

The mention of thunder evokes the theme of the New Year festival, the Kingship of God in what we regard as its original setting in the great seasonal festival at the turn of the year in late autumn, as in ancient Canaan, to which the Baal myth of Ras Shamra was relevant. Here the theme was the revival and epiphany of Baal-Hadad as king, whose ascendancy was signalized by thunder as the herald of the winter rains. With the sober theme of the triumph of cosmos over chaos the Canaanite liturgy was adapted in the liturgy of the New Year festival in Israel (Kapelrud 1940; J. Gray 1956; 1961).

10. *ʿᵃḏēh* means 'put on adornment' (e.g. Isa. 61.10; Jer. 31.4; Ezek. 16.11; etc.); cf. *ʿᵃḏî* 'adornment' (2 Sam. 1.24).

Verse 10a recalls *hôḏ wᵉhāḏār lāḇāštā* in Ps. 104.1, which refers to the characteristic vestments of God. This is contrasted with 'pride' (*gā'ôn*) and 'exaltation' (*gāḇōah*), human presumption.

11. *ʿeḇrāh* means 'overflow, excess', derived from the verb *ʿāḇar*, which is used of a river overflowing its banks. It denotes human arrogance (*zādôn*) in Prov. 21.24 and rage of humans (Gen. 49.7; Amos 1.11) and of God (Isa. 14.6; Zeph. 1.16, *dies irae*; etc.). Job is challenged to match effectively the just wrath of God beyond his own presumption and incontrollable anger, evinced in his indignant outbursts in the Dialogue. In v. 11b LXX omits *ûrᵉ'ēh*, in which case its insertion would be under the influence of *rᵉ'ēh* in v. 12a. We prefer, however, to retain MT, seeing in the repetition of *rᵉ'ēh* God's ironical challenge to Job to quell presumption by a look. It is unlikely that *gē'eh* should be repeated in vv. 11b and 12a, and we suggest the emendation *gāḇōah* for MT *gē'eh* in v. 11b. This is more suitable with *hašpîl* in v. 11b than with *haḵnîaʿ* in v. 12a, where Duhm after LXX proposed the same emendation; cf. Isa. 5.15 (*ʿênê gᵉḇōhîm tišpalnāh*); 10.33 (*haggᵉḇōhîm yišpᵉlû*); but cf. Isa. 13.11, *ga'ᵃwaṯ ʿᵃrîṣîm 'ašpîl*. In vv. 11b and 12a *rᵉ'ēh* is the imperative in the conditional sense, the so-called hypothetical imperative, akin to the jussive in the protasis without a conditional particle; cf. GKC, §159d.

12. *hᵃḏōḵ* is a *hapax legomenon*, for which Dhorme cites the Arab. cognate *hadaka* ('to pull down').

taḥtām ('in their place', i.e. possibly 'in respect to their place') might be an adverbial accusative, but may better be emended to *mittaḥtām* ('from their place'), assuming haplography of *m* after the previous word *rᵉšāʿîm*.

13. *ḥābaš* in parallelism with *ṭāman* ('to hide') must be cognate with Arab. *ḥabaśa* ('to confine'); cf. *ḥabśu*(*n*) ('prison'). We should find a word-play between *ṭāman* ('to hide') in v. 13a and *ṭāmûn* in v. 13b, which, as parallel with *ʿāpār*, must be cognate with Arab. *muṭmā'inu*(*n*) ('flat, or depressed, ground').

Job 40.3-5; 42.2-6

Job's Submission

Job's submission in two strophes (40.3-5; 42.2-3, 5-6) corresponds partly to the forensic tradition, where a litigant cedes his case, especially in 40.3-5, and partly to the response of the subject to the reassuring oracle in the Plaint of the Sufferer, especially in 42.2-3. There Job emerges from doubt to certainty, declared in the introductory *yāḏa'tî* ('I know'; cf. Pss. 20.7 [EVV 6]; 140.13 [EVV 12]), assured by the evidences of God's omnipotence and positive purpose (42.2) in the Divine Declaration, which corresponds to the oracle in the Plaint of the Sufferer. In this new dimension Job admits that his arguments for his personal case in the Dialogue have been inadequate. In the final strophe, after the acceptance of the revelation of the living God ('now my eye has seen you'), in the convention of the Plaint of the Sufferer Job finally emphasizes his submission and due repentance for his challenge of the divine economy (v. 6).

Job's final response to God in all humility is quickened by the significant encouragement of the personal experience of God who has condescended to address him (v. 5) and *ipso facto* has assured him that he is neither forgotten nor treated with indifference.

In this section 42.4 seems to be contradicted by Job's statement that he will say no more (40.5), and we treat it as Job's confession of his presumption in questioning God, quoting God's challenge to him in 38.3b and 40.7b, thus admitting that in communication between God and humans the initiative is with God and the human part is strictly response.

Chapters 40.3-5; 42.2-6

40.3. And Job answered Yahweh and said:

4. 'Lo, I am too insignificant to answer you;[1]
I have put my hand to my mouth;
5. I have said one thing and will not repeat it,[2]
Yea, two, and will say no more.

42.2. I know (for certain) that you are omnipotent
And there is no purpose beyond you.
3. "Who is this that obscures (your) purpose
With words[3] without knowledge?"
So I declared without understanding
Things too wonderful for me that I did not know, (saying),

4. "Hear, I pray you, and I will speak,
I shall question you, and do you inform me".
5. As the ear hears I had heard of you,
But now my eye has seen you.
6. Wherefore I demean myself and yield,[4]
Reduced[5] to dust and ashes.'

Textual Notes to Chapters 40.3.5; 42.2-6

1. Reading *mēhᵃšîḇᵉḵā* for MT *māh 'ᵃšîḇᵉḵā.*
2. Reading *'ešneh* for MT *'e'ᵉneh.* See Commentary *ad loc.*
3. Reading *bᵉmillîm* with LXX, S and one Heb. MS, completing the citation of 38.2. See Commentary *ad loc.*
4. Reading *'al-kēn 'emmā'ēs wᵉ'emmas*, following LXX and 11QtargJob. See Commentary *ad loc.* and the General Introduction, Text and Versions, pp. 76-91.
5. Reading *wᵉnimhē'ṯî* in colon b for *wᵉniḥamtî* in colon a of MT after 11QtargJob. See Commentary *ad loc.* and the General Introduction, Text and Versions, p. 76.

Commentary on Chapters 40.3-5 and 42.2-6

On the unity of this passage on Job's submission, broken up after the secondary insertion on Behemoth and Leviathan, with consequent adjustment in the insertion of 42.1, see the General Introduction (p. 35).

40.4. We adopt Ehrlich's emendation *mēhᵃšîḇᵉḵā* for MT *māh 'ᵃšîḇᵉḵā*, the infinitive construct Hiphil with the comparative *min*, which gives a smoother reading than MT. *qal* is used here in the primary sense 'to be light'. In the Piel it means 'to curse', lit. 'to make light', to divest of weight or substance (*kāḇôḏ*, lit. 'weight'). It denotes here someone conscious of his own insignificance. The hand upon the mouth indicates both silence and deference to a superior; cf. the worshipper before a god in Mesopotamian sculpture, for example Hammurabi before the sun-god on the famous stele with his code of laws (*ANEP*, pl. 246); and cf. the Legend of King Krt in the Ras Shamra texts (Gordon, *UT* 125, 41-42):

qḥ 'apk byd (b)r(l)tk bm ymn	Hold thy hand over thy nose, thy right hand over my throat.

The gesture may signify the acknowledgment that the very breath of life depended on the grace of the superior. On the other hand B. Couroyer (1960) adduces the gesture in forensic convention that a litigant has no more to say.

5. The parallelism indicates the reading *'ᵉšneh* for MT *'e'ᵉneh*, though *'e'ᵉneh* is not unintelligible in the sense 'to speak up again'. But after *'aḥaḏ dibbartî* the number two is expected in the convention of numerical climax noting multitude, frequency or repetition in epic convention and wisdom literature.

42.2. In Job's final submission the recurrence of the verb *yāḏa'* is to be noted, denoting at once Job's insufficient knowledge of the whole range and significance of the divine economy (v. 3b, d), of which he had been convicted in the Divine Declaration (38.2, 4-5, 18, 21; 39.1-2), and the firm conviction to which he has now attained of what faith had asserted regarding the nature and will of God (v. 2). The verb in the latter sense in Job's submission corresponds significantly to the recurrence of *yāḏa'* in the moment of assurance, or anticipation of the plea of the sufferer being heard, as Fohrer (1989: 532) has well noted at, e.g., Pss. 41.12 (EVV 11); 54.10 (EVV 9); 141.13 (EVV 12).

Verse 2b is Job's quotation from God's challenge from 38.2 in the introduction to 'marvels beyond marvels', which convinces Job that in questioning the divine economy he is *ultra vires*. In v. 2b MT *wᵉlō'-yibbāṣēr mimmᵉḵā mᵉzimmāh*, *mᵉzimmāh* may be supported against the proposal to read *mᵉ'ûmāh* (so Hoffmann, Graetz, Beer after LXX) by Gen. 11.6, *lō' yibbāṣēr mēhem kol-'ᵃšer yāzᵉmû* (read *yāzōmmû*). The verb *bāṣar* is attested in the sense 'to make inaccessible', e.g. *'îr mibṣār* ('fortified city', lit. 'cut off' by escarpment and high walls). *mᵉzimmāh* ('purpose'; see on 21.17) is considered as an objective to which access is barred, though not by God. Lévêque has noticed (1970: 524) that besides this passage *mᵉzimmāh* is applied to God only thrice (Jer. 33.30; 30.24; 51.11), always in reference to God's retributive purpose, contrasting the sinister contrivance and purpose of the wicked. Here the purpose of God is more positive.

3. We regard v. 3ab as Job's citation of God's indignant question in 38.2, *mî zeh maḥᵃšîḵ 'ēṣāh bᵉmillîm bᵉlî-ḏa'aṯ*, indicating that *bᵉmillîm* should be read in 42.3b after LXX, which the metre demands. *niplā'ôṯ mimmennî* recalls the statement of the suppliant who declares his faith in Ps. 131.1. *nip̄lā'ôṯ* denotes the immediate activity of God in which he gives no evidence of secondary causes by which humans can reason from natural cause to effect independent of the power of God.

4. On the significance of this verse recalling God's challenge in 40.7b, see the introduction to this section.

5. There is no reason to believe, as Tur-Sinai suggests, that *wᵉ'attāh 'ênî rᵉ'āṯᵉḵā* indicates the source of the Book. The verb here, as frequently in Arab., denotes mental as well as physical perception. *'ênî* in this context emphasizes actual experience without specifying its actual nature beyond Job's firm conviction as the result of his appreciation of the evidence of God's activity and providence. The full import of the verb *rā'āh* in Job's declaration is conveyed by the experience of Isaiah of Jerusalem, who declares, 'With my eyes I have seen the King, the Lord of Hosts' (Isa. 6.5). The prophet expresses at once his dread of the presence of the living God, his debasement, and his full realization of the divine nature and will, which it is now his imperative

duty to proclaim. The assurance of the efficacy of the living God in all contingencies and the security of his fellowship is expressed in Ps. 34.9 (EVV 8): 'Taste and see that the Lord is good; happy the one who finds refuge in him'. Here Job contrasts the conventional assertions about God based on the traditions of his society and accepted *theologoumena* with the personal experience of God. The contrast is between theology and religion. His declaration significantly echoes his assurance of vindication, *'ênay rā'ôh* (MT *rā'û*) in 19.27. See above *ad loc*.

6. MT *'em'as* without an object has suggested to LXX, S and V that the verb was reflexive *'emmā'ēs*. LXX gives a double interpretation, 'I demean myself' (*'emmā'ēs*) and 'I melt' (*'emmas*), so NEB. It has been proposed to take MT *'em'as* as 'I reject', understanding 'my case' or 'my words' as the object of the transitive verb (so G.B. Gray, Mowinckel, Fohrer, Pope, Kuyper 1959: 91-94), which might be supported by MT *w^{e}niḥamtî*. If this verb, contrary to MT, is taken with colon b it would indicate the utter submission and deepest humiliation of Job 'on dust and ashes'. But under stylistic and metrical considerations and after LXX and 11QtargJob we read:

> *'al-kēn 'emmā'ēs w^e'emmas*
> *w^{e}nimhē'ṯî 'al-'āp̄ār w^e'ēp̄er*

> Therefore I demean myself and yield,
> And am reduced to dust and ashes.

For a detailed justification of this text and translation, see the General Introduction, Text and Versions (pp. 86-87). We note the word-play so characteristic of the Book of Job in *'emmā'ēs w^e'emmas* and *'āp̄ār w^e'ēp̄er*.

Job 40.15–41.26 (EVV 34)

Wisdom Poems on Natural Themes

Job 40.15–41.26 contains Poems on the Beast (Behemoth), the Hippopotamus (40.15-24, 31-32; 41.1-3 [EVV 40.15-24; 41.7-11]) and the Crocodile (Leviathan) (40.25-30; 41.4-26 [EVV 41.1-6, 12-34]). The latter is a composite work of two poems (40.25-30 [EVV 41.1-6], and 41.4-26 [EVV 12-34]), 40.25-30 being drafted in MT from after 39.30 and subsequently expanded.

These are wisdom poems on natural themes, descriptive of characteristic features of natural phenomena like the shorter passages on the wild creatures in ch. 39, to which 40.25-30 belongs, and like them emphasizing the untameable nature and extraordinary strength and ferocity of the hippopotamus and the crocodile, which has made their hunting by humans a most dangerous enterprise, if not indeed, as in the second poem on the crocodile (41.4-26 [EVV 12-34]), impossible. They probably belonged to the same category of encyclopaedic work as the passages in ch. 39, and were added later to the Book of Job by one familiar with such a work. In spite of the lengthy and detailed description of the two great beasts, which digresses from the main point, the representation of two such formidable forces defying human power, and even, perhaps, as symbols of the powers of chaos defying God, would have been a fine climax to the list of beasts in ch. 39, as Richter has maintained (1958a: 5-20). The citation of the passages on the various beasts in ch. 39; 40.25-30, however, culminates in the conclusion to the Divine Declaration in 40.2, 7-14, after which the passages on the hippopotamus and the crocodile in 41.4-26 (EVV 12-34) are probably an addition, differing markedly from the shorter, more pointed passages on the other beasts in ch. 39 except for the passage on the horse (39.19-25) and possibly the expansion on the ostrich (39.14-17). H.H. Schmid (1966: 183n) regards Behemoth and Leviathan as mythological on the grounds that the names never signify the hippopotamus and the crocodile elsewhere in the OT, whereas Behemoth, identified with Rahab, is a manifestation of Chaos in Isa. 30.6; cf. the association of Behemoth and Leviathan in *1 En.* 60.7ff. and *4 Esd.* 6.49. The mythological significance of Leviathan at least is apparently assumed by LXX, which renders Leviathan as *ho drakōn*. Schmid admits that naturalistic features are lent to both creatures, perhaps under the influence of sapiential lists of natural phenomena such as that indicated in ch. 9. We consider it more likely that the creatures were primarily the hippopotamus and the crocodile, and that the mythological aspects, which we do not deny, were secondary. Leviathan is *ltn* of the Baal myth of Ras Shamra, identified with the forces of primaeval chaos overcome according to one version by Baal, the power of providence in nature, and according to another by Baal's sister and supporter in the maintenance of Order, the goddess Anat. The hippopotamus was a manifestation of Seth in Egyptian religion, the inveterate enemy of Horus, the champion of cosmos in the myth and ritual of the temple at Edfu in Upper Egypt in a twelfth-century text from Thebes (*ANET*, 14-17, esp. XII). Both the hippopotamus and the crocodile are kings in their own realm (40.19, see textual note and Commentary *ad loc.*, and 41.34), but they do not challenge the power of God; they lord it over the beasts of the jungle, each in its own element.

Chapter 40.15-24, 31-32; 41.1-3 (EVV 40.15-24; 41.7-11): Poem on Behemoth (the Huge Beast, i.e. the Hippopotamus)

15. Consider now the Beast before you,[1]
Which eats grass like an ox.
16. See the strength in his loins,
And the force in the muscles of his belly.
17. His tail is as stiff as a cedar,
The sinews of his thighs are close-knit;
18. His bones are brazen tubes,
His limbs are like bars of iron;
19. He is the first of God's ordered creation,
[2]Made to lord it over the pool,
20. Where the beasts of the mountains take their ease,
And all the wild creatures sport.[3]
21. He lies down where the mud is dry,
In the covert of reeds and mud,
22. Sheltered by the shade[4] of the lotus trees,
Encompassed by the willows of the wadi.
23. If the river is in flood he is not startled,
He is confident though the river swells;
24. Into his mouth[5] with open eyes he takes it in;
(Alone) among the river animals his snout protrudes.[6]

31. Will you fill his skin with barbs,
Or his head with whizzing harpoons?
32. Lay but your hand on him,
You will think no more of fight!
41.2 There is none so bold as to stir him up,[7]
And who can stand before him?[8]
1. See, one's hope is an illusion;
Even[9] at the sight of him one is prostrated.
3. Who confronts him[10] and comes off whole?[11]
Under all the heavens, who?[12]

Textual Notes to Chapter 40.15-24, 31-32; 41.1-3 (EVV 40.15-24; 41.7-11)

1. Omitting *'ašer 'āśîṯî* with LXX. See Commentary *ad loc.*
2. Reading *he'āśûy nôḡēś habbᵉrēḵāh* for MT *hā'ōśô yāggēš ḥarbô* and taking MT *kî* of v. 20 as a corruption of *-kāh* in the Old Heb. script, this being the end of *habbᵉrēḵāh* at the end of v. 19. See Commentary *ad loc.*
3. Reading *bûl hārîm yišlāyû šām / wᵉḵol-ḥayyaṯ haśśaḏeh yiśḥaq* for MT *bûl hārîm yiśᵉ'û-lô / wᵉḵol-ḥayyaṯ haśśaḏeh yᵉśaḥᵃqû-šām*. See Commentary *ad loc.*
4. Reading *ṣilᵉlām* for MT *ṣilᵃlô* in agreement with the subject, *m* being corrupted to *w* in the Old Heb. script. See Commentary *ad loc.*
5. Considerations of metre demand that *'el-pîhû* (v. 23) be read with v. 24.
6. Reading *yiqqōḇ 'appô* for MT *yinqaḇ-'ap̄*. See Commentary *ad loc.*
7. Reading *yᵉ'îrennû* or *yᵉ'ôrᵉrennû* for MT *yᵉ'ûrennû.*
8. Reading *lᵉp̄ānāyw* with certain Heb. MS for MT *lᵉp̄ānay.*
9. Reading *gam* for MT *hᵃgam.*
10. Reading *mî yaqdîmennû* for MT *mî hiqdîmanî.*
11. Reading *wᵉyišlām* with LXX for MT *wa'ᵃšallēm.*
12. Reading *mî-hû* for MT *lî-hû*, *m* being corrupted to *l* in the Old Heb. script.

Commentary on Chapter 40.15-24, 31-32; 41.1-3 (EVV 40.15-24; 41.7-11)

15ff. The occurrence of Leviathan (*ltn*), the mythical sea-monster of primaeval chaos in the Ras Shamra texts, has suggested to Pope that *bᵉhēmôṯ*, in which the plural is the plural of excellence, may be similarly a mythical land-creature, and he cites the bovine monsters who brought about the downfall of Baal in a Ras Shamra fragment (Gordon *UT* 75), with a presumed reference to a 'supernatural bullock' in another text (Gordon *UT* 'nt III, 41; 67, 4). There is no suggestion in Job that Behemoth is a horned beast, as the description of Baal's adversaries in Gordon *UT* 75 explicitly states, nor indeed is there any indication in the description of Leviathan in Job 40.25ff. that the creature is mythical rather than natural. The descriptions of both, if poetic, are as detailed as natural history. If it is true that Behemoth is taken as the chief of the beasts of the dry land as Leviathan is of the reptiles, that does not mean that the role of Behemoth and Leviathan as the mythical monsters of the dry land and waters respectively in post-biblical eschatology (e.g. 1 En. 60.7-9 and *4 Ezra* 6.49-52) was prior to the natural significance of Behemoth, which means simply 'beasts of the field' in Ps. 8.8; 73.22; Isa. 30.6; Joel 1.20; 2.22; Hab. 2.17. If there had been a mythical monster Behemoth, as Pope assumes, it is strange that like Leviathan it should not appear with Rahab and Tannin, the other monsters of primaeval chaos in Enthronement Psalms and other reflections of the liturgy of the New Year festival in the Psalms and the Prophets. Nor do we admit Pope's reference to 'the supernatural bullock' in the Ras Shamra texts, *'gl 'el*, which he so translates. We take *'gl 'el* as an adverbial accusative after the participle *'tk*, describing the 'prodigious haste' of the onset (*'tk*) of Death (*mt*). In the case of Leviathan, which is undoubtedly the crocodile, we have the natural particularization of a mythical monster. The natural monster, the Beast *par excellence*, which is what the plural *b^ehēmôṯ* signifies, has become with Leviathan the symbol of the brute creation, the antithesis of humans and their God-given nature and destiny in post-biblical apocalyptic. Behemoth, though meaning the Beast *par excellence*, may be a popular adaptation of Egyptian *pꜣ-ꜣ'iḥ-mw* ('water-ox'). We are prepared to admit that the description of both beasts has mythical overtones (so Mowinckel), but they are primarily natural. See the Introduction to the section.

In v. 15a LXX omits *'ašer 'āśîṯî*, with which we agree *metri causa 'immāḵ* means 'before you', indicating an example brought to one's notice. The eating of grass refers to the food of the hippopotamus, which is notoriously destructive of crops (Erman 1927: 188 ff.).

16. The loins (*moṯnayim*) denote both strength and virility; cf. Deut. 33.11. The plural *š^erîrîm* is a *hapax legomenon*. The adjective *š^erîr*, better known in Aram. and Syr., means 'firm, hard', and *š^erîrîm* may be the abstract plural 'hardness', that is, of flesh or rather muscle.

17. If *zānāḇ* means, as it does in the OT and cognate Semitic languages, 'tail', the comparison with the cedar is strange. The passage poses, moreover, the problem of the meaning of the verb *ḥāp̄aṣ* in the context. Ball suggested that it is cognate with Arab. *ḥafaḍa*, one meaning of which is 'to remain long in one place', thus referring to the stiffness of the short tail of the hippopotamus, the only point of comparison with the cedar being its stillness or rigidity and certainly not its length (so Dhorme, Friedrich Delitzsch, Budde, Duhm, Strahan, Szczygiel, Buttenwieser, Hölscher, Steinmann, Larcher).

But the normal meaning of Arab. *ḥafaḍa* is 'to lower', and so the reference may be to the erection of the penis of the hippopotamus, which, though exaggerated, would suit the simile (so Fohrer). We cannot, however, attest this meaning of *zanaḇ* in Heb. or any cognate language, but S evidently understood this meaning of the passage, as also evidently LXX and V, which renders *stringit*. Erection in the case of a quadruped would be lowering. The only possible incidence of *ḥāp̄aṣ* in a physical sense in the OT is in Ps. 37.23:

mēyhwh miṣ'^aḏê-geḇer kônānû w^eḏarkô yeḥpāṣ

By Yahweh a man's steps are established,
And his way is firm.

Here it must be admitted that the parallel with *kônānû* indicates the meaning of *ḥāp̄aṣ* as 'is firm' (so NEB), which would support Ball's interpretation, if indeed the verb is the same as *ḥāp̄aṣ* in Job 40.17. The rigidity of the short tail of the hippopotamus would compare not inaptly with the cedar, which in its trunk and branches is not pliant. *paḥ^aḏāyw* (Qere) is a *hapax legomenon* in the

OT, being cognate with Arab. *faḫadu*(*n*) ('thigh'), as understood by S and Saadyah, or as 'testicles' (V), which renders *'ešeḵ* with this meaning in Lev. 21.10. The meaning of *śārag̃* is practically certain; cf. *śārîg̃* 'vine-tendril' (Gen. 40.10, 12), Syr. *śrîgṯā'* means 'lattice', hence the verb would be 'to be close-knit'.

18. *'āpîq* means 'stream' or 'bed of a stream', hence here 'pipe' or 'tube'. *m^eṭîl*, another *hapax legomenon*, is probably cognate with Arab. *mamṭūlu*(*n*) ('a beaten strip of iron').

19. In *dar^eḵê, 'ēl, dereḵ* has the nuance of 'ordered government'; cf. 26.14, as *drkt* in the Ras Shamra texts. This is particularized in God's ordered creation. The phrase recalls the statement in Prov. 8.22 that Wisdom is *rē'šîṯ darkô*. Pope would therefore see a reference in Job 40.19 to Behemoth the chief of God's primordial works. This would conflict with the conception that Wisdom was *rē'šîṯ darkô*, and we suggest that the phrase refers rather to the hippopotamus as the culmination of God's brute creation, humans, as being created 'in the image of God', being considered apart.

In v. 19b *hā'ōśô yaggēš ḥarbô* is obviously wrong. In retaining MT and translating 'his maker may bring near his sword', Pope does not attempt to explain the grammar of *hā'ōśô*, the construct of the participle with the pronominal suffix *and* the definite article! Pope seems determined to secure a correspondence between his assumed mythical Behemoth in Job and Behemoth in post-biblical eschatology, where Behemoth is to provide sport for the faithful and to be slain by the sword of God. We believe that the corrupt text of v. 19b may have been the source of the eschatological conception in *Midrash Rabba*, Lev. 13.3 and Talmud Babli, *Baba Bathra* 75a (so also Larcher). This would be an abrupt reference without precedent in the Book of Job. The parallelism supports Giesebrecht's emendation *he'āśûy nōg̃ēś ḥ^aḇērāyw* ('which is made as the ruler of its fellows'). In this emendation certainly every word of MT is emended, as Pope alleges, but no emendation is drastic or arbitrary. All the corruptions assumed are natural errors at one stage or another of the transmission of the text. The reading *he'āśûy* is attested in LXX. Giesebrecht's reading and interpretation is accepted by Duhm, Strahan, Dhorme, Hölscher, Weiser, Steinmann, Mowinckel, Fohrer. Gunkel proposed the variation *he'āśûy nōg̃ēś ḥāreḇ* (pausal form), 'which is made ruler of the dry land', which might be supported by the description of Leviathan as 'king over all the reptiles' (41.26 [EVV 34]). The reading we suggest is *he'āśûy nōg̃ēś habb^erēḵāh* ('which is created lord of the pool'). Here alone the hippopotamus may lord it over the beasts. This makes *šām* in v. 20 explicable, which in MT is isolated without an antecedent. In this connection it is noteworthy that in the myth of the conflict between Horus and Seth, the Edfu version of the conflict of cosmos and chaos, Seth was incarnate in the hippopotamus, and a text relating to this theme on a papyrus from the eleventh century BCE describes how Horus took a gigantic harpoon and 'threw it at the majesty of Seth' (A.H. Gardiner, *The Chester Beatty Papyrus No. 1*, 1931, Chapter 13, 11.9-10). Fuller details of the myth of this conflict, where Horus sustains the Order of his father Re the sun-god against the menace of his enemies, particularly Seth in the guise of a hippopotamus, by means of the ritual of the ceremonial harpooning of the hippopotamus in the cult at Edfu are presented by H.W. Fairman (1935; Fairman and Blackman 1942, 1943, 1944). In one passage the vanquished enemies (unspecified) of Horus and Re are consigned to the river and become hippopotami and crocodiles, an important detail which made it easy to assimilate the crocodile to Leviathan, or Ugaritic *ltn*, the monster of primaeval chaos. The emendation we propose anticipates the difficulties in v. 20 not only by supplying an antecedent to *šām*, but in accounting for the difficult *kî* in v. 20a, by taking it as the last two consonants of *habbᵉrēḵāh* with scribal corruption of *h* to *k* in the Old Heb. script. On *nōgēś* see on 3.18.

20. We continue the text, reading *bûl hārîm yišlāyû šām* / *wᵉḵol-ḥayyaṯ haśśāḏeh yiṣḥaq* for MT *kî-bûl hārîm yiśᵉʾû-lô* / *wᵉḵol-ḥayyaṯ haśśāḏeh yᵉśaḥᵃqû-ṣām*. We follow Tur-Sinai in taking *bûl hārîm* as corresponding to Akk. *bul ṣeri* ('the beasts of the steppe'). In reading *yišlāyû* (pausal form) we follow the suggestion of Pope. No other reading which takes MT as meaning 'for the mountains give him *tribute* (Dhorme), or *produce*' (reading *yᵉḇûl*), or reading 'the rivers' (*nᵉhārîm*) for MT *hārîm*, sustains the parallelism.

21-22. *ṣeʾᵉlîm* is a *hapax legomenon* in the OT. In v. 22a it obviously signifies a tree, probably the lotus tree, so understood by Saadya, who rendered it by the Arab. *dallu*(*n*). But the apparent repetition in v. 21a is suspect. In v. 22a the word-play between *ṣeʾᵉlîm* and *ṣillô* indicates that *ṣeʾᵉlîm* is genuine here. In v. 21a we suspect a homonym or at least a near-homonym of *ṣeʾᵃlîm*, which we find in Arab. *ṣalālu*(*n*) ('dry mud', possibly 'a mud-bank'). This gives a parallel to *biṣṣāh* ('mud') in v. 21b as well as affording a word-play with *ṣeʾᵉlîm* ('lotus-trees'). *taḥat* in v. 21a does not necessarily mean 'under' but rather 'where', lit. 'the place of'; cf. Gordon, *UT* 2 Aqht V, 6-7: *tḥt ʾadrm* ('in the place of the notables').

23. Dhorme takes *yaʿᵃšōq nāhār* as 'the river is violent', citing Ass. *ešêqu* ('to be strong', so Hölscher, Mowinckel, Fohrer, Pope). This is possible, but it is also possible that *yaʿᵃšōq* is a corruption of *yišqaʿ* ('subsides'; cf. Amos 9.3), indicating the amphibious nature of the hippopotamus (so Gunkel and Budde). But already the land-habits of the hippopotamus have been mentioned, and on the principle of *difficilior lectio potior* the *hapax legomenon yaʿᵃšōq* is to be preferred, giving a synonymous, not antithetic, parallel to *yāḡîaʿ* ('swells, gushes'; see on 38.8). *hēn* is the Aram. particle 'if'; cf. Arab. *ʾinna*.

ḥāpaz is found as a synonym of *yārēʾ* in Deut. 20.3. Though this verb, as the antithetic parallel to *yiḇṭaḥ* indicates, suggests that the latter verb means 'is confident', there is probably a *double entendre*, implying a homonym; cf. Arab. *baṭaḥa*, meaning in the VII form 'to lie outstretched' (cf. Guillaume 1963: 128). In characteristic word-play this is elaborated in the sequel, which refers to the beast lying comfortably in the water with its snout protruding.

In v. 23a *yardēn* does not mean Jordan, but is a common noun 'river' in parallel with *nāhār*; cf. *hayyardēn hazzēh* in Gen. 32.11; Deut. 3.27; 31.32; etc., and the phrase *yardēn yᵉrîḥô* in Num. 26.3, 63; 31.12; 33.48; 50; etc. In Mandaean *yardēn* is a common noun. The suggestion to omit *yiḇṭaḥ* (Pope) or *yardēn* (Fohrer) shows strange disregard for the parallelism and is not justified metrically, especially if *'el-pîhû* is taken with v. 34a as the metre demands.

24. Reading *'el-pîhû bᵉ'ēnāyw yiqqāḥennû* ('into his mouth, up to the eyes, he takes it in') conjures up the picture of the gaping hippopotamus 'up to the eyes' in the river. The picture is amplified if with Guillaume (1963: 126) we read MT with two slight emendations, *'appô* for *'ap* and *yiqqaḇ* or *yiqqōḇ* (from *qāḇaḇ*), assuming the intrusion of *n* in MT *yinqaḇ* by dittography before *q* in the Old Heb. script, giving the translation '(alone) among the river animals his snout protrudes'. We follow Guillaume in taking *môqᵉšîm* as the masc. plur. participle of a verb cognate with Arab. *maqaśa* ('to plunge into water', transitive) and *qāḇaḇ* cognate with Arab. *qabba*, meaning in the V form 'to protrude', whence *qubbatu*(*n*) ('dome', lit. 'protuberance').

The unassailability of the hippopotamus by any tackle indicates that 40.31-32; 41.1-3 (EVV 40.31-32; 41.7-11) on this theme belongs here to the passage on the hippopotamus and not as in MT to that on the crocodile.

31. *śukkôṯ* is a *hapax legomenon* in the OT. Its general sense of 'barbs' is not in doubt, and Dhorme cites Akk. *śakâtu* ('to be pointed'); cf. Arab. *šikkatu(n)* ('weapon') from *šakka* ('to pierce'), cited as cognate in BDB, though the phonetic correspondence is irregular. *ṣilṣal* parallel with *śukkôṯ* may mean a pointed missile. Connected with the verb *ṣālal* ('to tingle', e.g. the ears [2 Kgs 21.12]; cf. Arab. *ṣalṣalatu[n]* ['a resounding voice']), it might denote the whirring harpoon.

32. We take *zᵉḵōr* as the infinitive construct, the verbal noun, the object of *tôsîp̄*.

41.1. The 3rd masc. sing. pronom. suffix refers probably to the indefinite subject 'one'. *hᵃ* in MT *hᵃgam* is probably a dittograph of the last consonant of the preceding word. Pope sees a Masoretic suppression of a mythological allusion in v. 1b, translating 'Were not the gods cast down at the sight of him?'; cf. Sym. and S, which read *'ēl* ('God' or 'a god') for the preposition *'el*, but we prefer to take the subject of *yuṭal* as that implied in the pronom. suffix in *tōḥaltô*, taking *gam* with MT *'el-mar'āyw* ('even at the sight of him'). *yuṭāl* (pausal form), Hophal form of *ṭûl*, is found most commonly in the Pilpel, meaning ‘to cast’. It is attested in Ps. 37.24, where it denotes a more drastic action than ‘throw down’, that is, ‘utterly cast down’. MT *mar’āyw* (‘the sight of him’) may be retained as an abstract plural.

2. *’aḵzār* in the OT means ‘cruel, fierce’. Here the sense is rather ‘bold’ or ‘rash’, as in Ben Sira 8.15.

Chapter 40.25-30; 41.4-26 (EVV 41.1-6, 12-34)
(40.25-30 secondarily drafted from after 39.30)

40.25. ‘Can you draw out Leviathan with a hook
Or contend with him with a line in despite of his teeth?
24. Can you put a bridle on his snout,
Or pierce his jaws with a hook?
27. Will he make supplications to you,
Or speak softly to you?
28. Will he make a compact with you,
That you should take him as a servant for ever?
29. Could you make a pet of him like a bird,
And put him on a string for your little girls?
30. Will the wholesale merchants haggle over him?
Will they divide him among the retailers?’

(For textual notes and commentary, see above, pp. 471, 480-81.)

41.4. I will not keep silence concerning his limbs,
And I will declare[1] his strength beyond compare.[2]
5. Who has come within the surface of his outer garment?
Who can penetrate the overlappings of his breastplate?[3]
6. Who has opened the doors of his mouth?[4]
About his teeth is terror.

7. His back[5] is as tanned shields,
His breast is sealed with flint.[6]
8. Each one (of the shield-scales) comes so close together
That no air can come between them;
9. Each one cleaves to the other,
They are interlocked and cannot be separated.
10. His sneezing[7] makes the sunlight flash,
And his eyes are like the eyes of the dawn.
11. Out of his mouth go torches,
And sparks of fire leap forth;
12. Out of his nostrils smoke issues,
As of a pot (on a fire) blown into a blaze.[8]

13. His breath sets coals ablaze;
And a flame comes forth from his mouth.
14. In his neck reposes strength,
And before him dances dismay.
15. The flakes of his flesh are joined together,

Welded[9] to him, immovable.[10]
16. His breast is firm as a stone,
As tight as a nether millstone.
17. At his uprising[11] strong men are in dread,
From his gaping jaws[12] they turn back.
18. If one would attack him the sword it is of no avail,
Nor with the spear, the shaft, the dart.
19. He accounts iron as straw,
Bronze as rotten wood.
20. The arrow cannot put him to flight;
With him sling-stones become mere chaff.
21. He will consider[13] a club as chaff,
And he will laugh at the hurtling javelin.
22. His belly is as a plough-sock making a furrow,[14]
He lies like[15] a sharp-studded threshing-sledge on the mud.
23. He makes the deep boil as a pot,
He makes the 'sea' as an ointment-pot.
24. In his wake he makes a bright path;
One would think the deep was hoary.
25. He has not his peer[16] on the earth,
Made without fear.
26. Of him all that is high is afraid;[17]
He is king over all the great beasts.

Textual Notes to Chapter 41.4-26 (EVV 12-34)

1. Reading *wa'^{a}ḏabbēr* for MT *ûḏ^{e}bar.*
2. Reading *'ên 'ereḵ* for MT *w^{e}ḥîn 'erkô*, ' being corrupted to *ḥ* in the Old Heb. script, and final *w* in MT *'erkô* being a dittograph after *k* or before *m* of the following word in the same script.
3. Reading *śiryōnô* after LXX for MT *risnô*. See Commentary *ad loc.*
4. Reading *pîw* with S for MT *pānāyw.*
5. Reading *gēwôh* with LXX, Aq and V for MT *ga'^{a}wāh*. See Commentary *ad loc.*
6. Reading *s^{e}ḡôrô ḥāṯûm ṣôr* for MT *sāḡûr ḥôṯam ṣār*. See Commentary *ad loc.*
7. Reading *'^{a}ṭîšāṯāyw* for MT *'aṭîšôṯāyw* in agreement with the verb.
8. Reading *'ôḡēm* after LXX and V for MT *w^{e}'agmōn.*
9. Reading *yûṣāqû* for MT *yāṣûq* in agreement with the plural subject. See Commentary *ad loc.*
10. Reading *yimmôṭ* for MT *yimmôṯ* in agreement with the plural subject.
11. Reading *miśśē'ṯô* with certain Heb. MSS for MT *miśśē̱ṯô*. See Commentary *ad loc.*
12. Reading *mišš^{e}ḇārāyw* for MT *mišš^{e}ḇārîm*, *w* being corrupted to *m* in the Old Heb. script.
13. Reading *neḥšaḇ lô* for MT *neḥš^{e}ḇû.*
14. Reading *taḥtāyw k^{e}ḥāḏûḏ yaḥ^{a}rōš* for MT *taḥtāyw ḥaddûḏê ḥāreś*. See Commentary *ad loc.*
15. Reading *yirkaḏ* for MT *yirpaḏ*. See Commentary *ad loc.*
16. Reading *m^{e}šālô* for MT *môš^{e}lô* with LXX.
17. Reading *'ōṯô kol-gāḇôah yîrā'* for MT *'eṯ-kol-gāḇōah yir'eh*. See Commentary *ad loc.*

Commentary on Chapter 41.4-26 (EVV 12-34)

For text and Commentary on 40.25-30 (EVV 41.1-7), see above p. 480, 490-91.

4. The parallelism with *g^e^ḇûrōṯ* ('his strength') indicates that *baddāyw* means 'his limbs' and not 'his boasting' or 'idle talk', as Pope proposes. For MT *ûḏ^e^ḇar g^e^ḇûrōṯ w^e^ḥîn 'erkô* Houbigant's proposal *wa'^a^ḏabbēr g^e^ḇurāṯô* is supported by the parallel *lō' 'aḥ^a^rîš baddāyw*. MT *w^e^ḥîn 'erkô* might be a corruption of *w^e^ḥêl 'erkô*, taking *n* as a scribal corruption of *l* in the Old Heb. script, and *'ereḵ* in the sense of 'frame', arrangement of members (so NEB). But equally feasible graphically would be *'ên 'ereḵ* ('without comparison'), final *w* in MT *'erkô* being a dittograph after *k* or before the following *m* in the Old Heb. script. We follow this suggestion of Ehrlich, which preserves the meaning of the root *'arāḵ* in respect of comparison, which is actually attested in 28.17, 19; cf. *'^e^nôš k^e^'erkî* ('a man like me', Ps. 55.14).

5. *kep̄el* means 'doubling', hence 'overlapping' (i.e. the folds of skin), here compared to scale armour, which is illustrated by excavations in the palace at Ras Shamra and elsewhere in the Near East. MT *risnô* ('his bridle') is an obvious corruption of *širyōnô* (so LXX), 'his breastplate', as the parallelism demands. The familiar spelling is *širyôn*, but *siryon* is also attested (Jer. 46.4; 51.3). The phonetic variation indicates a non-Semitic loanword. The armour *širyôn*, a breast-plate both for men and horses, is known from an administrative text from the palace at Ras Shamra (RS 15.83, Virolleaud 1957: 123, 5-6). The verb *gillāh* parallel to *bô'* here recalls the similar collocation of those verbs in the conventional description of entering in the Ras Shamra texts, for example, *tgly šd 'il wtb'û* ('she cleared the threshold of El and entered'). The root is used regularly in Heb. of going into captivity; cf. Arab *jala(y)* ('to emigrate', pass over'); and see on 38.17. In all cases it means going beyond a certain point, whether going out or in. In the present passage 'uncover his outer covering', assuming the familiar use of *gillāh* in Heb., or 'pass within his outer covering' would be equally suitable, with the parallel *bô'* suggesting the latter.

7. In MT *ga'^a^wāh '^a^p̄îqê māḡinnîm*, which we find unintelligible, *gēwôh* ('his back') should be read with LXX, Aq and V. *'^a^p̄îqê* immediately suggests water-courses, and Dhorme thinks of the depressions between the scales resembling watercourses; cf. Isa. 8.7, where it has this meaning parallel with 'banks'. The word in Job 41.7, however, may rather be cognate with Arab. *'afaqa* ('to tan leather'), giving the meaning 'tanned work of shields', that is, 'tanned shields'. *sāḡûr* recalls the noun *sāḡôr* in the phrase *s^e^ḡôr libbām* ('their rib-cage') in Hos. 13.8 and is so taken here by LXX. If the word is retained as a noun it may be emended to *s^e^ḡōrô* ('his breast'), which the parallel *gēwôh* would suggest, and MT *ḥôṯām ṣār* might be then emended to *ḥāṯûm ṣûr* ('sealed with flint').

8. In v. 8b *rewaḥ* is proposed for MT *rûaḥ* ('wind, air'), but *rûaḥ*, though usually feminine, may also be masculine, here the subject of *yāḇô'*.

9. The verb *yeḏubbāqû*, describing scale-armour, recalls *deḇāqîm*, the overlapping joints of the scale-amour of the king of Israel in 1 Kgs 22.34. On *yiṯlakkeḏû* (lit. 'seize hold of one another'), cf. its use of water frozen to ice (see 38.30).

10. The singular *'aṭîšāṯô* should be read with LXX in agreement with the verb. The word, a *hapax legomenon* in the OT, is onomatopoeic with an Arab. cognate. *'ôr* here probably means 'sun', as the parallel colon with 'dawn' (*šaḥar*), suggests. The reference is to the reflection of the sun in the humid sneezing of the crocodile. The comparison of its eyes to the 'eyes of the dawn' (see above on 3.9) is then said to be in respect of the reddish glow of the crocodile's eyes under the water, but it may also refer to the submersion of the crocodile up to its eyes, suggesting the sun rising above the horizon. Fohrer (1989: 530 n. 9) notes that the eyes of the crocodile represented the dawn in ancient Egyptian hieroglyphics.

11. *kîḏôḏîm* is a *hapax legomenon*, but the association with *'ēš* ('fire') and the Arab. *kāda, yakîdu* ('to emit fire or sparks') indicates 'sparks'.

12. *neḥîrîm* is a *hapax legomenon* in the OT, but is known from the verbal noun *naḥar* ('snorting') in 39.20 and from Akk., Aram. and Arab. cognates. Here *'āšān*, usually 'smoke', means 'vapour'. *'aḡmôn* may be a corruption of *'āḡûm* or *'ōḡēm* ('made to blaze'); cf. Ass. *agâmu* and Arab. *'ajama* ('to be fierce', of flame). LXX and S support the reading *'ōḡēm*. *dûḏ* means 'basket', but also 'cooking pot' (1 Sam. 2.14). *dûḏ nāp̄ûaḥ* recalls *sîr nāp̄ûaḥ* of Jer. 1.15.

13. The parallelism with *pîw* in v. 13b might support the meaning 'throat' for *nap̄šô*, as Pope proposes, but in this case *geḥālîm* ('glowing coals'; cf. *gaḥalê 'ēš* in Lev. 16.12; Ps. 18.9), would be difficult. Hence we prefer the conventional translation 'his breath sets coals ablaze', which still preserves the parallelism, if not quite so mechanically.

14. The neck is the seat of strength, as in 15.26. In *tāḏûṣ de'āḇāh*, *dûṣ* is a *hapax legomenon* in Heb. but known from, Syr., Aram. and Mandaean cognates meaning 'to dance'. MT *de'āḇāh*, another *hapax legomenon*, means 'faintness' or 'dismay'; cf. *da'aḇôn nep̄eš* (Deut. 28.65). The inception may be suggested by the imagery in Hab. 3.5 of pestilence (*deḇer*) and plague (*rešep̄*), attendants on Yahweh in the theophany; cf. 'Vine' and 'field', minor deities attendant on Baal, and *qdš* and *'amr*, the attendants on the Mother-goddess in the Baal myth at Ras Shamra. LXX offers a variant of *dāḇe'āh* ('destruction').

As another variant *dāḇe'āh* might be suggested, cognate with Ugar. *db'at* ('strength'), which would give a formal parallel to *'ōz* (Cross 1952: 152-54). We prefer to retain MT *de'āḇāh*, primarily the effect of 'dismay', but implying also the power to cause that effect.

15. *mappelô beśārô* (lit. 'falling pieces of his flesh' or 'body'), would suggest folds of skin, the plural suggesting the emendation of MT *yāṣûq* to *yuṣāqû* (Hophal) and of MT *yimmôṭ* in v. 15b to *yimmôṭû*. The verbs seem to suggest something like scales rather than the folds of skin or flesh, but these probably have already been mentioned in vv. 7-9. Here the meaning is probably that even the parts of the beast such as the joints, which have no scales, are still protected by folds of skin that are loose enough, yet compact enough to cushion a blow. The verb *yāṣaq* has already occurred, meaning 'to smelt' or 'pour', and means here 'to fuse' or 'weld'.

16. Formally, *yāṣûq* could be the passive participle of *yāṣaq*, meaning 'moulded', so 'firmly set', hence 'hard' as ice; cf. 37.10, where the Hophal is used. Normally, however, we should expect a homonym, or near-homonym, of *yāṣaq*, which is used in v. 15, and *yāṣûq* in v. 16a may be the imperfect of *ṣûq* ('to be pressed hard'). This might mean that the crocodile imposes hard restraint on his feelings, but probably, as the simile 'as the nether millstone' indicates, means simply 'hard' in the sense of 'compact', or 'tight'.

lēḇ here (lit. 'heart'), probably means 'breast', as in Akk. and Ugar.

17. The simplest solution of the difficulty in v. 17a is to emend MT *missēṯô* to *miśśē'ṯô*. It is noted that *miśśē'ṯ* is found in the same context as 'fear' here and in 13.11 and 31.23 (cf. *šō'āh* in Prov. 3.25), which prompts Tur-Sinai to postulate a root *šā'āh* ('fear'), which, however, is not attested, though T and S render 'by fear of him'. We take *miśśē'ṯô* to mean 'when he comes up on land'.

'ēlîm is ambiguous. Pope, sustaining his thesis of the gods terrified by the monsters of chaos, renders 'gods'. Alternatively we understand *'ēlîm* as 'strong ones', *scriptio defectiva* of *'ēlîm*. The Hithpael of *ḥāṭā'* is found only in Num. 8.21; 19.1, 12f., 20; 31.23, meaning 'to purify from sin'. Thus we must understand the verb in v. 17b as the cognate of Arab. *ḥaṭa'a* ('to turn back').

missebārîm, the 'breakers of the 'sea' or 'pool' (reading *mišberê yām*), could only mean the waves caused by the crocodile's rising out of the water. Pope proposes that the 'breaking' is a reference to the 'breaking of the loins' as a sign of fear, as is assumed in the Ras Shamra texts (e.g. Gordon, *UT* 51, II, 17). This depends on the acceptance of the hypothetical meaning of *śē'ṯ* in the parallel colon. Actually there is another possible Ugar. parallel in the word *ṯbrn* ('the open jaws'); cf. Arab *ṯabaratu*(*n*) ('cavity'), and see also Gordon, *UT* 51, VIII:

'al tqrbn lbn 'ilm mt	Come not near to Mot the son of El
'al y'dbkm k'imr bph	Lest he make you like a sheep in his mouth,
kll'i bṯbrn qnh	Like a goat in his jaws.

18. LXX, T, V and one Heb. MS read *t*[e]*śîḡēhû* for MT *maśśîḡēhû*, treating the verb as a jussive in the protasis of a conditional sentence without the conditional particle. MT, however, may be retained as a case of the *casus pendens* in the protasis in the conditional sentence, 'If one would attack him, the sword does not avail'; cf. 1 Sam. 2.13 *kol-'îš zōḇēaḥ zeḇaḥ ûḇā' na'ar hakkōhēn*... ('if any man offered sacrifice, the priest's lad would come...'). See GKC, §16w.

The verb *qûm* means literally 'to stand', Hiphil 'to establish', that is, to bring one's purpose to effect, hence *tāqûm* here means 'will be of (no) avail'. This verse contains two *hapax legomena, massā'* and *širyāh*. Both are obviously weapons, specifically missiles. *massā'* seems most obviously a derivative of the verb *nāsa'* ('to pull out', e.g. tent-pegs), so that here it may possibly denote a javelin discharged from a slinging apparatus such as a stiff leather pouch attached to the arm. *širyāh* is cognate with Arab. *śirwatu*(*n*) ('arrow').

20. The arrow is described as 'the son of the bow'. The expression *ben qešeṯ* is chosen for the sake of word-play with *'aḇ*[e]*nê-qela'* ('sling-stones'). *nehp*[e]*ḵû* is a very strong expression, denoting complete change.

21. For MT *neḥš*[e]*ḇû* read *neḥšaḇ lô* with the sing. subject *tôṯāḥ*, understood by Theod., V and T as 'club', cognate with Arab. *mîtaḥatu*(*n*) from the root *wataḥa* ('to strike with a stick'). *ra'aš* signifies both the quivering motion of the javelin (*kîḏôn*) in flight and the whirring sound.

22. We consider the verb *yirpaḏ* in v. 22b doubtful. It is found in MT 17.3 of spreading a bed, more usually *rāḇaḏ*, but *rāpaḏ* is a possible orthographic variant. But in the present passage we suggest *yirkaḏ* cognate with Arab. *rakada* ('to be still'), translating 'lying like a studded threshing-sledge'. *ḥārûṣ* (lit. 'sharp-edged') describes the metal or sharp stone studs on the heavy boards of the threshing-sledge; cf. Amos 1.3.

ḥaddûdê ḥāreś, possibly 'sharp pieces of pottery', might just refer to the studs of the threshing-sledge, but we would see rather a reference to another agricultural implement, the sock of a plough; cf. Arab. *ḥadîcatu, 'lḥarṯ*, the iron tip, or 'sock' of the wooden plough. We read *taḥtāyw k*[e]*ḥāḏûḏ yaḥ*[a]*rōš*, 'his belly is as a plough-sock making a furrow').

23. The verb *rāṯaḥ* is known in the OT only here and at 30.27, where it describes figuratively the state of Job's bowels as 'boiling'. *m*[e]*ṣûlāh*, 'the abyss' or lower depths, the place of chaos in Mesopotamian mythology, is also

used of the depth of the sea in Exod. 15.5; Ps. 107.24; Jon. 2.4. *yām* may have local reference to the habitat of the crocodile in the Nile, as in Isa. 18.2; 19.5; Ezek. 32.2; Nah. 3.8; cf. Arab. *baḥru'nnîl*. *merqāḥāh* means both 'perfumed ointment' (Ezek. 24.10) and, as here, 'ointment-pot'. The verb *rāqaḥ* is used of the compounding of perfumed oil for the sanctuary in Exod. 30.23.

24. The comparison of the wake of the crocodile to 'hoariness' (*śēḇāh*) recalls *poliē thalassē* ('the hoary sea') of Homer.

25. In v. 25a *'āpār* (lit. 'dust') is simply a synonym of 'earth' (*'ereṣ*). It means in certain contexts (e.g. 7.21; 10.9; 17.16; 20.11; 34.15; Isa. 26.19; Ps. 22.16, 30) the dust of the grave and the underworld; hence its meaning 'earth' must be noted in view of the danger of drawing unwarranted doctrinal conclusions from other passages where *'āpār* occurs, for example, 19.25ff. MT *mošᵉlô* ('his mastery', sc. means of mastering him), was read and understood by Sym. and T. 'His like' (*mᵉšālô*; cf. Arab. *miṯluhu*), was read by the rest of the versions. The word may well have been intentionally ambiguous, according to the style of the writer, as indicated by the reference to the crocodile as king (*meleḵ*), for which *mōšēl* is a synonym, over all the big game in v. 25b. Here the chiastic parallelism of vv. 25-26 may be noted in support of this interpretation. So far as the intentional ambiguity of *mošᵉlô* or *mᵉšālô* may be expressed in English, we may suggest 'he has not his match'.

26. In *'eṯ-kol-gāḇōah yir'eh* ('he looks on all that is high'), we see an antithesis to v. 25b in the chiasmus of vv. 25-26, and so read *'ōṯô kol-gāḇōah yîrā'* ('him all that is high fears'; so Gunkel, Duhm, Budde, Hölscher, G.B. Gray, Mowinckel, Fohrer). The emphatic position of *'ōṯô* must be noted. This reading is supported by v. 26b.

In v. 26b MT *bᵉnê-šaḥaṣ* recalls the phrase describing the great beasts in 28.8. LXX 'creatures in the water', T 'little fishes' and S and 11QtargJob (*rḥš*, 'reptiles') might support a reading *bᵉnê-šereṣ* ('reptiles'). It is doubtful, however, after the unqualified statements in v. 25a and v. 26a if the dominion of the crocodile should have been so limited. On *šaḥaṣ*, a cognate of Arab. *šaḥaṣa* ('to be elevated'), see on 28.8. The expression, confined to those two passages in Job, may describe big game, but in the present passage naturally includes all beasts and reptiles. The reference to the crocodile as king over all the great beasts, though a natural metaphor, may also be a local allusion to the fact that the crocodile was the hieroglyphic sign for 'king', as Fohrer (1989: 531) notes, following Erman (1894: 180).

Job 42.7-17

The Epilogue

The epilogue falls into two parts, vv. 7-11 and 12-17. In the first part, vv. 7-9 consists of God's condemnation of Eliphaz and his friends, v. 10 of Job's intercession for them and the general statement of Job's rehabilitation, and v. 11 of his reintegration with society. The second part describes the details of Job's rehabilitation (vv. 12-17).

After the source of the Book had given Yahweh's answer to Job introduced in 38.1 before its development in 38.2–40.14, and Job's response, also developed to suit the theme of the Book, Yahweh again speaks 'after these words to Job' (42.7), presumably conveying the divine approval of Job's submissive response in the original of 40.3-5; 42.1-6. What the friends have said is condemned in Yahweh's censure of Eliphaz (v. 7). Formally this might refer to what may have been said in the source to impair the orthodox faith upheld in the spirit of his firm faith in divine providence expressed in 1.21 and 2.10. Or, however that may have been, it might have been the author's adaptation of his source in the Dialogue in the too facile assertion of the current doctrine of the theodicy, which limited the power and purpose of God, in contrast to Job's maintenance of his integrity, realism and indeed honest doubt. This remains, however, an unsolved problem, one that is in the state of the evidence insoluble.

Source material may be detected in the divine name Yahweh (vv. 7, 9, 10, 11, 12), as in the introduction to the Divine Declaration (38.1) and the Prologue. Job's intercession for his friends (cf. Abraham's intercession, Gen. 18.23; 20.7) seems to reflect the Israelite adaptation of the source in the early monarchy and the burnt offering of expiation (v. 8) agrees with Job's sacrifice for his family in the Prologue (1.5).

In the rehabilitation of Job, two-fold restitution surely reflects the source, likewise the reunion with his community after he had emerged from the cloud, or what they apprehended as the wrath of God (v. 11). The presentation of a piece of money and a gold ring also reflects source material, with reflections of patriarchal tradition. *qᵉśiṭāh*, for instance, is mentioned in Gen. 33.19 (J), while a ring of gold, while familiar in all ages in the Near East as female adornment (Isa. 3.2; Prov. 11.22), was a gift which Abraham's servant took to Nahor (Gen. 24.22 [J]).

The specific details of the two-fold restitution of Job's property is in the vein of midrashic expansion, recalling the Aramaic midrash on Genesis from Cave 1 at Qumran. To this belongs the names of Job's three daughters (v. 14), while the age of Job, twice the normal life-span of 70 years, reflects the ages of the patriarchs (Gen. 25.8, Abraham; 50.26, Joseph) in the Pentateuch in the nature of midrashic expansion. Here it may be noted that after the note on the two-fold restitution of Job's property after his intercession for his friends (v. 10) 11QtargJob ends with the condolence of family and friends and their tokens of his reintegration in society (v. 11).

Chapter 42.7-17

7. And it came to pass after Yahweh had spoken these words to Job that Yahweh said to Eliphaz the Temanite, 'I am angry with you and your two friends because you did not speak right concerning me[1] like my servant Job. 8. But now take for yourselves seven bullocks and seven rams and go to my servant Job and offer up a whole burnt-offering on behalf of yourselves, and let my servant Job intercede for you; for I will accept[2] his petition that I may not act according to your obtuseness[3] in that you have not spoken concerning me[4] what was right like my servant Job 9. So Eliphaz the Temanite and Bildad the Shuhite and[5] Zophar the Naamathite went and did as Yahweh had told them, and Yahweh accepted Job. 10. And Yahweh rehabilitated[6] Job when he had interceded for his friends,[7] and Yahweh increased all that Job had two-fold. 11. And all his brothers and all his sisters and all who formerly knew him ate and drank[8] with him, and they showed their sorrow for him and comforted him for all the calamity that Yahweh had brought upon him, and they gave him each one *qešiṭāh* and one gold ring.

12. And Yahweh blessed the latter part of Job's life more than the former part. He had 14,000 small cattle and 6000 camels and 1000 yoke of oxen and 1000 she-asses. 13. And he had (twice) seven sons and three daughters, 14. And he called the first Yemîmāh and the second Qeṣî'āh and the third Qeren-happûk. 15. And women as beautiful as the daughters of Job were not to be found[9] in all the earth; and their father[10] gave them[11] an inheritance among their brothers.[12] 16. And Job lived after this a hundred and forty years, and he saw[13] his sons and his sons' sons (to) four generations. 17. And Job died old and full of years.

Textual Notes to Chapter 42.7-17

1. Reading *'ālay* for MT *'ēlay*.
2. Reading *'et-pānāyw* for MT *'im-pānāyw*.
3. Reading *'im nebālekem* for MT *'immaḵem nebālāh*.
4. Reading *'ālay* for MT *'ēlay*.
5. Reading *weṣôp̄ar* with LXX, S and V and many Heb. MSS.
6. Reading *šāḇ šeḇûṯ* (Qere). See Commentary *ad loc*.
7. Reading *rē'āyw* for MT *rē'ēhû*, *y* being corrupted to *h* in the Old Heb. script.
8. Reading *wayyištû* with LXX and one Heb. MS and omitting *leḥem beḇêṯô* ('bread in his house') with LXX and two Heb. MSS. 11QtargJob, however, follows MT.
9. Reading *nimṣe'û* with LXX, S, and V and two Heb. MSS for MT *nimṣā'*, final *w* being omitted by haplography before the following *n* in the Old Heb. script.

10. Insert *'ᵃbîhen* with five Heb. MSS.
11. Reading *lāhen* for MT *lāhem* with five Heb. MSS.
12. Reading *'ᵃḥêhen* for MT *'ᵃḥêhem* with three Heb. MSS.
13. Reading *wayyar'* (Kethib).

Commentary on Chapter 42.7-17

7. *'aḥar dibbēr* indicates Late Heb. prose. Classical Heb. would have used the infinitive construct after *'aḥar*.

nᵉḵônāh (lit. 'that which is adjusted') means 'proper, right'.

8. In MT *kî 'im* Budde omitted *'im*, and Dhorme, closer to MT, read *kî 'eṯ-...*, which we accept.

On *nāśā' pānîm* ('to raise the face'), hence LXX *prosōpolambanein*, 'to show favour', see above on 11.15.

The designation of Job as 'my servant', as in 1.8 and 2.3, is significant. The term indicates the confidant, mediator and executor of the will of the master, for example the king in Canaan, called in royal legends from Ras Shamra *'bd 'il* or *ġlm 'il*, and in Israel 'my servant David', as well as the atoning servant in Deutero-Isaiah (Isa. 52.13–53.12). Here it is peculiarly apt because of Job's unique, personal experience of God with relation to his friends, his unqualified submission and his intercessory office, which he exercises like Abraham, the friend of God. The amount of the expiatory sacrifices (cf. Lev. 4), conventionally sevenfold, indicates the popular style of this part of the Book of Job.

yiṯpallēl is used in its primary sense of intercessory prayer.

nᵉḇālāh, which generally indicates conduct which respects neither reason nor social convention—nor religion—is surprising, with reference to God's treatment of humans. Here, if it really refers to God's conduct, it would have a secondary sense of 'rough handling', treating humans with as little consideration as they had shown to God and their fellows. In the context of Wisdom literature, however, it generally signifies moral and intellectual obtuseness, and MT may be a corruption of *'im niḇlāṯᵉḵem* ('according to your obtuseness'), the pronominal suffix in the noun having been omitted by haplography before *kî* in the Old Heb. script. In this case *'im* could have the comparative sense 'in proportion to', as regularly in Heb. Wisdom literature.

10. *šāḇ šᵉḇûṯ* (Qere) means 'rehabilitated', which in the context includes the healing of Job, though that is probably not specifically visualized, as Budde and Alt (1937: 267) suggested. In cases like Jer. 29.14; 30.3, 18; 49.29; Ezek. 16.53; 39.25; etc., it refers to the rehabilitation of a people, and it was eventually applied to the rehabilitation *par excellence*, the restoration from exile or captivity (*šᵉḇîṯ*), from the verb *šāḇāh* ('to be captive'), but the pointing *šᵉḇûṯ* indicates that the phrase refers to 'rehabilitation' with no implication of return from exile. The phrase, apparently with an internal accusative *šᵉḇûṯ*,

may owe its anomalous form in Classical Heb. to the fact that it was an archaic survival from the liturgy of the New Year festival as is indicated by its use in the eschatological passage Joel 4.1 (EVV 3.1). The flexibility of the phrase is indicated in Lam. 2.14, where *hēšîḇ šeḇûṯ* refers to repentance effected by the prophets.

11. With LXX and one Heb. MS we should read *wayyištû* after *wayyō'ḵelû*. Job's ritual seclusion imposed by the apparent alienation of the sufferer from God is over, and the eating and drinking of his friends with him symbolizes this fact, so inaugurating reintegration of Job with society. The occasion, though not to be compared with mourning rites, was not the occasion for hilarity, so Job's friends 'nodded the head' or 'rocked to and fro' (*wayyānuḏû*) for him, like Eliphaz, Bildad and Zophar at the beginning of Job's calamity (2.11), which may indeed indicate that the present passage has been influenced by the former. MT *qešîṭāh* is spelled *qeśîṭāh* in Gen. 33.19 and Josh. 24.32, but the noun *qošṭ* is found in Prov. 22.21, where it qualifies 'words of truth'; cf. *qešîṭ* in Palestinian Aram. It is attested in Arab. *qiśṭu*(*n*) ('justice'), for example, a just measure of grain in its container. Coinage is not known in the ancient Near East until its introduction in Asia Minor in the sixth century BCE. *qešîṭāh* therefore is a piece of silver of guaranteed weight. The word here may represent the archaizing of the narrative in the source cast in patriarchal times when a hundred *qeśîṭôt* is given as the price of the ground acquired by Jacob at Shechem (Gen. 33.19). *nezem* denotes an earring in Gen. 35.4 and Judg. 8.24, and a nose-ring in Gen. 24.47; Isa. 3.21.

13. In the fashion of folk-tale and midrash Job's property is doubled. According to T this extends to his sons, taking *šiḇ'ānāh* as 'fourteen'; so also Pope, assuming the ending *-ānāh* as the archaic dual for Classical Heb. *–ayim*; cf. Arab. *-ani*. Alternatively *-ana* may be a scribal corruption of the adverbial ending *m*, giving the reading *šeḇa'-m* ('seven-fold'). Both are understood by the variants *šeḇ'āh* and *šiḇ'ān* in different Heb. MSS. On the proportion of sons to daughters, reflecting their respective social significance, see on 3.21.

14. The names of Job's daughters reflect the popular folk-tale or midrash. *yemîmāh* ('turtle-dove') is known in Arab. *yamāmatu*(*n*), and is mentioned in Song 2.14; 5.2; 6.9. *qeṣî'āh* is possibly mentioned in Ps. 45.9 with myrrh and aloes. It is said to be a fragrant bark, powdered for cosmetics. *qeren-happûḵ* is 'horn of antimony', hence Larcher's 'mascara' (JB). Antimony was powdered and used as eye-cosmetic (Arab. *kuḥlu[n]*), which was used by Jezebel in her last 'make-up' (2 Kgs 9.30).

15. A portion to daughters when sons were alive was exceptional in antiquity. Indeed, in the case of Zelophehad's daughters, who had no brothers alive, was rare enough to merit special notice in Heb. tradition. The case of Job's

daughters may be designed to indicate his superabundant affluence, or it may reflect the status of women in the Jewish community when the Book of Job was completed. The situation is analogous to that of women in the Jewish military colony at Elephantine in the fifth century BCE (*ANET*, 222f.).

In the style of folk-tale or midrash Job is said to have lived 140 years, twice the normal life-span (Ps. 90.10). His life, like his property, is doubled. The statement of LXX that Job lived 240 years (248 according to LXX^{B}) and further details of his family and descendants, which LXX gives on the authority of 'a Syriac Book', indicate that the midrashic tendency to expand the Job tradition was active.

17. 'And Job died old and full of years' shows the influence of the patriarchal narratives in the Pentateuch, for example, Gen. 25.8; 35.29 (both P).

BIBLIOGRAPHY

Aistleitner, J. *Wörterbuch der ugaritischen Sprache.* Berlin: Akademie Verlag, 1963.

Albright, W.F. 'The Oldest Chaldaean Inscriptions in Proto-Arabic Script.' *BASOR* 179 (1965) 39-45.

Alt, A. 'Zur Vorgeschichte des Buches Hiob.' *ZAW* 55 (1937) 265-86.

—'Die Weisheit Salomos.' In *Kleine Schriften zur Geschichte des Volkes Israels.* Vol. 2. Munich: Beck, 1953. 90-99.

Ball, C.J. *The Book of Job. A Revised Text and Version.* Oxford: Clarendon Press, 1922.

Barr, J. *Comparative Semitic Philology and the Text of the Old Testament.* Oxford: Clarendon Press, 1968.

Bauer, H. 'Safonisches.' *OLZ* 38 (1935) 129-33.

Baumgärtel, F. *Der Hiobdialog. Aufriss und Deutung.* BZAW, 4/9. Stuttgart: Kohlhammer, 1933.

Baumgartner, W. *Israelitische und altorientalische Weisheit.* SGV, 166. Tübingen: J.C.B. Mohr (Paul Siebeck), 1933.

—'The Wisdom Literature.' In *The Old Testament and Modern Study.* Ed. H.H. Rowley. Oxford: Oxford University Press, 1951. 210-37.

—'Was wir heute von der hebrâischen Sprache und ihrer Geschichte wissen.' In his *Zum Alten Testament und seiner Umwelt.* Leiden: E.J. Brill, 1959. 208-39.

Beek, G.W. van and A. Jamme. 'An Inscribed South Arabian Clay Stamp from Bethel.' *BASOR* 151 (1958) 9-16.

Beeston, A.F.L. *A Descriptive Grammar of Epigraphic South Arabian.* London: Luzac, 1962.

Bentzen, A. *Introduction to the Old Testament.* Copenhagen: G.E.C. Gad, 1958.

Bickell, Gustav. *Das Buch Job nach Anleitung der Strophik und der Septuaginta auf seine ursprüngliche Form zurückgeführt und in Versmasse des Urtextes übersetzt.* Vienna: Carl Gerold's Sohn, 1894.

Branden, A. van den. *Les textes thamoudéens de Philby.* Louvain: Publications universitaires, 1956.

Breasted, J.H. (ed.). *Ancient Records of Egypt.* Chicago: University of Chicago Press, 1906.

Brockelmann, C. *Grundriss der vergleichenden Grammatik der semitischen Sprachen.* 2 vols. Berlin: Reuther & Reichard, 1908, 1913.

—*Lexicon syriacum.* Halle: Niemeyer, 1928.

Bruston, E. 'La littérature sapientiale dans le livre de Job.' *ETR* 3 (1928) 297-305.

Buck, Adriaan de. *De egyptische voorstellingen betreffende den oerheuvel.* Leiden: Eduard IJdo, 1922.

Budde, Karl. *Das Buch Hiob übersetzt und erklärt.* GHAT 2/1. Göttingen: Vandenhoeck & Ruprecht, 1896; 2nd edn, 1913.

Buhl, F. 'Zur Vorgeschichte des Buches Hiob.' In *Vom Alten Testament. Karl Marti zum siebzigsten Geburtstage gewidmet von Freunden, Fachgenossen und Schülern*. Ed. Karl Budde. BZAW, 41. Giessen: A. Töpelmann, 1925. 52-61.
Burney, C.F. *Notes on the Hebrew Text of the Books of Kings*. Oxford: Clarendon Press, 1903.
Buttenwieser, Moses. *The Book of Job*. London: Hodder & Stoughton, 1922.
Cantineau J., 'La langue de Ras Shamra.' *Syria* 13 (1932) 13-25.
Carlyle, T. *The Hero as Prophet, Man of Letters, and King*. London, 1908.
Chiera, E. *Sumerian Lexical Texts from the Temple School of Nippur*. Chicago: University of Chicago Press, 1929.
Clarke, E.C. 'Reflections on Some Obscure Hebrew Words in the Biblical Job in the Light of XI Q Tg Job.' In *Studies in Philology in Honour of Ronald James Williams: A Festschrift*. Ed. Gerald E. Kadish and Geoffrey E. Freeman. SSEA, 3. Toronto: Benben Publications, 1982. 17-30.
Clines, D.J.A. *Job 1–20*. WBC 17. Waco, TX: Word Books, 1989.
Cornill, C.H. *Introduction to the Canonical Books of the Old Testament*. Theological Translation Library, 23. Trans. G.H. Box. London: Williams & Norgate, 1907.
Cowley, A. *Aramaic Papyri of the Fifth Century BC*. Oxford: Clarendon Press, 1923.
Craigie, P.C. 'The Problem of Parallel Word Pairs in Ugaritic and Hebrew Poetry.' *Sem* 5 (1979) 45-58.
—*Psalms 1–50*. WBC 19. Waco, TX: Word Books, 1983.
Cross, F.M. 'Papyri of the Fourth Century BC from Dâliyeh.' In *New Directions in Biblical Archaeology*. Ed. D.N. Freedman and J.C. Greenfield. Garden City, NY: Doubleday, 1969. 41-62.
Dahood, M. 'The Value of Ugaritic for Textual Criticism.' *Bib* 40 (1959) 160-70.
—'Northwest Semitic Philology and Job.' In *The Bible in Current Catholic Thought*. Ed. J.L. McKenzie. New York: Herder & Herder, 1962.
—'Qoheleth and Northwest Semitic Philology.' *Bib* 43 (1962) 349-65.
—'Hebrew–Ugaritic Lexicography I.' *Bib* 44 (1963) 289-303.
—'Hebrew–Ugaritic Lexicography II.' *Bib* 45 (1964) 311-32.
—'Hebrew–Ugaritic Lexicography IV.' *Bib* 47 (1966) 403-19.
—*Psalm I, 1–50*. AB, 16. Garden City, NY: Doubleday, 1966.
—'Hebrew–Ugaritic Lexicography V.' *Bib* 48 (1967) 421-38.
—*Psalm II, 51–100*. AB, 17. Garden City, NY: Doubleday, 1968.
—*Psalm III, 101–150*. AB, 17A. Garden City, NY: Doubleday, 1970.
Dalman, G.H. *Palästinischer Diwan*. Leipzig: J.C. Hinrichs, 1901.
—*Arbeit und Sitte in Palästina*. 8 vols. Gütersloh: C. Bertelsmann, 1920–37 [repr. Hildesheim: Georg Olms, 1964].
—*Aramäisch-neuhebräisches Handwörterbuch zu Targum, Talmud, und Midrasch*. Göttingen: Pfeiffer, 1938.
Danby, Hope, and Moses H. Segal. *A Concise Hebrew–English Dictionary*. Tel Aviv: Dvir, 1930.
Delitzsch, Franz J. *Das Buch Iob. Mit Beiträgen von Prof. Dr Fleischer und Consul Dr Wetzstein, nebst einer Karte und Inschrift*. Leipzig: Dörfling & Francke, 1864 [= *Biblical Commentary on the Book of Job*. Trans. F. Bolton. 2 vols. Edinburgh: T. & T. Clark, 1866].
Dell, Katharine J. *The Book of Job as Sceptical Literature*. BZAW, 1991. Berlin: de Gruyter.

Dennefeld, L. 'Les discours d'Elihou.' *RB* 48 (1939) 163-80.

Dhorme, E. *Le livre de Job.* Paris: Gabalda, 1926 [= *A Commentary on the Book of Job.* Trans. H. Knight. London: Thomas Nelson & Sons, 1967].

—'Job.' In *La Bible de la Pléiade.* Paris: Gallimard, 1959.

Dijk, Johannes J.A. van. *La sagesse suméro-accadienne.* Commentationes orientales, 1. Leiden: E.J. Brill, 1953.

Dillmann, A. *Lexicon linguae aethiopicae.* Leipzig: T.O. Weigel, 1865.

Doughty, Charles M. *Travels in Arabia deserta.* 2 vols. London: Jonathan Cape, 1926.

Driver, G.R. *Canaanite Myths and Legends.* Edinburgh: T. & T. Clark, 1956.

—'Ezekiel: Linguistic and Textual Problems.' *Bib* 35 (1954) 145-59, 299-312.

—'Hebrew Notes.' *JRAS* 1944 165-71.

—'Hebrew Notes.' *ZAW* 52 (1934) 51-56.

—'Hebrew Poetic Diction.' In *Congress Volume: Copenhagen, 1953.* Ed. J.A. Emerton *et al.* VTSup, 1. Leiden: E.J. Brill, 1953. 26-39.

—'L'interprétation du texte masorétique à la lumière de la lexicographie hébraïque.' *ETL* 26 (1950d) 337-53.

—'Misreadings in the Old Testament.' *WO* 1 (1948) 234-38.

—'Problems in Job.' *AJSL* 52 (1936) 160-70.

—'Problems in the Hebrew Text of Job.' In *Wisdom in Israel and in the Ancient Near East, Presented to Professor Harold Henry Rowley ... in Celebration of his Sixty-Fifth Birthday* VTSup, 3. Leiden: E.J. Brill, 1955. 72-93.

—'Problems of the Hebrew Text and Language.' In *Alttestamentliche Studien Friedrich Nötscher zum sechzigsten Geburtstage 19. Juli 1950 gewidmet.* BBB, 1. Ed. Hubert Junker and Johannes Botterweck. Bonn: Hanstein, 1950. 46-61.

—*Semitic Writing: From Pictograph to Alphabet.* London: Oxford University Press, 1976.

—'Some Hebrew Medical Expressions.' *ZAW* 65 (1954) 255-62.

—'Studies in the Vocabulary of the Old Testament. V.' *JTS* 34 (1933) 33-44.

—'Ugaritic and Hebrew Problems.' *AfO* 17 (1949) 153-57.

Driver, S.R. *The Book of Job in the Revised Version. Edited with Introductions and Brief Annotations.* Oxford: Clarendon Press, 1906.

Driver, S.R., and G.B. Gray. *The Book of Job.* ICC. Edinburgh: T. & T. Clark, 1921.

Dubarle, A.E. *Les sages d'Israël.* Lectio divina, 1. Paris: Cerf, 1946.

Duesberg, H. *Les scribes inspirés.* Paris: Desclée, 1939.

Duhm, Bernhard. *Das Buch Hiob erklärt.* KHC, 16. Freiburg i.Br.: J.C.B. Mohr (Paul Siebeck), 1897.

Dupont-Sommer, A. *Les Araméens.* L'Orient ancient illustré, 2. Paris: A. Maisonneuve, 1949.

—'Sur 11QtgJob, col. XXXIII.' *Sem* 15 (1965) 70-74.

Eerdmans, B.D. *Studies in Job.* Leiden: Burgersdijk & Niermans, 1939.

—*Randglossen zur hebräischen Bibel.* VI. *Psalmen, Sprüche, und Hiob.* Leipzig: J.C. Hinrichs, 1918 [repr. Hildesheim: Georg Olms, 1968].

Eissfeldt, O. *The Old Testament: An Introduction.* Trans. P.R. Ackroyd. New York: Harper & Row, 1965.

Eitan, Israel. *A Contribution to Biblical Lexicography.* New York: Columbia University Press, 1924.

Erman, Adolf. *Ägyptische Grammatik.* Porta linguarum orientalium, 15. Berlin: Reuther & Reichard, 1894.

Ewald, Georg Heinrich August von [Heinrich Ewald]. *Commentary on the Book of Job, with Translation.* Trans. J. Frederick Smith. London: Williams & Norgate, 1882.

Fichtner, J. *Die altorientalische Weisheit in ihrer israelitisch-jüdischen Ausprägung.* BZAW, 62. Giessen: A. Töpelmann, 1933.

Fisher, Loren R. (ed.) *Ras Shamra Parallels: The Texts from Ugaritic and the Hebrew Bible.* AnOr, 49–50. Rome: Pontifical Biblical Institute, 1972, 1975.

Fitzmyer, J.A. 'Some Observations on the Targum of Job from Qumran Cave 11.' *CBQ* 36 (1974) 503-24 [= 'The First-Century Targum of Job from Qumran Cave XI.' In his *A Wandering Aramean: Collected Aramaic Essays.* SBLMS, 25. Missoula, MT: Scholars Press, 1979. 161-82].

Fohrer, Georg. *Studien zum Buche Hiob.* BZAW, 159. Gütersloh: Gerd Mohn, 1963 [2nd edn, *Studien zum Buche Hiob (1956–1979).* Berlin: de Gruyter, 1983].

—*Das Buch Hiob.* KAT, 16. Gütersloh: Gütersloher Verlagshaus Gerd Mohn, 1963 [2nd edn, 1989].

Frankfort, Henri. *Kingship and the Gods: A Study of Ancient Near Eastern Religion as the Integration of Society and Nature.* Chicago: University of Chicago Press, 1948.

Freedman, David N. 'The Elihu Speeches in the Book of Job.' *HTR* 61 (1968) 51-59.

Freytag, Georg W. *Lexicon arabico-latinum.* 4 vols. Berlin: C.A. Schwetschke, 1830–37.

Friedrich, Johannes. *Phönizisch-punische Grammatik.* AnOr, 32. Rome: Pontifical Biblical Institute, 1951.

Fries, Karl. *Das philosophische Gespräch von Hiob bis Plato.* Tübingen: J.C.B. Mohr, 1904.

Fullerton, Kember. 'The Original Conclusion to the Book of Job.' *ZAW* 42 (1924) 116-35.

Gadd, C.J. 'The Harran Inscriptions of Nabonidus.' *AnatSt* 8 (1958) 35-92.

Gardiner, Alan H. *Ancient Egyptian Onomastica.* 3 vols. London: Oxford University Press, 1947.

Gemser, Berend. *Sprüche Salomos.* HAT, 16. Tübingen: J.C.B. Mohr (Paul Siebeck), 1937 [2nd edn, 1963].

Gerleman, Gillis. *Studies in the Septuagint.* I. *The Book of Job.* Lunds universitets årsskrift 1/43.2. Lund: C.W.K. Gleerup, 1946.

Gese, Hartmut. *Lehre und Wirklichkeit in der alten Weisheit. Studien zu den Sprüchen Salomos und zu dem Buche Hiob.* Tübingen: Mohr, 1958.

Gevirtz, Stanley. *Patterns in the Early Poetry of Israel.* Studies in Ancient Oriental Civilization, 32. Chicago: University of Chicago Press, 1963.

Gibson, John C.L. *Textbook of Syrian Semitic Inscriptions.* Vol. 2, Aramaic. Oxford: Clarendon Press, 1975.

—*Canaanite Myths and Legends.* OTS, 3. Edinburgh: T. & T. Clark, 2nd edn, 1978.

—*Job.* Daily Study Bible. Edinburgh: St Andrews Press, 1985.

Goetze, Albrecht. 'Is Ugaritic a Canaanite Dialect?' *Language* 17 (1941) 127-38.

Gordis, Robert. *Koheleth: The Man and his World.* New York: Bloch Publishing Co., 1955.

—*The Book of God and Man: A Study of Job.* Chicago: University of Chicago Press, 1965.

Gordon, Cyrus H. 'Belt-Wrestling in the Bible World.' *HUCA* 23 (1950–51) 131-36.

—*Ugaritic Textbook.* AnOr, 38. Rome: Pontifical Biblical Institute, 1965.

Gordon, E.I. *Sumerian Proverbs: Glimpse of Everyday Life in Ancient Mesopotamia.* Philadelphia: University of Pennsylvania, 1959.

Graetz, H. 'Lehrinhalt der "Weisheit" in den biblischen Büchern.' *MGWJ* 35 (1886) 289-99, 402-10, 544-49 [pp. 402-10, 544-49 often cited as 'Register der corrumpierten Stellen in Hiob und Vorschläge zur Verbesserung'].

Gray, J. 'The Rephaim.' *PEQ* 81 (1949) 127-39.

—'The Hebrew Conception of the Kingship of God: Its Origin and Development.' *VT* 6 (1956) 268-85.

—*The Legacy of Canaan: The Ras Shamra Texts and their Relevance to the Old Testament.* VTSup, 5. Leiden: E.J. Brill, 2nd edn, 1965.

—'The Book of Job in the Context of Near Eastern Literature.' *ZAW* 82 (1970) 251-69.

—'The Massoretic Text of the Book of Job, the Targum and the Septuagint Version in the Light of the Qumran Targum (11Qtarg Job).' *ZAW* 86 (1974) 331-50.

Gressmann, Hugo. *Altorientalische Texte und Bilder zum Alten Testament.* Tübingen: J.C.B. Mohr, 1909.

—'Die neugefundene Lehre des Amen-em-ope und die vorexilische Spruchdichtung Israels.' *ZAW* 42 (1924) 272-96.

Guillaume, Alfred. 'The Unity of the Book of Job.' *ALUOS* 4 (1962) 26-46.

—'The Arabic Background of the Book of Job.' In *Promise and Fulfilment: Essays Presented to S.H. Hooke.* Ed. F.F. Bruce. Edinburgh: T. & T. Clark, 1963. 106-27.

—*Studies in the Book of Job, with a New Translation.* ALUOS, 2. Leiden: E.J. Brill, 1968.

Gunkel, Herman. *Schöpfung und Chaos in Urzeit und Endzeit.* Göttingen: Vandenhoeck & Ruprecht, 3rd edn, 1922.

Habel, Norman C. *The Book of Job: A Commentary.* OTL. London: SCM Press; Philadelphia: Westminster Press, 1985.

Hartley, John E. *The Book of Job.* NICOT. Grand Rapids: Eerdmans, 1988.

Hempel, Johannes. *Die althebräische Literatur und ihr hellenistisch-jüdisches Nachleben.* Wildpark-Potsdam: Akademische Verlagsgesellschaft Athenaion, 1930.

Herdner, A. *Corpus des tablettes en cunéiformes alphabétiques.* Paris: Imprimerie nationale, 1963.

Hertzberg, H.W. 'Der Aufbau des Buches Hiob.' In *Festschrift Alfred Bertholet zum 80. Geburtstag gewidmet von Kollegen und Freunden.* Ed. Walter Baumgartner, Otto Eissfeldt, Kurt Elliger, and Leonhard Rost. Tübingen: J.C.B. Mohr (Paul Siebeck), 1950. 233-58.

Hesse, Franz. *Hiob.* Zürcher Bibelkommentar. Zurich: Theologischer Verlag, 1978.

Hitzig, Ferdinand. *Das Buch Hiob übersetzt und ausgelegt.* Leipzig and Heidelberg: C.F. Winter, 1874.

Hoffmann, Johann Georg Ernst [Georg]. *Hiob.* Kiel: C.F. Haeseler, 1891.

—'Ergänzungen und Berichtigungen zu Hiob.' *ZAW* 49 (1931) 141-45, 270-73.

Hölscher, Gustav. *Das Buch Hiob.* HAT, 1/17. Tübingen: J.C.B. Mohr (Paul Siebeck), 1937.

Hontheim, Joseph. *Das Buch Hiob als strophisches Kunstwerk nachgewiesen, übersetzt und erklärt.* Biblische Studien, 9/1-3. Freiburg i.Br.: Herder, 1904.

Horst, Friedrich. *Hiob.* I [chaps. 1-19]. BKAT, 16/1. Neukirchen: Neukirchener Verlag, 1960–69.

Houbigant, Carolus Franciscus. *Notae criticae in universos Veteris Testamenti libros cum hebraice, tum graecae scriptos cum integris ejusdem prolegomenis.* 2 vols. Frankfurt: Varrentrapp Filius & Wenner, 1777. Vol. 2. 155-218.

Humbert, Paul. *Recherches sur les sources égyptiennes de la littérature sapientiale d'Israël.* Mémoires de l'Université de Neuchâtel 7. Neuchâtel: Secrétariat de l'Université, 1929.

Hupfeld, Hermann. *Quaestionum in Jobeidos locos vexatos specimen. Commentatio ...* Halle: E. Anton, 1853.

Irwin, William A. 'The Elihu Speeches in the Criticism of the Book of Job.' *JR* 17 (1937) 37-47.

—'Job.' In *Peake's Commentary on the Bible*. Ed. Matthew Black and H.H. Rowley. London: Thomas Nelson & Sons, 1962. 391-408.

Jastrow, Morris. *The Religion of Babylonia and Assyria*. Boston: Ginn & Company, 1898.

—*A Dictionary of the Targumim, Talmud Bavli, Talmud Yerushalmi, and Midrashic Literature*. New York: Jastrow Publishers, 1903.

—*The Book of Job. Its Origin, Growth and Interpretation, together with a New Translation Based on a Revised Text*. Philadelphia: Lippincott, 1920.

Jean, Charles F., and Jacob Hoftijzer. *Dictionnaire des inscriptions sémitiques de l'ouest*. Leiden: E.J. Brill, 1960.

Jepsen, Alfred. *Das Buch Hiob und seine Deutung*. Aufsätze und Vorträge zur Theologie und Religionswissenschaft, 28. Berlin: Evangelische Verlagsanstalt, 1963 [=*Arbeiten zur Theologie*, 1/14. Ed. Alfred Jepsen, Otto Michel, and Theodor Schlatter. Stuttgart: Calwer Verlag, 1964].

Junker, Hubert. *Das Buch Job*. EchB. Würzburg: Echter-Verlag, 1951.

Kaiser, Otto. *Die mythische Bedeutung des Meeres in Ägypten, Ugarit und Israel*. Berlin: A. Töpelmann, 1962.

Kallen, Horace M. *The Book of Job as a Greek Tragedy Restored*. New York: Moffat, Yard & Co., 1918.

Kautzsch, Emil. *Die Aramaismen im Alten Testament*. Halle: Niemeyer, 1902.

Kautzsch, Karl. *Das sogenannte Volksbuch von Hiob und der Ursprung von Hiob cap. I. II. XLII, 7-17: Ein Beitrag zur Frage nach der Integrität des Buches Hiob*. Tübingen: J.C.B. Mohr, 1900.

Kissane, Edward J. *The Book of Job Translated from a Critically Revised Hebrew Text with Commentary*. Dublin: Browne & Nolan, 1939; New York: Sheed & Ward, 1946.

Klostermann, A. 'Hiob.' *RE*. 3rd edn, 1900. Vol. 8. 97-126.

Knabenbauer, Joseph. *Commentarius in librum Iob*. Cursus scripturae sacrae; Commentarii in Vetus Testamentum, 2,1. Paris: P. Lethielleux, 1886.

Köhler, Ludwig Hugo. *Der hebräische Mensch*. Tübingen: J.C.B. Mohr, 1953.

König, Eduard. *Das Buch Hiob eingeleitet, übersetzt und erklärt*. Gütersloh: C. Bertelsmann, 1929.

Kopf, L. 'Das arabische Wörterbuch als Hilfsmittel für die hebräische Lexikographie.' *VT* 6 (1956) 286-302.

Kraeling, Emil G. *The Book of the Ways of God*. London: SPCK, 1938.

Kramer, Samuel Noah. 'Man and his God: A Sumerian Variation on the "Job" Motif.' In *Wisdom in Israel and in the Ancient Near East, Presented to Professor Harold Henry Rowley*. Ed. M. Noth and D. Winton Thomas. VTSup, 3. Leiden: E.J. Brill, 1955. 170-82.

Kraus, Hans Joachim. *Psalmen*. BKAT, 15. Neukirchen: Neukirchener Verlag, 1961.

Kuhl, Curt. 'Neuere Literarkritik des Buches Hiob.' *TRu* NF 21 (1953) 163-205, 257-317.

—'Vom Hiobbuche und seinen Problemen.' *TRu* NF 22 (1954) 261-316.

Kuschke, A. 'Altbabylonische Texte zum Thema "Der leidende Gerechte".' *ThLZ* 81 (1956) 69-76.

Lambert, W.G. *Babylonian Wisdom Literature*. Oxford: Clarendon Press, 1960.

Lamparter, Helmut. *Das Buch der Anfechtung, übersetzt und ausgelegt*. BotAT. Stuttgart: Calwer, 1951.

Lane, Edward William. *Arabic–English Lexicon*. 8 vols. London: Williams & Norgate, 1863–93.

Langhe, R. de. 'L'enclitique cananéenne m(a).' *Muséon* 49 (1946) 89-111.

—*De taal van Ras Sjamra-Ugarit.* Nijmegen: Dekker & van de Vegt, 1948.
Larcher, C. *Le Livre de Job.* La Sainte Bible. Paris: Cerf, 1950, 2nd edn, 1957.
Le Fèvre, A. *Supplément au Dictionnaire de la Bible.* Vol. IV. Ed. H. Cazelles and A. Feuillet. Paris: Letouzey & Ané, 1949.
Leslau, Wolf. *Ethiopic and South Arabic Contributions to the Hebrew Lexicon.* Berkeley, CA: University of California Press, 1958.
Lévêque, Jean. *Job et son Dieu. Essai d'exégèse et de théologie biblique.* 2 vols. Paris: Gabalda, 1970.
—'La datation du livre de Job.' In *Congress Volume: Vienna 1980.* Ed. J.A. Emerton. VTSup, 32. Leiden: E.J. Brill, 1981. 206-19.
Ley, Julius. *Das Buch Hiob nach seinem Inhalt, seiner Kunstgestaltung und religiösen Bedeutung. Für gebildete Leser dargestellt.* Halle: Waisenhaus, 1903.
Lindblom, Johannes. 'Job and Prometheus. A Comparative Study.' In *Dragma. Martino P. Nilsson A.D. IV Id. Iul. anno MCMXXXIX dedicatum.* Acta Instituti Romani Regni Sueciae, 2/1. Lund: H. Ohlssons, 1939. 280-87.
—*Boken om Job och hans idande.* Lund: C.W.K. Gleerup, 1940.
—*La composition du livre de Job.* Lund: C.W.K. Gleerup, 1945.
Lods, A. 'Recherches récentes sur le livre de Job.' *RHPR* 14 (1934) 501-33.
Löhr, M. 'Die drei Bildad-Reden im Buche Hiob.' In *Karl Budde zum siebzigsten Geburtstag am 13. April 1920, überreicht von Freunden und Schülern und in ihrem Namen.* Ed. K. Marti. BZAW, 34. Giessen: A. Töpelmann, 1920. 107-12.
Lowth, Robert. 'De poemati Jobi argumento et fine.' Praelectio 37 in his *De sacra poesi hebraeorum. Praelectiones academicae.* Oxford: Clarendon Press, 1753 [= *Lectures on the Sacred Poetry of the Hebrews.* Trans. G. Gregory. London, 1789; Praelectio 33 is reprinted as 'Of the Poem of Job' in *The Dimensions of Job: A Study and Selected Readings.* Ed. Nahum H. Glatzer. New York: Schocken Books, 1969. 132-40].
MacKenzie, R.A.F. 'The Purpose of the Yahweh Speeches in the Book of Job.' *Bib* 40 (1959) 435-45.
Marshall, J.T. *Job and his Comforters: Studies in the Theology of the Book of Job.* London: James Clarke & Co., 1905.
Matous, Lubor. *Die lexikalischen Tafelserien der Babylonier und Assyrer in den Berliner Museen.* Berlin: Staatliche Museen, 1933.
May, Herbert Gordon. 'Prometheus and Job. The Problem of the God of Power and the Man of Wrath.' *ATR* 34 (1952) 240-46.
Milik, J.T. '"Prière de Nabonide" et autres écrits d'un cycle de Daniel: Fragments araméens de Qumrân 4.' *RB* 63 (1956) 407-15.
Möller, Hans. *Sinn und Aufbau des Buches Hiob.* Berlin: Evangelische Verlagsanstalt, 1955.
Montgomery, James A., and Zellig S. Harris. *The Ras Shamra Mythological Texts.* Memoirs of the American Philosophical Society, 4. Philadelphia: American Philosophical Society, 1935.
Morrow, Francis J. '11 Q Targum Job and the Massoretic Text.' *RevQ* 8 (1972–75) 253-56.
Moscati, Sabatino (ed.). *An Introduction to the Comparative Grammar of the Semitic Languages: Phonology and Morphology.* Porta linguarum orientalium, 6. Wiesbaden: Harrassowitz, 1964.
Mowinckel, Sigmund. 'Hiobs *gōʾēl* und Zeuge im Himmel.' In *Vom Alten Testament: Karl Marti zum siebzigsten Geburtstage gewidmet von Freunden, Fachgenossen und Schülern in ihrem Namen.* Ed. K. Budde. BZAW, 41. Giessen: A. Töpelmann, 1925. 207-12.

—'Diktet om Ijob.' In *Det gamle Testament.* Trans. S. Michelet, Sigmund Mowinckel and N. Messe. Oslo: H. Aschehoug & Co. (W. Nygaard), 1955. Vol. IV. 293-384.
—*The Psalms in Israel's Worship.* Trans. D.R. Ap-Thomas. Oxford: Basil Blackwell, 1962.
Müller, Hans-Peter. *Das Hiobproblem: seine Stellung und Entstehung im alten Orient und im Alten Testament.* Erträge des Forschung, 84. Darmstadt: Wissenschaftliche Buchgesellschaft, 1978; 3rd edn, 1995.
Nichols, H.H. 'The Composition of the Elihu Speeches.' *AJSL* 27 (1911) 97-186.
Nöldeke, Theodor. 'Wörter mit Gegensinn (Addad).' In his *Neue Beiträge zur semitischen Sprachwissenschaft.* Strasbourg: Trübner, 1910. 67-108.
Nougayrol, Jean. *Le palais royal d'Ugarit 2.* Mission de Ras Shamra. Paris: Imprimerie nationale, 1951.
—'Une version ancienne du "juste souffrant".' *RB* 59 (1952) 237-50.
—*Le palais royal d'Ugarit 5.* Mission de Ras Shamra. Paris: Imprimerie nationale, 1965.
—'(Juste) souffrant (R.S. 25.460).' *Ugaritica* 5 (1968) 265-83.
Olshausen, Justus. *Hiob erklärt.* KEH, 2. 2nd edn. Leipzig: S. Hirzel, 1852.
Orlinsky, Harry M. 'Studies in the Septuagint of the Book of Job.' *HUCA* 28 (1957) 53-74; 29 (1958) 229-71; 30 (1959) 153-57; 32 (1961) 239-68; 33 (1962) 119-51; 35 (1964) 57-78; 36 (1965) 37-47.
Peake, Arthur S. *Job: Introduction, Revised Version.* CB. London: T.C. &. E.C. Jack, 1904.
—*The Problem of Suffering in the Old Testament.* London: Robert Bryant, 1904; repr. London: Epworth Press, 1947.
Pedersen, Johannes. *Israel: Its Life and Culture.* London: Oxford University Press, 1926.
Perles, Felix. *Analekten des Alten Testaments.* Munich: Ackermann, 1895.
—*Analekten zur Textkritik des Alten Testaments. Neue Folge.* Leipzig: Engel, 1922.
Peters, Norbert. *Das Buch Hiob übersetzt und erklärt.* EHAT. Münster: Aschendorff, 1928.
Pfeiffer, R.H. 'The Priority of Job over Is. 40–55.' *JBL* 46 (1927) 202-206.
—*Introduction to the Old Testament.* New York: Harper & Brothers, 1941.
—*The Books of the Old Testament* [an abridgment of *Introduction to the Old Testament.* New York: Harper & Brothers, 1957].
Ploeg, J.P.M. van der. *Le Targum de Job de la Grotte 11 de Qumran (11QtgJob). Première communication.* Akademie van Wetenschappen, Amsterdam. Mededelingen. Afd. Letterkunde. N.R. 25/9. Amsterdam: Noord-Hollandsche Uitgevers Maatschappij, 1962.
Ploeg, J.P.M. van der and A.S. van der Woude. *Le targum de Job de la grotte XI de Qumran.* Leiden: E.J. Brill, 1971.
Pope, Marvin H. *Job: Introduction, Translation and Notes.* AB, 15. Garden City, NY: Doubleday, 1973. 2nd edn, 1965; 3rd edn, 1973.
Porten, Bezalel. *Archives from Elephantine: The Life of an Ancient Jewish Military Colony.* Berkeley, CA: University of California Press, 1968.
Pritchard, James B. (ed.). *Ancient Near Eastern Texts relating to the Old Testament.* Princeton, NJ: Princeton University Press, 2nd edn, 1955.
Rabin, Chaim. *Ancient West-Arabia: A Study of the Dialects of the Western Highlands of Arabia in the Sixth and Seventh Centuries A.D.* London: Taylor's Foreign Press, 1951.
Rad, Gerhard von. 'Josephgeschichte und ältere Chokma.' In *Congress Volume: Copenhagen, 1953.* Ed. J.A. Emerton *et al.* VTSup, 1. Leiden: E.J. Brill, 1953. 120-27.
—'Hiob xxxviii und die altägyptische Weisheit.' In *Wisdom in Israel and in the Ancient Near East.* Festschrift H.H. Rowley. Ed. M. Noth and D. Winton Thomas. VTSup, 3. Leiden: E.J. Brill, 1955. 293-301.

—*Theologie des Alten Testaments*. 2 vols. Munich: Kaiser, 1957, 1960 (= *Old Testament Theology*. 2 vols. London: SCM Press, 1975].

Rankin, Oliver S. *Israel's Wisdom Literature*. Edinburgh: T. & T. Clark, 1936.

Renan, Ernest. *Le livre de Job, traduit de l'hébreu.* [with] *Etude sur l'age et le caractère du poème.* Paris: Michel Lévy Frères, 1860 [repr. Paris: Arlea, 1991; in his *Oeuvres complètes.* VII. Paris: Calmann-Lévy, 1955; = *The Book of Job Translated from the Hebrew with a Study upon the Age and Character of the Poem.* Trans. A.F.G. [H.F. Gibbons] and W.M. T[homson]. London: W.M. Thomson, 1899].

Richter, Heinz. 'Die Naturweisheit des Alten Testaments im Buche Hiob.' *ZAW* 70 (1958) 1-20.

—*Studien zu Hiob. Der Aufbau des Hiobbuches, dargestellt an den Gattungen des Rechtslebens.* Berlin: Evangelische Verlagsanstalt, 1958, 1959.

Rignell, L.G. 'Notes on the Peshitta of the Book of Job.' *ASTI* 9 (1973) 98-106.

Ringgren, Helmer. *Word and Wisdom: Studies in the Hypostatization of Divine Qualities and Functions in the Ancient Near East.* Lund: H. Ohlssons, 1947.

—*Sprüche, Prediger.* Das Alte Testament Deutsch, 16/1. Göttingen: Vandenhoeck & Ruprecht, 1962.

Roberts, Bleddyn J. *The Old Testament Text and Versions.* Cardiff: Cardiff University Press, 1951.

Robinson, H. Wheeler. *The Cross of Job.* London: SCM Press, 1916 [reprinted in *The Cross in the Old Testament.* London: SCM Press, 1955].

Robinson, Theodore H. *Job and his Friends.* London: SCM Press, 1954.

Rodd, Cyril R. *The Book of Job.* Epworth Commentaries. London: Epworth Press, 1990.

—*The Book of Job.* Narrative Commentaries. Philadelphia: Trinity Press International, 1990.

Rowley, H.H. 'The Book of Job and its Meaning.' *BJRL* 41 (1958–59) 167-207 [= his *From Moses to Qumran: Studies in the Old Testament.* London: Lutterworth, 1963. 139-83.

Rowley, H.H. *Job.* NCB. London: Thomas Nelson & Sons, 1970.

Sarna, Nahum M. 'Epic Substratum in the Prose of Job.' *JBL* 76 (1957) 13-15.

Säve-Söderberg, T. *On Egyptian Representations of Hippopotamus Hunting as a Religious Motive.* Lund: C.W.K. Gleerup, 1953.

Sawyer, J.F.A. 'The Authorship and Structure of the Book of Job.' In *Studia biblica 1978.* I. *Papers on Old Testament and Related Themes.* Ed. E.A. Livingstone. JSOTSup, 11. Sheffield: JSOT Press, 1979. 253-57.

Schmid, Hans H. *Wesen und Geschichte der Weisheit.* BZAW, 101. Berlin: A. Töpelmann, 1966.

Schmidt, H. *Das Gebet der Angeklagten im Alten Testament.* BZAW, 49. Giessen: A. Töpelmann, 1928.

Scott, R.B.Y. 'Solomon and the Beginnings of Wisdom in Israel.' In *Wisdom in Israel and in the Ancient Near East, Presented to Professor Harold Henry Rowley.* Ed. M. Noth and D. Winton Thomas. VTSup, 3. Leiden: E.J. Brill, 1955. 262-79.

—*The Way of Wisdom in the Old Testament.* New York: Macmillan, 1971.

Szczygiel, Paul. *Das Buch Job, übersetzt under erklärt.* HSAT, 5/1. Bonn: Peter Hanstein, 1931.

Sekine, Masao. 'Schöpfung und Erlösung im Buche Hiob.' In *Von Ugarit nach Qumran: Beiträge zur alttestamentlichen und altorientalischen Forschung. Otto Eissfeldt zum 1. September 1957 dargebracht von Freunden und Schülern.* BZAW, 77. Berlin: A. Töpelmann, 1958. 213-23.

Sellin, Ernst. *Das Problem des Hiobbuches. Vortrag gehalten auf dem theologischen Lehrkursus für Feldgeistliche in Riga am 13. März 1918*. Leipzig: A. Deichert, 1919.

Siegfried, C. *The Book of Job. Critical Edition of the Hebrew Text*. SBOT. Baltimore: Johns Hopkins Press, 1893.

Skehan, P.W. 'Job's Final Plea (Job 29–31) and the Lord's Reply (Job 38–41).' *Bib* 45 (1964) 51-62.

Snaith, Norman H. *The Book of Job: Its Origin and Purpose*. SBT, 2/11. London: SCM Press; Naperville: Allenson, 1968.

Soden, W.B. von. *Akkadisches Handwörterbuch*. 3 vols. Wiesbaden: Harrassowitz, 1959–65.

Spiegel, Shalom. 'Noah, Daniel and Job: Touching on Canaanite Relics in the Legends of the Jews.' In *Louis Ginzberg Jubilee Volume. On the Occasion of his Seventieth Birthday*. New York: American Academy for Jewish Research. 1945. Vol. 1. 305-35.

Stamm, Johann J. *Das Leiden des Unschuldigen in Babylon und Israel*. Zurich: Zwingli Verlag, 1946.

Staples, William E. *The Speeches of Elihu: A Study of Job XXXII–XXXVII*. Toronto: Toronto University Press, 1925.

Steinmann, Jean. *Le Livre de Job*. Lectio divina. Paris: Cerf, 1955.

Steuernagel, Carl. 'Das Buch Hiob.' In *Die Heilige Schrift des Alten Testaments*. Ed. E. Kautzsch and A. Bertholet. 4th edn. Tübingen: J.C.B. Mohr, 1923. Vol. 2. 323-89.

Stevenson, William Barron. *The Poem of Job: A Literary Study with a New Translation*. London: Oxford University Press, 1947.

—*Critical Notes on the Hebrew Text of the Poem of Job*. Aberdeen: Aberdeen University Press, 1951.

Studer, G.L. 'Über die Integrität des Buches Hiob.' *JPTh* 1 (1875) 688-723.

Susman, Margarete. *Das Buch Hiob und das Schicksal des jüdischen Volkes*. Zurich: Steinberg Verlag, 1946. 2nd edn. Basel: Herder, 1968.

Sutcliffe, Edmund F. *Providence and Suffering in the Old and New Testaments*. London: Thomas Nelson, 1955.

Swete, Henry B. *The Old Testament in Greek according to the Septuagint*. 3 vols. Cambridge: Cambridge University Press, 1887–91.

Terrien, Samuel. *Job*. Commentaire de l'Ancien Testament, 13. Neuchâtel: Delachaux & Niestlé, 1963; 2nd edn, Geneva: Labor & Fides, 2005.

—'Quelques remarques sur les affinités de Job avec le Deutéro-Esaïe.' In *Volume du Congrès: Genève 1965*. VTSup, 15. Leiden: E.J. Brill, 1965. 295-310.

Thomas, D. Winton. 'The Language of the Old Testament.' In *Record and Revelation: Essays on the Old Testament*. Ed. H. Wheeler Robinson. Oxford: Oxford University Press, 1938. 374-402.

Thomson, William. *The Land and the Book*. London: Nelson & Sons, 1860.

Tournay, R. 'L'ordre primitif des chapitres xxiv–xxvii du livre de Job.' *RB* 64 (1957) 321-34.

Tsevat, Matitiahu. 'The Meaning of the Book of Job.' *HUCA* 37 (1966) 73-106 [= his *The Meaning of the Book of Job and Other Biblical Studies: Essays on the Literature and Religion of the Hebrew Bible*. New York: Ktav, 1980. 1-37].

Tur-Sinai, N.H. [Torczyner, H.]. ספר איוב עם פירוש חדש. Tel Aviv: Yavneh, 1954 [= *The Book of Job: A New Commentary*. Jerusalem: Kiryath-Sepher, 1957, 2nd edn, 1967].

Ullendorff, E. 'The Contribution of South Semitics to Hebrew Lexicography.' *VT* 6 (1956) 190-98.

Volz, Paul. 'Ein Beitrag aus den Papyri von Elephantine zu Hiob Kap. 31.' *ZAW* 32 (1912) 156ff.

—*Hiob und Weisheit (Das Buch Hiob, Sprüche und Jesus Sirach, Prediger).* Göttingen: Vandenhoeck & Ruprecht, 1921.

Wagner, Max. *Die lexikalischen und grammatikalischen Aramaismen im alttestamentlichen Hebräisch.* BZAW, 96. Berlin: A. Töpelmann, 1966.

Weber, Jean-Julien. *Le Livre de Job. L'Ecclésiaste. Texte et commentaire.* Paris: Desclée, 1947.

Weiser, Artur. *Das Buch Hiob übersetzt und erklärt.* ATD, 13. Göttingen: Vandenhoeck & Ruprecht, 1951, 3rd edn, 1968 [= *Giobbe: Traduzione e commento.* Brescia: Paideia, 1975].

Wellhausen, Julius. *Israelitische und jüdische Geschichte.* Berlin: G. Reimer, 1914.

Westermann, Claus. *Der Aufbau des Buches Hiob.* Tübingen: J.C.B. Mohr (Paul Siebeck), 1956.

Witte, Markus. *Vom Leiden zu Lehre: Der dritte Redegang (Hiob 21–27) und die Redaktionsgeschichte des Hiobbuches.* BZAW, 230. Berlin: de Gruyter, 1994.

Wright, G.H. Bateson. *The Book of Job. A New, Critically Revised Translation, with Essays on Scansion, Date, etc.* London: Williams & Norgate, 1883.

Würthwein, Ernst. *The Text of the Old Testament.* Trans. P.R. Ackroyd. Oxford: Basil Blackwell, 1957.

www.ingramcontent.com/pod-product-compliance
Lightning Source LLC
Chambersburg PA
CBHW051802230426
43672CB00012B/2597